The Paralegal's Introduction
to Business Organizations

The Paralegal's Introduction to Business Organizations

Lynn T. Slossberg

ASPEN LAW & BUSINESS
A Division of Aspen Publishers, Inc.

This publication is designed to provide accurate and authoritative information in regard to the subject matter covered. It is sold with the understanding that the publisher is not engaged in rendering legal, accounting, or other professional services. If legal advice or other professional assistance is required, the services of a competent professional person should be sought.

—From a *Declaration of Principles* jointly adopted by a Committee of the American Bar Association and Committee of Publishers and Associations.

1 2 3 4 5

To my family, with love

Summary of Contents

Table of Contents

4   *Limited Partnerships*   105

5 | Limited Liability Companies   *147*

8 | *Financial Structure of a Corporation*   *281*

11 | *Employment and Compensation*   *387*

Appendices   *513*

Preface

The purpose of this text is to provide the paralegal student with the necessary substantive and procedural background to work effectively in the realm of corporate law. The text is written with the entry-level paralegal in mind, although a more experienced paralegal may find helpful pointers as well. Each chapter begins with clearly defined chapter objectives setting both the tone and agenda and ends with chapter summaries, review questions, and lists of key terms, reinforcing the presented material. Because the underlying impetus is to present a guide to the paralegal's function in the day-to-day representation of business clients, the majority of the chapters include a section entitled *Client Simulation,* which simulates a client's case, showing a paralegal performing each required task.

The text is divided into 13 chapters. The first chapter covers both the legal and practical aspects of selecting the appropriate business entity to suit a client's needs. It looks generally at such factors as expense, tax consequences, personal liability, management, and transferability. The chapter provides questions that attorneys must ask while interviewing clients to best advise them on the appropriate business structure. It also focuses on the ethical responsibilities of all legal professionals when dealing with clients and suggests various methods for opening and organizing a business client's file with an emphasis on client confidentiality.

The text then proceeds to discuss the substantive law and procedural tasks involved in the formation and maintenance of each business entity, starting with the simplest, sole proprietorships, and continuing chapter by chapter with general partnerships, limited partnerships, and limited liability companies, until reaching its major concentration on corporations. Corporate law is covered in Chapters 6 through 13, starting with an introductory chapter and moving through such topics as formation, financial structure, meetings, shareholders' rights and liabilities, employment, corporate changes, and dissolution. Included within these materials is a chapter on trademark registration. Trademark application filing and trademark protection are major concerns of both large and small business entities, and proficiencies in this area provide a window of opportunity for the corporate paralegal.

The student workbook places the student in a fictional law office. All workbook exercises are designed based on this premise. Students will be adapting checklists and worksheets in the text to meet state law requirements. They will compile state-specific telephone and address listings for quick reference. Using intake provided by the supervising attorney, students will create various client documents, such as articles of incorporation, minutes of corporate meetings, shareholders' agreements, employment agreements, partnership agreements, certificates of limited partnership, fictitious name applications, SS-4 forms, articles of organization, operating agreements, federal trademark applications, and more. The workbook's perforated pages facilitate instructor grading and subsequent filing in a three-ring binder for quick reference on the job. Suggestions for binder divisions and additions, such as photocopies of often-used statutes, are included. The overall objective is to build competency while providing a resource tool that will be referred to time and time again.

As a final note, with the exception of Exhibit 8.1, all names of individuals, entities, and locations are purely fictional. Further, all tax information and tax forms provided are current as of the date this text was submitted for final review to the publisher. However, please note that changes in the area of tax law are rampant and the reader is advised to check the appropriate statutes for any subsequent changes.

Lynn T. Slossberg

Acknowledgments

I would like to express my gratitude to several people for their assistance in the preparation of this text. First, I would like to thank all those at Little, Brown and Company who believed in this project for their guidance and patience. Special thanks to Carolyn Merrill, Joan Horan, and Thomas Tuttle.

Additionally, I would like to thank Richard Vittenson of the American Bar Association and Debra Rand Perelman of The National Conference of Commissioners on Uniform State Laws for their assistance in obtaining permission for the reproduction of the Uniform and Model Acts found in the Appendices of the text. Thanks also to Martha Sneed and Mandy Putnam of the Patent and Trademark Office for their assistance with the trademark materials found in Chapter 12 of the text and with the Trademark Depository Library List found in the student workbook.

Lastly, I would like to thank all the reviewers of this book for their invaluable input, including Bernadette Agresti, Brian J. McCully, Judith M. Maloney, Kathleen Mercer Riggs, Mark S. Milker, Larry Nordick, Jeannine Pellettiere, James C. Ray, Nicholas W. Riggs, Marybeth W. Rutledge, and Richard S. Shaffran.

The Paralegal's Introduction to Business Organizations

1 | *Representation of the Business Client*

Upon completion of this chapter, the student will:

- understand the matters to consider when selecting a business entity
- know how to gather and analyze information in light of the client's business objectives
- understand the role of professional ethics in all dealings with the business client
- know the various billing methods available in billing business clients
- know how to open a new business client file

INTRODUCTION

The entrepreneurial spirit is more alive than ever in the United States. As the economic structure of the country and the composition of the American workforce change, more individuals are striking out on their own, gathering together their experience and drive, which may be underutilized as employees, and expanding opportunities by starting their own fledgling businesses. What form these businesses initially take depends on various factors. There are five major forms or legal structures from which one may choose to organize a business: a sole proprietorship, a general partnership (often referred to simply as a partnership), a limited partnership, a corporation, and a limited liability company.

A **sole proprietorship** is exactly what the term implies, a business owned and operated by a single individual. Although a sole proprietor may hire several employees and even a business manager to aid him or her, it is the sole proprietor who is totally responsible for the success or failure of the business, who is entitled to all profits, and is liable for all losses.

A **general partnership** simply is the joining together of two or more individuals (or entities) acting as co-owners of a business. Profits and losses, as well as management responsibilities, are shared among the partners according to the terms of a partnership agreement. Each partner in a general partnership is personally responsible for the financial obligations of the partnership.

A **limited partnership** is similar to a general partnership, requiring the joining of two or more individuals or entities to run a business based on the terms set forth in a partnership agreement. However, in a limited partnership, there must be at least one general partner and one limited partner. The limited partner is limited in terms of both personal liability and managerial responsibility. The limited partner only is liable personally for business losses up to the amount of the capital the limited partner put into the business. As a trade-off, the limited partner may not actively participate in the everyday running of the business.

A **corporation** is a business structure that is a legal entity separate from the owners of the business and is created according to the dictates of state statutes. The owners are termed **shareholders** and their share of the profits are apportioned by the number and types of shares of stock they hold in the corporation. An important feature of a corporation is the shielding from personal liability of the owners for the debts of the corporation.

The most recently recognized business structure is the **limited liability company**, which shares aspects of a partnership and aspects of a corporation. It typically requires at least two members (like a partnership and unlike a corporation which, in many states requires only one shareholder), is a legal entity separate from its owners, is created by state statute, and limits the personal liability of its owners from business debts.

This chapter will explore the matters an attorney should discuss with a client to enable the client to select the business structure that best suits his or her needs, as well as introduce the ethical responsibilities of all legal professionals inherent in representation of a client and the tasks to be performed by you as a paralegal in ensuring the efficient handling of the initial client conference.

MATTERS TO CONSIDER WHEN SELECTING A BUSINESS ENTITY

Which form of business structure is most appropriate is determined by examining the individual circumstances and needs of a client. Some forms may be excluded as possibilities simply because of the number of owners involved in the business. For example, if a client is to be the sole owner, he or she cannot form a general partnership or limited partnership for obvious reasons. A limited liability company probably will not be an option either because, as stated above, most state statutes require two or more members (owners) when forming the company. In this circumstance, then, the client has a choice between a sole proprietorship and a corporation.

A.   Taking Over an Existing Business

Sometimes a client is taking over an existing business. The client may need to know whether the presently existing structure of the business should be maintained or changed. For example, the former owners may have run the business as a general partnership. The client and his or her colleagues may choose to do the same or may find that this structure does not best serve their needs. Perhaps one of the client's colleagues simply wants to invest in return for a share of the profits and does not want to be involved in the day-to-day operations of the business. Additionally, this colleague is concerned about personal liability for business debts and has considerable personal property that is not exempt from collection by a business creditor. A general partnership may not be the most appropriate option in this case, and others should be considered. A limited partnership could be set up with this colleague as a limited partner. If that were done, the limited partner would be liable only to the extent of his or her capital investment in the business. If the client and the other colleagues expressed similar concerns regarding personal liability, then a corporation or limited liability company would be more suitable, because in a limited partnership the general partner or partners remain personally liable. Clearly, these concerns may arise both when purchasing an ongoing concern as well as when starting up a new business.

B.   Personal Liability

The issue of personal liability is more complex than first appears. Theoretically, the law provides more shelter from personal liability for corporations and limited liability companies which are considered legal entities separate from their owners. When it comes to lenders and certain other creditors, however, they may require that the owners of a business sign personal guarantees, regardless of the business's legal structure. Many corporations are undercapitalized and lenders will not risk financing unless the owners are personally responsible for the loan. Other long-term creditors are starting to follow suit. Thus, it is becoming harder to escape personal liability for major financial contractual obligations. If one's greatest concern in the area of personal liability is not the payment of business debts but is instead tort liability (liability for personal injuries to customers or the wrongful actions of employees, for example), it may be possible to purchase insurance to safeguard against personal exposure. Additionally, most businesses, regardless of legal structure, purchase theft and fire insurance coverage. In a situation where a business is engaged in hazardous activities or where the nature of a business causes the expense of acquiring adequate insurance coverage to be prohibitive, it is wise to incorporate.

C.   Raising Capital

How is the business going to raise capital? Are the owners going to be raising the capital internally, looking to outside lenders, or looking for financing from trade creditors? A sole proprietor may only look to himself or herself as an internal capital source. If his or her capital is inadequate as start-up capital, a loan will become necessary. If the sole proprietor has little to offer by way of collateral for the loan, and/or if his or her credit history is weak, raising capital could become a problem. In a partnership, whether general or limited, the business has an aggregate capital source with which to start. Should additional capital be required, a lender will look at the partners' creditworthiness as a group when evaluating a business loan. Corporations initially sell shares of stock to owners to raise capital. In theory, if a corporation wants to raise more capital, it may sell more shares. In practice, however, if it is a small private business that has incorporated, its shares are not traded on a stock exchange and the value of the shares to outsiders is difficult to determine. The original shareholders-owners may inject additional capital or the corporation may look to commercial lenders.

As discussed above, if the business is going to be looking to outside lenders for financing, the increasingly frequent requirement of personal guarantees indicates that choosing a corporate structure will not necessarily shield an owner from personal liability for a major loan. However, if most of the capital is going to be raised by the owners themselves without recourse to outside lenders, a corporation provides more varied methods for structuring the financial arrangements (discussed in later chapters).

D.   Daily Operations

How will the business be managed and how much control over daily operations does the client wish to maintain? In a sole proprietorship, the owner is typically the manager as well, although it is possible to hire someone with more expertise if necessary. Nonetheless, the owner is ultimately responsible for the business's success or failure. For someone who prefers to make all decisions independently, this structure may seem ideal. If the business will involve more than one participant, exactly how much involvement does each want? Does each participant want an equal share of management responsibility? A general partnership is an attractive option. Can the same thing be achieved in a corporation or a limited liability company? Yes, if there are few participants. In a situation where a large number of participants is anticipated, a corporate structure may be the best option because management is centralized in a board of directors and the board can make many decisions without consulting each participant. This is an especially important consideration if participants are dispersed all over the country. It would be unduly burdensome to require a vote on each business decision under these circumstances.

E. Business Duration

Does the client anticipate a long-term business operation or one of a short duration? Corporations provide the most long-term continuity because state statutes allow a corporation to have a perpetual existence. A sole proprietorship's existence is based on the life of the sole proprietor. The sole proprietorship ceases to exist when the owner does. While it is possible for an heir to take the business assets of a sole proprietorship and form a new sole proprietorship with them, one must remember that there may be adverse estate tax consequences because the business assets are deemed the personal assets of the deceased sole proprietor and are treated as such by the Internal Revenue Service. Partnerships may terminate by operation of law upon the death, disability, bankruptcy, or retirement of a partner unless other provisions for continued existence are set forth in the partnership agreement. The duration of limited liability companies is dictated by state statute and is of a definite duration, usually 30 years. One should remember that the longer the projected life of the business, the more flexible the chosen business structure should be in order to allow expansion to occur. For example, a sole proprietor cannot take on new business colleagues to expand the business without changing the structure of the business from a sole proprietorship to one of the other possible business structures.

F. Transferability of Interest in the Business

Duration issues lead one to another consideration, namely, how freely may an interest in a business be transferred? Interest in a business is an owner's share of the business. In a sole proprietorship, interest in the business cannot be transferred at all without creating a new entity. If the client is seeking free transferability of interest in the business, a corporation allows for this because an owner's interest in the business is translated into the owner's shares of stock. In the absence of a shareholders' restrictive agreement, if the owner wants to sell or give his or her interest in part or in its entirety, to someone else, he or she may do so simply by transferring those shares of stock. As will be discussed in later chapters, if a partner wants to transfer his or her interest in the partnership to another, it is more problematic. His or her share of the profits may be transferred, but the transferee does not automatically become a partner. One may only become a partner if all other partners agree. The same is true of limited liability companies. If the client desires to restrict transferability of interest in the business, the client may choose any of the business entities, including a corporation, for an agreement between the shareholders may be drafted to limit the shareholders' rights in transferring stock.

G.　*Tax Considerations*

The client may have many questions about tax matters that will influence the choice of business structure. (The Internal Revenue Service publishes a helpful pamphlet entitled *Tax Guide for Small Business*, Publication 334, which can be ordered over the telephone and is available in most offices across the country.) In a sole proprietorship, all profits and losses are treated as personal profits and losses, and are shown as such on the sole proprietor's personal 1040 income tax return. The same is true of general partnerships and limited partnerships. Each partner's share of profits and losses is reflected on the partner's own tax return. Annual informational forms must be filed, but neither a general partnership nor a limited partnership files a separate income tax return for the business itself.

How a corporation is taxed depends on the type of corporation formed. Later chapters will discuss the various types of corporations and discuss the special tax concerns of corporations in greater detail. In this preliminary discussion, it is important to know that the Internal Revenue Service makes a distinction between a corporation called a "C" corporation and one called an "S" corporation. A C corporation is taxed as a separate entity. This means that a corporate tax return must be filed each year of the corporation's existence indicating the income of the corporation as well as allowable deductions. If the owners of the business, the shareholders, receive a portion of the profits in any given year (paid out in dividends), each shareholder must report this on his or her personal tax return as income. In effect, what is happening is that the profits of the business are being taxed twice: once as income of the corporation, then as income of the individual shareholders. This concept is known as **double taxation** and most clients seek to avoid this consequence if possible. Keep in mind that many states also impose a state tax on corporations.

S corporations are taxed differently. If the corporation meets various requirements set forth by the Internal Revenue Service (discussed in later chapters) it may file an application to be considered an S corporation. S corporations are not taxed as separate entities. The shareholders report all earnings and losses on their individual returns and double taxation is avoided.

If a client is leaning toward incorporating for other reasons, but is concerned about tax implications, it may be possible to reduce the amount of tax paid at the corporate level. Salaries are legitimate deductible business expenses. If the majority of the payout of dividends would be going to a small group of shareholders who actually run the daily operations of the corporation, the corporation may compensate these individuals by paying them salaries instead. While the shareholders will have to report these salaries as income on their individual returns, they would also have had to report dividends as income, so either way they would be taxed individually, but dividends paid out to shareholders are profits (certainly not a tax deduction) while salaries are expenses to the corporation.

At the present time, the Internal Revenue Service is taxing limited liability companies in the same manner in which partnerships are taxed, and therefore each member's share of income is reflected on his or her individual return. It must be noted, however, that each state may choose differently when it comes to imposing state income tax on business entities and may treat limited liability companies the same as corporations in this regard.

Additionally, prior to setting up a business, a client needs to consider retirement plans and employee benefit plans. If a client chooses to incorporate and run the business as a C corporation, employee health and welfare benefits may be listed as corporate tax deductions. Other business entities may not take such deductions. Retirement plans may be set up for any of the business entities discussed.

H.   *Complexity of Organization*

If ease of organization and low set-up costs are major concerns, a sole proprietorship is the easiest of the business structures to start. A sole proprietorship does not require the drafting of partnership or other agreements, nor the drafting and filing of other official documents with the state (although *some* documentation may be required, such as the SS-4 application for a tax identification number and a fictitious-name application, both of which are discussed in the next chapter). Indeed, many people start sole proprietorships without prior consultation with an attorney, sparing themselves legal fees.

Following sole proprietorships, general partnerships are next favored for their ease in organization. The main document to be drafted is a partnership agreement. While it is advisable that a client use the services of an attorney for the drafting of this agreement, the legal expenses incurred should be much less than for the creation of a limited partnership, corporation, or limited liability company. No documents are filed with the Secretary of State in order to create a general partnership nor to terminate one.

Limited partnerships, corporations, and limited liability companies are all creatures of statute and as such require more paperwork to create and maintain. Initial filings must be made with the secretary of state's office (or other applicable governmental authority) to create these entities, and there are many statutory maintenance procedures to be performed. The costs are greater, not only in legal expenses but in other fees as well, such as incorporation fees and franchise taxes.

I.   *Operating in Foreign States*

Is the business going to be operating in more than one state? This consideration may influence which business structure is chosen. A sole proprietorship or a general partnership may be conducted in more than one state without much fuss (with the exception of acquiring appropriate occupational and other licenses required by each state). Limited partnerships, corporations, and limited liability companies require the filing of an application with each state in which business will be conducted, together with the paying of fees, before they may expand in this way. In addition, most states will require these entities to appoint a resident of the state to be available to accept **service of process** (the serving of legal papers initiating a lawsuit) on the business. That person is called a **registered agent**.

ETHICAL AND OTHER PROFESSIONAL DUTIES WHEN FIRST MEETING WITH THE CLIENT

A paralegal may become involved with a law firm's business clients as early as the first client meeting. Today's law firms understand that well-trained paralegals can, under the direction and supervision of an attorney, efficiently and cost-effectively provide many services for clients, including detailed client interviewing, drafting documents for attorney review, monitoring corporate maintenance procedures, and providing follow-up with clients. In fact, the paralegal often is the client's major contact in the firm. Once clients understand the role of a paralegal in a law firm, as well as the fact that paralegal services are billed at a lower rate than attorney services, clients welcome the assistance of paralegals with their legal matters.

Usually, the first contact with a client will be over the telephone. The receptionist will turn the client over to you, the paralegal, to set up an appointment. When a client calls to make an appointment, be sure to check your attorney's calendar for availability. Provide the client with clear directions to the office and advise him or her of appropriate documents to bring to a first meeting. For example, the client may need the attorney to review a lease for office space, business loan documents, a proposed partnership agreement, or a business plan. It is a good practice to note the date, time, client's name, and telephone number directly on the attorney's calendar for ease in reviewing a day's client schedule first thing in the morning. Immediate access to the telephone number allows for quick rescheduling should it be necessary.

A. Checking for Conflict of Interest

Prior to the first appointment, it is common practice to check a new client's name against the firm's current client case listings for a conflict of interest. Situations giving rise to conflicts of interest are set forth in the American Bar Association's Model Code of Professional Responsibility and Model Code of Professional Conduct (sometimes referred to as **ABA standards**), as well as each state's adopted code of professional responsibility. A broad definition of a **conflict of interest** is any situation in which an attorney's professional judgment might be affected because of business or personal interests. Taking on a new client who wishes to sue a current client is an obvious example of this. In this situation, the attorney cannot properly represent one party without adversely affecting the other. Checking your own attorney's client list is not sufficient if the firm consists of more than one attorney. You must check the case listings for all attorneys because the professional code of ethics treats the entire body of attorneys in a firm as one for conflict of interest purposes. A thorough check may reveal, for instance, that another attorney in the firm is representing an established client in a lawsuit against the individual for whom you set up an initial appointment. This is a conflict of interest and must be brought to your attorney's attention. When checking for conflicts of interest, note that a business client will be the business, not the person who represents the business, yet both names must be checked. For example, the new client may be Adam Andrews of XYZ, Inc. A thorough check includes both names. Some businesses conduct business under several names, in which event all need to be checked.

B.   *Confidentiality of Client Files*

Assuming no conflict appears, a file must be opened for the new client. Your firm may be using a new client data form to initiate this. This form will include the basic background information on the client, the nature of the client matter, the names of the persons to be handling the file, and the pertinent billing information. A sample of such a form appears in Exhibit 1.1. The form will be

---

EXHIBIT 1.1

New Client Data Form

DATE: _____
REFERRED BY: _____   INITIATING ATTORNEY: _____
ASSIGNED ATTORNEY(S): _____
ASSIGNED PARALEGAL(S): _____
CLIENT NUMBER: _____
MATTER NUMBER: _____
TYPE OF CASE: _____
(Supply one of the following):

01	Bankruptcy	07	Other Professional Malpractice
02	Commercial Litigation	08	Personal Injury
03	Contracts	09	Products Liability
04	Corporate	10	Real Estate
05	Divorce	11	Trusts and Estates
06	Medical Malpractice	12	Workers' Compensation
		13	Other

BILLING METHOD: _____
(Supply one of the following):

01   Contingency fee: standard rate
02   Contingency fee: special rate
03   Flat fee: (supply fee in special rate line below)
04   Hourly fee: standard rate
05   Hourly fee: special rate

EXHIBIT 1.1   *Continued*

SPECIAL RATE (Please describe in detail): _____

_____

RETAINER FOR COSTS: _____
BILLING FREQUENCY (FEES): _____
(Supply one of the following):
    01   Annually   02   Semi-Annually   03   Quarterly
    04   Monthly   05   End of Case   06   Other
BILLING FREQUENCY (COSTS): _____
(Supply one of the following):
    01   Annually   02   Semi-Annually   03   Quarterly
    04   Monthly   05   End of Case   06   Other
CLIENT NAME: _____
CLIENT BILLING ADDRESS: _____

_____

CLIENT PHONE: OFFICE: _____   HOME: _____   FAX: _____
CASE NAME: _____
OPPOSING PARTY (PARTIES): _____

_____

ADDRESS(ES) OF OPPOSING PARTY (IES): _____

_____

_____

_____

OPPOSING COUNSEL: _____

_____

ADDRESS OF OPPOSING COUNSEL: _____

_____

_____

_____

OPPOSING COUNSEL'S PHONE: _____   FAX: _____
COURT: _____   CASE NUMBER: _____
JUDGE: _____   JUDICIAL ASSISTANT: _____

provided to the legal secretary for data entry and to the billing department and will be put in the client file. An important step in processing such a form is the assignment of a **client number** and a **matter number**. Each new client is assigned his or her own number. The number may be numeric, such as 3702. Alternatively, the client number may be alphanumeric, such as W3702 in which the letter may refer to the client's name or the responsible attorney's name, depending upon the preferred office procedure of your firm.

This procedure not only helps in file organization, but also helps to preserve the **confidentiality** of a client. All legal professionals understand that communications with their clients (including potential clients coming to the office for a consultation as well as former clients) are strictly confidential. A corollary to this ethical rule is that the names of clients are also confidential and must not be made known to others coming into the law office. Client files commonly circulate throughout a firm and may be piled on someone's desk. It is important that no other client know whose names appear on those files. While it is always best practice to clear a desk of files before a client enters your office, this is not always possible. This system preserves the confidentiality of client names. Because the firm may end up handling several different matters for the client, a client matter number must be assigned to each and added to the end of the client number (3702.0001, for instance, in which the 0001 refers to the first client matter the firm is handling for this client).

C.   *Retainer Agreements*

A second initial document is a **retainer agreement**. Should the client hire the attorney, the client and the attorney must reach an agreement on how the client will be billed for the attorney's work. The three basic billing methods are contingency fees, flat fees, and hourly fees.

Contingency fees are most commonly used in personal injury cases (as well as certain other tort cases) and the collection of such a fee is dependent upon the client reaching settlement or winning in court. The payment the attorney receives is set forth as a percentage of the settlement or court award. The contingency fee refers only to payment to a lawyer for the time he or she has spent on the case and does not include any costs incurred on behalf of the client, such as filing fees, payment of a court reporter for depositions, et cetera. Such fees are the responsibility of the client whether or not he or she settles, wins, or loses. Most states impose caps on the percentage of contingency fees and require detailed contingency fee agreements spelling out all rights of the client.

Flat fees (sometimes referred to as **fixed fees**) are often used for routine legal matters where the amount of work involved is relatively easy to determine. Such matters might include uncontested divorces, real estate closings, preparation of a simple will, bankruptcies, and the incorporation of a business.

The most often used billing method is the **hourly fee**, in which a client pays for the attorney's services based upon the amount of time the attorney spends on the client matter. Hourly fee structures within a firm are often hierarchical, with a client paying more per hour for the services of a senior partner than for those of an associate, and still less for those of a paralegal. It is crucial to keep meticulous track of time when working on a client matter. Most firms bill in tenths of an hour (i.e., six-minute intervals) and each attorney and paralegal is required to record time spent on each matter on **time slips**, detailing the time the task was started, ended, and a description of the work done.

It is common for an attorney to request a certain amount to be paid upon hiring as a retainer. This sum must be deposited in the firm's **client trust account**, not in the firm's regular business account. Very strict rules are imposed by state professional codes of ethics for the handling of client trust accounts and it is important to understand thoroughly the manner in which your firm's accounts are administered. A sample retainer agreement for an hourly employment agreement appears in Exhibit 1.2.

EXHIBIT 1.2

Retainer Agreement

I, _____ (hereinafter referred to as "Client"), do hereby retain and employ the law firm of _____
to represent me in the matter described as _____

_____

_____.

I hereby agree to pay all necessary expenses incurred by the above firm in the handling of this matter and shall be billed for said expenses _____ (e.g., monthly, quarterly). I further agree to pay the above firm the following fees for attorneys' and paralegals' services in the handling of this matter and shall be billed for said fees _____ (e.g., monthly, quarterly):

EXHIBIT 1.2   *Continued*

$_____ per hour for partners;
$_____ per hour for associates;
$_____ per hour for paralegals

I understand that if I do not reasonably keep current with the payment of attorneys' fees set forth above, an advance on fees may be required.

Upon the signing of this Agreement, I shall pay a retainer sum of $_____ to be held in the above firm's trust account. This retainer sum shall be applied in the following manner: _____.

DATED this _____ day of _____, 19_____.

_____
(Client signature)

_____
(Attorney signature)

D.   Information Gathering

A third item to include and have ready for the initial client conference is an **interview information worksheet**. If the client has informed you over the telephone of the type of business entity he or she plans on starting, your firm may have specialized worksheets that aid in obtaining the particular information needed to prepare the initial documents for that entity (see Chapters 3, 4, 5, and 7). If the client is not clear on which entity best suits his or her needs and is consulting your firm prior to making this decision, a worksheet which addresses more general information, such as the one found in Exhibit 1.3, would be appropriate.

EXHIBIT 1.3

Interview Information Worksheet

DATE OF INTAKE: _____
ATTORNEY: _____
PARALEGAL: _____
CLIENT NUMBER: _____
MATTER NUMBER: _____
PERSON RESPONSIBLE FOR INTAKE: _____

1. CLIENT NAME: _____
2. SOCIAL SECURITY #: _____
3. CITIZENSHIP/RESIDENCY: _____
4. ADDRESS: _____

   _____

5. TELEPHONE: _____ FAX: _____
6. NAME OF BUSINESS (inform client that certain suffixes must be included for corporations, e.g., Inc., Corp., or Co.; limited partnerships, e.g., Ltd., and limited liability companies; e.g., L.C.)
   First choice: _____
   Second choice: _____
   Third choice: _____
7. STATE OF FORMATION: _____
8. LIST ANY OTHER STATES IN WHICH CLIENT WILL CONDUCT BUSINESS: _____

   _____

   _____

9. PRINCIPAL OFFICE OF BUSINESS: _____
10. OTHERS INVOLVED IN BUSINESS:
    NAME: _____ SOCIAL SECURITY #: _____
    CITIZENSHIP/RESIDENCY: _____
    ADDRESS: _____

    _____

    TELEPHONE: _____ FAX: _____
    NAME: _____ SOCIAL SECURITY #: _____
    CITIZENSHIP/RESIDENCY: _____

EXHIBIT 1.3   *Continued*

ADDRESS: _____

_____

TELEPHONE: _____ FAX: _____
NAME: _____ SOCIAL SECURITY #: _____
CITIZENSHIP/RESIDENCY: _____
ADDRESS: _____

_____

TELEPHONE: _____ FAX: _____
NAME: _____ SOCIAL SECURITY #: _____
CITIZENSHIP/RESIDENCY: _____
ADDRESS: _____

_____

TELEPHONE: _____ FAX: _____
11. BUSINESS PURPOSE: _____

_____

12. ACCOUNTANT: _____
13. HAS APPLICATION BEEN MADE FOR A FEDERAL EMPLOYER'S IDEN-
TIFICATION NUMBER?
YES _____   NEED TO DO _____
14. HAS APPLICATION BEEN MADE FOR A STATE TAX NUMBER FOR
WITHHOLDING PURPOSES?
YES _____   NEED TO DO _____
15. LIST NECESSARY PROFESSIONAL LICENSES TO CONDUCT BUSINESS:
(indicate name of licensee and whether license is current and in good standing):

_____

_____

_____

16. LIST NECESSARY STATE LICENSES TO CONDUCT BUSINESS:
(indicate name of licensee and whether license is current and in good standing):

_____

_____

_____

EXHIBIT 1.3 *Continued*

17. LIST NECESSARY OCCUPATIONAL LICENSES TO CONDUCT BUSI-
     NESS: (indicate name of licensee and whether license is current and in good
     standing):

     _____

     _____

     _____

18. IF CLIENT IS PURCHASING ONGOING BUSINESS:
     (A) CURRENT OWNER:
          NAME: _____
          ADDRESS: _____

          _____
     (B) PREVIOUS TRADE NAME OF BUSINESS: _____
     (C) PREVIOUS TAXPAYER IDENTIFICATION NUMBER: _____
     (D) ARE THERE ANY LIENS AGAINST THE BUSINESS?
          (if yes, describe, including name of creditor and amount of debt):

          _____

          _____

          _____
     (E) DID OWNER SIGN/WILL OWNER SIGN A COVENANT NOT TO
          COMPETE? _____
     (F) DATE OF PURCHASE: _____

19. INITIAL CAPITAL:
     (A) TOTAL ESTIMATED AMOUNT OF INITIAL CAPITAL: _____
     (B) SOURCES OF CAPITAL:
          1. PROSPECTIVE OWNERS
          (list each name and amount each is contributing):

          _____

          _____

          _____

          _____

EXHIBIT 1.3 *Continued*

2. OUTSIDE LENDERS
(list each and the amount of each loan, including all necessary terms, such
as length of loan, interest, etc.):

_____

_____

_____

_____

3. COLLATERAL FOR LOANS: _____

_____

20. PROSPECTIVE EMPLOYEES:
    (A) OWNERS: Salaried _____ Unsalaried _____
    (B) SALES PERSONNEL:
         Salaried _____ Commission _____ Both _____
    (C) ADMINISTRATIVE/MANAGEMENT PERSONNEL:
         Salaried _____ Commission _____ Both _____
    (D) INDEPENDENT CONTRACTORS: _____
    (E) OTHER: _____
21. INSURANCE NEEDS:
    (A) FIRE/THEFT: _____
    (B) TORT LIABILITY: _____
    (C) WORKERS' COMPENSATION: _____
    (D) OTHER: _____
22. ANY TRADEMARK/SERVICE MARK REGISTRATIONS NEEDED?
    (describe):

_____

_____

_____

_____

23. DOCUMENTS TO BE PREPARED/REVIEWED:
    (A) Fictitious Name Affidavit/Certificate:
         To be prepared: _____ To be reviewed: _____

EXHIBIT 1.3 *Continued*

(B) Incorporation documents:
To be prepared: _____   To be reviewed: _____
(C) Partnership agreements:
To be prepared: _____   To be reviewed: _____
(D) Limited partnership documents:
To be prepared: _____   To be reviewed: _____
(E) Limited liability company documents:
To be prepared: _____   To be reviewed: _____
(F) Employment contracts:
To be prepared: _____   To be reviewed: _____
(G) Loan documents:
To be prepared: _____   To be reviewed: _____
(H) Contracts for goods and/or services:
To be prepared: _____   To be reviewed: _____
(I) Leases:
To be prepared: _____   To be reviewed: _____
(J) Franchise agreements:
To be prepared: _____   To be reviewed: _____
(K) Profit-sharing and/or pension plans:
To be prepared: _____   To be reviewed: _____
(L) Fringe benefit plans:
To be prepared: _____   To be reviewed: _____
(M) Other: _____

This information greatly aids both the attorney and the client in determining the appropriate business structure based on the nature and scope of the business, the client's capital structure, the number of owners involved, the number of prospective employees, and so forth. An essential document for obtaining a business loan from an outside lender is a well-prepared **business plan**. Some clients will arrive at the initial attorney conference with such a plan, which will include some of the above items plus a detailed analysis of the estimated start-up expenses, market research, and profit objectives of the business. If the client has put in the time and effort to formulate a business plan, the client has reached an evaluation of the potential success of the business and will come into the law office with clearer objectives in mind.

E.   Client Conferences

A well-organized paralegal will have prepared an **initial conference folder** containing the new client data form, a retainer agreement, and the appropriate client interview worksheet, and have this sitting on the attorney's desk prior to the initial conference. All initial conferences with a client will start with a discussion between the client and the attorney, although a paralegal may be asked to sit in and may later be asked to take the client into a conference room to obtain further details on the client matter after the attorney and client have worked out the basic client objectives. If you, as a paralegal, are included in the initial conference, the attorney should introduce you to the client and explain your status in the firm.

The initial **consultation fee** may have been discussed over the telephone. The attorney should advise the client that he or she will discuss fee arrangements in detail before the client must pay anything additional to this consultation fee and that both the client and the attorney are free to reserve judgment about going forward with the client matter until the end of the conference.

If the client hires the attorney, the attorney will collect the agreed-upon retainer and the client will receive a copy of the retainer agreement upon its signing. Prior to the client leaving the office, the attorney or paralegal should review with the client any additional information the client must provide before the client matter can be handled. A **follow-up letter** should be sent as a reminder to the client. Some clients provide only sketchy information in an initial interview, yet wish to pursue the matter further. If this is the case, make a photocopy of the partially completed worksheet and send it home with the client with an addressed, stamped envelope, indicating that the client should return the completed form to the designated paralegal. In this instance as well, a reminder letter should be sent.

A reminder letter is not only a courtesy, it is insurance against miscommunication between attorney and client and possible malpractice. In many states, the most common reason for attorney discipline by an ethics committee tribunal is attorney neglect of a client matter. Often, this situation could easily have been remedied through better communication channels between attorney and client. Without a reminder letter, a client may assume that his or her attorney has taken care of a legal matter when, in fact, the client file has remained inactive waiting for further information from the client. A paralegal should always follow-up the reminder letter with a telephone call, hopefully prompting the client to action, and allowing the paralegal to address any further procedural questions the client may have.

Sometimes the client is not certain that he or she wants to proceed after the initial conference and wants some time to think about the matter. Here, the client has neither accepted nor declined representation. The initial file should be retained as an inactive file for a prescribed period of time (e.g., 90 days, 120 days) before closing it. As the prescribed time period draws near, a letter should be sent to the prospective client, indicating that the firm will be closing the file on the client if it does not hear from the client by a set date. If the client decides not to hire the attorney, the file will be closed. No file should be closed, however, without first sending the client a letter confirming that the client met with the attorney and declined representation.

Chapter Summary

1. The five basic legal structures for a business are a sole proprietorship, a general partnership, a limited partnership, a corporation, and a limited liability company.

2. In order to determine the best structure for a client, the attorney must look at the needs and desires of the client, weighing the advantages and disadvantages of each structure in light of these needs.

3. Matters to consider in choosing a business structure include, but are not limited to, the number of owners involved in the business, the nature of the business, protection from personal liability, complexity of organization, the capital structure of the business, interstate activity, transferability of interest in the business, and tax considerations.

4. In general terms, sole proprietorships and general partnerships are riskiest in terms of personal liability, while corporations and limited liability companies provide the best shield from personal liability. Limited partnerships only shield the limited partner; general partners within a limited partnership retain unlimited personal liability.

5. Corporations may exist perpetually, and thus provide the greatest continuity of existence, while sole proprietorships provide the least.

6. C corporations are subject to double taxation, meaning that a tax is imposed on the corporation as a separate legal entity, and imposed additionally on individual shareholders when they receive their share of the profits, known as dividends. In S corporations, general partnerships, limited partnerships, and sole proprietorships, profits are taxed on each owner's individual income tax return.

7. Before accepting a new client, a search must be done of the listing of all of the firm's cases to check for a possible conflict of interest.

8. It is good practice to prepare an initial client folder prior to the client's first conference at the law office. This folder should include a new client data form, a retainer agreement, and a client interview worksheet. Each new client should be assigned a client number and each client project should be assigned its own matter number. This maintains efficiency in handling client files as well as client confidentiality.

9. There are three basic methods of billing a client: contingency fee, flat fee, and hourly fee. The most commonly used method is the hourly fee method, requiring all legal staff working on a client matter to keep meticulous records of time spent.

10. Upon the completion of the initial client conference, the client folder may become active, inactive, or closed. Certain procedures must be followed in each instance. If the client accepts attorney representation, the client should receive a copy of the retainer agreement and additional information to be proffered by the client should be reviewed, followed by a reminder letter. If the client remains undecided about representation, the folder should be labeled inactive and retained as such for the firm's prescribed inactive period, toward the close of which a letter should be sent to the client indicating the firm's intentions to close the file. If the client declines representation, the file will be closed and a letter must be sent to the client reaffirming the client's decision.

Review Questions

1. Which of the five business structures presented would be most suitable for a client who:
    (i)   is a sole owner of a business and wants to limit his or her personal liability for business debts?
    (ii)   is primarily concerned with the flexibility of transfer of interest in the business?
    (iii) simply wants to invest in a business and does not want any management responsibilities?
    (iv)   wants to avoid personal liability for business debts, avoid double taxation, and wants to actively participate in the management of the business?

2. Outline the tasks to be performed by a paralegal from the initial telephone contact with a potential client to the end of the initial client conference.

3. Which of the three billing options (contingency fee, flat fee, hourly fee) would be most appropriate for the following matters:
    (i)   a complex corporate merger
    (ii) a trademark infringement lawsuit
    (iii) incorporation of a business

KEY TERMS

ABA standards	contingency fees
business plan	flat fees
client number	hourly fees
client trust account	matter number
confidentiality	retainer agreement
conflict of interest	time slips

2 Sole Proprietorships

Overview of Objectives

Upon completion of this chapter, the student will:

- understand the advantages and disadvantages of choosing a sole proprietorship as a business format
- know the various financing options available to a sole proprietor
- know how to form a sole proprietorship
- know the retirement plan options available to a sole proprietor and any employees he or she might hire

INTRODUCTION

A **sole proprietorship** is an unincorporated business owned by one person. It is important to include "unincorporated" in this definition, for it is possible in many states to form a one-person corporation. An individual who chooses to run his or her business as a sole proprietor may or may not choose to incorporate at some later date, but initially chooses to run his or her business with few legal formalities. The concept of one-person ownership is key. A sole proprietor may hire employees and may even hire an assistant manager, but may never share ownership of the business with someone else. If this happens, the business ceases to be a sole proprietorship.

This chapter will discuss the advantages and disadvantages of choosing this form of business structure including, but not limited to, the tax treatment sole proprietorships receive and the types of financing that are available and are not available to a sole proprietor. Should a client choose this business structure, he or she may choose to consult an attorney to determine the licenses and documentation necessary to start the business and to inquire about the retirement plans available to a sole proprietor and any potential employees. Consequently, as a paralegal working in a law firm, you must be acquainted with the minimal formalities necessary to start a sole proprietorship and the available retirement plan options, which are topics discussed in detail in this chapter.

NATURE OF A SOLE PROPRIETORSHIP

A sole proprietorship cannot be separated from the identity of its owner. The owner *is* the business. The owner has ultimate responsibility for all business profits and losses. There is no separation of business and personal assets. This means, in effect, that the sole proprietor's financial risk is not limited to his or her business investments. This financial risk may take the form of debts to creditors (the most common risk) or lawsuits based on torts committed by the sole proprietor or by his or her employees. Creditors (as well as those who have obtained a money judgment in court against the sole proprietor in a tort or breach of contract action) have the ability to reach any of the sole proprietor's personal nonexempt assets. Exemption here refers to those assets that state or federal law determines may not be used to pay off creditors. Although liability insurance may be purchased to limit some risks, an individual owning significant nonexempt assets in his or her own name may prefer to incorporate rather than expose himself or herself to such risks. Before commencing a business as a sole proprietor, a determination should be made as to how creditor-proof one's assets are.

It is possible to hold legal title to assets in such a manner as to limit the potential risk. For example, in many states a husband and wife can hold title to property (property referred to here as both real and personal property) as tenants by the entireties. This means not only that they jointly own the property, but that it cannot be severed because each owns 100 percent of the property. This property could not be touched by the husband's creditors, for instance, if he were a sole proprietor owing business debts, because his wife is a 100 percent owner of the property and she is not legally responsible for the debt. It should be noted, however, that some creditors not only require collateral that can be reached in the event of lack of payment on a debt obligation, but some additionally require guarantors.

Because the individual owner cannot be separated from the sole proprietorship, the business can only exist as long as the owner does. Upon the death of a sole proprietor, the personal representative of his or her estate generally has authority to continue the business for a short duration. This allows the personal representative to either hand the business over to a named beneficiary in the proprietor's will (or to the appropriate heir if the proprietor died without leaving a will), sell the business as a going concern, or liquidate it and disperse the proceeds according to the terms of the will or state law. Whether the business is inherited or sold, in most states it technically is no longer the same business—the sole proprietorship terminates and a new sole proprietorship or other business entity must be created to continue on in its stead. In this manner, sole proprietorships tend to lack the potential continuity and longevity available to other business entities.

Many individuals see the disadvantages discussed above, as well as the limited methods of raising capital discussed below, as trade-offs for several advantages to be gained by becoming a sole proprietor. All profits belong to the sole proprietor. All profits and losses show up as individual profits and losses on the sole proprietor's individual income tax return and thus a sole proprietorship is not subjected to the double taxation of a C corporation, as discussed in the previous chapter. Additionally, in years when the business is operating at a loss (typically the first year or so), these losses can be applied to offset the proprietor's personal income.

A sole proprietor has full authority and responsibility for the daily operations of the business. No one need be consulted in management decisions. This allows for optimal flexibility and little delay in implementing ideas, as decisions do not have to be funneled through partners or bureaucratic structures such as a board of directors of a corporation or the managers of a limited liability company. If the sole proprietor needs help in managing the business, he or she can always hire someone with the appropriate expertise while maintaining total control of the business.

The formalities to start up operations are minimal. Because a sole proprietorship is considered simply an extension of the individual owner, it is not deemed a separate legal entity created by state statutes: it therefore does not need to file documents with the state and is subject to less governmental interference than other business entities. As a result of having minimal formalities to follow, legal and organizational expenses are relatively low. While limited partnerships, corporations, and limited liability companies must meet statutory qualifications to conduct business in other states and receive authority from the secretary of state or other appropriate governmental authority within those states, a sole proprietorship is not subjected to these formalities.

FINANCING

A.   *Equity Financing versus Debt Financing*

The sole proprietor's outlets for start-up capital are limited. A partner in a general partnership or limited partnership can look to other existing partners or take on additional partners to increase capital contributions. A member of a limited liability company likewise can look to other members for additional financing. A corporation can raise capital through the sale of stock or the issuing of bonds and debentures. These resources are not available to the sole proprietor. A sole proprietor may not raise capital through **equity financing** (the raising of capital by selling ownership interest in the business). A sole proprietor's two major sources of capital are his or her own savings and **debt financing** (loans to be paid back, usually with interest). In many instances, raising the necessary funds through debt financing is difficult unless the sole proprietor has considerable personal assets.

Debt financing may be short-term, intermediate-term, or long-term. **Short-term financing** generally consists of a loan term of one year or less, **intermediate-term financing** consists of a loan term of one to five years, and **long-term financing** consists of a loan term of more than five years. While it may be possible to obtain an **unsecured** short-term loan (one in which no collateral is required to secure the debt), some sort of security is almost always required for a long-term commercial loan, be it in the form of equipment, inventory, personal assets, receivables of the business, or any combination of these. If the sole proprietor is fortunate, he or she may be able to secure a loan from family or friends on advantageous terms, but most sole proprietors seek business loans from commercial establishments.

In order to obtain commercial financing, the sole proprietor must have a well-prepared business plan and be ready to field such questions as how much he or she needs, for how long, what he or she plans to do with the loan money, and how he or she plans on paying back the loan. The shorter the proposed term of the loan, the smaller the risk of the venture, the more contingency plans the sole proprietor has in place for paying back the loan, and the more likely he or she will obtain financing.

B.   Special Financing Mechanisms

Other available financing mechanisms are the use of finance companies, trade credit, accounts receivable financing, and factoring. **Finance companies** may be more willing to make a loan to a new business that a bank deems too risky a venture, but they typically charge higher interest rates than those charged by a bank. They will require the pledging of collateral, be it equipment, inventory, receivables, or a combination of these. Most new businesses, including sole proprietorships, should be able to obtain some sort of **trade credit** from suppliers, allowing them to take anywhere from 30 to 90 days to pay their accounts. **Accounts receivable financing** is a method of obtaining a short-term bank loan by pledging a business's receivables as collateral for the loan and is based on a discounted value of the pledged receivables. **Factoring** is a method of obtaining financing in which, instead of pledging a business's accounts receivable as collateral, the business's accounts receivable are sold at a discounted value to a finance company or a factoring company which then collects on the accounts. The last two financing methods are more suited to businesses providing goods rather than services and factoring in particular has become more popular with manufacturing businesses. An individual desiring to start a business as a sole proprietor should investigate each of these avenues to determine whether adequate financing can be obtained to keep the business afloat until the business is turning a profit. The major reason small businesses fail is undercapitalization, and a sole proprietorship is more likely to find itself in this position because of its limited sources of capital.

TAX CONSIDERATIONS

All business profits and losses of a sole proprietorship are reported on the sole proprietor's 1040 tax return and all income is taxed at the individual's tax rate. The sole proprietor includes this information on one of two schedules: Schedule C (see Exhibit 2.1) or Schedule C-EZ (see Exhibit 2.2). Schedule C-EZ is used if the gross receipts from the business amount to $25,000 or less and business expenses amount to $2,000 or less; otherwise, Schedule C must be used. The Internal Revenue Service only considers those business expenses deemed to be ordinary and necessary as deductible expenses. An ordinary and necessary expense is one that is commonly accepted, helpful, and appropriate to the sole proprietor's business.

Excluded from this definition are capital expenses. A **capital expense** is one incurred in getting started in the business, in acquiring a business asset

EXHIBIT 2.1

| SCHEDULE C
(Form 1040)

Department of the Treasury
Internal Revenue Service　(O) | **Profit or Loss From Business**
(Sole Proprietorship)
▶ Partnerships, joint ventures, etc., must file Form 1065.
▶ Attach to Form 1040 or Form 1041.　▶ See Instructions for Schedule C (Form 1040). | OMB No. 1545-0074
19⁢95
Attachment
Sequence No. **09** |

Name of proprietor | Social security number (SSN)

A Principal business or profession, including product or service (see page C-1) | **B** Enter principal business code
(see page C-6) ▶ | | | |

C Business name. If no separate business name, leave blank. | **D** Employer ID number (EIN), if any | | | | | | | |

E Business address (including suite or room no.) ▶ ....
City, town or post office, state, and ZIP code

F Accounting method:　(1) ☐ Cash　(2) ☐ Accrual　(3) ☐ Other (specify) ▶ ....

G Method(s) used to
value closing inventory:　(1) ☐ Cost　(2) ☐ Lower of cost
or market　(3) ☐ Other (attach
explanation)　(4) ☐ Does not apply (if
checked, skip line H) | Yes | No

H Was there any change in determining quantities, costs, or valuations between opening and closing inventory? If "Yes," attach
explanation

I Did you "materially participate" in the operation of this business during 1995? If "No," see page C-2 for limit on losses.

J If you started or acquired this business during 1995, check here . . . . ▶ ☐

Part I	**Income**

1	Gross receipts or sales. **Caution:** *If this income was reported to you on Form W-2 and the "Statutory* *employee" box on that form was checked, see page C-2 and check here* . . . . ▶ ☐	**1**	
2	Returns and allowances	**2**	
3	Subtract line 2 from line 1	**3**	
4	Cost of goods sold (from line 40 on page 2)	**4**	
5	**Gross profit.** Subtract line 4 from line 3	**5**	
6	Other income, including Federal and state gasoline or fuel tax credit or refund (see page C-2) . . .	**6**	
7	**Gross income.** Add lines 5 and 6 . . . . ▶	**7**	

Part II	**Expenses.** Enter expenses for business use of your home **only** on line 30.

8	Advertising	**8**			19	Pension and profit-sharing plans	**19**	
9	Bad debts from sales or services (see page C-3) . .	**9**			20	Rent or lease (see page C-4):		
					a	Vehicles, machinery, and equipment .	**20a**	
10	Car and truck expenses (see page C-3)	**10**			b	Other business property . .	**20b**	
11	Commissions and fees. . .	**11**			21	Repairs and maintenance . .	**21**	
12	Depletion.	**12**			22	Supplies (not included in Part III) .	**22**	
13	Depreciation and section 179 expense deduction (not included in Part III) (see page C-3) . .	**13**			23	Taxes and licenses	**23**	
					24	Travel, meals, and entertainment:		
14	Employee benefit programs (other than on line 19) . . .	**14**			a	Travel	**24a**	
15	Insurance (other than health) .	**15**			b	Meals and en- tertainment .		
16	Interest:				c	Enter 50% of line 24b subject to limitations (see page C-4)		
a	Mortgage (paid to banks, etc.) .	**16a**						
b	Other	**16b**			d	Subtract line 24c from line 24b .	**24d**	
17	Legal and professional services	**17**			25	Utilities	**25**	
					26	Wages (less employment credits) .	**26**	
					27	Other expenses (from line 46 on page 2)	**27**	
18	Office expense	**18**						

28	**Total expenses** before expenses for business use of home. Add lines 8 through 27 in columns . . ▶	**28**	
29	Tentative profit (loss). Subtract line 28 from line 7	**29**	
30	Expenses for business use of your home. Attach **Form 8829**	**30**	
31	**Net profit or (loss).** Subtract line 30 from line 29.		
	• If a profit, enter on **Form 1040, line 12,** and ALSO on **Schedule SE, line 2** (statutory employees, see page C-5). Estates and trusts, enter on Form 1041, line 3. • If a loss, you MUST go on to line 32.	**31**	
32	If you have a loss, check the box that describes your investment in this activity (see page C-5).		
	• If you checked 32a, enter the loss on **Form 1040, line 12,** and ALSO on **Schedule SE, line 2** (statutory employees, see page C-5). Estates and trusts, enter on Form 1041, line 3.	**32a** ☐ All investment is at risk.	
	• If you checked 32b, you MUST attach **Form 6198.**	**32b** ☐ Some investment is not at risk.	

For Paperwork Reduction Act Notice, see Form 1040 instructions. | Cat. No. 11334P | Schedule C (Form 1040) 1995

EXHIBIT 2.1 *Continued*

Schedule C (Form 1040) 1995

Page **2**

Part III Cost of Goods Sold (see page C-5)

33	Inventory at beginning of year. If different from last year's closing inventory, attach explanation . .	33	
34	Purchases less cost of items withdrawn for personal use	34	
35	Cost of labor. Do not include salary paid to yourself	35	
36	Materials and supplies	36	
37	Other costs	37	
38	Add lines 33 through 37	38	
39	Inventory at end of year	39	
40	**Cost of goods sold.** Subtract line 39 from line 38. Enter the result here and on page 1, line 4 . .	40	

Part IV **Information on Your Vehicle.** Complete this part **ONLY** if you are claiming car or truck expenses on line 10 and are not required to file Form 4562 for this business. See the instructions for line 13 on page C-3 to find out if you must file.

41 When did you place your vehicle in service for business purposes? (month, day, year) ▶ ..../........../....... .

42 Of the total number of miles you drove your vehicle during 1995, enter the number of miles you used your vehicle for:

a Business .... b Commuting .... c Other ....

43 Do you (or your spouse) have another vehicle available for personal use? . . . . ☐ Yes ☐ No

44 Was your vehicle available for use during off-duty hours? . . . . ☐ Yes ☐ No

45a Do you have evidence to support your deduction? . . . . ☐ Yes ☐ No
b If "Yes," is the evidence written? . . . . ☐ Yes ☐ No

Part V **Other Expenses.** List below business expenses not included on lines 8–26 or line 30.

....	
....	
....	
....	
....	
....	
....	
....	
....	
....	

46	**Total other expenses.** Enter here and on page 1, line 27	46	

Printed on recycled paper

*U.S.GPO:1995-389-198

EXHIBIT 2.2

SCHEDULE C-EZ (Form 1040)	**Net Profit From Business**	OMB No. 1545-0074
	(Sole Proprietorship)	19**95**
Department of the Treasury Internal Revenue Service (O)	▶ Partnerships, joint ventures, etc., must file Form 1065. ▶ Attach to Form 1040 or Form 1041. ▶ See instructions on back.	Attachment Sequence No. **09A**
Name of proprietor		Social security number (SSN)

Part I   General Information

You May Use This Schedule Only If You:	• Had gross receipts from your business of $25,000 or less. • Had business expenses of $2,000 or less. • Use the cash method of accounting. • Did not have an inventory at any time during the year. • Did not have a net loss from your business. • Had only one business as a sole proprietor.	And You:	• Had no employees during the year. • Are not required to file **Form 4562**, Depreciation and Amortization, for this business. See the instructions for Schedule C, line 13, on page C-3 to find out if you must file. • Do not deduct expenses for business use of your home. • Do not have prior year unallowed passive activity losses from this business.

A	Principal business or profession, including product or service	**B Enter principal business code** (see page C-6) ▶
C	Business name. If no separate business name, leave blank.	**D Employer ID number (EIN), if any**
E	Business address (including suite or room no.). Address not required if same as on Form 1040, page 1.	
	City, town or post office, state, and ZIP code	

Part II   Figure Your Net Profit

1	**Gross receipts.** If more than $25,000, you **must** use Schedule C. **Caution:** *If this income was reported to you on Form W-2 and the "Statutory employee" box on that form was checked, see* **Statutory Employees** *in the instructions for Schedule C, line 1, on page C-2 and check here* . . . . ▶ ☐	1	
2	**Total expenses.** If more than $2,000, you **must** use Schedule C. See instructions	2	
3	**Net profit.** Subtract line 2 from line 1. If less than zero, you **must** use Schedule C. Enter on **Form 1040, line 12,** and ALSO on **Schedule SE, line 2.** (Statutory employees **do not** report this amount on Schedule SE, line 2. Estates and trusts, enter on Form 1041, line 3.)	3	

Part III   Information on Your Vehicle. Complete this part **ONLY** if you are claiming car or truck expenses on line 2.

4   When did you place your vehicle in service for business purposes? (month, day, year) ▶ ..... / ..... / ..... .

5   Of the total number of miles you drove your vehicle during 1995, enter the number of miles you used your vehicle for:

a Business .... b Commuting .... c Other ....

6   Do you (or your spouse) have another vehicle available for personal use? . . . .   ☐ Yes   ☐ No

7   Was your vehicle available for use during off-duty hours? . . . .   ☐ Yes   ☐ No

8a Do you have evidence to support your deduction? . . . .   ☐ Yes   ☐ No

b If "Yes," is the evidence written? . . . .   ☐ Yes   ☐ No

For Paperwork Reduction Act Notice, see Form 1040 instructions.   Cat. No. 14374D   Schedule C-EZ (Form 1040) 1995

(such as real property, machinery, trucks, intellectual property rights), or in making improvements to a business asset (such as new plumbing, new floors). Although the sole proprietor may not list capital expenses as deductions, it may be possible to take partial deductions through depreciation, amortization, or depletion. **Depreciation** pertains to business assets that have a useful life of more than one year. The total cost of the asset may not be deducted on the income tax return for the year in which the asset is bought; rather, the cost must be spread over the useful life of the asset. The Internal Revenue Service also allows **amortization** of certain intangible properties acquired by a business. Amortization works in a manner similar to depreciation, allowing deductions to be spread over a certain time frame which, for intangible capital expenses, is 15 years. **Depletion** is relevant only to businesses related to the acquisition and utilization of mineral property (such as oil and gas wells) and timber and allows deductions to be calculated by one of two formulas. A helpful IRS publication which provides detailed guidelines of all permissible business deductions is Publication 535 entitled *Business Expenses*, which is freely provided by the Internal Revenue Service.

In recent years, there has been a big move toward individuals working out of their homes. While many corporations are allowing employees to do this under appropriate circumstances, many sole proprietors in service businesses are finding this an attractive alternative to renting office space, provided doing so does not violate any city or county zoning ordinances. The Internal Revenue Service does allow an individual to deduct expenses for business use of a home and requires anyone wanting to claim such deductions to file a Form 8829 (see Exhibit 2.3). The Internal Revenue Service only allows deductions pertaining to that part of the home that is used *exclusively* for business on *a regular basis*. Further, deductions are permitted only if the part of the home for which one is claiming the deduction is either (1) the individual's principal place of business, or (2) used as a place of business in which the individual meets with patients, clients, or customers, or (3) used in connection with the individual's business and is a separate structure not attached to the home. (Please note that special rules apply to the storage of inventory and to use of the home as a day-care facility.)

A sole proprietor who hires employees is required to withhold federal income tax, and in most circumstances social security and Medicare taxes, from the wages of such employees. Additionally, sole proprietors are personally liable for self-employment tax and typically are required to make estimated tax payments. Internal Revenue Service Publications 937 and 533 provide helpful information in these areas. In addition to these federal tax considerations, the sole proprietor's business profits and losses will appear as personal profits and losses on state income tax returns (in states imposing such taxes). State income

EXHIBIT 2.3

Form **8829**

Department of the Treasury
Internal Revenue Service (O)

Expenses for Business Use of Your Home

▶ File only with Schedule C (Form 1040). Use a separate Form 8829 for each home you used for business during the year.

▶ See separate instructions.

OMB No. 1545-1266

1995

Attachment
Sequence No. **66**

Name(s) of proprietor(s)

Your social security number

Part I   Part of Your Home Used for Business

1	Area used regularly and ... ...iness, regularly for day care, or for inventory storage. See instructions	1
2	Total area of home	2
3	Divide line 1 by line 2. Enter the result as a percentage	3 %

- For day-care facilities not used exclusively for business, also complete lines 4–6.
- All others, skip lines 4–6 and enter the amount from line 3 on line 7.

4	Multiply days used for day care during year by hours used per day	4	hr.
5	Total hours available for use during the year (365 days × 24 hours). See instructions	5	8,760 hr.
6	Divide line 4 by line 5. Enter the result as a decimal amount	6	.
7	Business percentage. For day-care facilities not used exclusively for business, multiply line 6 by line 3 (enter the result as a percentage). All others, enter the amount from line 3 ▶	7	%

Part II   Figure Your Allowable Deduction

8	Enter the amount from Schedule C, line 29, **plus** any net gain or (loss) derived from the business use of your home and shown on Schedule D or Form 4797. If more than one place of business, see instructions		8

See instructions for columns **(a)** and **(b)** before completing lines 9–20.

		(a) Direct expenses	(b) Indirect expenses	
9	Casualty losses. See instructions	9		
10	Deductible mortgage interest. See instructions	10		
11	Real estate taxes. See instructions	11		
12	Add lines 9, 10, and 11	12		
13	Multiply line 12, column (b) by line 7		13	
14	Add line 12, column (a) and line 13			14
15	Subtract line 14 from line 8. If zero or less, enter -0-			15
16	Excess mortgage interest. See instructions	16		
17	Insurance	17		
18	Repairs and maintenance	18		
19	Utilities	19		
20	Other expenses. See instructions	20		
21	Add lines 16 through 20	21		
22	Multiply line 21, column (b) by line 7		22	
23	Carryover of operating expenses from 1994 Form 8829, line 41		23	
24	Add line 21 in column (a), line 22, and line 23			24
25	Allowable operating expenses. Enter the **smaller** of line 15 or line 24			25
26	Limit on excess casualty losses and depreciation. Subtract line 25 from line 15			26
27	Excess casualty losses. See instructions		27	
28	Depreciation of your home from Part III below		28	
29	Carryover of excess casualty losses and depreciation from 1994 Form 8829, line 42		29	
30	Add lines 27 through 29			30
31	Allowable excess casualty losses and depreciation. Enter the **smaller** of line 26 or line 30			31
32	Add lines 14, 25, and 31			32
33	Casualty loss portion, if any, from lines 14 and 31. Carry amount to **Form 4684**, Section B			33
34	Allowable expenses for business use of your home. Subtract line 33 from line 32. Enter here and on Schedule C, line 30. If your home was used for more than one business, see instructions ▶			34

Part III   Depreciation of Your Home

35	Enter the **smaller** of your home's adjusted basis or its fair market value. See instructions	35
36	Value of land included on line 35	36
37	Basis of building. Subtract line 36 from line 35	37
38	Business basis of building. Multiply line 37 by line 7	38
39	Depreciation percentage. See instructions	39 %
40	Depreciation allowable. Multiply line 38 by line 39. Enter here and on line 28 above. See instructions	40

Part IV   Carryover of Unallowed Expenses to 1996

41	Operating expenses. Subtract line 25 from line 24. If less than zero, enter -0-	41
42	Excess casualty losses and depreciation. Subtract line 31 from line 30. If less than zero, enter -0-	42

For Paperwork Reduction Act Notice, see page 1 of separate instructions. ✚ *Printed on recycled paper* Cat. No. 13232M Form **8829** (1995)

*U.S. Government Printing Office: 1995 - 389-468

taxes imposed on an individual are not deductible by the individual as a business expense, but the Internal Revenue Service does allow them to be deducted in computing the individual's income tax liability if deductions are itemized.

RETIREMENT PLANS

A. *Defined Contribution Plans*

Many potential sole proprietors have concerns about future retirement needs and how they may best be met. In fact, there are several options available to a sole proprietor and his or her employees. The Internal Revenue Service considers a sole proprietor an employee of his or her own business and therefore considers a sole proprietor an employee participant under a retirement plan. If the sole proprietor hires employees to assist in the business, retirement plans may be set up that are funded either exclusively by employer contributions or by a mix of employer and employee contributions (the latter being either mandatory or voluntary). In general, employer contributions to an employer-sponsored retirement plan are tax-deductible.

Retirement plans may be qualified plans or nonqualified plans, or they may be individual retirement arrangements (IRAs), which are frequently referred to as individual retirement accounts. A **qualified plan** is a written plan that the employer (here, the sole proprietor) establishes for the exclusive benefit of his or her employees and their beneficiaries. The most typical qualified plans are known as **defined contribution plans**, which fall into three categories:

1. **profit-sharing plans**, which must include a definite formula for allocating contributions,
2. **stock bonus plans**, which are similar to profit-sharing plans and are only available to corporations, and
3. **money purchase pension plans**, which are based on a stated formula that is not based on profits.

The Internal Revenue Service requires that annual returns be filed for employee benefit or pension plans, including one-participant plans that are often set up by sole proprietors. A **one-participant plan** would be a pension plan set up by and for the owner of his or her own business and may include his or her spouse. If the plan qualifies as a one-participant plan, the simplified Form 5500-EZ may be used (see Exhibit 2.4) and the return must be filed commencing the year in which plan assets exceed $100,000 and for each year thereafter.

EXHIBIT 2.4

Form **5500-EZ**	**Annual Return of One-Participant (Owners and Their Spouses) Retirement Plan** This form is required to be filed under section 6058(a) of the Internal Revenue Code. ▶ See separate instructions.	OMB No. 1545-0956 **1995**

Department of the Treasury
Internal Revenue Service

Please type or print

This Form Is Open to Public Inspection

For the calendar plan year 1995 or fiscal plan year beginning , 1995, and ending , 19

This return is: *(i)* ☐ the first return filed *(ii)* ☐ an amended return *(iii)* ☐ the final return *(iv)* ☐ a short plan year (less than 12 mos.)

Check here if you filed an extension of time to file and attach a copy of the approved extension . . . . ▶ ☐

Use IRS label. Otherwise, please type or print.	**1a** Name of employer	**1b** Employer identification number	
	Number, street, and room or suite no. (If a P.O. box, see instructions for line 1a.)	**1c** Telephone number of employer	
		1d Business activity code	
	City or town, state, and ZIP code	**1e** If plan year has changed since last return, check here . . . . . ▶ ☐	

2a Is the employer also the plan administrator? ☐ Yes ☐ No (If "No," see instructions.)

2b *(i)* Name of plan ▶ ....

(ii) ☐ Check if name of plan has changed since last return

2c Date plan first became effective
Month Day Year

2d Enter three-digit plan number ▶

3 Type of plan: **a** ☐ Defined benefit pension plan (attach Schedule B (Form 5500)) **b** ☐ Money purchase plan (see instructions)
c ☐ Profit-sharing plan **d** ☐ Stock bonus plan **e** ☐ ESOP plan (attach Schedule E (Form 5500))

4a If this is a master/prototype, or regional prototype plan, enter the opinion/notification letter number . .
b Check if this plan covers: *(i)* ☐ Self-employed individuals, *(ii)* ☐ Partner(s) in a partnership, or *(iii)* ☐ 100% owner of corporation
5a Enter the number of qualified pension benefit plans maintained by the employer (including this plan). . ▶
b Check here if you have more than one plan and the total assets of all plans are more than $100,000 (see instructions) . . . ▶ ☐

6 Enter the number of participants in each category listed below:

		Number
a Under age 59½ at the end of the plan year	**6a**	
b Age 59½ or older at the end of the plan year, but under age 70½ at the beginning of the plan year	**6b**	
c Age 70½ or older at the beginning of the plan year	**6c**	

7a *(i)* Is this a fully insured pension plan which is funded entirely by insurance or annuity contracts? . . ▶ ☐ Yes ☐ No
If "Yes," complete lines 7a(ii) through 7f and skip lines 7g through 9d.

(ii) If 7a(i) is "Yes," are the insurance contracts held? . . . . ▶ ☐ under a trust ☐ with no trust

b Cash contributions received by the plan for this plan year	**7b**	
c Noncash contributions received by the plan for this plan year	**7c**	
d Total plan distributions to participants or beneficiaries	**7d**	
e Total nontaxable plan distributions to participants or beneficiaries	**7e**	
f Transfers to other plans	**7f**	
g Amounts received by the plan other than from contributions	**7g**	
h Plan expenses other than distributions	**7h**	
8a Total plan assets at the end of the year	**8a**	
b Total plan liabilities at the end of the year	**8b**	

9 Check "Yes" and enter amount involved if any of the following transactions took place between the plan and a disqualified person during this plan year. Otherwise, check "No."

	Yes	No	Amount
a Sale, exchange, or lease of property **9a**			
b Payment by the plan for services **9b**			
c Acquisition or holding of employer securities **9c**			
d Loan or extension of credit **9d**			

If 10a is "No," do not complete line 10b and line 10c. See the specific instructions for line 10b and line 10c.

		Yes	No
10a Does your business have any employees other than you and your spouse (and your partners and their spouses)? ▶	**10a**		
b Total number of employees (including you and your spouse and your partners and their spouses) ▶			
c Does this plan meet the coverage requirements of Code section 410(b)? . . . . ▶	**10c**		
11a Did the plan distribute any annuity contracts this plan year? . . . . ▶	**11a**		
b During this plan year, did the plan make distributions to a married participant in a form other than a qualified joint and survivor annuity or were any distributions on account of the death of a married participant made to beneficiaries other than the spouse of that participant? . . . . ▶	**11b**		
c During this plan year, did the plan make loans to married participants? . . . . ▶	**11c**		

Under penalties of perjury and other penalties set forth in the instructions, I declare that I have examined this return, including accompanying schedules and statements, and to the best of my knowledge and belief, it is true, correct, and complete.

Signature of employer (owner) or plan administrator ▶ Date ▶

For Paperwork Reduction Act Notice, see page 1 of the instructions. Cat. No. 63263R Form **5500-EZ** (1995)
✪ *Printed on recycled paper* *U.S.GPO:1995-389-408

Sole proprietors are allowed to set up certain qualified retirement plans, usually known as **Keogh** or **HR-10 plans**. This may be done even if the sole proprietor has no hired employees but simply wants to set up the plan for himself or herself. Contributions made to such plans are not taxed until the plan benefits are distributed. Deduction limits differ depending upon which type of defined contribution plan is chosen as the Keogh plan and depending upon whether the contributions are made on behalf of employees other than the sole proprietor or on the sole proprietor's behalf. At the time of this writing, deduction limits for each employee (other than the sole proprietor) is the lesser of $30,000 or 15 percent of the employee's taxable compensation (if the plan is a profit-sharing plan) or the lesser of $30,000 or 25 percent of the employee's taxable compensation (if the plan is a money purchase pension plan). Deductions for contributions made on behalf of the sole proprietor himself or herself are limited to the lesser of $30,000 or 13.0435 percent of net earnings, or the lesser of $30,000 or 20 percent of net earnings if the plan is a money purchase pension plan.

B.   *Simplified Employee Pensions and Individual Retirement Arrangements*

Another pension plan available to a sole proprietor and his or her employees is a **simplified employee pension (SEP).** This is a written plan that can be used in place of or in addition to other plans. The SEP allows the sole proprietor to make deductible contributions toward his or her own retirement as well as toward each qualifying employee's retirement by setting up individual retirement arrangements (**IRAs** or, in this instance, SEP-IRAs) for each participant with a bank, insurance company, or other qualified financial institution. Under Internal Revenue Service rules, all eligible employees must be allowed to participate in the SEP. The Internal Revenue Service defines an eligible employee as one who is at least 21 years old and has performed service for the employer in at least three of the immediately preceding five years. Some employees are considered excludable employees and Section 408(k) of the Internal Revenue Code should be consulted for details on such employees.

Internal Revenue Service Form 5305-SEP may be used to establish an agreement to provide SEP benefits (see Exhibit 2.5), but please note that this form is not to be filed with the Internal Revenue Service, nor does it set up IRA accounts. To establish an IRA, one may use Form 5305 which is a model trust account agreement automatically approved by the Internal Revenue Service, but again, this form is not filed with the IRS (see Exhibit 2.6).

EXHIBIT 2.5

Form **5305-SEP** (Rev. March 1994) Department of the Treasury Internal Revenue Service	**Simplified Employee Pension-Individual Retirement Accounts Contribution Agreement** (Under section 408(k) of the Internal Revenue Code)	OMB No. 1545-0499 Expires 2-28-97 **DO NOT File with the Internal Revenue Service**

_____ makes the following agreement under section 408(k) of the
(Name of employer)
Internal Revenue Code and the instructions to this form.

Article I—Eligibility Requirements (Check appropriate boxes—see **Specific Instructions.**)

The employer agrees to provide for discretionary contributions in each calendar year to the individual retirement account or individual retirement annuity (IRA) of all employees who are at least _____ years old (not to exceed 21 years old) and have performed services for the employer in at least _____ years (not to exceed 3 years) of the immediately preceding 5 years. This simplified employee pension (SEP) ☐ includes ☐ does not include employees covered under a collective bargaining agreement, ☐ includes ☐ does not include certain nonresident aliens, and ☐ includes ☐ does not include employees whose total compensation during the year is less than $396*.

Article II—SEP Requirements (See **Specific Instructions.**)

The employer agrees that contributions made on behalf of each eligible employee will be:

A. Based only on the first $150,000 of compensation.
B. Made in an amount that is the same percentage of total compensation for every employee.
C. Limited annually to the smaller of $30,000* **or** 15% of compensation.
D. Paid to the employee's IRA trustee, custodian, or insurance company (for an annuity contract).

_____   _____
Employer's signature and date   Name and title

Paperwork Reduction Act Notice

The time needed to complete this form will vary depending on individual circumstances. The estimated average time is:

Recordkeeping	7 min.
Learning about the law or the form	26 min.
Preparing the form	20 min.

If you have comments concerning the accuracy of these time estimates or suggestions for making this form more simple, we would be happy to hear from you. You can write to both the **Internal Revenue Service,** Attention: Reports Clearance Officer, PC:FP, Washington, DC 20224; and the **Office of Management and Budget,** Paperwork Reduction Project (1545-0499), Washington, DC 20503. **DO NOT** send this form to either of these addresses. Instead, keep it for your records.

A Change To Note

For years beginning after December 31, 1993, the Revenue Reconciliation Act of 1993 (the Act) reduced to $150,000 the annual compensation of each employee to be taken into account in making contributions to a SEP. The $150,000 amount will be indexed for inflation after 1994 in increments of $10,000 that will be rounded to the next lowest multiple of $10,000. See Act section 13212 for different effective dates and the transition rules that apply to governmental plans and plans under a collective bargaining agreement.

General Instructions

Section references are to the Internal Revenue Code unless otherwise noted.

Purpose of Form.—Form 5305-SEP (Model SEP) is used by an employer to make an agreement to provide benefits to all eligible employees under a SEP described in section 408(k). **Do not** file this form with the IRS. See **Pub. 560,** Retirement Plans for the Self-Employed, and **Pub. 590,** Individual Retirement Arrangements (IRAs).

Specific Instructions

Instructions to the Employer

Simplified Employee Pension.—A SEP is a written arrangement (a plan) that provides you with a simplified way to make contributions toward your employees' retirement income. Under a SEP, you can contribute to an employee's individual retirement account or annuity (IRA). You make contributions directly to an IRA set up by or for each employee with a bank, insurance company, or other qualified financial institution. When using Form 5305-SEP to establish a SEP, the IRA must be established on an IRS form or a master or prototype IRA for which the IRS has issued a favorable opinion letter. Making the agreement on Form 5305-SEP does not establish an employer IRA described in section 408(c).

When Not To Use Form 5305-SEP.—Do not use this form if you:

1. Currently maintain any other qualified retirement plan. This does not prevent you from also maintaining a Model Elective SEP (Form 5305A-SEP) or other SEP to which either elective or nonelective contributions are made.

2. Previously maintained a defined benefit plan that is now terminated.

3. Have any eligible employees for whom IRAs have not been established.

4. Use the services of leased employees (described in section 414(n)).

5. Are a member of an affiliated service group (described in section 414(m)), a controlled group of corporations (described in section 414(b)), or trades or businesses under common control (described in sections 414(c) and 414(o)), unless all eligible employees of all the members of such groups, trades, or businesses, participate in the SEP.

6. Will not pay the cost of the SEP contributions. Do not use Form 5305-SEP for a SEP that provides for elective employee contributions even if the contributions are made under a salary reduction agreement.

Use Form 5305A-SEP, or a nonmodel SEP if you permit elective deferrals to a SEP.

Eligible Employees.—All eligible employees must be allowed to participate in the SEP. An eligible employee is any employee who: (1) is at least 21 years old, and (2) has performed "service" for you in at least 3 of the immediately preceding 5 years. **Note:** *You can establish less restrictive eligibility requirements, but not more restrictive ones.*

Service is any work performed for you for any period of time, however short. If you are a member of an affiliated service group, a controlled group of corporations, or trades or businesses under common control, service includes any work performed for any period of time for any other member of such group, trades, or businesses.

Excludable Employees.—The following employees do not have to be covered by the SEP: (1) employees covered by a collective bargaining agreement whose retirement benefits were bargained for in good faith by you and their union, (2) nonresident alien employees who did not earn U.S. source income from you, and (3) employees who received less than $396* in compensation during the year.

Contribution Limits.—The SEP rules permit you to make an annual contribution of up to 15% of the employee's total compensation or $30,000*, whichever is less. Compensation, for this purpose, does not include employer contributions to the SEP or the employee's compensation in excess of $150,000. If you also maintain a Model Elective SEP or any other SEP that permits employees to make elective deferrals, contributions to the two SEPs together may not exceed the smaller of $30,000* or 15% of compensation for any employee.

Contributions cannot discriminate in favor of highly compensated employees. You are not required to make contributions every year. But you must contribute to the SEP-IRAs of all of the eligible employees who actually performed services during the year of the contribution. This includes eligible employees who die or quit working before the contribution is made.

This amount reflects the cost-of-living increase under section 408(k)(8), effective January 1, 1994. The amount is adjusted annually. Each January, the IRS announces the increase, if any, in a news release and in the Internal Revenue Bulletin.

Cat. No. 11825J   Form **5305-SEP** (Rev. 3-94)

EXHIBIT 2.6

Form **5305** (Rev. October 1992) Department of the Treasury Internal Revenue Service	**Individual Retirement Trust Account** (Under Section 408(a) of the Internal Revenue Code)	**DO NOT File** **with the Internal** **Revenue Service**

Name of grantor	Date of birth of grantor	Identifying number (see instructions)
Address of grantor		
		Check if Amendment ▶ ☐
Name of trustee	Address or principal place of business of trustee	

The Grantor whose name appears above is establishing an individual retirement account under section 408(a) to provide for his or her retirement and for the support of his or her beneficiaries after death.

The Trustee named above has given the Grantor the disclosure statement required under Regulations section 1.408-6.

The Grantor has assigned the trust..dollars ($...) in cash.

The Grantor and the Trustee make the following agreement:

Article I

The Trustee may accept additional cash contributions on behalf of the Grantor for a tax year of the Grantor. The total cash contributions are limited to $2,000 for the tax year unless the contribution is a rollover contribution described in section 402(c) (but only after December 31, 1992), 403(a)(4), 403(b)(8), 408(d)(3), or an employer contribution to a simplified employee pension plan as described in section 408(k). Rollover contributions before January 1, 1993, include rollovers described in section 402(a)(5), 402(a)(6), 402(a)(7), 403(a)(4), 403(b)(8), 408(d)(3), or an employer contribution to a simplified employee pension plan described in section 408(k).

Article II

The Grantor's interest in the balance in the trust account is nonforfeitable.

Article III

1. No part of the trust funds may be invested in life insurance contracts, nor may the assets of the trust account be commingled with other property except in a common trust fund or common investment fund (within the meaning of section 408(a)(5)).

2. No part of the trust funds may be invested in collectibles (within the meaning of section 408(m)) except as otherwise permitted by section 408(m)(3) which provides an exception for certain gold and silver coins and coins issued under the laws of any state.

Article IV

1. Notwithstanding any provision of this agreement to the contrary, the distribution of the Grantor's interest in the trust account shall be made in accordance with the following requirements and shall otherwise comply with section 408(a)(6) and Proposed Regulations section 1.408-8, including the incidental death benefit provisions of Proposed Regulations section 1.401(a)(9)-2, the provisions of which are herein incorporated by reference.

2. Unless otherwise elected by the time distributions are required to begin to the Grantor under paragraph 3, or to the surviving spouse under paragraph 4, other than in the case of a life annuity, life expectancies shall be recalculated annually. Such election shall be irrevocable as to the Grantor and the surviving spouse and shall apply to all subsequent years. The life expectancy of a nonspouse beneficiary may not be recalculated.

3. The Grantor's entire interest in the trust account must be, or begin to be, distributed by the Grantor's required beginning date, April 1 following the calendar year end in which the Grantor reaches age 70½. By that date, the Grantor may elect, in a manner acceptable to the trustee, to have the balance in the trust account distributed in:

(a) A single sum payment.

(b) An annuity contract that provides equal or substantially equal monthly, quarterly, or annual payments over the life of the Grantor.

(c) An annuity contract that provides equal or substantially equal monthly, quarterly, or annual payments over the joint and last survivor lives of the Grantor and his or her designated beneficiary.

(d) Equal or substantially equal annual payments over a specified period that may not be longer than the Grantor's life expectancy.

(e) Equal or substantially equal annual payments over a specified period that may not be longer than the joint life and last survivor expectancy of the Grantor and his or her designated beneficiary.

4. If the Grantor dies before his or her entire interest is distributed to him or her, the entire remaining interest will be distributed as follows:

(a) If the Grantor dies on or after distribution of his or her interest has begun, distribution must continue to be made in accordance with paragraph 3.

(b) If the Grantor dies before distribution of his or her interest has begun, the entire remaining interest will, at the election of the Grantor or, if the Grantor has not so elected, at the election of the beneficiary or beneficiaries, either

(i) Be distributed by the December 31 of the year containing the fifth anniversary of the Grantor's death, or

(ii) Be distributed in equal or substantially equal payments over the life or life expectancy of the designated beneficiary or beneficiaries starting by December 31 of the year following the year of the Grantor's death. If, however, the beneficiary is the Grantor's surviving spouse, then this distribution is not required to begin before December 31 of the year in which the Grantor would have turned age 70½.

(c) Except where distribution in the form of an annuity meeting the requirements of section 408(b)(3) and its related regulations has irrevocably commenced, distributions are treated as having begun on the Grantor's required beginning date, even though payments may actually have been made before that date.

(d) If the Grantor dies before his or her entire interest has been distributed and if the beneficiary is other than the surviving spouse, no additional cash contributions or rollover contributions may be accepted in the account.

Cat. No. 11810K   Form **5305** (Rev. 10-92)

EXHIBIT 2.6   *Continued*

Form 5305 (Rev. 10-92)   Page **2**

5. In the case of a distribution over life expectancy in equal or substantially equal annual payments, to determine the minimum annual payment for each year, divide the Grantor's entire interest in the trust as of the close of business on December 31 of the preceding year by the life expectancy of the Grantor (or the joint life and last survivor expectancy of the Grantor and the Grantor's designated beneficiary, or the life expectancy of the designated beneficiary, whichever applies). In the case of distributions under paragraph 3, determine the initial life expectancy (or joint life and last survivor expectancy) using the attained ages of the Grantor and designated beneficiary as of their birthdays in the year the Grantor reaches age 70½. In the case of a distribution in accordance with paragraph 4(b)(ii), determine life expectancy using the attained age of the designated beneficiary as of the beneficiary's birthday in the year distributions are required to commence.

6. The owner of two or more individual retirement accounts may use the "alternative method" described in Notice 88-38, 1988-1 C.B. 524, to satisfy the minimum distribution requirements described above. This method permits an individual to satisfy these requirements by taking from one individual retirement account the amount required to satisfy the requirement for another.

Article V

1. The Grantor agrees to provide the Trustee with information necessary for the Trustee to prepare any reports required under section 408(i) and Regulations section 1.408-5 and 1.408-6.

2. The Trustee agrees to submit reports to the Internal Revenue Service and the Grantor as prescribed by the Internal Revenue Service.

Article VI

Notwithstanding any other articles which may be added or incorporated, the provisions of Articles I through III and this sentence will be controlling. Any additional articles that are not consistent with section 408(a) and related regulations will be invalid.

Article VII

This agreement will be amended from time to time to comply with the provisions of the Code and related regulations. Other amendments may be made with the consent of the persons whose signatures appear below.

Note: *The following space (Article VIII) may be used for any other provisions you want to add. If you do not want to add any other provisions, draw a line through this space. If you do add provisions, they must comply with applicable requirements of state law and the Internal Revenue Code.*

Article VIII

Grantor's signature .... Date ....

Trustee's signature .... Date ....

Witness ....
(Use only if signature of the Grantor or the Trustee is required to be witnessed.)

General Instructions

(Section references are to the Internal Revenue Code unless otherwise noted.)

Purpose of Form

Form 5305 is a model trust account agreement that meets the requirements of section 408(a) and has been automatically approved by the IRS. An individual retirement account (IRA) is established after the form is fully executed by both the individual (Grantor) and the trustee and must be completed no later than the due date of the individual's income tax return for the tax year (without regard to extensions). This account must be created in the United States for the exclusive benefit of the Grantor or his or her beneficiaries.

Individuals may rely on regulations for the Tax Reform Act of 1986 to the extent specified in those regulations.

Do not file Form 5305 with the IRS. Instead, keep it for your records.

For more information on IRAs, including the required disclosure you can get from your trustee, get **Pub. 590**, Individual Retirement Arrangements (IRAs).

Definitions

Trustee.—The trustee must be a bank or savings and loan association, as defined in section 408(n), or any person who has the approval of the IRS to act as trustee.

Grantor.—The grantor is the person who establishes the trust account.

Identifying Number

The Grantor's social security number will serve as the identifying number of his or her IRA. An employer identification number is required only for an IRA for which a return is filed to report unrelated business taxable income. An employer identification number is required for a common fund created for IRAs.

IRA for Nonworking Spouse

Form 5305 may be used to establish the IRA trust for a nonworking spouse.

Contributions to an IRA trust account for a nonworking spouse must be made to a separate IRA trust account established by the nonworking spouse.

Specific Instructions

Article IV.—Distributions made under this article may be made in a single sum, periodic payment, or a combination of both. The distribution option should be reviewed in the year the Grantor reaches age 70½ to ensure that the requirements of section 408(a)(6) have been met.

Article VIII.—Article VIII and any that follow it may incorporate additional provisions that are agreed to by the grantor and trustee to complete the agreement. They may include, for example, definitions, investment powers, voting rights, exculpatory provisions, amendment and termination, removal of the trustee, trustee's fees, state law requirements, beginning date of distributions, accepting only cash, treatment of excess contributions, prohibited transactions with the grantor, etc. Use additional pages if necessary and attach them to this form.

Note: *Form 5305 may be reproduced and reduced in size for adoption to passbook purposes.*

☆ U.S. GPO: 1992-343-034/60161

A sole proprietor may contribute up to $30,000 or 15 percent of the employee's compensation, whichever is smaller, each year. These contributions are not included in the participant's income when contributed. Each employee may also contribute up to $2,000 each year to this IRA, independent of the employer's contributions. The SEP can include an elective deferral called a **salary reduction arrangement** under certain circumstances, which means that employees can choose to have the sole proprietor as employer contribute part of their salary to their SEP-IRA. The tax on the salary contributed in this way is deferred. There are limits on the amount of total income that can be contributed in this manner. At the time of this writing, the limit is the lesser of $9,240 or 15 percent of the employee's compensation, but note that this limit refers only to amounts contributed under a salary reduction arrangement and not to any contributions from employer's funds. SEP contributions under a salary reduction arrangement are included on the employee's Form W-2 for Social Security and Medicare tax purposes only. SEP contributions not made under such an arrangement are not included on the employee's Form W-2. A sole proprietor may make contributions to his or her own SEP-IRA under a special computation, limiting the contribution to 13.0435 percent of his or her compensation.

Finally, a sole proprietor may choose to simply set up a regular IRA account. The Internal Revenue Service allows one to make contributions to an IRA if one has received taxable compensation during the year in which the contribution is made and if one has not reached the age of 70½ by the end of that year. For a sole proprietor, compensation is net self-employment income reduced by the deduction for contributions on the sole proprietor's behalf to retirement plans and the allowable deduction for one-half of the self-employment tax. The maximum contribution that may be made to an IRA in a given year is $2,000 or the sole proprietor's taxable compensation, whichever is smaller.

FORMATION

Once the decision has been made to start a business as a sole proprietor, the few formal requirements to be seen to are easily accomplished, and many individuals attend to these matters themselves rather than incurring the additional expense of hiring an attorney to do so. An individual needs to check state statutes to determine if he or she meets a state's requirements for any applicable professional licenses or permits. Certain businesses, other than those considered professions, may also require the obtaining of special permits. An example is the restaurant business, in which a liquor license is often considered key for obtaining financial success.

Once these requirements are researched and met, the prospective sole proprietor must determine under what name he or she plans on running the business. If the sole proprietor wishes to conduct business under any name other than his or her legal name, most states require the filing of a **fictitious** (or trade or assumed) **name registration**, certificate, or affidavit. For example, if Elizabeth Miller wishes to open a florist's shop and chooses to call it "Betsy's Blossoms," this name would be considered a fictitious name and it would have to be registered with the secretary of state or other appropriate governmental authority in her state. Generally, a sole proprietor may operate his or her business under any lawful name that is not deceptively similar to the name of another business operating or registered in the area. To curtail the possibility of more than one business operating under the same or deceptively similar names in a given territory, many states require that a notice be published in a newspaper of general circulation in the county in which the business is to be conducted, either prior to or after registration. In some states, a business is prevented from bringing or defending a lawsuit until its fictitious name has been registered and lack of registration may subject a business to monetary penalties. Please note that fictitious name statutes vary considerably in their specifics from state to state and must be reviewed carefully.

If the sole proprietor plans on hiring employees, plans on starting a Keogh plan, or is required to file excise, alcohol, tobacco, or firearms returns, he or she must obtain a federal **employer identification number**, also known as a **taxpayer identification number** (if none of these situations apply, the sole proprietor uses his or her social security number as a taxpayer identification number). This may be done by submitting a **SS-4 form** (see Exhibit 2.7) by mail and waiting for notification of an assigned number or it may be done by completing the form, phoning in the required information to the Internal Revenue Service, and receiving an employer identification number over the telephone. If the latter method is utilized, it is nonetheless necessary to mail in the form with the number inserted in the right-hand corner of the form. Once a federal employer identification number is obtained, it should be included on all tax returns, statements, or documents filed with the Internal Revenue Service, which imposes a penalty for failure to do so. In addition to a federal employer identification number, some states require that an employer obtain a state employer (or tax) identification number. Further, a sole proprietor hiring employees must investigate his or her responsibilities concerning unemployment insurance and workers' compensation. It is possible to request forms for reporting payroll taxes, social security taxes, and unemployment compensation funds over the telephone.

EXHIBIT 2.7

| Form **SS-4**
(Rev. December 1993)
Department of the Treasury
Internal Revenue Service | **Application for Employer Identification Number**
(For use by employers, corporations, partnerships, trusts, estates, churches,
government agencies, certain individuals, and others. See instructions.) | EIN
OMB No. 1545-0003
Expires 12-31-96 |

Please type or print clearly.

1 Name of applicant (Legal name) (See instructions.)

2 Trade name of business, if different from name in line 1 | **3** Executor, trustee, "care of" name

4a Mailing address (street address) (room, apt., or suite no.) | **5a** Business address, if different from address in lines 4a and 4b

4b City, state, and ZIP code | **5b** City, state, and ZIP code

6 County and state where principal business is located

7 Name of principal officer, general partner, grantor, owner, or trustor—SSN required (See instructions.) ▶

8a Type of entity (Check only one box.) (See instructions.)
☐ Sole Proprietor (SSN) _____
☐ REMIC ☐ Personal service corp.
☐ State/local government ☐ National guard
☐ Other nonprofit organization (specify) _____
☐ Other (specify) ▶ _____
☐ Estate (SSN of decedent) _____ ☐ Trust
☐ Plan administrator-SSN _____ ☐ Partnership
☐ Other corporation (specify) _____ ☐ Farmers' cooperative
☐ Federal government/military ☐ Church or church controlled organization
(enter GEN if applicable) _____

8b If a corporation, name the state or foreign country (if applicable) where incorporated ▶ | State | Foreign country

9 Reason for applying (Check only one box.)
☐ Started new business (specify) ▶ _____
☐ Hired employees
☐ Created a pension plan (specify type) ▶ _____
☐ Banking purpose (specify) ▶ _____
☐ Changed type of organization (specify) ▶ _____
☐ Purchased going business
☐ Created a trust (specify) ▶ _____
☐ Other (specify) ▶ _____

10 Date business started or acquired (Mo., day, year) (See instructions.) | **11** Enter closing month of accounting year. (See instructions.)

12 First date wages or annuities were paid or will be paid (Mo., day, year). **Note:** If applicant is a withholding agent, enter date income will first be paid to nonresident alien. (Mo., day, year) . . . . ▶

13 Enter highest number of employees expected in the next 12 months. **Note:** If the applicant does not expect to have any employees during the period, enter "0." . . . . . . ▶ | Nonagricultural | Agricultural | Household

14 Principal activity (See instructions.) ▶

15 Is the principal business activity manufacturing? . . . . ☐ Yes ☐ No
If "Yes," principal product and raw material used ▶

16 To whom are most of the products or services sold? Please check the appropriate box. ☐ Business (wholesale)
☐ Public (retail) ☐ Other (specify) ▶ ☐ N/A

17a Has the applicant ever applied for an identification number for this or any other business? . . . . ☐ Yes ☐ No
Note: If "Yes," please complete lines 17b and 17c.

17b If you checked the "Yes" box in line 17a, give applicant's legal name and trade name, if different than name shown on prior application.

Legal name ▶ | Trade name ▶

17c Enter approximate date, city, and state where the application was filed and the previous employer identification number if known.
Approximate date when filed (Mo., day, year) | City and state where filed | Previous EIN

Under penalties of perjury, I declare that I have examined this application, and to the best of my knowledge and belief, it is true, correct, and complete. | Business telephone number (include area code)

Name and title (Please type or print clearly.) ▶

Signature ▶ | Date ▶

Note: Do not write below this line. For official use only.

| Please leave blank ▶ | Geo. | Ind. | Class | Size | Reason for applying |

For Paperwork Reduction Act Notice, see attached instructions. | Cat. No. 16055N | Form **SS-4** (Rev. 12-93)

If the sole proprietor is in the business of selling goods, most states require the collection of state and/or local sales tax and therefore a sales tax permit or certificate must be obtained from the appropriate authorities. A sales tax number will be issued to the proprietor, who will then be responsible for filing the required sales tax reports. It is advisable that prior to commencing business the proprietor send a letter to the appropriate state authority detailing his or her type of business, requesting information on requirements for filing sales tax reports, and requesting copies of the requisite official state forms.

An occupational license usually is necessary to operate a business in most cities and counties. If the sole proprietor plans on operating his or her business within city limits, it may be necessary to obtain both city and county licenses. Local authorities should be consulted to ascertain if, and which, occupational licenses are required. When doing so, it is advisable to determine what documents the city and/or county require copies of in order to issue these licenses. Some authorities require detailed information pertaining to floor plans, square footage, building permits for building alterations, and the like and may require copies of leases, state licenses, fictitious name certificates, and other documentation.

Once these steps are taken, it is important for the sole proprietor to create an efficient method of bookkeeping. Although no statutory recordkeeping procedures are imposed upon sole proprietors, accurate and complete records are essential to good management and may be examined by the Internal Revenue Service. Records supporting items reported on a tax return must be kept for a period of either three years after the date the return is due or filed, or two years after the date the tax was paid, whichever is later. Keeping a detailed record of business expenses as they occur serves as a guarantee not to forget any when sitting down to prepare a tax return.

A separate bank account should be established in which all business receipts are deposited and from which all business checks are disbursed. A filing method should be established to retain and organize all invoices, sales slips, canceled checks, and any other documents related to entries made in the business's account books. Separate records should be kept of employment taxes (if applicable) and must be kept for a minimum of four years after the due date of the return or after the date the tax is paid, whichever is later.

CLIENT SIMULATION

Caroline Matthews wants to open an educational testing and consulting business. She has a master's degree in education and is a licensed teacher in the state of Any State. She will provide tutoring services, skills testing, college admissions guidance, and general academic counseling services. She wants to name her business Ability Plus Educational Testing and Consulting Services. Initially, she will be the only full-time staff person but may hire a part-time assistant and she plans on using instructors as independent contractors for the tutoring work she cannot handle herself. Caroline has scouted out potential office space in an executive suite services building and is eager to sign a lease and get started as she already has received many student referrals. However, she has received mixed advice from family, friends, and former colleagues on the issue of incorporating before opening her business. She feels she would like to run the business as a sole proprietorship initially and perhaps incorporate at a later date if appropriate. Seeking professional guidance in this matter she chooses to consult an attorney.

Caroline has been referred to the law firm of Trumbull and McDonald, P.A. by a friend and has set up an appointment to meet with attorney Thomas Trumbull, who handles most of the firm's corporate work. Caroline outlines her plans for Thomas and expresses an interest in keeping the formalities of setting up her business as simple as possible. After discussing both the possibility of a sole proprietorship and a corporation, Thomas asks about Caroline's personal assets and her start-up capital. Caroline informs Thomas that few of her assets are in her individual name, title to her home and bank accounts are held as tenancies by the entirety with her husband. The only major asset in her individual name is her car. Her start-up capital comes from a combination of savings and money lent by her husband's parents, who have encouraged her to start a business of her own. Her business is a service business so her capital needs are less than if she had a business in which she had to stock inventory. Her husband's income is satisfactory to tide them both over in the event that the business does not realize a profit in the first two years and Caroline is realistic in believing that most businesses need such a period in which to establish themselves.

Having conversed about the matter for a half hour, Thomas and Caroline both agree that she is taking little personal risk in starting her business as a sole proprietorship and Thomas suggests that Caroline can handle the few required formalities herself, although the firm would be at her disposal if she encountered any difficulties. Thomas calls Karen Greer into his office. Karen is a paralegal who has been working with Thomas for three years. After introducing Karen as his legal assistant, he asks Karen to take Caroline into her office and review the forms she will need to complete and file to get her business started.

The first form Karen pulls out for Caroline is a SS-4 form. Caroline will need to obtain a federal employer identification number because she anticipates hiring employees. She would also like to start a Keogh plan, something

EXHIBIT 2.8

Form **SS-4**	**Application for Employer Identification Number**		**EIN** 98–7654321

Form **SS-4**
(Rev. December 1993)
Department of the Treasury
Internal Revenue Service

Application for Employer Identification Number

(For use by employers, corporations, partnerships, trusts, estates, churches, government agencies, certain individuals, and others. See instructions.)

EIN 98–7654321

OMB No. 1545-0003
Expires 12-31-96

Please type or print clearly.

1 Name of applicant (Legal name) (See instructions.)
Caroline Matthews

2 Trade name of business, if different from name in line 1
Ability Plus Educational Testing

3 Executor, trustee, "care of" name
and Consulting Services

4a Mailing address (street address) (room, apt., or suite no.)
334 Prestwick Ave., #351

5a Business address, if different from address in lines 4a and 4b

4b City, state, and ZIP code
Any City, Any State

5b City, state, and ZIP code

6 County and state where principal business is located
Any County, Any State

7 Name of principal officer, general partner, grantor, owner, or trustor—SSN required (See instructions.) ► 000–00–0000
Caroline Matthews

8a Type of entity (Check only one box.) (See instructions.)
☒ Sole Proprietor (SSN) _____
☐ REMIC   ☐ Personal service corp.
☐ State/local government   ☐ National guard
☐ Other nonprofit organization (specify) _____
☐ Other (specify) ► _____

☐ Estate (SSN of decedent) _____
☐ Plan administrator-SSN _____
☐ Other corporation (specify) _____
☐ Federal government/military   ☐ Church or church controlled organization
_____ (enter GEN if applicable) _____

☐ Trust
☐ Partnership
☐ Farmers' cooperative

8b If a corporation, name the state or foreign country (if applicable) where incorporated ►

State

Foreign country

9 Reason for applying (Check only one box.)
☒ Started new business (specify) ► _____
☐ Hired employees
☐ Created a pension plan (specify type) ► _____
☐ Banking purpose (specify) ► _____

☐ Changed type of organization (specify) ► _____
☐ Purchased going business
☐ Created a trust (specify) ► _____
☐ Other (specify) ► _____

10 Date business started or acquired (Mo., day, year) (See instructions.)
February 12, 1997

11 Enter closing month of accounting year. (See instructions.)
December 31

12 First date wages or annuities were paid or will be paid (Mo., day, year). **Note:** If applicant is a withholding agent, enter date income will first be paid to nonresident alien. (Mo., day, year) . . . . ► April 1, 1997

13 Enter highest number of employees expected in the next 12 months. **Note:** If the applicant does not expect to have any employees during the period, enter "0." . . . . ►

Nonagricultural	Agricultural	Household
2		

14 Principal activity (See instructions.) ►   educational testing and consulting

15 Is the principal business activity manufacturing? . . . . ☐ Yes ☒ No
If "Yes," principal product and raw material used ►

16 To whom are most of the products or services sold? Please check the appropriate box.
☒ Public (retail)   ☐ Other (specify) ►
☐ Business (wholesale)   ☐ N/A

17a Has the applicant ever applied for an identification number for this or any other business? . . . . ☐ Yes ☐ No
Note: If "Yes," please complete lines 17b and 17c.

17b If you checked the "Yes" box in line 17a, give applicant's legal name and trade name, if different than name shown on prior application.

Legal name ►

Trade name ►

17c Enter approximate date, city, and state where the application was filed and the previous employer identification number if known.

Approximate date when filed (Mo., day, year)	City and state where filed	Previous EIN

Under penalties of perjury, I declare that I have examined this application, and to the best of my knowledge and belief, it is true, correct, and complete.

Business telephone number (include area code)
(000) 251–5369

Name and title (Please type or print clearly.) ► Caroline Matthews

Signature ► Caroline Matthews   Date ► 2/12/97

Note: Do not write below this line.   For official use only.

Please leave blank ►	Geo.	Ind.	Class	Size	Reason for applying

For Paperwork Reduction Act Notice, see attached instructions.   Cat. No. 16055N   Form **SS-4** (Rev. 12-93)

she mentioned to Thomas briefly during their discussion. Karen suggests that Caroline complete the SS-4 form and that before sending it to the Internal Revenue Service telephoning the Service to obtain the number over the phone. Because the Service will ask over the phone for the information requested in the form, it is wise to complete the form first. After a number is assigned to Caroline, she should write the number in the upper right-hand corner of the form and mail it to the Internal Revenue Service. Once assigned a number, she can begin using it right away. Karen reviews the form with Caroline to determine if Caroline has any questions.

Next, Karen pulls out a Notice Under Fictitious Name Law form and tells Caroline to complete the form and send it to a newspaper of general circulation in the county with the applicable fee. Under applicable state laws, the Notice must be published once, after which the paper will provide Caroline with a Proof of Publication and an Application for Fictitious Name Registration. Caroline is instructed to send a copy of the Proof of Publication together with the application and the applicable filing fee to the Division of Corporations, which is the governmental body handling fictitious name registration in the state. Karen provides Caroline with the appropriate address and filing fee amount. She informs Caroline that a fictitious name registration is valid for five years under state law and must then be refiled to keep the registration active.

Finally, Karen asks Caroline if she has found office space and whether she has filed for or acquired an occupational license. Caroline responds that she has found a possible location and is anxious to sign the lease. Karen instructs Caroline to go down to City Hall with a copy of the lease after signing and apply for an occupational license in person. In her city, an occupational license must be applied for in person. Once the license is obtained, Caroline must display it in a prominent place.

Karen quickly jots down a checklist and gives it Caroline. It reads as follows:

1. Federal Employer Identification Number
    (i)   Fill out SS-4 form
    (ii)   Call the IRS to obtain number over the phone
    (iii) Mail form
2. Notice Under Fictitious Name Law
    (i)   Fill out form to be mailed (or hand-delivered) to major local newspaper, such as The Herald
    (ii)   Send form together with fee (The Herald presently charges $65)
    (iii) Obtain Proof of Publication and application form (should be provided by the newspaper)

3.   Fictitious Name Registration Application
  (i)   Fill out form to be mailed to:
        Division of Corporations, Department of State
        P.O. Box 1000
        Capitol City, Any State
  (ii)   Mail with statutory filing fee of $100
4.   Occupational License
  (i)   Take lease to City Hall
  (ii)   Complete application (they will want to know the square foot-age and the name and address of the lessor, so have this infor-mation available. They will also ask for a copy of your fictitious name registration.)
  (iii)   Pay license fee of $125

Having thanked both Thomas and Karen for their assistance, Caroline follows the steps outlined above. She is able to negotiate and sign a lease with CCC Commercial Group, Inc. for office space in an executive suites building, so Caroline has an office address to use on her forms. Her completed SS-4 form is found above in Exhibit 2.8. Having received her employer identification

---

EXHIBIT 2.9

Notice Under Fictitious Name Law

NOTICE IS HEREBY GIVEN that the undersigned, desiring to engage in business under the fictitious name of __Ability Plus Educational Testing and Consulting Services__, located at ___334 Prestwick Avenue, Suite 351___, in the City of __Any City__, County of __Any County__, Any State, __00000__ intends to register the said name with the Division of Corporations of the Department of State.

Dated: ___February 12, 1997___

_____Caroline Matthews_____
      Owner's Name

Phone: ___(000) 251-5369___

Send Proof of Publication to: ___Caroline Matthews___
966 Clayton Street, Any City, Any State 00000

number over the phone, she can include it when requested on any subsequent form work. She decides to use the services of The Herald in publishing her fictitious name. Her completed notice form and subsequent registration application are set out in Exhibits 2.9 and 2.10.

Because her city requires proof of fictitious name registration prior to ob-

---

EXHIBIT 2.10

Application for Registration of Fictitious Name

SECTION I:

1. Fictitious Name to be Registered: Ability Plus Educational Testing and Consulting Services

2. Mailing Address of Business: 334 Prestwick Avenue, Suite 351 Any City, Any State 00000

3. FEI Number: 98-7654321   _____ Applied For

    _____ Not Applicable

SECTION II: OWNER OF FICTITIOUS NAME IF INDIVIDUAL:

1. Matthews   Caroline   E.
    Last   First   Middle Initial

2. 966 Clayton Street, Any City, Any State 00000
    Home Address

3. SS#:   000-00-0000

SECTION III: OWNER OF FICTITIOUS NAME IF PARTNERSHIP, CORPORATION, OR OTHER BUSINESS ENTITY:

1. Name of Business Entity: Not Applicable

2. Address: _____

3. FEI Number: _____

EXHIBIT 2.10   *Continued*

SECTION IV:

I the undersigned, being the party owning interest in the above fictitious name, certify that the information indicated on this form is true and accurate. I further certify that the fictitious name shown in Section I of this form has been advertised at least once in a newspaper as defined in Chapter 40, Statutes of Any State, in the county where the applicant's principal place of business is located. I understand that the signature below shall have the same legal effect as if made under oath.

Caroline Matthews	March 2, 1997
Signature of Owner or Owner's Representative	Date

(000) 251-5369
Telephone Number

taining an occupational license if one is doing business under a name other than one's legal name, Caroline waits until she receives a certificate of fictitious name registration before filing her occupational license application, which reads as follows in Exhibit 2.11:

EXHIBIT 2.11

Application for Occupational License
Any City

CONTACT PERSON: Caroline Matthews

TELEPHONE: (000) 277-0909

CHECK ONE: __X__ New Business   _____ Change Address

_____ Change Ownership   _____ Other (specify) _____

COMPANY NAME: Ability Plus Educational Testing and Consulting Services

BUSINESS TEL.: (000) 251-5369

EXHIBIT 2.11 *Continued*

BUSINESS ADDRESS: 334 Prestwick Avenue, Suite 351
Any City, Any State 00000

MAILING ADDRESS (If different from business address): Same as above

DESCRIBE EXACT NATURE OF BUSINESS: Providing educational testing and consulting services

CHECK ONE: __X__ Sole Proprietorship   _____ Partnership

_____ Limited Partnership   _____ Corporation

_____ Limited Liability Company

FEDERAL EMPLOYER I.D. NO: 98-7654321

IF CHANGE OF BUSINESS ADDRESS, LIST PREVIOUS BUSINESS ADDRESS:
Not applicable

SQUARE FOOTAGE: 200 square feet

NUMBER OF EMPLOYEES (including self): __2__

ARE THERE ANY INTERIOR/EXTERIOR BUILDING ALTERATIONS TO BE PERFORMED PRIOR TO OCCUPANCY? _____ Yes __X__ No

If yes, please describe: _____

PROPERTY OWNER FOR BUSINESS ADDRESS:

NAME: CCC Commercial Group, Inc.

ADDRESS: 8500 Executive Drive
Any City, Any State 00000

COUNTY PROPERTY IDENTIFICATION NUMBER: 00-01-02-03-04-05678

I AFFIRM THAT THE INFORMATION GIVEN ON THIS DOCUMENT IS TRUE TO THE BEST OF MY KNOWLEDGE AND BELIEF.

Caroline Matthews   March 15, 1997

Signature of Authorized Representative   Date

Chapter Summary

1. A sole proprietorship is an unincorporated business owned by one person which is considered an extension of that individual and does not exist as a separate entity in its own right. It offers simplicity and low cost of organization, individual control, flexibility, and favorable tax treatment. It also carries with it unlimited personal liability, limited means of raising capital, and no framework for continuity.

2. A sole proprietor typically looks to some form of debt financing to raise start-up capital for his or her business. This may take the form of a short-term, intermediate-term, or long-term loan from a bank or finance company. Other financing mechanisms include trade credit, accounts receivable financing, and factoring.

3. All business profits and losses are recorded as part of the sole proprietor's individual 1040 tax return on Schedule C or Schedule C-EZ. Ordinary and necessary business expenses may be deducted and capital expenses may be depreciated, amortized, or depleted. If the sole proprietor works out of his or her home, he or she may deduct business expenses that apply to those portions of the home that are used exclusively for business, and these expenses must be recorded and submitted on Form 8829.

4. A sole proprietor who hires employees must withhold federal income, social security, and Medicare taxes, and must file estimated tax returns for self-employment tax.

5. A sole proprietor is considered an employee for purposes of participating in a retirement plan and may choose among several options, including an IRA, an SEP-IRA, and a Keogh plan. The allowable maximum contributions for each plan varies, as does the contribution for an employee versus a self-employed individual.

6. The few formalities most sole proprietors must meet prior to opening a business include obtaining the necessary professional, occupational, and special licenses or permits; filing a fictitious name registration, certificate, or affidavit; and acquiring a federal employer identification number (if hiring employees, creating a Keogh plan, or filing alcohol, firearms, or other special returns).

7. A sole proprietor must set up meticulous bookkeeping methods from the start, keeping track of personnel records, tax records, and accounting records.

Review Questions

1. A client is a landscape designer who has worked for a landscape design company for four years and now wants to start her own business. She is not certain whether to incorporate or run her business as a sole proprietorship. What information would aid in evaluating her best alternative?

2. List in order the steps to be taken to set up a business as a sole proprietorship.

3. A client is a computer software consultant who wants to run his business out of his home. What steps must he take in order to deduct expenses for business use of a home?

4. If a sole proprietor wishes to set up a retirement plan for herself and her spouse, what options are available besides an IRA?

5. What insurance needs might a sole proprietor have?

KEY TERMS

accounts receivable financing

amortization

capital expense

debt financing

depletion

depreciation

equity financing

factoring

fictitious name registration

finance company

form SS-4

intermediate-term financing

IRA

Keogh plan

long-term financing

money purchase pension plan

one-participant plan

profit-sharing plan

qualified plan

salary reduction arrangement

secured loan

short-term financing

simplified employee pension

sole proprietorship

stock bonus plan

trade credit

unsecured loan

3 | *General Partnerships*

Upon completion of this chapter, the student will:

- understand the advantages and disadvantages of choosing a general partnership as a business format
- understand the role uniform laws play in general partnership law and know the distinctions between the Uniform Partnership Act and the Revised Uniform Partnership Act
- know how to form a general partnership, including how to draft a general partnership agreement
- know the distinction between dissociation and dissolution and the resulting impact of each on the continuance or termination of a general partnership
- know the various options available for valuation of a partnership business and partner buyout

INTRODUCTION

In the last chapter we looked at the simplest of the available business structures, a sole proprietorship. Should a client desire to start a business together with one or more associates, one possibility is the formation of a general partnership.

A **general partnership** (often simply referred to as a "partnership") consists of a voluntary association of two or more persons for the purpose of conducting a for-profit enterprise. Each component of this definition has legal significance. The term "persons" as used in this context includes not only individuals, but also general and limited partnerships, limited liability companies, corporations, and other entities. Thus, it is possible to form a partnership in which a general partnership and a corporation are partners. A minor may be a partner (this most often occurs in **family partnerships**, discussed below in the section dealing with tax considerations) although the minor's capacity to act as a partner may be restricted. Some partners may be governed not only by partnership law but other laws or documents as well. For example, a corporation as a general partner is governed not only by partnership law and the terms of the partnership agreement, but also by its articles of incorporation and its state's corporate statutes. Because the association of the partners is voluntary, any partner may withdraw at will, subject to the terms of the partnership agreement. The proviso that the enterprise in which the business is engaged must be for-profit eliminates the possibility of nonprofit organizations adopting this type of business structure.

This chapter will focus on the statutory and common law principles governing partnerships as well as the advantages and disadvantages of this business structure. Additionally, this chapter will outline the steps that you, as a paralegal, must take in assisting a client with the formalities required for a general partnership.

NATURE OF A GENERAL PARTNERSHIP

General partnerships are governed by state statutes and common law principles including contract law, the latter owing to the fact that general partnerships exist and operate under the terms of a partnership agreement. Unless state statutes dictate to the contrary, a partnership agreement does not have to be written to be legally valid. At present, most state statutes require few formalities for the creation of a general partnership and do not subject them to the same formalities as limited partnerships, limited liability companies, or corporations in terms of public filings or statutory qualifications to conduct business in other states. This provides general partnerships with greater privacy and flexibility, as well as fewer organizational costs than most other business structures. It should be noted, however, that this lack of formality may change. Under the Revised Uniform Partnership Act (discussed in detail below), public filing statements have been made optional for state adoption and states may move toward requiring or permitting various documents to be filed with the secretary of state.

Each partner in a general partnership has the right to participate in the management and operation of the business. Unless the partnership agreement states otherwise each partner has an equal voice and responsibility in the carrying out of partnership affairs and matters are decided by a majority vote.

Each partner also has a proportionate share, or **partnership interest** in the business, with partners sharing profits and losses equally unless the partnership agreement provides for some other apportionment. This partnership interest does not entitle any partner to particular partnership property. Rather, it typically reflects that partner's equity interest in the business. A partner usually acquires this interest by making a capital contribution to the partnership. However, a partner may contribute property and/or services instead of or in addition to a capital contribution. A partnership interest is considered a personal property right. Although the creditor of a specific partner may not attach or obtain a judgment on partnership property, the creditor may make a request to a court for a charging order (a lien) against that partner's partnership interest in the business.

A partnership interest may be freely transferred or assigned to another unless the partnership agreement specifically imposes restrictions on such a transfer. The transfer of a partnership interest does not make the transferee a partner. Because a partnership is a voluntary association, a new or different partner cannot be forced on the others. The Roman law concept of *delectus personae*, choice of persons, prevails. Thus, all partners must unanimously consent before the transferee is conferred partner status. Until or unless that is done, the transferee simply is entitled to the share of profits reflected by the transferor's partnership interest.

The partnership structure enables a business to raise capital through either equity or debt financing, or a combination of the two. Additional capital contributions may be required of existing partners or new partners added as the business expands. This allows for some flexibility. The same debt financing resources available to a sole proprietor are available to a partnership. When a financing institution looks at a partnership as a potential customer and calculates its risk, it looks at the aggregation of the partners' credit history and collateral. This may fare well or ill for the partnership, depending on the creditworthiness of each partner.

Partners in a general partnership have unlimited personal liability for partnership debts and obligations. Creditors of the general partnership are required, however, under the rule of **marshaling of assets**, to look to partnership property first in the satisfaction of debts. If these prove inadequate, only then may the creditors seek satisfaction by proceeding against the individual assets of the partners. A new, incoming partner typically is not personally responsible for any debts or obligations acquired prior to his or her admission unless he or she expressly agrees to assume them. The capital contribution of the incoming partner may, however, be applied to partnership debts. Conversely, a withdrawing partner may remain liable for partnership debts incurred while a partner as well as those incurred after his or her withdrawal unless the partnership agrees to release that partner from those obligations and partnership creditors are so informed.

General partnerships are not taxed as an entity and thus not subject to the double taxation quandary of corporations. Each partner pays income tax, on his or her proportionate share of income in the business, reflected in an informational return the general partnership is required to file with the Internal Revenue Service.

A general partnership's continuity may be determined by state law or the partnership agreement. Most state law acts as a default measure in this area, requiring a partnership to terminate under certain enumerated circumstances unless the partnership agreement states otherwise. Traditionally, a general partnership terminated whenever a partner retired, died, was adjudicated insane or bankrupt, or was expelled. While this no longer is necessarily the case (see detailed discussion below), a general partnership's life is of a more limited duration than that of a corporation, which can continue perpetually.

Some partnerships, **term partnerships**, are specifically structured to exist for a limited term and then terminate at the end of the specified term. **Joint ventures**, which have many of the legal characteristics of general partnerships, and indeed are governed by general partnership law, are similar but are designed to carry out a particular venture, and then terminate upon its completion. The phrase "term partnership" is sometimes used to embrace both concepts. Joint ventures are common in real estate acquisition and mineral prospecting, but may be created to carry out other activities.

PARTNERS AND THE LAW OF AGENCY

The concept of **agency** is one in which one party (the **agent**) acts for or represents another party (the **principal**) through the implied or actual consent of the principal. The agent may be a general partner in a partnership, an officer in a corporation, a manager in a limited liability company, an employee of a business, an owner of a business, and in some instances an independent contractor.

Thus, the concept and law of agency is not the exclusive province of general partnerships. However, both case law and statutory law seem to indicate that it is here that it plays its most considerable role.

A partner in a general partnership is an agent of that partnership (and of the other partners) with the **apparent authority** (sometimes referred to as **ostensible authority**) to bind the partnership by his or her acts. Apparent authority is authority a principal (in this case, the partnership) either knowingly or negligently allows an agent (the partners) to assume or authority which a principal holds an agent out as possessing. A partner additionally has the **actual authority** to bind the partnership, meaning that a partner is given authority by agreement. This agreement may be express (put into words, written or oral) or implied (not put into words but implied by the relationship between the parties, here the partner and the partnership). Providing partners with agency authority is necessary for the proper functioning of the partnership. Partners are co-agents, in that each partner shares authority with the other(s) in transacting business on behalf of the partnership.

The partner, acting as an agent for the partnership (as principal) is typically acting on behalf of a **disclosed principal**. This means that the third party knows on whose behalf the partner, as agent, is acting. While one seldomly comes across the circumstances when dealing with partnerships as principals and partners as agents, it is possible for agents to transact on behalf of **partially disclosed** or even **undisclosed principals**. If a third party knows that someone is acting as an agent for a principal but does not know who the principal is, the principal is considered **partially disclosed**. As the term implies, when an agent is acting on behalf of an **undisclosed** principal, the third party is unaware of the fact that an agency relationship exists.

Although this term is not specifically used in either the Uniform Partnership Act nor the Revised Uniform Partnership Act (discussed below), a partner is considered a general agent of the partnership and the other partners in matters concerning the partnership business. A **general agent** is one given authority to act on behalf of the principal in all matters concerning the principal's business. This is contrasted with a **special agent**, one given authority to act in a specific transaction or with regard to a specific matter only. Because partners are general agents, the potential for liability on behalf of the partnership and each partner is greater. The partnership is liable not only for contractual transactions entered into by a partner, but also for the torts of a partner committed while acting in the ordinary course of the business of the partnership.

It should be noted that the partnership is also liable through the doctrine of **vicarious liability** (indirect legal responsibility) for torts committed by employees of the partnership acting within the scope of employment. Although the general law of agency, which applies to all agency relationships and not just that of partners as agent, deems that agents and principals have **fiduciary duties** (duties brought about by the special relationship of trust) with regard to each other, partnership law has created its own statutory fiduciary duties which apply to partners in a general partnership. These duties are discussed in the next section.

THE UNIFORM PARTNERSHIP ACT AND THE REVISED UNIFORM PARTNERSHIP ACT

Although each state has its own statutes governing the law of partnerships, every state, with the exception of Louisiana, has patterned these statutes on a uniform law of partnership, be it the original Uniform Partnership Act or the more recent Revised Uniform Partnership Act. (A **uniform law** is a law in a particular subject area, in this instance, partnerships, that is approved by the Commissioners on Uniform State Laws and is adopted in whole or in part by individual states.) A uniform law of partnership was considered by the National Conference of Commissioners as early as 1902, with the first Uniform Partnership Act finally approved in 1914. This original **Uniform Partnership Act** (to be referred to hereinafter in this chapter as the **UPA**) underwent very few changes until a drafting committee was appointed in 1987 to update and revise it. This drafting committee was created as a response to the American Bar Association's recommendation that extensive revisions to the UPA were needed. The result was a restyled Uniform Partnership Act (1994), which is often referred to as the "Revised Act" or the **Revised Uniform Partnership Act** (to be referred to hereinafter in this chapter as the **RUPA**).

The RUPA was approved by the American Bar Association in 1994 and as of the time of this writing has been enacted by a handful of states and introduced into the state legislatures of several more, with the likelihood of still more following suit. Because presently the majority of states are operating under statutes paralleling the UPA while many are considering revising their statutes in keeping with the RUPA, the differences between the two uniform acts must be considered.

A.   *Entity Theory versus Aggregate Theory*

One significant change in the uniform law is the move toward an "entity" theory of partnerships. The question asked by the drafters of the original act was "What is a partnership?" Is a partnership a legal entity separate and apart from its owners, as is the case with a corporation? Or is a partnership truly an aggregate of its owners? Prior to the creation of the UPA, there existed the mercantile tradition, which espoused the **entity theory** of partnerships, as well as the common law, which espoused the **aggregate theory** of partnerships. (Mercantile law, based on the customs of trade, was an area of law that arose in medieval England and developed separately from the common law of the main English courts. Much of early English partnership law was an outgrowth of mercantile law.)

Under the entity theory, a partnership is a legal entity having an existence separate from the existence of the individual partners, possessing legal rights (such as owning property in the business name) as well as legal obligations (such as the mandatory filing of an annual informational return with the Internal Revenue Service in the business name). Under the aggregate theory, a partnership is an association of persons. This theory is bolstered by the fact that each partner is individually liable for partnership debts and that all partnership income is realized by the individual partners and taxed accordingly. Both the entity and aggregate theories had merit and what resulted was adoption of a uniform law, the UPA, encompassing aspects of both.

The RUPA more strongly embraces the entity theory than its predecessor by distinctly stating, in Section 201, that a partnership is an entity distinct from its partners. It also contains a new provision, Section 307, providing that a partnership may sue and be sued in the partnership name, as well as another new provision, Section 405(a), allowing a partnership itself to maintain an action against a partner for any breach of the partnership agreement or violation of a duty owed, thus following the entity theory. Section 25(1) of the UPA states that partnership property is held as a tenancy in partnership, with all partners as co-owners, reflecting the aggregate theory of partnership. Section 501 of the RUPA, adopting the entity theory, states that partnership property is owned by the entity, partners are not co-owners and have no interest in partnership property that can be transferred, either voluntarily or involuntarily.

Nonetheless, the RUPA does still recognize the aggregate approach toward partners' liability, holding partners jointly and severally liable (meaning that a third party may bring suit against the partners collectively or individually or both). As a matter of fact, in this regard the RUPA, in Section 306, goes further than the UPA, imposing joint and several liability on the partners for all partnership obligations. Section 15 of the UPA imposes joint and several liability on the partners for torts, but imposes only joint, not several, liability for contracts.

B. Governing of Limited Partnerships

A second significant difference between the UPA and the RUPA is that the RUPA does not encompass limited partnerships. Although limited partnerships, discussed at length in the next chapter, have their own uniform laws, the UPA provided for the governing of limited partnerships in cases not provided for in the Uniform Limited Partnership Act and the Revised Uniform Limited Partnership Act. In its definitional section, the RUPA's definition of "partnership" explicitly excludes limited partnerships by defining a partnership as one formed under Section 202 of the RUPA (the section governing the formation of general partnerships).

C.   Public Filing Statements

A third distinction between the UPA and the RUPA is the addition in the RUPA of a section pertaining to the execution, filing, and recording of "statements." Historically, general partnerships have not been required to submit public filing statements with governmental agencies in the manner of limited partnerships, limited liability companies, and corporations. This lack of requirement afforded a partnership greater privacy and fewer formalities in formation. The drafters of the RUPA added this provision in the belief that partnerships may soon find themselves forced to discard their prior informalities as lenders, transferees of partnership property, and others push for the public filing of statements. What the RUPA does in Section 105 is make the filing of statements voluntary, but nevertheless provides procedures to follow in the event they are required. It anticipates that any state adopting a public filing requirement will assign the responsibility to the secretary of state. Thus, partnerships wishing to expand business into other states will now have to check into the reporting and filing requirements of those states to ascertain if filing is required or permitted.

D.   Internal Matters

There are some differences in the way the UPA and the RUPA address internal matters such as choice of law in resolving internal affairs, the authority a partner has to bind the partnership, and the resolving of financial disputes through an accounting. The RUPA adds a provision not contained in the UPA pertaining to a partnership's internal relations, providing that the law of the jurisdiction in which a partnership has its principal office is the law by which the partnership will govern its internal affairs. This new provision is meant to be a default provision, in the event that the partnership agreement is silent on this matter.

Under both the UPA and the RUPA, a partner is an agent of the partnership, but there are some differences. The UPA specifically lists certain acts that require the unanimous consent of the partners before the partnership is bound. The RUPA omits such a listing, leaving this area more flexible.

The RUPA provides for an **accounting** (a formal rendition of account) as to partnership business in Section 405(b), as does the UPA in Section 22, but the RUPA embraces a new attitude which allows partners access to the courts when resolving partnership claims and does not require that an accounting be done as a prerequisite to such access.

E.   Transfer of Partnership Property

Section 302 of the RUPA governs the transfer of partnership property. While the UPA, in Section 10, provides for the transfer of real property that is partnership property, it does not make provision for the transfer of personal property. The RUPA governs both the transfer of real property and the transfer of personal property acquired by instrument and held in the name of the partnership or in the name of one or more of the partners. Additionally, the RUPA makes provision for the situation in which all of the partners' interests are held by one person, such as a surviving partner. The UPA does not address this situation. Under the RUPA, the surviving partner receives clear record title.

F.   Statement of Authority

The RUPA, influenced by trends in California and Georgia, adds a new provision, Section 303, allowing the optional filing of a **statement of authority**. Such a statement specifies the names of the partners authorized to carry out certain activities, such as the execution of instruments transferring real property and the transaction of other business on behalf of the partnership. This statement of authority may also limit partners' authority. The incentive is to facilitate the transfer of real property in the name of the partnership. The UPA does not include such a provision. A complementary Section 304 has been added to the RUPA providing for the optional filing of a **statement of denial**, allowing one to deny any factual allegation asserted in the statement of authority, including the denial of one's own status as a partner or of another's status or authority as a partner. Note that Section 303 of the RUPA only concerns the authority of partners to bind the partnership to third parties and that it does not affect relations among the partners, which are governed by the partnership agreement.

An additional word of caution is advised when drafting a statement of authority because tax implications may result. The Internal Revenue Service presently does not tax a general partnership as a separate entity. One of the determining factors in the tax status of a business is the concept of centralization of management. Clearly, this is not the only determining factor. The Internal Revenue Service looks at other factors as well, such as continuity of life, limited liability, and free transferability of interests. However, if centralization of management exists, the Service may be more likely to consider the business a separate entity for tax purposes. One indication of centralized management is the limitation on agency authority. While listing partners' names on a statement of authority to act on behalf of the partnership should present no problem, limiting and/or extending agency power to some partners and not to others may be interpreted as an attempt to centralize management.

G. Fiduciary Duties

Although the UPA indicates that a partner is a fiduciary (a person holding a special obligation of trust), it touches only briefly on the matter. The RUPA, in Section 404, provides more extensive treatment of the fiduciary duties of partners. It states that a partner owes to the partnership and to the other partners a duty of loyalty, and then provides specific rules comprising a partner's duty of loyalty. Further, it establishes a statutory duty of care absent from the UPA. The RUPA adopts gross negligence as the imposed standard of care and states that the duty of care may be reduced, but not eliminated by agreement. The RUPA also provides for the obligation of good faith and fair dealing, which is a contract concept. This is not included in the UPA. Again, this obligation may not be eliminated by agreement, although a partnership agreement may set forth the standards by which this obligation is met. Finally, Section 404 of the RUPA makes it clear that a partner is not a trustee, and thus cannot be held to the same standards. This means that acting in one's own individual interest does not, of itself, make a partner's conduct improper.

H. Termination of the Partnership

The RUPA makes a major departure from the UPA when it comes to partnership dissolution. The RUPA in Section 601 utilizes (but does not define) a new term, "dissociation," instead of the term "dissolution" which, under the RUPA is retained but used in a different fashion. Under the RUPA, a partner's dissociation from the partnership does not necessarily cause a dissolution of the partnership. Section 601 lists the events that cause a partner's voluntary dissociation and expulsion and states the residual rights and duties of a dissociated partner.

While the UPA in Section 31(1)(d) only allows expulsion of a partner if so provided in the partnership agreement, Section 601(4) of the RUPA allows expulsion by unanimous vote, even if the partnership agreement does not so authorize. Further, while the UPA in Section 31(4) requires dissolution of a partnership upon the death of a partner in absence of an agreement by the remaining partners to continue, the RUPA in Section 601(7)(i) provides that such an event causes dissociation of the deceased partner rather than dissolution of the partnership. Under Section 603 of the RUPA, a partner's dissociation, caused by whatever means, results in either a buyout of that partner's interest or the dissolution and winding up of partnership business. Under Section 38 of the UPA, on the other hand, every withdrawal and expulsion from the partnership results in a dissolution unless the partnership agreement provides otherwise. Because of this change, a new Article 7 was added to the RUPA, providing for the buyout of a dissociated partner's interest.

Under the RUPA, a partnership is bound by a dissociated partner's acts with regard to the partnership for two years after that partner's dissociation. However, this is the case if, and only if, the third party to the transaction reasonably believed that the dissociated partner was still a partner in the partnership and did not have notice indicating the contrary. Section 704 of the RUPA allows the filing of a **statement of dissociation** which destroys a dissociated partner's authority. Ninety days after the filing of this statement, third parties are deemed to have notice of the dissociation. The UPA makes no such provision. Further, Section 805(a) of the RUPA provides that after dissolution of a partnership, any partner who has not been wrongfully dissociated may file a **statement of dissolution**, which serves as notice of the limitations of a partner's authority. The same ninety-day rule applies here as it does with a statement of dissociation. A more detailed discussion of dissociation and dissolution is provided further along in this chapter.

The RUPA does not make the distinction made in Section 40(b) of the UPA regarding distribution of a partner's capital contribution and a partner's profit. Section 807(b) of the RUPA speaks only in general terms of a partner's right to his or her distribution during the liquidation of the partnership.

I. *Conversions and Mergers*

Finally, the RUPA adds a new Article 9 addressing the topics of conversions and mergers, which are not found in the UPA, providing statutory authority for these transactions. The purpose of Article 9 is to provide guidance and guidelines, but its provisions are not mandatory. Note that unlike elsewhere in the RUPA, Article 9 necessarily deals with both general and limited partnerships, because it allows conversion of a general partnership to a limited partnership and conversion of a limited partnership to a general partnership. Further, Section 905, dealing with merger, allows the surviving entity to be either a general or a limited partnership. Section 907(a) allows for the filing of a statement of merger containing the name of each party to the merger, the name and address of the surviving entity, and whether it is a general or limited partnership. Exhibit 3.1 provides a comparison chart of the UPA and the RUPA.

EXHIBIT 3.1

Comparison Chart of the UPA and the RUPA

	UPA	RUPA
1. THEORIES OF PARTNERSHIP:	Applies both the entity and aggregate theories.	Adopts the entity theory.
2. PARTNERS' INTEREST IN PARTNERSHIP PROPERTY:	Partners are co-owners as tenants in partnership.	Partners have no interest.
3. PARTNERS' LIABILITY:	Joint and several for torts; joint but not several for contracts.	Joint and several for all partnership obligations.
4. LIMITED PARTNERSHIPS:	Covers them in areas not covered by the ULPA or the RULPA.	Does not govern them.
5. PUBLIC FILINGS:	No provision.	Provides for voluntary filings and establishes procedures.
6. INTERNAL RELATIONS:	No provision.	Governed by the law of the jurisdiction of the principal office.
7. AGENCY:	Lists certain acts requiring unanimous consent of partners to bind the partnership.	Omits listing of certain acts requiring unanimous consent of partners to bind the partnership.

EXHIBIT 3.1   *Continued*

	UPA	RUPA
8. TRANSFER OF PART-NERSHIP PROPERTY:	Governs only real property.	Governs real and personal property. Gives surviving partner clear record title.
9. STATEMENT OF AUTHORITY:	No provision.	Makes provision for optional filing. Also allows optional filing of statement of denial.
10. FIDUCIARY DUTIES:	Partner is a fiduciary.	Extensive treatment. Duty of loyalty and care (standard of care is gross negligence). Obligation of good faith and fair dealing. A partner is not a trustee.
11. ACCOUNTING:	Prerequisite to court action in resolving partnership disputes.	Not a prerequisite to court action in resolving partnership disputes.
12. DISSOLUTION:	Partnership is dissolved when a partner leaves.	Provides for "dissociation" when a partner leaves; does not necessarily result in dissolution.
13. STATEMENT OF DISSOCIATION:	No provision.	Allows for the filing of such statement which cuts off dissociated partner's authority and provides constructive notice to third parties.
14. STATEMENT OF DISSOLUTION:	No provision.	Allows for the filing of such statement which limits a partner's authority and provides constructive notice to third parties.
15. CONVERSION AND MERGER:	No provision.	Provides specific statutory authority for both. Allows for the filing of a statement of merger.

TAX CONSIDERATIONS

A.   *Tax Filings*

Although a partnership is considered an "entity" under the Revised Uniform Partnership Act, the Internal Revenue Service does not tax it as such. The partnership, as an entity, is required to file an informational tax return, a Form 1065 (see Exhibit 3.2), each year but the partnership itself does not pay federal or state income taxes. Each partner reports his or her share of profits and losses on his or her own individual tax return. The informational tax return, signed by a general partner, supplies the names and addresses of each partner, all partnership income and deductions, and each partner's distributive share. This return, when filed by the partnership, enables the Internal Revenue Service to determine whether each partner has reported accurately his or her distributive share of the earnings from the business.

A partnership begins filing this return the first year in which it has realized income or incurred deductions and continues filing it each subsequent tax year even if it has not realized income for the year. The partnership must provide each partner with a Schedule K-1 (see Exhibit 3.3) on or before the date the Form 1065 must be filed, indicating each partner's share of income, deductions and credits. The Schedule K-1 also indicates where to include each item on the partner's individual 1040.

A partnership may choose its tax year; however, if all partners are individuals, the tax year is generally the calendar year. According to the Internal Revenue Service, the required tax year is the majority interest tax year. If one or more partners having the same tax year own a majority interest in partnership profits and capital, the partnership must use the tax year of those partners. In the event that there is no majority interest tax year, the partnership must use the tax year of all its principal partners. A principal partner is one who has a 5 percent or more interest in the partnership. If the partnership can show an acceptable business purpose for using a tax year other than its required tax year, the Internal Revenue Service will allow use of a different tax year. The partnership informational tax return must be filed by the fifteenth day of the fourth month following the close of the partnership tax year. Failure to file the return in a timely fashion results in assessed penalties. At present, the penalty is $50 times the total number of partners in the partnership during any part of the tax year for each month (or part of a month) the return is late or incomplete, up to five months.

Each partner is required to pay any required estimated taxes on his or her distributive share of partnership profits. As of the date of this writing, the

EXHIBIT 3.2

Form **1065**	**U.S. Partnership Return of Income**	OMB No. 1545-0099
Department of the Treasury Internal Revenue Service	For calendar year 1995, or tax year beginning .... , 1995, and ending .... , 19 .... . ▶ **See separate instructions.**	**1995**

A Principal business activity	Use the IRS label. Other-wise, please print or type.	Name of partnership	D Employer identification number
B Principal product or service		Number, street, and room or suite no. (If a P.O. box, see page 10 of the instructions.)	E Date business started
C Business code number		City or town, state, and ZIP code	F Total assets (see page 10 of the instructions) $

G Check applicable boxes: **(1)** ☐ Initial return **(2)** ☐ Final return **(3)** ☐ Change in address **(4)** ☐ Amended return
H Check accounting method: **(1)** ☐ Cash **(2)** ☐ Accrual **(3)** ☐ Other (specify) ▶ ....
I Number of Schedules K-1. Attach one for each person who was a partner at any time during the tax year ▶ ....

Caution: *Include **only** trade or business income and expenses on lines 1a through 22 below. See the instructions for more information.*

Income	1a	Gross receipts or sales	1a		
	b	Less returns and allowances	1b		1c
	2	Cost of goods sold (Schedule A, line 8)			2
	3	Gross profit. Subtract line 2 from line 1c			3
	4	Ordinary income (loss) from other partnerships, estates, and trusts *(attach schedule)*. . .			4
	5	Net farm profit (loss) *(attach Schedule F (Form 1040))*			5
	6	Net gain (loss) from Form 4797, Part II, line 20			6
	7	Other income (loss) *(attach schedule)*			7
	8	**Total income (loss).** Combine lines 3 through 7			8

Deductions (see page 11 of the instructions for limitations)	9	Salaries and wages (other than to partners) (less employment credits)			9
	10	Guaranteed payments to partners			10
	11	Repairs and maintenance			11
	12	Bad debts			12
	13	Rent			13
	14	Taxes and licenses			14
	15	Interest			15
	16a	Depreciation (if required, attach Form 4562)	16a		
	b	Less depreciation reported on Schedule A and elsewhere on return	16b		16c
	17	Depletion (**Do not deduct oil and gas depletion.**)			17
	18	Retirement plans, etc.			18
	19	Employee benefit programs			19
	20	Other deductions *(attach schedule)*			20
	21	**Total deductions.** Add the amounts shown in the far right column for lines 9 through 20 .			21

	22	**Ordinary income (loss)** from trade or business activities. Subtract line 21 from line 8 . .	22

Please Sign Here
Under penalties of perjury, I declare that I have examined this return, including accompanying schedules and statements, and to the best of my knowledge and belief, it is true, correct, and complete. Declaration of preparer (other than general partner or limited liability company member) is based on all information of which preparer has any knowledge.

▶ Signature of general partner or limited liability company member   ▶ Date

Paid Preparer's Use Only	Preparer's signature ▶	Date	Check if self-employed ▶ ☐	Preparer's social security no.
	Firm's name (or yours if self-employed) and address ▶		EIN ▶	
			ZIP code ▶	

For Paperwork Reduction Act Notice, see page 1 of separate instructions.   Cat. No. 11390Z   Form **1065** (1995)

EXHIBIT 3.2 *Continued*

Form 1065 (1995)   Page **2**

Schedule A   Cost of Goods Sold (see page 13 of the instructions)

1	Inventory at beginning of year	1
2	Purchases less cost of items withdrawn for personal use	2
3	Cost of labor	3
4	Additional section 263A costs *(attach schedule)*	4
5	Other costs *(attach schedule)*	5
6	**Total.** Add lines 1 through 5	6
7	Inventory at end of year	7
8	**Cost of goods sold.** Subtract line 7 from line 6. Enter here and on page 1, line 2	8

9a Check all methods used for valuing closing inventory:
    (i) ☐ Cost as described in Regulations section 1.471-3
    (ii) ☐ Lower of cost or market as described in Regulations section 1.471-4
    (iii) ☐ Other (specify method used and attach explanation) ▶ ....
  b Check this box if there was a writedown of "subnormal" goods as described in Regulations section 1.471-2(c). . . . ▶ ☐
  c Check this box if the LIFO inventory method was adopted this tax year for any goods *(if checked, attach Form 970)* . . ▶ ☐
  d Do the rules of section 263A (for property produced or acquired for resale) apply to the partnership? . . ☐ **Yes** ☐ **No**
  e Was there any change in determining quantities, cost, or valuations between opening and closing inventory? ☐ **Yes** ☐ **No**
    If "Yes," attach explanation.

Schedule B   Other Information

		Yes	No
1	What type of entity is filing this return?		
	Check the applicable box ▶ ☐ General partnership ☐ Limited partnership ☐ Limited liability company		
2	Are any partners in this partnership also partnerships?		
3	Is this partnership a partner in another partnership?		
4	Is this partnership subject to the consolidated audit procedures of sections 6221 through 6233? If "Yes," see **Designation of Tax Matters Partner** below		
5	Does this partnership meet **ALL THREE** of the following requirements?		
a	The partnership's total receipts for the tax year were less than $250,000;		
b	The partnership's total assets at the end of the tax year were less than $600,000; **AND**		
c	Schedules K-1 are filed with the return and furnished to the partners on or before the due date (including extensions) for the partnership return.		
	If "Yes," the partnership is not required to complete Schedules L, M-1, and M-2; Item F on page 1 of Form 1065; or Item J on Schedule K-1		
6	Does this partnership have any foreign partners?		
7	Is this partnership a publicly traded partnership as defined in section 469(k)(2)?		
8	Has this partnership filed, or is it required to file, **Form 8264,** Application for Registration of a Tax Shelter? . .		
9	At any time during calendar year 1995, did the partnership have an interest in or a signature or other authority over a financial account in a foreign country (such as a bank account, securities account, or other financial account)? (See page 14 of the instructions for exceptions and filing requirements for Form TD F 90-22.1.) If "Yes," enter the name of the foreign country. ▶		
10	Was the partnership the grantor of, or transferor to, a foreign trust that existed during the current tax year, whether or not the partnership or any partner has any beneficial interest in it? If "Yes," you may have to file Forms 3520, 3520-A, or 926		
11	Was there a distribution of property or a transfer (e.g., by sale or death) of a partnership interest during the tax year? If "Yes," you may elect to adjust the basis of the partnership's assets under section 754 by attaching the statement described under **Elections Made By the Partnership** on page 5 of the instructions		

Designation of Tax Matters Partner (see page 14 of the instructions)
Enter below the general partner designated as the tax matters partner (TMP) for the tax year of this return:

Name of designated TMP ▶		Identifying number of TMP ▶	
Address of designated TMP ▶			

EXHIBIT 3.2 *Continued*

Form 1065 (1995)

Page **3**

Schedule K — Partners' Shares of Income, Credits, Deductions, etc.

	(a) Distributive share items		(b) Total amount
Income (Loss)	**1** Ordinary income (loss) from trade or business activities (page 1, line 22)	**1**	
	2 Net income (loss) from rental real estate activities *(attach Form 8825)*	**2**	
	3a Gross income from other rental activities — **3a**		
	b Expenses from other rental activities *(attach schedule)* — **3b**		
	c Net income (loss) from other rental activities. Subtract line 3b from line 3a	**3c**	
	4 Portfolio income (loss): **a** Interest income	**4a**	
	b Dividend income	**4b**	
	c Royalty income	**4c**	
	d Net short-term capital gain (loss) *(attach Schedule D (Form 1065))*	**4d**	
	e Net long-term capital gain (loss) *(attach Schedule D (Form 1065))*	**4e**	
	f Other portfolio income (loss) *(attach schedule)*	**4f**	
	5 Guaranteed payments to partners	**5**	
	6 Net gain (loss) under section 1231 (other than due to casualty or theft) *(attach Form 4797)*	**6**	
	7 Other income (loss) *(attach schedule)*	**7**	
Deductions	**8** Charitable contributions *(attach schedule)*	**8**	
	9 Section 179 expense deduction *(attach Form 4562)*	**9**	
	10 Deductions related to portfolio income (itemize)	**10**	
	11 Other deductions *(attach schedule)*	**11**	
Investment Interest	**12a** Interest expense on investment debts	**12a**	
	b (1) Investment income included on lines 4a, 4b, 4c, and 4f above	**12b(1)**	
	(2) Investment expenses included on line 10 above	**12b(2)**	
Credits	**13a** Low-income housing credit:		
	(1) From partnerships to which section 42(j)(5) applies for property placed in service before 1990	**13a(1)**	
	(2) Other than on line 13a(1) for property placed in service before 1990	**13a(2)**	
	(3) From partnerships to which section 42(j)(5) applies for property placed in service after 1989	**13a(3)**	
	(4) Other than on line 13a(3) for property placed in service after 1989	**13a(4)**	
	b Qualified rehabilitation expenditures related to rental real estate activities *(attach Form 3468)*	**13b**	
	c Credits (other than credits shown on lines 13a and 13b) related to rental real estate activities	**13c**	
	d Credits related to other rental activities	**13d**	
	14 Other credits	**14**	
Self-Employment	**15a** Net earnings (loss) from self-employment	**15a**	
	b Gross farming or fishing income	**15b**	
	c Gross nonfarm income	**15c**	
Adjustments and Tax Preference Items	**16a** Depreciation adjustment on property placed in service after 1986	**16a**	
	b Adjusted gain or loss	**16b**	
	c Depletion (other than oil and gas)	**16c**	
	d (1) Gross income from oil, gas, and geothermal properties	**16d(1)**	
	(2) Deductions allocable to oil, gas, and geothermal properties	**16d(2)**	
	e Other adjustments and tax preference items *(attach schedule)*	**16e**	
Foreign Taxes	**17a** Type of income ▶ .... **b** Foreign country or U.S. possession ▶		
	c Total gross income from sources outside the United States *(attach schedule)*	**17c**	
	d Total applicable deductions and losses *(attach schedule)*	**17d**	
	e Total foreign taxes (check one): ▶ ☐ Paid ☐ Accrued	**17e**	
	f Reduction in taxes available for credit *(attach schedule)*	**17f**	
	g Other foreign tax information *(attach schedule)*	**17g**	
Other	**18** Section 59(e)(2) expenditures: **a** Type ▶ .... **b** Amount ▶	**18b**	
	19 Tax-exempt interest income	**19**	
	20 Other tax-exempt income	**20**	
	21 Nondeductible expenses	**21**	
	22 Distributions of money (cash and marketable securities)	**22**	
	23 Distributions of property other than money	**23**	
	24 Other items and amounts required to be reported separately to partners *(attach schedule)*		

Analysis	**25a** Income (loss). Combine lines 1 through 7 in column (b). From the result, subtract the sum of lines 8 through 12a, 17e, and 18b				**25a**	

b Analysis by type of partner:	(a) Corporate	(b) Individual		(c) Partnership	(d) Exempt organization	(e) Nominee/Other
		i. Active	ii. Passive			
(1) General partners						
(2) Limited partners						

EXHIBIT 3.2   *Continued*

Form 1065 (1995)   Page **4**

Note: *If Question 5 of Schedule B is answered "Yes," the partnership is not required to complete Schedules L, M-1, and M-2.*

Schedule L   **Balance Sheets**

	Beginning of tax year		End of tax year	
Assets	(a)	(b)	(c)	(d)
1 Cash				
2a Trade notes and accounts receivable				
b Less allowance for bad debts				
3 Inventories				
4 U.S. government obligations				
5 Tax-exempt securities				
6 Other current assets *(attach schedule)*				
7 Mortgage and real estate loans				
8 Other investments *(attach schedule)* . . .				
9a Buildings and other depreciable assets . . .				
b Less accumulated depreciation				
10a Depletable assets				
b Less accumulated depletion				
11 Land (net of any amortization)				
12a Intangible assets (amortizable only). . . .				
b Less accumulated amortization				
13 Other assets *(attach schedule)*				
14 **Total** assets				
Liabilities and Capital				
15 Accounts payable				
16 Mortgages, notes, bonds payable in less than 1 year.				
17 Other current liabilities *(attach schedule)* . . .				
18 All nonrecourse loans				
19 Mortgages, notes, bonds payable in 1 year or more .				
20 Other liabilities *(attach schedule)*				
21 Partners' capital accounts				
22 **Total** liabilities and capital				

Schedule M-1   **Reconciliation of Income (Loss) per Books With Income (Loss) per Return**
(see page 23 of the instructions)

1 Net income (loss) per books	**6** Income recorded on books this year not included on Schedule K, lines 1 through 7 (itemize):
2 Income included on Schedule K, lines 1 through 4, 6, and 7, not recorded on books this year (itemize):	**a** Tax-exempt interest $ ....
....	....
3 Guaranteed payments (other than health insurance)	**7** Deductions included on Schedule K, lines 1 through 12a, 17e, and 18b, not charged against book income this year (itemize):
4 Expenses recorded on books this year not included on Schedule K, lines 1 through 12a, 17e, and 18b (itemize):	**a** Depreciation $ ....
a Depreciation $	....
b Travel and entertainment $	....
....	**8** Add lines 6 and 7 . . . . . .
....	**9** Income (loss) (Schedule K, line 25a). Subtract line 8 from line 5 . . . . . .
5 Add lines 1 through 4	

Schedule M-2   **Analysis of Partners' Capital Accounts**

1 Balance at beginning of year	**6** Distributions: **a** Cash . . . . . .
2 Capital contributed during year	**b** Property . . . . . .
3 Net income (loss) per books	**7** Other decreases (itemize): ....
4 Other increases (itemize):	....
....	**8** Add lines 6 and 7 . . . .
5 Add lines 1 through 4	**9** Balance at end of year. Subtract line 8 from line 5

✿ *Printed on recycled paper*

EXHIBIT 3.3

SCHEDULE K-1 (Form 1065)	**Partner's Share of Income, Credits, Deductions, etc.**	OMB No. 1545-0099
Department of the Treasury Internal Revenue Service	▶ See separate instructions. For calendar year 1995 or tax year beginning , 1995, and ending , 19	**19 95**

Partner's identifying number ▶

Partnership's identifying number ▶

Partner's name, address, and ZIP code

Partnership's name, address, and ZIP code

A This partner is a ☐ general partner ☐ limited partner
☐ limited liability company member
B What type of entity is this partner? ▶ ....
C Is this partner a ☐ domestic or a ☐ foreign partner?
D Enter partner's percentage of:

	(i) Before change or termination	(ii) End of year
Profit sharing	...........%	.........%
Loss sharing	...........%	.........%
Ownership of capital	...........%	.........%

E IRS Center where partnership filed return:

F Partner's share of liabilities (see instructions):
Nonrecourse . . . . $ ....
Qualified nonrecourse financing . $ ....
Other . . . . $ ....
G Tax shelter registration number . ▶ ....
H Check here if this partnership is a publicly traded partnership as defined in section 469(k)(2) . . . . ☐
I Check applicable boxes: **(1)** ☐ Final K-1 **(2)** ☐ Amended K-1

J Analysis of partner's capital account:

(a) Capital account at beginning of year	(b) Capital contributed during year	(c) Partner's share of lines 3, 4, and 7, Form 1065, Schedule M-2	(d) Withdrawals and distributions	(e) Capital account at end of year (combine columns (a) through (d))
			( )	

		(a) Distributive share item		(b) Amount	(c) 1040 filers enter the amount in column (b) on:
Income (Loss)	1	Ordinary income (loss) from trade or business activities . . .	1		See pages 5 and 6 of Partner's Instructions for Schedule K-1 (Form 1065).
	2	Net income (loss) from rental real estate activities	2		
	3	Net income (loss) from other rental activities	3		
	4	Portfolio income (loss):			
	a	Interest	4a		Sch. B, Part I, line 1
	b	Dividends	4b		Sch. B, Part II, line 5
	c	Royalties	4c		Sch. E, Part I, line 4
	d	Net short-term capital gain (loss)	4d		Sch. D, line 5, col. (f) or (g)
	e	Net long-term capital gain (loss)	4e		Sch. D, line 13, col. (f) or (g)
	f	Other portfolio income (loss) *(attach schedule)*	4f		Enter on applicable line of your return.
	5	Guaranteed payments to partner	5		See page 6 of Partner's Instructions for Schedule K-1 (Form 1065).
	6	Net gain (loss) under section 1231 (other than due to casualty or theft)	6		
	7	Other income (loss) *(attach schedule)*	7		Enter on applicable line of your return.
Deductions	8	Charitable contributions (see instructions) *(attach schedule)* . .	8		Sch. A, line 15 or 16
	9	Section 179 expense deduction	9		See page 7 of Partner's Instructions for Schedule K-1 (Form 1065).
	10	Deductions related to portfolio income *(attach schedule)* . . .	10		
	11	Other deductions *(attach schedule)*	11		
Investment Interest	12a	Interest expense on investment debts	12a		Form 4952, line 1
	b	**(1)** Investment income included on lines 4a, 4b, 4c, and 4f above	b(1)		See page 7 of Partner's Instructions for Schedule K-1 (Form 1065).
		(2) Investment expenses included on line 10 above	b(2)		
Credits	13a	Low-income housing credit:			
		(1) From section 42(j)(5) partnerships for property placed in service before 1990	a(1)		Form 8586, line 5
		(2) Other than on line 13a(1) for property placed in service before 1990	a(2)		
		(3) From section 42(j)(5) partnerships for property placed in service after 1989	a(3)		
		(4) Other than on line 13a(3) for property placed in service after 1989	a(4)		
	b	Qualified rehabilitation expenditures related to rental real estate activities	13b		See page 8 of Partner's Instructions for Schedule K-1 (Form 1065).
	c	Credits (other than credits shown on lines 13a and 13b) related to rental real estate activities	13c		
	d	Credits related to other rental activities	13d		
	14	Other credits	14		

For Paperwork Reduction Act Notice, see Instructions for Form 1065. Cat. No. 11394R **Schedule K-1 (Form 1065) 1995**

EXHIBIT 3.3   *Continued*

Schedule K-1 (Form 1065) 1995   Page **2**

	(a) Distributive share item		(b) Amount	(c) 1040 filers enter the amount in column (b) on:
Self-em-ployment	**15a** Net earnings (loss) from self-employment	15a		Sch. SE, Section A or B
	b Gross farming or fishing income	15b		See page 8 of Partner's Instructions for Schedule K-1 (Form 1065).
	c Gross nonfarm income	15c		
Adjustments and Tax Preference Items	**16a** Depreciation adjustment on property placed in service after 1986	16a		
	b Adjusted gain or loss	16b		See pages 8 and 9 of Partner's Instructions for Schedule K-1 (Form 1065) and Instructions for Form 6251.
	c Depletion (other than oil and gas)	16c		
	d **(1)** Gross income from oil, gas, and geothermal properties	d(1)		
	(2) Deductions allocable to oil, gas, and geothermal properties	d(2)		
	e Other adjustments and tax preference items *(attach schedule)*	16e		
Foreign Taxes	**17a** Type of income ▶			Form 1116, check boxes
	b Name of foreign country or U.S. possession ▶			
	c Total gross income from sources outside the United States *(attach schedule)*	17c		Form 1116, Part I
	d Total applicable deductions and losses *(attach schedule)*	17d		
	e Total foreign taxes (check one): ▶ ☐ Paid ☐ Accrued	17e		Form 1116, Part II
	f Reduction in taxes available for credit *(attach schedule)*	17f		Form 1116, Part III
	g Other foreign tax information *(attach schedule)*	17g		See Instructions for Form 1116.
Other	**18** Section 59(e)(2) expenditures: **a** Type ▶			See page 9 of Partner's Instructions for Schedule K-1 (Form 1065).
	b Amount	18b		
	19 Tax-exempt interest income	19		Form 1040, line 8b
	20 Other tax-exempt income	20		See page 9 of Partner's Instructions for Schedule K-1 (Form 1065).
	21 Nondeductible expenses	21		
	22 Distributions of money (cash and marketable securities)	22		
	23 Distributions of property other than money	23		
	24 Recapture of low-income housing credit:			
	a From section 42(j)(5) partnerships	24a		Form 8611, line 8
	b Other than on line 24a	24b		

Supplemental Information	**25** Supplemental information required to be reported separately to each partner *(attach additional schedules if more space is needed)*:	

♻ *Printed on recycled paper*   *U.S. Government Printing Office: 1995 - 389-267 required estimated tax payment for individuals is 90 percent of the total expected tax for the current year, or 100 percent of the total tax shown on the prior year's tax return, whichever is smaller. An individual with an adjusted gross income of more than $150,000 ($75,000 if married and filing a separate return) must pay an estimated tax payment of 90 percent of the total expected tax return for the year, or 110 percent of the total tax shown on the prior year's tax return, whichever is smaller. In addition, each partner must include with his or her 1040 tax return, Form SE for self-employment tax, as a partner is considered a self-employed person. Each partner must report his or her share whether or not any or all of this share actually is distributed to the partner as income during the reporting tax year. Thus, even if all profit is retained in the business in any given year, each partner must declare and pay taxes on his or her share. The result of this tax treatment is that there is little incentive to retain earnings for business expansion.

According to the Internal Revenue Code, a partner's income can be considered either "active" or "passive." A partner's income is considered active if he or she regularly and substantially participates in the running of the partnership business. If a partner simply invests in the business and does not participate in the operations of the business, his or her share of partnership income is considered passive. In the typical general partnership in which all partners materially participate, a partner's income is considered active. This means that a partner's share of the losses may be applied against any income earned from other active personal income sources.

B.   *Computing a Partner's Distributive Share for Tax Purposes*

The partnership agreement determines a partner's distributive share of partnership profits. The agreement may set forth a general division of profits and losses or it may set up a detailed arrangement of allocating particular income, losses, depreciation, and/or credits. Partners are allowed to modify the partnership agreement for a particular tax year after the close of the year but not later than the date for filing the partnership return for that year (extensions are not included). However, it should be noted that although the Internal Revenue Service accepts the terms of a partnership agreement as controlling in computing a partner's distributive share, it will disregard any provision in a partnership agreement that lacks "substantial economic effect." A provision lacks substantial economic effect if the allocation set forth in the agreement does not substantially affect the dollar amount of the partner's share independent of tax consequences and if the partner to whom the allocation is made does not actually receive the economic benefit or burden of the allocation. If the Internal

Revenue Service determines that a partnership provision lacks substantial economic effect, it will allocate distributive shares according to the partners' ownership interest in the partnership.

The situation in which this problem most often arises is in a family partnership. A **family partnership** is one in which all partners are spouses, ancestors, and/or lineal descendants (or any trust for the primary benefit of those persons). These partnerships are looked at with much scrutiny by the Internal Revenue Service, which has set up criteria to determine whether family members truly are partners or whether they have been included in the agreement simply for tax considerations. To make this determination, the Internal Revenue Service looks to see if capital is a material income-producing factor in the partnership business. It is a material income-producing factor if a large part of the gross income of the business comes from the use of capital. This is the case in partnership businesses that require substantial inventories or major investments in plants, machinery, or equipment. Capital generally is not a material income-producing factor if the business is a service business in which remuneration consists principally of fees or commissions or for personal services performed.

If the family partnership is one in which capital is a material income-producing factor, in order for a family member to be considered a partner, that member must acquire his or her capital interest in the business in a bona fide transaction (even if by gift or purchase from another family member), actually own the partnership interest, and actually control the interest. In this scenario, if a family member acquires a capital interest in the partnership as a gift (as a donee), the Internal Revenue Service places limits on that member's distributive share of partnership income. Before calculating that member's distributive share, the donor's compensation for services rendered to the partnership must be subtracted from partnership income. After this is done, the donee's distributive share must not be proportionately greater than the donor's share attributable to the donor's capital.

For example, suppose a mother takes her two daughters into her business, giving each a one-third interest. The business is considered to be one in which capital is a material income-producing factor. This year, the partnership has a profit of $120,000 and the mother has performed services for the partnership worth $30,000. This $30,000 must be allocated to the mother and subtracted from the $120,000 profit before determining the share of each daughter. Of the remaining $90,000, the mother's one-third distributive share is $30,000 and each daughter's distributive share is $30,000.

If the family partnership is one in which capital is not a material income-producing factor, the family members must have joined together in good faith to conduct a business, must have agreed that contributions of each entitle them to a share in the profits, and must each provide some capital or service to the business.

Note that if spouses carry on a business together and share in the profits and losses, the Internal Revenue Service considers them to be partners whether or not they have a formal partnership agreement. This means that they must report all income or loss from the business on Form 1065, report each spouse's partnership share on Schedule K-1, and allocate each spouse's partnership share accordingly on their 1040 tax returns, whether they file individually or jointly. Additionally, each spouse must calculate his or her self-employment tax and declare it on a separate Schedule SE (Form 1040). Doing so will give each spouse credit for social security earnings on which retirement benefits are based.

The Internal Revenue Service states that it is up to the partnership, not the individual partners, to make the determination about how to compute income. The partnership itself determines the accounting method and depreciation method used, the accounting for specific items, and the amortization of certain organizational fees and start-up costs. Thus, each partner's individual return will reflect this consensus.

C.   *Other Tax Considerations*

A partnership is allowed to amortize those expenses that are incident to the creation of the partnership. Expenses falling into this category must have been incurred during the period before the partnership actually began business and ended by the date for filing the partnership return (not including extensions) for the tax year in which the partnership began business. The Internal Revenue Service makes a distinction between those expenses incurred in the creation of the partnership and those expenses incurred in starting the operation of the partnership business, only allowing amortization of the former. Further, the amortizable expenses must be of a nature normally expected to benefit the partnership throughout the entire life of the partnership. Allowable amortizable expenses include legal fees for negotiation and preparation of a partnership agreement, accounting fees for services incident to the organization of the partnership, and any required filing fees. If a partnership decides to amortize these expenses, it must attach a statement to the partnership's return for the tax year the partnership begins its business. The statement must provide (1) a description of each organizational expense, (2) the amount of each expense, (3) the date each expense was incurred, (4) the month the partnership began its business, and (5) the number of months (not less than 60) over which the expenses are to be amortized.

Most joint ventures are treated similarly to partnerships for tax purposes and thus they also need to file an informational tax return. An exception is made for certain real estate joint ventures which do not have to file informational returns. As with partnerships, the joint venture, not its individual participants, determines the tax year (typically the same as that of any principal partner), accounting methods, depreciation methods, and the like. A participant's distributive shares of income or losses are determined by the joint venture agreement, which can be modified, just like a partnership agreement, after the close of that tax year but before the filing of that year's informational tax return. If a joint venture is not operating as an active business, but rather, simply is a method of passive investment for the participants, the joint venture can elect to be excluded from partnership tax treatment if all participants of the joint venture so agree.

Partnerships have the same retirement plan options as sole proprietorships. Partnerships may adopt simplified employee pension plans in which the partnership contributes to the individual IRA account of each partner and employee, or self-employed retirement plans.

All partnerships must obtain a federal employer identification number (details for obtaining this number are found in the previous chapter). Partnerships hiring employees must comply with federal and state labor and tax laws, including compliance with minimum wage and hour requirements, withholding of federal income and social security tax, matching social security tax contributions for each employee, and filing quarterly withholding returns.

State law should be checked to determine whether a state employer identification number is required. State unemployment insurance and disability insurance taxes are typical requirements. The state department of employment should be contacted for instructional information and appropriate forms. Additionally, most states have a state income tax on wages and require income withholding. Finally, most states require collection of sales tax by all non-exempt businesses, requiring the business to obtain a sales permit and to remit collected taxes and requisite forms.

FORMATION

A.   Preliminary Matters

A general partnership takes more care to form than a sole proprietorship. All general partnerships must obtain a federal employer identification number, whether or not outside employees are to be hired. A general partnership must register a fictitious name application or affidavit if the business will be conducted in any name other than the surnames of all of the partners. Thus, if the surnames of less than all of the partners are used, this document must be filed. Note that state law may limit the use of certain terms, such as "company," when referring to a partnership, allowing their use only in the name of a corporation. Just as in the case of sole proprietorships, all requisite professional and occupational licenses must be obtained. State statutes should be checked to determine if the state in which the partnership is formed requires any public filings. As noted above, the RUPA now makes such filings optional (meaning that a state that adopts the RUPA may choose or choose not to require or permit it). If the partnership plans expansion into other states, those state statutes should be checked as well.

B. Partnership Agreements

In addition to these customary matters, a **partnership agreement** (sometimes referred to as **articles of partnership**) must be drafted. While neither the UPA nor the RUPA requires a written partnership agreement, the agreement is the foundation upon which the business is conducted. Therefore it is imperative that the agreement should be well thought-out, with attention to details and contingencies. A partnership agreement is a contract, governed by contract law, and need not be drafted by an attorney in order to be valid. Nonetheless, an attorney is experienced in the pitfalls that may befall a partnership down the road and is thus in a better position to practice "preventive medicine." While partners start out optimistically and do not want to envision future trouble, much damage control can be handled by providing for such matters as partners' duties and rights, profits and losses, circumstances and procedures for withdrawal of partners, partnership dissolution, and other matters in the partnership agreement. Paralegals often participate in the process of drafting such agreements and must be well-versed in this area. Unlike the preparation of form documents, which often are skeletal and standard in their requirements, a partnership agreement must speak to the individual needs of the client.

1. Recitals

A partnership agreement often begins in the same manner of many other contracts, with recitals. These passages "recite," or set forth the background and objectives of the parties. The recitals provide an introduction to the agreement and are not considered an actual provision of the agreement. At a minimum, the recitals set forth the names of the parties to the agreement and may provide "name tags" by which the parties will be referred throughout the body of the agreement. Often, the recitals include the date upon which the agreement is made and takes effect. The purpose of the partnership agreement may be included in the recitals or set forth as a separate provision in the agreement. Many attorneys advise their clients to outline the business purpose in general terms, as the business may grow and expand into areas not originally envisioned. However, if it best suits the objectives of the parties to state the business purpose in specific terms, as would be the case in a joint venture agreement, then this should be done.

2.   Name and Duration

The first provision should set forth the name under which the partnership shall be conducted. This typically is followed by a provision setting forth the term or planned duration of the enterprise. A joint venture has a set objective, the attaining of which brings a logical end to the enterprise. Many other partnerships, however, plan to continue for an indefinite duration. If this is the case in the client's situation, a simple statement of the effective date (the date the partnership agreement takes legal effect) followed by a statement that the partnership shall continue until terminated by conditions set forth in the agreement should suffice. The principal place of business is often included as a preliminary matter as well. These preliminary matters are then followed by the substantive provisions of the agreement.

3.   Partners' Contributions

The contributions of each partner must be set forth with particularity. The type of contribution each partner is making and its valuation should be spelled out. If the contribution is monetary, its value is clear. If the contribution is being made in property or services, the value is less clear and an agreed-upon monetary valuation of such property or services should be reached. The time at which the initial contribution must be made should be included, as well as the timing, amounts, notification requirements, and circumstances under which any additional contributions are to be made. If a partner makes an excess contribution, this may be construed as an advance and treated as a loan by the firm. If so, specifics need to be set forth as to the terms of the loan. On the other hand, an excess contribution may be considered an event that triggers a redistribution of proportionate interest of the partners. This would also have to be addressed.

4. Rights Regarding Specific Property, Salary, and Profits

Any partner's rights to specific property held by the partnership should be addressed. Recall that while under the UPA partners hold title to partnership property as tenants in partnership, under the RUPA the property is owned by the partnership as an entity and they are not co-owners of the property. If a partner is to retain individual rights in partnership property, such rights should be clearly indicated.

Partners ordinarily are not entitled to salaries. However, there are many circumstances in which the payment of salaries may be appropriate. A situation in which one partner is acting as managing partner with the consequent additional workload and duties is one example. Any authority to pay salaries should be contained in the agreement. Salaries may either be fixed or contingent upon profits. Expense accounts and a procedure for reimbursement of business expenses may be established in the agreement as well.

Often partners find it valuable to set up drawing accounts from which a partner may withdraw monies. If the client wishes to establish such accounts, it must first be determined whether limits will be placed on withdrawal amounts and how such limits will be determined. Any requirements for repayment of withdrawn capital contributions should be stated. A partner's proportionate share of net losses and profits may be deducted and credited to these accounts. Although the UPA and the RUPA presume that profits and losses are shared equally among partners unless the partnership agreement specifies otherwise, it is good practice to spell out such apportionment. Partners may want to provide for the adjustment of profit entitlement in circumstances in which a partner's benefits (expense account, other perks) exceed a specified maximum.

5. Management

A provision should address the management duties and other duties of the partners. Again, unless the agreement states otherwise, the UPA and the RUPA presume equal sharing of management responsibilities and authority. This may be perfectly acceptable in some partnerships, but not in others in which some partners do not want to devote full time to the business. The partners may want to designate a managing partner and describe his or her specific duties. Additionally, the partners may want to require bonding of a managing partner to protect against possible negligence in the management of partnership affairs. If so, this should be included in the agreement. Any limitations on the partners' ability to enter into other businesses as either owners or employees should be stated.

As noted above, the UPA lists those acts that require the unanimous consent of the partners while the RUPA does not. It is advisable to list in the partnership agreement those acts that require unanimous consent to bind the partnership. These may include extending credit, pledging partnership property, hiring and firing of employees, and releasing partnership debts. Understand that even when this is done, it does not insulate the partnership from liability to third parties when a partner breaches this provision. This simply allows grounds for suit by the partnership against the offending partner.

Although many partnerships are loosely structured when it comes to daily operations, it is a good idea to include a provision providing for partnership meetings. Neither the UPA nor the RUPA require them and the client may balk at the formality of setting up scheduled meeting times, yet this added structure adds a framework for partners to discuss and reevaluate existing partnership policies, plans, and trouble spots.

6.   Transfer of Partnership Interests and New Partners

If the partners wish to restrict transfers of a partner's interest in the partnership, this should be specified. Certain consent requirements may be indicated as well as the right of first refusal of the other partners to purchase a partner's interest at a fixed price. Additionally, the conditions under which and procedures for admitting new partners should be included in the partnership agreement. There are many reasons for a partnership to consider taking on new partners. The partnership may need or desire additional capital to continue or expand the business, capital that the existing partners may not readily have available, and may not wish to incur further debt through a loan to acquire. A new partner may bring new skills to the partnership or new markets for the business. As noted in the introduction to this chapter, the transfer of a partnership interest does not automatically make the transferee a partner. Typically, unanimous consent of the partners is required. It is usually required to take on additional partners as well. If special procedures or circumstances are applicable in your client's situation, these should be spelled out in the agreement. Note that the partnership agreement will need to be revised once a new partner is added to the partnership as certain changes must be made, including the redistribution of proportionate interest in the partnership, but the original partnership agreement should provide for the mechanics of adding new partners as well as the new incoming partner's liability for existing partnership debts. Traditionally, a new partner is liable for partnership debts incurred prior to his or her inclusion in the partnership up to his or her share of contribution and no more. If the client wishes to deviate from this, the partnership agreement should so provide.

7.   Bookkeeping Procedures

Partnership records and accounting procedures should be included in the agreement. A fiscal year should be fixed and an **accounting method** (cash or accrual) should be established. With the **cash method**, expenses and income are listed in the appropriate ledger when received. This method is commonly used in service businesses. The **accrual method** is typically used in retail businesses with large inventories because this method is generally required for income tax purposes when a business regularly buys and sells goods. Under this method, income is recorded as received when the customer is billed. Likewise, expenses are recorded when incurred rather than when paid. All partnership records should be accessible to the partners for inspection, typically at the principal office of the partnership.

The partnership will need to set up one or several bank accounts. The partnership agreement should set forth those partners (or other persons, if so desired, such as a hired manager) authorized to sign checks on these accounts. If cosignatories are to be required, this should be indicated. Note that although cosignatures may seem a good idea as an added precaution, the client's business may not be conducive to such an arrangement, for example, in a partnership of two partners where one partner is traveling a great deal of the time on buying trips for the business.

8.   Indemnification and Insurance

It is customary to include an **indemnification** provision in partnership agreements. Such a provision assures reimbursement to a partner for losses or expenses incurred by that partner that truly are obligations of the partnership.

Insurance matters may be included in the partnership agreement. Most partnerships will need liability insurance and, where applicable, malpractice insurance. Additionally, many partnerships are now purchasing life insurance policies on the life of each partner. This can be accomplished in one of two ways. Either the partnership itself can purchase the policies (an **entity plan**) or the individual partners can each purchase policies (a **cross-purchase plan**). The proceeds of the policies are used to pay the estate of a deceased partner for that partner's partnership interest. Most businesses do not have readily available assets with which to pay a deceased partner's proportionate interest in the business and find themselves in the unfortunate position of forced liquidation to fulfill this obligation. The purchasing of life insurance safeguards against forced liquidation and allows the partnership to carry on.

9.   Dispute Resolution

The manner in which partnership disputes are to be settled is an important provision. Traditionally, as noted earlier, the UPA provided that partners ask for an accounting before resorting to court action. The RUPA has eliminated an accounting as a prerequisite. Nonetheless, the circumstances under which a partner has a right to an accounting may be addressed in this provision. Other methods of dispute resolution should be considered as well. Many courts are requesting, and in some instances requiring, civil disputes to be brought to mediation or arbitration before a court action is commenced. Even if this is not the case in your client's state, mediation or arbitration may be appropriate tools for dispute resolution. They allow the matter of the dispute to be handled expeditiously and many times in a less costly manner than if the matter were to be handled by the court system.

10.   Withdrawal or Expulsion of a Partner

The withdrawal of a partner is an issue requiring great consideration. A partnership is a voluntary association of partners and thus a partner is free, under both the UPA and the RUPA, to withdraw from a partnership at will. This may cause problems for the existing partnership. Under the UPA, the partnership dissolves when a partner leaves unless there is an agreement by the remaining partners to the contrary. Under the RUPA, the withdrawing partner is a dissociated partner whose interest must be bought out or the partnership dissolved. In either situation, it is wise to include a provision indicating that the withdrawal of a partner does not bring about the dissolution of the partnership, that the remaining partners are free to continue the partnership, and to provide for the buyout of the withdrawing partner. A decision should also be made as to whether the withdrawing partner's future activities should be limited by a noncompetition clause. Case law has generally upheld such clauses when drafted reasonably as to geographic and time limitations.

Who gets the right to continue use of the partnership name may become an issue. Over time, the name may very well have considerable goodwill value attached to it. Although the RUPA does not dictate that a partnership continued after the withdrawal of a partner has the right to use the name, Section 705 of the RUPA (an edited version of the UPA Section 41[10]), does state that a withdrawing partner is not liable for the debts of the continuing business simply because the partnership continues to operate under the same partnership name. Very often a partnership name will include the names of the partners. Section 705 of the RUPA states that even in this instance, the partnership may continue using the name and the withdrawing partner will not incur liability simply because his or her name continues to be associated with the business. Notice the use of the term "simply": a withdrawing partner may incur continued liability for other reasons. Thus, in addition to providing for the forfeiture or right to continue the use of the partnership name, the partnership agreement should indemnify a withdrawing partner from all existing and future liabilities incurred by the remaining partners.

The grounds for expulsion should be described and the procedures for any hearing or appeal process should be explained. For example, grounds for expulsion may include commission of a felony, adjudication of insanity, breach of the partnership agreement and failure to rectify the breach after proper notification, or any action taken that could be considered detrimental to the partnership. The erring partner should be given proper notification spelling out the reason for expulsion and should be allowed an opportunity to be heard before a final decision to expel is reached.

11. Termination of the Partnership

The circumstances under which the partnership may be terminated should be addressed. The winding up procedures, liquidation of assets, and distribution of assets, should all be covered. It is often advisable to appoint one partner as the liquidating partner to handle the details of the liquidation and distribution process. That partner's authority and responsibilities should be addressed in this provision.

12. Miscellaneous Provisions

Finally, the partnership agreement may include "**boilerplate**" provisions. These are provisions that are not specific to partnership agreements and are found in most contracts. They cover such matters as the jurisdictional law governing the agreement, the necessity of reducing to written form any amendments to the agreement, the fact that the possible invalidity of any particular provision in the agreement will not invalidate the entirety of the agreement, and other matters of general contract principles. Please note that even boilerplate provisions may require modification to comply with a client's particular needs.

It is easy to see that a partnership agreement is a detailed document and the client's particular circumstances must be addressed and embodied in it. Often the client will come into a law office with a general idea of the issues he or she wants covered, but rarely does the client grasp the complexity of contingencies provided for in a well-drafted agreement. Therefore, it is a good idea to use a partnership agreement worksheet when discussing the agreement with the client. This assures that neither the law firm nor the client overlooks an important issue. A sample worksheet is provided in the Client Simulation at the end of the chapter.

DISSOCIATION AND DISSOLUTION

As noted in the discussion of the differences between the UPA and the RUPA, a new term has been created to define the status of partners withdrawing from a partnership: **dissociation**. The drafters of the RUPA noted a need to make it easier for a partnership to continue in business after a partner's leave-taking. Under Section 29 of the UPA, the term **dissolution** was defined as the change in the relation of the partners caused by any partner ceasing to be associated in the carrying on of the business. Thus, under the UPA the leave-taking of any partner, under any circumstance, would trigger a dissolution of the partnership, requiring the remaining partners to terminate the business and liquidate its assets unless the partnership agreement stated otherwise. Under the RUPA, this is no longer the case because the new rules provide for the continued existence of the partnership after the dissociation of a partner, including provisions for the buyout of a dissociated partner's interest in the partnership.

Under the RUPA, a partner is dissociated from a partnership under the following circumstances:

1. the partner's notification to the partnership of a desire to withdraw,
2. the partner's proper expulsion according to the terms of the partnership agreement or by unanimous vote of the other partners, or by judicial determination,
3. the partner's becoming a debtor in bankruptcy,
4. the partner's executing an assignment for the benefit of creditors,
5. the partner's death,
6. the partner's incapacity,
7. termination of a partner that is not an individual (i.e., a partnership, corporation, trust, or estate), or
8. an event agreed to in the partnership agreement as causing the dissociation of a partner.

A partner has the power to dissociate at any time by expressing a desire to withdraw, even if such withdrawal is deemed "wrongful." Under Section 602(b) of the RUPA, a wrongful dissociation occurs if:

1. it breaches a provision of the partnership agreement, or
2. in a term partnership, before the expiration of the term
    (i)   a partner voluntarily withdraws,
    (ii)   a partner is expelled for misconduct, or
    (iii) a partner becomes bankrupt.

The significance of wrongful dissociation is that the dissociated partner is not entitled to participate in winding up the business (should the remaining partners choose to terminate rather than continue the business) and may be required to compensate the partnership for any damages caused by the wrongful dissociation. This compensation may be offset against the amount of the buyout price due the dissociated partner. Further, if the dissociated partner wrongfully dissociated in a term partnership, the partnership need not pay out the partner until the term of the partnership expires.

Under Section 603(a) of the RUPA, after a partner's dissociation from the partnership, the partnership may either buy out the partner (buyout rules are found in Article 7) and continue operating or it may dissolve and proceed to wind up the business (covered in Article 8). Under the RUPA, a partnership must dissolve if it is carrying on an illegal business or is dissolved by court decree. Otherwise, the partnership agreement governs. If the agreement is silent, Section 801 of the RUPA indicates those circumstances under which dissolution is indicated. The enumerated events causing dissolution include an agreement by the partners to dissolve the partnership or a partner's withdrawing from a term partnership prior to the expiration of the term (unless the majority of the partners agree to continue within 90 days of the dissociated partner's withdrawal). Section 801 further provides that a partnership must dissolve if a partner indicates an express desire to withdraw in a **partnership at will** (defined in the RUPA as "a partnership in which the partners have not agreed to remain partners until the expiration of a definite term or the completion of a particular undertaking"). In effect, this subsection of Section 801 states that a partner in a partnership at will has the right to force a liquidation of the partnership. Dissociation under any circumstance other than those enumerated in Section 801, however, provides the partnership with the choice of continuance or dissolution and winding up the business.

As noted above, the term dissolution under the UPA refers to a change in the status quo that occurs when a partner ceases to be associated with the partnership. The cause may be the expiration of a term partnership; the death, bankruptcy, retirement, or incapacity of a partner; the desire of one partner to leave the business; or the agreement of all the partners to end the association. Additionally, any partner may apply to the courts for dissolution by decree. Grounds for such a court order include the adjudicated insanity, incapacity, or misconduct of a partner; breach of the partnership agreement; continued loss of business revenues; or any other reasonable circumstance. As may be observed, some of these enumerated circumstances would indicate a necessary termination of the partnership while others would not.

Under the UPA, any of the "trigger" events (voluntary or not) listed above brings about automatic dissolution that requires winding up the partnership business unless the partnership agreement states otherwise or the dissolution was wrongful. A wrongful dissolution is one caused by a partner's expulsion, misconduct, or breach of the partnership agreement. Under these circumstances, the remaining partners have the right to continue the business as long as they properly compensate the departing partner and provide appropriate indemnification. If the dissolution was not wrongful and the partnership agreement does not specify otherwise, the winding up process commences.

Under both the UPA and the RUPA, during a dissolution no new partnership business may be conducted. The winding up may be handled by all of the partners or the task may be designated to a particular partner, the liquidating partner. This liquidating partner is given the authority to liquidate partnership assets, settle partnership affairs, and make proper distribution of remaining proceeds.

Under the UPA, distribution of liquidated assets are paid out in a certain order. The first to be paid are nonpartner creditors. If there are proceeds remaining after these debts are paid, then monies owing to any partner for loans made by that partner to the partnership are paid out next. After this, each partner receives his or her capital contribution, and finally, his or her respective share of the profits. Note that typically interest is not paid on capital contributions unless the partnership agreement indicates otherwise. Note also that under the RUPA, partners who are creditors of the partnership are treated on parity with nonpartner creditors in terms of distribution of liquidated assets and that the RUPA does not distinguish between return of capital contribution and profits. Should the liquidation of partnership assets prove inadequate to pay partnership debts, each partner must make additional contributions, proportionate to his or her interest in the partnership. Once distribution is made, the business is considered terminated and no partnership business of any kind is legally authorized. At this point, notice of dissolution should be made to all persons previously extending credit to the partnership to relieve the partners of any potential future liability.

BUYOUT PROCEDURES

Should dissolution not occur, either because a partner's withdrawal does not trigger it under the RUPA or the partnership agreement permits continuation, a buyout of the withdrawing partner becomes necessary. The RUPA sets forth buyout procedures, including a method of calculating a buyout price, in Article 7. Article 7 is meant to work as a default provision to go into effect if the partnership agreement is silent on this matter. According to Section 701(b) of the RUPA, the buyout price is the amount the partner would have received if the partnership assets were sold at a price equal to the greater of **liquidation value** (a hypothetical selling price presuming a willing and informed seller selling to a willing and informed buyer) or **going concern value** (the price of selling the business as a going concern).

Under Section 701(e) of the RUPA, if no buyout agreement is reached within 120 days of the dissociated partner's written demand for payment, the partnership must pay out in cash to the dissociated partner the undisputed minimum value of that partner's partnership interest. If the dissociated partner is not satisfied with this amount, he or she may bring suit to have the proper amount determined by the court.

Both the UPA and the RUPA allow the partnership agreement to specify terms of the buyout of a departing partner, and retaining the right to buy out the partner and continue the business is wise considering the fact that liquidation of the business typically means that much less money will be realized by all of the partners. A buyout provision should specify the right to continue the business, should provide a procedure to be used in determining the worth of the business and/or the departing partner's interest in the business, and should provide a procedure for paying out this share to the departing partner. If the agreement has not so provided in another section, it should also restrict the transfer of the partner's interest to outsiders, or at the minimum allow the remaining partners the right of first refusal. Although a transferee of the departing partner's interest would not become a partner without the unanimous consent of the remaining partners, a transferee may still be a burdensome interference in the smooth running of the business.

A buyout provision also aids in the area of income and estate taxes. In the case of a deceased partner, the income representing that partner's interest in the partnership is included as part of that partner's estate when calculating estate taxes. A partner voluntarily withdrawing must include the buyout proceeds as income on his 1040 return. In either case, the proper valuation for tax purposes is easy to determine when its worth has been carefully calculated in this manner.

The value of the partnership for purposes of a buyout provision is its net worth on the date a partner withdraws. Because a partner's interest in a partnership business does not have an outside marketplace value as shares of publicly traded stock have, any value placed on that business necessarily will be artificial. The value is only one consideration here. The remaining partners must structure the buyout in such a way as to be able to have funds available to carry on the business. Thus, a system of manageable installment payments is advisable, even if the trade-off is a higher buyout price.

There are various valuation methods that may be chosen. The simplest, of course, is the **set dollar amount method**, in which the partners all agree to a set price which will be reevaluated and reset each year (or other specified interval). Another method is the **book value method**. Under this method, the book value of the partnership is derived by looking to the partnership assets and liabilities as they appear in the partnership's accounting records. The **market value method** is that espoused by the UPA and the RUPA, looking to the current market value of all of the partnership's assets and liabilities. The **capitalization of earnings method** may be more appropriate for a business that has been running successfully for several years. Under this method, the partnership's average yearly net earnings (expenses and current market wages for partners' services are deducted to arrive at this figure) are calculated for a set period (typically three to five years) and then are multiplied by a figure aptly called a multiplier to calculate the current value of the partnership. If none of these methods are deemed appropriate, the partners could agree to hire an independent appraiser to come in and appraise the value of the business. With most of these methods, a big problem is the calculation of the value of **goodwill** (the probability of continued customer patronage that comes from a well-established reputation), an intangible, but often valuable asset. It is a subjectively calculated asset, so any valuation placed on it is artificial.

Finally, recall the discussion of life insurance earlier in the chapter. The purchase of life insurance policies on the lives of each of the partners aids in the timely payment of a deceased partner's interest to his or her estate and does not tie up partnership capital.

CLIENT SIMULATION

Karen checks her tickler file to determine what her priorities should be this morning and sees that she has scheduled a block of time this morning to attend to the drafting of a general partnership agreement for a new client. Karen and Tom met with Brian Baker yesterday and Karen conferred at length with Brian after the initial meeting to complete a general partnership agreement work-sheet. Brian Baker has recently graduated with a doctorate in veterinary medi-cine. He and two other classmates wish to form a general partnership and open a practice together. They believe their interests and skills are complementary rather than competitive, and each can aid the other in the practice of veteri-nary medicine. Brian is a generalist and prefers working with common pets (cats and dogs) in a traditional medical framework. His colleague Angela Romero prefers to practice avian and exotic animal medicine, while another colleague, Stuart Feaman, is interested in holistic veterinary medicine. Karen pulls the client file and takes out the completed worksheet, which reads as follows:

EXHIBIT 3.4

General Partnership Agreement Worksheet

DATE OF INTAKE: February 14, 1997

ATTORNEY: Thomas Trumbull

PARALEGAL: Karen Greer

CLIENT NUMBER: 1592

MATTER NUMBER: 0001

PERSON RESPONSIBLE
FOR INTAKE: Karen Greer

1. CLIENT NAME: Brian Baker, for client partnership

2. ADDRESS: 166 N.W. 22nd Avenue

   Any City, Any State

3. TELEPHONE: (000) 499-5550 FAX: None yet

4. NAME OF PARTNERSHIP: Today's Vet

5. STATE OF FORMATION: Any State

6. LIST ANY OTHER STATES IN WHICH BUSINESS WILL BE CONDUCTED:
   None at this time

7. ARE PUBLIC FILINGS REQUIRED IN ANY OF THE ABOVE-NAMED
   STATES (SPECIFY): None required

EXHIBIT 3.4   *Continued*

8. PRINCIPAL OFFICE OF PARTNERSHIP:

166 N.W. 22nd Avenue

Any City, Any State

9. OTHER OFFICES: None at this time

10. PURPOSE: The practice of veterinary medicine and any other lawful, related business.

11. EFFECTIVE DATE: Upon the signing of this agreement. Partnership shall continue until terminated as per this agreement.

12. FISCAL YEAR: Calendar year

13. ACCOUNTANT: Gene Pierce, C.P.A.

455 S.W. 43rd Street

Any City, Any State

(000) 280-8741

14. ACCOUNTING METHOD: Cash method

15. NAMES AND ADDRESSES OF PARTNERS:

Brian Baker	554 Meadows Lane
	Any City, Any State
Angela Romero	623 Exeter Street
	Any City, Any State
Stuart Feaman	184 Lancaster Avenue
	Any City, Any State

16. ADDITIONAL PARTNERS: Only by unanimous consent of the partners.

17. INITIAL CAPITAL CONTRIBUTION OF EACH PARTNER AND PERCENTAGE OF INTEREST IN THE PARTNERSHIP:

Brian Baker	$35,000	33⅓% interest
Angela Romero	$35,000	33⅓% interest
Stuart Feaman	$35,000	33⅓% interest

EXHIBIT 3.4   *Continued*

18. ADDITIONAL CONTRIBUTIONS: None at this time. Partners may lend funds to partnership in excess of equal proportions; this to be evidenced by promissory note bearing prevailing interest rate at time of loan.

19. PARTNERS' CONTRIBUTIONS OTHER THAN CAPITAL: SPECIFY PROPERTY AND DESIGNATED VALUE): None at this time

20. PARTNERS' RIGHTS IN SPECIFIC PROPERTY: (SPECIFY): None

21. APPORTIONMENT OF PROFITS AND LOSSES: Partners shall share equally

22. RESTRICTIONS ON TRANSFERS OF INTEREST IN THE PARTNERSHIP: Partners have right of first refusal. Transferee does not become partner without unanimous consent.

23. WITHDRAWAL OF CAPITAL: Capital and drawing accounts to be established. Withdrawal limits to be set annually by majority vote.

24. SALARIES: No salaries to be paid at this time.

25. DUTIES OF PARTNERS: Partners shall have equal voice in management and shall devote full time to partnership. No managing partner to be designated at this time.

26. LIMITATIONS ON POWERS OF PARTNERS: Partners may not do the following without consent of others: (1) borrow or lend money, (2) execute mortgage, bond, or lease, (3) assign, transfer, or pledge partnership property, or (4) compromise a partnership claim.

27. BANK ACCOUNTS: Partnership account to be opened at Patriot Bank, 3500 Capitol Avenue, Any City, Any State. Signatures of any two partners required on each check.

EXHIBIT 3.4   *Continued*

28. MEETINGS OF PARTNERS: Regular meetings to be held the first Tuesday of each month. Special meetings may be called by any partner giving reasonable notice.

29. INDEMNIFICATION: Standard indemnification provision

30. INSURANCE: Malpractice insurance shall be maintained by partnership and on the individual partners. Public liability insurance shall be carried on the premises. Partnership shall purchase life insurance on the life of each partner insuring for $50,000 initially, to be increased as needed. Upon withdrawal of partner, life insurance policy on that partner's life to become his/her separate property.

31. DISSOCIATION OF PARTNERS:

  (a) VOLUNTARY WITHDRAWAL OF PARTNER:

    (i) CIRCUMSTANCES: Partner may withdraw at any time after the first year of the partnership by giving one month's notice. No effect on continuation of partnership.

    (ii) PROCEDURES: Partner giving notice gives others right of first refusal to purchase shares. Notification given in writing within 30 days by departing partner of decision. Buyout method is set price method, to be redetermined annually. Payment shall be 25% cash and balance in quarterly installments over 3 years. No allowance to be made for goodwill. Partnership may continue use of partnership name.

  (b) EXPULSION OF PARTNER:

    (i) CIRCUMSTANCES: Partner may be expelled on affirmative vote of partners if partner: (1) commits a felony, (2) is adjudicated

EXHIBIT 3.4   *Continued*

insane, (3) commits act detrimental to the partnership, or (4) breaches agreement.

(ii) PROCEDURES: Expelled partner provided written notification. May request hearing by all partners within 10 days of notification. Outcome of hearing is final. Buyout of expelled partner is the same as that of voluntary withdrawal.

32. NONCOMPETITION CLAUSE: Client does not want one.

33. TERMINATION OF THE PARTNERSHIP: Partnership will not be dissolved upon voluntary withdrawal, death, or expulsion of a partner. Will occur upon majority vote of the partners. No liquidating partner appointed.

34. MEDIATION: Partnership disputes to be settled by mediation. Any partner may submit request for mediation. Mediation to commence within 10 days of notice. Costs to be shared equally.

35. ARBITRATION: To be used if mediation fails. To commence within 10 days of unresolved mediation. Costs to be shared equally.

36. AMENDMENTS: Made in writing; attached to original agreement.

37. ADDITIONAL PROVISIONS: None.

Having reviewed this information and with the worksheet in front of her, Karen pulls up a skeletal general partnership agreement on her computer. This agreement has the typical recitals, provision headings, and boilerplate clauses. Karen will flesh out and customize this agreement according to the information supplied on the worksheet. The completed agreement reads as follows:

EXHIBIT 3.5

General Partnership Agreement of Today's Vet

BY THIS AGREEMENT dated this _____ day of _____, 19_____, between BRIAN BAKER, ANGELA ROMERO, and STUART FEAMAN (the "Partners"), all of the City of Any City, State of Any State, the parties hereby form a general partnership, on the following terms and conditions:

I. *Name.* The name of the partnership shall be TODAY'S VET.

II. *Purpose.* The purpose of the partnership shall be to engage in the practice of veterinary medicine and any other lawful, related business.

III. *Principal Place of Business.* The partnership's principal office shall be located at 166 N.W. 22nd Avenue and may be changed from time to time as so designated by the Partners.

IV. *Term.* The partnership shall begin on the date written above and shall continue until terminated as herein provided.

V. *Capital.* The initial capital shall be contributed in equal amounts by each partner as follows:

Name	Amount
Brian Baker	$35,000
Angela Romero	$35,000
Stuart Feaman	$35,000

No interest shall be paid to any Partner on his or her capital account, except that upon the agreement of all the Partners, any Partner may lend funds to the partnership in excess of equal proportions and in such instance, such excess shall be evidenced by a promissory note of the partnership payable to such partner bearing interest at the then-prevailing interest rate.

VI. *Profit and Loss.* Net profits and losses of the partnership shall be charged to the Partners equally.

VII. *Capital Accounts and Drawing Accounts.* The capital accounts of the Partners shall be maintained at all times in the proportions of their interests in profits or losses of the partnership, and individual drawing accounts shall be maintained for each Partner. All withdrawals by a Partner shall be charged to that Partner's drawing account.

EXHIBIT 3.5   *Continued*

Withdrawals during the year shall be limited to such amounts as the Partners, by a majority vote, shall determine from time to time. Each partner's share of any partnership net loss shall be charged to that Partner's drawing account, unless the Partners, by a majority vote, agree to charge such loss to the capital accounts of the Partners. Each partner's share of partnership profits shall be credited to that Partner's drawing account.

VIII. *Management Duties and Restrictions.* Each partner shall have an equal voice in the management of the partnership business. Each partner shall devote his or her full time to the partnership business with such exceptions as may be agreed upon a majority vote of the Partners. No partner, without the consent of the others, shall:

1. Borrow or lend money on behalf of the partnership.
2. Execute any mortgage, bond or lease.
3. Assign, transfer or pledge any debts due the partnership or release any such debts due, except upon payment in full.
4. Compromise any claim due to the partnership.

IX. *Bank Accounts.* The partnership shall maintain checking or other bank accounts in such bank or banks as the Partners shall agree upon. Withdrawals shall be on the signatures of any two Partners.

X. *Partnership Accounting Procedures.* All partnership bookkeeping shall be done by the cash method. All books, records, and accounts of the partnership shall be maintained at the office of the partnership and shall be open to inspection at all times by the Partners. For the purpose of partnership accounting and for income tax reporting, the partnership fiscal year shall end on the 31st day of December.

XI. *Insurance.* Malpractice insurance shall be maintained by the partnership and on the individual Partners. Liability insurance shall be carried on the partnership premises in amounts to be agreed upon by the Partners.

XII. *Life Insurance.* The partnership shall promptly obtain and maintain in force for the duration of this Agreement, as owner and as beneficiary, a policy of life insurance insuring the life of each Partner for $50,000. The principal purpose of such life insurance is to fund the purchase of a deceased Partner's interest in the partnership. The partnership shall increase the amount of life insurance on the life of each Partner on an as needed basis so as to be reasonably certain of having sufficient net proceeds to redeem said deceased Partner's interest. On the withdrawal of any Partner for any reason other than his or her death, any life insurance policy on his or her life for which the partner-

EXHIBIT 3.5   *Continued*

ship paid the premiums shall be delivered to that Partner and become his or her separate property.

XIII. *Indemnification.* The partnership shall indemnify each Partner for all obligations incurred by each Partner in the ordinary course of partnership business.

XIV. *Valuation of the Partnership Business.* The partnership shall use a set dollar amount method of valuation. Within 60 days after the end of each fiscal year of the partnership, the Partners shall determine the partnership's value by unanimous written agreement, said agreement remaining in effect until the next unanimous written agreement. Should the Partners fail to reach a unanimous agreement, the partnership's value shall be the value last established under this provision.

XV. *Voluntary Withdrawal.* Any Partner shall have the right to withdraw from the partnership after the first year this Agreement is in effect, providing one month's notice of his or her intention to withdraw. The withdrawal of any Partner shall have no effect upon the continuation of the partnership business.

The remaining Partners shall have first right of refusal to purchase the withdrawing Partner's interest. If the remaining Partners elect to purchase the interest of the withdrawing Partner, they shall serve notice in writing of such election upon the withdrawing Partner at the office of the partnership within 30 days after receipt of the notice of intention to withdraw.

The purchase price to be paid for the withdrawing Partner's interest in the partnership shall be as set forth in Paragraph XIV. Said purchase price shall be payable 25 percent in cash and the balance in quarterly installments over a period of three years. No allowance shall be made for goodwill, trade name, patents, or other intangible assets. If the remaining Partners refuse to purchase the withdrawing Partner's interest, the withdrawing Partner may seek a buyer outside the partnership or may demand a dissolution of the partnership and liquidation of its assets.

XVI. *Death of a Partner.* Upon the death of any Partner, the partnership shall pay the deceased Partner's estate his or her share of the partnership, the sum to be taken from the life insurance policy proceeds as set forth in Paragraph XII. Should it be determined that said proceeds exceed the set dollar value of the deceased Partner's share, said excess proceeds shall remain partnership property.

XVII. *Expulsion of a Partner.* A Partner may be expelled, upon the affirmative vote of the other Partners, if said Partner commits any of the following acts:

EXHIBIT 3.5 *Continued*

1. Commits a felony;
2. Is adjudicated insane;
3. Commits an act deemed detrimental to the partnership;
4. Breaches this Agreement and fails to promptly rectify said breach when notified.

The Partners voting for expulsion shall provide written notice of intent to expel. A Partner receiving said notice may request a hearing of all the Partners on the matter no later than ten days from receipt of said notice. The final vote taken at said hearing shall be binding. Expulsion of a Partner shall not result in dissolution of the partnership and the partnership may continue in business. The partnership shall pay the expelled Partner his or her partnership share in the manner set forth in Paragraph XV.

XVIII. *Voluntary Dissolution.* The partnership may be dissolved at any time upon majority vote of all the Partners. Upon any voluntary dissolution, the partnership shall immediately commence to wind up its affairs. The Partners shall continue to share profits and losses during the period of liquidation in the same proportions as before dissolution. Any gain or loss on disposition of partnership properties in the process of liquidation shall be credited or charged to the Partners in the proportion of their interests in profit or loss.

XIX. *Mediation and Arbitration.* The Partners agree that any dispute arising out of this Agreement or the partnership business shall be resolved by mediation. The mediation shall be conducted by a single mediator agreed upon by the Partners. The Partners agree to cooperate fully and fairly with the mediator in an attempt to reach a mutually satisfactory resolution. Any Partner believing a partnership dispute cannot be resolved by the Partners themselves may request mediation by submitting a notice of request for mediation in writing. The mediation shall commence within ten days of said notice. Any decision reached by mediation shall be reduced to writing and signed by all Partners as binding. The costs of mediation shall be shared equally by the Partners.

If a decision cannot be reached by mediation, then the dispute shall be brought to arbitration. The arbitration shall be conducted by a single arbitrator agreed upon by the Partners. Arbitration shall commence within ten days of the termination of the unresolved mediation. The decision of the arbitrator shall be reduced to writing and shall be considered binding on all Partners. The costs of arbitration shall be shared equally by the Partners.

EXHIBIT 3.5   *Continued*

XX. *Representatives, Successors, and Assigns.* This Agreement shall be binding upon the representatives, successors, and assigns of the parties.

XXI. *Headings.* The headings of the provisions in this Agreement are for convenience only. They form no part of this Agreement and shall not affect its interpretation.

XXII. *Entire Agreement.* This document contains the entire agreement and understanding of the parties and may not be altered except by an agreement in writing.

XXIII. *Possible Invalidity.* In the event that any provision of this Agreement is found to be unenforceable, the Agreement shall continue in full force and effect and shall be construed as if such unenforceable provision had never been contained herein.

XXIV. *Governing Law.* This Agreement shall be governed by and construed in accordance with the laws of the State of Any State.

IN WITNESS WHEREOF, the parties have executed this Agreement the day and year first above written.

_____
Brian Baker, Partner

_____
Angela Romero, Partner

_____
Stuart Feaman, Partner

After review of the agreement by Thomas, Karen will schedule a time for Brian to come into the office and read it. In the interim, she will have prepared an SS-4 form for federal employer identification number as well as a Notice Under Fictitious Name Law form and fictitious name registration application form for Brian to sign before sending each to the proper authority.

Chapter Summary

1. A general partnership is an unincorporated business comprised of two or more persons (be they individuals or entities) carried out for profit in which

each partner shares in the management as well as profits and losses of the business. It is governed by common law, state statutory law, and the terms of the partnership agreement, the latter controlling unless it is in direct conflict with the former.

2. A general partnership provides the same tax advantages as a sole proprietorship, as well as the same disadvantage of unlimited personal liability. However, it provides more options in terms of capital raising and greater (although not perpetual) continuity. Because general partners are agents of the partnership and of each other, the acts of one binds them all. This increases the potential risk factor of the business.

3. Most state statutes are patterned after the Uniform Partnership Act or the Revised Uniform Partnership Act. The latter attempts to simplify certain areas of partnership law and provide stability for those partnerships that have continuation provisions in their agreements. It covers the fiduciary duties of partners more extensively than the original act and includes entirely new areas, such as conversions and mergers. Additionally, it reflects the trend among lenders and other institutions of requiring greater access to partnership information by making provision for the public filing of statements, such filings at the present time remaining optional.

4. The same formalities are required to form a general partnership as are required to form a sole proprietorship. Acquisition of a federal employer identification number is mandatory even if the partnership does not hire outside employees because of the added requirement of the filing of annual informational returns with the Internal Revenue Service. Additionally, there is the requirement of a partnership agreement (oral or written).

5. A paralegal's responsibilities often include the drafting of partnership agreements. A well-drafted agreement should include provisions covering the contributions of the partners, management of the partnership, apportionment of profits and losses, insurance requirements, accounting procedures, voluntary withdrawal and expulsion of a partner, termination of the partnership, and dispute resolution. A partnership agreement is not a standard form; it should address any unique needs of the partnership.

6. The Revised Uniform Partnership Act has introduced the concept of "dissociation," referring to a departing partner. Under the RUPA, the departure of a partner does not necessarily lead to the dissolution of the partnership. Typically, the remaining partners have the choice to continue in business by buying out the departing partner or dissolving and winding up the business. Under the original act, the departing of a partner is a "triggering" event for the dissolution of the partnership, unless the partnership agreement states otherwise.

7. If a partnership chooses to buy out a partner, several methods of valuation of the partnership business are available. These include the set dollar

amount method, the book value method, the market value method, and the capitalization of earnings method. Additionally, the Revised Uniform Partnership Act provides a method of valuation as a default method if the partnership agreement is silent on this matter.

Review Questions

1. Explain the concept of agency and provide an example of a circumstance in which a partner might act as an agent of a general partnership.
2. Compare and contrast the UPA and the RUPA with regard to the following:
   (i)   joint and several liability of the partners
   (ii)   public filing statements
   (iii) transfer of partnership property
   (iv)   fiduciary duties
3. Compare sole proprietorships and general partnerships with regard to the following:
   (i)   raising of capital
   (ii)   tax filing requirements
   (iii) personal liability of the owner(s)
   (iv)   formality requirements
4. Distinguish between the concept of dissociation and the concept of dissolution.
5. Discuss the strengths and weaknesses of the various methods that may be used in determining the value of a business.

KEY TERMS

accounting
accrual method
actual authority
agency
agent
aggregate theory

apparent authority
boilerplate
book value method
capitalization of earnings
   method
cash method

cross-purchase plan
delectus personae
disclosed principal
dissociation
dissolution
entity plan
entity theory
family partnership
fiduciary duty
general agent
general partnership
going concern value
goodwill
indemnification
joint venture

liquidation value
marshaling of assets
partnership agreement
partnership at will
partnership interest
RUPA
set dollar amount
   method
special agent
statement of authority
statement of denial
term partnership
uniform law
UPA
vicarious liability

4 | *Limited Partnerships* —

no good laws
since tax laws
changed 1986

Overview of Objectives

Upon completion of this chapter, the student will:

- know the advantages and disadvantages of a limited partnership as a chosen business format
- understand the role uniform laws play in the governing of limited partnerships and the distinctions between the original Uniform Limited Partnership Act, the Revised Uniform Limited Partnership Act, and the Revised Act with the 1985 Amendments
- understand the role securities laws may play in the operation of a limited partnership
- know the key documents of a limited partnership and how to draft them

INTRODUCTION

A general partnership may be a preferred business structure for a client wishing to fully participate in the daily operations of a business yet share responsibility with his or her associates. Some clients, however, are looking for a way to invest in a business with no managerial responsibilities or personal liability. The limited partnership is one option in meeting these needs. It is a popular method of investment for those seeking the possibility of greater returns than offered by many other investment alternatives.

A **limited partnership** is a partnership in which there is at least one general partner and at least one limited partner. A partner in a limited partnership may be, just as in a general partnership, an individual, a general partnership, a limited partnership, a limited liability company, a corporation, a trust, or an estate.

This chapter focuses on the advantages and disadvantages of the limited partnership as a business structure, as well as on the state and federal laws that pertain to limited partnerships. As a paralegal, you may play an active role in assisting your attorney in the formation of limited partnerships for business clients, performing such tasks as reserving the limited partnership name, drafting the documents to be filed with the secretary of state, and researching the laws of other states in which a limited partnership may conduct business. This chapter will take you through each step of the formation process.

NATURE OF A LIMITED PARTNERSHIP

Each general partner in a limited partnership has the same rights, duties, and liability as each would have in a general partnership. The general partners in a limited partnership manage the partnership business, are considered agents and fiduciaries of the business, and are subject to unlimited personal liability. Each limited partner in a limited partnership has chosen a trade-off: limitations on managerial control of the business for limitations on liability for business debts. A limited partner's liability for such debts is limited to the extent of that partner's actual and promised contributions to the business. Business creditors may not touch a limited partner's personal assets to satisfy the limited partnership's debts.

The curtailment of a limited partner's interaction with the business goes hand in hand with certain rights. A limited partner is permitted to inspect and copy the books. Additionally, a limited partner is entitled to an accounting of partnership activities. Because limitations are placed on a limited partner's managerial control of the business, a limited partner is not deemed an agent or fiduciary of the limited partnership. Not being held to the standards of a fiduciary, a limited partner cannot be prevented from taking part in other business opportunities, including those in competition with the limited partnership. There are instances in which a limited partner may lose his or her status as such. Should a limited partner participate in the managerial control of the business, that partner's shield from personal liability vanishes and that partner will be treated as a general partner. Further, a limited partner's surname may not appear in the name of the limited partnership unless it is also the surname of a general partner. If this rule is not followed, the limited partner whose surname appears forfeits his or her limited liability status. Finally, if there are defects in the formation of the limited partnership, a limited partner may lose his or her status until such defects are corrected.

A limited partnership is a business structure that provides an option for those who would like to invest in a business and limit their risk (i.e., enter as a limited partner). Because a limited partner's role is that of an investor, a limited partner typically may assign his or her partnership interest in the business freely. This provides greater flexibility than a general partnership structure, which often imposes restrictions on the assignment of partnership interests. For those who wish to play a more active role in a business, a limited partnership, although fraught with more formalities than a general partnership, allows for additional equity financing without worries over sharing control of the business or the creation and distribution of shares of stock. Should the limited partnership seek some form of debt financing, lenders will look to the aggregate of the partners' collateral and credit risk in making a determination as they would in the case of a general partnership.

It is possible to be both a limited partner and a general partner in the same limited partnership. As a general partner, the partner is subject to the same rights and obligations as any other general partner. However, the partnership interest attributable to those contributions made as a limited partner is as freely transferable as that of any other limited partner and distributions made on these contributions share the same preference as those made to other limited partners.

More options are available for structuring the return on contribution the limited partner will receive than are available for the return on contribution for a general partner. In the latter instance, it is usually a proportionate share of the profits. In the case of a limited partner, he or she may receive a set return on his or her investment, similar to that of a lending institution. However, unlike a lending institution, this return will not be realized if the limited partnership fails to flourish. Instead of a set return, the limited partner may receive a proportionate share of the profits for a set period of time or continuously until the termination of the limited partnership. Note, however, that in any of these scenarios, the limited partnership may not make distributions unless the remaining assets will cover all business liabilities.

Limited partnerships are created and terminated by state statute. They come into existence when a **certificate of limited partnership** (sometimes referred to as a **registration statement**) is filed with the appropriate state authority, usually the secretary of state. In this circumstance, they differ from general partnerships which presently are not required to file documents for public record. Similar to general partnerships, state statutes governing limited partnerships are drawn from uniform laws. However, the uniform laws governing limited partnerships require many more formalities than those governing general partnerships (a detailed discussion is provided below). These formalities include but are not limited to the requirement that a limited partnership wishing to conduct business in states other than its state of formation (**domicile**) file an application to operate as a **foreign limited partnership** within those states. At present, this typically is not required of general partnerships. As is the case with general partnerships, the details pertaining to the running of a limited partnership are generally found in the partnership agreement. Limited partnerships are also subject to federal and state securities laws. The documentation required for the creation and maintenance of a limited partnership means that more legal fees may be incurred than with a sole proprietorship or a general partnership.

A limited partner's passive role means that the death or withdrawal of a limited partner does not automatically dissolve the limited partnership (provided the business continues to have at least one limited partner). Further, most state statutes provide that the death or withdrawal of a general partner will not automatically dissolve a limited partnership as long as there remains at least one general partner and the certificate of limited partnership or the limited partnership agreement makes provision for continuance. Absent such a provision, the limited partnership may continue if all the partners consent in writing within 90 days of such death or withdrawal to the continuance of the business.

A limited partnership is treated like a general partnership for tax purposes. It is not treated as a separate tax-paying entity, but it is a reporting entity, filing an annual informational return with tax authorities. Thus, as in a general partnership, each partner includes income and losses on his or her own tax return reflecting his or her proportionate share of the business. Please note, however, that unlike a general partner whose partnership income is typically considered "active" income, a limited partner's income is considered **"passive"** (derives from an activity in which one does not materially participate during the tax year). Because of this, any losses apportioned to a limited partner's share may be used only to offset income produced by other passive investments.

COMPARISONS TO LIMITED LIABILITY PARTNERSHIPS

A limited partnership should not be confused with a limited liability partnership. The latter is the newest form of partnership, first recognized by the state of Texas in 1991. At the time of this writing, over 30 states have enacted legislation recognizing limited liability partnerships. A **limited liability partnership** is a general partnership designed for professionals in which the partners are shielded from personal liability for certain partnership debts, most specifically those involving the malpractice or negligence of fellow partners. In return for this protection, most states recognizing limited liability partnerships require the acquisition of liability coverage. The letters "R.L.L.P.," "RLLP," "L.L.P.," "LLP," or the words "Registered Limited Liability Partnership" or "Limited Liability Partnership" must be included in the partnership name indicating to third parties that the partnership is a limited liability partnership.

In a limited liability partnership, the partners remain personally liable for all other business debts and each partner remains personally liable for debts arising from his or her own malpractice or negligence (as well as those caused by the acts of employees under his or her direct supervision). In contrast, a limited partnership shields each limited partner from personal liability for any and all debts of the partnership while general partners in a limited partnership receive no protection whatsoever.

The National Conference of Commissioners on Uniform State Laws approved an amendment to the RUPA in July 1996 which adopted the Limited Liability Partnership Act as part of the RUPA. Under these new amendments, a partnership may become a limited liability partnership by filing a **statement of qualification**. Limited liability partnerships are required, as are other partnerships, to file annual reports. Further, a limited liability partnership must file an application, called a **statement of foreign qualification**, to be qualified to transact business as a foreign limited liability partnership in any state other than its state of formation.

THE UNIFORM LIMITED PARTNERSHIP ACT, THE REVISED UNIFORM LIMITED PARTNERSHIP ACT, AND THE 1985 AMENDMENTS

A. *The Uniform Limited Partnership Act*

The first statutes enacted pertaining to limited partnerships were enacted in New York at the beginning of the nineteenth century. Over the next 30 years, several other states adopted nearly identical provisions. These early statutes were considered rigid and contained so many pitfalls subjecting limited partners to potential unlimited liability that many investors avoided limited partnerships as possible investment opportunities. These statutes reflected the basic distrust of their times in limited liability businesses. In response to a call for change in the existing laws, in 1916 the National Conference of State Commissioners on Uniform Laws adopted the **Uniform Limited Partnership Act (ULPA)**.

The ULPA, although retaining many of the restrictions of the earlier statutes, was nonetheless considered a great improvement. Comprised of 31 sections, it was designed to cover all the major provisions deemed appropriate for governing the internal affairs of a limited partnership. The ULPA was adopted by every state (except Louisiana) plus the District of Columbia, and remained essentially unchanged for 60 years. The ULPA in its original form is still being used as the basis for the limited partnership statutes of Vermont.

Section 2 of the ULPA sets forth the requirements of a certificate of limited partnership. Under this Act, the certificate set forth very detailed information, including: the name of the limited partnership, the general character of the business, its office address, the name and address of all partners, the type and amount of contribution of each partner, trigger events for additional contributions, distribution rights, powers of limited partners to assign their interests, trigger events for dissolution, the right of continuing the business after death or withdrawal of a general partner, the latest date upon which the limited partnership is to dissolve, and any other relevant matter the general partners wish to include in the certificate. This certificate had to be signed by all of the partners. Inasmuch as a certificate of limited partnership is a publicly recorded document, under the ULPA outsiders were privy to considerable information about the limited partnership and no anonymity was provided for the limited partners. Additionally, any time any of the above information changed, such as a change in capital contribution or a change in a partner, the certificate had to be amended and refiled. It was common practice for the general partners to be given power of attorney by the limited partners to make such amendments to the certificate on their behalf since the signatures of all the partners were required.

According to Section 3 of the ULPA, a limited partner's contributions to the limited partnership were restricted to cash and/or property. Although general partners were allowed to make contributions in the form of services, limited partners were not.

Under the ULPA, only general partners were allowed to maintain an action on behalf of the limited partnership. However, general partners had no authority to perform certain acts without the written consent of all the limited partners. These acts included the admission of additional general partners, admission of additional limited partners (unless otherwise indicated in the certificate of limited partnership), the assignment rights in specific partnership property, the confession of a judgment against the partnership, the continuance of the business after the death or withdrawal of a general partner (unless otherwise indicated in the certificate of limited partnership), or the performance of any act in contravention of the certificate.

Section 9 of the ULPA allowed for free transferability of a limited partner's interest, unless the limited partnership agreement provided otherwise, and disallowed a flat prohibition against transfer of such interest.

Section 13 of the ULPA prohibited a limited partner from holding any partnership property as collateral. The ULPA did allow a limited partner the right to demand a complete return of his or her contribution on the date set forth in the certificate of limited partnership or, if the certificate was silent, six months after giving written notice to the limited partnership. However, it prohibited a limited partner from receiving any distribution from the limited partnership if remaining assets would be insufficient to pay outside creditors.

Just as important as those areas covered by the ULPA are those areas glaringly absent. The ULPA contained no provisions regarding the limited partnership agreement, deeming the certificate of limited partnership as the most important document of formation. It contained no provisions for the sharing of profits and losses, nor for the sharing of distributions. It contained no provisions for name reservation, registered agent, nor filing with the secretary of state's office. It contained no list of documents required to be kept for inspection. No provision was included to address voting rights of limited partners nor for the winding up of the business.

B. The Revised Uniform Limited Partnership Act

As businesses grew and became more sophisticated, the ULPA as originally adopted became problematic. It did not foresee the expansion of limited partnerships' transactions into other states and countries (and thus made no provision for the registration of a limited partnership as a foreign limited partnership), nor their use as vehicles for increasingly complex ventures. In 1976, the National Conference of Commissioners on Uniform State Laws adopted a revised Act (sometimes referred to as the **RULPA**, but herein referred to as the **1976 Act** to distinguish it from the amendments made in 1985). It made provision for many areas not addressed in the ULPA. First, it provided definitions for terms used throughout the 1976 Act, thus providing more clarity in the uniform laws. Additionally, it acknowledged the partnership agreement as the most important document governing a limited partnership.

While retaining the ULPA's very detailed requirements for the contents of the certificate of limited partnership, the 1976 Act abolished the requirement of notarization of the certificate. Further, it included provisions for a registered agent and registered agent's office, name registration, and the filing of documents with the office of the secretary of state. The 1976 Act also expanded the acceptable contributions of limited partners to include services. It addressed the manner of sharing of profits and losses as well as the sharing of distributions as was specified in the limited partnership agreement.

While not defining what is meant by taking part in the control of the business, the 1976 Act devised a list of activities in which a limited partner might safely participate without being considered as taking part in control of the business. This list is sometimes referred to as the **safe harbor list** or **safe harbor rule**. It allowed a limited partner to act as a contractor, agent, or employee of the limited partnership; consult and advise the general partners; act as a surety; and vote on various matters, including the removal of a general partner, a change in the nature of the business, sale of substantially all the assets, and the dissolution and winding up of the limited partnership.

The 1976 Act added further rights and guidelines. It set forth a detailed list of required records to be kept in a specified office. It required that limited partners be provided with a copy of the certificate of limited partnership and that voting was to be conducted in the manner prescribed in the limited partnership agreement. It designated that general partners or, if none, limited partners are to wind up partnership affairs; but also allowed any partner, partner's legal representative, or partner's assignee to apply to have a court wind up the business.

Another innovation was the recognition of the right of limited partners to bring **derivative actions** (lawsuits brought to enforce rights derived from ownership of the injured entity, in this instance, the limited partnership). Under Article 10 of the 1976 Act, a limited partner was given the right to bring an action to recover a judgment in favor of the limited partnership if the general partners have refused to take such an action or if an effort to cause the general partners to bring the action is not likely to succeed. In order to bring a derivative action, the limited partner must have been a partner at the time of the wrongdoing giving rise to the action.

The 1976 Act retained certain characteristics of the original ULPA. As stated above, it retained all of the requirements of the certificate of limited partnership enumerated above. It retained the provision that all limited partners consent to the admission of a new or additional general partner. Further, it retained the provision that limited partners may be added only through the amendment of the certificate of limited partnership.

C.   *The 1985 Amendments*

The 1976 Act was considered a significant improvement over the ULPA and was widely adopted without much alteration. Some states, however, such as California and Delaware, embraced the basic tenets of the 1976 Act but added several modifications. These modifications were instrumental in the further revision of the Act in 1985. Today, a minority of state statutes still follow the 1976 Act, the majority (plus the District of Columbia) having incorporated the 1985 revisions (referred to herein as the **1985 Act**). The 1985 Act leaves the basic structure of the 1976 Act unchanged, retaining the format of eleven articles. The Committee acting for the National Conference of Commissioners on Uniform State Laws kept what were considered the best aspects of the 1976 Act and added the best of the modifications made to it by various states.

The 1985 Act streamlines the information required in the certificate of limited partnership. In so doing, it deletes, among other requirements, the requirement that the certificate include the name, address, and capital contribution of each limited partner. Additionally, it requires that the certificate be signed by only the general partners and amendments to the certificate to be signed by only one general partner. In this way, the limited partners are able to protect their anonymity. The 1985 Act also makes it easier to add limited partners. Recall that under the 1916 and 1976 Acts, additions of limited partners required the amending and refiling of the certificate of limited partnership. Under the 1985 Act, limited partners may be admitted through the limited partnership agreement. Although the 1985 Act adds the requirement of keeping records of the dates on which each limited partner was admitted, it eliminates much administrative work and costs by negating the requirement of amending the certificate. Most of the information formerly required in the certificate, if not included in the limited partnership agreement, is now to be kept in the business records of the limited partnership. Thus, one finds that the list of records to be kept in Section 105 of the 1985 Act is significantly expanded.

Because of the significant changes in the certificate of limited partnership, and in keeping with the premise that the limited partnership agreement is the controlling document, many provisions pertaining to the limited partnership agreement in the 1976 Act were revised by inserting the word "written" before the term "partnership agreement." Although the 1985 Act does not maintain that a limited partnership agreement must be in writing, it provides that, to protect the partners from fraud, significant provisions must be set forth in a written limited partnership agreement if they are to be enforceable under the terms of the Act. These significant provisions include the sharing of profits and losses, the sharing of distributions, the right to demand distribution in a form other than cash, the withdrawal of a limited partner, the admission or withdrawal of a general partner, and the continuance of the limited partnership after withdrawal of a general partner.

The 1985 Act expanded the safe harbor list of activities included in Article 3 of the 1976 Act. In addition to the above-enumerated list of activities in which limited partners may take part without losing their protective shield of limited liability, the 1985 Act allows a limited partner to be an officer, director, or shareholder of a general partner that is a corporation; to guarantee or assume specific financial obligations of the limited partnership; and to request or attend a meeting of the partners. Under the same provision, the 1985 Act also allows limited partners to propose and vote on matters not included in the 1976 Act, such as the admission of a general partner, the admission or removal of a limited partner, transactions involving actual or potential conflicts of interest between a general partner and the limited partnership, amendments to the limited partnership agreement or certificate, and any other matters contained in the limited partnership agreement which call for the approval or disapproval of the limited partners.

A departure from the 1916 and 1976 Acts which required the consent of all limited partners before additional general partners could be admitted, Section 401 of the 1985 Act provides that the written limited partnership agreement determines the procedure for authorizing the admission of additional general partners. Under this section, the written consent of all partners is required only when the limited partnership agreement fails to address the question.

Finally, Section 903 pertaining to the registration of foreign limited partnerships was changed from the original provision adopted in 1976. The changes reflect the move toward more skeletal information being provided in the certificate of limited partnership. Under the 1985 Act, the application for registration as a foreign limited partnership no longer requires a statement of the general character of the business nor a list of names and addresses of all of the partners. Instead, it requires the address of the office in which such a list (together with other records) is kept. Exhibit 4.1 provides a summarized comparison of the 1916, 1976, and 1985 Acts.

EXHIBIT 4.1

Comparison of the 1916, 1976, and 1985 Acts

		1916 Act	1976 Act	1985 Act
1.	Definitions	No provision	Provides for	Provides for
2.	Basic Document	Certificate of limited partnership	Partnership agreement	Partnership agreement
3.	Certificate	Very detailed. Signed by all partners. Notarization required.	Very detailed. Signed by all partners. Notarization not required.	Skeletal. Signed by general partners only. No notarization required.
4.	Registered Office and Agent	No provision	Provides for	Provides for
5.	Name Registration	No provision	Provides for	Provides for

EXHIBIT 4.1 *Continued*

		1916 Act	1976 Act	1985 Act
6.	Filing in Secretary of State's Office	No provision	Provides for	Provides for
7.	Partnership Interest	Not defined	Defined	Defined
8.	Limited Partner's Contributions	Cash, property, no services. Requires contributions to be set forth in the certificate.	Cash, property, services. Requires contributions to be set forth in the certificate.	Cash, property, services. Contributions to be set forth in the partnership agreement and/or records.
9.	Sharing of Profits and Losses	No provision	Provides for	Provides for
10.	Sharing of Distributions	No provision	Provides for	Provides for
11.	Limited Partner's Participation	No participation in control of business allowed.	Provides safe harbor list of activities not considered taking part in control of business.	Expands safe harbor list.
12.	Partnership Records	No detailed list of required records.	Detailed list of required records.	Expands list of required records; however allows information to be in partnership agreement instead.
13.	Delivery of Certificate to Limited Partners	No provision	Provides for	Provides for
14.	Voting	No provision	Provides for	Provides for
15.	Admission of Limited Partners	Requires amended certificate.	Requires amended certificate.	Provides for admission through partnership agreement. Business records must record date each limited partner admitted.

EXHIBIT 4.1   *Continued*

		1916 Act	*1976 Act*	*1985 Act*
16.	Admission of Additional General Partners	Requires that all limited partners consent.	Requires that all limited partners consent.	Written partnership agreement determines procedure.
17.	Derivative Actions by Limited Partners	No provision	Provides for	Provides for
18.	Foreign Limited Partnerships	No provision	Provides for	Provides for
19.	Winding Up	No provision	Provides for	Provides for

LIMITED PARTNERSHIPS AND SECURITIES LAW

As stated in the introduction to this chapter, a limited partner's role in a limited partnership primarily is the role of an investor. A limited partner invests capital with an expectation of a return on this investment. This return, if it materializes, will be brought about by the efforts of the general partners who manage the business. Therefore, a limited partner's interest in the business fits within the definition of a **security** (an investment in a business enterprise managed by others in which expectation of a profitable return depends on the efforts of others). Taking this one step further, the sale of a limited partner's interest may be considered the sale of a security. Because of this, state and federal securities law must be checked and, if applicable, complied with when forming a limited partnership.

Historically, securities laws in the United States developed in response to a perceived need to protect the unwary public from purchasing interests in fraudulent businesses. The most significant federal security laws were enacted in the 1930s and early 1940s, during the Depression following the stock market crash of 1929: the **Securities Act of 1933**, the **Securities and Exchange Act of 1934** (both of which are discussed below and which give federal regulatory agencies such as the Securities Exchange Commission supervisory authority over the sale of securities), and the **Investment Advisors Act of 1940** (a federal statute which regulates activities of those who provide investment advice). States followed suit, enacting their own securities laws, sometimes referred to as **blue sky laws** (protecting against the unscrupulous sale of shares in the "blue sky," i.e., nonexistent entities).

Compliance with federal securities laws is not required if a limited partnership qualifies for one of two exemptions. The first exemption applies to intrastate offerings. If all interests in the limited partnership are offered and sold only in the state of formation, the limited partnership qualifies for this exemption. A word of caution is advisable here. To qualify under this exemption, all funds used to purchase an interest in the limited partnership must come from the limited partnership's state of formation as well. Thus, if a limited or general partner is utilizing out-of-state funds to finance all or part of an interest, the limited partnership falls outside this exemption.

The second exemption applies to private offerings. Private offerings are not subject to federal securities laws. To determine whether an offering is deemed a private offering, several factors are considered. The number of persons or entities to whom an offer is made is one factor. There is no federal statutory numerical limit. Rather, one must look to state law to determine this. There is a requirement that the enterprise offering an interest in the business be able to identify each offeree. Other factors considered include the manner in which the offering is made, the size of the offering, the offeree's access to pertinent information about the business, and the sophistication of the offerees. State securities regulations vary. Some states only provide exemptions to intrastate offerings. Others may provide exemptions for certain types of securities and not for others. Often, states simply allow exemptions by capping the specified number of sales of interests in the business that may be made during a particular time period or place a limitation on the number of offers that may be made within a particular time period.

FORMATION

A limited partnership is more complex than either a sole proprietorship or a general partnership and thus may require considerably more legal assistance in its formation. In addition to meeting applicable state licensing and permit requirements, filing for a federal employer identification number, and preparing a partnership agreement, there are other formalities to be met.

A.   Name Selection and Reservation

The first consideration is the name of the limited partnership. Unlike a general partnership or sole proprietorship, the name of a limited partnership may be reserved. As stated earlier in the chapter, the surname of a limited partner may not be included in the name of the limited partnership unless it is also the surname of one of the general partners. The name of the limited partnership must include a word or an abbreviation identifying the business as a limited partnership. The exact required wording differs from state to state so local statutes need to be checked. Some states do not allow the use of abbreviations and require "limited partnership" to be attached to the name while others allow the single word "limited." Many allow the abbreviations "L.P." or "Ltd." In some states, the name chosen must not be deceptively similar to that of any other limited partnership, limited liability company, or corporation. In others, the requirement is that the name be "distinguishable" from others filed with the office of the secretary of state. Additionally, the chosen name must not mislead the public by containing words (such as "Company," "Incorporated," or the like) that would indicate that the business is organized other than as a limited partnership.

The best practice is to obtain the client's top three choices of name prior to checking name availability with the secretary of state or other appropriate governmental authority. In most states, verification of name availability may be done over the telephone prior to sending in an application for name reservation.

Although name reservation is not mandatory, it definitely is advisable. It assures that the certificate of limited partnership will not be returned due to name conflict with another business on file. It also allows the client to proceed with ordering business cards, stationery, and other items on which the name of the business is required. Most states require that the actual reservation of a name be done through a written application and limit the period of time for which a name may be reserved and many do not allow a name reservation to be renewed. Thus, a certificate of limited partnership should be filed closely following the name reservation. When sending in a name reservation application, be aware of the requisite filing fees. An application sent without the accompanying fee (or the wrong fee) is usually sent back or ignored. Please note that a limited partnership may conduct business under an assumed, or fictitious, name (a name other than the name under which it has filed its certificate of limited partnership), and if business is to be conducted under a fictitious name, a fictitious name application or affidavit must be prepared and filed as well.

B.   *Registered Agent*

Next, the client must choose a **registered agent** for service of process. This is a requirement under both the 1976 and 1985 Acts, which state that the name and office address of the registered agent must be included in the certificate of limited partnership. The registered agent may be, but need not be, a partner. The agent must be a resident of the state of formation. If the agent is a business entity, then it must be authorized to do business in the limited partnership's state of formation. The purpose of a registered agent is to provide someone upon whom legal papers may be served. Some states have requirements that the office of a registered agent must be open on weekdays during specified hours to facilitate this. It is not unusual for an attorney to act as the initial registered agent of a client.

The chosen registered agent must keep statutorily required business records at the registered office and make them available to the partners for inspection. These include a current alphabetical listing of the names and last known mailing addresses of each partner; a copy of the certificate of limited partnership and any amendments; copies of any executed powers of attorney; copies of the limited partnership's federal, state, and local income tax reports for the three most recent years; a copy of the written limited partnership agreement; and copies of any financial statements for the three most recent years. In states that have adopted the 1985 Act, there is an additional requirement that unless set forth in the written limited partnership agreement, the records must contain a description of each partner's actual and promised contribution; the times or events on the happening of which any additional contributions agreed to be made are to be made; any right of a partner to receive a distribution of property, including cash, from the partnership; and the events upon the happening of which the partnership is to be dissolved and wound up.

If any of the general partners in the limited partnership is a limited partnership, limited liability company, or corporation, make sure that it is qualified to conduct business in the state in which the limited partnership will be formed. If the general partner is a domestic entity (was created under the laws of that state) there is no problem. However, if it is a foreign entity (created under the laws of another state or country) it must qualify to do business and the governmental authority with which the certificate is filed may ask for an authenticated copy of a **certificate of authority** (sometimes referred to as a **certificate of registration**), which authorizes a foreign entity to conduct business in the state, to accompany the certificate of limited partnership.

C. *Certificate of Limited Partnership*

Once the limited partnership's name is reserved, a registered agent is chosen, and the status of all general partners is checked, one can draft the certificate of limited partnership. Some states require that a governmental form be used. If this is the case, this form may be obtained by contacting the appropriate governmental authority (usually the secretary of state) and requesting copies. Other states do not use forms but require that the prepared certificate contain all the information detailed in state statutes. This information will vary depending upon whether the state statutes follow the 1976 or 1985 Act. (Recall that only one state, Vermont, follows the original ULPA and Louisiana does not codify any version of the uniform law). As mentioned above, the 1985 Act streamlined the information to be set forth. State statutes patterned after the 1985 Act require the following information to be included in the certificate of limited partnership:

1. the name of the limited partnership;
2. the office address and the name and address of the agent for service of process;
3. the name and business address of each general partner;
4. the latest date upon which the limited partnership is to dissolve; and
5. any other matters the general partners desire to include in the certificate.

With regard to the fifth point, although one is permitted to include other matters in the certificate, it is a better practice to limit its contents to these minimal requirements and include all other pertinent matters in the limited partnership agreement for two reasons: (1) the certificate of limited partnership is a document of public record and the partners may wish to keep the internal affairs of the limited partnership private, and (2) if one chooses to change any of the information in the certificate, an amended certificate must be filed and additional fees paid.

Note that the certificate must be signed by all of the general partners. Additionally, the registered agent designated in the certificate must accept his or her appointment. In some states that utilize forms, provision is made for the registered agent's signature indicating acceptance right on the form. In other states, it will be necessary to attach an acceptance of designation of registered agent to the certificate.

In those states whose limited partnership statutes closely follow the 1976 Act, more detailed information is required. As noted earlier, certificates in these states must include the following information:

1. the name of the limited partnership;
2. a brief description of the character, or purpose, of the business;
3. the address of the office and the name and address of the agent for service of process;

4. the name and the business address of each partner (specifying separately the general partners and the limited partners);

5. the amount of cash and a summary description and the agreed value of any other property or services contributed by each partner and which each partner has agreed to contribute in the future;

6. the times at which or events upon the happening of which any additional contributions agreed to be made by each partner are to be made;

7. any power granted to a limited partner to assign any part of his or her partnership interest to another;

8. if agreed upon, the time at which or the events on the happening of which a partner may terminate his or her membership in the limited partnership and the amount of, or the method of determining, the distribution to which he or she may be entitled respecting his or her partnership interest, and the terms and conditions of the termination and distribution;

9. any right of a partner to receive distributions of property or cash from the limited partnership;

10. any right of a partner to receive, or of a general partner to make, distribution to a partner, including a return of all or any part of a partner's contribution;

11. any time at which or events upon the happening of which the limited partnership is to be dissolved and its affairs wound up;

12. any right of the remaining general partners to continue the business on the withdrawal of a general partner; and

13. any other matters the partners desire to include in the certificate.

Typically, states requiring this information further require that the certificate be signed by all partners, both general and limited. Again, a designation of acceptance of the appointment as registered agent must be included.

After the certificate is drafted, reviewed, and executed, copies should be made before it is sent to the secretary of state or other appropriate governmental authority. Some states require that the certificate be filed in more than one place, such as with the secretary of state and the town clerk's office. Some may also require that the certificate be published in a local newspaper of general circulation or a local legal newspaper, so it is necessary to check state statutes. As with the name reservation noted above, filing fees must be paid at the time the certificate is filed. Often there are separate fees for filing the certificate and for designation of the registered agent. If certified copies of the certificate are desired (it is advisable to obtain at least one certified copy), additional fees must be paid. The cover letter that will be sent together with the check and the certificate should indicate the fees the check is to cover. The cover letter also should indicate the contact person at the law firm, should any questions arise.

D.   *Limited Partnership Agreement*

The next document to be prepared is the limited partnership agreement. The uniform laws do not specify the contents of this agreement, allowing maximum flexibility in drafting. Many of the provisions contained in it will be similar to those found in a general partnership agreement, such as provisions describing the general purpose of the business, the bookkeeping procedures used, indemnification of general partners, insurance, meeting requirements, and so forth. Other provisions, such as those pertaining to contributions, distributions, and withdrawal from the partnership, may require more intricacy than provisions found in a general partnership agreement. Even in those states requiring detailed information in the certificate of limited partnership, it is desirable to make sure that the limited partnership agreement defines all aspects of the relationship among the partners.

As well as setting forth the rights and duties of the general partners, particular attention should be paid to the rights of the limited partners. As can be gleaned from the earlier discussion of safe harbor rules, limited partners statutorily are afforded certain voting, inspection, and limited participation rights, none of which will constitute taking part in the control of the business. Any rights granted limited partners in the limited partnership agreement should be specifically enumerated rather than generalized to avoid any potential reading of such rights as participation in the running of the business.

The limited partnership agreement should address not only the initial capital contributions to be made by each general and limited partner, but also the timing or events upon which additional contributions are to be made. Under the 1985 Act, a promise by a limited partner to contribute to the partnership only is enforceable if the promise is in a writing signed by the limited partner. The timing of the return of a contribution made by a limited partner should be included. Profits and losses may be allocated in whatever manner desired by the parties. As noted earlier, the limited partnership agreement may specify that the limited partners will receive a set return, or a proportion of the profits for a set period, or share profits in the manner of the general partners. Under both the 1976 and 1985 Acts, the limited partnership agreement is controlling. The manner in which any loan made to the limited partnership by a general or limited partner will be paid back should be detailed and the creditor status of the partner indicated. Under Section 804 of both the 1976 and 1985 Acts, partners who are creditors of the limited partnership have the same rights as nonpartner creditors. If the client desires a different result, it must be so specified in the agreement.

Provision should be made for both the admission and removal (or expulsion) of a general partner. The limited partnership agreement should indicate the requisite voting requirements and any other admissions procedures desired. In the case of removal of a general partner, it should specify the circumstances under which a general partner may be removed, the procedure for such removal, and the procedure for replacing a general partner should the situation require it. Voluntary withdrawal of both general and limited partners is an important issue, necessitating specification of notice requirements and buyout provisions. Section 603 in 1976 and 1985 Acts states in that unless otherwise specified in the limited partnership agreement, a limited partner may not withdraw without first providing six months' notice in writing. However, the Acts do permit free transferability of a limited partner's interest in the partnership. The circumstances under which an assignee becomes a limited partner should be detailed in the limited partnership agreement. Should the parties choose to restrict such transfer, the particulars of such restriction should be spelled out. As with the admission of additional general partners, the limited partnership agreement should address the admission of additional limited partners, specifying voting requirements and any other admissions requirements that must be met.

A limited partnership typically is created for a specific venture or series of ventures and thus is in existence for a limited duration. The time frame for its existence or the events upon the happening of which the limited partnership will be terminated should be set forth. If priorities will be given to certain partners in distribution upon dissolution of the limited partnership, they should be set forth as well.

E. Additional Considerations

In addition to drafting the limited partnership agreement, a few additional matters must be addressed. In those states requiring all partners to sign the certificate of limited partnership, any amendments to the certificate must be signed by all partners as well. Therefore, it is advisable to obtain powers of attorney given by each limited partner to a general partner to facilitate any future amendment process. Further, having researched the Securities and Exchange Commission regulations, a determination should be made by the attorney as to whether the client limited partnership meets any of the exemptions. If the client does not, then registration with the Securities and Exchange Commission and the state securities commissioner may be required. Additionally, if the client wishes to operate in other states, the appropriate applications to qualify to transact business as a foreign limited partnership must be prepared (this is discussed in the next section).

To keep track of the various tasks that may be required of you as a paralegal in aiding the client in the formation process, a checklist is helpful. If none presently exists in the law office, one may be devised along these lines:

Limited Partnership Checklist

- Check name availability (obtain at least three choices from client)
- Reserve name: send reservation form and fee
- Research SEC exemptions to determine whether filing with the SEC is required
- Research qualifications in other states and reserve name in those states (if applicable)
- Prepare certificate of limited partnership
- Have certificate signed by appropriate partners and registered agent designation signed by registered agent
- After photocopying, send cover letter, certificate, and filing fee to state filing official
- Prepare limited partnership agreement to be signed by all partners
- Prepare powers of attorney to be signed by limited partners (if applicable)
- Prepare foreign limited partnership applications for those foreign states in which client will conduct business (if applicable)
- Prepare any required fictitious name documents (if applicable)
- If not handled by client or client's accountant, apply for federal employer identification number, sales tax permit (if applicable), and any other pertinent permits and licenses

In addition to a checklist of tasks to be completed, a limited partnership formation worksheet is essential to guarantee all relevant information is obtained from the client before any of the above documents are drafted. This can be approached in one of two ways; separate worksheets can be created for the certificate and for the limited partnership agreement, or one master worksheet can be created and highlighters (or some other chosen technique) used to discern the information necessary for each document. A completed sample master worksheet is found in the Client Simulation at the end of the chapter. Additionally, it is a timesaver if various forms can be pulled up on the firm's computers. In states that do not prescribe state-authorized forms, the time taken to create name reservation and certificate of limited partnership forms based on your state's statutory guidelines will be time well spent. In those states requiring the use of official forms, check with the office of the secretary of state to see if they will allow a computer-generated form copying the official form's format. If your office has a scanning device, you may be able to generate an exact replica of the official form to appear on your computer screen. Another timesaving device is to keep a listing of all phone numbers for the various divisions of the secretary of state's office, the Internal Revenue Service, city hall, and so forth on a laminated card or on a bulletin board for easy access. These are numbers you will call time and time again in connection with the formation and maintenance of various business entities, so quick access is advisable.

LIMITED PARTNERSHIP IN A FOREIGN STATE

A limited partnership is a foreigner in every state except its state of formation (domicile). Because transacting business is considered a privilege rather than a right, permission is required to transact business as a foreign limited partnership. Permission is granted when application to register as a foreign limited partnership has been made and a certificate of authority has been issued. Typically, a foreign limited partnership transacting business in a state may not bring suit or defend an action in any court of that state until registration has been completed. Additionally, some states assess penalties against a foreign limited partnership for the period during which it conducted unauthorized business in the state. The statutory requirements of each state in which the client desires to conduct business must be researched.

The first thing that must be considered is how a state's statutes define the term "transacting business." There may be certain activities in which a limited partnership may partake that are not considered "transacting business" and thus would not require registration. What one usually will find is that state statutes, rather than defining transacting business, will provide a detailed list of those activities that fall *outside* its scope. Such a list often includes:

1. Maintaining, defending, or settling any suit or similar proceeding within the state.
2. Maintaining bank accounts within the state.
3. Selling within the state through the use of independent contractors.
4. Owning, without more, personal or real property in the state.
5. Holding meetings of the partners within the state or carrying on other activities concerning internal partnership affairs of the limited partnership.

6. Maintaining offices or agencies within the state for the transfer, exchange, and registration of the partnership's own securities or maintaining trustees or depositaries with respect to those securities.
7. Soliciting or obtaining orders within the state, whether by mail or through employees or agents or otherwise, if the orders require acceptance outside the state before they become contracts.
8. Securing or enforcing collection of debts within the state, including mortgages and other security interests.
9. Creating or acquiring indebtedness in either real or personal property located within the state.
10. Conducting an isolated transaction within the state that is completed within 30 days and that is not one of a course of repeated transactions of a like nature.
11. Transacting business in interstate commerce.

Although this list would appear to allow many liberties, if there is any question as to whether a client's proposed transactions would fall outside the permitted list of activities, it is prudent to have the client register as a foreign limited partnership. Registration is typically done through the office of the secretary of state. Many states require the application to be submitted in duplicate. Although the contents of the registration application varies from state to state, the usual requirements are skeletal:

1. The name of the foreign limited partnership and, if different, the name under which it proposes to register and transact business in the state.
2. The date and state of its formation.
3. The general character of the business it proposes to transact in the state (this is often omitted).
4. The name and address of a registered agent and office in the state (the agent must be an individual resident of the state, a domestic corporation, or a foreign corporation having a place of business in the state).
5. A statement that the secretary of state is appointed as the registered agent if no agent has been appointed or the agent's authority is revoked.
6. The address of the office required to be maintained in the state of its organization by the laws of that state or, if not so required, of the principal office of the foreign limited partnership.
7. The name and business address of each general partner. (Some states require the name and address of each limited partner as well.)
8. The address of the recordkeeping office maintained in the state of domicile.

As in the domiciliary state, a foreign limited partnership must comply with the name requirements in the foreign state. Verifying name availability and reserving the desired name should be done. As noted in the enumerated list of requirements above, a registered agent and office must be designated in the foreign state. Some states may require a **certificate of existence** (sometimes referred to as a **certificate of good standing**), a statement that the applicant limited partnership is existing legally as a limited partnership from the domicile state. A few states require a copy of the certificate of limited partnership. Once the application is completed, it must be signed and sworn to by a general partner (some states may require all the general partners or all partners). After it is sent to the secretary of state's office with the appropriate filing fee and processed, a certificate of authority will be provided. See Exhibit 4.2 for a sample application.

EXHIBIT 4.2

Application by Foreign Limited Partnership for Authorization to Transact Business in the State of Any State

1. _____
   (Name of limited partnership as it is in the home state)

2. _____
   (If name is unavailable, name under which the limited partnership proposes to register or transact business in Any State; must contain "Limited Partnership," "Limited," or "Ltd.")

3. _____
   (State of Formation)

4. _____
   (Date of Formation)

5. _____
   (Name of Registered Agent for Service of Process)

6. _____
   (Street Address of Registered Office)

   _____, Any State _____
   (City)   (Zip Code)

EXHIBIT 4.2   *Continued*

7. Acceptance by the Registered Agent for Service of Process.

_____

(Agent must sign on this line)

8. _____

(Address of Registered Office required in State of Formation or, if not required, Address of Principal Office.)

9. NAMES OF GENERAL PARTNERS   BUSINESS ADDRESSES

_____   _____

_____   _____

_____   _____

10. _____

(Office where Names, Addresses and Contributions of Limited Partners are kept.)

11. The limited partnership will undertake to keep the records listing the addresses and capital contributions of the limited partner or limited partners until the limited partnership's registration in Any State is canceled or withdrawn.

12. _____

(Mailing Address of Limited Partnership)

This _____ day of _____, 19_____.

_____

General Partner

STATE OF _____

COUNTY OF _____

THE FOREGOING instrument was acknowledged and sworn to before me this

_____ day of _____, 19_____, by _____ (Name of

General Partner) of _____

EXHIBIT 4.2 *Continued*

(Name of Limited Partnership) a _____ (State or Country) Limited Partnership, on behalf of the Limited Partnership.

_____
        Notary Public

State of _____ at Large

(SEAL) My Commission Expires: _____

DISSOLUTION

Under the 1976 and 1985 Acts, dissolution of a limited partnership may occur
in one of several ways: (1) by the occurrence of events specified in the limited
partnership agreement, (2) by the expiration of the period of duration specified
in the certificate of limited partnership or in the limited partnership agreement,
(3) by written unanimous consent of the partners, (4) by judicial decree, or
(5) by the withdrawal of a general partner. In this last case, the dissolution need
not occur if at least one general partner remains and the limited partnership
agreement allows continuance of the business. If the limited partnership agreement is silent, the limited partnership may still continue in operation if, within
90 days of a general partner's withdrawal, the remaining partners unanimously
consent in writing to do so (in this situation, if no general partner is left, one
or more additional general partners may be appointed). Withdrawal or death of
a limited partner does not typically dissolve a limited partnership unless there
are no limited partners remaining (in which instance the limited partnership
may be dissolved and a general partnership formed if the parties so desire).

Upon dissolution, the winding up of a limited partnership follows the dictates of the limited partnership agreement. If no such provision is made, the
task is left to the general partners or, if none exist, to the limited partners.
Section 804 of both the 1976 and 1985 Acts states the manner in which distribution of assets is to occur, unless otherwise provided in the agreement. All
creditors of the limited partnership are to be paid off first. As noted earlier, no
distinction is made between nonpartner and partner creditors. Should anything
remain after these obligations are met, partners receive a return of contributions and lastly, their share of distributions.

Section 203 of both the 1976 and 1985 Acts provides that upon commencement of winding up of the limited partnership a **certificate of cancellation** must be filed. This certificate sets forth the name of the limited partnership, the date of filing the certificate of limited partnership, the reason for filing the certificate of cancellation, the effective date of cancellation if it is not to be effective upon the filing of the certificate, and any other information the general partners desire to include. Section 204 of both Acts provides that the certificate of cancellation must be signed by all of the general partners.

CLIENT SIMULATION

Earlier in the day, Karen and Thomas met with a new client, Leslie Osborne, president of Osborne Construction Corporation who, together with four other parties, desires to form a limited partnership. The parties are joining together to buy an older office building which, when renovated, they plan on turning into a medical office complex which they will rent out and then sell. The estimated cost to purchase and renovate is $1.5 million and the prospective lender wants at least 30 percent down ($450,000). Osborne Construction Corporation, in charge of the renovations, will be one of two general partners. The other general partner is Nicholas Stark, a plastic surgeon who plans on opening an office in the complex. The three limited partners are Madeline Holmes, Edward Corbett, and Frank Emeroy.

Having returned from lunch, Karen pulls out the limited partnership formation worksheet completed earlier so she may begin to prepare the necessary documents. The completed worksheet reads as follows:

EXHIBIT 4.3

Limited Partnership Formation Worksheet

DATE OF INTAKE:	February 17, 1997
ATTORNEY:	Thomas Trumbull
PARALEGAL:	Karen Greer
CLIENT NUMBER:	1608

EXHIBIT 4.3   *Continued*

MATTER NUMBER: 0001

PERSON RESPONSIBLE
FOR INTAKE: Karen Greer

1. CLIENT NAME: Leslie Osborne of Osborne Construction Corporation for
client limited partnership

2. ADDRESS: 7353 Grantham Road
Any City, Any State

3. TELEPHONE: (000) 331-2263   FAX: (000) 331-2277

4. NAME OF LIMITED PARTNERSHIP (THREE CHOICES):
1st choice: Equity Capital Investments, Ltd.
2nd choice: Prestige Capital Investments, Ltd.
3rd choice: Premiere Capital Investments, Ltd.

5. STATE OF FORMATION: Any State

6. LIST ANY STATES THAT RESERVATION OF NAME IS NEEDED:
Any State
Client does not have plans to become a foreign limited
partnership in any other state at this time.

7. IS SEC FILING REQUIRED? _____ Yes   X   No

8. REGISTERED AGENT: Thomas Trumbull, Esquire

9. REGISTERED OFFICE: Trumbull and McDonald, P.A.
2500 Jefferson Street
Any City, Any State

10. PRINCIPAL OFFICE OF THE LIMITED PARTNERSHIP: 145 Ventnor Street
Any City, Any State

11. OTHER OFFICES: None at this time

12. LATEST DATE UPON WHICH THE LIMITED PARTNERSHIP IS TO
DISSOLVE: December 31, 2025

EXHIBIT 4.3   *Continued*

13. PURPOSE: Real estate investment and any other lawful business

permitted under the laws of the United States and

Any State

14. EFFECTIVE DATE: Upon filing of the certificate of limited partnership

15. FISCAL YEAR: Calendar year

16. ACCOUNTANT: Avtar Singh, C.P.A.

216 Larkspur Road

Any City, Any State

(000) 721-8181

17. ACCOUNTING METHOD: Cash method

18. NAMES AND BUSINESS ADDRESSES OF GENERAL PARTNERS:

Osborne Construction Corporation

7353 Grantham Road, Any City, Any State

Dr. Nicholas Stark

268 St. Albans Drive, Any City, Any State

19. ADDITIONAL GENERAL PARTNERS: May be added by majority vote of

all partners

20. INITIAL CAPITAL CONTRIBUTION OF EACH GENERAL PARTNER AND
PERCENTAGE OF INTEREST IN THE LIMITED PARTNERSHIP:

Osborne Const. Corp. $100,000   20% interest

Dr. Nicholas Stark $100,000   20% interest

21. ADDITIONAL CONTRIBUTIONS OF GENERAL PARTNERS: Each general

partner shall make such additional capital contributions

as may be agreed upon from time to time by the general

partners. Any loans made by a general partner shall be

evinced by a promissory note indicating the terms and

EXHIBIT 4.3 *Continued*

conditions of repayment, which shall be agreed upon by all the general partners.

22. GENERAL PARTNERS' CONTRIBUTIONS OTHER THAN CAPITAL: (SPECIFY PROPERTY AND DESIGNATED VALUE):   None

23. GENERAL PARTNERS' RIGHTS IN SPECIFIC PROPERTY: (SPECIFY):
None

24. NAMES AND BUSINESS ADDRESSES OF LIMITED PARTNERS:

Madeline Holmes

679 Crescent Circle, Any City, Any State

Edward Corbett

226 N.W. 7th Avenue, Any City, Any State

Frank Emeroy

550 S.W. 3rd Street, Any City, Any State

25. ADDITIONAL LIMITED PARTNERS: May be added by a majority vote of all partners

26. INITIAL CAPITAL CONTRIBUTION OF EACH LIMITED PARTNER AND PERCENTAGE OF INTEREST IN THE LIMITED PARTNERSHIP:

Madeline Holmes	$100,000	20% interest
Edward Corbett	$100,000	20% interest
Frank Emeroy	$100,000	20% interest

27. ADDITIONAL CONTRIBUTIONS OF LIMITED PARTNERS: Each limited partner shall make such additional capital contributions as may be agreed upon from time to time by the general partners. Any loans made by a limited partner shall be evinced by a promissory note indicating the terms and conditions of repayment, which shall be agreed upon by all the general partners.

EXHIBIT 4.3   *Continued*

28. LIMITED PARTNERS' CONTRIBUTIONS OTHER THAN CAPITAL: (SPECIFY PROPERTY AND DESIGNATED VALUE): None

29. LIMITED PARTNERS' RIGHTS IN SPECIFIC PROPERTY: (SPECIFY): None

30. TIMING OF RETURN OF CONTRIBUTION TO LIMITED PARTNERS: No contribution or any part thereof made by a limited partner shall be returned to said partner without the consent of all general partners.

31. RIGHT OF LIMITED PARTNERS TO DEMAND AND RECEIVE PROPERTY OTHER THAN CASH IN RETURN FOR CONTRIBUTION: None

32. APPORTIONMENT OF PROFITS AND LOSSES: Profits shall be shared in proportion to each partner's percentage interest in the limited partnership. Limited partners shall be liable for obligations of the limited partnership only to the extent of any contributions made or promised to the limited partnership.

33. RESTRICTIONS ON TRANSFER OF INTEREST IN LIMITED PARTNERSHIP: Each partner's interest in the limited partnership is assignable; however, no assignee shall become either a general or limited partner except by a majority vote of all partners.

34. WITHDRAWAL OF CAPITAL BY A GENERAL PARTNER: No general partner shall withdraw capital from the limited partnership without first obtaining consent from all other general partners.

35. WITHDRAWAL OF CAPITAL BY A LIMITED PARTNER: No limited partner shall withdraw capital from the limited partnership without first obtaining consent from all general partners.

EXHIBIT 4.3 *Continued*

36. RIGHTS AND DUTIES OF GENERAL PARTNERS: All management powers, unless otherwise set forth in this agreement, shall vest in the general partners. The general partners shall have all rights granted by law in the carrying out of their managerial duties.

37. LIMITATIONS ON POWERS OF GENERAL PARTNERS: No general partner may, without the unanimous consent of all partners: (1) borrow or lend money on behalf of the limited partnership; (2) assign, transfer, or pledge any debts due the limited partnership or release any such debts due, except upon payment in full; (3) compromise any claim due to the limited partnership.

38. COMPENSATION OF GENERAL PARTNERS: Osborne Construction Corporation shall receive compensation for the development or renovation of any real estate purchased by the limited partnership according to the terms set forth in a separate agreement between Osborne Construction Corporation and the limited partnership. Other than the terms set forth in said separate agreement, no other compensation shall be paid any general partner.

39. RIGHTS AND LIMITATIONS OF LIMITED PARTNERS: No limited partner may take part in the control of the limited partnership. Limited partners may vote in accordance with the terms set forth elsewhere in the limited partnership agreement. Additionally, they may: (1) consult with the general partners with respect to the business of the limited part-

EXHIBIT 4.3   *Continued*

nership; (2) act as surety for the limited partnership; and (3) request or attend a meeting of the partners.

40. POWER OF ATTORNEY: Client does not want this.

41. VOTING: In accordance with the terms set forth elsewhere in the limited partnership agreement.

42. BANK ACCOUNTS: The limited partnership shall maintain a bank account at Millenium Bank, 3400 Commercial Drive, Any City, Any State. Withdrawals shall be on the signature of two general partners.

43. MEETINGS OF GENERAL PARTNERS: The general partners shall meet twice a month at the principal office of the limited partnership at such times and on such dates as the general partners may from time to time decide. A special meeting may be called by any partner upon written notice to all other partners.

44. INDEMNIFICATION: The limited partnership shall indemnify each general partner with respect to payments reasonably made or liabilities reasonably incurred on behalf of the limited partnership.

45. INSURANCE: Client does not want this.

46. VOLUNTARY WITHDRAWAL OF A LIMITED PARTNER:

(a) CIRCUMSTANCES: A limited partner may not withdraw unless first providing no less than six months' notice to the limited partnership.

(b) PROCEDURES: The withdrawing limited partner shall be paid the appraised value of said partner's share and the remaining partners' interests shall be proportionately increased. The

EXHIBIT 4.3   *Continued*

withdrawal of a limited partner shall not cause the dissolution of the limited partnership.

47. VOLUNTARY WITHDRAWAL OF A GENERAL PARTNER:

    (a) CIRCUMSTANCES: A general partner may not withdraw unless first
obtaining the consent of all of the partners.

    (b) PROCEDURES: The withdrawing general partner shall be paid the
appraised value of said partner's share and the remaining
partners' interests shall be proportionately increased. The
withdrawal of a general partner shall not cause the dissolution of the limited partnership unless no general partner
remains and the remaining limited partners fail to substitute the withdrawing general partner within 90 days from
said withdrawal.

48. EXPULSION OF A GENERAL PARTNER:

    (a) CIRCUMSTANCES: A general partner may be removed by a majority vote
of all of the partners.

    (b) PROCEDURES: The general partner sought to be removed shall be given
30 days' written notice of intent to remove which shall
state the grounds for removal. Should removal of said
partner result in the necessity of substituting a new general
partner, removal of said partner shall become effective
upon such substitution, but in no event prior to above-
mentioned notice. The expelled partner shall be paid his
or her interest in accordance with the provisions set forth
for payment of a withdrawing partner.

49. NONCOMPETITION CLAUSE FOR GENERAL PARTNERS: (IF DESIRED,
    SPECIFY):   Client does not want this.

EXHIBIT 4.3   *Continued*

50. TERMINATION OF LIMITED PARTNERSHIP: The limited partnership shall be dissolved and its affairs wound up by the date set forth in the certificate of limited partnership or sooner upon (1) the unanimous consent of all of the partners or (2) the withdrawal or expulsion of a general partner with no successor general partner elected within 90 days.

51. MEDIATION: Client does not want this.

52. ARBITRATION: All disputes that may arise between the partners shall be settled by arbitration, with the parties choosing a single arbitrator to hear the dispute. The decision of the arbitrator shall be binding.

53. AMENDMENTS: All amendments to this agreement shall be made in writing.

54. ADDITIONAL PROVISIONS: None

After reviewing the worksheet, Karen turns to her list of frequently called numbers she keeps on the bulletin board by her desk and finds the number for the Any State Secretary of State's office. Surprisingly, she gets through right away and is informed that the client's first choice of name is unavailable, but the second choice, Prestige Capital Investments, Ltd., is available and may be reserved for a nonrenewable period of 120 days. After hanging up, Karen turns to her computer and pulls up a form for name reservation and commences to fill in the requisite information. She then sends the form along with the applicable filing fee to the Secretary of State's office.

Karen next turns her attention to the certificate of limited partnership. Her state's statutes closely follow the provisions of the 1985 Act. Karen pulls up a copy of the required official form and reviews the worksheet once more. She has highlighted on the worksheet those items that must be included in the certificate of limited partnership and thus can quickly complete the form, which she does as set out in Exhibit 4.4:

EXHIBIT 4.4

Certificate of Limited Partnership of Prestige Capital Investments, Ltd.

1. Prestige Capital Investments, Ltd.
   (Name of Limited Partnership; must contain a suffix such as
   "Limited," "Ltd.," or "Limited Partnership")

2. 145 Ventnor Street, Any City, Any State
   (The Business Address of Limited Partnership)

3. Thomas Trumbull, Esquire
   (Name of Registered Agent for Service of Process)

4. Trumbull and McDonald, P.A., 2500 Jefferson Street, Any City, Any State
   (Street Address for Registered Agent)

5. _____
   (Registered Agent must sign here to accept designation as Registered Agent for
   Service of Process)

6. 145 Ventnor Street, Any City, Any State
   (Mailing Address of the Limited Partnership)

7. The latest date upon which the Limited Partnership is to be dissolved is
   December 31, 2025.

8. NAME OF GENERAL PARTNER(S)   BUSINESS ADDRESS
   Osborne Construction Corporation   7353 Grantham Road

                                       Any City, Any State
   Dr. Nicholas Stark   268 St. Albans Drive

                                       Any City, Any State

Signed this _____ day of _____, 19_____.

Signature of all general partners:

By: _____
    Dr. Nicholas Stark, General Partner

By: _____
    President, Osborne Construction Corporation, General Partner

Karen proofreads the certificate for errors and prepares a cover letter to send along with the certificate and the appropriate fees after the certificate is reviewed and signed by Thomas as registered agent and the general partners.

With the aid of the detailed worksheet, Karen can competently draft a limited partnership agreement according to her client's specifications. She pulls up a skeletal agreement form containing only an outline agreement and several boilerplate provisions. From this outline, she will flesh out a customized limited partnership agreement. When she is done, it reads as follows:

EXHIBIT 4.5

Limited Partnership Agreement of Prestige Capital Investments, Ltd.

BY THIS AGREEMENT, the signers form a limited partnership under the laws of the State of Any State as of the _____ day of _____, 19_____, and agree to the following terms and conditions:

I. Partners. The general partners are **Osborne Construction Corporation** and **Dr. Nicholas Stark** (hereinafter referred to as "general partners"). The limited partners are **Madeline Holmes, Edward Corbett,** and **Frank Emeroy** (hereinafter referred to as "limited partners").

II. Place of Business. The partnership's principal place of business shall be at 145 Ventnor Street, Any City, Any State, or such other place as the general partners determine in the future.

III. Purpose. The purpose of the limited partnership shall be to engage in real estate investment and any other lawful business permitted under the laws of the United States and Any State.

IV. Term. The limited partnership shall begin on the date first above written and shall continue until terminated as herein provided.

V. Registered Agent and Office. For the term of this Agreement, the limited partnership shall maintain a registered agent and office in full force and effect as set forth in the certificate of limited partnership.

VI. Capital Contributions of General Partners. The initial capital contribution and percentage interest of each general partner are as follows:

Osborne Construction Corporation	$100,000	20% interest
Dr. Nicholas Stark	$100,000	20% interest

EXHIBIT 4.5   *Continued*

VII. Capital Contributions of Limited Partners. The initial capital contribution and percentage interest of each limited partner are as follows:

Madeline Holmes	$100,000	20% interest
Edward Corbett	$100,000	20% interest
Frank Emeroy	$100,000	20% interest

VIII. Additional Contributions. Each partner shall make such additional capital contributions as may be agreed upon from time to time by all of the general partners. Any loans made by a partner shall be evinced by a promissory note indicating the terms and conditions of repayment, which shall be agreed upon by all of the general partners.

IX. Right of a Limited Partner to Demand Return of Contribution. No contribution or any part thereof made by a limited partner shall be returned to said partner without the consent of all general partners.

X. Profit and Loss. Profits shall be shared in proportion to each partner's percentage interest in the limited partnership. Limited partners shall be liable for obligations of the limited partnership only to the extent of any contributions, made or promised, to the limited partnership.

XI. Withdrawal of Capital. No partner shall withdraw capital from the limited partnership without first obtaining the consent of all general partners.

XII. Rights and Limitations of General Partners. All managerial powers, unless otherwise set forth in this Agreement, shall vest in the general partners. The general partners shall have all rights granted by law in the carrying out of their managerial duties. No general partner may, without the unanimous consent of all of the partners:

1. borrow or lend money on behalf of the limited partnership;
2. assign, transfer, or pledge any debts due the limited partnership, or release any such debts due, except on payment in full;
3. compromise any claim due the limited partnership.

XIII. Rights and Limitations of Limited Partners. No limited partner may take part in the control of the limited partnership. Limited partners may vote in accordance with the terms set forth elsewhere in this Agreement. Additionally, they may:

1. consult with the general partners;
2. act as surety for the limited partnership;
3. request or attend meetings of the partners.

EXHIBIT 4.5   *Continued*

XIV. Compensation of General Partners. Osborne Construction Corporation shall receive compensation for the development and/or renovation of any real estate purchased by the limited partnership according to the terms set forth in a separate agreement between Osborne Construction Corporation and the limited partnership. Other than the terms set forth in said separate agreement, no other compensation shall be paid any general partner.

XV. Bank Accounts. The limited partnership shall maintain a bank account at Millenium Bank or at such other banks as may from time to time be agreed upon by the general partners. Withdrawals from said bank account shall be on the signature of two general partners.

XVI. Fiscal Year. The fiscal year of the limited partnership shall end on the 31st day of December.

XVII. Records. The limited partnership shall maintain, at the office of the registered agent, all records as are statutorily required. These records shall be open to inspection at all times by all partners.

XVIII. Meetings of the General Partners. The general partners shall meet twice a month at the principal office of the limited partnership at such times and on such dates as the general partners may from time to time decide. A special meeting may be called by any partner upon written notice to all other partners.

XIX. Indemnification. The limited partnership shall indemnify each general partner with respect to payments reasonably made or liabilities reasonably incurred on behalf of the limited partnership.

XX. Restrictions on Transfer of Interest in the Limited Partnership. Each partner's interest in the limited partnership is assignable; however, no assignee shall become either a general or limited partner except by a majority vote of all partners.

XXI. Voluntary Withdrawal of a Limited Partner. A limited partner may not withdraw without first providing no less than six months' written notice to the limited partnership. The withdrawal of any limited partner shall not cause the dissolution of the limited partnership. The withdrawing limited partner shall be paid the appraised value of said partner's share, and the remaining partners' interests shall be proportionately increased.

EXHIBIT 4.5   *Continued*

XXII. Voluntary Withdrawal of a General Partner. A general partner may not withdraw without first obtaining the consent of all of the partners. The withdrawal of a general partner shall not cause the dissolution of the limited partnership unless there is no remaining general partner and the limited partners fail to substitute the withdrawing general partner within 90 days from said withdrawal. The withdrawing general partner shall be paid the appraised value of said partner's share, and the remaining partners' interests shall be proportionately increased.

XXIII. Expulsion of a General Partner. A general partner may be removed by a majority vote of all of the partners. The general partner sought to be removed shall be given 30 days' written notice of intent to remove, which shall state the grounds for removal. Should removal of said partner result in the necessity of substituting a new general partner, removal of said partner shall become effective upon such substitution, but in no event prior to the above-mentioned notice. The expelled partner shall be paid his or her interest in the limited partnership in accordance with the provisions set forth for payment of a withdrawing partner.

XXIV. Termination. The limited partnership shall be dissolved and its affairs wound up by the date set forth in the certificate of limited partnership or sooner upon (1) the unanimous consent of all of the partners, or (2) the withdrawal or expulsion of a general partner with no successor general partner elected within 90 days.

XXV. Arbitration. All disputes that may arise between partners shall be settled by arbitration, with the parties choosing a single arbitrator to hear the dispute. The decision of the arbitrator shall be binding.

XXVI. Amendments. Any amendments to this Agreement shall be made in writing and shall be attached to this original Agreement.

XXVII. Governing Law. This Agreement shall be governed by and construed in accordance with the laws of the State of Any State.

XXVIII. Severability. In the event that any provision herein shall be unenforceable, the Agreement shall continue in full force and effect and be construed as if such unenforceable provision had never been contained herein.

XXIX. Entire Agreement. This writing represents the entire agreement and understanding of the partners.

EXHIBIT 4.5   *Continued*

IN WITNESS WHEREOF, the parties to this limited partnership agreement have executed it effective as of the day and year first above written.

General Partners:

_____

President, Osborne Construction Corporation

_____

Dr. Nicholas Stark

Limited Partners:

_____

Madeline Holmes

_____

Edward Corbett

_____

Frank Emeroy

After Thomas reviews these documents, Karen will schedule a time for Leslie Osborne to come to the office to meet with Thomas to go over them. Before Leslie takes the documents to be signed by the other partners, photocopies should be made. Upon return by Leslie of the certificate of limited partnership, Karen will send it with the prepared cover letter and applicable fees to the office of the Any State Secretary of State. To facilitate Leslie's returning the original certificate and the limited partnership agreement, Karen provides her with a self-addressed, stamped envelope.

Chapter Summary

1. A limited partnership is a statutorily created entity comprised of at least one limited partner and at least one general partner. It is an advantageous business format for those parties wishing both to invest in a business and limit their risk. For general partners, it provides additional flexibility in raising capital.

Although fraught with more formalities and legal expenses than either a sole proprietorship or a general partnership, it avoids the double taxation bind of corporations.

2. Unlike a general partnership, a limited partnership must register to transact business in any state other than its state of domicile. Most states define "transacting business" in the negative by enumerating those activities not considered as such.

3. The 1916, 1976, and 1985 Acts show the evolution in uniform laws pertaining to limited partnerships from more restrictive to less restrictive, from greater reliance on the certificate of limited partnership to greater reliance on the limited partnership agreement, and from state boundary limitations to expansion of business into other states.

4. Limited partners may lose their protective shield of limited personal liability for partnership debts if their surnames are included in the partnership name or if they take part in the control of the partnership business. The 1976 Act devised a safe harbor list, later expanded by the 1985 Act, of acceptable activities in which limited partners may participate safely.

5. A limited partner's interest is considered a security and will be subject to federal and state securities regulations unless the limited partnership meets the qualifications for one of the allowable exemptions. Intrastate offerings and private offerings are exempt under the SEC regulations. States, enacting their own blue sky laws, vary in their securities filing requirements.

6. A limited partnership does not exist legally until a certificate of limited partnership is filed. Under the 1985 Act, this document has been streamlined down to skeletal requirements and needs to be signed only by the general partners. Under the 1976 Act, a more detailed certificate must be filed and signed by all of the partners. In both instances, a registered agent must be designated and a registered office kept in full force and effect throughout the term of the limited partnership.

7. The limited partnership agreement now is considered the key document for the operation of the internal affairs of the limited partnership. In addition to drafting the certificate and the agreement, a legal assistant may be asked to prepare any required fictitious name affidavits, federal employer identification forms, and foreign limited partnership registration applications.

Review Questions

1. Compare and contrast a limited partnership with:
    (i)   a general partnership
    (ii) a limited liability partnership

2. List the types of activities in which a limited partner may participate without being considered as taking part in the control of the business.
3. What are the major differences between:
    (i)   the 1916 Act and the 1976 Act?
    (ii) the 1976 Act and the 1985 Act?
4. Explain the intrastate offering exemption and the private offering exemption.
5. List the steps to be taken in forming a limited partnership.

KEY TERMS

blue sky law
certificate of authority
certificate of
    cancellation
certificate of existence
certificate of limited
    partnership
derivative actions
domicile
foreign limited
    partnership
Investment Advisors
    Act of 1940
limited liability
    partnership

limited partner
limited partnership
registered agent
RULPA
safe harbor list
security
Securities Act of
    1933
Securities Exchange
    Act of 1934
statement of foreign
    qualification
statement of
    qualification

5 | *Limited Liability Companies*

Overview of Objectives

Upon completion of this chapter, the student will:

- understand the similarities and differences between limited liability companies and other business entities
- understand the major factors determining the tax status of a limited liability company
- know the key documents of a limited liability company and how to draft them
- know how to amend the key documents of a limited liability company

INTRODUCTION

On any given day, if one were to ask a business client what would be the best possible world in which to function as a business entity, the answer would contain the following characteristics: protection from personal liability, full participation rights, no statutorily imposed restrictions on membership, favorable tax treatment, and managerial flexibility. Can an accommodating attorney oblige such a client? Perhaps. The limited liability company is a legislative attempt to provide all of the above characteristics. It remained an unknown possibility until 1977 when Wyoming became the first state to adopt legislative provisions creating the Wyoming Limited Liability Company Act. Florida followed Wyoming's lead in 1982, but most state legislatures failed to recognize this entity as a viable alternative until the early 1990s. At present, almost every state has recognized this business entity and has enacted limited liability statutes or is in the process of considering enactment of such statutes.

This chapter compares and contrasts limited liability companies with other business entities and introduces terminology particular to a limited liability company with which a paralegal should be acquainted. Further, this chapter explains the steps you would take in assisting a client in forming a limited liability company, amending documents, and, if need be, in dissolving the company.

NATURE OF A LIMITED LIABILITY COMPANY

A **limited liability company** is an artificial entity, legally separate from its owners, and created by state statute. The National Conference of Commissioners on Uniform State Laws approved a **Uniform Limited Liability Company Act** in August of 1994 (the **ULLCA**), which was subsequently amended in August 1995 and approved in amended form by the American Bar Association in February 1996. The ULLCA, discussed throughout this chapter, grew out of the perceived need for uniform legislation due to the great variation in state law governing limited liability companies. At the time of this writing, no state has officially adopted the ULLCA, although a movement toward widespread adoption is likely.

The most outstanding characteristic of the limited liability company is its hybrid nature, combining the primary advantages of a corporation and a partnership. A limited liability company combines the limited personal liability and broad powers of a corporation with the advantageous federal tax treatment of a partnership.

A.   Comparisons to Sole Proprietorships and General Partnerships

Limited liability companies allow the owners of the company (called **members**) full participation in the daily operations of the business, if they so desire. In this manner, they are similar to sole proprietorships and general partnerships. It also is possible for a limited liability company, like a general partnership, to dissolve upon the occurrence of a "triggering" event, such as the death, bankruptcy, disability, insanity, or retirement of a member, unless the other members decide to continue the business. As noted in Chapter 3, if a partner assigns or sells his or her partnership interest to another, the assignment or sale of the partnership interest does not automatically make the assignee or buyer a partner. Typically, one may not become a partner unless all other partners agree. Membership in a limited liability company usually works the same way. Further, just as partners have no property interest in the property owned by a partnership, the members of a limited liability company have no property interest in the property owned by a limited liability company.

The members of a limited liability company have a distinct advantage, however, when it comes to personal liability. Unlike a sole proprietor or general partner, a member of a limited liability company is not individually liable for business obligations. A member's liability is limited to the extent of his or her current and promised contributions to the company. Some exceptions exist, however, such as holding members and managers personally liable for violation of environmental and federal tax laws.

Not-for-profit organizations are precluded from becoming general partnerships or limited partnerships. Under the ULLCA, a limited liability company may be organized to engage in an activity either for or not for profit. State laws may vary on this, however, and should be checked.

B.   Comparisons to Limited Partnerships

As noted in the last chapter, a limited partner in a limited partnership has a distinct advantage over a general partner when it comes to insulation from unlimited personal liability for business debts. The price paid by the limited partner for such protection is the relinquishment of full participation in the business. A limited liability company allows all members the same protection as well as equal participation rights.

Under Section 902 of the ULLCA, a general partnership or a limited partnership may be converted to a limited liability company. In order to convert, the conversion must be approved by all of the partners or the requisite number of partners specified in the partnership agreement.

C.   Comparisons to Corporations

The limited liability company statutes of some states require at least two members, unlike the corporate statutes of most states which permit single-shareholder corporations. Under the ULLCA, single-member limited liability companies are permitted. Both business entities provide limited liability for their owners. While corporations may have a perpetual existence, a number of states presently impose a limitation of 30 years on limited liability companies. This limitation may be changing, however. The ULLCA makes a distinction between **term companies** (i.e., those companies whose legal duration is for a specified term, such as 30 years) and **at-will companies** (i.e., those existing for an unspecified duration). This distinction has important ramifications when it comes to dissociation and dissolution, as discussed below.

When a shareholder of a corporation wants to sell stock, representing his or her ownership interest in the corporation, the shareholder usually may do so freely, unless a restrictive shareholders' agreement is in place (discussed in later chapters). In selling those shares, the shareholder is also selling voting rights, giving the new shareholder the same authority as his or her predecessor. When a member of a limited liability company sells his or her membership interest, the buyer does not typically become a member unless all other members agree.

In a corporation, the board of directors may not pay out distributions to shareholders if the corporation's total assets would be less than its total liabilities or the corporation would not be able to pay its debts as they became due in the ordinary course of business. Distributions paid under these circumstances would be considered unlawful distributions, and the directors of the corporation would be personally liable to the corporation. The same is true with a limited liability company. In a limited liability company, the persons who manage the company (be they members or hired managers) incur personal liability for the payment to members of unlawful distributions.

A shareholder in a corporation may bring a lawsuit, called a derivative suit or derivative action, on behalf of the corporation if the board of directors has the authority to do so and refuses to take action. (The concept of derivative action was mentioned in the previous chapter and is discussed in detail in Chapter 10.) Similarly, a member of a limited liability company may bring a derivative suit on behalf of the limited liability company if the members or managers having authority to do so refuse to take action.

The major advantage of a limited liability company over a regular corporation (a "C" corporation, discussed in the next chapter), is in its federal tax treatment. If formed properly, a limited liability company will be taxed as a partnership, thus avoiding a concept called "double taxation." This means that the individual members will be taxed on their proportionate profits and losses, but the business will not be federally taxed as a separate entity.

Many businesses seek to avoid the double taxation problem by forming a type of corporation called an "S" corporation (discussed in the next chapter). Although S corporations receive the favorable tax treatment of a partnership, many restrictions apply to forming such an entity which do not apply to forming a limited liability company. Limited liability companies do not have the same restrictions imposed on the number or types of members permitted. Limited liability companies are permitted to own 80 percent or more of a corporation, unlike S corporations. The Internal Revenue Code has provisions allowing special allocation of income, gains, losses, deductions, and credits for limited liability companies, as well as provisions allowing greater flexibility regarding contributions and distributions of appreciated property.

TERMINOLOGY

A. *Members*

Members are the owners of the limited liability company. In most states, members can be natural persons, partnerships, corporations, or other business entities. In many states, members are allowed to manage a limited liability company directly and have equal management rights (reflected in equal voting rights), regardless of each member's proportionate capital contribution. In some states, management rights of members are determined in proportion to each member's capital contribution. According to Section 404(a) of the ULLCA, in a **member-managed company**, each member has equal management rights and any business-related matter may be decided by a majority vote of the members, unless the operating agreement provides otherwise.

A member's capital contribution may be made in terms of cash contributions, property, services, or legally binding promises to contribute any of the above. A member exercises managerial power through voting, whether it be at a duly convened meeting of the members, or through a written unanimous consent of the members, which most states allow. If the articles of organization (described in the next section) state that the company will be managed by managers, the members exercise control by electing and voting for managers. If the articles of organization are silent on the matter of managers, the members manage the company directly.

In a member-managed company, a member owes other members the duty of loyalty and the duty of care (see discussion of these duties in Chapter 6). Under Section 301 of the ULLCA, each member is an agent of the company in a member-managed company. However, if the company is managed by appointed managers (i.e., a **manager-managed company**), members are not considered agents of the company and do not, as members, have the apparent authority to bind the company to third parties.

Section 404(c) of the ULLCA provides that the following matters require the consent of all members (regardless of whether the limited liability company is member-managed or manager-managed):

1.   the amendment of the operating agreement (unless the operating agreement states otherwise);
2.   the authorization or ratification of acts or transactions which would otherwise violate the duty of loyalty;
3.   an amendment to the articles of organization (unless the operating agreement states otherwise);
4.   the compromise of an obligation to make a contribution;
5.   the compromise, as among members, of an obligation of a member to make a contribution or return money or other property paid or distributed in violation of this Act;
6.   the making of interim distributions, including the redemption of an interest;
7.   the admission of a new member;
8.   the use of the company's property to redeem an interest subject to a charging order;
9.   the consent to dissolve the company;
10. a waiver of the right to have the company's business wound up and the company terminated;
11. the consent of the members to merge with another entity; and
12. the sale, lease, exchange, or other disposal of all, or substantially all, of the company's property with or without goodwill.

If a member chooses to resign, the member must provide proper written notice. If the resigning member violates any terms of the company's operating agreement (discussed below), the member may be liable for damages to the company. New members usually are not allowed unless all other existing members agree.

B. Organizers

Organizers execute a document called the **articles of organization**, which formally creates the limited liability company. A limited liability company is not legally created until this document is signed by one or more organizers and filed with the filing official in the state of creation (usually the secretary of state's office). An organizer may be a member of the limited liability company, but need not be. In most states, the only requirement of organizers is that they be natural persons of lawful age. It may be that the attorney drafting the articles of organization for the client company will act as organizer.

C. *Board of Governors*

A few states require a limited liability company to have a body called a board of governors. This board's function is similar to that of a board of directors of a corporation (discussed in the next chapter).

D. *Managers*

In most states, the management of a limited liability company may be placed in the hands of managers. The managers may or may not be members of the limited liability company and need not be state residents. Their function is to manage the daily operations of the company and, if the company does not have a board of governors, to establish the broad policy structure of the company. Section 404(b) of the ULLCA states that in a manager-managed company, each manager has equal management rights and business-related matters may be decided by a majority vote of the managers. In some states, a limited liability company must have at least two members and one manager. A manager must be a natural person of lawful age.

Managers are voted into office by the members at an annual meeting, typically by a majority vote, unless the articles of organization or operating agreement indicate otherwise. While state statutory law requires that managers be voted in each year, most states allow for staggered terms. This can be accomplished by dividing managers into classes and having the members vote in at least one class each year. This provides an overlap of new and old management and prevents an entirely new group of managers from being voted in at one time. An attorney drafting the articles of organization of a limited liability company must find out from the client whether this precaution is desired prior to filing the document.

Just as managers are voted into office by a majority vote of the members, a manager may be removed from office by a majority vote of the members, unless the articles of organization or the operating agreement state otherwise. Should a vacancy occur between elections, the vacancy may be filled by the majority of the managers.

Managers are agents of the limited liability company, similar to general partners in a partnership, and have the same fiduciary duties to the company as general partners do to the partnership. They sign the important company documents and their actions legally bind the company. It is therefore important when drafting the articles of organization and/or the operating agreement to detail any limitations the members desire to place on the managers' authority to act. If a manager acts in contravention of these limitations, he or she will have breached his or her fiduciary duties and will be liable for such breach to the company and the members.

E.   Articles of Organization

This document officially creates the limited liability company. It is signed by one or more organizers and is filed with the state filing official, usually the secretary of state. It contains basic information about the company and its members, although the statutory requirements regarding the information the articles must contain varies from state to state.

F.   Regulations

Some states require that a limited liability company have a document called **regulations** which acts as the internal governing document of the company, similar to the bylaws of a corporation.

G.   Operating Agreement

The **operating agreement** is a contract between the members of the limited liability company, similar to a partnership agreement, which is binding on all members and thus must be agreed to by all members of the limited liability company. Under the ULLCA, an operating agreement may be oral, although it is advisable to have a written agreement. Because it is not filed with the state and therefore remains an internal document, it usually contains more detailed information than the articles of organization.

It is advisable that there be no conflict between the articles of organization and the operating agreement of a limited liability company. However, should a conflict exist, the ULLCA provides that the operating agreement controls as to members but the articles of organization control as to third parties.

TAX CONSIDERATIONS

One of the primary advantages of forming a limited liability company is the prevention of double taxation to which many corporations are subject. By carefully drafting the articles of organization and operating agreement, a "pass through" entity will be created. This means that the profits and losses of the entity will pass through to the members, who are the owners, and will bypass federal taxation at the entity level.

The Internal Revenue Service first looked at the federal tax status of a limited liability company in 1988 when it issued Revenue Ruling 88-76, classifying a Wyoming limited liability company as a partnership for federal tax purposes based on a determination that it lacked certain corporate characteristics. The primary characteristic lacking was continuity of life.

At present, a thorough understanding of Treasury Regulation 301.7701-2 is required in order to successfully create a limited liability company that works as a pass through entity. This federal regulation determines whether an entity will be taxed as a corporation. It sets forth a list of characteristics considered corporate characteristics, which include the following:

- Continuity of life
- Centralized management
- Limited liability — *all LLC's have this*
- Free transferability of interests

The Internal Revenue Service will classify an entity as a partnership if it is lacking two or more of the above characteristics.

Subsection (b)(1) of the regulation pertains to continuity of life. Most corporations have a perpetual existence. They may continue to function indefinitely, regardless of the death, retirement, or expulsion of a shareholder. A limited liability company must lack this characteristic if it wants to be taxed as a partnership. Many state statutes limit the life of a limited liability company to a set number of years, such as 30 years. Additionally, a "triggering" event for dissolution of the company, such as death, bankruptcy, retirement, resignation, expulsion, or insanity of a member, will negate the continuity of the entity. This is the case even if a provision is included giving the remaining members the right to continue the business after such a triggering event if all remaining members consent to do so. One must be careful, however, in drafting such a provision, to require the unanimous consent of the remaining members rather than a simple majority, which may not be sufficient for Internal Revenue Service purposes.

Subsection (c)(1) pertains to centralized management. A corporation is deemed to have centralized management because its management is in the hands of the board of directors. The Internal Revenue Service considers an entity to possess this characteristic if any group that does not include all the members has exclusive authority to make management decisions.

Subsection (d)(1) concerns limited liability. An entity possesses this characteristic if no member is personally liable for the entity's debts. All limited liability companies contain this characteristic.

Subsection (e)(1) treats free transferability of interests. As noted above, shareholders in corporations may freely transfer their ownership interest to another by selling their stock, unless a shareholders' restrictive agreement prevents such a transfer. With the transfer of the stock comes the transfer of ownership rights in the corporation. The Internal Revenue Service considers an entity to possess the characteristic of free transferability of interests if each member has the ability, without the consent of other members, to transfer his or her membership rights to another. Conversely, an entity will lack this characteristic if the consent of other members must first be obtained before such transfer can take place. Unanimous consent is not required; the consent of the majority capital interests in the company will suffice.

When drafting the articles of organization and the operating agreement for a client limited liability company, one must be aware of these interpretations to provide the client with the desired federal tax treatment. The Internal Revenue Service issues **private letter rulings** (written statements issued to taxpayers interpreting and applying tax laws to a specific set of facts) on the tax classification of limited liability companies and an attorney should request one if he or she has any doubt about the prospective tax status of a client. Additionally, one must understand that the above regulation refers only to federal tax treatment; states differ on whether a limited liability is subject to state corporate income tax. Therefore, a thorough review of state tax statutes is essential.

FORMATION

A paralegal can be an active participant in the formation of a limited liability company. Utilizing information obtained from the client and a checklist of tasks to be performed, a legal assistant can smoothly assist the attorney and client through the formation process. A checklist of tasks to be performed may look something like this:

Checklist

- Check name availability
- Reserve name: send reservation form and fee
- Research qualifications in other states (if applicable)
- Prepare articles of organization

- Have articles signed by organizer(s), and registered agent designation signed by registered agent
- Make photocopies of articles
- Send articles and photocopy to state filing official together with cover letter and filing fee
- Prepare operating agreement
- Have operating agreement signed by all members

A.   Name Selection and Reservation

The first step in forming a limited liability company is securing the name under which the client wishes to operate. Under most state statutes, the name of a limited liability company must contain the words "limited liability company" or the abbreviations "L.C." or "L.L.C." Some states simply allow the use of the word "limited" or its abbreviation. In other states, such designations would indicate a limited partnership, so state statutes must be checked carefully.

The name of the limited liability company may not be deceptively similar to (and must be distinguishable in records from) the name of any existing corporation, limited partnership, other limited liability company, or any other registered or reserved name. Additionally, the name must not mislead the public by implying that the company is engaged in a business other than that stated in its articles of organization.

In most states, verification of name availability may be done over the phone, usually by calling the appropriate telephone number at the secretary of state's office. When checking on name availability, remember that a client may wish to do business in more than one state, operating under the same name. Therefore, it might be necessary to verify name availability (and reserve or register the name) with each state in which the client wishes to operate. It is advisable to obtain several choices of name from the client, listed in order of preference, before telephoning to avoid repeated telephone calls. (Please note, however, that to register a name in a foreign state, some states may first require a certificate of existence from the state of organization. Thus, registration in these states may not be accomplished until the company is legally created by the filing of articles of organization in the state of domicile.)

Typically, a name reservation cannot be made over the phone. The telephone verification is a preliminary step to sending in a name reservation application along with the appropriate reservation fee. The name of the limited liability company will be reserved for the client for a specified number of days upon receipt of the application. Thus, it is necessary to have prepared and filed the articles of organization within this reserved time period to safeguard use of the name. A limited liability company may conduct business under an assumed, or fictitious, name and the appropriate filings of a fictitious name application must be considered as well.

B. Articles of Organization

Once the desired name for the limited liability company is secured, the articles of organization must be prepared. A paralegal working in the business organizations department of a law firm should take the time to prepare a worksheet of items that must be included in articles of organization to satisfy state statutory requirements. The worksheet, which should be reviewed on a regular basis and compared with any changes in state statutory law, will be a timesaver in the long run because it will negate the necessity of duplicative research prior to drafting.

Most states require only skeletal articles of organization, stating minimum requirements. It should be noted that because articles of organization are filed with the state filing official, they become a matter of public record. Therefore, the client may choose to limit the articles to these minimum requirements and include more detailed information about the company's operational structure in the operating agreement, which is an internal document and thus, not a matter of public record.

Most state statutes require that the articles of organization contain the name of the limited liability company, the address of its principal place of business, the name and address of its registered agent, and the limited liability company's duration. The ULLCA states that unless a limited liability company is designated a term company with the duration of its term specified in the articles of organization, the limited liability company will be considered an at-will company. (Please note that under Section 411 of the ULLCA, if a term company is continued after expiration of the specified term, the company becomes an at-will company, with the rights and duties of members and managers remaining the same.)

Some states require additional information such as the purpose of the company (usually a broadly stated purpose will suffice), the names and addresses of the members, a statement indicating whether the company will be operated by managers (and, if so, their names and addresses), the company's initial capitalization, and voting requirements. Other states allow some or all of these matters to be provided in the operating agreement instead. If the limited liability company's date of commencement is to be delayed, the articles of organization may also set forth the delayed effective date. Sections 203(a) and (b) of the ULLCA provide:

(a) Articles of organization of a limited liability company must set forth:

(1) the name of the company;

(2) the address of the initial designated office;

(3) the name and street address of the initial agent for service of process;

(4) the name and address of each organizer;

(5) whether the company is to be a term company and, if so, the term specified;

(6) whether the company is to be manager-managed, and, if so, the name and address of each initial manager; and

(7) whether one or more of the members of the company are to be liable for its debts and obligations under Section 303(c).

(b) Articles of organization of a limited liability company may set forth:

(1) provisions permitted to be set forth in an operating agreement; or

(2) other matters not inconsistent with law.

The necessity for understanding the state statutory requirements in the state in which the client wishes to organize is clear.

Once the articles of organization are prepared, they must be signed by the organizer or organizers. A member of the company may choose to act as organizer, or the responsible attorney may play this role. A registered agent also must be chosen and must sign the designation accepting the position of registered agent. As discussed in Chapter 4, a registered agent's role is to accept service of process of legal papers on behalf of the entity. The registered agent must be a resident of the state of creation. Some states have requirements that the registered agent be available at the designated office during certain hours to fulfill this role. Again, a member or manager may choose to act as registered agent, or the responsible attorney may agree to fulfill this obligation. When providing the address of the registered agent, one must provide a street address as opposed to a post office box. The registered agent's position and office must be continuously maintained or the company will be in contravention of state statutes and the company may be dissolved by the state. If a change in registered agent or registered office is made at some later date, the state filing official must be promptly notified, usually on a change-of-status form.

Once the articles of organization are signed by the organizer(s) and registered agent, copies should be made before sending them to the state filing official. An office copy should be kept in the client file. The state may require not only the original articles, but a certain number of copies as well. Even if the state does not require copies to be sent along with the original articles, many law offices send a copy to be certified by the state and sent back to the client or law office. Every state has a filing fee requirement and there usually is an additional charge for designation of registered agent and certified copies. The cover letter that will be sent together with the check and the articles should indicate the fees the check is to cover. The cover letter should also provide the contact person at the law firm, should any questions arise.

C.   Applications to Transact Business in a Foreign State

If the client desires to operate in other states, the paralegal must prepare the appropriate applications to qualify to transact business as a foreign limited liability company. These applications must be obtained from the state filing authority in the foreign state and foreign state statutes must be researched prior to filing the applications and filing fees. Most states will require a certificate of status from the state of creation to accompany the application, providing proof of good standing. All states will require that the limited liability company provide a registered agent and office in the foreign state. In states that have not yet adopted limited liability company acts, the client may have to qualify as a foreign corporation.

D.   Operating Agreement

The next document of major importance is the **operating agreement**. This agreement is similar to a partnership agreement and outlines the terms and conditions binding upon the members of the limited liability company. These include the initial and future capital contributions of the members, if such terms are not required to be set forth in the articles of organization. Also included will be provisions for distribution of profits and losses, accounting methods, conditions under which a member may resign or be expelled, as well as conditions under which new members may be added. In some respects, the operating agreement is similar to the bylaws of a corporation as well because it details voting procedures, rights and duties of managers, indemnification of managers, meeting requirements, and so forth.

While some state statutes itemize required provisions for the operating agreement, most states allow great flexibility in the drafting of the agreement. The key requirement in drafting such an agreement is that the terms of the operating agreement be consistent with both the articles of organization and state statutes. Just as an attorney must customize any contract to suit the client's specific needs, so too must the operating agreement reflect the specific requirements of the members of the client company.

Once a final draft of the operating agreement is prepared, all members of the client limited liability company must sign it, just as all partners sign a partnership agreement. The operating agreement is not filed with the state. A copy of the agreement should be kept in the law firm's client files.

E.   Maintenance Records

In addition to the documents necessary to create the company, maintenance records must be kept for the company. Periodic reports (annual in most states) must be filed with the state filing official, together with any annual fees or franchise taxes. Section 211(a) of the ULLCA provides that the annual report must set forth:

> (1) the name of the company and the State or country under whose law it is organized;
> (2) the address of its designated office and the name and address of its agent for service of process in this State;
> (3) the address of its principal office; and
> (4) the names and business addresses of any managers.

Internal records must reflect up-to-date lists of all members, their addresses, and their ownership percentages. All amendments to documents, as well as minutes of meetings and unanimous consent resolutions must be maintained, together with all accounting records.

A limited liability company may request the state filing authority to furnish a certificate of existence or a certificate of authority (the latter for a foreign limited liability company) to evidence the company's current good standing. These documents should be kept with the other company records. Under Section 208 of the ULLCA:

> (a) A person may request the Secretary of State to furnish a certificate of existence for a limited liability company or a certificate of authorization for a foreign limited liability company.
> (b) A certificate of existence for a limited liability company must set forth:
> > (1) the company's name;
> > (2) that it is duly organized under the laws of this State, the date of organization, whether its duration is at-will or for a specified term, and, if the latter, the period specified;

(3) if payment is reflected in the records of the Secretary of State and if nonpayment affects the existence of the company, that all fees, taxes, and penalties owed to this State have been paid;

(4) whether its most recent annual report required by Section 211 has been filed with the Secretary of State;

(5) that articles of termination have not been filed; and

(6) other facts of record in the office of the Secretary of State which may be requested by the applicant.

(c) A certificate of authority for a foreign limited liability company must set forth:

(1) the company's name used in this State;

(2) that it is authorized to transact business in this State;

(3) if payment is reflected in the records of the Secretary of State and if nonpayment affects the authorization of the company, that all fees, taxes, and penalties owed to this State have been paid;

(4) whether its most recent annual report required by Section 211 has been filed with the Secretary of State;

(5) that a certificate of cancellation has not been filed; and

(6) other facts of record in the office of the Secretary of State which may be requested by the applicant.

(d) Subject to any qualification stated in the certificate, a certificate of existence or authorization issued by the Secretary of State may be relied upon as conclusive evidence that the domestic or foreign limited liability company is in existence or is authorized to transact business in this State.

To aid in the drafting of the essential documents necessary for the formation of a limited liability company, a worksheet should be used to assure that all relevant information is obtained from the client. A completed sample worksheet is found in the Client Simulation at the end of the chapter.

AMENDMENTS

Any amendment to the articles of organization requires a formal procedure. The first step is the recommendation of a change or addition to the articles by the managers of the limited liability company. Such recommendations must then be put to the vote of the members. Usually a majority vote will suffice to adopt an amendment, unless the articles or operating agreement specify otherwise. State law may vary as to the requisite contents of the **articles of amend-**

ment. Under Section 204(a) of the ULLCA, the articles of amendment must set forth the name of the limited liability company, the date of the filing of the articles of organization, and the text of any amendments to the articles of organization. Before an amendment to the articles can have full force and effect, the amended articles must be filed with the state filing official. A filing fee typically is charged for such a filing.

Amending an operating agreement typically requires the unanimous consent of all members, because it operates like a partnership agreement and is signed by all members. Because it is an internal document, amendments to the operating agreement are not filed with the state.

DISSOCIATION AND DISSOLUTION

A. Dissociation

Dissociation of a member occurs when a member ceases to be associated with the conduct of the limited liability company's business. Under Section 601 of the ULLCA, a member is dissociated when any of the following occurs:

(1) the company's having notice of the member's express will to withdraw upon the date of notice or on a later date specified by the member;

(2) an event agreed to in the operating agreement as causing the member's dissociation;

(3) upon transfer of all of a member's distributional interest, other than a transfer for security purposes or a court order charging the member's distributional interest which has not been foreclosed;

(4) the member's expulsion pursuant to the operating agreement;

(5) the member's expulsion by unanimous vote of the other members if:

(i) it is unlawful to carry on the company's business with the member;

(ii) there has been a transfer of substantially all of the member's distributional interest, other than a transfer for security purposes or a court order charging the member's distributional interest which has not been foreclosed;

(iii) within 90 days after the company notifies a corporate member that it will be expelled because it has filed a certificate of dissolution or the equivalent, its charter has been revoked, or its right to conduct business has been suspended by the jurisdiction of its incorporation, the member fails to obtain a revocation of the certificate of dissolution or a reinstatement of its charter or its right to conduct business; or

(iv) a partnership or a limited liability company that is a member has been dissolved and its business is being wound up;

(6) on application by the company or another member, the member's expulsion by judicial determination because the member:

(i) engaged in wrongful conduct that adversely and materially affected the company's business;

(ii) willfully or persistently committed a material breach of the operating agreement or of a duty owed to the company or the other members under Section 409; or

(iii) engaged in conduct relating to the company's business which makes it not reasonably practicable to carry on the business with the member;

(7) the member's:

(i) becoming a debtor in bankruptcy;

(ii) executing an assignment for the benefit of creditors;

(iii) seeking, consenting to, or acquiescing in the appointment of a trustee, receiver, or liquidator of the member or of all or substantially all of the member's property; or

(iv) failing, within 90 days after the appointment, to have vacated or stayed the appointment of a trustee, receiver, or liquidator of the member or of all or substantially all of the member's property obtained without the member's consent or acquiescence, or failing within 90 days after the expiration of a stay to have the appointment vacated;

(8) in the case of a member who is an individual:

(i) the member's death;

(ii) the appointment of a guardian or general conservator for the member; or

(iii) a judicial determination that the member has otherwise become incapable of performing the member's duties under the operating agreement;

(9) in the case of a member that is a trust or is acting as a member by virtue of being a trustee of a trust, distribution of the trust's entire rights to receive distributions from the company, but not merely by reason of the substitution of a successor trustee;

(10) in the case of a member that is an estate or is acting as a member by virtue of being a personal representative of an estate, distribution of the estate's entire rights to receive distributions from the company, but not merely the substitution of a successor personal representative; or

(11) termination of the existence of a member if the member is not an individual, estate, or trust other than a business trust.

B.   Member-Managed and Manager-Managed Companies

Under the ULLCA, how a member's dissociation will affect the limited liability company is determined by (1) whether the company is member-managed or manager-managed, and (2) whether the company is an at-will company or a term company. If a member is dissociated in a member-managed at-will company, the limited liability company will be dissolved unless a specified percentage of the remaining members agree to continue the business. If the company continues the business, it must purchase the dissociated member's interest at its fair market value as of the date of dissociation.

In a member-managed term company, only subsections (7) through (11) of Section 601 act as triggering events to bring about dissolution of a limited liability company, and even then the company need not dissolve if the specified percentage of members agree to continue the business. If the members of a member-managed term company decide to continue in business, the company does not have to purchase the dissociated member's interest until the expiration of the specified term that existed on the date of the member's dissociation. To clarify, the ULLCA allows a term company to become an at-will company if it continues to operate after its specified term expires. If a term company with a dissociated member chooses to do this, it must first pay the dissociated member the fair market value for his or her (or its) interest in the company at the end of the originally specified term in order to continue in operation.

Under the ULLCA, if a limited liability company is manager-managed, a member's dissociation does not dissolve the company unless the member is also a manager. Even then, the company may continue if the specified percentage of members agree.

C.   Dissolution

Dissolution of a limited liability company may also occur due to the expiration of the specified term of duration or by vote to terminate by the requisite number of members specified in the operating agreement. Upon dissolution of the company, assets must be distributed in a particular fashion. Any assets of the company must first be distributed to creditors of the limited liability company. The company must provide notice to all creditors of its intended dissolution and may be required by state statute to publish a notice of dissolution in a newspaper of general circulation in the county in which the company's principal office is located. If any assets remain after this distribution, remaining assets are first applied to pay back capital contributions of the members. Finally, any remaining profits are proportionately distributed.

After this is done, articles of termination are filed with the appropriate state filing authority. Under Section 805(a), **the articles of termination** must state the name of the company, the date of the dissolution, and that the company's business has been wound up and the legal existence of the company has been terminated. Please note that state law on dissociation and dissolution varies and state statutes should be consulted.

CLIENT SIMULATION

In the past several months, as more business journals have been running articles on the limited liability company as an increasingly popular business entity, Karen's firm, Trumbull and McDonald, P.A., has seen a corresponding interest expressed by clients who are looking to start up a business.

Two months ago, Thomas asked Karen to review the state's limited liability company statutes and compile a worksheet inclusive of all significant items to be covered in drafting articles of organization and an operating agreement that would meet state statutory requirements. The firm now uses this worksheet for client intake when interviewing a client interested in forming a limited liability company. Reviewing the applicable statutes and obtaining pertinent information from the secretary of state's office, Karen also has prepared a form for articles of organization on her computer which she customizes according to the information provided by the client.

Today, Karen has been asked to sit in on an interview with a new client, Ann Michaels. Ann is interested in starting a business providing language translation services for businesses with international clientele. Ann has three colleagues who will be running the business with her. Ann mentions that she and her colleagues do not want to be personally liable for business debts and do not want the double taxation consequences of forming a corporation, so they looked into the possibility of forming an S corporation, but were discouraged upon learning that no shareholders may be nonresident aliens.

One of Ann's colleagues, Nobuko Hattori, is not a United States citizen and she does not have a green card. Ann explains that Nobuko's husband is here on a L-1 visa as an intracompany transferee of an international firm and

Nobuko has a L-2 visa as his spouse. Nobuko and her husband may eventually become residents, as both are interested in remaining in the United States. Nonetheless, because of Nobuko's current immigration status, she is prevented from becoming a shareholder in an S corporation.

Ann asks Thomas if any other possibilities are available that would allow Nobuko active participation, prevent double taxation consequences and, most importantly, limit personal liability. Thomas suggests the formation of a limited liability company and proceeds to explain its characteristics and the documents that must be drafted. Ann believes this is the best option available and wants Thomas to start on the necessary documents right away. Thomas asks Karen to escort Ann to the conference room and obtain all necessary client information. Karen takes out a worksheet and tells Ann that she will be using it as a guideline to ask questions to assure all relevant information is covered. The first thing Karen needs to know is the proposed name of the business, which must include the words "Limited Company" or the abbreviation "L.C." according to state statutes. Karen asks Ann for her top three choices, explaining that Ann's first choice may not be available and that she will be telephoning the Secretary of State's office for name availability and reservation. Karen proceeds through each item on the worksheet. After the conference is concluded, Karen reviews the completed worksheet, which reads as follows:

EXHIBIT 5.1

Limited Liability Company Formation Worksheet

DATE OF INTAKE:	February 18, 1997
ATTORNEY:	Thomas Trumbull
PARALEGAL:	Karen Greer
CLIENT NUMBER:	1610
MATTER NUMBER:	0001
PERSON RESPONSIBLE FOR INTAKE:	Karen Greer
1. CLIENT NAME:	Ann Michaels for client company
2. ADDRESS:	1000 Lincoln Avenue
	Any City, Any State

EXHIBIT 5.1   *Continued*

3. TELEPHONE: ___(000) 235-7273___   FAX: ___(000) 235-7219___

4. NAME OF COMPANY (THREE CHOICES):

1st choice: Multilingual Services, L.C.

2nd choice: Global Translation Services, L.C.

3rd choice: Multinational Translations, L.C.

5. STATE OF FORMATION: Any State

6. LIST ANY STATES THAT RESERVATION OF NAME IS NEEDED:

Any State

Client does not have plans to become a foreign limited

liability company in any other state at this time.

7. ORGANIZER(S): Ann Michaels

1000 Lincoln Avenue

Any City, Any State

(000) 235-7273

8. REGISTERED AGENT: Thomas Trumbull, Esquire

9. REGISTERED OFFICE: Trumbull and McDonald, P.A.

2500 Jefferson Street

Any City, Any State

10. PRINCIPAL OFFICE OF COMPANY: 1000 Lincoln Avenue

Any City, Any State

11. OTHER OFFICES: None at this time.

12. TERM OF EXISTENCE: 30 years

13. PURPOSE: Translation services and any other lawful business per-

mitted under the laws of the United States and Any State.

14. EFFECTIVE DATE: Upon filing of Articles of Organization.

15. FISCAL YEAR: Calendar year

EXHIBIT 5.1   *Continued*

16. ACCOUNTANT: Cynthia Howard, C.P.A.

4085 Roosevelt Avenue

Any City, Any State

(000) 848-7694

17. ACCOUNTING METHOD: Cash method

18. NAMES AND ADDRESSES OF MEMBERS:

Ann Michaels	545 N. W. 10th Street
	Any City, Any State
Nobuko Hattori	5541 Maple Lane
	Any City, Any State
David Pearce	1361 Longwood Lane
	Any City, Any State
Craig Lanson	126 S. W. 40th Street
	Any City, Any State

19. ADDITIONAL MEMBERS: Only by unanimous consent of members.

20. INITIAL CAPITAL CONTRIBUTION OF EACH MEMBER AND PERCENTAGE OF INTEREST IN THE COMPANY:

Ann Michaels	$10,000	25% interest
Nobuko Hattori	$10,000	25% interest
David Pearce	$10,000	25% interest
Craig Lanson	$10,000	25% interest

21. ADDITIONAL CONTRIBUTIONS: To be decided by a majority vote of the members.

22. APPORTIONMENT OF PROFITS AND LOSSES: Based on percentage of interest in the company.

EXHIBIT 5.1   *Continued*

23. RESTRICTIONS ON TRANSFERS OF INTEREST IN THE COMPANY:
    A member may transfer his/her interest only with the
    consent of all other members.

24. MEETINGS OF MEMBERS:
    (A) ANNUAL MEETING: Date to be determined by managers each fiscal year
    (B) QUORUM: Majority of members
    (C) SPECIAL MEETINGS: May be called by managers or at least ¼ members
    entitled to vote; reasonable notice to be given
    (D) QUORUM: Majority of members
    (E) MEMBER ACTION BY UNANIMOUS WRITTEN CONSENT: Yes

25. DISSOCIATION OF MEMBERS: Retirement of member: must give 90 days'
    notice; expulsion by unanimous vote of members for
    cause; bankruptcy; insanity; breach of operating agreement

26. INITIAL MANAGERS: NAMES AND BUSINESS ADDRESSES:
    Ann Michaels   1000 Lincoln Avenue
                      Any City, Any State
    Nobuko Hattori   1000 Lincoln Avenue
                      Any City, Any State
    David Pearce   1000 Lincoln Avenue
                      Any City, Any State
    Craig Lanson   1000 Lincoln Avenue
                      Any City, Any State

27. TOTAL NUMBER OF MANAGERS: May be increased or decreased by majority
    vote of the members.

28. ELECTION OF MANAGERS:
    (A) ANNUALLY: Yes
    (B) STAGGERED: No

EXHIBIT 5.1 *Continued*

29. MEETINGS OF MANAGERS:

   (A) REGULAR MEETINGS: To be determined as needed.

   (B) QUORUM: Majority of managers

   (C) SPECIAL MEETINGS: May be called by any manager giving reasonable notice.

   (D) QUORUM: Majority of managers

   (E) MANAGER ACTION BY UNANIMOUS WRITTEN CONSENT: Yes

30. INDEMNIFICATION: Managers shall not be liable to the Company for any mistake or error in judgment or any act or omission believed in good faith to be within scope of authority. Company shall indemnify each manager for claims made against him or her if manager acted within scope of authority. Managers shall be liable for intentional wrongdoing or gross negligence. No member shall be liable for debts, expenses, or liabilities of Company except to extent of his or her interest in the Company.

31. TERMINATION OF THE COMPANY: Termination triggered by bankruptcy or legal incapacity of any member, unless within 30 days from the date of filing of any such bankruptcy petition, or the finding of incapacity by an appropriate court, the members vote by a majority vote to continue the operation of the Company.

32. BANK ACCOUNTS: Company account to be opened at National Bank, 1200 Main Street, Any City, Any State. Signatures of any two managers required on each check.

33. AMENDMENTS: By majority vote of the members.

EXHIBIT 5.1   *Continued*

34. ADDITIONAL PROVISIONS: Life insurance provision to purchase deceased member's interest; Company to be owner of policies; proceeds to be paid to deceased member's estate within 30 days from receipt by Company.

Karen looks at the list of frequently called numbers she keeps on the bulletin board by her desk and finds the number for the Secretary of State's office. While waiting on the line, Karen turns to her computer and pulls up a form for name reservation. She fills in the requisite information, leaving the company name blank. Karen is put through to appropriate party and finds out that the name Multilingual Services, L.C. is available. She fills this in on the name reservation form, prints the form, and sends the form along with the applicable filing fee to the Secretary of State's office. According to state statute, the name Multilingual Services, L.C. will be reserved for 120 days.

Next, Karen turns to the task of preparing the articles of organization. Karen reviews the worksheet once more. She has taken a highlighter and has highlighted in green the items on the form that must appear in the articles according to state statutes. She pulls up the articles of organization form on her computer, skims through the worksheet for items highlighted in green, and inserts the information in the form. She proofreads for typographical errors before printing, and finally prints the Articles for Thomas's review. The articles of organization read as follows in Exhibit 5.2:

EXHIBIT 5.2

Articles of Organization of Multilingual Services, L.C.

I, the undersigned natural person, of the age of eighteen years or more, acting as organizer of a Limited Liability Company under the Limited Liability Company Act of the State of Any State, hereby adopt the following Articles of Organization for the Limited Liability Company:

EXHIBIT 5.2 *Continued*

ARTICLE ONE

The name of the Limited Liability Company is Multilingual Services, L.C.

ARTICLE TWO

The address of the principal place of business of the Limited Liability Company is 1000 Lincoln Avenue, Any City, Any State.

ARTICLE THREE

The Limited Liability Company is organized for the purpose of providing translation services and for the purpose of transacting any lawful business for which a limited liability company may be organized.

ARTICLE FOUR

The period of duration of the Limited Liability Company shall be (30) years from its effective date.

ARTICLE FIVE

The address of the registered office and the name and business residence, or mailing address of the registered agent for service of process is Thomas Trumbull, Esquire, Trumbull and McDonald, P.A., 2500 Jefferson Street, Any City, Any State.

ARTICLE SIX

The name and business address of each initial manager of the Limited Liability Company is:

Ann Michaels	1000 Lincoln Avenue Any City, Any State
Nobuko Hattori	1000 Lincoln Avenue Any City, Any State
David Pearce	1000 Lincoln Avenue Any City, Any State

EXHIBIT 5.2   *Continued*

Craig Lanson   1000 Lincoln Avenue
                       Any City, Any State

The above-named managers shall serve as managers until the first annual meeting of members or until their successors are elected and qualify.

ARTICLE SEVEN

The Limited Liability Company may continue to operate its business following the death, retirement, resignation, expulsion, bankruptcy, or dissolution of a member or upon the occurrence of any other event which terminates the continued membership of a member if all remaining members consent to its continuation.

ARTICLE EIGHT

The effective date of the formation of the Limited Liability Company shall be the date of the filing of these Articles of Organization.

ARTICLE NINE

The name and address of the organizer is as follows:

Ann Michaels
1000 Lincoln Avenue
Any City, Any State

IN WITNESS WHEREOF, the undersigned organizer has executed these Articles of Organization of Multilingual Services, L.C., this _____ day of _____, 19_____, on behalf of the parties who shall be its members.

_____
Ann Michaels, Organizer

A certificate of designation of registered agent and registered office is required in her state to indicate that the named registered agent agrees to accept service of process on behalf of the limited liability company. The registered agent for Multilingual Services, L.C. will be Thomas. Thomas had explained to Ann during her office visit that the registered agent need not be a member of the limited liability company and that clients often use their attorneys as registered agents to accept any litigation papers that may be filed against the company. Using an attorney as a registered agent assures that these papers are not misplaced and can be dealt with expeditiously. Karen prepares the certificate for Thomas's signature which reads as follows:

EXHIBIT 5.3

Certificate of Designation of Registered Agent and Registered Office

Pursuant to the provisions of the statutes of Any State, the undersigned limited liability company, organized under the laws of the state of Any State, submits the following statement in designating the registered agent and registered office in the state of Any State.

The name of the limited liability company is:

Multilingual Services, L.C.

The name and address of the registered agent and office is:

Thomas Trumbull, Esquire
Trumbull and McDonald, P.A.
2500 Jefferson Street
Any City, Any State

Signature: _____
Ann Michaels, Organizer

Date: _____

Having been named as registered agent and to accept service of process for the above stated limited liability company at the place designated in this certificate, I hereby accept the appointment as registered agent and agree to act in this capacity. I further agree to comply with the provisions of all statutes relating to the proper and complete performance of my duties as registered agent.

Signature: _____
Thomas Trumbull

Date: _____

Karen next turns her attention to preparing the operating agreement. She has highlighted in pink the worksheet items that must be included in the agreement. Recalling that she prepared an operating agreement a month ago for another client, she reviews that document, using it as a guideline for the agreement she is to prepare for Multilingual Services, L.C. This enables her to create efficiently a document that is customized to her client's needs without starting from scratch. Certain provisions are boilerplate provisions that are found in most contracts and Karen can utilize the same language in this agreement. This is true of the controlling law and severability provisions found within the agreement. Other provisions will contain specific information obtained from the client intake. For example, in her conversation with Thomas, Ann was advised that the company should take out life insurance on each of its members. By doing so, the company will have accessible funds to use in purchasing a deceased member's interest in the company. If the company did not have the capital available to pay out a deceased member's estate, it might be forced into liquidation. Still other provisions, while not "boilerplate," will be taken from previously approved examples by Thomas. For example, the wording of the transfer of interest provision must be drafted carefully to avoid giving the appearance of a corporate entity, as discussed above. After completion, the operating agreement created by Karen reads as follows:

EXHIBIT 5.4

Operating Agreement of Multilingual Services, L.C.

THIS AGREEMENT, dated and adopted this _____ day of _____, 19_____, by and between the undersigned members of the Multilingual Services, L.C. (hereinafter "the Company"), a limited liability company organized under the laws of the State of Any State, who agree as follows:

I. Offices. The Company shall designate a registered office and maintain said office in accordance with the laws of the State of Any State. The Company may have offices at such other places within and without the state as the members may from time to time designate in writing.

II. Purpose. The purpose of the Company is to provide translation services and its permitted activities shall include any activities permitted under the laws of the United States and Any State.

EXHIBIT 5.4   *Continued*

III. *Members.* The managers of the Company may designate any place, either within or without the State of Any State, as the place of meeting for any meeting of the members. If no designation is made, then the place of meeting shall be the principal office of the Company. The purpose of the annual meeting of the members is to elect managers and to transact such other business as may properly come before the members. The annual meeting of the members shall be held at such time and place as shall be determined by a resolution of the managers during each fiscal year of the Company. Special meetings of the members may be called by a majority of managers then in office or by at least one-fourth of all of the members entitled to vote at the meeting. A majority of the members entitled to vote shall constitute a quorum for both annual and special meetings of the members. All decisions shall be made by majority vote at a meeting at which a quorum is present, unless specified otherwise in this Agreement. Alternatively, decisions may be made by unanimous written consent of the members.

IV. *Managers.* The affairs of the Company shall be managed by managers. The Company initially shall have four managers. The initial managers of the Company shall be Ann Michaels, Nobuko Hattori, David Pearce, and Craig Lanson, who shall serve until the first annual meeting of the members and until their successors are elected and qualified. The managers of the Company shall be elected by a majority vote of the members at the annual meeting of the members. The number of managers may be increased or decreased by a majority vote of the members. Vacancies may be filled by a majority vote of the members. A manager chosen to fill a vacancy shall serve the unexpired term of his or her predecessor in office. A manager may be removed from office, with or without cause, by a majority vote of the members.

The duties of the managers shall include all duties and activities necessary to operate and manage the Company as provided in this Agreement. Each manager shall have an equal voice in the operation and management of the Company. Regular meetings of the managers may be held at such time and place as shall be determined from time to time by the managers. Special meetings of the managers may be called by any manager, said manager fixing a reasonable time and place for the holding of the meeting. A majority of the managers entitled to vote shall constitute a quorum at a meeting of the managers. Except as otherwise provided in this Agreement, questions related to Company matters shall be determined by a majority vote of the managers at a meeting at which a quorum is present. Alternatively, decisions may be made by unanimous written consent of the managers.

EXHIBIT 5.4   *Continued*

V. *Capital Contributions.* The members shall make the following capital contributions to the Company:

Member	Form of Contribution	Value	Percentage of Interest
Ann Michaels	cash	$10,000	25%
Nobuko Hattori	cash	$10,000	25%
David Pearce	cash	$10,000	25%
Craig Lanson	cash	$10,000	25%

If at any time or from time to time, by a majority vote of the members, the members determine that further capital is required in the interest of the Company, the additional capital shall be contributed by the members in accordance with their respective interests as set forth above.

VI. *Profits and Losses.* The profits and losses of the Company shall be allocated among the members in accordance with their percentage interests as set forth above.

VII. *Membership Changes.* A new member may be admitted to the Company only with the written consent of all existing members. A member may retire from the Company by delivering ninety (90) days' prior written notice of such retirement to the managers and to each member. A member may be expelled from the Company only for cause and only upon the unanimous vote of all other members. Cause includes a willful and substantial breach of this Agreement, bankruptcy of a member, and conduct prejudicial to the Company and its members. A retiring, bankrupt, or expelled member shall be compensated as provided below.

VIII. *Transfers of Interests.* A member may not transfer his or her interest in the Company without first obtaining the written consent of all other members.

IX. *Life Insurance.* The Company shall contract for life insurance on the lives of each of the members, in an amount proportionate to the value of each member's interest in the Company. The insurance proceeds shall be used to fund the purchase of a deceased member's interest in the Company; accordingly, the Company shall, as and when appropriate, increase the amount of life insurance on each member to assure sufficient net proceeds to redeem completely a deceased member's interest. The Company shall pay all premiums on the policies. Payment of the proceeds shall be made to the deceased member's estate within thirty (30) days following their receipt by the Company.

EXHIBIT 5.4 *Continued*

X. *Indemnification.* The managers shall not be liable to the Company or to any member for any mistake or error in judgment or for any act or omission believed in good faith to be within the scope of authority conferred by this Agreement. The Company shall indemnify each manager for claims made against him or her, provided said manager was acting within the scope of his or her authority. Each manager shall be liable to the Company only for acts and/or omissions involving intentional wrongdoing or gross negligence.

No member shall be liable for the debts, expenses, or liabilities of the Company except to the extent of the member's interest in the Company. In the event that any member is held liable for a debt, expense or liability of the Company and is required to pay or does pay more than his or her percentage interest in that debt, expense, or liability, said member shall have a right of indemnification against the other members for that amount in excess of his or her interest.

XI. *Accounting, Records, and Reports.* The fiscal year of the Company shall be the calendar year. The Company shall maintain full and accurate accounting records, which shall be kept at the Company's principal office. The accounting method applied shall be the cash method. Members shall receive periodic reports on the financial status of the Company. Each member shall have the right to inspect and copy the books and records of the Company during normal business hours.

XII. *Bank Accounts.* The Company shall maintain one or more bank accounts in which all monies received by the Company shall be deposited. The funds in these accounts shall be subject to withdrawal by checks, notes, drafts, bills of exchange, and/or other instruments made in the Company's name, when signed by any two managers.

XIII. *Continuation of Business.* The Company shall dissolve upon the bankruptcy or legal incapacity of any member, unless within thirty (30) days from the date of filing of any such bankruptcy petition, or the finding of incapacity by an appropriate court, as the case may be, the members, by a majority vote, have voted to continue the operation of the Company. A departing member, or the estate of a deceased or bankrupt member, shall be compensated in cash for the membership interest of such member in an amount equal to the member's outstanding capital contribution plus the member's proportionate share of any accrued net Company profits, or less the member's proportionate share of any accrued net Company losses. Company assets shall be valued at book value for purposes of this provision, with no value attributed to goodwill.

EXHIBIT 5.4   *Continued*

XIV. *Termination*. Upon the dissolution of the Company, when the business will not be continued as provided above, the managers, or the members if there are no managers, shall promptly wind up the business and affairs of the Company and the assets of the Company shall be distributed as follows:

(a) First, to the creditors of the Company, including members who are creditors, in satisfaction of the liabilities of the Company other than liabilities for distribution to members.

(b) Second, proportionately to members and former members as distributions owed as stated above in this Agreement.

(c) Third, proportionately to members as distributions for the return of their respective capital contributions.

(d) Fourth, to members as distributions in respect to their membership interests in proportion to their respective capital contributions.

XV. *Amendment*. This Agreement and the Articles of Organization may be amended by a majority vote of the members, except that any provision in this Agreement or in the Articles of Organization that specifies a membership voting or consent requirement of greater than a majority may be amended only by a membership vote that is equal to the voting or consent requirement specified in the provision sought to be amended.

XVI. *Notices*. All notices, consents, and other instruments hereunder shall be in writing and hand delivered or mailed by certified mail, return receipt requested, postage prepaid, and shall be directed to the parties' last known addresses.

XVII. *Binding Effect*. All rights, obligations, duties, restrictions and qualifications provided in this Agreement are binding upon all parties and each of their heirs, personal representatives, successors, and assigns.

XVIII. *Severability*. If any provision of this Agreement or the application thereof to any person or circumstance shall be determined to be invalid or unenforceable, the remaining provisions of the Agreement or the application of such provision to persons or circumstances other than those to which it is held invalid or unenforceable shall not be affected thereby and shall be valid and enforceable to the fullest extent permitted by law.

XIX. *Controlling Law*. All questions with respect to the construction of this Agreement, and the rights and liabilities of the parties, shall be determined in accordance with the provisions of the laws of the State of Any State. To the extent not specifically addressed in this Agreement, the operation of the Company and the conduct of its

EXHIBIT 5.4 *Continued*

affairs shall be governed by the provisions of the Any State Limited Liability Company Act, and any terms of this Agreement violative of the Act shall be of no force and effect.

IN WITNESS WHEREOF, the parties have executed this Agreement as of the date first above written.

_____
Ann Michaels, Member

_____
Nobuko Hattori, Member

_____
David Pearce, Member

_____
Craig Lanson, Member

After review of these documents by Thomas, Karen will schedule a time for Ann to come to the office to read and sign them. Karen will photocopy the documents for the file, provide a photocopy of the Articles of Organization for Ann, and will send the Articles of Organization to the Secretary of State's office with a cover letter and a check for the filing fees certified mail, return receipt requested. To facilitate Ann's returning a copy of the operating agreement to the office after it is signed by all the members, Karen provides her with a self-addressed, stamped envelope.

Chapter Summary

1. A limited liability company is a separate legal entity, apart from its owners, created by state statute. It combines features of a partnership and a corporation to provide maximum flexibility, limited liability, and favorable federal tax treatment.

2. The owners of a limited liability company are called members. Their personal obligations to business creditors is limited to the extent of their actual and promised capital contributions to the company.

3. Unlike limited partners in a limited partnership, members of a limited liability company are free to fully participate in the management of the company without losing their limited liability status.

4. For federal taxation purposes, a limited liability company will be considered a "pass through" entity, and not taxed as a corporation if it lacks two or more corporate characteristics. These characteristics include limited liability, continuity of life, centralized management, and free transferability of interests.

5. A limited liability company may be managed by its members, or may be managed by managers who may or may not also be members of the company. In some states, a limited liability company must have at least two members and one manager. Managers are elected annually by the members. A manager is an agent of the company and owes a fiduciary duty to the company and its members.

6. The name of a limited liability company must include the term "limited liability company," its abbreviation, or some other similar designation. It cannot be deceptively similar to (and must be distinguishable in the records from) the name of any other limited liability company, corporation, or limited partnership. In most states, the name may be reserved by filing an application and paying a reservation fee.

7. The document which creates the limited liability company is the articles of organization, which must be filed with the state filing official. It includes basic information about the company, such as its name, its period of existence, its principal address, the name and address of its registered agent, and any other statutorily required information. It is signed by a person called an organizer.

8. Members of limited liability companies sign an operating agreement, which is similar to a partnership agreement. This document is not of public record, but must be consistent with the articles of organization as well as state statutory law. It includes provisions specifying the duties of managers and members, meetings, contributions, distributions, and any other provisions the members may desire.

9. Both the articles of organization and the operating agreement may be amended. The articles of organization may be amended when a change is recommended by the managers and put to a majority vote of the members. The amended articles must be filed with the state filing official. The operating agreement may be amended by unanimous consent of the members and, as the amended agreement is an internal document, the amendments are not filed with the state.

10. A limited liability company may be dissolved by the unanimous written consent of the members; by dissociation of a member, unless the specified number of members agree to continue the business; or by expiration of its stated term of existence. If a limited liability company continues in business after the

expiration of its stated term, it becomes an at-will company. Upon dissolution, creditors must be paid first from the assets, capital contributions of the members are repaid next, and finally, any remaining assets are distributed as profits on a pro rata basis.

Review Questions

1. Compare and contrast a limited liability company with the following business structures:
   (i)   general partnership
   (ii) limited partnership
   (iii) corporation
2. List the steps to be taken to form a limited liability company.
3. Explain the importance of the following characteristics in determining the tax status of a business entity:
   (i)   continuity of life
   (ii) centralized management
   (iii) limited liability
   (iv) free transferability of interests
4. List the information to be contained in articles of organization.
5. Discuss the distinctions made between member-managed companies and manager-managed companies with regard to dissociation and dissolution.

KEY TERMS

articles of amendment

articles of organization

articles of termination

at-will companies

board of governors

limited liability company

manager

manager-managed
   companies

member

member-managed
   companies

operating agreement

organizer

regulations

term companies

ULLCA

6

Introduction to Corporations

Overview of Objectives

Upon completion of this chapter, the student will:

- understand the advantages and disadvantages of choosing a corporation as a business format
- know the key "players" in a corporation and the duties assigned to each
- know the various types of corporations and the statutory law governing each
- know the requirements for becoming an S corporation
- understand the requisite steps to be taken for a corporation to become a public corporation

INTRODUCTION

Thus far, our exploration of business structures has moved progressively from the most simple (sole proprietorships) to increasingly more complex structures. The concentration of the remainder of this text shall be on the corporate structure, the most varied of the business entities in terms of financial structure and in terms of selection of type (e.g., C corporations, S corporations, closely held corporations, professional corporations, public corporations, and nonprofit corporations, each of which is discussed below).

This chapter introduces the corporate structure, the laws which govern it, the role of various individuals involved in its creation and daily operation, and corporate tax considerations. Additionally, this chapter describes the various types of corporations you may assist in creating for a client, with special emphasis on the creation of S corporations and the steps that must be taken to transform a private corporation into a public corporation.

NATURE OF A CORPORATION

A **corporation** is a business structure having a legal existence separate from that of its owners (**shareholders**). It is considered a legal entity or "person" (albeit an artificial one) in its own right for most purposes. Being a creature of statute, it cannot exist until its articles of incorporation are filed with the appropriate state filing authority (typically the secretary of state). As a legal entity, it can continue to exist regardless of the departure of its original shareholders. It can sue and be sued in its own name. Shareholders are not personally liable for corporate debts (except in unusual circumstances, as discussed in Chapter 10). Further, a corporation is taxed as a separate entity, unless it meets the requirements and files for status as an S corporation.

Most corporate activities are governed by state statutory law. Historically, great disparity existed among these statutes, with some states adopting provisions much more liberal and "business-friendly" than others. Delaware was noted for its permissive stance and many corporations chose to incorporate there even if their primary business activities were conducted in other states. Although state statutes continue to vary, many states have modernized their corporate statutes to attract businesses to their territories. Most state statutes are modeled after the Model Business Corporation Act adopted in 1950 by the American Bar Association's Committee on Corporation, Banking, and Business Law. Originally based on Illinois statutes, this Model Act underwent major revisions in 1984 and is continuing to undergo revision. A model act is precisely what the term implies, a model for states to follow when adopting legislation rather than an act to be adopted in its entirety by a state legislature. A corporation is governed by the statutes of its state of **domicile** (the state in which it is incorporated), but additionally may be governed by the statutes of any state in which it conducts business as a **foreign corporation** (a corporation incorporated in one state which conducts business in another).

Section 3.02 of the Revised Model Business Corporation Act sets forth broad rights granted to corporations to enable them to carry out their business, including the right of a corporation to exist perpetually. Historically, a number of states limited corporate existence to a specified duration. Now, most states allow for perpetual existence. Other rights granted not only by this section but by most state statutes are:

1. the right to have a corporate seal;
2. the right to make (and amend) bylaws;
3. the right to acquire and sell both real and personal property (some states require shareholder approval);
4. the right to borrow and lend money (some states place certain restrictions on this, such as requiring shareholder approval or prohibiting certain types of loans such as those to directors, officers, or employees);
5. the right to be a member of another business entity;
6. the right to provide various benefits to employees;
7. the right to donate to educational, scientific, and charitable endeavors (some states impose dollar amount limitations);
8. the right to engage in activities that aid government policy; and
9. the right to do any act not in conflict with state and federal law which furthers the business of the corporation.

If a corporation's shareholders wish to curtail these rights by placing restrictions on the corporation's authority, such restrictions must be included in the corporation's articles of incorporation.

A corporation's major operative document is its **articles of incorporation**. This document sets forth basic mandatory information concerning the corporation, such as its name, its purpose, the name and address of its registered agent, the classes and number of shares of stock it is authorized to issue, and the name and address of the incorporators. Each state's statutes put forth the matters that must be contained in the articles. Some state statutes require more than these skeletal provisions and all states allow a corporation to include additional provisions. Once this document is filed with and approved by the state filing authority, a corporation comes into legal existence.

A corporation's **bylaws** are the rules by which the internal affairs of the corporation are governed. Unlike articles of corporation which, upon filing, become part of the public record, bylaws are not filed and remain an internal document. For this reason, a corporation's bylaws are more detailed than the articles of incorporation. They set forth the procedures by which corporations regulate themselves and include provisions for such matters as board of directors' meetings, the duties of the board, the duties of the corporate officers, election procedures, and the like. The bylaws, usually adopted by a corporation's board of directors, may not be in conflict with either the corporation's articles of incorporation or state or federal law. Both the articles of incorporation and the bylaws are discussed in detail in the next chapter. Here, it is important to note that these two documents, together with state statutes and any applicable federal securities regulations, govern the conduct of corporations.

Most people are attracted to the corporate business format because of the limited liability afforded its owners (shareholders). The same freedom from personal liability for business debts and obligations is afforded shareholders in a corporation as is afforded to limited partners in a limited partnership or to members in a limited liability company. This protection pertains also to a corporation's directors and officers who may or may not be shareholders in the corporation. Please remember, however, as stated in earlier chapters, that many financial institutions require personal guarantees from the owners of small businesses, including small corporations, before dispensing loans and may require a shareholder to pledge his or her personal assets as collateral for a corporate loan.

A corporate format provides great possibilities for equity financing through the sale of shares of stock or the issuance of bonds or debentures. A potential shareholder may be more attracted to this method of business investment than becoming a partner or a member of a limited liability company because of the free transferability of interest in the business by the selling of his or her stock. In the absence of a shareholders' restrictive agreement, shares of stock in a corporation are freely transferable. Unlike the assignment of a partner's interest in a partnership, the transfer of shares of stock by sale, gift, bequest, or other disposition transfers all rights pertaining to that stock, including voting rights should the shares be voting shares.

A corporation must abide by many formalities, not only in its creation, but in its maintenance as a viable business entity. One such formality is the creation of a centralized management to oversee corporate affairs. The management of a corporation is given to a board of directors elected by the shareholders. The board, in turn, hands over the daily operations to appointed officers. In a corporation composed of few shareholders, this means that the same people wear a variety of hats and must act within the appropriate scope of authority each time they change hats. Thus, in a corporation comprised of three shareholders, the shareholders will be the directors on the board of directors as well as the officers (unless state statutes allow for the absence of a board of directors by including a provision in the articles of incorporation that the corporation shall be managed by the shareholders). These three will have to hold directors' meetings and officers' meetings (or, in states with statutes that so provide, sign unanimous consents in lieu of meetings) just as a large corporation would, and will have to keep minutes of meetings, records of resolutions, annual reports, and so forth.

As stated above, in addition to complying with formalities dictated by state statutes of its state of incorporation, a corporation wishing to expand its business activities outside state boundaries must qualify to do business in each state in which it desires to engage in business activities. This means additional filing and legal fees, as well as compliance with whatever formalities are required of foreign corporations in those states as dictated by their statutes.

Corporations generally are subject to more kinds of taxes than other business entities. A corporation that does not qualify as an S corporation (a C corporation) must pay federal income tax as a separate entity. Most states also tax corporations as a separate entity and thus corporations may end up paying not only state income tax in their state of incorporation but also in other states in which they operate as a foreign corporation. Additionally, any **dividends** (profits paid out to shareholders in proportion to each shareholder's interest in the corporation) are taxable income to the recipient shareholders. This creates a situation of **double taxation**. Further, many states impose **franchise taxes** (imposed for the right to do business as a corporation in that state) and **share transfer taxes** (imposed when stock transfers hands). On the other hand, employees' salaries as well as qualified employee benefit plans and fringe benefits (both discussed in detail in Chapter 11) may be tax deductible to the corporation as legitimate expenses. Further, qualified employee benefit plans and fringe benefits are nontaxable benefits passed on to employees, including shareholder-employees. Finally, a corporation (other than an S corporation) is afforded greater latitude by the Internal Revenue Service in selecting its fiscal year and therefore may select a tax year that favors its particular business cycle.

TERMINOLOGY

There are many "players" in a corporation. There are those who are involved in preincorporation transactions, such as **promoters** who lay the groundwork by scoping out appropriate business opportunities and developing them into viable business ventures by coordinating ideas and capital raising, and **subscribers** who pledge the necessary capital to start the business by promising to purchase shares in the yet-to-be-formed corporation. Other players enter the stage once the corporation has legally been created, such as the **directors** who function as managers of the business and the **officers** who oversee the daily operations. Often, the same person or persons will play many or all of these roles. Yet each role is distinct in its scope of authority and its obligations to the corporation.

A.   Promoters

A **promoter** is a person who takes and develops a business idea from inception to its birth as a newly created business. The promoter's activities commence with the finding and development of a business opportunity; continue with the conducting of a feasibility analysis to determine economic viability; proceed to the raising of capital, property, and personnel for the enterprise; and end with the formation of the corporation. Upon incorporation, the promoter's role as promoter is finished. Should the promoter wish to invest personally, he or she may become a subscriber, and later, a shareholder. Should the promoter wish to play an active management role, he or she may be elected to the board of directors. However, his or her role as promoter ends with the birth of the corporation. Prior to the corporation's legal creation, the promoter has a fiduciary duty to the soon-to-be-created corporation to act on its behalf in good faith and may incur liability for breach of this duty.

A promoter often enters into contracts on behalf of the inchoate corporation, such as leasing agreements, sales agreements, and employment agreements, just to name a few. When entering into such contracts, the promoter is under a duty to fully disclose to third parties his or her role and authority to act on behalf of the yet-to-be-created corporation. A corporation is not obligated under a contract entered into on its behalf by a promoter unless, after incorporation, the contract is assigned by the promoter to the corporation and is formally adopted by the corporation. Until this occurs, the promoter is personally obligated under the terms of the contract. Further, the promoter will remain personally obligated, even after the contract is so assigned, unless a novation occurs. A **novation** is an agreement between all parties (the original parties to the contract and the corporation which agrees to take the place of the promoter) allowing the substitution of a party to the agreement by releasing an original party (in this instance, the promoter) from liability on the contract and substituting a new party (the corporation) in its place. Note that any expenses incurred by a promoter in connection with the formation of the corporation must likewise be adopted by the corporation before the promoter may be compensated.

B.   Subscribers

A **subscriber**, as stated above, is an individual or business entity agreeing to purchase shares of stock in the yet-to-be-created corporation. A subscriber becomes a shareholder once the business is incorporated. Often, subscribers enter into written preincorporation subscription agreements in which they promise to buy a stipulated number of shares of stock for a specified price. Some states consider such an agreement to be irrevocable for a statutorily prescribed time, such as six months, unless the subscriber is released from the agreement by all other subscribers. The underlying principle for such a requirement is that the corporation was formed in reliance on this agreement and thus the subscriber should be held to his or her promise. An example of a simple stock subscription agreement is found in Exhibit 6.1.

EXHIBIT 6.1

Stock Subscription Agreement

FOR VALUE RECEIVED, the undersigned hereby subscribes for the purchase of Ten Thousand (10,000) Shares of TRIDENT METALWORKS, INC. (Corporation) for the total purchase price of One Hundred Thousand ($100,000.00) Dollars.

The undersigned understands that said shares shall have full voting rights and upon issue shall constitute five percent of the total outstanding shares of the Corporation, all classes inclusive.

Said shares are further issued subject to such rights and obligations as are contained in the bylaws or articles of incorporation. The subscription price shall be fully paid upon demand of the treasurer of the Corporation and delivery of said shares.

DATED: January 21, 1997

Roger Bowles
Subscriber

James O'Connell
On behalf of the Corporation

C. *Incorporators*

An **incorporator** is a person who executes and files the articles of incorporation. The majority of states require only one incorporator. An incorporator may be someone who has a vested financial interest in the corporation, such as a future shareholder, or may (in most states) be someone with no such interest. Most state statutes allow anyone 18 or more years of age to be an incorporator and place no residency requirements upon incorporators. Many states also allow an incorporator to be a business entity. Often, the attorney hired to draft the articles of incorporation for the business will act as incorporator. While state statutes vary, many states provide that incorporators may meet to conduct the initial organizational meeting of the corporation, may call the first meeting of the board of directors if the initial board is named in the articles of incorporation, and may amend the articles of incorporation by unanimous consent or, conversely, voluntarily dissolve the corporation, if the corporation has not issued shares or commenced business.

D.   Shareholders

The **shareholders** (sometimes referred to as **stockholders**) are the owners of the corporation. They may or may not have been subscribers prior to incorporation. They receive an equity interest in the corporation by purchasing shares of stock, either from the corporation or from another shareholder. A shareholder may be a natural person, a trust, an estate, or a business entity. Shareholders holding voting stock in a corporation vote to elect the corporate board of directors. It is through their voting power that shareholders indirectly run their business. Unless otherwise provided in the corporation's articles of incorporation or bylaws, shareholders may remove a director from the board of directors at any time with or without cause. In addition to electing the board of directors, shareholders vote on other important corporate matters, such as merger, consolidation, sale of substantially all the business assets, and dissolution. Besides voting rights, shareholders have the right to dividends when the board of directors chooses to distribute dividends, as well as the right to a proportionate share of liquidated assets (after the payment of corporate obligations) should the corporation liquidate. The role of shareholders is discussed in detail in Chapter 10.

E.   Board of Directors

A corporation's policies and their implementation are the province of the board of directors. The requisite minimum number of directors on the board is determined by state statute. Historically, most states required at least three directors, but now approximately half of the states permit a board of one director and some state statutes permit one or two directors in corporations with fewer than three shareholders. Some state statutes, as noted above, allow for the elimination of a board of directors in corporations with few shareholders if the articles of incorporation provide that the corporation will be managed by the shareholders. Directors do not have to be shareholders in the corporation unless the articles of incorporation so provide. Some states require that a certain percentage of the board be comprised of directors who are residents of the state of incorporation. Even in the absence of such a statutory requirement, the articles of incorporation may stipulate various qualifications that must be met by directors, including a residency requirement, if so desired.

The board of directors acts as a unit. Directors meet to discuss and vote on measures that become corporate resolutions. (For a discussion of election of directors and directors' meetings, see Chapter 9.) Directors are not agents of the corporation and no director has the authority to act alone on behalf of the board or the corporation. The board of directors elects corporate officers. It also decides when to issue shares of stock, the value which must be paid for these shares, and when to distribute dividends. The articles of incorporation or the bylaws impose restrictions on these rights. Additionally, the board of directors typically has the authority to amend the bylaws and may initiate certain actions which may later require a vote of approval by the shareholders, such as a merger, consolidation, sale of substantially all of the corporate assets, and the voluntary dissolution of the corporation.

The directors of a corporation owe fiduciary duties to the corporation. Directors must perform their duties with such care as an ordinarily prudent person in a like position would use in similar circumstances. Directors must exercise their **duty of care** both in their own undertakings and in their selection and supervision of officers. If a director fails to use such care, he or she may be held personally liable for resulting damages. In order to exercise due care, directors must acquaint themselves generally with the affairs of the corporation. They are allowed to rely on information and reports supplied by officers and professionals hired by the corporation, such as attorneys and accountants. To assure that due care has been exercised, it is advisable for directors not only to attend all meetings, but to keep their own notes on the meetings and to review the corporate minutes. Because hindsight is always better than foresight, decisions made by directors are governed by a doctrine called the **business judgment rule**. Under this doctrine, a director will be shielded from liability for a poor business decision if, at the time the decision was made, the decision was reasonable, rational, and informed, even if other reasonable persons might disagree with the decision.

Directors of a corporation also owe a fiduciary **duty of loyalty** to the corporation and must perform their duties in good faith in a manner which serves the best interests of the corporation. Should a director have a personal interest in a matter coming before the board, he or she should make full disclosure and should refrain from voting on the matter. Courts scrutinize transactions in which a director has a significant financial interest to determine whether the transaction is fair to the corporation. In accordance with the duty of loyalty, the **corporate opportunity doctrine** requires that a director (or officer) inform the corporation of any business opportunity that comes the director's way in which the corporation might reasonably be interested. Should the director fail to do so and personally take advantage of the opportunity, he or she will be deemed to have breached his or her fiduciary duty of loyalty and may be forced to transfer any profits realized by the transaction to the corporation. This transfer is justified under the theory that the director engaged in this business activity as a constructive trustee on behalf of the corporation.

Although directors are shielded from personal liability for most purposes, there are situations in which personal liability may arise. Directors may be held personally liable for payment of dividends to shareholders in excess of the amount legally available for such payment. Recall that dividends are paid out of profits realized by the corporation. If the directors call for the distribution of dividends before assuring that corporate funds are available to meet current obligations, the directors who have distributed illegal dividends may be held personally accountable. Similarly, should a corporation go into dissolution and liquidate its assets, any distribution of liquidated assets to shareholders prior to assuring adequate provision for corporate debts is an illegal distribution of such assets and the directors may be personally liable to the corporation's creditors. Please note that in a minority of states, directors may be absolved from paying monetary damages to the corporation for a breach of fiduciary duty if the articles of incorporation so provide. Statutory law in many states entitles directors to indemnification by the corporation for legal fees and other expenses incurred in the successful defense of any action brought in a shareholder derivative action or a third-party action.

In most states, unless the articles of incorporation or bylaws provide for the contrary, the board of directors may determine their own compensation as long as such compensation is reasonable. What is considered reasonable will vary depending upon the amount of director involvement with the corporation. If a director holds many positions within the corporation (for example, the director is a majority shareholder, president of the corporation, and a full-time employee of the corporation) the director may not be compensated at all for his or her services as director (or may receive only a nominal compensation) because he or she receives adequate compensation for his or her other positions, either by way of salary or profits, or both. On the other hand, some corporations recruit directors from outside of the corporation. These directors typically are compensated for their services, either through payment for each meeting attended or by payment of an annual fee. Some states require the amount of director compensation to be set forth in the articles or the bylaws, or to be approved by a shareholder resolution. It is advisable to include a provision determining director compensation in the bylaws for under common law, if the articles or bylaws were silent in this regard, it was implied that the directors were to serve without compensation. It is preferable to include a provision in the bylaws rather than in the articles because it is easier to amend the bylaws than it is to amend the articles.

F.   Officers

Officers, elected by the board of directors (typically by a majority vote), manage the daily affairs of the corporation. State statutory law rarely provides a detailed description of their duties and authority beyond requiring a minimum number of officers. Many states require, at a minimum, a president, a secretary, and a treasurer. Some include the position of vice president as well. Most states allow one person to hold more than one office, although some prohibit the same person from holding both the positions of president and secretary. Some states allow all offices to be held by one person, while others follow a more modern trend and do not specify officer positions in their statutes or permit the inclusion of (or substitution by) the positions of **chief executive officer** and **chief financial officer**. The Revised Model Business Corporation Act does not specify officer positions and permits the bylaws of a corporation to determine the requisite positions. The articles of incorporation usually are silent on the matter of officers. The bylaws typically enumerate the positions to be held, powers and duties delegated to each position, the qualifications to be met in order to hold each position, and the term to be served. Although the roles of corporate officers may vary depending upon their description in the bylaws, certain general characteristics apply.

The **president** is the principal officer of the corporation, unless the board has selected a chief executive officer. He or she controls the corporation's business affairs and is the appropriate officer to execute documents on behalf of the corporation, including share certificates. The **vice president** may share the responsibilities of the president and fills the president's shoes should he or she become incapacitated or resign. In most corporations, the vice president has joint authority with the president to execute corporate documents. The **secretary** is custodian of the corporate records (including the stock transfer books and shareholder register) and the corporate seal, as well as being responsible for keeping accurate minutes of corporate meetings. The **treasurer** is custodian of the corporate funds and is responsible for all financial records of the corporation. Because of the nature of a treasurer's duties, the corporation may require that the treasurer be bonded. In some corporations, the chief financial officer replaces or serves in addition to the treasurer. If a corporation has both a chief financial officer and a treasurer, the treasurer usually holds the lesser role.

Unlike directors, officers are agents of the corporation. As such, they owe a duty of obedience to act within their respective authority. Similar to the fiduciary duties owed by directors, officers must exercise due care, good faith, and diligence in their dealings and must subordinate their personal interests to those of the corporation. An officer may be liable to the corporation if that officer exceeds his or her actual authority in a transaction with a third party, unless the corporation ratifies the transaction. Note that a corporation may be found to have ratified such a transaction if it has knowledge of the transaction and fails to disaffirm it. Further, if a corporation retains the benefits of the transaction, the corporation may be found to have ratified the transaction. In most states, officers may be removed from their positions with or without cause by the board of directors. Bear in mind, however, that if an officer has been hired on as a key employee of the corporation any employment agreement entered into by the corporation with that officer as employee must be checked prior to that officer's removal, for a removal without cause could well be considered a breach under the terms of the agreement. Likewise, although state statutes typically allow an officer to resign at will, if that officer has been hired under an employment agreement, his or her resignation may be deemed a breach under the terms of the agreement. Although courts will not require that officer to stay on, the officer may be required to compensate the corporation for the breach.

TYPES OF CORPORATIONS

A.   Closely Held Corporations

A **closely held corporation** is sometimes referred to as a **close corporation**, a **statutory close corporation**, or a **small business corporation**. Although the first three terms generally are synonymous, the term small business corporation includes corporations other than closely held corporations. The Internal Revenue Code in Sections 1244(c)(3)(A) and 1361(b)(1)(A) defines a small business corporation as an incorporated business that has fewer than 100 employees, 35 or fewer owners, and a net worth of less than $1 million.

Close corporation codes or acts governing closely held corporations are operative in a minority of states while in the majority of states closely held corporations are governed by the state's general corporation statutes. A few states have included a number of special provisions pertaining to closely held corporations within their general corporation statutes rather than enact a separate code or act. Although the definition of a closely held corporation will be variously defined by states that have special statutory provisions pertaining to them, most definitions share common characteristics. A closely held corporation is a private corporation whose stock is not publicly traded; rather, its stock is owned by few shareholders (in those states following the Revised Model Business Corporation Act, the number is 50 or fewer shareholders) and stock transfer restrictions are normally imposed on its stock shares. In many ways, a closely held corporation acts like an incorporated partnership. Typically, the shareholders hold all the major positions in the corporate structure and often are permitted to dispense with the traditional corporate hierarchy and manage the corporation directly. Often they are even permitted to dispense with bylaws and formal shareholders' meetings, using written consents to replace formal resolutions.

In states that have close corporation codes or acts, close corporation elections must be held. In these states, the articles of incorporation must contain a separate statement declaring the corporation to be a statutory close corporation as defined in that state's close corporation code or act. The election to be classified as such must be approved by a statutorily prescribed percentage of the shareholders (or subscribers). Once this is done, the corporation is governed by the state's close corporation statutes rather than its general corporation statutes. General requirements under these statutes include the requirements that all of the corporation's issued and outstanding stock be subject to specified restrictions, that the stock certificates include a legend indicating that the corporation is a statutory close corporation and share transfer restrictions apply, and that stock may be held by a statutorily limited number of persons. The corporation's status as a close corporation is retained as long as the above requirements are in place or until the shareholders decide to terminate this status by shareholder vote. In states that include close corporation provisions within their general corporation statutes, the corporation's status as a closely held corporation typically is indicated by a statutorily authorized shareholders' agreement.

If a corporation qualifies as a close corporation, it may dispense with or limit the authority of the board of directors. In states that permit a close corporation to be formed by a shareholders' agreement, the agreement may include provisions permitting direct shareholder management or, in the alternative, provisions specifying the directors and officers of the corporation, the method of selection, their term, and the grounds for their removal. Often, these agreements remain valid for a limited number of years. Under either arrangement, dissolution of the corporation is considerably easier than it is for other corporations. Dissolution may occur by the occurrence of a specified event or upon the desire of the shareholders to dissolve. Often, such a desire by one shareholder may bring about a dissolution, just as may occur when a partner wishes to dissolve a partnership.

B. S Corporations

S corporations are those which qualify and apply for special tax status under the provisions of subchapter S of the Internal Revenue Code. S corporations

are taxed similarly to partnerships. All income and deductions are passed through to the shareholders of the corporation who report their proportionate share (based on their proportionate stock ownership in the corporation) on their individual tax returns. The corporation itself does not pay federal income tax although it must file an annual income tax return using Form 1120S (see Exhibit 6.3 at the end of this chapter) and remains responsible for other pertinent taxes, such as employment taxes, franchise taxes, and the like. A corporation can become an S corporation if it meets the requirements of S corporation status, if all its shareholders consent to the S corporation status, if it uses a permitted tax year, and if it files a **Form 2553** with the Internal Revenue Service to indicate its election to become an S corporation (Form 2553 is found in Exhibit 6.2).

To qualify for S corporation status, a corporation must meet all the following requirements:

1. The corporation must be a domestic corporation. Please note that the Internal Revenue Service is using the term "domestic corporation" in a manner other than its normal usage. Typically, a corporation is considered a domestic corporation to its state of incorporation. However, for the purposes of subchapter S, a domestic corporation is any corporation that is either organized in the United States or organized under federal or state law.

2. It must have only one class of stock. A corporation is considered to have only one class of stock if all outstanding shares confer identical rights to dividend distributions and identical rights to liquidation proceeds. Stock may have differences in voting rights and nonetheless be considered one class of stock for purposes of subchapter S.

3. It must have no more than 35 shareholders. For the purposes of this requirement, a husband and a wife count as one unit rather than as two shareholders when calculating the number of shareholders in a corporation.

4. It must have as shareholders only individuals, estates (including estates of individuals in bankruptcy), and certain trusts. Partnerships, limited liability companies, and corporations cannot be shareholders of an S corporation.

5. All of its shareholders must be citizens or residents of the United States.

Certain domestic corporations are ineligible to elect S corporation status. They are:

1. A member of an affiliated group of corporations. An affiliated group is defined by the Internal Revenue Code as one or more chains of corporations connected through stock ownership with a common parent corporation that is also part of the group. To be classified in this manner, the common parent must directly own stock that possesses at least 80 percent of the total voting power of the stock of at least one of the corporations and which has a value equal to at least 80 percent of the total value of the stock of that same corporation. In addition, the stock the common parent owns must have a value equal to at least 80 percent of the total value of the stock of that same corporation.
2. A DISC (domestic international sales corporation), which is a U.S. corporation deriving its main income from exports, or former DISC.
3. A corporation that takes the Puerto Rico and possessions tax credit for doing business in a United States possession.
4. A financial institution that is a bank, including mutual savings banks, cooperative banks, and domestic building and loan associations.
5. An insurance company taxed under subchapter L of the Internal Revenue Code.

Only certain trusts can qualify as shareholders of an S corporation. They are:

1. A trust that is treated as entirely owned by an individual who is a United States citizen or resident. The individual, not the trust, is treated as the shareholder.
2. A trust that qualified under (1) above immediately before the owner's death, and continues to exist after the owner's death, may continue to be an S corporation shareholder for stock held by the trust when the owner died. Note that under the Internal Revenue Code this is valid only for a period of 60 days, beginning on the day of the owner's death. However, if the entire corpus (i.e., property) of the trust is included in the owner's gross estate, the sixty-day period becomes a two-year period. The owner's estate is treated as the shareholder.
3. A trust created primarily to exercise the voting power of stock transferred to it, with each beneficiary of the trust treated as a shareholder.
4. Any trust to which stock is transferred under the terms of a will, for a sixty-day period only, beginning with the day the stock was transferred to the trust. The estate of the person leaving the will is treated as the shareholder.

EXHIBIT 6.2

Form 2553
(Rev. September 1993)

Department of the Treasury
Internal Revenue Service

Election by a Small Business Corporation
(Under section 1362 of the Internal Revenue Code)
► For Paperwork Reduction Act Notice, see page 1 of instructions.
► See separate instructions.

OMB No. 1545-0146
Expires 8-31-96

Notes: 1. This election, to be an "S corporation," can be accepted only if all the tests are met under **Who May Elect** on page 1 of the instructions; all signatures in Parts I and III are originals (no photocopies); and the exact name and address of the corporation and other required form information are provided.

2. Do not file **Form 1120S**, U.S. Income Tax Return for an S Corporation, until you are notified that your election is accepted.

Part I	**Election Information**		
Please Type or Print	Name of corporation (see instructions)	**A** Employer identification number (EIN)	
	Number, street, and room or suite no. (If a P.O. box, see instructions.)	**B** Date incorporated	
	City or town, state, and ZIP code	**C** State of incorporation	

D Election is to be effective for tax year beginning (month, day, year) . . . . ►   /   /

E Name and title of officer or legal representative who the IRS may call for more information   **F** Telephone number of officer or legal representative ( )

G If the corporation changed its name or address after applying for the EIN shown in **A**, check this box . . . . ► ☐

H If this election takes effect for the first tax year the corporation exists, enter month, day, and year of the **earliest** of the following: (1) date the corporation first had shareholders, (2) date the corporation first had assets, or (3) date the corporation began doing business . . . . ►   /   /

I Selected tax year: Annual return will be filed for tax year ending (month and day) ► . . . .

If the tax year ends on any date other than December 31, except for an automatic 52-53-week tax year ending with reference to the month of December, you **must** complete Part II on the back. If the date you enter is the ending date of an automatic 52-53-week tax year, write "52-53-week year" to the right of the date. See Temporary Regulations section 1.441-2T(e)(3).

J Name and address of each shareholder, shareholder's spouse having a community property interest in the corporation's stock, and each tenant in common, joint tenant, and tenant by the entirety. (A husband and wife (and their estates) are counted as one shareholder in determining the number of shareholders without regard to the manner in which the stock is owned.)	**K** Shareholders' Consent Statement. Under penalties of perjury, we declare that we consent to the election of the above-named corporation to be an "S corporation" under section 1362(a) and that we have examined this consent statement, including accompanying schedules and statements, and to the best of our knowledge and belief, it is true, correct, and complete. (Shareholders sign and date below.)*		**L** Stock owned		**M** Social security number or employer identification number (see instructions)	**N** Share-holder's tax year ends (month and day)
	Signature	Date	Number of shares	Dates acquired		

*For this election to be valid, the consent of each shareholder, shareholder's spouse having a community property interest in the corporation's stock, and each tenant by the entirety, joint tenant, and tenant in common must either appear above or be attached to this form. (See instructions for Column K if a continuation sheet or a separate consent statement is needed.)

Under penalties of perjury, I declare that I have examined this election, including accompanying schedules and statements, and to the best of my knowledge and belief, it is true, correct, and complete.

Signature of officer ►   Title ►   Date ►

See Parts II and III on back.   Cat. No. 18629R   Form **2553** (Rev. 9-93)

EXHIBIT 6.2 *Continued*

Form 2553 (Rev. 9-93)   Page **2**

Part II **Selection of Fiscal Tax Year (All corporations using this part must complete item O and one of items P, Q, or R.)**

O Check the applicable box below to indicate whether the corporation is:

    1. ☐ A new corporation adopting the tax year entered in item I, Part I.

    2. ☐ An existing corporation retaining the tax year entered in item I, Part I.

    3. ☐ An existing corporation changing to the tax year entered in item I, Part I.

P Complete item P if the corporation is using the expeditious approval provisions of Revenue Procedure 87-32, 1987-2 C.B. 396, to request: **(1)** a natural business year (as defined in section 4.01(1) of Rev. Proc. 87-32), or **(2)** a year that satisfies the ownership tax year test in section 4.01(2) of Rev. Proc. 87-32. Check the applicable box below to indicate the representation statement the corporation is making as required under section 4 of Rev. Proc. 87-32.

    1. Natural Business Year ▶ ☐ I represent that the corporation is retaining or changing to a tax year that coincides with its natural business year as defined in section 4.01(1) of Rev. Proc. 87-32 and as verified by its satisfaction of the requirements of section 4.02(1) of Rev. Proc. 87-32. In addition, if the corporation is changing to a natural business year as defined in section 4.01(1), I further represent that such tax year results in less deferral of income to the owners than the corporation's present tax year. I also represent that the corporation is not described in section 3.01(2) of Rev. Proc. 87-32. (See instructions for additional information that must be attached.)

    2. Ownership Tax Year ▶ ☐ I represent that shareholders holding more than half of the shares of the stock (as of the first day of the tax year to which the request relates) of the corporation have the same tax year or are concurrently changing to the tax year that the corporation adopts, retains, or changes to per item I, Part I. I also represent that the corporation is not described in section 3.01(2) of Rev. Proc. 87-32.

Note: *If you do not use item P and the corporation wants a fiscal tax year, complete either item Q or R below. Item Q is used to request a fiscal tax year based on a business purpose and to make a back-up section 444 election. Item R is used to make a regular section 444 election.*

Q Business Purpose—To request a fiscal tax year based on a business purpose, you must check box Q1 and pay a user fee. See instructions for details. You may also check box Q2 and/or box Q3.

    1. Check here ▶ ☐ if the fiscal year entered in item I, Part I, is requested under the provisions of section 6.03 of Rev. Proc. 87-32. Attach to Form 2553 a statement showing the business purpose for the requested fiscal year. See instructions for additional information that must be attached.

    2. Check here ▶ ☐ to show that the corporation intends to make a back-up section 444 election in the event the corporation's business purpose request is not approved by the IRS. (See instructions for more information.)

    3. Check here ▶ ☐ to show that the corporation agrees to adopt or change to a tax year ending December 31 if necessary for the IRS to accept this election for S corporation status in the event: (1) the corporation's business purpose request is not approved and the corporation makes a back-up section 444 election, but is ultimately not qualified to make a section 444 election, or (2) the corporation's business purpose request is not approved and the corporation did not make a back-up section 444 election.

R Section 444 Election—To make a section 444 election, you must check box R1 and you may also check box R2.

    1. Check here ▶ ☐ to show the corporation will make, if qualified, a section 444 election to have the fiscal tax year shown in item I, Part I. To make the election, you must complete **Form 8716,** Election To Have a Tax Year Other Than a Required Tax Year, and either attach it to Form 2553 or file it separately.

    2. Check here ▶ ☐ to show that the corporation agrees to adopt or change to a tax year ending December 31 if necessary for the IRS to accept this election for S corporation status in the event the corporation is ultimately not qualified to make a section 444 election.

Part III **Qualified Subchapter S Trust (QSST) Election Under Section 1361(d)(2)****

Income beneficiary's name and address	Social security number
Trust's name and address	Employer identification number

Date on which stock of the corporation was transferred to the trust (month, day, year) . . . . ▶   /   /

In order for the trust named above to be a QSST and thus a qualifying shareholder of the S corporation for which this Form 2553 is filed, I hereby make the election under section 1361(d)(2). Under penalties of perjury, I certify that the trust meets the definitional requirements of section 1361(d)(3) and that all other information provided in Part III is true, correct, and complete.

Signature of income beneficiary or signature and title of legal representative or other qualified person making the election	Date

**Use of Part III to make the QSST election may be made only if stock of the corporation has been transferred to the trust on or before the date on which the corporation makes its election to be an S corporation. The QSST election must be made and filed separately if stock of the corporation is transferred to the trust after the date on which the corporation makes the S election.

✪ *Printed on recycled paper*   *U.S. Government Printing Office: 1993 — 301-828/80271

Beneficiaries may have their trusts qualify as **qualified subchapter S trusts (QSSTs)** if certain requirements are met. To qualify as a QSST, all trust income must be distributed to one beneficiary, the beneficiary must be a citizen or resident of the United States, and the same person must remain the beneficiary until death.

In addition to meeting all requirements for subchapter S status, all existing shareholders must sign a written consent to the election of such status. Although a husband and wife are considered to be a single shareholder for qualification purposes, each must sign a written consent. At first blush, it would appear that having the shareholders sign such a consent (Form 2553 includes a shareholders' consent statement with appropriate signature blocks) would not be a problem because all shareholders would want to reap the benefits of avoiding double taxation. However, once subchapter S status is elected, all shareholders must pay taxes on their proportionate share of the income of the corporation, even if they do not receive dividends for a particular year because the generated income was retained by the corporation as working capital. Many shareholders do not realize this and become disgruntled about paying taxes on income they have not personally received.

The election of subchapter S status must be made by the fifteenth day of the third month of the current tax year for the election to be effective for the current year. An election filed after this date will become effective for the following year. Once the election becomes effective, it is automatically renewed each year, even if the number of shareholders increases, as long as the cap is not exceeded. Because the year in which the election becomes effective is determined by the corporation's tax year, the corporation must specify its tax year on Form 2553. A corporation must have a tax year that meets the definition of a "permitted year," as defined in Section 1378 of the Internal Revenue Code (i.e., the calendar year or any other accounting period for which the corporation establishes a business purpose to the satisfaction of the Treasury Secretary).

C.   *Professional Corporations*

State legislatures recognize the desire of persons in various professions to incorporate their practices rather than forming partnerships. While historically incorporation of professional businesses was prohibited, the 1960s saw a move toward recognition of **professional corporations** (sometimes referred to as **professional service corporations**) in a minority of states. The number of states recognizing professional corporations grew after 1969 when the Internal Revenue Service recognized these corporations by declaring that they were to be taxed as other corporations were taxed. Now, every state recognizes professional corporations and most have special statutes governing the incorporation of certain professions which are found either within the general corporation statutes, as a separate professional corporations act, or within the statutes regulating each applicable profession. A number of states model their professional corporation statutes after the Model Professional Corporation Act, adopted in 1979. Some states recognize a business entity called a **professional association**, which is similar to a professional partnership but is taxed like a corporation. The professions most often included in all of these statutory provisions are law, medicine, veterinary medicine, dentistry, psychology, accountancy, engineering, and architecture. Some states recognize other professions as well, such as physical therapy, chiropractic, acupuncture, optometry, podiatry, nursing, and certain types of counseling. Other states do not enumerate permissible professions but instead permit a professional corporation to be formed by individuals of any profession duly licensed within the state. In a majority of states, professional corporations (or professional associations) are statutorily limited to the practice of a single profession. However, this limitation does not preclude a professional corporation from investing in real estate, stocks, bonds, and other investment activities available to general corporations.

Most states place restrictions on the qualifications of shareholders of professional corporations, requiring that all shareholders be licensed to practice the profession of the corporation. In these states, the spouse of a licensed professional, for example, would be prohibited from owning stock in the corporation unless the spouse was also licensed to practice that profession. In that same vein, the stock of a deceased shareholder in a professional corporation can only pass to a qualified professional. Therefore, it is good practice for professional corporations to have restrictive shareholders' agreements (discussed in detail in Chapter 10) which restrict the transfer of shares and which include buyout provisions providing that should a shareholder wish to sell his or her shares of stock, the corporation or the other shareholders will purchase those shares; further, should a shareholder die, the corporation or the other shareholders will purchase those shares from his or her estate. Such an agreement would act as preventive medicine, avoiding an involuntary dissolution of the corporation due to the inclusion of a disqualified shareholder.

Similarly, most states require that the directors and/or officers of a professional corporation be licensed to practice the profession of the corporation. Some states require that all directors and/or officers be so licensed while others require that a certain percentage be so licensed. In the latter instance, those states typically provide that nonlicensed directors and officers have no decision-making power over professional matters. It is advisable, therefore, to include in the corporate bylaws a provision pertaining to the qualifications of the directors and officers which parallels the state statutory qualifications for directors and officers of professional corporations. Professional corporations must include in their name words indicating their status, such as "professional corporation" or its abbreviation "P.C.," "professional association" or its abbreviation "P.A.," "service corporation" or its abbreviation "S.C.," or similar designations. In some states, the surname of one or more of the shareholders must be included in the name.

Shareholders wishing to form a professional corporation share the same concern about personal liability as ordinary shareholders. While shareholders in a professional corporation may be shielded from personal liability to corporate creditors, they remain personally liable for professional malpractice, negligence, and other misconduct. Some states limit personal liability if the corporation carries malpractice and other liability insurance or if the corporation has a surety bond. Other states hold all shareholders liable for the malpractice, negligence, or misconduct of any shareholder and those persons under their supervision, while still others hold only the culpable shareholder personally liable.

Many professions are governed by their own codes of professional and ethical conduct. All regulations governing such conduct remain applicable to licensed professionals regardless of the business format under which they choose to provide their services. Thus, for example, the rules of confidentiality pertaining to many professions must be complied with by shareholders of professions which require the protection of confidential information.

A professional corporation desiring to expand its business into other states is presented with special problems. It must do more than simply register as a foreign corporation in the states in which it wants to do business. It can only conduct business in a foreign state through persons licensed to practice that profession in those states. Further, it must comply not only with all regulations governing corporations but also those governing that particular profession in those states.

D.   Nonprofit Corporations

A **nonprofit corporation** (sometimes referred to as a **not-for-profit corporation**) typically is defined as a corporation which meets the requisite criteria set forth in the Internal Revenue Code Section 501(c) to receive special tax status. The term "nonprofit" is something of a misnomer, because a nonprofit corporation can realize profits. However, the profits are not paid out to shareholders as dividends. Indeed, nonprofit corporations do not have shareholders, for they do not sell shares of stock. Rather, they have members and all profits realized by the corporation are used exclusively for charitable, educational, scientific, religious, or civic purposes. They are governed by the nonprofit statutes of their state of incorporation, many of which are modeled after the Model Nonprofit Corporation Act.

The articles of incorporation of a nonprofit corporation typically state as the corporation's purpose the raising, administering, and distributing of funds together with any interest such funds generate, exclusively for charitable, religious, or educational purposes. Further, the articles or bylaws often contain provisions for membership eligibility and may set forth membership fees and dues. In addition, the articles of incorporation explicitly may prohibit the corporation, its board of directors, and/or its officers from engaging in certain activities which would jeopardize the corporation's nonprofit status. Thus, the articles of incorporation may include a provision prohibiting the corporation from attempting to influence legislation as a substantial part of its activities (including participation in political campaigns), or from allowing any part of its net income to inure to the benefit of officers, directors, or members of the corporation except in the furtherance of its charitable purposes. The articles of incorporation may also include a catchall provision prohibiting the conduct of any activities not permitted to be carried on by organizations exempt under Section 501(c) of the Internal Revenue Code.

E. Public Corporations

Public corporations are corporations whose shares of stock are traded in a public market and which are subject to state and federal securities regulations. Stock traded on a **stock exchange** is traded at a market or similar facility by members of the exchange. **Over-the-counter trading** activities are not conducted at a physical trading facility but rather, through brokers utilizing computer networks.

Public corporations most commonly start out as private corporations whose shareholders and board of directors decide to "go public" in order to increase both capital investments and public exposure to products and services. Once such a decision is made, numerous statutorily mandated steps must be taken before the corporation's **securities** (stocks, bonds, debentures, or other certificates evincing a financial interest in the corporation) may be publicly traded. The legal costs are often high and the disclosure requirements are rigorous.

The two most important federal acts regulating public corporations are the **Securities Act of 1933**, which governs the initial registration of securities sold through interstate commerce, and the **Securities Exchange Act of 1934**, which governs public disclosures and other reporting requirements after initial registration. Recall that both of these acts were discussed in Chapter 4. The exemptions to these two acts discussed in Chapter 4 (i.e., the private offering exemption and the intrastate exemption) relate not only to securities of limited partnerships but also to corporations. In addition to the exemptions discussed in that chapter, the following exemptions, listed in Section 3 of the Securities Act, are noteworthy:

1. Certain securities issued or guaranteed by:
   (i)   federal, state, or local governments;
   (ii) banks; or
   (iii) savings and loan associations, building and loans associations, cooperative banks, and similar loan institutions
2. Short-term commercial paper
3. Insurance policies, annuity contracts, and optional annuity contracts
4. Industrial development bonds
5. Interests in railroad equipment trusts
6. Securities of nonprofit issuers
7. Certificates issued by receivers or trustees under the Bankruptcy Code
8. Certain securities exchanged without commission paid to the broker or other facilitator of the exchange

The first step in making the transition from a private to a public corporation is the preparation of a **registration statement** to be submitted on SEC Form S-1, in triplicate, together with the requisite filing fee, to the Securities and Exchange Commission. Schedule A of the Securities Act specifies the information that must be included in the registration statement. The registration statement consists of two parts. The first part is called the **prospectus**, which includes requisite disclosures of information on the corporate directors and officers, corporate assets, and other pertinent information. The second part of the registration includes information on the actual securities being offered, as well as information on the underwriters. An **underwriter** is an individual or entity engaged in the business of purchasing and selling securities, often a securities broker or financial institution. It is possible for a corporation to enter into agreements with more than one underwriter.

A gap period of 20 days exists between the filing of a registration statement and its effective date. During this period, a corporation may offer its securities for sale through preliminary prospectuses (sometimes referred to rather colorfully as **red herring prospectuses** due to the warning on their cover, printed in red ink, that the registration is not yet effective) but may not consummate their sale. Upon the effective date, the sale of securities may proceed. If the sale of securities is to be conducted through a stock exchange, the Securities Exchange Act of 1934 requires not only registration with the Securities and Exchange Commission, but also with the exchange on which the securities will be traded by filing an application with each applicable exchange (as well as submission of duplicate originals of the application(s) with the Securities and Exchange Commission), registration with said exchange(s) typically becoming effective 30 days after the filing of the application(s).

Section 13 of the Securities Exchange Act of 1934 specifies requisite periodic reporting requirements that must be met by filing periodic disclosure forms with the Securities Exchange Commission. **Form 8-K** must be filed whenever any material information contained within the corporation's registration statement changes. **Form 10-K** is an annual report that must be filed within 90 days from the end of the corporation's fiscal year. Similar to the registration statement, this form contains two parts and requires detailed information pertaining to the corporation's last five fiscal years or, if the corporation has been registered for less than five years, information bringing the registration up to date. **Form 10-Q** is a quarterly report that must be submitted within 45 days of the end of a quarter for the first three quarters of each fiscal year.

Special federal regulations pertain to proxies of public corporations. A **proxy** is a shareholder's authorization turning over to another his or her voting rights. Section 14(a) of the Securities Exchange Act of 1934 governs proxies of all corporations that either (a) are registered on a national securities exchange or (b) have assets in excess of $1 million and a class of equity security held by 500 or more shareholders of record. Section 14(a) provides that all proxy solicitations must be accompanied by a proxy statement setting forth detailed information about the persons making the solicitation as well as detailed information about the directors of the corporation and the nominees. Further, the proxy statement must be accompanied or preceded by the distribution of the corporation's annual report. Five copies of the proxy statement and proxy form must be submitted to the Securities and Exchange Commission at least ten days prior to the mailing of the proxy solicitation to the corporation's shareholders.

Section 10(b) of the Securities Exchange Act of 1934 is the anti-fraud provision which prohibits deceptive practices, including insider trading. **Insider trading** is the sale or purchase of securities of a public corporation by a party with "insider" knowledge that gives that party a distinct advantage over a less-informed public.

In addition to federal regulations, public corporations are subject to state securities regulations, commonly referred to as **blue sky laws**. Most states have adopted either the **Uniform Securities Act of 1956** or the **Revised Uniform Securities Act of 1985** (with the **1988 amendments**). State statutes should be checked for applicable exemptions. Whereas federal regulations typically pertain to interstate sales of securities, blue sky laws pertain to intrastate sales of securities by both domestic and foreign corporations, requiring registration of publicly traded securities at the state level. States following the original uniform act provide for registration by coordination, while states following the revised act with the 1988 amendments provide for registration by filing. The former is accomplished by submission of a detailed statement (the requisite information detailed in the state statute) together with the applicable filing fee, to the appropriate state filing authority. The latter similarly is accomplished by submitting a statement, together with the applicable filing fee, of eligibility for filing (transacting business in the United States for a specified number of years), information about the corporation, information about the registered securities, and a copy of the latest prospectus filed with the Securities and Exchange Commission. The difference between the two types of registration is in the amount of information required, the former generally requiring more information than the latter.

TAX CONSIDERATIONS

A.   General Considerations

Choosing a corporate structure for a business implies consideration of numerous tax-related considerations. The most obvious consideration is that of double taxation. As noted in this as well as earlier chapters, a C corporation (one not qualifying for subchapter S status) is caught in the bind of double taxation. The corporation is taxed at the corporate tax rate on income realized by the corporation. If the corporation then pays out a portion of its profits to its shareholders as dividends, those shareholders pay taxes on their proportionate share. Many corporations attempt to avoid, or at least minimize, these results through distributing profits in a manner other than through the payment of dividends. One such method is through compensation for personal services provided by shareholders to the corporation by the payment of salary and the implementation of tax-qualified benefit plans (discussed in detail in Chapter 11). Although section 162(a) of the Internal Revenue Code imposes certain limitations, a corporation generally may take deductions for salaries and such plans. The shareholder-recipients are still responsible for including the salaries as income on their individual tax returns, but taxation at the corporate level is avoided and the shareholder-recipient's taxation on the qualified benefit plans is deferred. Another method of distributing earnings to shareholders is through rental payments. This is achieved by having shareholders lease equipment to the corporation, the rental payments being tax-deductible by the corporation.

B.   Accumulated Earnings, Personal Holding Company, and Collapsible Corporation Taxes

In addition to potential double taxation as well as state corporate income taxes, franchise taxes, and share transfer taxes (mentioned at the beginning of the chapter), certain other taxes are applicable to corporations that are not applicable to other business entities. These taxes include the **accumulated earnings tax**, the **personal holding company tax**, and the **collapsible corporation tax**. The Internal Revenue Code, in its efforts to force corporations to distribute their earnings to shareholders, has included special tax provisions in Sections 531 through 535. In capsule form, these sections state that a corporation which accumulates earnings and profits in excess of a specified amount (at the time of this writing, $250,000) for the purpose of avoiding income tax imposed on its shareholders, is subject to an accumulated earnings tax on its accumulated taxable income. At present, under Section 535, a $150,000 accumulated earnings limitation is imposed on certain types of corporate businesses. The accumulated earnings tax does not apply to tax-exempt corporations or to personal holding companies.

Sections 542 and 543 of the Internal Revenue Code define a **personal holding company** as either a corporation in which more than 50 percent of outstanding corporate stock is owned by not more than five individuals, or as a corporation in which at least 60 percent of the corporation's adjusted gross income is derived from dividends, interest, royalties, annuities, trusts, estates, and certain personal service contracts. Under Section 541 of the Internal Revenue Code, personal holding companies pay, in addition to any other applicable taxes, a penalty tax on undistributed income.

Section 341 of the Internal Revenue Code defines a **collapsible corporation** as one used primarily for the manufacture, construction, production, or purchase of certain kinds of property with the principal aim of distribution to the corporation's shareholders prior to the realization by the corporation of a substantial portion of taxable income from the property. The Internal Revenue Code considers such gains as ordinary income to the shareholders and taxes it as such.

C.   Elections Under Sections 248 and 1244

Corporations are allowed to choose to amortize certain organizational expenses over a period of not less than 60 months (five years). Section 248 of the Internal Revenue Code allows the following expenses to be amortized:

1. legal and accounting services incident to incorporation
2. expenses of temporary directors and incorporators
3. fees paid to the state for incorporation
4. expenses of organizational meetings of directors and shareholders

If a corporation takes a **Section 248 election**, it must attach a statement of such election to the corporation's first federal tax return.

Section 1244 of the Internal Revenue Code allows shareholders to treat their financial investment in a corporation as an ordinary loss rather than a capital loss if certain qualifications are met. This allows each shareholder to deduct from his or her personal income any loss sustained from his or her stock investment up to a maximum of $50,000 per year for an individual and $100,000 for a joint return. For a corporation to qualify for a **Section 1244 election**, the total amount to be received by the corporation for the issued stock and the entire net capitalization of the corporation at the time of the election cannot exceed $1 million.

D.   Miscellaneous Tax Considerations

A newly formed C corporation is permitted to select its own tax year. Section 441(f) of the Internal Revenue Code allows such a corporation to select, without prior approval from the Internal Revenue Service, a tax year ending with the close of any of its first 12 months of existence. However, once the election is made, it may not be changed within the first ten calendar years of the corporation's existence without approval of the Treasury Secretary. In selecting a tax year, a corporation should consider such factors as the timing of compensation payments to shareholder-employees and seasonal variations in income or inventory of the business.

Corporations are permitted to pay **alternative minimum tax (AMT)**. The AMT rate for corporations at the time of this writing is 20 percent. There is an exemption of up to $40,000. This amount is reduced by 25 percent of the amount by which the alternative minimum taxable income exceeds $150,000. Internal Revenue Form 4626 (see Exhibit 6.4 at the end of this chapter) is used for calculating AMT.

Every corporation, unless specifically exempt, must file an annual corporate tax return (either Form 1120-A or Form 1120, Exhibits 6.5 and 6.6 respectively at the end of this chapter) by the fifteenth day of the third month following the close of the corporation's fiscal year. The short-form return, Form 1120-A, may be used by corporations having gross receipts under $500,000, total income under $500,000, total assets under $500,000, and which meet certain other requirements. Additionally, any corporation making nondividend contributions to shareholders must file a Form 5452 (Exhibit 6.7 at the end of this chapter) with its income tax return due for the tax year in which the nondividend distributions were made. As noted previously, S corporations file Form 1120S.

Chapter Summary

1. A corporation is a business entity legally existing separate from its owners. It is created and regulated by statute. Most states have adopted corporate statutes modeled after the Model Business Corporation Act. A corporation must follow not only the statutory law of its state of domicile but also the statutory law of each state in which it conducts business as a foreign corporation. Further, should a corporation qualify as one dealing in securities, it must abide by the rules set forth in the Securities Act of 1933, the Securities Exchange Act of 1934, and any other related securities laws.

2. The two most important corporate documents are the articles of incorporation, which are filed with the state filing authority, and the bylaws, which are not. The articles of incorporation, typically a skeletal document setting forth the most basic information about the corporation, must be filed in order for the corporation to come into legal existence. Once filed, the articles become a matter of public record. The bylaws are the rules governing the internal operations of the corporation and remain an internal document, thus shielded from public scrutiny.

3. A corporate format is considered advantageous for those persons seeking limited personal liability and free transferability of their interest in the business should they wish to depart it. It also provides an avenue for increased working capital through the sale of stock shares and the issuance of bonds and debentures. Many corporate expenses are not only tax deductible to the corporation but also income producing yet nontaxable for the employees, including shareholder-employees.

4. Corporations that do not qualify as S corporations are subject to double taxation should they realize a profit and wish to pass it on to their shareholders through the payment of dividends. Additionally, corporations are subject to state income taxes and often franchise and share transfer taxes. Additional costs are incurred through filing fees and legal fees.

5. In preincorporation matters, the major "players" are the promoters, the subscribers, and the incorporators. Promoters bring about the creation of the corporation by investigating business opportunities and assembling the necessary components, such as business plans, capital, and personnel, to establish the business. Upon incorporation, the promoter's role is completed. Subscribers are investors who promise to purchase a specified number of shares of stock at a predetermined price once the corporation is formed. Incorporators bridge the gap between pre- and post-incorporation matters. Incorporators execute the articles of incorporation and file them with the state filing authority. Additionally, they may hold the first organizational meeting of the corporation.

6. Upon incorporation, the major players are the shareholders, directors, and officers. The shareholders are the owners of the corporation. They manage their enterprise indirectly by electing directors to the board of directors. They also vote on major corporate changes such as mergers, consolidations, and dissolution. If state statutes so allow, the shareholders may manage directly in lieu of a board of directors. The directors of a corporation are responsible for setting and implementing corporate policies. Elected by the shareholders, they serve at the shareholders' pleasure and generally can be removed with or without cause. The directors, in turn, elect the officers of the corporation. Both the directors and the officers of a corporation have fiduciary duties to the corporation. These include the duties of due care, diligence, and loyalty. Unlike directors, officers are also agents of the corporation. Their authority to act on behalf of the corporation may be restricted by inclusion of restrictive language in the bylaws. Although traditionally a corporation had to have, at a minimum, a president, a secretary, and a treasurer, the modern trend is to allow the bylaws to specify the requisite officers and their respective duties.

7. A closely held corporation is one in which corporate stock is subject to specified share transfer restrictions and remains in the hands of few shareholders. Many states permit such corporations greater flexibility in their management structure and allow them to dispense with many of the formalities pertaining to other corporations, such as the election of a board of directors and the holding of formal meetings. In states which have enacted close corporation codes, the articles of incorporation must declare the corporation to be a statutorily close corporation before the close corporation code will apply.

8. An S corporation is taxed like a partnership and thus pays no federal income taxes. Instead, the income and deductions of the corporation are passed

through to the shareholders and are reflected proportionately on their individual tax returns. To qualify as an S corporation, a corporation must be a domestic corporation as such term is defined by subchapter S, must have only one class of stock, and must have 35 or fewer shareholders, all of whom are United States citizens or residents and all or whom are either individuals, estates, or certain trusts.

9. Professional corporations are corporations formed for the purpose of providing professional services to the public while affording their shareholders limited liability for business debts and favorable tax treatment for certain expenses. Most states require that all shareholders as well as all (or a designated percentage of) directors and officers be licensed members of the profession of the corporation. Professional corporations must include statutorily mandated words or abbreviations in their names to inform the public of their status.

10. Public corporations are corporations whose securities are publicly traded. Unless exempt, a corporation must comply with both state and federal securities regulations. Before a corporation's securities may be sold to the public at large, a registration statement (Form S-1) must be filed with the Securities and Exchange Commission, the registration typically becoming effective 20 days after the filing. Once properly registered, a public corporation must meet various periodic reporting requirements by submitting quarterly (10-Q) and annual (10-K) reports, as well as keeping the Securities and Exchange Commission abreast of any changes through the submission of 8-K reports.

Review Questions

1. Explain the concept of double taxation.
2. Define the role of each of the following:
    (i)   promoters
    (ii) shareholders
    (iii) directors
    (iv) officers
3. Explain the steps a private corporation must take to become a public corporation.
4. Compare and contrast the following:
    (i)   C corporations and S corporations
    (ii) professional corporations and limited liability partnerships
    (iii) nonprofit corporations and for-profit corporations

5. List the various taxes to which a corporation and/or its shareholders
    may be subjected.

KEY TERMS

accumulated earnings
articles of incorporation
board of directors
business judgment rule
bylaws
C corporation
closely held corporation
corporate opportunity
   doctrine
corporation
dividends
double taxation
foreign corporation
Form 8-K
Form 10-K
Form 10-Q
franchise tax
incorporator
insider trading
nonprofit corporation
novation
officer
over-the-counter trading

personal holding
   company
professional association
professional corporation
promoter
prospectus
proxy
public corporation
red herring prospectus
registration statement
S corporation
Section 248 election
Section 1244 election
shareholder
share transfer tax
small business
   corporation
stock exchange
subscriber
underwriter
Uniform Securities Act
   of 1956
Uniform Securities Act
   of 1985

EXHIBIT 6.3

Form **1120S**	U.S. Income Tax Return for an S Corporation	OMB No. 1545-0130
	► Do not file this form unless the corporation has timely filed Form 2553 to elect to be an S corporation.	19**95**
Department of the Treasury Internal Revenue Service	► See separate instructions.	

For calendar year 1995, or tax year beginning _____ , 1995, and ending _____ , 19 ___

A Date of election as an S corporation	Use IRS label. Other-wise, please print or type.	Name	C Employer identification number
		Number, street, and room or suite no. (If a P.O. box, see page 9 of the instructions.)	D Date incorporated
B Business code no. (see Specific Instructions)		City or town, state, and ZIP code	E Total assets (see Specific Instructions) $

F Check applicable boxes: (1) ☐ Initial return (2) ☐ Final return (3) ☐ Change in address (4) ☐ Amended return
G Check this box if this S corporation is subject to the consolidated audit procedures of sections 6241 through 6245 (see instructions before checking this box) . ► ☐
H Enter number of shareholders in the corporation at end of the tax year . . . . ►

Caution: Include **only** trade or business income and expenses on lines 1a through 21. See the instructions for more information.

Income

1a	Gross receipts or sales		b Less returns and allowances		c Bal ►	1c	
2	Cost of goods sold (Schedule A, line 8)					2	
3	Gross profit. Subtract line 2 from line 1c					3	
4	Net gain (loss) from Form 4797, Part II, line 20 (attach Form 4797)					4	
5	Other income (loss) (attach schedule)					5	
6	**Total income (loss).** Combine lines 3 through 5 . . . . ►					6	

Deductions (see page 10 of the instructions for limitations)

7	Compensation of officers			7	
8	Salaries and wages (less employment credits)			8	
9	Repairs and maintenance.			9	
10	Bad debts			10	
11	Rents			11	
12	Taxes and licenses.			12	
13	Interest			13	
14a	Depreciation (if required, attach Form 4562)	14a			
b	Depreciation claimed on Schedule A and elsewhere on return . .	14b			
c	Subtract line 14b from line 14a			14c	
15	Depletion (**Do not deduct oil and gas depletion.**)			15	
16	Advertising			16	
17	Pension, profit-sharing, etc., plans			17	
18	Employee benefit programs			18	
19	Other deductions (attach schedule)			19	
20	**Total deductions.** Add the amounts shown in the far right column for lines 7 through 19 . ►			20	
21	Ordinary income (loss) from trade or business activities. Subtract line 20 from line 6			21	

Tax and Payments

22	**Tax: a** Excess net passive income tax (attach schedule). . .	22a			
b	Tax from Schedule D (Form 1120S)	22b			
c	Add lines 22a and 22b (see page 13 of the instructions for additional taxes)			22c	
23	**Payments: a** 1995 estimated tax payments and amount applied from 1994 return	23a			
b	Tax deposited with Form 7004	23b			
c	Credit for Federal tax paid on fuels (attach Form 4136) . . .	23c			
d	Add lines 23a through 23c			23d	
24	Estimated tax penalty. Check if Form 2220 is attached . . . . ► ☐			24	
25	**Tax due.** If the total of lines 22c and 24 is larger than line 23d, enter amount owed. See page 3 of the instructions for depositary method of payment . . . . ►			25	
26	**Overpayment.** If line 23d is larger than the total of lines 22c and 24, enter amount overpaid ►			26	
27	Enter amount of line 26 you want: **Credited to 1996 estimated tax** ► _____ **Refunded** ►			27	

Please Sign Here

Under penalties of perjury, I declare that I have examined this return, including accompanying schedules and statements, and to the best of my knowledge and belief, it is true, correct, and complete. Declaration of preparer (other than taxpayer) is based on all information of which preparer has any knowledge.

► _____ _____ ► _____
Signature of officer   Date   Title

Paid Preparer's Use Only

Preparer's signature ►		Date	Check if self-employed ► ☐	Preparer's social security number
Firm's name (or yours if self-employed) and address ►			EIN ►	
			ZIP code ►	

For Paperwork Reduction Act Notice, see page 1 of separate instructions.   Cat. No. 11510H   Form **1120S** (1995)

EXHIBIT 6.3   *Continued*

Form 1120S (1995)   Page **2**

Schedule A   **Cost of Goods Sold** (see page 14 of the instructions)

1 Inventory at beginning of year	**1**	
2 Purchases	**2**	
3 Cost of labor	**3**	
4 Additional section 263A costs *(attach schedule)*	**4**	
5 Other costs *(attach schedule)*	**5**	
6 **Total.** Add lines 1 through 5	**6**	
7 Inventory at end of year	**7**	
8 **Cost of goods sold.** Subtract line 7 from line 6. Enter here and on page 1, line 2	**8**	

9a Check all methods used for valuing closing inventory:
  (i) ☐ Cost as described in Regulations section 1.471-3
  (ii) ☐ Lower of cost or market as described in Regulations section 1.471-4
  (iii) ☐ Other (specify method used and attach explanation) ▶ ....
b Check if there was a writedown of "subnormal" goods as described in Regulations section 1.471-2(c) . . . . . . ▶ ☐
c Check if the LIFO inventory method was adopted this tax year for any goods *(if checked, attach Form 970)*. . . . . ▶ ☐
d If the LIFO inventory method was used for this tax year, enter percentage (or amounts) of closing
  inventory computed under LIFO . . . . | **9d** | |
e Do the rules of section 263A (for property produced or acquired for resale) apply to the corporation? . . . ☐ Yes ☐ No
f Was there any change in determining quantities, cost, or valuations between opening and closing inventory? . . ☐ Yes ☐ No
  If "Yes," attach explanation.

Schedule B   **Other Information**

	Yes	No
1 Check method of accounting: **(a)** ☐ Cash **(b)** ☐ Accrual **(c)** ☐ Other (specify) ▶		
2 Refer to the list on page 24 of the instructions and state the corporation's principal:		
(a) Business activity ▶ .... **(b)** Product or service ▶		
3 Did the corporation at the end of the tax year own, directly or indirectly, 50% or more of the voting stock of a domestic corporation? (For rules of attribution, see section 267(c).) If "Yes," attach a schedule showing: **(a)** name, address, and employer identification number and **(b)** percentage owned.		
4 Was the corporation a member of a controlled group subject to the provisions of section 1561?		
5 At any time during calendar year 1995, did the corporation have an interest in or a signature or other authority over a financial account in a foreign country (such as a bank account, securities account, or other financial account)? (See page 14 of the instructions for exceptions and filing requirements for Form TD F 90-22.1.) . . . . If "Yes," enter the name of the foreign country ▶		
6 Was the corporation the grantor of, or transferor to, a foreign trust that existed during the current tax year, whether or not the corporation had any beneficial interest in it? If "Yes," the corporation may have to file Forms 3520, 3520-A, or 926		
7 Check this box if the corporation has filed or is required to file **Form 8264,** Application for Registration of a Tax Shelter . . . . ▶ ☐		
8 Check this box if the corporation issued publicly offered debt instruments with original issue discount . . ▶ ☐		
If so, the corporation may have to file **Form 8281,** Information Return for Publicly Offered Original Issue Discount Instruments.		
9 If the corporation: **(a)** filed its election to be an S corporation after 1986, **(b)** was a C corporation before it elected to be an S corporation **or** the corporation acquired an asset with a basis determined by reference to its basis (or the basis of any other property) in the hands of a C corporation, and **(c)** has net unrealized built-in gain (defined in section 1374(d)(1)) in excess of the net recognized built-in gain from prior years, enter the net unrealized built-in gain reduced by net recognized built-in gain from prior years (see page 14 of the instructions) . . . . . ▶ $		
10 Check this box if the corporation had subchapter C earnings and profits at the close of the tax year (see page 15 of the instructions) . . . . ▶ ☐		

Designation of Tax Matters Person (see page 15 of the instructions)

Enter below the shareholder designated as the tax matters person (TMP) for the tax year of this return:

Name of designated TMP ▶	Identifying number of TMP ▶

Address of designated TMP ▶

EXHIBIT 6.3 *Continued*

Form 1120S (1995)   Page **3**

Schedule K   **Shareholders' Shares of Income, Credits, Deductions, etc.**

	(a) Pro rata share items		(b) Total amount
Income (Loss)	**1** Ordinary income (loss) from trade or business activities (page 1, line 21)	**1**	
	2 Net income (loss) from rental real estate activities *(attach Form 8825)*	**2**	
	3a Gross income from other rental activities	**3a**	
	b Expenses from other rental activities *(attach schedule)*.	**3b**	
	c Net income (loss) from other rental activities. Subtract line 3b from line 3a	**3c**	
	4 Portfolio income (loss):		
	a Interest income	**4a**	
	b Dividend income	**4b**	
	c Royalty income	**4c**	
	d Net short-term capital gain (loss) *(attach Schedule D (Form 1120S))*	**4d**	
	e Net long-term capital gain (loss) *(attach Schedule D (Form 1120S))*.	**4e**	
	f Other portfolio income (loss) *(attach schedule)*	**4f**	
	5 Net gain (loss) under section 1231 (other than due to casualty or theft) *(attach Form 4797)*	**5**	
	6 Other income (loss) *(attach schedule)*	**6**	
Deductions	**7** Charitable contributions *(attach schedule)*	**7**	
	8 Section 179 expense deduction *(attach Form 4562)*.	**8**	
	9 Deductions related to portfolio income (loss) (itemize)	**9**	
	10 Other deductions *(attach schedule)*	**10**	
Investment Interest	**11a** Interest expense on investment debts	**11a**	
	b (1) Investment income included on lines 4a, 4b, 4c, and 4f above	**11b(1)**	
	(2) Investment expenses included on line 9 above	**11b(2)**	
Credits	**12a** Credit for alcohol used as a fuel *(attach Form 6478)*	**12a**	
	b Low-income housing credit:		
	(1) From partnerships to which section 42(j)(5) applies for property placed in service before 1990	**12b(1)**	
	(2) Other than on line 12b(1) for property placed in service before 1990.	**12b(2)**	
	(3) From partnerships to which section 42(j)(5) applies for property placed in service after 1989	**12b(3)**	
	(4) Other than on line 12b(3) for property placed in service after 1989	**12b(4)**	
	c Qualified rehabilitation expenditures related to rental real estate activities *(attach Form 3468)*	**12c**	
	d Credits (other than credits shown on lines 12b and 12c) related to rental real estate activities	**12d**	
	e Credits related to other rental activities.	**12e**	
	13 Other credits	**13**	
Adjustments and Tax Preference Items	**14a** Depreciation adjustment on property placed in service after 1986	**14a**	
	b Adjusted gain or loss	**14b**	
	c Depletion (other than oil and gas)	**14c**	
	d (1) Gross income from oil, gas, or geothermal properties	**14d(1)**	
	(2) Deductions allocable to oil, gas, or geothermal properties	**14d(2)**	
	e Other adjustments and tax preference items *(attach schedule)*	**14e**	
Foreign Taxes	**15a** Type of income ▶		
	b Name of foreign country or U.S. possession ▶		
	c Total gross income from sources outside the United States *(attach schedule)*	**15c**	
	d Total applicable deductions and losses *(attach schedule)*	**15d**	
	e Total foreign taxes (check one): ▶ ☐ Paid ☐ Accrued	**15e**	
	f Reduction in taxes available for credit *(attach schedule)*	**15f**	
	g Other foreign tax information *(attach schedule)*	**15g**	
Other	**16** Section 59(e)(2) expenditures: **a** Type ▶		
	b Amount	**16b**	
	17 Tax-exempt interest income	**17**	
	18 Other tax-exempt income	**18**	
	19 Nondeductible expenses	**19**	
	20 Total property distributions (including cash) other than dividends reported on line 22 below	**20**	
	21 Other items and amounts required to be reported separately to shareholders *(attach schedule)*		
	22 Total dividend distributions paid from accumulated earnings and profits	**22**	
	23 **Income (loss).** (Required only if Schedule M-1 must be completed.) Combine lines 1 through 6 in column (b). From the result, subtract the sum of lines 7 through 11a, 15e, and 16b.	**23**	

EXHIBIT 6.3   *Continued*

Form 1120S (1995)   Page **4**

Schedule L	Balance Sheets	Beginning of tax year		End of tax year	
	Assets	(a)	(b)	(c)	(d)
1	Cash				
2a	Trade notes and accounts receivable . .				
b	Less allowance for bad debts				
3	Inventories				
4	U.S. Government obligations				
5	Tax-exempt securities				
6	Other current assets *(attach schedule)* . .				
7	Loans to shareholders				
8	Mortgage and real estate loans . . .				
9	Other investments *(attach schedule)* . .				
10a	Buildings and other depreciable assets .				
b	Less accumulated depreciation				
11a	Depletable assets				
b	Less accumulated depletion				
12	Land (net of any amortization) . . .				
13a	Intangible assets (amortizable only) . . .				
b	Less accumulated amortization				
14	Other assets *(attach schedule)*				
15	Total assets				
	Liabilities and Shareholders' Equity				
16	Accounts payable				
17	Mortgages, notes, bonds payable in less 1 year				
18	Other current liabilities *(attach schedule)*				
19	Loans from shareholders				
20	Mortgages, notes, bonds payable in 1 year or more				
21	Other liabilities *(attach schedule)* . . .				
22	Capital stock				
23	Paid-in or capital surplus				
24	Retained earnings				
25	Less cost of treasury stock	(	)	(	)
26	Total liabilities and shareholders' equity . .				

Schedule M-1 — **Reconciliation of Income (Loss) per Books With Income (Loss) per Return** (You are not required to complete this schedule if the total assets on line 15, column (d), of Schedule L are less than $25,000.)

1	Net income (loss) per books	5	Income recorded on books this year not included on Schedule K, lines 1 through 6 (itemize):	
2	Income included on Schedule K, lines 1 through 6, not recorded on books this year (itemize):	a	Tax-exempt interest $	
	....			
3	Expenses recorded on books this year not included on Schedule K, lines 1 through 11a, 15e, and 16b (itemize):	6	Deductions included on Schedule K, lines 1 through 11a, 15e, and 16b, not charged against book income this year (itemize):	
a	Depreciation $	a	Depreciation $	
b	Travel and entertainment $		....	
	....		....	
	....	7	Add lines 5 and 6	
4	Add lines 1 through 3	8	Income (loss) (Schedule K, line 23). Line 4 less line 7	

Schedule M-2 — **Analysis of Accumulated Adjustments Account, Other Adjustments Account, and Shareholders' Undistributed Taxable Income Previously Taxed** (see page 22 of the instructions)

		(a) Accumulated adjustments account	(b) Other adjustments account	(c) Shareholders' undistributed taxable income previously taxed
1	Balance at beginning of tax year . . .			
2	Ordinary income from page 1, line 21 . .			
3	Other additions			
4	Loss from page 1, line 21	( )		
5	Other reductions	( )	( )	
6	Combine lines 1 through 5			
7	Distributions other than dividend distributions .			
8	Balance at end of tax year. Subtract line 7 from line 6			

*U.S. Government Printing Office: 1995 - 389-315

EXHIBIT 6.4

Form **4626**	**Alternative Minimum Tax—Corporations** (including environmental tax) ▶ See separate instructions. ▶ Attach to the corporation's tax return.	OMB No. 1545-0175 **1995**
Department of the Treasury Internal Revenue Service		

Name		Employer identification number

1	Taxable income or (loss) before net operating loss deduction. **(Important:** If the corporation is subject to the environmental tax, see the instructions for line 16 on page 6.**)**	**1**	
2	**Adjustments and preferences:**		
a	Depreciation of post-1986 property	**2a**	
b	Amortization of certified pollution control facilities	**2b**	
c	Amortization of mining exploration and development costs	**2c**	
d	Amortization of circulation expenditures (personal holding companies only) . .	**2d**	
e	Adjusted gain or loss	**2e**	
f	Long-term contracts	**2f**	
g	Installment sales	**2g**	
h	Merchant marine capital construction funds	**2h**	
i	Section 833(b) deduction (Blue Cross, Blue Shield, and similar type organizations only)	**2i**	
j	Tax shelter farm activities (personal service corporations only)	**2j**	
k	Passive activities (closely held corporations and personal service corporations only)	**2k**	
l	Loss limitations	**2l**	
m	Depletion	**2m**	
n	Tax-exempt interest from specified private activity bonds	**2n**	
o	Charitable contributions	**2o**	
p	Intangible drilling costs	**2p**	
q	Reserves for losses on bad debts of financial institutions	**2q**	
r	Accelerated depreciation of real property (pre-1987)	**2r**	
s	Accelerated depreciation of leased personal property (pre-1987) (personal holding companies only)	**2s**	
t	Other adjustments	**2t**	
u	Combine lines 2a through 2t	**2u**	
3	Preadjustment alternative minimum taxable income (AMTI). Combine lines 1 and 2u	**3**	
4	**Adjusted current earnings (ACE) adjustment:**		
a	Enter the corporation's ACE from line 10 of the worksheet on page 8 of the instructions	**4a**	
b	Subtract line 3 from line 4a. If line 3 exceeds line 4a, enter the difference as a negative amount (see page 4 of the instructions for examples)	**4b**	
c	Multiply line 4b by 75% (.75). Enter the result as a positive amount	**4c**	
d	Enter the excess, if any, of the corporation's total increases in AMTI from prior year ACE adjustments over its total reductions in AMTI from prior year ACE adjustments (see page 5 of the instructions). **Note:** *You **must** enter an amount on line 4d (even if line 4b is positive).*	**4d**	
e	ACE adjustment: • If you entered a positive number or zero on line 4b, enter the amount from line 4c here as a positive amount. • If you entered a negative number on line 4b, enter the smaller of line 4c or line 4d here as a negative amount.	**4e**	
5	Combine lines 3 and 4e. If zero or less, stop here; the corporation does not owe alternative minimum tax	**5**	
6	Alternative tax net operating loss deduction (see page 5 of the instructions)	**6**	
7	**Alternative minimum taxable income.** Subtract line 6 from line 5	**7**	

For Paperwork Reduction Act Notice, see separate instructions.   Cat. No. 12955I   Form **4626** (1995)

EXHIBIT 6.4 *Continued*

Form 4626 (1995)   Page **2**

8   Enter the amount from line 7 (alternative minimum taxable income) . . . . | **8** |

9   **Exemption phase-out computation** (if line 8 is $310,000 or more, skip lines 9a and 9b and enter -0- on line 9c):

a Subtract $150,000 from line 8 (if you are completing this line for a member of a controlled group, see page 5 of the instructions). If zero or less, enter -0- . . . | **9a** |

b Multiply line 9a by 25% (.25). . . . . | **9b** |

c Exemption. Subtract line 9b from $40,000 (if you are completing this line for a member of a controlled group, see page 5 of the instructions). If zero or less, enter -0- . . . . | **9c** |

10 Subtract line 9c from line 8. If zero or less, enter -0- . . . . | **10** |

11 Multiply line 10 by 20% (.20). . . . . | **11** |

12 Alternative minimum tax foreign tax credit. See page 5 of the instructions for limitations. . . . . | **12** |

13 Tentative minimum tax. Subtract line 12 from line 11. . . . . | **13** |

14 Regular tax liability before all credits except the foreign tax credit and possessions tax credit . . . | **14** |

15 **Alternative minimum tax.** Subtract line 14 from line 13. Enter the result on the appropriate line of the corporation's income tax return (e.g., Form 1120, Schedule J, line 9a). If zero or less, enter -0- . | **15** |

16 **Environmental tax.** Subtract $2 million from line 5 (figured without the corporation's environmental tax deduction). Multiply the excess, if any, by 0.12% (.0012). Enter the result here and on the appropriate line of the corporation's income tax return (e.g., Form 1120, Schedule J, line 9b). If you are completing this line for a member of a controlled group, see page 6 of the instructions. . . . . | **16** |

✿ *Printed on recycled paper*   *U.S.GPO:1995-389-375

EXHIBIT 6.5

Form **1120-A**	**U.S. Corporation Short-Form Income Tax Return**	OMB No. 1545-0890

Department of the Treasury
Internal Revenue Service

See separate instructions to make sure the corporation qualifies to file Form 1120-A.
For calendar year 1995 or tax year beginning .... , 1995, ending .... , 19 .....

1995

A Check this box if the corp. is a personal service corp. (as defined in Temporary Regs. section 1.441-4T—see instructions) ▶ ☐	Use IRS label. Other-wise, print or type.	Name	**B** Employer identification number
		Number, street, and room or suite no. (If a P.O. box, see page 6 of instructions.)	**C** Date incorporated
		City or town, state, and ZIP code	**D** Total assets (see page 6 of instructions) $

E Check applicable boxes: **(1)** ☐ Initial return **(2)** ☐ Change of address

F Check method of accounting: **(1)** ☐ Cash **(2)** ☐ Accrual **(3)** ☐ Other (specify) . . ▶

Income

1a Gross receipts or sales	**b** Less returns and allowances	**c** Balance ▶	**1c**
2 Cost of goods sold (see page 12 of instructions).			**2**
3 Gross profit. Subtract line 2 from line 1c			**3**
4 Domestic corporation dividends subject to the 70% deduction			**4**
5 Interest			**5**
6 Gross rents			**6**
7 Gross royalties			**7**
8 Capital gain net income (attach Schedule D (Form 1120))			**8**
9 Net gain or (loss) from Form 4797, Part II, line 20 (attach Form 4797)			**9**
10 Other income (see page 7 of instructions).			**10**
11 **Total income.** Add lines 3 through 10 . . . . ▶			**11**

Deductions (See instructions for limitations on deductions.)

12 Compensation of officers (see page 8 of instructions)			**12**
13 Salaries and wages (less employment credits)			**13**
14 Repairs and maintenance			**14**
15 Bad debts			**15**
16 Rents			**16**
17 Taxes and licenses			**17**
18 Interest			**18**
19 Charitable contributions (see page 9 of instructions for 10% limitation)			**19**
20 Depreciation (attach Form 4562)	**20**		
21 Less depreciation claimed elsewhere on return	**21a**		**21b**
22 Other deductions (attach schedule)			**22**
23 **Total deductions.** Add lines 12 through 22 . . . . ▶			**23**
24 Taxable income before net operating loss deduction and special deductions. Subtract line 23 from line 11			**24**
25 **Less: a** Net operating loss deduction (see page 11 of instructions) .	**25a**		
b Special deductions (see page 11 of instructions)	**25b**		**25c**

Tax and Payments

26 **Taxable income.** Subtract line 25c from line 24					**26**
27 **Total tax** (from page 2, Part I, line 7)					**27**
28 **Payments:**					
a 1994 overpayment credited to 1995	**28a**				
b 1995 estimated tax payments .	**28b**				
c Less 1995 refund applied for on Form 4466	**28c**	(	) Bal ▶	**28d**	
e Tax deposited with Form 7004			**28e**	
f Credit from regulated investment companies (attach Form 2439) .			**28f**	
g Credit for Federal tax on fuels (attach Form 4136). See instructions			**28g**	
h **Total payments.** Add lines 28d through 28g . . . . ▶					**28h**
29 Estimated tax penalty (see page 12 of instructions). Check if Form 2220 is attached . . . ▶ ☐					**29**
30 **Tax due.** If line 28h is smaller than the total of lines 27 and 29, enter amount owed . . .					**30**
31 **Overpayment.** If line 28h is larger than the total of lines 27 and 29, enter amount overpaid . . .					**31**
32 Enter amount of line 31 you want: **Credited to 1996 estimated tax** ▶			Refunded ▶		**32**

Sign Here

Under penalties of perjury, I declare that I have examined this return, including accompanying schedules and statements, and to the best of my knowledge and belief, it is true, correct, and complete. Declaration of preparer (other than taxpayer) is based on all information of which preparer has any knowledge.

▶ _____ _____ ▶ _____
Signature of officer   Date   Title

Paid Preparer's Use Only

Preparer's signature ▶		Date	Check if self-employed ▶ ☐	Preparer's social security number
Firm's name (or yours if self-employed) and address	▶		EIN ▶	
			ZIP code ▶	

For Paperwork Reduction Act Notice, see page 1 of the instructions.   Cat. No. 11456E   Form **1120-A** (1995)

EXHIBIT 6.5 *Continued*

Form 1120-A (1995)   Page **2**

Part I   Tax Computation (See page 14 of instructions.)

1   Income tax. If the corporation is a qualified personal service corporation (see page 15), check here ▶ ☐   **1**

2a   General business credit. Check if from: ☐ Form 3800 ☐ Form 3468 ☐ Form 5884
     ☐ Form 6478 ☐ Form 6765 ☐ Form 8586 ☐ Form 8830 ☐ Form 8826 ☐ Form 8835
     ☐ Form 8844 ☐ Form 8845 ☐ Form 8846 ☐ Form 8847 . . . .   **2a**

b   Credit for prior year minimum tax (attach Form 8827) **2b**

3   **Total credits.** Add lines 2a and 2b **3**

4   Subtract line 3 from line 1 . . . .   **4**

5   Recapture taxes. Check if from: ☐ Form 4255 ☐ Form 8611 . . . . .   **5**

6   Alternative minimum tax (attach Form 4626) **6**

7   **Total tax.** Add lines 4 through 6. Enter here and on line 27, page 1 . . . . .   **7**

Part II   Other Information (See page 17 of instructions.)

1   See page 19 of the instructions and state the principal:
   a   Business activity code no. ▶ ....
   b   Business activity ▶ ....
   c   Product or service ▶ ....

2   Did any individual, partnership, estate, or trust at the end of the tax year own, directly or indirectly, 50% or more of the corporation's voting stock? (For rules of attribution, see section 267(c).) . . . . ☐ Yes ☐ No
If "Yes," attach a schedule showing name and identifying number.

3   Enter the amount of tax-exempt interest received or accrued during the tax year . . . . . ▶ |$

4   Enter amount of cash distributions and the book value of property (other than cash) distributions made in this tax year . . . . . ▶ |$

5a   If an amount is entered on line 2, page 1, see the worksheet on page 12 for amounts to enter below:
   (1)   Purchases . . . .
   (2)   Additional sec. 263A costs (attach schedule)
   (3)   Other costs (attach schedule) .

b   Do the rules of section 263A (for property produced or acquired for resale) apply to the corporation? . . . . . . ☐ Yes ☐ No

6   At any time during the 1995 calendar year, did the corporation have an interest in or a signature or other authority over a financial account in a foreign country (such as a bank account, securities account, or other financial account)? If "Yes," the corporation may have to file Form TD F 90-22.1 . . . . ☐ Yes ☐ No
If "Yes," enter the name of the foreign country ▶ ....

Part III   Balance Sheets

		(a) Beginning of tax year		(b) End of tax year	
Assets	1 Cash				
	2a Trade notes and accounts receivable				
	b Less allowance for bad debts	(	)	(	)
	3 Inventories				
	4 U.S. government obligations . .				
	5 Tax-exempt securities (see instructions)				
	6 Other current assets (attach schedule) .				
	7 Loans to stockholders				
	8 Mortgage and real estate loans . .				
	9a Depreciable, depletable, and intangible assets				
	b Less accumulated depreciation, depletion, and amortization	(	)	(	)
	10 Land (net of any amortization) . .				
	11 Other assets (attach schedule) . .				
	12 Total assets				
Liabilities and Stockholders' Equity	13 Accounts payable				
	14 Other current liabilities (attach schedule)				
	15 Loans from stockholders . . .				
	16 Mortgages, notes, bonds payable .				
	17 Other liabilities (attach schedule) . .				
	18 Capital stock (preferred and common stock) . .				
	19 Paid-in or capital surplus . . .				
	20 Retained earnings				
	21 Less cost of treasury stock . . .	(	)	(	)
	22 Total liabilities and stockholders' equity . .				

Part IV   Reconciliation of Income (Loss) per Books With Income per Return *(You are not required to complete Part IV if the total assets on line 12, column (b), Part III are less than $25,000.)*

1   Net income (loss) per books . . . . .

2   Federal income tax . . . .

3   Excess of capital losses over capital gains .

4   Income subject to tax not recorded on books this year (itemize) ....

5   Expenses recorded on books this year not deducted on this return (itemize)

6   Income recorded on books this year not included on this return (itemize)...............

7   Deductions on this return not charged against book income this year (itemize)...............

8   Income (line 24, page 1). Enter the sum of lines 1 through 5 less the sum of lines 6 and 7 . .

✪ *Printed on recycled paper*   *U.S. Government Printing Office: 1995 - 389-292

EXHIBIT 6.6

Form **1120**	**U.S. Corporation Income Tax Return**	OMB No. 1545-0123
Department of the Treasury Internal Revenue Service	For calendar year 1995 or tax year beginning .... , 1995, ending .... , 19 ... ▶ Instructions are separate. See page 1 for Paperwork Reduction Act Notice.	19**95**

A Check if a: 1 Consolidated return (attach Form 851) ☐ 2 Personal holding co. (attach Sch. PH) ☐ 3 Personal service corp. (as defined in Temporary Regs. sec. 1.441-4T— see instructions) ☐	**Use IRS label. Otherwise, print or type.**	Name	**B** Employer identification number
		Number, street, and room or suite no. (If a P.O. box, see page 6 of instructions.)	**C** Date incorporated
		City or town, state, and ZIP code	**D** Total assets (see page 6 of instructions) $

E Check applicable boxes: (1) ☐ Initial return (2) ☐ Final return (3) ☐ Change of address | $

Income	**1a**	Gross receipts or sales	**b** Less returns and allowances	**c** Bal ▶	**1c**
	2	Cost of goods sold (Schedule A, line 8)	**2**
	3	Gross profit. Subtract line 2 from line 1c	**3**
	4	Dividends (Schedule C, line 19)	**4**
	5	Interest	**5**
	6	Gross rents	**6**
	7	Gross royalties	**7**
	8	Capital gain net income (attach Schedule D (Form 1120))	**8**
	9	Net gain or (loss) from Form 4797, Part II, line 20 (attach Form 4797)	**9**
	10	Other income (see page 7 of instructions—attach schedule)	**10**
	11	**Total income.** Add lines 3 through 10 ▶	**11**
Deductions (See instructions for limitations on deductions.)	**12**	Compensation of officers (Schedule E, line 4)	**12**
	13	Salaries and wages (less employment credits)	**13**
	14	Repairs and maintenance	**14**
	15	Bad debts	**15**
	16	Rents	**16**
	17	Taxes and licenses	**17**
	18	Interest	**18**
	19	Charitable contributions (see page 9 of instructions for 10% limitation)	**19**
	20	Depreciation (attach Form 4562)	**20**	
	21	Less depreciation claimed on Schedule A and elsewhere on return	**21a**		**21b**
	22	Depletion	**22**
	23	Advertising	**23**
	24	Pension, profit-sharing, etc., plans	**24**
	25	Employee benefit programs	**25**
	26	Other deductions (attach schedule)	**26**
	27	**Total deductions.** Add lines 12 through 26 ▶	**27**
	28	Taxable income before net operating loss deduction and special deductions. Subtract line 27 from line 11	**28**
	29	**Less:** **a** Net operating loss deduction (see page 11 of instructions)	**29a**	
		b Special deductions (Schedule C, line 20)	**29b**		**29c**
Tax and Payments	**30**	**Taxable income.** Subtract line 29c from line 28	**30**
	31	**Total tax** (Schedule J, line 10)	**31**
	32	**Payments: a** 1994 overpayment credited to 1995	**32a**	
	b	1995 estimated tax payments	**32b**	
	c	Less 1995 refund applied for on Form 4466	**32c** ( )	**d** Bal ▶	**32d**
	e	Tax deposited with Form 7004	**32e**
	f	Credit from regulated investment companies (attach Form 2439)	**32f**
	g	Credit for Federal tax on fuels (attach Form 4136). See instructions	**32g**		**32h**
	33	Estimated tax penalty (see page 12 of instructions). Check if Form 2220 is attached ▶ ☐	**33**
	34	**Tax due.** If line 32h is smaller than the total of lines 31 and 33, enter amount owed	**34**
	35	**Overpayment.** If line 32h is larger than the total of lines 31 and 33, enter amount overpaid	**35**
	36	Enter amount of line 35 you want: **Credited to 1996 estimated tax** ▶	**Refunded** ▶	**36**

Sign Here	Under penalties of perjury, I declare that I have examined this return, including accompanying schedules and statements, and to the best of my knowledge and belief, it is true, correct, and complete. Declaration of preparer (other than taxpayer) is based on all information of which preparer has any knowledge.	
	▶ Signature of officer	Date	▶ Title

Paid Preparer's Use Only	Preparer's signature ▶	Date	Check if self-employed ☐	Preparer's social security number
	Firm's name (or yours if self-employed) and address ▶		EIN ▶	
			ZIP code ▶	

Cat. No. 11450Q

EXHIBIT 6.6   *Continued*

Form 1120 (1995)   Page **2**

Schedule A   **Cost of Goods Sold** (See page 12 of instructions.)

1	Inventory at beginning of year	1
2	Purchases	2
3	Cost of labor	3
4	Additional section 263A costs (attach schedule)	4
5	Other costs (attach schedule)	5
6	**Total.** Add lines 1 through 5	6
7	Inventory at end of year	7
8	**Cost of goods sold.** Subtract line 7 from line 6. Enter here and on page 1, line 2	8

9a Check all methods used for valuing closing inventory:
   (i) ☐ Cost as described in Regulations section 1.471-3
   (ii) ☐ Lower of cost or market as described in Regulations section 1.471-4
   (iii) ☐ Other (Specify method used and attach explanation.) ▶ ....
 b Check if there was a writedown of subnormal goods as described in Regulations section 1.471-2(c) . . . . ▶ ☐
 c Check if the LIFO inventory method was adopted this tax year for any goods (if checked, attach Form 970) . . . . ▶ ☐
 d If the LIFO inventory method was used for this tax year, enter percentage (or amounts) of closing
    inventory computed under LIFO . . . . | 9d |
 e Do the rules of section 263A (for property produced or acquired for resale) apply to the corporation? . . . . . ☐ Yes ☐ No
 f Was there any change in determining quantities, cost, or valuations between opening and closing inventory? If "Yes,"
    attach explanation . . . . ☐ Yes ☐ No

Schedule C   **Dividends and Special Deductions** (See page 13 of instructions.)

		(a) Dividends received	(b) %	(c) Special deductions (a) × (b)
1	Dividends from less-than-20%-owned domestic corporations that are subject to the 70% deduction (other than debt-financed stock)		70	
2	Dividends from 20%-or-more-owned domestic corporations that are subject to the 80% deduction (other than debt-financed stock)		80	
3	Dividends on debt-financed stock of domestic and foreign corporations (section 246A)		see instructions	
4	Dividends on certain preferred stock of less-than-20%-owned public utilities . . .		42	
5	Dividends on certain preferred stock of 20%-or-more-owned public utilities . . .		48	
6	Dividends from less-than-20%-owned foreign corporations and certain FSCs that are subject to the 70% deduction		70	
7	Dividends from 20%-or-more-owned foreign corporations and certain FSCs that are subject to the 80% deduction		80	
8	Dividends from wholly owned foreign subsidiaries subject to the 100% deduction (section 245(b))		100	
9	**Total.** Add lines 1 through 8. See page 13 of instructions for limitation			
10	Dividends from domestic corporations received by a small business investment company operating under the Small Business Investment Act of 1958		100	
11	Dividends from certain FSCs that are subject to the 100% deduction (section 245(c)(1))		100	
12	Dividends from affiliated group members subject to the 100% deduction (section 243(a)(3))		100	
13	Other dividends from foreign corporations not included on lines 3, 6, 7, 8, or 11 . .			
14	Income from controlled foreign corporations under subpart F (attach Form(s) 5471) .			
15	Foreign dividend gross-up (section 78)			
16	IC-DISC and former DISC dividends not included on lines 1, 2, or 3 (section 246(d)) .			
17	Other dividends			
18	Deduction for dividends paid on certain preferred stock of public utilities			
19	**Total dividends.** Add lines 1 through 17. Enter here and on line 4, page 1 . . ▶			
20	**Total special deductions.** Add lines 9, 10, 11, 12, and 18. Enter here and on line 29b, page 1 . . . . . ▶			

Schedule E   **Compensation of Officers** (See instructions for line 12, page 1.)
Complete Schedule E only if total receipts (line 1a plus lines 4 through 10 on page 1, Form 1120) are $500,000 or more.

		(b) Social security number	(c) Percent of time devoted to business	Percent of corporation stock owned		(f) Amount of compensation
	(a) Name of officer			**(d) Common**	**(e) Preferred**	
1			%	%	%	
			%	%	%	
			%	%	%	
			%	%	%	
			%	%	%	
2	Total compensation of officers					
3	Compensation of officers claimed on Schedule A and elsewhere on return					
4	Subtract line 3 from line 2. Enter the result here and on line 12, page 1					

EXHIBIT 6.6   *Continued*

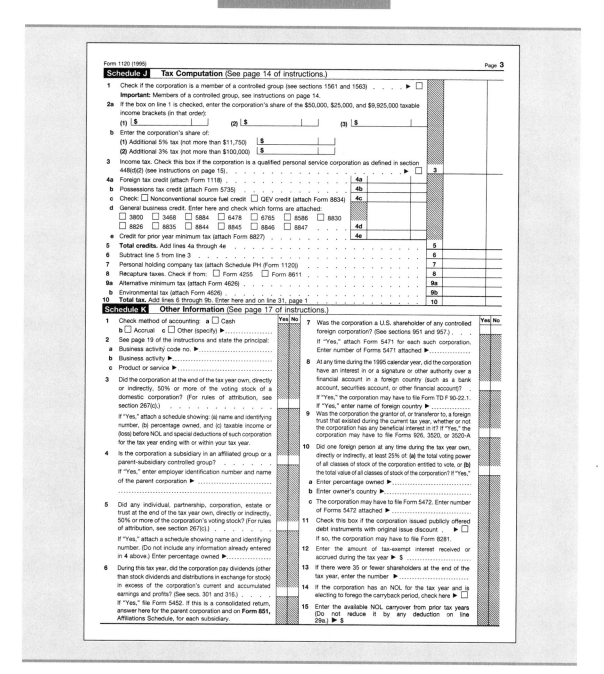

Form 1120 (1995)   Page **3**

Schedule J   Tax Computation (See page 14 of instructions.)

1   Check if the corporation is a member of a controlled group (see sections 1561 and 1563) . . . . ▶ ☐
     Important: Members of a controlled group, see instructions on page 14.

2a   If the box on line 1 is checked, enter the corporation's share of the $50,000, $25,000, and $9,925,000 taxable
     income brackets (in that order):
     (1) ☐ $ _____   (2) ☐ $ _____   (3) ☐ $ _____

 b   Enter the corporation's share of:
     (1) Additional 5% tax (not more than $11,750) ☐ $ _____
     (2) Additional 3% tax (not more than $100,000) ☐ $ _____

3   Income tax. Check this box if the corporation is a qualified personal service corporation as defined in section
     448(d)(2) (see instructions on page 15) . . . . ▶ ☐ | **3** |

4a   Foreign tax credit (attach Form 1118) . . . . | **4a** |
 b   Possessions tax credit (attach Form 5735) . . . . | **4b** |
 c   Check: ☐ Nonconventional source fuel credit ☐ QEV credit (attach Form 8834) | **4c** |
 d   General business credit. Enter here and check which forms are attached:
     ☐ 3800   ☐ 3468   ☐ 5884   ☐ 6478   ☐ 6765   ☐ 8586   ☐ 8830
     ☐ 8826   ☐ 8835   ☐ 8844   ☐ 8845   ☐ 8846   ☐ 8847 . . . . | **4d** |
 e   Credit for prior year minimum tax (attach Form 8827) . . . . | **4e** |

5   **Total credits.** Add lines 4a through 4e . . . . | **5** |
6   Subtract line 5 from line 3 . . . . | **6** |
7   Personal holding company tax (attach Schedule PH (Form 1120)) . . . . | **7** |
8   Recapture taxes. Check if from: ☐ Form 4255 ☐ Form 8611 . . . . | **8** |
9a   Alternative minimum tax (attach Form 4626) . . . . | **9a** |
 b   Environmental tax (attach Form 4626) . . . . | **9b** |
10   **Total tax.** Add lines 6 through 9b. Enter here and on line 31, page 1 . . . . | **10** |

Schedule K   Other Information (See page 17 of instructions.)

		Yes	No
1   Check method of accounting: **a** ☐ Cash
     b ☐ Accrual **c** ☐ Other (specify) ▶ ....
2   See page 19 of the instructions and state the principal:
 a   Business activity code no. ▶ ....
 b   Business activity ▶ ....
 c   Product or service ▶ ....
3   Did the corporation at the end of the tax year own, directly
     or indirectly, 50% or more of the voting stock of a
     domestic corporation? (For rules of attribution, see
     section 267(c).)
     If "Yes," attach a schedule showing: (a) name and identifying
     number, (b) percentage owned, and (c) taxable income or
     (loss) before NOL and special deductions of such corporation
     for the tax year ending with or within your tax year.
4   Is the corporation a subsidiary in an affiliated group or a
     parent-subsidiary controlled group? . . . . .
     If "Yes," enter employer identification number and name
     of the parent corporation ▶ ....
     ....
5   Did any individual, partnership, corporation, estate or
     trust at the end of the tax year own, directly or indirectly,
     50% or more of the corporation's voting stock? (For rules
     of attribution, see section 267(c).)
     If "Yes," attach a schedule showing name and identifying
     number. (Do not include any information already entered
     in 4 above.) Enter percentage owned ▶ ....
6   During this tax year, did the corporation pay dividends (other
     than stock dividends and distributions in exchange for stock)
     in excess of the corporation's current and accumulated
     earnings and profits? (See secs. 301 and 316.) . . . .
     If "Yes," file Form 5452. If this is a consolidated return,
     answer here for the parent corporation and on **Form 851,**
     Affiliations Schedule, for each subsidiary.

		Yes	No
7   Was the corporation a U.S. shareholder of any controlled
     foreign corporation? (See sections 951 and 957.) . . .
     If "Yes," attach Form 5471 for each such corporation.
     Enter number of Forms 5471 attached ▶ ....
8   At any time during the 1995 calendar year, did the corporation
     have an interest in or a signature or other authority over a
     financial account in a foreign country (such as a bank
     account, securities account, or other financial account)?
     If "Yes," the corporation may have to file Form TD F 90-22.1.
     If "Yes," enter name of foreign country ▶ ....
9   Was the corporation the grantor of, or transferor to, a foreign
     trust that existed during the current tax year, whether or not
     the corporation has any beneficial interest in it? If "Yes," the
     corporation may have to file Forms 926, 3520, or 3520-A
10   Did one foreign person at any time during the tax year,
     directly or indirectly, at least 25% of: **(a)** the total voting power
     of all classes of stock of the corporation entitled to vote, or **(b)**
     the total value of all classes of stock of the corporation? If "Yes,"
 a   Enter percentage owned ▶ ....
 b   Enter owner's country ▶ ....
 c   The corporation may have to file Form 5472. Enter number
     of Forms 5472 attached ▶ ....
11   Check this box if the corporation issued publicly offered
     debt instruments with original issue discount . ▶ ☐
     If so, the corporation may have to file Form 8281.
12   Enter the amount of tax-exempt interest received or
     accrued during the tax year ▶ $ ....
13   If there were 35 or fewer shareholders at the end of the
     tax year, enter the number ▶ ....
14   If the corporation has an NOL for the tax year and is
     electing to forego the carryback period, check here ▶ ☐
15   Enter the available NOL carryover from prior tax years
     (Do not reduce it by any deduction on line
     29a.) ▶ $ ....

EXHIBIT 6.6 *Continued*

Form 1120 (1995)   Page **4**

Schedule L	Balance Sheets	Beginning of tax year		End of tax year	
	Assets	(a)	(b)	(c)	(d)
1	Cash				
2a	Trade notes and accounts receivable . . .				
b	Less allowance for bad debts	( )		( )	
3	Inventories				
4	U.S. government obligations				
5	Tax-exempt securities (see instructions) . .				
6	Other current assets (attach schedule) . .				
7	Loans to stockholders				
8	Mortgage and real estate loans				
9	Other investments (attach schedule) . . .				
10a	Buildings and other depreciable assets . .				
b	Less accumulated depreciation	( )		( )	
11a	Depletable assets				
b	Less accumulated depletion	( )		( )	
12	Land (net of any amortization)				
13a	Intangible assets (amortizable only)				
b	Less accumulated amortization	( )		( )	
14	Other assets (attach schedule)				
15	Total assets				
	Liabilities and Stockholders' Equity				
16	Accounts payable				
17	Mortgages, notes, bonds payable in less than 1 year				
18	Other current liabilities (attach schedule) . .				
19	Loans from stockholders				
20	Mortgages, notes, bonds payable in 1 year or more				
21	Other liabilities (attach schedule)				
22	Capital stock: a Preferred stock . . .				
	b Common stock . . .				
23	Paid-in or capital surplus				
24	Retained earnings—Appropriated (attach schedule)				
25	Retained earnings—Unappropriated . . .				
26	Less cost of treasury stock		( )		( )
27	Total liabilities and stockholders' equity . .				

Note: *You are not required to complete Schedules M-1 and M-2 below if the total assets on line 15, column (d) of Schedule L are less than $25,000.*

Schedule M-1	Reconciliation of Income (Loss) per Books With Income per Return (See page 18 of instructions.)

1	Net income (loss) per books		7	Income recorded on books this year not included on this return (itemize):	
2	Federal income tax				
3	Excess of capital losses over capital gains .			Tax-exempt interest $	
4	Income subject to tax not recorded on books this year (itemize):			. . . .	
	. . . .		8	Deductions on this return not charged against book income this year (itemize):	
5	Expenses recorded on books this year not deducted on this return (itemize):		a	Depreciation . . . . $	
a	Depreciation . . . . $		b	Contributions carryover $	
b	Contributions carryover $			. . . .	
c	Travel and entertainment $			. . . .	
	. . . .		9	Add lines 7 and 8	
6	Add lines 1 through 5		10	Income (line 28, page 1)—line 6 less line 9	

Schedule M-2	Analysis of Unappropriated Retained Earnings per Books (Line 25, Schedule L)

1	Balance at beginning of year		5	Distributions: a Cash	
2	Net income (loss) per books			b Stock	
3	Other increases (itemize):			c Property	
	. . . .		6	Other decreases (itemize):	
	. . . .		7	Add lines 5 and 6	
4	Add lines 1, 2, and 3		8	Balance at end of year (line 4 less line 7)	

♲   *Printed on recycled paper*   *U.S.GPO:1995-389-287

EXHIBIT 6.7

Form **5452** (Rev. December 1994) Department of the Treasury Internal Revenue Service	**Corporate Report of Nondividend Distributions** ▶ For calendar year ending December 31, 19 .... ▶ Attach to the corporation's income tax return.	OMB No. 1545-0205

Name	Employer identification number

A Has the corporation filed a Form 5452 for a prior calendar year? . . . . ▶ ☐ Yes ☐ No

   If "Yes," state which year(s) _____

B Are any of the distributions part of a partial or complete liquidation? . . . . ▶ ☐ Yes ☐ No

   If "Yes," discuss in a separate statement.

C **Earnings and Profits**
- Accumulated earnings and profits (since February 28, 1913) at the beginning of the tax year . . . ▶ $ _____

- Actual earnings and profits for the current tax year . . . . ▶ $ _____

D **Shareholders at Date of Last Dividend Payment**
- Number of individuals . . . . . . _____
- Number of partnerships . . . . . . _____
- Number of corporations and other shareholders . . . . _____

Note: *If there are 12 or fewer shareholders, attach copies of the Forms 1099-DIV (or the information from that form) that the shareholders received.*

E **Corporate Distributions** (See instructions.)

Date Paid	Total Amount Paid (Common (C), Preferred (P), Other (O))	Amount Per Share	Amount Paid During Calendar Year From Earnings & Profits Since February 28, 1913			Percent Taxable	Amount Paid During Calendar Year From Other Than Earnings & Profits Since February 28, 1913	Percent Nontaxable
			From the Current Year	Accumulated	Total			
	$	$	$	$	$	%	$	%
Totals	$		$	$	$		$	

For Paperwork Reduction Act Notice, see the instructions on page 2.   Cat. No. 11881T   Form **5452** (Rev. 12-94)

EXHIBIT 6.7   *Continued*

Form 5452 (Rev. 12-94)   Page **4**

Worksheet for Figuring Current-Year Earnings and Profits

Date Incorporated: _____

Method of Accounting: _____

	Retained Earnings Shown in Books		Earnings and Profits Current Year		Accumulated Earnings and Profits Credit Balance	Key
	Debit	Credit	Debit	Credit		
Balance forward 12/31/____						
19 ____						
1 Taxable income from Form 1120, line 28 (or comparable line of other income tax return) . .						
2 Federal income taxes per books and tax return						
3 Excess of capital losses over capital gains (tax basis)						
4 Depreciation adjustment on earnings and profits (section 312(k))						
5 Depreciation adjustment on sale of property . . .						
6 Total itemized expenses from line 5, Schedule M-1						
a Travel and entertainment						
b Life insurance premium greater than cash surrender value (CSV)						
c Nondeductible interest paid for tax-exempt bonds						
d Contributions carryover						
e Other (list separately)						
7 Total itemized income from line 7, Schedule M-1						
a Life insurance proceeds greater than CSV . . .						
b Bad debt recovery (not charged against taxable income)						
c Tax-exempt interest on municipal bonds . . .						
d Other (list separately).						
8 Refund of prior year Federal income taxes . . .						
9 Reserve for contingencies						
10 Additional adjustments:						
....						
....						
11 Totals						
Current-Year Earnings and Profits						
Cash Distributions:						
From current-year earnings and profits . . . ___%						
From accumulated earnings and profits . . ___%						
Total distribution from earnings and profits . ___%						
From other distribution . . . . ___%						
Total distribution 100%						
Total cash distributions						
Totals						
Current-year change.						
Balance forward 12/31/____						

*U.S. Government Printing Office: 1994 — 387-095/00300

7 Formation of Corporations

Overview of Objectives

Upon completion of this chapter, the student will:

- understand the various tasks the paralegal may perform in the corporate formation process
- know how to draft articles of incorporation
- know the key provisions in corporate bylaws and how to draft them
- know how to qualify a corporation as a foreign corporation
- understand the maintenance procedures required of corporations

INTRODUCTION

Once a client decides to incorporate a business, several factors determine where that business should be incorporated. These factors should be considered carefully prior to starting the incorporation process. Historically, many corporations chose Delaware as the favored state of domicile due to that state's corporate-friendly statutes. Today, many states have relaxed restrictions, attempting to attract corporate business and all the economic advantages to be reaped from such businesses. Factors to consider in choosing a state of incorporation include, but are not limited to:

1. the flexibility (or lack thereof) inherent in state corporate statutes
2. the state blue sky laws
3. the state in which the corporation will primarily operate
4. the state of residence of those parties who will be managing the corporation
5. the tax treatment of corporations by the state
6. the state reporting requirements
7. the costs of incorporating in the state

Once a state of domicile has been chosen, the paralegal will work closely with the client in gathering relevant information and preparing the required documents. This chapter focuses on the information-gathering process and the drafting of articles of incorporation and bylaws. This chapter also guides you in helping a client apply to transact business in a foreign state. Finally, this chapter enumerates the various tasks you may undertake in assisting a client with corporate maintenance procedures.

HOW TO INCORPORATE

There are a variety of tasks involved in the corporate formation process. Some of these tasks are similar to those performed when creating other business entities while others are exclusive to corporations. To keep track of the requisite tasks, a checklist, such as the one below, is helpful:

Checklist

- Check name availability
- Reserve name: send reservation form and fee
- Research qualifications in other states (if applicable)
- Order corporate kit
- Prepare articles of incorporation
- Have articles signed by incorporator(s) and registered agent designation signed by registered agent
- Make photocopies of articles
- Send articles and photocopy to state filing official together with cover letter and filing fee
- Prepare bylaws

- Prepare Form 2553 if subchapter S status is desired
- Prepare shareholders' restrictive agreement, if desired
- Prepare employment agreements, if desired
- Arrange organizational meeting(s) of incorporators, board of directors, and shareholders

A. *Preincorporation Procedures*

Prior to preparing any corporate documents, the availability of the proposed corporate name must be checked. Statutory law mandates that the name of a corporation must contain the word "corporation," "incorporated," or in some states "company" or "limited," or an abbreviation of any of these. State statutes should be checked to verify which of these words or abbreviations applies in a particular state. In addition to the inclusion of one of these words or abbreviations, statutory law further requires that the name of a corporation must not be deceptively similar to or must be distinguishable upon the records from the names of all other entities on file with the state. Several name choices should be solicited from the client because the client's first choice might not be available. If the client will be operating in more than one state, the name should be checked for availability in the other designated states as well. Verification of name availability may be done over the telephone, but note that verification and reservation are not one and the same thing. Reservation forms must be completed and sent with the applicable filing fee to assure that the name is secured. Reservation of a corporate name will be held for a limited time period and therefore the articles of incorporation should be filed within this time frame.

If a client seeks to operate in other states as a foreign corporation, registration of the corporate name may not be possible until the corporation is legally created in the state of domicile because the foreign state may require a certificate of existence or good standing from the state of domicile before registration can be accomplished. Both the reservation and registration requirements of these states should be checked carefully.

A corporation wishing to operate under a name other than its legal name must file an assumed or fictitious name application. If the client's choice of name is available in the state of domicile but not in targeted foreign states, it is possible for the client to operate in those states under an assumed or fictitious name.

Once the corporate name is secured, the corporate kit can be ordered and corporate documents can be drafted. A **corporate kit** contains the corporate seal, stock certificates, and a corporate **minute book** in which minutes of corporate meetings and corporate documents are to be kept. Most corporate kits provide a stock ledger, preprinted minutes for organizational meetings (with space for insertion of client-specific information), preprinted bylaws, and may also include a Form 2553, a Form SS-4, and other commonly used forms. When ordering a corporate kit, certain information must be supplied such as the name of the corporation, the state of incorporation, the type of stock, number of authorized shares, and par value of the stock.

Attorneys may prefer to have their own paralegals prepare corporate documents or may choose to use a **corporate service company** or **attorney service bureau**. These companies, for a fixed fee, will prepare standard articles of incorporation, file them, and may serve as the registered agent of the client corporation. Their offices are often located near the secretary of state's office and thus their staff can speedily walk through the filing procedure and deliver a certified copy of the articles of incorporation and the certificate of incorporation in minimal time (typically within 24 to 48 hours). Some attorneys use such services only when time is of the essence to a client and prefer in other circumstances to have their own paralegals prepare and file the articles.

B.   Articles of Incorporation

Prior to drafting the **articles of incorporation** (referred to in some states as the **charter**), a paralegal should prepare a worksheet of items that must be included to satisfy statutory requirements. As with any other area of law, corporate formation worksheets should be reviewed on a regular basis and modified, when necessary, to reflect changes in the law. Often, a paralegal will be asked to prepare corporate bylaws and minutes of organizational meetings as well. One comprehensive worksheet could be used to gather client information for all these documents, or separate worksheets may be preferred.

In general, most states require only skeletal information to be included in the articles of incorporation, although they do permit the articles to be more inclusive. Because the articles of incorporation, upon filing, become a public document, it is advisable to keep their contents to the statutory minimum, unless there is good reason to do otherwise, and include more detailed information about the management of the corporation in the corporate bylaws. (Please note that state statutory requirements are often different for special types of corporations, such as professional corporations and nonprofit corporations, and those specific statutes must be referred to when drafting articles of incorporation for such corporations. The following discussion pertains to general, for-profit corporations.) Although the actual requirements vary from state to state, most state statutes require the following information to be included in the articles of incorporation:

1. The name of the corporation;
2. the period of duration of the corporation, which may be perpetual (note that because most corporations indicate perpetual duration, some states have omitted the requirement of a statement of duration in the articles);
3. the capital stock structure of the corporation, including the number of authorized shares of stock, the type(s) of stock and relative rights and limitations assigned thereto, and the par value, if any, assigned to shares;
4. the name(s) and address(es) of the incorporator(s) and signature(s);
5. the name of the registered agent, the street address of the registered office, and the agent's acceptance of the position (the acceptance is sometimes included in a separate document).

In addition to the above, some states require inclusion of such information as the corporation's principal office and the purpose for which the corporation is organized. In states in which a recitation of corporate purpose is required, a broad purpose statement will often suffice. Care should be taken in drafting a purpose statement to assure the possibility of corporate expansion into activities other than those initially envisioned. A statement such as the following typically is appropriate:

> The purpose of this Corporation is to engage in any activities or business permitted under the laws of the United States and the State of Any State.

The attorney will have discussed with the client the pros and cons of assigning a par value to the capital stock of the corporation. **Par value** is a nominal amount which represents the face value of the stock but rarely indicates the actual value paid for the shares. Many states do not require that stock be assigned a par value. Nonetheless, in some instances it is advisable to assign par value to the stock. In some states, organizational taxes are imposed that are based on the aggregate value of the authorized stock of the corporation. If stock is assigned a par value, the tax will be computed based on the par value of the stock. If no par value is assigned, the tax may be computed at a higher valuation, in some instances based on the price actually paid for the stock. State law on this matter should be researched prior to drafting the capital stock structure provision of the articles.

Some states presume **preemptive** and/or **cumulative voting** rights are granted unless otherwise stated in the articles of incorporation, while other states require an express granting of these rights in the articles of incorporation if these rights are to exist. **Preemptive rights**, discussed in detail in Chapter 10 pertaining to shareholders' rights and liabilities, give original shareholders first rights in purchasing newly issued corporate shares of stock on a pro rata basis. This provides a method by which the original shareholders may protect their proportionate interests and exercise ownership control of the business. The following is an example of a preemptive rights provision which may be included in the articles of incorporation:

> The holders of the common stock of this Corporation shall have preemptive rights to purchase, at prices, terms and conditions that shall be fixed by the Board of Directors, those shares of the common stock of this Corporation which may be issued from time to time for money, property, or services in addition to that stock authorized and issued by the Corporation. The preemptive right of any holder is determined by the ratio of the authorized and issued shares of common stock held by the holder and all shares of common stock currently authorized and issued.

Cumulative voting, discussed in detail in the next chapter, is a method of applying votes in the election of directors. This method attempts to protect minority shareholders by allowing a shareholder to cast all of his or her votes for one director, thus increasing the chances of minority shareholder representation on the board. The following is an example of a cumulative voting provision:

> Shareholders of this Corporation may vote their stocks cumulatively. Each shareholder shall have the total number of votes which is equal to the number of shares of stock with voting rights which such shareholder holds multiplied by the number of directors to be elected. The shareholder may give all of his or her votes to one candidate or distribute them among as many candidates as the shareholder may wish. Notice must be given by any shareholder to the President or Vice President of the Corporation not less than 24 hours prior to the time set for holding of a shareholders' meeting for the election of directors that such shareholder intends to cumulate his or her vote at said election.

Articles of incorporation sometimes list the names and addresses of the initial board of directors of the corporation. While this is optional, in many states the inclusion of the initial board of directors in the articles allows the corporation to bypass an organizational meeting of the incorporators and simply hold an organizational meeting of the board of directors.

Once prepared, the articles of incorporation must be signed by one or more incorporators. The incorporator may be, but typically need not be, a shareholder, director, or officer of the corporation. The client's attorney may act as incorporator or, if one of the services described above is used, one of their staff members may act as incorporator. The registered agent must sign a statement accepting the position of registered agent. Some states allow a statement of acceptance to be added on at the end of the articles, whereas other states require a separate document called a certificate of designation of registered agent. Statutory law requires that a registered agent be a resident of the state and some states may set minimum age requirements for registered agents. Often, the client's attorney will act as registered agent. Should a change of registered agent or registered office be made at some later date, the state filing official should be notified promptly by filing a change of status form.

After the required signatures are obtained (and notarized in states in which notarization is required), the articles of incorporation must be photocopied. A copy should be kept in the client file, a copy given to the client, and a copy should be sent with the original to the state filing official to be certified by the state and returned to the law office. Filing fees should be scrutinized. Often a filing fee for the articles will be listed separately from the fee for designation of registered agent. An additional fee usually is required for a certified copy. The articles of incorporation, together with a cover letter and the total fees, should be sent certified mail, return receipt requested, to the state filing official, typically the secretary of state. In addition to filing the articles of incorporation with the state filing authority, some states require filing the articles of incorporation with the county in which the principal office of the corporation is located. Others require publication in a newspaper of general circulation in the county in which the principal corporate office is located. Still others require additional statutorily specified documents to be filed together with the articles of incorporation. Because of these variations, state statutes should be consulted.

Upon receipt and review of the articles of incorporation, the secretary of state's office will issue a **certificate of incorporation** recognizing the corporation as a corporation duly authorized under state law. When received, this certificate should be put into the corporate minute book, together with the certified copy of the articles.

C. *Other Applicable Documents*

Next, bylaws should be prepared for adoption at the organizational meeting. The attorney may choose to use the preprinted bylaws provided in most corporate kits, but often lawyers prefer to use a standard set of bylaws prepared by the firm to closely follow state statutory law and then customize them to suit the client's specifications. Bylaws are discussed below in detail.

An attorney usually will discuss the possibility of subchapter S election with a client at consultation and determine whether the client's corporation will qualify (refer back to Chapter 6 for a list of requirements). If subchapter S election is desired, then the names, addresses, and social security numbers of the initial shareholders should be obtained, together with the number of shares issued to each. This information will be needed to prepare the 2553 form to be sent to the Internal Revenue Service. Adoption of subchapter S election may be made by resolution at the organizational meeting of the board of directors. At the same meeting, the matters of 248 election and 1244 stock election (both discussed in Chapter 6) may be brought up and adopted by resolution of the board. Because the paralegal is often the person preparing the minutes of the organizational meeting, it is advisable to determine from the client prior to such meeting if such options are being considered.

The client may require the drafting of special corporate contracts, such as shareholders' restrictive agreements (discussed in Chapter 10) or employment agreements (discussed in Chapter 11). Often these contracts must be drafted at an early stage, prior to the issuance of stock. The attorney may choose to draft these documents or may solicit the paralegal's assistance. If the client has not done so on his or her own, an employer identification number for the corporation should be obtained. Finally, any necessary applications to qualify the corporation as a foreign corporation should be obtained from the appropriate states, together with instructions for completing such forms and the fees required for their filing.

As can be seen from the above discussion, a wealth of information must be gathered from the client. If a corporate formation worksheet is not readily available in the law office, you can use one similar to the completed worksheet found in the Client Simulation at the end of the chapter.

BYLAWS

The **bylaws** of a corporation contain the rules for internal management of the corporation. They should be prepared prior to the first organizational meeting of the corporation (be it the organizational meeting of the incorporators or the organizational meeting of the board of directors) so they may be reviewed prior to adoption at such meeting. The incorporators or the board of directors adopt the initial bylaws of a corporation unless that power is reserved to the shareholders in the articles of incorporation. Most state statutes do not dictate the contents of the bylaws; rather, they tend to state that the bylaws of a corporation must be consistent with state statute and with the articles of incorporation. The bylaws remain an internal document not subject to public scrutiny and are typically easier to amend than the articles of incorporation. Often, the board of directors is given the power to amend the bylaws without a vote of the shareholders.

In some states, unless the articles of incorporation provide otherwise, the board of directors may adopt another set of bylaws to be effective only in an emergency. **Emergency bylaws** are subject to amendment or repeal by the shareholders. They include all necessary provisions for managing the corporation during an emergency, such as procedures for calling a meeting of the board of directors, quorum requirements, and designation of additional or substitute directors. All provisions of the regular bylaws, together with the emergency bylaws, remain effective during the period of emergency. Once the emergency ends, the emergency bylaws become ineffective.

A checklist of items typically included in bylaws (by no means exhaustive) reads as follows:

Bylaw Checklist

I. CORPORATE OFFICES
    A. Principal office
    B. Registered office
    C. Other offices
II. SHAREHOLDERS
    A. Annual meetings
    B. Special meetings
    C. Place of meetings
    D. Notice of meeting
    E. Waiver of notice
    F. Action without meeting
    G. Voting record
    H. Shareholder quorum and voting
    I. Inspectors of election (if desired)
    J. Proxies
III. BOARD OF DIRECTORS
    A. General powers
    B. Number and qualification of directors
    C. Election of directors

A.   Corporate Offices

The bylaws may include a statement regarding the **corporate offices**. Because the principal place of business may change over time, if such a statement is included it is advisable to keep it fairly general, stating that the principal office shall be within the state of domicile and permitting the corporation to open other offices both within and without the state, such as in the following provision:

> The principal office of the Corporation shall be in the State of Any State. The Corporation shall designate a registered office in accordance with state law and shall maintain it continuously. The Corporation may have offices at such other places within and without the State of Any State as the Board of Directors may from time to time determine.

B.   Shareholders' Meetings

The first major area to be covered in the bylaws concerns **shareholders' meetings**. The bylaws should address both annual and special meetings setting forth the procedures for calling the meetings (including requisite notice and permissible waiver of notice), the quorum requirements, whether a majority or supermajority vote is required for election of the board of directors, record voter lists, proxies, and other pertinent matters.

The section pertaining to **annual meetings of the shareholders** should state where such meetings shall take place or who will determine where they will take place. Many state statutes provide that the annual meeting must be held no later than 13 months after the last annual meeting. However, there may be instances when the failure to hold an annual meeting within this time frame is unavoidable. To protect the validity of any actions by either the board of directors or the officers that may be taken in the lapse between the statutorily prescribed time and the time the annual meeting actually takes place, it is advisable to include a statement in the bylaws indicating that failure to hold the meeting in a timely fashion shall not affect the validity of actions taken by the board of directors or the officers. A sample annual meeting provision reads as follows:

> The annual meeting of the shareholders of the Corporation, for the election of directors and for the transaction of other business, shall be held each year at the principal office of the Corporation or at such other place within or without the State of Any State as the board of directors shall determine. If the date chosen is a legal holiday in any year, the meeting shall be held at the same hour and place

on the next business day following. The annual meeting of the shareholders for any year shall be held no later than thirteen (13) months after the last annual meeting of shareholders. However, failure to hold an annual meeting in a timely fashion shall in no way affect the terms of Directors or Officers of the Corporation nor the validity of actions of the Corporation.

The provision pertaining to **special meetings of the shareholders** should indicate the persons who may call, as well as the procedure for calling, such meetings. Most state statutes allow special meetings of the shareholders to be called by the board of directors, one or more officers of the corporation, and by shareholders holding a certain percentage of voting shares. The notice for special meetings must include a statement of the purpose of the special meeting. For example:

Special meetings of the shareholders may be called by the Board of Directors, by the President, or by holders of not less than one-tenth of all shares entitled to vote at the meeting. Notice of a special meeting shall state the purpose or purposes for which the meeting is to be called. Special meetings shall be held at such time as the Board of Directors or the person(s) calling the meeting may determine and the meetings shall be held at the principal office of the Corporation or at such other place within or without the State of Any State as specified in the notice.

Most state statutes prescribe the time period within which notice for the annual shareholders' meeting must be sent and bylaws usually parallel the statutory notice requirements. The **notice provision** should indicate the prescribed period within which notice must be sent, the manner in which the notice must be delivered, and the items that must be included in the notice, such as the place, day, and hour of the meeting, as in the following sample provision:

Written notice of each meeting of shareholders shall be given, personally or by mail, not less than ten (10) and no more than sixty (60) days prior to the date of the meeting, to each shareholder entitled to vote at such meeting. If mailed, such notice shall be deposited in the United States mail with first-class postage prepaid, addressed to the shareholder at his or her address as it appears on the Corporation's stock transfer books. The notice shall state the place, day, and hour of the meeting and, in the case of a special meeting, the purpose or purposes for which the meeting is called. The business which may be conducted at a special meeting shall be confined to matters which are related to the purpose or purposes set forth in the notice.

It is common for state statutes to allow shareholders to waive their rights to formal notice of meetings. In small corporations, most or all of the shareholders are actively involved in running the business and have no need of such formalities. Nonetheless, statutory law often requires formal notice unless a waiver is signed. In a number of states, attendance at a meeting constitutes a waiver of notice of the meeting. The bylaws should include a **waiver of notice provision**, such as

> A written waiver of notice signed by a shareholder, whether before or after a meeting, shall be equivalent to the giving of such notice. Attendance of a shareholder at a meeting shall constitute a waiver of notice of such meeting, except when the shareholder attends for the express purpose of objecting, at the beginning of the meeting, to the transaction of any business because the meeting is not lawfully called or convened.

Again, in small corporations in which all of the shareholders are also the officers and directors, the shareholders may wish to legally adopt actions without the formality of meetings. Most states allow action by the shareholders without a meeting if a consent to action is signed by a prescribed number of shareholders. In some instances, unanimous consent may be required; in other instances, consent of the majority of shareholders or the number to pass the action had a duly convened meeting taken place may be required. If consent is not unanimous, statutory law typically requires that notice of the authorized action be given to those shareholders who did not give written consent, said notice including a statement of dissenter's rights, if any. For example:

> Any action of the shareholders may be taken without a meeting, without prior notice, and without a vote, if a consent in writing setting forth the action so taken is signed by holders of outstanding shares having not less than the minimum number of votes that would be necessary to authorize or take such action at a meeting at which all shares entitled to vote thereon were present and voted. If any class of shares is entitled to vote as a class, written consent shall be required of the holders of a majority of the shares of each class of shares entitled to vote as a class and of the total shares entitled to vote.
>
> Within ten (10) days after obtaining authorization by written consent, notice must be given to those shareholders who have not consented in writing. The notice shall fairly summarize the material features of the authorized action and, if the action is a merger, consolidation or sale or exchange of assets for which dissenters' rights are provided under law, the notice shall contain a clear statement of the right of dissenting shareholders to be paid the fair value of their shares upon compliance with the applicable statutory provisions.

C. *Shareholder Voting and Proxies*

Shareholders entitled to vote at the annual meeting of shareholders are called **record holders** and they are ascertained by looking at corporate records to determine which shareholders own voting shares on a specified date called the **record date** (discussed in greater detail in the next chapter). State statutes require that a corporation make a list of record holders within a certain number of days prior to the meeting and make that list available to the shareholders for inspection. The list must also be brought to the meeting. The bylaws usually include a provision pertaining to the **voting record** or **list of shareholders**:

> If the Corporation has ten (10) or more shareholders of record, the officers having charge of the stock transfer books for shares of the Corporation shall make, at least ten (10) days prior to each meeting of the shareholders, a complete list of shareholders entitled to vote at such meeting, with the address of each and the number, class and series, if any, of shares held by each. For a period of ten (10) days prior to such meeting, the list shall be subject to inspection by any shareholder at the principal place of business of the Corporation during regular business hours. The list shall also be subject to inspection by any shareholder at any time during the meeting.

The bylaws should include a provision indicating the number of shareholders necessary for a **quorum** as well as whether an affirmative vote of a majority or a supermajority of shareholders is required to authorize an action:

> At each meeting of shareholders for the transaction of any business, a quorum shall consist of a majority of holders of record entitled to vote at such meeting, whether in person or by proxy. If a quorum is present, unless otherwise provided by law or in the Articles of Incorporation, the affirmative vote of a majority of shares represented at the meeting shall be the act of the shareholders. After a quorum has been established at a shareholders' meeting, the subsequent withdrawal of shareholders so as to reduce the number required for a quorum shall not affect the validity of any action taken at the meeting or any adjournment thereof.

In larger corporations, **inspectors of election** are sometimes used to assure that an election of the board of directors runs smoothly. An inspector typically is chosen by the board of directors and his or her duties are to make sure all formalities are met, such as determining the number of outstanding shares of stock, which shareholders are entitled to vote, the existence of a quorum, the validity of proxies, and verification of vote tabulation. If a client foresees substantial growth in the number of shareholders of the corporation, it is advisable to include a provision allowing the board of directors to appoint inspectors of election, as in the following example:

> The Board of Directors may, in advance of any meeting of the shareholders, appoint one or more inspectors to act at the meeting. If inspectors are not so

appointed in advance of the meeting, the person presiding at such meeting may, and on the request of any shareholder entitled to vote shall, appoint one or more inspectors. In case any inspector appointed fails to appear or act, the vacancy may be filled by appointment made by the Board of Directors in advance of the meeting by the person presiding at such meeting. Each inspector, before entering upon the discharge of his or her duties, shall take and sign an oath to execute faithfully the duties of inspector at such meeting with strict impartiality to the best of his or her ability. No person who is a candidate for the office of director of the Corporation shall act as an inspector at any meeting of the shareholders at which directors are elected.

Completing the section on shareholders, the bylaws should include a provision pertaining to proxies. Every shareholder entitled to vote may either vote in person or by proxy. A **proxy** is a shareholder's written authorization of another person to act in his or her stead. Proxies are discussed in greater detail in the next chapter. A sample proxy provision reads as follows:

Every shareholder entitled to vote at a meeting of shareholders or to express consent or dissent without a meeting may authorize another person or persons to act for him or her by proxy. Any proxy shall be signed by such shareholder or his or her attorney-in-fact and shall be delivered to the Secretary of the meeting. No proxy shall be valid after the expiration of eleven (11) months from the date thereof unless otherwise provided in the proxy. Every proxy shall be revocable at the pleasure of the shareholder executing it, except as otherwise provided by law.

D.   *Board of Directors*

The next major section of the bylaws addresses the **board of directors**. Some drafters choose to include a **general powers** provision at the beginning of this section, which states that subject to the limitations set forth by statute, the articles of incorporation, or the bylaws, all corporate powers are to be exercised by or under the authority of the board of directors. The inclusion of such a provision is merely a formality, for the provision reiterates the statutory rights given to the board of directors.

The bylaws may set forth any requisite **qualifications** for directors. For example, state law may not require that a director be a resident of the corporation's state of domicile nor that a director be a shareholder of the corporation; however, the shareholders may desire such qualifications. If so, then these qualifications should be set forth in this section. The same provision may address the issue of the number of directors that may be elected and whether staggered elections are permissible. The purpose of staggered elections is to assure that some of the old cadre remain on the board each year. A sample provision follows:

> The Board of Directors of the Corporation shall consist of one or more directors. The number of directors may be increased or decreased from time to time by action of the shareholders or by vote of a majority of the entire Board of Directors. The directors need not be shareholders nor residents of Any State. All directors shall be at least twenty-one (21) years of age. Directors shall be elected by the shareholders at the annual meeting of shareholders and shall serve until the next succeeding annual meeting and until their successors have been elected and qualified.

As is the case with shareholders' meetings, provisions pertaining to directors' meetings should be detailed in the bylaws. There is no statutory requirement that directors hold annual directors' meetings, but if desired, the bylaws may so stipulate. The directors are expected to meet at regular intervals to discuss the internal affairs of the corporation. Most state statutes provide great leeway in choosing where and when such meetings take place, and most bylaw provisions relating to regular meetings are quite general, such as the following:

> Regular meetings of the Board of Directors may be held without notice at such time and at such place as shall be determined from time to time by the Board of Directors.

Special meetings of the directors usually may be called by any director and the president of the corporation, or other officers provided for in the special meetings provision. Here, as with shareholders, notice of meetings may be waived and a waiver of notice provision should be included, as well as an action without meeting provision, and a quorum provision.

In addition to meetings, the filling of vacancies on the board as well as the removal of directors from the board should be covered. Most statutes allow the board of directors to fill a board vacancy until the next annual meeting of the shareholders. However, the board may not remove one of their own. Directors may be removed with or without cause by a vote of the shareholders.

An important area to address is the issue of director compensation. Directors may be compensated for attending meetings and may be reimbursed for out-of-pocket, business-related expenses. In some instances, they may also be paid a salary for serving as directors. The amount of compensation is usually not stated in exact terms in the bylaws because the sum may change over the course of time and therefore the bylaws often state that the amount shall be determined by the board of directors. For example:

> Directors, including salaried officers who are directors, may receive compensation for their services as directors as well as traveling and other out-of-pocket expenses

incurred in attending any regular or special meeting of the board. The fee may be a fixed sum to be paid for attending each meeting of the board of directors or a fixed sum to be paid monthly, quarterly, or semi-annually, regardless of the number of meetings attended. The amount of compensation and the basis on which it shall be paid shall be determined by the board of directors. No payment shall preclude any director from serving the Corporation in any other capacity and receiving compensation therefor.

Before leaving the area of directors, the bylaws may want to address the right of indemnification to be provided to the directors. This provision verifies that the corporation will indemnify a director from and against liability, loss, or expense incurred by reason of any act or omission in the conduct of the business of the corporation, with the exception of those acts or omissions caused by the director's willful misconduct or gross negligence. The same provision may include indemnification of officers and shareholders as well. A sample indemnification provision follows:

Each director and officer of the Corporation shall be indemnified by the Corporation from and against any and all liability, loss, costs, expense (including legal fees) or damage incurred or sustained by reason of any act or omission in the conduct of the business of the Corporation. This indemnification shall cover governmental, civil or criminal actions or proceedings, or appeals therein, in accordance with and to the fullest extent permitted by law. Notwithstanding the above, no indemnification shall be provided for any liability, loss, cost, expense (including legal fees) or damage incurred in connection with an officer's or director's fraud, willful misconduct, or gross negligence.

E.   Officers

Many of the topics addressed in the bylaws section pertaining to directors will need to be addressed in the section pertaining to officers. This section should include provisions pertaining to the election of officers by the board of directors and the length of term for which the officers will serve, the filling of vacancies and the procedure for removal of officers, and compensation of officers. Additionally, this section should include the titles of offices to be held. This provision may simply list the titles or it may provide a detailed description of each office, such as the following description of the treasurer's office:

The Treasurer shall have the care and custody of all monies and securities of the Corporation. He or she shall cause to be entered in the books of the Corporation a full and accurate account of all monies received and paid on account of the Corporation. He or she shall make and sign such reports, statements, and instruments as may be required of him or her by the board of directors or by law, and shall perform such other duties as usually pertain to this office.

If a detailed description of each office is not included, then a provision outlining the general duties of officers should be provided. This provision may indicate whether or not such duties may be delegated.

> The officers of the Corporation shall have such powers and duties as usually pertain to their respective offices and such additional powers and duties specifically conferred by law, by the Articles of Incorporation, by the bylaws, or as may be assigned to them from time to time by the Board of Directors. In case of the absence of disability of any officer of the Corporation, or for any other reason deemed sufficient by the Board of Directors, the Board of Directors may delegate such officer's powers or duties to any other officer or to any other director.

F.   Committees

After providing the requisite information on corporate officers, the bylaws should include a section on executive and other committees. Statutory law permits the board of directors to create executive committees and any other committees the board deems helpful in the running of corporate affairs. The authority to create such committees should be included in the bylaws, as well as provisions covering committee meetings and compensation of committee members. A sample provision authorizing the creation of such committees follows:

> The Board of Directors, by resolution passed by a majority of the entire board, may designate an Executive Committee and one or more other committees. In the interim between meetings of the Board of Directors, the Executive Committee shall have all the authority of the Board of Directors except as otherwise provided by law. Each other committee so designated shall have such name as may be provided by resolution and may exercise such power as lawfully delegated by the Board of Directors.

G.   Stock Certificates, the Corporate Seal, and the Transfer of Shares

The bylaws also address the stock certificates to be issued by the corporation. This provision describes the certificates, including all the information to be stated on each certificate, and states which officers are authorized to sign the certificates:

> The shares of the Corporation shall be represented by certificates signed by the President or a Vice President and by the Secretary or an Assistant Secretary. The

signatures of the officers upon a certificate may be facsimiles if the certificate is manually signed on behalf of a transfer agent or a registrar other than the Corporation itself or its employees. Each stock certificate shall be numbered and shall be entered in the records of the Corporation as it is issued. Each certificate shall state the following: (a) the name of the Corporation; (b) that the Corporation is organized under the laws of the State of Any State; (c) the name of the person or persons to whom issued; (d) the number and class of shares and the designation of the series, if any, which such certificate represents; and (e) the par value of each share represented by such certificate or a statement that the shares are without par value.

Following the provision describing the corporation's stock certificates is typically a provision concerning the transfer of shares. This provision details the method of transferring and the recording of such transfers:

Shares of the Corporation shall be transferable on the books of the Corporation by the holder thereof, in person or by duly authorized attorney, upon the surrender of the certificates representing the shares to be transferred, properly endorsed. The Board of Directors may appoint one or more transfer agents or transfer clerks and one or more registrars as custodians of the transfer books and may require all transfers to be made with and all stock certificates to bear the signatures of any of them. For all corporate purposes including the voting of shares and the issuance and payment of dividends on shares, the Corporation shall have the absolute right to recognize as the owner of any shares of stock issued by it the person or persons in whose name the certificate representing such shares stands on its books.

The manner in which lost or destroyed stock certificates are to be replaced usually is provided for in the bylaws. This provision may simply leave the issuance of new certificates to the discretion of the directors or may require more formality, such as the submission of an affidavit and bond by the shareholder to indemnify the corporation against any claim that may be made against it concerning the lost or destroyed certificate(s). For example:

The Board of Directors shall cause a new stock certificate to be issued by the Corporation in the place of any certificate previously issued if the holder of record of the certificate: (a) makes proof in affidavit form that it has been lost, destroyed, or stolen; (b) requests the issuance of a new certificate before the Corporation has notice that the certificate has been acquired by a purchaser for value in good faith and without notice of any adverse claim; (c) gives bond in such form as the Corporation may direct to indemnify the Corporation against any claim that may be made against it on account of the alleged loss or destruction of any such certificate or the issuance of any such new certificate; and (d) satisfies any other reasonable requirements imposed by the Corporation.

Just as the corporation's stock certificates are described in the bylaws, so is the corporate seal. This provision states that the seal shall bear the name of the corporation and the year of incorporation.

H.   Records

The records section of the bylaws contains provisions pertaining to such matters as recordkeeping, inspection of records, and reporting requirements. Corporate records are usually kept at the principal office of the corporation, but may be kept at the registered office of the corporation. Shareholders as owners of the business have the right to inspect corporate records during normal business hours and may make copies of portions of the corporate records if done for a proper purpose. State statutes may allow inspection of the records to be limited to shareholders who have held stock for a certain period of time (e.g., six months) or who hold a certain percentage of the outstanding corporate stock (e.g., at least 5 percent), as set forth in the following provision:

> Any person who has been a holder of record of shares or of voting trust certificates for shares of the Corporation for at least six (6) months immediately preceding his or her demand, or is the holder of record of shares, or the holder of record of voting trust certificates, for at least five (5) percent of the outstanding shares of any class or series of the Corporation, shall have the right, for any proper purpose and at any reasonable time, on written demand stating the purpose thereof, to examine and make copies from the relevant books and records of accounts, minutes, and records of shareholders of the Corporation.

Corporations generally send annual reports to shareholders without requiring prior written demand by the shareholders. The bylaws may contain a provision stating when such reports are to be sent and what such reports are to contain.

I.   Financial Matters

The financial section of the bylaws may include provisions indicating the corporation's fiscal year, the bank in which corporate funds are to be deposited and the procedure for their withdrawal, loans to employees and officers of the corporation, and the declaration of dividends by the board of directors. This latter provision states when dividends may be declared and the manner of payment of such dividends. Cash dividends are commonly paid out of the corporation's earned surplus or capital surplus (for a discussion of these concepts, see Chapter 8) but dividends may also be paid out in property or shares of stock. A sample dividend provision reads as follows:

> The Board of Directors may from time to time declare, and the Corporation may pay, dividends on its outstanding shares of capital stock in the manner and upon the terms and conditions provided by the Articles of Incorporation and by law. Dividends may be paid in cash, in property, or in shares of stock, subject to the provisions of the Articles of Incorporation and applicable law.

J. Amendments

Finally, the bylaws include a provision addressing the amending of the bylaws. Unless state statute disallows it, amendment of the bylaws may be made by the board of directors rather than by a vote of the shareholders. This facilitates the amendment process. If there is some concern that allowing the amendment of the bylaws without consultation of the shareholders is giving too much discretion to the board, then providing for amendment by a shareholder vote may be preferable, or the provision may allow the shareholders to alter or repeal an amendment adopted by the board of directors, such as in the following provision:

> These bylaws may be altered, amended, or replaced and new bylaws may be adopted by the Board of Directors; provided that any bylaws or amendments thereto as adopted by the Board of Directors may be altered, amended, or repealed by vote of the shareholders, or a new bylaw in lieu thereof may be adopted by the shareholders.

CORPORATIONS IN A FOREIGN STATE

Should a client wish to expand corporate business outside of the boundaries of the state of domicile, it may be necessary to register the corporation as a foreign corporation in other states. Not all activities fall within the category of "transacting business," which requires registration as a foreign corporation. Problematically, most state statutes do not list activities which constitute transacting business; rather they list activities which do *not* constitute transacting business within the state. While this list will vary from state to state, the following activities (representational but by no means exhaustive) are often listed as those that do not constitute transacting business:

1. maintaining bank accounts
2. transacting business in interstate commerce
3. selling through independent contractors
4. maintaining, defending, or settling any proceeding
5. holding corporate meetings
6. maintaining officers or agents for the transfer, exchange, and registration of corporate securities
7. creating, securing, or collecting debts (including mortgages)
8. conducting an isolated transaction that is completed within a statutorily specified time period
9. owning or controlling a subsidiary corporation within the state
10. owning, without more, real or personal property in the state

From this listing one can see that it is not always easy to determine whether corporate activities are going to require foreign registration. This determination thus should ultimately be left to the attorney.

Should authority to transact business in a foreign state be required, an application for a certificate of authority should be obtained. As noted in earlier chapters, a certificate of authority is issued by the state filing authority and evinces the state's granting of permission to transact business in the state. Although the contents of these applications vary from state to state, many follow Section 15.03(a) of the Model Business Corporation Act, which provides:

(a) A foreign corporation may apply for a certificate of authority to transact business in this state by delivering an application to the secretary of state for filing. The application must set forth:

(1) the name of the foreign corporation or, if its name is unavailable for use in this state, a corporate name that satisfies the requirements of section 15.06;

(2) the name of the state or country under whose law it is incorporated;

(3) its date of incorporation and period of duration;

(4) the street address of its principal office;

(5) the address of its registered office in this state and the name of its registered agent at that office; and

(6) the names and usual business addresses of its current directors and officers.

As noted above, the client must maintain a registered agent and office in the foreign state. That agent must be an individual or entity that is a resident of that state. A corporate service agency is often used to act as registered agent if the corporation does not plan to open a permanent office in the state. Often foreign states will require that a certificate of existence from the corporation's state of domicile be submitted together with the application. This certificate may be obtained by sending a letter of request, together with the appropriate fee, to the state filing authority. Please note that these certificates may "go stale" (i.e., become invalid after a specified time period) so they should be requested shortly before the application is to be submitted. Some states may also require submission of a certified copy of the articles of incorporation.

Once the application, certificate, application fee, and any other requisite documents are obtained, the foreign state will issue a certificate of authority which grants the same rights and responsibilities to the foreign corporation as are enjoyed by that state's domestic corporations. These responsibilities may include annual reporting requirements, the payment of franchise taxes, and the payment of state income tax and sales tax. Should the corporation change its name, period of duration, or state of incorporation, the corporation must apply for an amended certificate of authority reflecting such change. If a corporation transacts business in the foreign state without first obtaining a certificate of authority, the corporation will be subject to stiff monetary penalties and will be precluded from maintaining a proceeding in any court of that state until the certificate is acquired.

MAINTENANCE

Once incorporated, a corporation must maintain certain formalities in order to retain its legal status. An organizational meeting must be held (either by the shareholders, incorporators, or board of directors, depending on state statute and whether an initial board of directors was named in the articles of incorporation). Minutes of the organizational meeting, as well as all subsequent meetings of shareholders, directors, and committees must be meticulously taken and kept in the corporate minute book. Notices and waivers of notices of all meetings should be kept as well. Corporate actions must be approved by the requisite body (the shareholders or board) and recorded as resolutions (corporate meetings and resolutions are discussed in detail in Chapter Nine).

Annual reports must be filed with the state filing official in the state of domicile, and where applicable, in other states, together with any annual fees or franchise taxes, and copious corporate records must be kept. These records include stock and bond records, canceled stock certificates and transfer lists, and proxies.

In addition to corporate records, the corporation has to keep the same accounting and business operation records as is required of other businesses, all of which may be subject to inspection by the shareholders. Accounting records include audit reports, general ledgers, canceled dividend checks, bank statements, payroll checks, accounts payable and receivable, and expense reports. Business operations records include all corporate contracts; copyright, trademark, and patent registrations; tax records; and leases, deeds, and mortgages.

CLIENT SIMULATION

Yesterday afternoon Oliver Spires, a new client, consulted with Thomas about incorporating an advertising, marketing, and public relations business he wishes to start with his wife, Amanda, and her brother, Lawrence. Oliver has worked in the advertising field for seven years. Amanda has eight years' experience as a graphic designer and Lawrence was a vice president of a public relations firm in Chicago. Oliver's accountant helped him formulate a viable business plan. Oliver, Amanda, and Lawrence are agreeable to contributing $20,000 each toward start-up expenses. There is a possibility that a former colleague from Lawrence's Chicago firm, John, may join their business in a year or two if all goes well. Oliver, as promoter, has signed a lease for office space with the provision that a novation will be signed substituting the corporation for Oliver as lessee once the business is incorporated.

Oliver, Amanda, and Lawrence all concur that they want the corporation to be an S corporation and Oliver's accountant has explained the desirability of qualifying their stock as 1244 stock (which allows shareholders to treat their financial investment in the corporation as an ordinary loss rather than a capital loss, as discussed in detail in Chapter 6) and of amortizing certain organizational expenses under Section 248 of the Internal Revenue Code (also discussed in detail in Chapter 6). Thomas explained the corporate formalities which must be complied with, such as the filing of articles of incorporation, the preparation of bylaws, the organizational meetings, the records that must be kept, and so forth. Thomas also explained that the State of Any State imposes a high organizational tax valuation on no par shares of stock and thus encouraged Oliver to set a par value of $1.00 on the corporate stock. After his consultation with Thomas, Oliver spent some time with Karen completing a corporate formation worksheet covering the relevant information necessary for the drafting of the articles of incorporation and the bylaws as well as the minutes of the organizational meeting of the directors which will be held once the certificate of incorporation and certified copy of the articles of incorporation are received from the Secretary of State's office. Similar to the worksheet the firm uses for limited liability companies (Chapter 5), Karen has formulated one comprehensive worksheet to include all of the above-mentioned matters.

This morning Karen's first task is to prepare the articles of incorporation and bylaws for Oliver's corporation. Opening his file on her desk, she skims the completed worksheet, which reads as follows:

EXHIBIT 7.1

Corporation Formation Worksheet

DATE OF INTAKE: February 20, 1997

ATTORNEY: Thomas Trumbull

PARALEGAL: Karen Greer

CLIENT NUMBER: 1614

MATTER NUMBER: 0001

PERSON RESPONSIBLE
FOR INTAKE: Karen Greer

1. CLIENT NAME: Oliver Spires for client company

2. ADDRESS: 1440 Adams Avenue

   Any City, Any State

3. TELEPHONE: (000) 222-3333   FAX: (000) 222-3307

4. TYPE OF CORPORATION:

   ___X___ PROFIT

   _____ NOT-FOR-PROFIT

   _____ PROFESSIONAL

5. NAME OF CORPORATION (THREE CHOICES):

   1st choice: Future Visions, Inc.

   2nd choice: The Graphic Image, Inc.

   3rd choice: Creative Strategies, Inc.

EXHIBIT 7.1 *Continued*

6. STATE OF FORMATION: Any State

7. LIST ANY STATE IN WHICH RESERVATION OF NAME IS NEEDED:

Any State

Client does not have plans to become a foreign corpora-

tion in any other state at this time

8. INCORPORATOR(S): Oliver Spires

1440 Adams Avenue

Any City, Any State

(000) 222-3333

9. REGISTERED AGENT: Thomas Trumbull, Esquire

10. REGISTERED OFFICE: Trumbull and McDonald, P.A.

2500 Jefferson Street

Any City, Any State

11. PRINCIPAL OFFICE OF CORPORATION:

1440 Adams Avenue

Any City, Any State

12. OTHER OFFICES: None at this time

13. TERM OF EXISTENCE: Perpetual

14. PURPOSE: Advertising business and any other activities or

business permitted under the laws of the United States

and Any State

15. EFFECTIVE DATE: Upon filing Articles of Incorporation

16. FISCAL YEAR: Calendar year

17. ACCOUNTANT: Gerald Moss, C.P.A.

1295 State Street

Any City, Any State

(000) 848-0077

EXHIBIT 7.1 *Continued*

18. ACCOUNTING METHOD: Cash method

19. CAPITAL STOCK:

    (A) 1. TYPE OF STOCK: Common stock

         2. NUMBER OF AUTHORIZED SHARES: 100,000

         3. PAR VALUE (IF ANY): $1.00

    (B) 1. TYPE OF STOCK: Not applicable

         2. NUMBER OF AUTHORIZED SHARES: _____

         3. PAR VALUE (IF ANY): _____

    (C) 1. TYPE OF STOCK: Not applicable

         2. NUMBER OF AUTHORIZED SHARES: _____

         3. PAR VALUE (IF ANY): _____

20. NAMES, ADDRESSES, AND SOCIAL SECURITY NUMBERS OF INITIAL SHAREHOLDERS:

Name	SSN	Address
Oliver Spires	000-11-3232	235 Willow Lane
		Any City, Any State
Amanda Spires	000-21-3190	235 Willow Lane
		Any City, Any State
Lawrence Macklin	000-34-0055	366 N.W. 20th Terrace
		Any City, Any State

21. TYPE OF STOCK AND NUMBER OF SHARES OF STOCK TO BE ISSUED TO EACH SHAREHOLDER AND THE CONSIDERATION RECEIVED FOR THE SHARES:

Oliver Spires	20,000 shares common stock,	$20,000
Amanda Spires	20,000 shares common stock,	$20,000
Lawrence Macklin	20,000 shares common stock,	$20,000

22. RESTRICTIONS ON TRANSFERS OF SHARES OF STOCK (IF ANY):

Client desires a shareholders' restrictive agreement

EXHIBIT 7.1   *Continued*

23. MEETINGS OF SHAREHOLDERS:

    (A) PLACE OF MEETINGS: The Board of Directors may designate any place, either within or without the State of Any State. If no designation is made, then place of meeting shall be the principal office of the corporation.

    (B) ANNUAL MEETINGS: Date to be determined by directors; annual meeting to be held no later than 13 months after last annual meeting of shareholders; notice of meeting to be delivered not less than 10 days nor more than 60 days before the meeting date; waiver of notice permitted.

    (C) QUORUM: Majority of shareholders

    (D) SPECIAL MEETINGS: May be called by president, majority of the board of directors, or by shareholders owning one-quarter or more of the outstanding voting shares of the corporation.

    (E) QUORUM: Majority of shareholders

    (F) PROXIES: Proxies to be signed by shareholder or shareholder's attorney-in-fact. No proxy to be valid after the expiration of 11 months from the date thereof unless otherwise provided in the proxy. Proxies are revocable at pleasure of the shareholder.

    (G) SHAREHOLDER ACTION BY WRITTEN CONSENT: Permitted if a consent in writing setting forth the action so taken is signed by shareholders of a majority of the outstanding voting shares of the corporation.

    (H) INSPECTOR OF ELECTIONS: Not applicable

EXHIBIT 7.1 *Continued*

24. NAMES AND ADDRESSES OF INITIAL DIRECTORS:

Oliver Spires	1440 Adams Avenue
	Any City, Any State
Amanda Spires	1440 Adams Avenue
	Any City, Any State
Lawrence Macklin	1440 Adams Avenue
	Any City, Any State

25. TOTAL NUMBER OF DIRECTORS: May be increased or decreased by election in accordance with the bylaws

26. IS THE INITIAL BOARD OF DIRECTORS TO BE NAMED IN THE ARTICLES OF INCORPORATION? __X__ YES

_____ NO

27. QUALIFICATIONS OF DIRECTORS: The directors need not be shareholders of the corporation or residents of Any State.

28. ELECTION OF DIRECTORS:

   (A) ANNUALLY: __yes__

   (B) STAGGERED: __no__

29. DIRECTOR VACANCIES: May be filled by affirmative vote of a majority of the remaining directors. A director elected to fill a vacancy shall hold office only until the next election of directors by the shareholders.

30. REMOVAL OF DIRECTOR(S): A director may be removed from office, with or without cause, by vote of holders of a majority of the outstanding shares then entitled to vote at an election of directors. New directors may be elected by the shareholders for the unexpired term of a director removed from

EXHIBIT 7.1   *Continued*

office. If the shareholders fail to elect new directors, the unfilled vacancy shall be filled in accordance with bylaw provisions for vacancies.

31. COMPENSATION OF DIRECTORS: Directors may be repaid their expenses. They may also be paid for attendance at each meeting and may be paid a stated salary.

32. INDEMNIFICATION OF DIRECTORS: Directors and officers are indemnified against liability incurred in connection with any proceeding (other than an action by, or in right of, the corporation), including any appeal thereof, if they acted in good faith and in a manner they reasonably believed to be in, or not opposed to, the best interests of the corporation.

33. MEETINGS OF DIRECTORS:

(A) REGULAR MEETINGS: The board of directors shall hold its annual meeting at the same place as and immediately following each annual meeting of the shareholders. Regular meetings may be held without notice at such time and at such place as shall be determined from time to time by the board. Telephone meetings are permitted.

(B) QUORUM: Majority of the directors

(C) SPECIAL MEETINGS: May be called by the chairperson, the president, or any director. The person calling the meeting may fix a reasonable time and place for holding the meeting. At least three days' written notice required (unless waived by signing waiver of notice).

(D) QUORUM: Majority of directors

EXHIBIT 7.1   *Continued*

(E) DIRECTOR ACTION BY WRITTEN CONSENT: Permitted if a consent in writing setting forth the action is signed by all of the directors.

34. NAMES, TITLES, AND ADDRESSES OF OFFICERS:

Oliver Spires	President	1440 Adams Avenue
		Any City, Any State
Amanda Spires	Vice President	1440 Adams Avenue
	Secretary	Any City, Any State
Lawrence Macklin	Treasurer	1440 Adams Avenue
		Any City, Any State

35. ELECTION AND TERM OF OFFICE OF OFFICERS: To be elected annually by the board of directors at its meeting after each annual meeting of shareholders. Each officer shall hold office until a successor is duly elected.

36. DUTIES OF OFFICERS: The chairperson or president shall preside at all meetings of the board of directors and of the shareholders. The president shall be the chief executive officer. The officers shall have such powers as usually pertain to their respective offices and such additional powers and duties specifically conferred by law, by the articles, by the bylaws, or as may be assigned by the board of directors.

37. OFFICER VACANCIES: May be filled at any time by election by the board of directors for the unexpired terms of such offices.

38. REMOVAL OF OFFICERS: May be removed at any time, with or without cause on the affirmative vote of a majority of the board of directors whenever, in its judgment, removal serves the best

EXHIBIT 7.1 *Continued*

interests of the corporation. Removal shall be without prejudice to any contract rights of the persons so removed, but election of an officer shall not of itself create contract rights.

39. COMPENSATION OF OFFICERS: To be fixed from time to time by the board of directors, and no officer shall be prevented from receiving such salary by reason of the fact that he or she is also a director of the corporation.

40. EXECUTIVE AND OTHER COMMITTEES: The board of directors may, by resolution, passed by a majority of the whole board, designate an executive committee and other committees. The executive committee (if formed) will consult with and advise the officers of the corporation in the management of its business. Other committees (if formed) will have such functions as delegated by board of directors.

41. COMMITTEE MEETINGS: Regular meetings of the executive committee and other committees may be held without notice at such time and at such place as shall from time to time be determined by the executive committee or other committees. Special meetings can be called by any committee member upon two days' notice to the other members of the committee or on such shorter notice as may be agreed to in writing by each of the other members of the committee. Committees shall keep regular minutes of their meetings.

42. COMMITTEE VACANCIES: To be filled by the board of directors

EXHIBIT 7.1   *Continued*

43. COMPENSATION OF COMMITTEE MEMBERS: Committee members may be compensated in accordance with the bylaw provisions pertaining to compensation of directors.

44. BANK ACCOUNTS: Corporate account to be opened at Capitol Bank, 1325 Congress Avenue, Any City, Any State. Signatures of any two officers required on each check.

45. LOANS TO EMPLOYEES AND OFFICERS: The corporation may lend money to, guarantee an obligation of, or otherwise assist any officer or other employee of the corporation, including any officer or employee who is a director of the corporation whenever, in the judgment of the board of directors, such loan, guarantee, or assistance may reasonably be expected to benefit the corporation.

46. AMENDMENT OF BYLAWS: May be amended by a majority vote of the directors.

47. ARE PREEMPTIVE RIGHTS DESIRED?   YES __X__
                                     NO _____

48. IS CUMULATIVE VOTING DESIRED?   YES _____
                                    NO __X__

49. IS SUBCHAPTER S ELECTION DESIRED?   YES __X__
                                        NO _____

50. IS 1244 STOCK QUALIFICATION DESIRED?   YES __X__
                                           NO _____

51. IS 248 ELECTION DESIRED?   YES __X__
                               NO _____

52. ADDITIONAL PROVISIONS: All other provisions should be patterned after the corporate statutes of the State of Any State.

Karen's first step is to determine availability of the proposed corporate name. To do this, she must call the Secretary of State's office. Oliver's first choice, Future Visions, Inc., is not available but his second choice, The Graphic Image, Inc., is available. Karen pulls up the corporate name reservation form on her computer, completes it, and checks her list of corporate fees to determine the filing fee for name reservation. She then requisitions a check to be made out in the appropriate amount and as soon as the check is cut, she will send the form with the fee by certified mail to the Secretary of State's office. Under state statute, the name The Graphic Image, Inc. will be reserved for 120 days.

Karen's next step is to order a corporate kit for the corporation. She calls the company most often used by the law firm and provides them with the name of the corporation, the type of stock, number of authorized shares, par value, and any other information required.

The Secretary of State's office provides forms one may use for drafting the articles of incorporation. In Any State, it is permissible to submit the forms or to prepare customized articles of incorporation as long as the latter include all requisite provisions provided in the forms. In her computer files, Karen has both the scanned official form and a firm-generated form which parallels the official form but includes commonly added provisions, such as a provision naming the initial board of directors, a provision for cumulative voting, and a provision for preemptive rights.

Reviewing the worksheet, Karen recalls that Oliver has chosen to include the names of the first directors in the articles of incorporation so that the organizational meeting of incorporators or shareholders may be bypassed and the corporation need only hold an organizational meeting of the directors. Further, having consulted with Thomas about his concern in keeping the corporate control in the hands of the original shareholders (with the possible exception of the inclusion of John at a later stage), Oliver desires preemptive rights. In the State of Any State, preemptive rights are not presumed and therefore a provision providing for preemptive rights must be included expressly in the articles of incorporation. In this instance, cumulative rights are not desired. From this review, Karen determines that she should work with the firm-generated form for the articles of incorporation, and she pulls it up on the computer. Taking a green highlighter, she highlights the items on the worksheet that must be included in the articles of incorporation and then inserts this information in the form. Having checked for typographical errors, she then prints out the articles of incorporation, which read as follows:

EXHIBIT 7.2

Articles of Incorporation
of
The Graphic Image, Inc.

The undersigned incorporator, for the purpose of forming a corporation under the laws of the State of Any State, hereby adopts the following Articles of Incorporation.

ARTICLE I.   NAME

The name of the corporation shall be: THE GRAPHIC IMAGE, INC.

ARTICLE II.   PRINCIPAL OFFICE

The principal place of business and mailing address of this corporation shall be:

1440 Adams Avenue
Any City, Any State

ARTICLE III.   CAPITAL STOCK

The number of shares of stock that this corporation is authorized to have outstanding at any one time is One Hundred Thousand (100,000) shares of common stock having a par value of One ($1.00) Dollar per share.

ARTICLE IV.   INITIAL REGISTERED AGENT AND ADDRESS

The name and address of the initial registered agent is:

Thomas Trumbull, Esquire
Trumbull and McDonald, P.A.
2500 Jefferson Street
Any City, Any State

EXHIBIT 7.2   *Continued*

ARTICLE V.   INITIAL BOARD OF DIRECTORS

The initial Board of Directors shall consist of three directors. The number of directors may be increased or decreased from time to time by vote of the shareholders, as specified in the bylaws. The names and business addresses of the directors constituting the initial Board of Directors are:

Name	*Address*
Oliver Spires	1440 Adams Avenue Any City, Any State
Amanda Spires	1440 Adams Avenue Any City, Any State
Lawrence Macklin	1440 Adams Avenue Any City, Any State

ARTICLE VI.   PREEMPTIVE RIGHTS

The holders of the common stock of this corporation shall have preemptive rights to purchase, at prices, terms and conditions that shall be fixed by the Board of Directors, those shares of the common stock of this corporation which may be issued from time to time for money, property, or services in addition to that stock authorized and issued by the corporation. The preemptive right of any holder is determined by the ratio of the authorized and issued shares of common stock held by the holder and all shares of common stock currently authorized and issued.

ARTICLE VII.   INCORPORATOR

The name and street address of the person signing these Articles of Incorporation is:

Name	*Address*
Oliver Spires	1440 Adams Avenue Any City, Any State

Oliver Spires, Incorporator

EXHIBIT 7.2   *Continued*

STATE OF ANY STATE   :
                            : SS
COUNTY OF ANY COUNTY :

The foregoing Articles of Incorporation of The Graphic Image, Inc., were acknowledged before me this _____ day of _____, 19_____ by Oliver Spires as incorporator.

_____
Notary Public, State of Any State
My Commission Expires:

ACCEPTANCE OF REGISTERED AGENT

Having been named to accept service of process for The Graphic Image, Inc., at the place designated in the Articles of Incorporation, Thomas Trumbull, Esquire agrees to act in this capacity, and agrees to comply with the laws of the State of Any State relative to keeping open such office.

Date: _____   _____
                                         Thomas Trumbull, Registered Agent

Note that in Any State, the designation of registered agent need not be submitted as a separate certificate and may be attached at the end of the articles of incorporation. Thomas will be acting as registered agent of the corporation. As noted in earlier chapters, using an attorney as a registered agent assures that any litigation matters are immediately brought to the attention of the attorney so they may be dealt with promptly. Oliver will have to sign the articles of incorporation as incorporator and Thomas must sign as registered agent before the articles of incorporation are sent to the Secretary of State's office. Karen has scheduled Oliver to come into the office the next day to review the articles for signature and prepares a cover letter to submit with the articles of incorporation so they may be sent as soon as they are signed and photocopied. Looking at her list of corporate fees, the State of Any State charges a $40 filing fee for the filing of the articles of incorporation, a $25 fee for designation of registered agent, and a $50 fee for a certified copy of the articles of incorporation. Although a certified copy of the articles of incorporation is not required, it is advisable to keep a certified copy in the corporate minute book and Thomas has encouraged Oliver to do so.

February 21, 1997

CERTIFIED MAIL #P221173454
RETURN RECEIPT REQUESTED

Department of State
Division of Corporations
P.O. Box 1234
Any City, Any State

RE: The Graphic Image, Inc.

Enclosed please find an original and one (1) copy of the articles of incorporation for the above corporation and check in the amount of $115.00 to cover the fees for filing the articles of incorporation, the registration of registered agent, and a certified copy of the articles of incorporation. Please send the Certificate of Incorporation and the certified copy of the articles of incorporation for the above corporation to the following:

Trumbull and McDonald, P.A.
2500 Jefferson Street
Any City, Any State
attn: Karen Greer

Very truly yours,
Karen Greer, Legal Assistant

Enc.

    The corporate minute book will come with preprinted bylaws. In some instances, the use of preprinted bylaws is perfectly acceptable. Thomas prefers that Karen use the bylaws in the firm's computer file, which closely parallel state statutes, and then customize them according to the information provided by the client. Certain bylaw provisions, such as the provisions pertaining to the form of stock certificates and corporate seal are considered "boilerplate" provisions and usually are left unchanged. Other provisions, such as those pertaining to meetings, amendment of the articles of incorporation and bylaws, and other crucial provisions must be customized.

For example, on the worksheet Oliver has indicated that special meetings of the shareholders may be called by the president, the majority of the board of directors, or by shareholders owning one-quarter or more of the outstanding voting shares of the corporation. Initially, there will be only three shareholders in the corporation; however, John may join the corporation at a later date and Oliver does not want to amend the bylaws at that time to reflect John's participation as a major shareholder, so the special meeting provision will anticipate John's later inclusion by using the one-fourth fraction rather than one-third. Karen takes her pink highlighter and highlights those items to be included in the bylaws. Certain items, such as subchapter S election, 1244 stock qualification, and others will not be included in the bylaws but will be put to resolution at the organizational meeting of the directors. After completion, the bylaws created by Karen read as follows:

EXHIBIT 7.3

Bylaws of
The Graphic Image, Inc.

ARTICLE I.   OFFICES

The principal office of the Corporation shall be in the State of Any State. The Corporation shall designate a registered office in accordance with the laws of Any State and shall maintain it continuously. The Corporation may have offices at such other places within and without the State of Any State as the Board of Directors may from time to time determine.

ARTICLE II.   SHAREHOLDERS

Section 1.   Annual Meetings.   The purpose of the annual meeting of shareholders is to elect directors and to transact such other matters as may properly come before the shareholders. The annual meeting of the shareholders of the Corporation shall be held at the times and places designated by the Board of Directors or the President of the Corporation. The annual meeting of shareholders for any year shall be held no later than thirteen (13) months after the last annual meeting of shareholders. However, the failure to hold an annual meeting in a timely fashion shall in no way affect the terms of officers or directors of the Corporation or the validity of actions of the Corporation.

Section 2.   Special Meetings.   Special meetings of shareholders may be called by the President or by a majority of the Board of Directors then in office or by shareholders

EXHIBIT 7.3   *Continued*

owning one-fourth (¼) or more of the outstanding voting shares of the Corporation. The purpose of each special meeting shall be stated in the notice and may only include purposes which are lawful and proper for shareholders to consider.

Section 3.   Place of Meeting.   The Board of Directors may designate any place, either within or without the State of Any State, as the place of meeting for any meeting of shareholders. If no designation is made, then the place of meeting shall be the principal office of the Corporation in the State of Any State.

Section 4.   Notice of Meeting.   Written or printed notice stating the place, day, and hour of the meeting and, in the case of a special meeting, the purpose or purposes for which the meeting is called, shall be delivered personally or by mail not less than ten (10) days nor more than sixty (60) days before the date of the meeting. Notice shall be given by or at the direction of the President or the Secretary or the persons calling the meetings to each shareholder of record entitled to vote at the meeting. If mailed, such notice shall be deemed to have been delivered when deposited in the United States Mail addressed to the shareholder at his or her address as it appears on the records of the Corporation with postage thereon prepaid.

Section 5.   Waiver of Notice.   A written waiver of notice signed by a shareholder, whether before or after a meeting, shall be equivalent to the giving of such notice. Attendance of a shareholder at a meeting shall constitute a waiver of notice of such meeting, except when the shareholder attends for the express purpose of objecting, at the beginning of the meeting, to the transaction of any business because the meeting is not lawfully called or convened.

Section 6.   Action Without Meeting.   Any action of the shareholders may be taken without a meeting, without prior notice and without a vote, if a consent in writing setting forth the action so taken is signed by shareholders of a majority of the outstanding voting shares of the Corporation. Within ten (10) days after obtaining such authorization by written consent, notice must be given to those shareholders who have not consented in writing. The notice shall fairly summarize the merger, consolidation, or sale or exchange of assets for which dissenters' rights are provided by state statute, and shall contain a clear statement of the right of dissenting shareholders to be paid the fair value of their shares upon compliance with the applicable statutory provisions. Any certificate to be filed as a result of the shareholders' action under this section shall state that written consent was given in accordance with the laws of the State of Any State.

EXHIBIT 7.3   *Continued*

Section 7.   Voting Record.   If the Corporation has ten (10) or more shareholders of record, the officers having charge of the stock transfer book for shares of the Corporation shall make, at least ten (10) days before each meeting of shareholders, a complete list of the shareholders entitled to vote at such meeting or any adjournment thereof, with the address of each and the number, class and series, if any, of shares held by each. For a period of ten (10) days prior to such meeting, the list shall be kept on file at the registered office of the Corporation, at the principal place of business of the Corporation, or at the office of the transfer agent or registrar of the Corporation, and any shareholder shall be entitled to inspect the list at any time during usual business hours. The list shall also be produced and kept open at the time and place of the meeting and shall be subject to the inspection of any shareholder at any time during the meeting. If the requirements of this section have not been substantially complied with, then upon demand of any shareholder in person or by proxy, the meeting shall be adjourned until the requirements are complied with. If no such demand is made, failure to comply with the requirements of this section shall not affect the validity of any action taken at such meeting.

Section 8.   Shareholder Quorum and Voting.   Unless otherwise required in the Articles of Incorporation, a majority of the shareholders appearing in person or by proxy shall constitute a quorum at a meeting of shareholders. When a specified item of business is required to be voted on by a class or series of stock, unless otherwise required in the Articles of Incorporation, a majority of the shareholders of such class or series shall constitute a quorum for the transaction of such items of business by that class or series. If a quorum is present, unless otherwise provided by law or in the Articles of Incorporation, the affirmative vote of a majority of the shareholders at the meeting entitled to vote on the subject matter shall be the act of the shareholders. After a quorum has been established at a shareholders' meeting, the subsequent withdrawal of shareholders, so as to reduce the number of shareholders entitled to vote at the meeting below the number required for a quorum, shall not affect the validity of any action taken at the meeting or any adjournment thereof. If a quorum is not present when a meeting starts, then a majority of the shareholders at the meeting may adjourn the meeting from time to time without further notice until a quorum is present.

Section 9.   Votes.   Each outstanding share, regardless of class, shall be entitled to one vote on each matter submitted to a vote at a meeting of shareholders.

EXHIBIT 7.3   *Continued*

Section 10.   Proxies.   Every shareholder entitled to vote at a meeting of shareholders or to express consent or dissent without a meeting may authorize another person or persons to act for him or her by proxy. Every proxy shall be in writing and shall be signed by the shareholder or the shareholder's otherwise duly authorized attorney-in-fact. No proxy shall be valid after the expiration of eleven (11) months from the date thereof unless otherwise provided in the proxy. Every proxy shall be revocable at the pleasure of the shareholder executing it, except as otherwise provided by the law of the State of Any State.

ARTICLE III.   BOARD OF DIRECTORS

Section 1.   General Powers.   Subject to the limitations of the Articles of Incorporation, these bylaws, and state statutes concerning corporate action that must be authorized or approved by the shareholders of the Corporation, all corporate powers shall be exercised by or under the authority of the Board of Directors, and the business and affairs of the Corporation shall be controlled by the Board of Directors.

Section 2.   Number, Qualification, Election, and Tenure.   The number of directors shall be the number of directors elected from time to time in accordance with these bylaws. The number of directors may be increased or decreased from time to time by election in accordance with these bylaws. The directors need not be shareholders of this Corporation or residents of the State of Any State. Directors shall be elected by the shareholders at the annual meeting of shareholders and shall serve until the next succeeding annual meeting and until their successors have been elected and qualified.

Section 3.   Annual Meetings.   The Board of Directors shall hold its annual meeting at the same place as and immediately following each annual meeting of shareholders for the purpose of the election of officers and the transaction of such other business as may come before the meeting. If a majority of the directors are present at the annual meeting of shareholders, no prior notice of the annual meeting of the Board of Directors shall be required. However, another place and time for such meeting may be fixed by written consent of all of the directors.

Section 4.   Meetings.   Regular meetings of the Board of Directors may be held without notice at such time and at such place as shall be determined from time to time by the Board of Directors.

EXHIBIT 7.3   *Continued*

Section 5.   Special Meetings.   Special meetings of the Board of Directors may be called by the Chairperson of the Board (if there is one), the President, or any director. The person or persons authorized to call special meetings of the Board of Directors may fix a reasonable time and place for holding them.

Section 6.   Telephone Meetings.   Directors may participate in meetings of the Board of Directors by means of a conference telephone or similar communications equipment by which all persons participating can hear each other at the same time, and participation by such means shall constitute presence in person at such a meeting.

Section 7.   Action Without Meeting.   Any action of the Board of Directors may be taken without a meeting if a consent in writing setting forth the action so taken signed by all of the directors is filed in the minutes of the Board of Directors. Such consent shall have the same effect as an unanimous vote.

Section 8.   Notice and Waiver.   Notice of any special meeting shall be given at least three (3) days prior thereto by written notice delivered personally, by mail, or by facsimile to each director at his or her address. If mailed, such notice shall be deemed to be delivered when deposited in the United States Mail with postage prepaid. Any director may waive notice of any meeting, either before, at, or after such meeting by signing a waiver of notice. The attendance of a director at a meeting shall constitute a waiver of notice of such meeting and a waiver of any and all objections to the place of such meeting or the manner in which it has been called or convened, except when a director states at the beginning of the meeting any objection to the transaction of business because the meeting is not lawfully called or convened.

Section 9.   Quorum and Voting.   A majority of directors in office shall constitute a quorum for the transaction of business. The vote of a majority of directors, present at a meeting at which a quorum is present shall constitute the action of the Board of Directors. If less than a quorum is present, then a majority of those directors present may adjourn the meeting from time to time without notice until a quorum is present.

Section 10.   Indemnification.   Directors and officers are indemnified against liability incurred in connection with any proceeding (other than an action by, or in right of, the corporation) including any appeal thereof, if they acted in good faith and in a manner they reasonably believed to be in, or not opposed to, the best interests of the corporation.

EXHIBIT 7.3   *Continued*

Section 11.   Vacancies.   Any vacancy occurring in the Board of Directors may be filled by the affirmative vote of a majority of the remaining directors even though it is less than a quorum of the Board of Directors, unless otherwise provided by law or the Articles of Incorporation. A director elected to fill a vacancy shall hold office only until the next election of directors by the shareholders. Any directorship to be filled by reason of an increase in the number of directors shall be filled by election at an annual meeting of shareholders or a special meeting of shareholders called for that purpose.

Section 12.   Removal.   At any meeting of shareholders called expressly for that purpose, any director or directors may be removed from office, with or without cause, by vote of holders of a majority of the outstanding shares then entitled to vote at an election of directors. New directors may be elected by the shareholders for the unexpired terms of directors removed from office at the same meetings at which such removals are voted. If the shareholders fail to elect persons to fill the unexpired terms of removed directors, and if the shareholders did not intend to decrease the number of directors to serve on the board, then the vacancies unfilled shall be filled in accordance with provisions in these bylaws for vacancies.

Section 13.   Compensation.   By resolution of the Board of Directors, the directors may be repaid their expenses, if any, of attendance at each meeting of the Board of Directors; they may also be paid a fixed sum for attendance at each meeting of the Board of Directors; and they may also be paid a stated salary as directors. No payment shall preclude any director from serving the Corporation in any other capacity and receiving compensation therefor.

Section 14.   Presumption of Assent.   A director of the Corporation who is present at a meeting of the Board of Directors at which action on any corporate matter is taken shall be presumed to have assented to the action taken unless he or she votes against such action or abstains from voting because of an asserted conflict of interest.

ARTICLE IV.   OFFICERS

Section 1.   Officers.   The officers of this Corporation shall be a President, Vice President, Secretary, and Treasurer, each of whom shall be elected by the Board of Directors. A Chairperson of the Board and such other officers as may be deemed appropriate may be elected by the Board of Directors from time to time. Any two or more offices may be

EXHIBIT 7.3   *Continued*

held by the same person. A failure to elect a President, Vice President, Secretary, or Treasurer shall not affect the existence of the Corporation.

Section 2.   Election and Term of Office.   The officers of the Corporation shall be elected annually by the Board of Directors at its meeting after each annual meeting of shareholders. If the election of officers shall not be held at such meeting, such election shall be held as soon thereafter as conveniently may be. Each officer shall hold office until his or her successor shall have been duly elected and shall have qualified, or until his or her death, or until he or she shall resign, or shall have been removed in the manner hereinafter provided.

Section 3.   Removal.   Any officer may be removed from office at any time, with or without cause, on the affirmative vote of a majority of the Board of Directors whenever, in its judgment, the best interests of the Corporation will be served thereby. Removal shall be without prejudice to any contract rights of the person so removed, but election of an officer shall not of itself create contract rights.

Section 4.   Vacancies.   Vacancies in offices, however occasioned, may be filled at any time by election by the Board of Directors for the unexpired terms of such offices.

Section 5.   Duties.   The Chairperson of the Board, or the President if there is no Chairperson of the Board, shall preside at all meetings of the Board of Directors and of the shareholders. The President shall be the chief executive officer of the Corporation. Subject to the foregoing, the officers of the Corporation shall have such powers and duties as usually pertain to their respective offices and such additional powers and duties specifically conferred by law, by the Articles of Incorporation, by these bylaws, or as may be assigned to them from time to time by the Board of Directors.

Section 6.   Salaries.   The salaries of the officers shall be fixed from time to time by the Board of Directors, and no officer shall be prevented from receiving such salary by reason of the fact that he or she is also a director of the Corporation. Any payment made to an officer of the Corporation such as salary, commission, bonus, interest, rent, or travel or entertainment expense incurred by him or her, which shall be disallowed in whole or in part as a deductible expense by the Internal Revenue Service, shall be reimbursed by such officer to the Corporation to the full extent of such disallowance. It shall be the duty of the directors, as a Board, to enforce payment of each amount disallowed. In lieu of payment of the officer, subject to the determination of the Board of

EXHIBIT 7.3   *Continued*

Directors, proportionate amounts may be withheld from his or her future compensation payments until the amount owed to the Corporation has been recovered.

Section 7.   *Delegation of Duties.*   In the absence or disability of any officer of the Corporation or for any other reason deemed sufficient by the Board of Directors, the Board may delegate his or her powers or duties to any other officer or to any other director.

ARTICLE V.   EXECUTIVE AND OTHER COMMITTEES

Section 1.   *Creation of Committees.*   The Board of Directors may, by resolution passed by a majority of the whole Board, designate an executive committee and one or more other committees.

Section 2.   *Executive Committee.*   The executive committee (if there is one) shall consult with and advise the officers of the Corporation in the management of its business and shall have and may exercise, to the extent provided in the resolution of the Board of Directors creating such executive committee, such powers of the Board of Directors as can be lawfully delegated by the Board.

Section 3.   *Other Committees.*   Such other committees shall have such functions and may exercise such power of the Board of Directors as can be lawfully delegated and to the extent provided in the resolution or resolutions creating such committee or committees.

Section 4.   *Meetings.*   Regular meetings of the executive committee and other committees may be held without notice at such time and at such place as shall from time to time be determined by the executive committee or such other committees, and special meetings of the executive committee or such other committees may be called by any member thereof upon two (2) days' notice to the other members of such committee, or on such shorter notice as may be agreed to in writing by each of the other members of such committee, given either personally or in the manner provided in these bylaws pertaining to notice for directors' meetings.

Section 5.   *Vacancies.*   Vacancies on the executive committee or on other committees shall be filled by the Board of Directors then in office at any regular or special meeting of the Board of Directors.

EXHIBIT 7.3 *Continued*

Section 6. *Quorum.* At all meetings of the executive committee or other committees, a majority of the committee's members then in office shall constitute a quorum for the transaction of business.

Section 7. *Manner of Acting.* The acts of a majority of the members of the executive committee or other committees present at any meeting at which there is a quorum shall be the act of such committee.

Section 8. *Minutes.* The executive committee (if there is one) and the other committees shall keep regular minutes of their proceedings and report the same to the Board of Directors when required.

Section 9. *Compensation.* Members of the executive committee and the other committees may be paid compensation in accordance with the provisions of these bylaws pertaining to compensation of directors.

ARTICLE VI.   STOCK CERTIFICATES

Section 1. *Form and Issuance.* The shares of the Corporation shall be represented by certificates signed by the President or Vice President, and by the Secretary. If a certificate is manually signed on behalf of a transfer agent or registrar other than the Corporation itself or an employee of the Corporation, any other signatures or counter-signatures on the certificate may be facsimiles. Each share certificate shall also state the following: (a) the name of the Corporation; (b) that the Corporation is organized under the laws of the State of Any State; (c) the name of the person or persons to whom issued; (d) the number and class of shares and the designation of the series, if any, which such certificate represents; and (e) the par value of each share represented by such certificate or a statement that the shares are without par value. Each certificate shall also set forth or fairly summarize on the face or back thereof or shall state that the Corporation will furnish to any shareholder on request and without charge, a full statement of the designations, preferences, limitations, and relative rights of the shares of each class or series authorized to be issued. Any certificate representing shares that are restricted as to the sale, disposition, or other transfer of such shares, shall also state that such shares are restricted as to transfer and shall set forth or fairly summarize on the certificate or shall state that the Corporation will furnish to any shareholder on request and without charge, a full statement of such restrictions. No certificate shall be issued for any share until such share is fully paid.

EXHIBIT 7.3   *Continued*

Section 2.   Transfers.   Transfer of shares of the Corporation shall be made in the manner specified in the Uniform Commercial Code of Any State. The Corporation shall maintain stock transfer books, and any transfer shall be registered thereon only on request and surrender of the stock certificate representing the transferred shares. Additionally, the Board of Directors may appoint one or more transfer agents or transfer clerks and one or more registrars as custodians of the transfer books, and may require all transfers to be made with and all share certificates to bear the signatures of any of them. For all corporate purposes including the voting of shares and the issuance and payment of dividends on shares, the Corporation shall have the absolute right to recognize as the owner of any shares of stock issued by it the person or persons in whose name the certificate representing such shares stands on its books. However, if a transfer of shares is made solely for the purpose of furnishing collateral security, and if such fact is made known to the Secretary of the Corporation, or to the Corporation's transfer agent or transfer clerk, the record entry of such transfer shall state the limited nature thereof.

Section 3.   Lost, Stolen, or Destroyed Certificates.   The Corporation shall issue a new stock certificate in the place of any certificate previously issued if the holder of record of the certificate: (a) makes proof in affidavit form that it has been lost, destroyed, or stolen; (b) requests the issuance of a new certificate before the Corporation has notice that the certificate has been acquired by a purchaser for value in good faith and without notice of any adverse claim; (c) gives bond in such form as the Corporation may direct, to indemnify the Corporation, transfer agent, and registrar, if any, against any claim that may be made on account of the alleged loss, destruction, or theft of the certificate; and (d) satisfies any other reasonable requirements imposed by the Corporation.

ARTICLE VII.   BOOKS, RECORDS, AND REPORTS

Section 1.   Report to Shareholders.   The Corporation shall send an annual report to the shareholders of the Corporation not later than four (4) months after the close of each fiscal year of the Corporation. Such report shall include a balance sheet as of the close of the fiscal year of the Corporation and an income statement for the year ending on such closing date. Such financial statements shall be prepared from and in accordance with the books of the Corporation, in conformity with generally accepted accounting principles applied on a consistent basis.

Section 2.   Inspection of Corporate Records.   Any person who has been a holder of record of shares or of voting trust certificates for shares of the Corporation for at least six

EXHIBIT 7.3 *Continued*

(6) months immediately preceding his or her demand, or is the holder of record of shares, or the holder of record of voting trust certificates for at least five (5) percent of the outstanding shares of any class or series of the Corporation, shall have the right, for any proper purpose and at any reasonable time, on written demand stating the purpose thereof, to examine and make copies from the relevant books and records of accounts, minutes, and records of shareholders of the Corporation. Upon the written request of any shareholder or holder of voting trust certificate for shares, the Corporation shall mail to such shareholder or holder of voting trust certificate a copy of the most recent balance sheet and profit and loss statement. If such request is received by the Corporation before such financial statements are available for its last fiscal year, the Corporation shall mail such financial statements as soon as they become available. In any event, the financial statements must be mailed within four (4) months after the close of the last fiscal year. Additionally, balance sheets and profit and loss statements shall be filed in the registered office of the Corporation in Any State, shall be kept for at least five (5) years, and shall be subject to inspection during business hours by any shareholder or holder of voting trust certificate, in person or by agent.

ARTICLE VIII. FINANCES

Section 1. Corporate Accounts. The funds of the Corporation shall be deposited in its name with such banks, trust companies, or other depositories as the board of directors may from time to time designate. All checks, notes, drafts, and other negotiable instruments of the Corporation shall be signed by any two (2) officers of the Corporation.

Section 2. Fiscal Year. The fiscal year of the Corporation shall be the calendar year, unless otherwise provided by the board of directors or shareholders.

Section 3. Loans to Employees and Officers. The Corporation may lend money to, guarantee any obligation of, or otherwise assist any officer or other employee of the Corporation, including any officer or employee who is a director of the Corporation whenever, in the judgment of the Board of Directors, such loan, guarantee, or assistance may reasonably be expected to benefit the Corporation.

Section 4. Dividends. The Board of Directors may from time to time declare, and the Corporation may pay, dividends on its outstanding shares of capital stock in the manner and upon the terms and conditions provided by the Articles of Incorporation and by

EXHIBIT 7.3   *Continued*

law. Dividends may be paid in cash, in property, or in shares of stock, subject to the provisions of the Articles of Incorporation and applicable law.

ARTICLE IX.   SEAL

The corporate seal shall bear the name of the Corporation between two concentric circles and in the inside of the inner circle shall be the year of incorporation.

ARTICLE X.   AMENDMENTS

These bylaws may be altered, amended, or replaced and new bylaws may be adopted by an affirmative vote of the majority of directors of the Board of Directors.

Karen places the articles of incorporation and bylaws in a folder for review by Thomas. Once the articles of incorporation are signed, a photocopy will be sent with the original by certified mail to the Secretary of State's office, a photocopy will be kept in the client file, and a photocopy will be provided to Oliver. A copy of the bylaws will be provided to Oliver with the original remaining in the client file to be put into the corporate minute book once it is delivered. Oliver has stated that he and his colleagues desire the corporation to be an S corporation. The official election of S corporation status will be made by the passing of a resolution at the first meeting of the board of directors. Karen inserts a 2553 form in the client file with a note to complete the form and have all parties sign it at the meeting.

Finally, Karen runs off a worksheet the firm uses for shareholders' restrictive agreements and includes it in the folder with a note to have Thomas discuss it with Oliver when he comes in to sign the articles of incorporation (for a detailed discussion of these agreements and a copy of the form, see Chapter 10). During his consultation with Thomas, Oliver indicated that there was a strong desire to keep control of the corporation among the original shareholders (and John, should he later join), yet they want to leave themselves open to adding minor shareholders or providing shares to employees as an incentive at a later stage. Thomas had suggested a shareholders' restrictive agreement and had discussed the various provisions such an agreement would include. Oliver mentioned that he would discuss the possibility with Amanda and Lawrence and consult again with Thomas when the articles of incorporation were prepared.

Chapter Summary

1. A paralegal may be asked to perform a myriad of tasks in aiding the client in the corporate formation process. Having gathered all requisite information from the client, the paralegal will perform any necessary legal research of state statutes (both local and foreign), check for corporate name availability, reserve the corporate name, order the corporate kit, prepare the articles of incorporation for signature and filing, prepare the bylaws and other requested documents (e.g., shareholders' restrictive agreements), and arrange for organizational meetings.

2. The articles of incorporation typically contain a bare minimum of information about the corporation, the more detailed information residing in the corporate bylaws. If special rights are to be afforded (or, in instances where they are presumed, are to be denied), such as preemptive rights or cumulative voting, statements asserting (or denying) these rights should be included in the articles of incorporation.

3. The bylaws contain the rules and regulations for corporate management and should be comprehensive yet flexible enough to withstand corporate change and growth. Some provisions, such as those pertaining to quorum requirements, should be quite specific; others, such as those pertaining to regular meetings of the board of directors, may be drafted in rather broad terms.

4. While the specific contents of the bylaws will vary from corporation to corporation, bylaws generally contain provisions for shareholders' meetings; directors' meetings; election and duties of officers; vacancies and removal of directors and officers; compensation of directors and officers; executive and other committees; issuance, transfer, and replacement of stock certificates; corporate recordkeeping; corporate finances; and amendment of the bylaws.

5. A corporation only need qualify as a foreign corporation in those states (other than the state of domicile) in which it plans to transact business. Most state statutes fail to define "transacting business," preferring instead to list those activities which do not constitute transacting business within the state.

6. To qualify as a foreign corporation, a business must obtain a certificate of authority from the secretary of state of the foreign state. To do this, an application must be submitted, together with a certificate of good standing from the state of domicile, and the requisite filing fee. Once authorized, a foreign corporation is subject to the laws of the foreign state and must comply with all reporting and tax requirements.

7. Corporations are required to maintain records of all activities, from the holding of meetings and passing of resolutions, to the accounting of all financial and business operations. These records are open to inspection by the sharehold-

ers. Additionally, corporations must file annual reports with the state of domicile (and states in which they are acting as foreign corporations) and pay all franchise, income, and other applicable taxes in order to maintain their good standing.

Review Questions

1. List the steps to be taken in forming a corporation.
2. Compare and contrast the information contained in the articles of incorporation and the information contained in the bylaws.
3. Which, if any, of the following is likely to constitute "transacting business" in a foreign state:
    (i)   a camping equipment company selling goods in a foreign state through mail order catalogs;
    (ii)   a clothing manufacturer opening a discount outlet in a foreign state;
    (iii) a cosmetics company selling products through independent contractors in a foreign state;
    (iv)   a development company owning a tract of real estate in a foreign state?
4. What steps must be taken before a corporation may transact business as a foreign corporation?
5. What documentation must be kept in a corporate minute book?

KEY TERMS

certificate of
  incorporation
corporate kit
corporate service
  company

cumulative voting
emergency bylaws
minute book
par value
preemptive rights

Financial Structure of a Corporation

Upon completion of this chapter, the student will:

- understand the difference between equity securities and debt securities
- understand the factors to be considered when formulating a corporation's capital stock structure
- understand the rights adherent to various types of stock
- know the mechanics of issuing stock certificates to shareholders
- know the various components of an annual report

INTRODUCTION

In discussing business entities in previous chapters, the ability to raise capital and the methods available for raising capital were considerations when selecting the appropriate business entity to meet a client's needs. One of the advantages of choosing a corporate structure is that it provides the greatest flexibility in these areas.

When a business chooses to incorporate, it has the ability to set up a capital structure providing for the raising of capital by various means. One method of raising capital is through the selling of shares of stock in the corporation. The shareholders purchasing shares in the corporation become holders of **equity**

securities in the form of either common stock or preferred stock. The term "equity" refers to the fact that the holder of shares has purchased an ownership interest in the corporation. Another method by which a corporation can raise working capital is by obtaining loans, either by applying for a business loan from a financial institution or through the sale of bonds and debentures. Bonds and debentures, discussed below, are types of **debt securities**. The holders of these instruments are considered creditors of the corporation, entitled to receive their investment back within a stipulated amount of time, together with interest, but are not considered owners of the corporation. Thus, the corporation's **capital structure** is comprised of a combination of all equity securities authorized to be issued by the corporation and all debt securities of the corporation.

This chapter focuses on the capital structure of a corporation, outlining the various types of equity and debt securities that may be utilized in the raising of capital. The chapter also discusses the options available to a corporation in making distributions to shareholders. Additionally, because paralegals may be asked by a corporate client to prepare stock certificates, a section of the chapter focuses on the proper method for preparing stock certificates. Finally, attorneys may be asked to compile or review annual reports for a client and consequently you may be asked to assist in these tasks. Therefore, the chapter concludes with a discussion of the components of a corporate annual report.

THE CAPITAL STRUCTURE

A.   Capital Stock

As discussed in the last chapter, when a business decides to incorporate it files articles of incorporation with the state filing authority. Included in the articles is a provision outlining the corporation's capital stock structure. **Capital stock** refers to all common stock and preferred stock the corporation is authorized to issue. The term **authorized shares** (sometimes called **authorized capital**) refers to the number and kind of shares of stock the corporation is lawfully permitted to issue to shareholders. **Issued shares** refers to shares sold to shareholders. A corporation always may issue fewer shares than are authorized by the articles of incorporation; however, the corporation can never issue more shares than are authorized. If the corporation wishes to increase the number of authorized shares, it must do so by amending its articles of incorporation. Once a corporation issues shares, they remain **outstanding shares** as long as they remain in the hands of the shareholders. Should the corporation buy back stock from the shareholders, the shares of stock returned to the corporation are referred to as **treasury shares**. In other words, treasury shares are shares that have been issued and then bought back. Once bought back, the shares are no longer outstanding. Treasury shares do not have voting rights or earn dividends until such time as they are resold by the corporation.

There are a number of considerations when formulating a corporation's capital stock structure. The corporation will attempt to raise a good portion of its working capital by selling shares. When deciding how many shares to divide the corporation into, the initial shareholders should consider not only how many shares each initial shareholder should receive for his or her investment in the corporation, but also how many shares should be retained by the corporation. These **unissued shares** may later be sold to raise additional capital, may be distributed to shareholders in the form of stock dividends (discussed below), or may be offered as stock options or bonuses to key employees (discussed in Chapter 11).

Additionally, the initial shareholders must consider whether all shareholders should be afforded the same ownership rights when purchasing shares. If control of management is to be kept in the hands of a select few, the shareholders may choose to issue both voting and nonvoting types of stock. Some potential investors may not be interested in participating in the running of the corporation but may require a certain percentage of return on their investment each year. Therefore the corporation may want to issue both common and preferred stock (discussed below). Section 6.01(c) of the Revised Model Business Corporation Act sets forth various ways in which to set up classes of stock:

> (c) The articles of incorporation may authorize one or more classes of shares that:
>
> (1) have special, conditional, or limited voting rights, or no right to vote, except to the extent prohibited by this Act;
>
> (2) are redeemable or convertible as specified in the articles of incorporation (i) at the option of the corporation, the shareholder, or another person or upon the occurrence of a designated event; (ii) for cash, indebtedness, securities or other property; (iii) in a designated amount or in an amount determined in accordance with a designated formula or by reference to extrinsic data or events;
>
> (3) entitle the holders to distributions calculated in any manner, including dividends that may be cumulative, noncumulative, or partially cumulative;
>
> (4) have preference over any other class of shares with respect to distributions, including dividends and distributions upon the dissolution of the corporation.

Stock can be further divided into series. A **series** is a subdivision of a class of stock, usually preferred stock. Each series of stock can be afforded different rights and limitations as long as these rights and limitations are identical for all shares within a series. Section 6.02 of the Revised Model Business Corporation Act states that:

(a) If the articles of incorporation so provide, the board of directors may determine, in whole or in part, the preferences, limitations, and relative rights (within the limits set forth in section 6.01) of (1) any class of shares before the issuance of any shares of that class or (2) one or more series within a class before the issuance of any shares of that series.

(b) Each series of a class must be given a distinguishing designation.

(c) All shares of a series must have preferences, limitations, and relative rights identical with those of other shares of the same series and, except to the extent otherwise provided in the description of the series, with those of other series of the same class.

(d) Before issuing any shares of a class or series created under this section, the corporation must deliver to the secretary of state for filing articles of amendment, which are effective without shareholder action, that set forth:

(1) the name of the corporation;

(2) the text of the amendment determining the terms of the class or series of shares;

(3) the date it was adopted; and

(4) a statement that the amendment was duly adopted by the board of directors.

State statute may allow a rather broad provision in the articles of incorporation providing that a named type of stock (common or preferred) be issued in one or more series, leaving the particular rights of each series to be determined by the board of directors at a later date and not requiring an amendment of the articles of incorporation for implementation. Because state law varies, statutes should be checked.

Another consideration is whether or not to give corporate stock a par value, a concept briefly mentioned in the last chapter. **Par value** is an arbitrary figure assigned to authorized shares of stock, such as $1 per share. Par value often is not the purchase price paid for stock. For example, 100 shares of common stock, par value $1 per share, may in fact be sold at $20 per share (or some other amount determined to be a reasonable valuation by the board of directors). Historically, par value was not arbitrary, it was the amount for which stock was actually issued. Its original purpose was providing a base for obtaining corporate credit (by providing potential lenders with an easily discernible way of calculating the equity investment in the business) and assuring equal contributions by all shareholders (by assuring that all shareholders paid the same price for shares). Today, corporations have the choice of issuing par value stock or no par stock. If stock is given a designated par value in the articles of incorporation, that stock may not be issued for less than par value.

Although par value appears to have lost its historical importance, the matter of assigning par value may have significance in some states. State statutes imposing franchise fees for the privilege of conducting business in the state may calculate the fees differently for par value stock and no par stock. Franchise fees may be in the form of a flat fee or may be calculated based on the aggregate value of the capital stock of the corporation. In the latter instance, if the corporate stock has a designated par value, the aggregate value usually is taken to be aggregate par value of the stock (e.g., a corporation with 100,000 shares of common stock, par value $1 per share, will pay a franchise fee based upon an aggregate value of $100,000). If corporate stock has no par value, state law assigns its own arbitrary figure for no par stock when calculating the franchise fee. The same dilemma may be encountered with the imposition of taxes imposed on the issuance or transfer of shares of stock which typically is calculated on the par value of the stock or, if no par value is given, then on the amount paid for the stock (see the discussion of the documentary stamp tax below).

B. Stated Capital, Capital Surplus, and Earned Surplus

Par value plays a further role in corporate accounting records. Corporate accounting typically divides capital into three accounts: stated capital, capital surplus, and earned surplus. The **stated capital** account represents the permanent investment capital of the corporation. The purpose of this account is to make provision for corporate creditors. In most states, the stated capital account is comprised of the par value of all shares issued by the corporation plus the portion of monies paid for all no par share issued that the board of directors allocates to stated capital. For example, suppose a corporation has issued 10,000 shares of stock with a par value of $1 per share. Those 10,000 shares actually sold for $15 per share. The aggregate par value of the shares is $10,000, and therefore this amount must be placed into the stated capital account. If those same 10,000 shares did not have a designated par value, then a portion of the aggregate purchase price of $150,000 would be allocated by the board of directors to be put into the stated capital account. Withdrawal restrictions are placed on the stated capital account to assure that a corporation retains a minimum capitalization for the benefit of creditors. Some state statutes mandate a prescribed minimum stated capital amount for incorporation.

The **capital surplus** account contains monies paid over the par value for par value stock plus the monies paid for no par stock that are not allocated by the board of directors to the stated capital account. Taking the above example, if the corporation sells 10,000 shares of stock, par value $1 per share, for $15 a share, $10,000 is allocated to the stated capital account and the remainder, $140,000, is allocated to the capital surplus account. If those 10,000 shares are no par shares, the board of directors may determine what percentage of the $150,000 should be allocated to the stated capital account and what percentage should be allocated to the capital surplus account. The **earned surplus** account contains the corporation's accumulated profits from the running of the business, minus dividends paid to shareholders (most states require that dividends be paid out of the earned surplus account rather than the capital surplus account).

Most small corporations have a simple capital stock structure, consisting of one type of stock: common stock. Nonetheless, every corporation has its own needs and these needs should be addressed at the initial stages of forming a corporation. A corporate attorney should spend adequate time at the early stages explaining the considerations discussed above and the various methods of setting up the capital structure of a corporation to arrive at the best approach for the client.

TYPES OF STOCK

A.   *Common Stock*

There are two major types of equity securities a corporation may issue: common stock and preferred stock. **Common stock** is ordinary stock which does not confer preferences to the shareholder. Holders of common stock typically have three basic rights: (1) voting rights, (2) dividend rights, and (3) liquidation rights.

Voting rights entitle shareholders to elect the board of directors and to vote on major corporate issues including, but not limited to, amendments to the articles of incorporation, mergers, and dissolution of the corporation. Every corporation must have at least one type of stock with voting rights, and therefore every corporation has at least one type of common stock. In some instances, a corporation may divide its common stock into two classes, voting and nonvoting shares. This is often the case when a corporation wishes to raise capital by selling shares on an international market but wants to retain domestic control of the corporation. Another variation is to provide that different classes of stock have a different number of votes. For example, Class A Common Stock may have two votes per share and Class B Common Stock may have one vote per share. A third variation is to allow one class of common stock, typically Class A, the right to vote on all matters and give Class B stock the right to vote only on certain matters.

The right of common shareholders to dividends is a residual right because the holders of common stock are entitled to receive dividends (when distribution of dividends is declared by the board of directors) only after preferred shareholders are paid. Dividends usually are declared annually but often are paid out quarterly. For example, if the dividend to be paid is $1 per share of common stock, a holder of common stock will be paid $.25 per share per quarter.

Additionally, the holders of common stock have a residual right to their pro rata share of corporate assets when a corporation liquidates. Creditors are paid off first, followed by preferred shareholders. If assets remain, these assets are divided proportionately among the common shareholders.

B. Preferred Stock

Preferred stock is stock given priority in certain matters over common stock (e.g., preference in liquidation and dividend rights as discussed above) but may also be subject to certain limitations (e.g., lack of voting rights). Holders of **straight preferred stock** are entitled to fixed-rate dividends. As noted above, these dividends must be paid before holders of common stock are entitled to their dividends. If the board of directors fails to distribute dividends in a particular quarter, the holders of straight preferred stock are not entitled to back payment of these missed dividends. Should the corporation dissolve and liquidate, the holders of straight preferred stock are paid a fixed percentage of the par value of their stock, plus any unpaid dividends, before common shareholders receive anything. Straight preferred stock appeals to potential investors desiring a known, fixed rate of return on their investment. This stock also appeals to individuals in a family-owned business desiring to shift a portion of business profits to family members in lower tax brackets. By issuing two types of stock, common stock and straight preferred stock, the management control remains with the family members holding the common stock while the holders of straight preferred stock receive profits but no voting rights.

Another type of preferred stock is **participating preferred stock**. Holders of this stock are accorded a fixed-rate dividend, just as is accorded the holders of straight preferred stock. In addition, holders of participating preferred stock share in the residual dividends on the same basis as holders of common stock. A less common form of participating preferred stock entitles the holder to the fixed-rate dividends and liquidation preferences of straight preferred stock and also allows "participation" in the running of the business by according limited voting rights. Please note, however, that in states with statutes patterned after the Revised Model Business Corporation Act, outstanding stock of any class is entitled to vote unless the articles of incorporation provide otherwise. Thus, if a corporation wishes to have both voting and nonvoting classes of preferred stock, this must be spelled out with particularity in the articles of incorporation.

Holders of **convertible preferred stock** have the right to convert their preferred shares into a stated amount of common stock under specified conditions. The convertibility option is attractive because common stock potentially has a higher yield than preferred stock. Although the holders of common stock are only accorded their pro rata share of residual profits and thus face a higher risk that they will not receive a favorable distribution in a given year, the rate of return on preferred stock is fixed whereas the rate of return on common stock is not fixed. As a corporation's profit margin increases, so does the potential for common shareholders to reap higher rewards than preferred shareholders.

As stated above, preferred shareholders ordinarily are not entitled to back dividends should the board of directors fail to make distribution of dividends in a quarter. However, if a shareholder holds **cumulative preferred stock**, that shareholder has the right to any accumulated back dividends. Further, the payment of cumulative dividends (the arrearages plus the present fixed dividends) take priority over the dividends of common stock.

The issuance of **redeemable preferred stock** (also referred to as **callable preferred stock**) allows a corporation to reacquire ("redeem" or "call back") these shares at a predetermined price. When issued, the certificates of redeemable preferred stock include a statement referring the holder to the terms of the redemption agreement. This agreement includes, at a minimum, the date upon which the corporation may redeem the shares, the notification procedures and deadline for informing the holder of the corporation's exercise of its redemption privilege, the price for which the shares may be redeemed, and the mechanics of surrendering the stock certificates. If a corporation's articles of incorporation authorize the issuance of redeemable preferred stock, the corporation should establish a sinking fund. A **sinking fund** is a reserve account set aside for the future redemption of redeemable preferred stock at a specified time. Periodic payments are deposited into the fund to assure that adequate monies are available when needed.

Finally, hybrids of the various types of preferred stock mentioned above may be authorized by the corporation's articles of incorporation. For example, a corporation may be authorized to issue cumulative convertible preferred stock, combining the preferences of cumulative preferred stock (entitlement to back dividends) with the preferences of convertible preferred stock (entitlement to convert preferred shares into common shares). Generally speaking, the more preferences accorded a type of preferred stock, the lower the fixed rate tends to be.

C. Options

An **option** is an agreement permitting an individual or entity to buy or to sell a specified number of shares of stock at a specified price within a specific period of time. There are two types of options: a call and a put. A **call** is an agreement permitting an individual or entity to buy stock at a specified price (this price is sometimes referred to as a **strike price** or the **exercise price**). Conversely, a **put** is an option agreement permitting an individual or entity to sell stock at a specified price. The person given the option to purchase the stock need only pay a small percentage of the stock price at the time of signing the agreement.

For example, suppose the price of stock of Universal Communications Corporation is currently $40 per share. An option agreement might provide that for a payment of $400 (the option fee) one has the right to purchase 100 shares of Universal Communications stock at the $40 per share price within the next four months. This is an example of a call option. If the price of the stock increases more than $4 per share within the four-month period, say to $50 per share, the holder of the option will most likely exercise the option ("call" it in), purchasing the 100 shares for a total of $4,000 and will be able to turn around and sell those shares for $5,000, realizing a $600 profit ($1,000 minus the option fee of $400). Another possibility available to the holder of the option is to sell the option to another investor. Using the same example, suppose an investor wanted to purchase the option from the holder for $600. The holder would realize a profit of $200. The holder receives a 50 percent profit on the $400 investment and does not have to put up the money to purchase the shares of stock. Although this is less than the $600 profit quoted above, remember that the price of the stock could remain the same or could decrease within the four-month period, leaving the holder with a useless option.

With a put option, the holder of the option purchases the right to sell stock at a specified price and within a specific time frame. Returning to the same example, suppose the option was a put option, the holder paying $400 for the right to sell 100 shares of stock at $40 per share within a four-month period. Suppose further that within the four-month period the price of the stock falls to $30 per share. The holder could exercise the option and again come out with a $600 profit ($1,000 minus the fee of $400).

CONSIDERATION AND ISSUANCE OF STOCK

A.   *Consideration for Shares*

Before stock certificates can be issued to shareholders, the board of directors must give its approval at a board of directors' meeting or by a unanimous written consent. The board of directors decides when to issue shares, to whom the shares will be issued, how many shares of stock authorized by the articles of incorporation will be issued, and the **consideration** (value) to be received in return for the shares of stock. A corporation can never issue more than the number of shares authorized by the articles of incorporation. Although subscription agreements may be accepted before the articles of incorporation are filed, the corporation cannot issue shares until the corporation is legally in existence and the issuance has been approved formally during or after the organizational meeting.

In deciding whether to approve the issuance of stock, the board must determine whether the consideration offered for the shares is adequate. Consideration offered can take many forms, such as cash, property, or services. Section 6.21(b) of the Revised Model Business Corporation Act provides that:

> The board of directors may authorize shares to be issued for consideration consisting of any tangible or intangible property or benefit to the corporation, including cash, promissory notes, services performed, contracts for services to be performed, or other securities of the corporation.

The price of the initial shares offered typically will coincide with the amount of starting capital required by the business as set forth in the proposed business plan. A corporation's articles of incorporation should be structured to include a greater number of authorized shares than will be initially issued to allow room for growth. It is a common practice for a corporation to issue a greater number of shares at a lower price per share than to issue a smaller number of shares at a high price (e.g., 1,000 shares at $1 per share rather than one share at $1,000 per share). This makes it easier for the shareholder to transfer all or some of his or her shares at a later date. Recall in the last chapter that The Graphic Image, Inc. was created with an authorized capital structure of 100,000 shares of common stock with a par value of $1 per share and that three shareholders, Oliver Spires, Amanda Spires, and Lawrence Macklin, were each agreeing to put $20,000 into the corporation for start-up expenses in return for 20,000 shares each of the corporate stock. Thus, they receive a large number of shares at a low price and the corporation is left with 40,000 shares to distribute should the board of directors decide to raise more capital by selling shares of stock. If the articles of incorporation (or state law) provide for preemptive rights (discussed briefly in the last chapter and in more detail in Chapter 10), as is the case with the articles of incorporation of The Graphic Image, Inc., then the initial shareholders must be afforded first rights to purchase new shares issued by the corporation in proportion to the percentage of ownership rights each presently holds in the corporation.

If cash is offered for shares of stock the amount offered must be at least equal to the par value of the stock, if the stock has a par value. Indeed, since par value is a purely arbitrary figure bearing no relation to the true value of the stock, stock is often sold at a price exceeding par. Stock sold for less than par value is called **watered stock** (also referred to as **discount stock**). The directors on the board will have breached their duty of due care in issuing stock for less than par and the shareholders holding watered stock will be liable to the corporation's creditors for the amount that should have been paid for the shares if the corporation should become insolvent (for a detailed discussion of shareholder liabilities, see Chapter 10). When stock is given no par value, the board of directors fixes a minimum value for stock shares, the **stated value**, which value is readjusted from time to time.

If the shareholder is offering property in return for stock shares, the board of directors must determine that the property offered is of a value at least equal to the par value or stated value. Property includes both tangible and intangible property, and thus can include (but is not limited to) such things as real property, office furniture and equipment, patents, and copyrights. Most states allow the board of directors simply to apply a good-faith determination of the adequacy of the property offered in exchange for the stock shares. A more cautious board may choose to hire an appraiser to give an official appraisal of the property.

If, on the other hand, stock is to be issued in return for services, some states may still make a distinction between services already performed and future services. All states recognize that a board of directors is permitted to issue stock in return for past services performed for the corporation. Many states have followed the Revised Model Business Corporation Act in expanding the acceptable forms of consideration to include future services to be performed for the corporation. State statute or the corporate bylaws may require a written employment agreement evidencing the services contracted for before allowing the board of directors to issue shares. Section 6.21(e) of the Revised Model Business Corporation Act permits the corporation to hold stock shares in escrow until the future services actually are performed, thereby providing protection for the corporation should the contracted services fail to be performed. If state law permits the issuance of stock shares in return for a promissory note, the corporation may treat the issuance similar to the issuance of shares in return for future services, requiring that the shares be held in escrow until the terms of the note have been satisfied.

B.   *Issuance of Stock Certificates*

If a corporation's board of directors determines that adequate consideration is being offered for shares of stock then it will authorize the exchange of **stock certificates** (sometimes referred to as **share certificates**) in return for the consideration. A stock certificate is a type of intangible property. It is not the stock itself, but rather a written statement providing evidence of the holder's share of ownership interest in the corporation. Because a stock certificate is only a writing evidencing the ownership of stock, the Revised Model Business Corporation Act, as well as the statutes of many states, allows for the issuance of **uncertified shares** (stock issued without stock certificates). Ownership of uncertified shares is recorded in the corporate stock ledger but the owner of the shares does not receive a certificate. The owner of uncertified shares has the same rights as holders of certificates of the same type, class, and series of stock. Uncertified shares are most commonly issued by public corporations in which shares of stock are transferred continuously, making the issuance of certificates burdensome.

Stock certificates must include, as a minimum, the following:

1. the name of the corporation issuing the stock;
2. a statement that the corporation is organized under the state of domicile;
3. the name of the person to whom the stock certificate is issued; and
4. the number and class of shares and the designation of the series, if any, represented by the certificate.

Stock certificates must be signed by one or more officers of the corporation as designated by state statute, the bylaws, or the board of directors and impressed with the corporate seal. The stock certificates may be signed manually or by facsimile. In large corporations, the mechanics of issuing certificates usually is conducted by a transfer agent.

If you, as a paralegal, are assigned the task of preparing stock certificates for issuance by the client corporation, you must follow certain steps. First, you must ascertain that the minutes of the organizational meeting of the corporation contain a resolution authorizing the directors of the corporation to issue stock shares. If such a resolution is contained in the minutes, it most likely will specify the type of stock, number of shares, par value, and purchase price for which shares will be issued to named individuals. If a resolution to this effect is not included in the minutes, the next step is to check to see if a sufficient resolution was adopted subsequent to the organizational meeting. (For a detailed discussion of corporate meetings, minutes, and resolutions see Chapter 9.) All initial shares of stock of the same type, class, and series typically are issued for the same price per share. As noted above, a corporation cannot issue more shares of stock than the number of shares authorized by the articles of incorporation.

The next step is to determine the manner in which the prospective shareholder(s) are to take title to the stock shares. If the shares are to be issued to an individual shareholder, then the shares presumably are to be issued to that individual in his or her own name. If shares are to be owned jointly, however, there are several ways in which title to those shares may be held, each with its own legal ramifications. For example, Alice Clark and Lyle Clark are purchasing 10,000 shares of stock together: they may be taking title as tenants by the entirety, tenants in common, or joint tenants with right of survivorship. A **tenancy by the entirety** is a manner of taking title to property that is only applicable to spouses. If title to property, including stock shares, is held in this manner, each spouse owns 100 percent of the shares, not 50 percent each. Thus, one spouse cannot sell the shares without the consent of the other. Further, this manner of holding title includes the right of survivorship, which means that when one spouse dies the other spouse obtains full title to the shares to do with as he or she pleases. If Alice and Lyle are husband and wife they may choose to hold title to the stock shares in this manner, but this should not be presumed. They may choose, instead, to hold title as **tenants in common**. This manner of holding title allows each co-owner to have an interest in the shares, but does not give the co-owners right of survivorship. Therefore, each tenant in common can dispose of his or her interest in the shares as he or she sees fit. If Alice and Lyle are not husband and wife (for example, they may be mother and son or sister and brother) they may take title to the shares as tenants in common or as **joint tenants with right of survivorship** (as may any nonmarried co-owners). In the latter instance, Alice and Lyle, as co-owners of the shares, each take title with right of survivorship, similar to that provided in a tenancy by the entirety. Unlike a tenancy by the entirety, however, should Alice sell her interest in the shares, then Lyle and the person to whom Alice has sold her interest become co-owners as tenants in common. Because of these legal

EXHIBIT 8.1

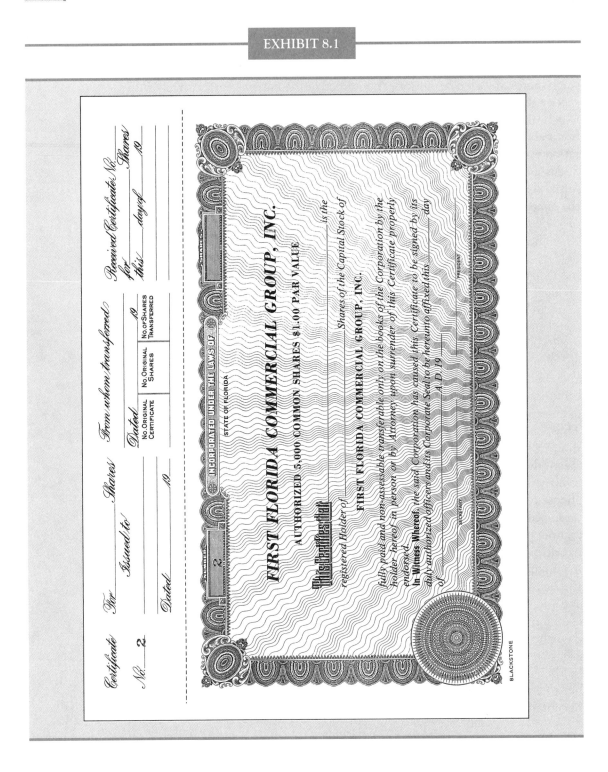

EXHIBIT 8.1 *Continued*

For Value Received, _____ hereby sell, assign and transfer unto

PLEASE INSERT SOCIAL SECURITY OR OTHER
IDENTIFYING NUMBER OF ASSIGNEE

_____ Shares
represented by the within Certificate, and do hereby
irrevocably constitute and appoint

_____ Attorney
to transfer the said Shares on the books of the within named
Corporation with full power of substitution in the premises.
Dated _____ 19____

In presence of

_____   _____

NOTICE: THE SIGNATURE OF THIS ASSIGNMENT MUST CORRESPOND WITH THE NAME AS WRITTEN UPON THE FACE OF THE CERTIFICATE, IN EVERY PARTICULAR, WITHOUT ALTERATION OR ENLARGEMENT OR ANY CHANGE WHATEVER.

distinctions, the manner of title holding must be accurately described on the stock certificates.

The stock certificates included in the corporate minute book contain two parts: the stock certificate and the certificate stub (see Exhibit 8.1). Both must be filled in completely. The certificates are numbered consecutively and the certificate number on the stub should correspond with the certificate number on the stock certificate. On the stub, fill in the person (or persons) to whom the shares are to be issued, the date of issuance, the number of the stock certificate to be issued, and the number of shares to be issued. Some certificate stubs include space for the address of the shareholder. Leave the section referring to transfer blank. That section is to be completed only when the original shareholder transfers the shares to another person. On the stock certificate, fill in the number of shares numerically in the box provided at the top of the certificate, the name of the person (or persons) to whom the certificate is issued, the number of shares (spelled out, e.g., One Thousand, which may be followed by numerals in parentheses, e.g., (1,000)), and the date of issuance. The certificate must be signed by the officers so designated (typically the president and secretary of the corporation) and the corporate seal must be impressed at the bottom of the certificate. Please note that if the shareholder is issued stock shares subject to a shareholders' restrictive agreement, then a statement to that effect must be included on the certificate, such as the following:

NOTICE OF STOCK TRANSFER RESTRICTIONS

The shares of stock represented by this certificate are subject to transfer and other restrictions as set forth in the Corporation's articles of incorporation or in the shareholders' restrictive agreement dated February 13, 1997, copies of which are on file at the Corporation's registered office. No transfer or other disposition of the shares represented by this certificate shall be valid or recognized by the Corporation unless the requirements set forth in the above-mentioned documents are first complied with to the Corporation's satisfaction.

As a method of raising revenue, states impose a tax on the act of issuing corporate stock. This tax is called a **documentary stamp tax** and it is imposed when original certificates of stock are issued. The tax paid is represented by stamps very similar in appearance to postage stamps, that are to be attached to the stock certificate stubs. The documentary stamp rates as well as information pertaining to the available denominations of documentary tax stamps can be obtained from the state's department of revenue. State law may provide differing methods of computation or differing rates of the applicable documentary stamp tax for par value shares and for no par shares.

To illustrate how the documentary stamp tax works, suppose in Any State that the documentary stamp tax rate that applies to shares with par value is $.25 on each $100 (or fraction thereof) of the total stated par value of the shares represented by each stock certificate. Recall in the last chapter that the corporate formation worksheet Karen completed for the client corporation, The Graphic Image, Inc., indicated that there were to be three initial shareholders, Oliver Spires, Amanda Spires, and Lawrence Macklin. Each were purchasing 20,000 shares of common stock, par value $1 per share for payment of $20,000 each. If Karen were to compute the documentary stamp tax for the issuance of 20,000 shares to Oliver, the computation would be as follows:

Step 1: total stated par value of the shares represented by Oliver's certificate equals $20,000 (20,000 shares multiplied by a par value of $1)

Step 2: $20,000 divided by 100 equals 200 (tax applied to each $100, or fraction thereof, of the total par value)

Step 3: 200 multiplied by $.25 equals $50

Thus, the documentary stamp tax of the $20,000 value of the stock is $50. Now suppose that the stock was no par stock and that Oliver paid $2 per share for 20,000 shares, or $40,000. Suppose further that in Any State the documentary stamp tax on no par stock is $.25 for each $100 of value of the consideration that a shareholder pays for his or her no par shares. Here, the consideration paid by Oliver is $40,000. It is divided by 100, leaving 400, and multiplied by the tax rate to arrive at a tax amount of $100.

Once the amount of the tax is determined, obtain the tax stamps in the appropriate denominations. They may be ordered from the state's department of revenue or, in some instances, may be available from the city or county clerk's office. Attach the stamps to the certificate stubs. The final steps for the issuance of stock certificates is the preparation of a shareholder receipt and the insertion of the specified information in the corporate stock ledger (e.g., name of shareholder, address, certificate numbers, shares issued, issuance date, amount paid for the shares, documentary stamp tax) (see Exhibit 8.2). If the certificate stub contains a receipt, the shareholder should be requested to sign the appropriate portion of the stub. If the certificate does not include a receipt, prepare a separate receipt to be signed and then stapled to the stub.

EXHIBIT 8.2

	NAME OF STOCKHOLDER	PLACE OF RESIDENCE	TIME BECAME OWNER	CERTIFICATES ISSUED		FROM WHOM SHARES WERE TRANSFERRED (If Original Issue Enter As Such)	
				CERTIF. NOS.	NO. SHARES		
A							
B							
C							
D							
E							
F							
G							

EXHIBIT 8.2 *Continued*

	AMOUNT PAID THEREON	DATE OF TRANSFER OF SHARES	TO WHOM SHARES ARE TRANSFERRED	CERTIFICATES SURRENDERED		NUMBER OF SHARES HELD (BALANCE)	VALUE OF STOCK TRANSFER TAX STAMP AFFIXED
				CERTIF. NOS.	NO. SHARES		

DISTRIBUTIONS TO SHAREHOLDERS

A shareholder, as an owner of the corporation, invests money, property, or services in the hope of receiving economic benefits down the road. When a corporation realizes profits, its shareholders want a distribution of a share of those profits. Although most shareholders understand that sometimes profits must be reinvested in the business in order for the corporation to grow, a board of directors which regularly fails to declare dividends will soon find itself voted out of office.

State statutes give the board of directors fairly broad discretion to make distributions to shareholders, subject to one major limitation: the corporation must be solvent. Dividends may not be paid out to shareholders by the board of directors if, after the dividends are so paid, the corporation would not have the ability to pay its debts as they become due in the ordinary course of business. In making a determination as to the corporation's solvency, the board of directors often uses the **balance sheet test**. Under this test, a corporation may make dividend distributions if, after payment of all liabilities, the corporation is left with net assets in excess of dissolution preferences to preferred shareholders. This means that the board of directors must look at the corporate financial records and consider whether the corporation at this moment in time has enough assets to not only pay off its creditors but also, should it dissolve right now, pay out to preferred shareholders the par value of their shares. Although the balance sheet test is the test most commonly used, state statutes may differ in their requirements and therefore should be checked.

Dividends are paid to all holders of stock on a designated date as set forth in the bylaws or determined by the board of directors, referred to as the **record date**. Note that "record date" in Chapter 9 refers to the holders of voting shares on a designated date because the phrase is used in two instances: determining those shareholders entitled to payment of dividends and determining those shareholders entitled to vote at a shareholders' meeting. If the board of directors decides to declare payment of dividends, the decision to do so should be evidenced by a resolution, such as the one provided in Exhibit 8.3 below.

EXHIBIT 8.3

Resolution of the Board of Directors of Magic Lantern Lighting Corp.

RESOLVED, that the quarterly dividend of the Magic Lantern Lighting Corp. be and hereby is declared payable to holders of record as of March 31, 1997, of the common

---

EXHIBIT 8.3   *Continued*

---

stock of the Corporation, in the amount of $.50 per share, and that the Treasurer is hereby ordered to draw on the corporate funds for the payment of this dividend on March 31, 1997.

I do hereby certify that I am the duly elected Secretary of Magic Lantern Lighting Corp. and that the above is a true and correct copy of a resolution duly adopted at a meeting of the Board of Directors held on March 31, 1997.

IN WITNESS WHEREOF, I have affixed my name as Secretary and have caused the corporate seal to be affixed on this 31st day of March, 1997.

[Corporate Seal]

_____
Thelma Waters, Secretary

If the corporation's board of directors determines that all income received in a particular year should be retained by the corporation to improve its financial condition, this decision should also be noted in a resolution, such as in the one found in Exhibit 8.4.

EXHIBIT 8.4

Resolution of the Board of Directors of F & R Electronics, Inc.

RESOLVED, that the Board of Directors of F & R Electronics, Inc., in its desire to improve the financial condition of the Corporation, has ordered that no dividends be declared on the common stock of the Corporation for the fiscal year 1997, and that the earnings of the Corporation of the year 1997 be credited to the Corporation's surplus account.

I do hereby certify that I am the duly elected Secretary of F & R Electronics, Inc. and that the above is a true and correct copy of a resolution adopted at a meeting of the Board of Directors held on March 31, 1997.

IN WITNESS WHEREOF, I have affixed my name as Secretary and have caused the corporate seal to be affixed this 31st day of March, 1997.

[Corporate Seal]

_____
Bruce Henderson, Secretary

Dividends are not considered a business expense, as they represent a portion of the profits accrued by the corporation. Therefore, if the corporation is a C corporation (refer to the discussion in Chapter 6), they are taxable to the corporation. Dividends are also taxable to the shareholders receiving them, whether the corporation is a C corporation or a subchapter S corporation. In addition, recall the discussion of subchapter S corporations in Chapter 6 in which it was stated that shareholders of a subchapter S corporation are responsible for paying their proportionate share of taxes on income realized by the corporation even if this income is not distributed to them in the form of dividends.

STOCK DIVIDENDS AND STOCK SPLITS

At times, a board of directors may choose, instead of declaring cash dividends, to declare the payment of stock dividends. A **stock dividend** is the distribution to shareholders of extra shares of stock or extra fractions of shares of stock. The par value, if any, of the stock of the corporation remains the same. A stock dividend proportionately increases the number of shares of stock of each shareholder holding shares on the record date on which stock dividends are declared. Thus, shareholders are left in the same position proportionately as they were in before the stock dividend was declared, although the value of their shares is diluted because the amount of their investment now is divided into a larger number of shares.

Before declaring a stock dividend the board of directors must first determine that there are available funds in the corporation's earned surplus account. Recall that shares may not be issued for less than par value or the stated value. The aggregate amount of par value (or stated value) must be available from earned surplus to be transferred to the stated capital account of the corporation. A sample resolution authorizing the declaration of a stock dividend and the setting aside of appropriate sums from earned surplus for this purpose is found in Exhibit 8.5 below.

EXHIBIT 8.5

Resolution of the Board of Directors of The Trident Group, Inc.

RESOLVED, that the Board of Directors of The Trident Group, Inc., having determined that the Corporation has undistributed surplus funds in the amount of Three

---

EXHIBIT 8.5   *Continued*

Hundred Thousand Dollars ($300,000), has ordered that One Hundred Thousand Dollars ($100,000) be set aside from the undistributed surplus funds for the purpose of declaring a stock dividend to be distributed to all holders of common stock of the Corporation as of March 31, 1997, and that the officers of the Corporation be directed to transfer this amount from the earned surplus account to the stated capital account.

FURTHER RESOLVED, that a stock dividend has been declared in the amount of one (1) share of common stock for each one hundred (100) shares of common stock issued and outstanding as of March 31, 1997, the record date, and that the officers of the Corporation be directed to pay out this stock dividend on said record date.

I do hereby certify that I am the duly elected Secretary of The Trident Group, Inc. and that the above is a true and correct copy of a resolution duly adopted at a meeting of the Board of Directors on March 31, 1997.

IN WITNESS WHEREOF, I have affixed my name as Secretary and have caused the corporate seal to be affixed this 31st day of March, 1997.

[Corporate Seal]
_____

Nancy Cummings, Secretary

At times, the declaration of a stock dividend may result in the issuance of **fractional shares** of corporate stock. For example, a board of directors may declare that the dividend shall be equal to one share of common stock for every 50 shares of issued and outstanding common stock. If a shareholder held 225 shares of common stock prior to the declaration of the stock dividend, then after the dividend the shareholder would be entitled to four and one-half additional shares of stock. The one-half additional share is a fractional share. This fractional share may be represented by scrip. **Scrip** is a written certificate which represents a fraction of a full share of stock. When a shareholder has enough scrip to represent a full share, the scrip can be exchanged for a full stock certificate.

A stock dividend is not taxable to the shareholder at the time it is received. Rather, the income represented by stock shares received through stock dividends is taxed to the shareholder when he or she sells those shares of stock. In this way, stock dividends may be considered more advantageous to a shareholder than cash dividends, which are taxed when received.

A **stock split** is an action declared by a corporation's board of directors (unless state statute, the articles of incorporation, or the bylaws require a vote of the shareholders) which divides the shares of a corporation into a larger number of shares with each shareholder receiving his or her proportionate number of additional shares. For example, if a corporation's board of directors declares a four-to-one stock split, the owner of 100 shares of stock will now own 400 shares. A stock split leaves each shareholder with the same percentage of ownership interest in the corporation as he or she had before the split occurred and is considered by the Internal Revenue Service to be a nontaxable event because the shareholders are left in the same financial position as before the declaration of the stock split. The purpose of a stock split is to bring down the price of each share of stock, thereby making the stock cheaper and more attractive to potential investors. If, for example, the stock of DataMax Corporation, a computer software company, was initially selling at $400 per share, after the stock split the stock would be valued at $100 per share. Investors rarely purchase one or two shares of stock, preferring to purchase in larger increments. At $100 per share, a potential investor may find DataMax stock more attractive.

To effectuate a stock split, the corporation must have an adequate number of authorized shares of stock. If the number of authorized shares set forth in the articles of incorporation is too low, the articles of incorporation must be amended. Amendment of the articles typically requires shareholder approval. Further, if the par value of the stock is to be reduced by the stock split, the articles likewise will have to be amended accordingly.

A **reverse stock split** is the division of the number of authorized shares of a corporation into a lesser number. Here again, the shareholders continue to maintain their proportionate ownership interests in the corporation but now these ownership interests are reflected by fewer shares (e.g., a shareholder owning 20,000 shares of common stock will own 5,000 shares after a four-to-one reverse stock split). Again, because the number of authorized shares is being altered, the articles of incorporation must be amended by a vote of the shareholders. Unlike a regular stock split in which shareholders are issued additional shares, in a reverse stock split shareholders must redeem their current stock certificates for new certificates reflecting the decrease of shares of stock owned.

BONDS AND DEBENTURES

As noted at the beginning of the chapter, bonds and debentures are types of debt securities. The corporation issues these instruments as a means of raising capital, pledging to pay the holder a stated percent of interest and to return the principal on the maturity date. The interest paid by the corporation to the holder of the bond or debenture is tax deductible to the corporation (whereas the distribution of dividends is not). Therefore, a corporation can avoid some of the perils of double taxation by having a certain percentage of the corporation's capital structure comprised of debt securities.

Essentially a bond (or debenture) is a type of loan. The difference between a bond and a debenture is that a **bond** is a secured debt instrument whereas a **debenture** is not. A bond is secured by a lien on specific corporate assets whereas a debenture is issued against the general creditworthiness of the corporation. Bonds are rated by credit rating services which rate the creditworthiness of the issuing corporations. The ratings relied upon most often are those provided by Moody's and by Standard & Poor's. Generally speaking, the lower the credit rating, the higher the interest rate the corporation pays as a trade-off for the degree of risk to the bondholder. Because the holder of a bond or debenture is a creditor rather than an owner of the corporation, the holder is not entitled to vote on corporate issues nor is the holder entitled to any share of the corporate profits. Should a corporation face financial difficulty and be forced to liquidate its assets, holders of bonds and debentures, as creditors of the corporation, receive the principal amount of the debt instrument before any assets are distributed to shareholders. Bondholders, as secured creditors, may collect the corporate assets pledged as collateral. Throughout the rest of this section, the discussion will refer simply to bonds, although most of the discussion will be applicable to debentures as well.

The terms of agreement between the issuing corporation and the holder are set forth on a written statement called an **indenture** or a **trust indenture**. This latter term reflects the fact that bonds quite often are handled by financial institutions named as trustees for the benefit of the bondholders. The indenture sets forth such items as the principal amount of the debt instrument, the amount of interest to be paid, the dates upon which the interest will be paid, and the **maturity date** (the date upon which the principal is returned to the bondholder). This list is by no means exhaustive. The interest rate paid on a bond is referred to as the **coupon rate**, and usually is paid semiannually. The bondholder "clips" the coupons attached to the bond and sends them to the corporation in order to collect the interest. The face of the bond includes the following:

1. the name of the issuing corporation;
2. the face value of the bond;
3. the name of the bondholder;
4. the trustee of the issue;
5. the coupon rate;
6. the maturity date;

7.   the signature of the authorized officer(s); and
8.   the impression of the corporate seal

Corporations can issue various types of bonds. Just as corporations can set up their capital stock structure to include convertible preferred stock, corporations can issue convertible bonds. A **convertible bond** is a bond which, like other bonds, receives a stated amount of interest each year and a repayment of principal on the maturity date, but also provides the holder with the option of converting the bond into a stated number of shares of stock in the corporation at a specified time. Suppose, for example, that a bondholder had a convertible bond with the face value of $3,000, with the option to convert the bond into 100 shares of common stock at a specified time. As long as the purchase price for the common stock is equal to or less than $30 a share the bondholder will not gain by converting the bond. However, supposing that the purchase price for the common stock increases to $45 per share, the bond would be worth $4,500 (100 shares of common stock multiplied by the purchase price of $45 per share) and the bondholder therefore may choose to convert the bond into the shares.

Another type of bond is a discounted bond. **Discounted bonds** are bonds sold for less than the face amount of the principal (e.g., the bondholder pays $4,000 for a bond with the face value of $5,000). The holder of a discounted bond receives a stated amount of interest at specified intervals, and receives the full face value (in this example, $5,000) upon maturity. A similar type of bond is the **zero-coupon bond**. This bond is also purchased at a discount (for less than face value). However, unlike the holder of a discounted bond, the holder of a zero-coupon bond does not receive interest until the maturity date of the bond (hence the name "zero-coupon" indicating that the holder has no coupons to "clip" and redeem). **Floating rate bonds** are bonds with adjustable interest rates, which rise or fall according to the rise and fall of the prime interest rate or other commonly used indicators.

A **redeemable** (or **callable**) **bond** is similar to redeemable preferred stock in that the issuing corporation may call it in on a call date. In the case of a bond, the **call date** is a date prior to the maturity date of the bond. The issuing corporation typically pays a premium for the option of calling the bond in. This premium is referred to as a **call premium**. A corporation will call in a redeemable bond when it sees an opportunity to sell new bonds at a lower interest rate.

A **mortgage bond** is precisely what its name implies, a bond secured by a mortgage on real property. Theoretically, the holder of such a bond can foreclose on the specified real property of the corporation should the corporation fail to repay the principal on the maturity date. However, the bondholder must ascertain if there are other parties with superior rights to the property, such as a financial institution which supplied a long-term loan in return for a first mortgage. If, for example, Capital Bank recorded a first mortgage against the property for a loan of $500,000 and the corporation defaults on the loan, Capital Bank has superior rights to foreclose on the property and all proceeds from the foreclosure must first go toward paying Capital Bank in full before any other party can receive monies from the sale.

ANNUAL REPORTS

An **annual report** is a comprehensive financial statement issued by a corporation on a yearly basis. Copies of these reports are provided to shareholders prior to the annual meeting of the shareholders. Because legal counsel may be consulted by corporate clients when compiling these reports, paralegals should understand the various components of an annual report. (Please note here that many corporations also distribute quarterly reports to their shareholders, the components of which are similar to those found in annual reports. Note also that corporations registered with the Securities and Exchange Commission are required to annually file a 10-K financial report with the Commission, as discussed in Chapter 6.)

The first section of an annual report is the **president's report** (sometimes referred to as the **president's letter to the shareholders**). This opening section provides an overview of the corporation's performance over the last year and may also include information on future goals and plans. If the corporation performed poorly in the last year, this section may enumerate the factors creating the poor performance and corrective action taken.

The president's report is followed by the balance sheet. The **balance sheet** provides a "snapshot" of the corporation on a designated day as an indicator of the corporation's financial condition. If a corporation has subsidiaries, then a **consolidated balance sheet** will be provided, combining figures for all subsidiaries plus the parent corporation. The balance sheet is divided into three parts: assets, liabilities, and shareholders' equity. When all items are added, the corporate assets should equal the total of the liabilities plus the shareholders' equity. Corporate assets are listed first, including current assets, securities, and fixed assets. **Current assets** are cash and all other assets that are easily convertible into cash within the course of the year (e.g., inventory and accounts receivable). **Securities** are instruments reflecting investments made by the corporation to earn a high rate of return (e.g., Treasury bills). **Fixed assets** are assets used to generate income for the corporation, such as factories and equipment.

The assets are followed by corporate liabilities. These include **current liabilities**, which are obligations that should be paid by the corporation within the year (e.g., accounts payable), and **fixed liabilities**, which are long-term loans plus bonds and debentures issued by the corporation.

Shareholders' equity is comprised of the par value of common stock, the par value of preferred stock, additional **paid-in capital** (the amount above par value which the corporation received from the sale of stocks), and **retained earnings** (the profit earned by the corporation after paying dividends). Note that paid-in capital is another name for capital surplus and retained earnings is another name for earned surplus. A sample balance sheet is provided in Exhibit 8.6.

EXHIBIT 8.6

Balance Sheet
Scherezade Rug Company
December 31, 1996

ASSETS

Cash	$ 150,000
Securities	$ 300,000
Inventory	$ 200,000
Current Assets	$ 650,000
Factory	$ 750,000
Equipment	$ 325,000
Total Assets	$1,725,000

LIABILITIES

Accounts payable	$ 75,000
Accrued taxes	$ 60,000
Bank note	$ 175,000
Current Liabilities	$ 310,000
Long-term loan	$ 500,000
Total Liabilities	$ 810,000

EXHIBIT 8.6   *Continued*

SHAREHOLDERS' EQUITY

Preferred stock ($10 par)	$ 300,000
Common stock ($5 par)	$ 400,000
Additional paid-in capital	$ 100,000
Retained earnings	$ 115,000
Total Shareholders' Equity	$ 915,000
Total Liabilities and Shareholders' Equity	$1,725,000

The next section of an annual report is the **income statement** (also referred to as the **profit and loss statement** or **earnings report**). In some annual reports, this statement will appear before the balance sheet. Whereas the balance sheet presents a *micro* view of the corporation's financial position by looking at one day, the income statement presents a *macro* view. The income statement is a cumulative report of the profits and losses accrued by the corporation's operations for the entire year, presented both as an aggregate figure and as a per share amount (earnings per share is calculated by dividing the net profit of the corporation by the total number of outstanding shares). Data is given for the last three years (or more) of operation to allow the shareholder to compare current performance with the performance of previous years. A sample income statement for one year is provided below in Exhibit 8.7. Remember that a completed report will provide data for at least three years. Note on the exhibit that among other items listed, the statement includes depreciation and amortization. Recall from earlier chapters that **depreciation** is a device to allocate the loss of value of a fixed asset (such as a piece of machinery) over a period of years, and that **amortization** is a device to allocate the loss of value of an intangible asset (such as a patent) over a period of years.

EXHIBIT 8.7

Income Statement
Bearhug Toy Company
For the Year Ended December 31, 1996

Net Sales		$20,000,000
Cost of Goods Sold	$5,200,000	
Marketing and Administrative		
Expenses	$3,250,000	
Depreciation	$ 600,000	
Amortization	$ 175,000	
Total Operating Expenses		$ 9,225,000
Operating Income		$ 3,500,000
Other Income		$ 200,000
Income Before Income Taxes		$ 3,700,000
Federal, State, and Local		
Taxes	$1,480,000	
Net Income		$ 2,220,000
Earnings per common share		$.52
Average number of common shares		4,250,000

In addition to these three major sections, an annual report may include a statement showing the increase or decrease in the working capital. This statement is often referred to as the **statement of changes in financial position**. The report will be illustrated with graphs and charts dissecting portions of the balance sheet or income statement. The annual report concludes with the **accountant's report**, which verifies that the figures presented in the report were reviewed by an independent certified accountant.

Chapter Summary

1. A corporation's capital structure may be comprised of both equity and debt securities. Equity securities are shares of stock and provide the holder with

an ownership interest in the corporation. Debt securities, such as bonds and debentures, confer creditor status on the holder. The return received by a holder of equity securities is a pro rata share of the corporation's profits paid out as dividends. The return received by the holder of debt securities is a stated rate of interest on the principal loaned by the holder to the corporation.

2. When formulating a corporation's capital stock structure, factors to be taken into account include the number of shares to be issued to the initial shareholders, the number of unissued shares to be held in reserve, the desirability (or lack thereof) of dividing shares into different classes with varying ownership rights, and the choice of assigning (or not assigning) a par value to the stock.

3. Small corporations often choose a simple capital stock structure, authorizing only one kind of stock, common stock, in their articles of incorporation. Holders of common stock enjoy three basic rights: voting rights, dividend rights, and liquidation rights. The last two common stock rights are residual rights inasmuch as preferred shareholders are paid dividends or liquidation distributions first, common shareholders only receiving their pro rata share out of the residual.

4. The basic rights accorded to holders of preferred stock are the right to fixed dividends and the right to a percentage of the par value of their aggregate shares of stock upon liquidation. Preferred stock may be authorized in many variations including, but not limited to, participating preferred (receiving the additional right to residual dividends), convertible preferred (receiving the additional right to convert preferred shares into a certain amount of common shares), and cumulative preferred (receiving the additional right to back dividends).

5. Before stock can be issued to a shareholder, the board of directors must find that the proffered consideration is of reasonable value (which may never be less than the par value of the stock). Having made this determination, the board of directors must formally approve the offer to purchase shares either at a board of directors' meeting or through written consent. The corporation's secretary (or a corporate paralegal) will then take the requisite steps for issuing stock certificates. The names of the shareholders and the method of title-holding will be verified, both the stock certificates and the certificate stubs will be filled in with the appropriate information, the certificates will be signed by designated officers (manually or by facsimile) and impressed with the corporate seal, the documentary stamp tax will be calculated, and the transactions will be recorded in the stock ledger.

6. A corporation's annual report is a yearly, comprehensive financial statement, providing both micro and macro examinations of the corporation's financial condition. The three main sections of the report are the president's report,

the balance sheet, and the income statement. The report also may include charts, graphs, and miscellaneous financial statements. The accountant's report is found at the end of the report, the accountant verifying the accuracy of the reported figures.

Review Questions

1. Compare and contrast the following:
    (i)   authorized shares
    (ii)   issued shares
    (iii) treasury shares
    (iv)   uncertified shares
2. Explain the concepts of stated capital, capital surplus, and earned surplus.
3. Why would a board of directors decide to assign a par value to corporate stock?
4. List the steps to be taken to prepare and issue a stock certificate.
5. Compare and contrast the following:
    (i)   convertible bond
    (ii)   discounted bond
    (iii) zero-coupon bond
    (iv)   floating rate bond

KEY TERMS

accountant's report	capital surplus
annual report	common stock
authorized shares	consolidated balance
balance sheet	sheet
balance sheet test	convertible bond
bond	coupon rate
call	cumulative preferred
call date	stock
call premium	current assets
capital stock	current liabilities
capital structure	debenture

debt securities
discounted bond
documentary stamp tax
earned surplus
equity securities
fixed assets
floating rate bond
fractional share
income statement
indenture
issued shares
maturity date
mortgage bond
option
outstanding shares
paid-in capital
participating preferred
    stock
preferred stock
president's report
put

redeemable preferred
    stock
retained earnings
reverse stock split
scrip
securities
series
shareholders' equity
sinking fund
stated capital
stated value
statement of changes
stock
stock certificate
stock dividend
stock split
straight preferred stock
treasury shares
uncertified shares
unissued shares
watered stock
zero-coupon bond

9 | *Corporate Meetings*

Overview of Objectives

Upon completion of this chapter, the student will:

- know how to prepare notices of meetings and waivers of notice
- know how to prepare minutes of organizational, shareholders', and board of directors' meetings as well as written consents in lieu of meetings
- understand the concept of cumulative voting
- know how to prepare certified resolutions

INTRODUCTION

As noted previously, a corporation must adhere to certain formalities in order to protect the limited liability of its owners, the shareholders. These formalities perpetuate the concept that a corporation is a legal entity separate from its owners. The holding of corporate meetings, beginning with the organizational meeting and continuing with other requisite meetings of shareholders and directors, plays a significant role in the maintenance of statutorily prescribed formalities. The drafting of **minutes** (a detailed record of all actions taken at a corporate meeting) is necessary as evidence that the meetings have taken place and that certain actions received approval by the appropriate authorities. Third parties having business with the corporation may request evidence of corporate approval for such matters as the sale of real property or authorization for a loan. Directors and officers want written records that actions taken by them on behalf of the corporation were approved. Written records of resolutions are required to protect certain tax benefits sought by the corporation and to avoid penalties.

Your role as a paralegal is considerable in assuring that these formalities are enforced and properly documented. This chapter addresses the purpose and conduct of corporate meetings as well as the tasks a paralegal may be asked to perform in arranging and documenting these meetings. These tasks include sending out applicable notices or obtaining waivers of notice, preparing written consents in lieu of meetings, preparing resolutions and meeting minutes, preparing other documents requiring approval at corporate meetings, handling stock transfers, and maintaining the corporate minute book by making sure that all necessary documents are inserted and organized for easy access.

ORGANIZATIONAL MEETINGS

The first meeting a paralegal must arrange is the **organizational meeting**, which is typically held directly after incorporation. The details attended to at this meeting allow the corporation to start transacting business. State statute dictates who must hold the organizational meeting (i.e., the incorporators, shareholders, or directors). In many states, the directors may hold the organizational meeting if the first board of directors is named in the articles of incorporation. If the directors are not so named, then two organizational meetings may be necessary. The first is the organizational meeting of the incorporators during which directors will be elected and the corporate bylaws approved, followed by a second meeting of the newly elected directors to conduct all other organizational business. In some states, all organizational business may be conducted at the organizational meeting of the incorporators. State statute may allow the organizational business of the corporation to be effected by written consent rather than the holding of an actual meeting.

At times a nominal board of directors may be named in the articles of incorporation (i.e., the attorneys and paralegals representing the client corporation or the employees of a corporate service bureau or agency). Once the corporation is created by the filing of the articles of incorporation, these directors must be replaced by those persons who actually intend to manage the corporation. One common method of effectuating the transition from nominal to actual directors is to have the nominal directors resign at the organizational meeting and have new directors elected to take their place.

The business typically conducted at an organizational meeting includes the following:

1. documentation of the filing of the articles of incorporation;
2. election of the first board of directors, if not named in the articles of incorporation;
3. adoption of the bylaws;
4. election of corporate officers;
5. approval of the corporate seal;
6. approval of the form of stock certificate;
7. adoption of the corporation's fiscal year;
8. approval of all expenses incurred to date by the promoter(s) and/or incorporator(s) in the formation of the corporation and authorization of the treasurer to reimburse appropriate parties for these expenditures;
9. authorization of the secretary to open and maintain the corporate books;
10. adoption of a banking resolution setting up the corporate bank account(s);
11. authorization of specified officers to sign documents on behalf of the corporation;
12. acceptance of any subscription agreements; and
13. issuance of shares of stock to the initial shareholders

In addition to the above matters, an organizational meeting is the appropriate time to consider the following matters:

1. adoption of subchapter S election;
2. adoption of a plan for offering common stock under Section 1244 of the Internal Revenue Code;
3. adoption of Section 248 of the Internal Revenue Code allowing for the amortization of certain organizational expenses;
4. appointment of an executive committee;
5. approval of a shareholders' restrictive agreement;
6. approval of any employment agreements; and
7. ratification of any agreements entered into by the promoter(s) on behalf of the corporation.

A.   *Preparation for an Organizational Meeting*

The first task of the paralegal is to determine who is required to attend the organizational meeting of the corporation and then to determine what notice is statutorily required to be given to those persons required to attend. State statutes usually specify that notice must be given in writing unless the articles of incorporation permit oral notice. If oral notice is permitted, it is considered effective when communicated in person or by telephone to the person required to be notified. If written notice is required, it is considered effective when mailed or, where permitted, sent by facsimile or electronic mail. It is common for incorporators or directors to waive notice. In either instance (where notice is given or waiver of notice occurs) the paralegal must prepare the appropriate documentation, such as found in Exhibits 9.1 and 9.2 below.

EXHIBIT 9.1

Notice of Organizational Meeting

To: All Directors

The organizational meeting of directors of National Commercial Enterprises, Inc. will be held at 10:00 A.M. on Wednesday, March 19, 1997, at the corporate offices located at 2970 Franklin Avenue, Suite 301, Any City, Any State. The purpose of this meeting shall be to approve corporate bylaws, elect officers of the corporation, and to conduct such other organizational business coming before the directors. Any director unable to attend should contact the law firm of Trumbull and McDonald, P.A. at (000) 555-1111 on or before March 4, 1997.

EXHIBIT 9.2

Waiver of Notice of Organizational Meeting

We, the undersigned, constituting all of the directors of National Commercial Enterprises, Inc., a corporation duly organized under the laws of the State of Any State, do hereby waive all statutory notice of the organizational meeting of directors and con-

---

EXHIBIT 9.2 *Continued*

---

sent that the meeting shall take place at 10:00 A.M. on Wednesday, March 19, 1997, at the corporate offices located at 2970 Franklin Avenue, Suite 301, Any City, Any State.

Dated: March 3, 1997

_____
Michael Halladay, Director

_____
Priscilla Bradley, Director

_____
Nathaniel Travis, Director

_____
Marion Driscoll, Director

A copy of the notice or the original signed waiver of notice should be placed in the corporate minute book.

If not attended to prior to the sending of notices or waivers, the paralegal should immediately thereafter determine what documents must be completed prior to the organizational meeting. In addition to the bylaws, the paralegal may be asked to prepare or assist in preparing a shareholders' restrictive agreement, employment agreements, and other documents to be approved at the organizational meeting. For example, a shareholders' restrictive agreement should be signed by all designated shareholders (and quite often, the corporation) and then approved at the organizational meeting before the issuance of the first shares of stock. Similarly, a banking **resolution** (a written statement authorizing that certain actions be taken by designated persons on behalf of the corporation) should be prepared to be signed by the directors authorizing the opening of a corporate bank account and all attendant banking matters. This resolution can then be approved at the organizational meeting. Most banks will not permit a corporate account to be opened unless a banking resolution is provided, together with a certified copy of the articles of incorporation. It is quite difficult for the corporation to transact business until a corporate bank account is opened.

B.   *Minutes of an Organizational Meeting*

If an organizational meeting is to be held (as opposed to a written consent in lieu of a meeting), the paralegal may be asked to attend the meeting and then prepare minutes or may be asked to customize "form" minutes provided in the corporate minute book or on file in the firm's computer form file. If corporate statutes allow a written consent in lieu of a meeting, the paralegal will be responsible for preparing the consent for signature. Exhibits 9.3 and 9.4 below provide examples of the minutes of the organizational meeting of incorporators and the organizational meeting of the board of directors, respectively.

EXHIBIT 9.3

Minutes of the Organizational Meeting of
Incorporators of TCS Pharmaceuticals, Inc.

A meeting of the incorporators of TCS Pharmaceuticals, Inc., a corporation duly authorized under the laws of the State of Any State, was held at the corporate offices located at 1300 Corporate Boulevard, Any City, Any State on February 21, 1997 at 3:00 P.M. pursuant to waiver of notice. The following persons, being all of the incorporators of the Corporation, were present at the meeting:

Theodore C. Strickland
Patrick K. Strickland

The meeting was called to order by Theodore C. Strickland and, upon motion duly made, seconded, and carried, Theodore C. Strickland was chosen to act as Chair of the meeting and Patrick K. Strickland was chosen to act as Secretary. The Secretary presented the waiver of notice of meeting and, there being no objection, the Chair indicated that the waiver be filed in the corporate minute book. The Chair then stated that the meeting was to be held in compliance with the statutes of the State of Any State.

The Secretary reported that the articles of incorporation of the Corporation had been filed with the Secretary of State's office on February 5, 1997 and that a Certificate of Incorporation had been issued by the Secretary of State on February 10, 1997. Upon motion duly made, seconded, and carried it was

EXHIBIT 9.3 *Continued*

RESOLVED, that the Certificate of Incorporation, together with a certified copy of the articles of incorporation are hereby approved and the Secretary be directed to insert these documents in the corporate minute book.

The Secretary next presented a proposed form of bylaws for the regulation and management of the Corporation's affairs which were then read and upon motion duly made, seconded, and carried it was

RESOLVED, that the proposed bylaws be adopted as the bylaws of the Corporation and that the Secretary be directed to insert a copy of the bylaws in the corporate minute book.

The Chair then stated that the bylaws provided for the election of directors of the Corporation and in keeping with such provision, called for nomination of directors whereupon, upon motion duly made, seconded, and carried, the following persons were nominated as directors:

Theodore C. Strickland

Patrick K. Strickland

Upon unanimous vote of the incorporators, the Chair declared that Theodore C. Strickland and Patrick K. Strickland were elected as directors of the Corporation, to hold office until the first annual meeting of the shareholders or until their respective successors are elected.

Upon motion duly made, seconded, and carried it was

RESOLVED, that the Board of Directors be authorized in its discretion to issue from time to time shares in the capital stock of the Corporation in such amounts and for such consideration as determined by the Board of Directors and as permitted by law.

There being no further business to come before the meeting, upon motion duly made, seconded, and carried the meeting was adjourned.

Dated: February 21, 1997

_____

Patrick K. Strickland, Secretary

EXHIBIT 9.4

Minutes of the First Meeting of the
Board of Directors of TCS Pharmaceuticals, Inc.

The first meeting of the Board of Directors of TCS Pharmaceuticals, Inc., a corporation duly authorized under the laws of the State of Any State, was held at the corporate offices located at 1300 Corporate Boulevard, Any City, Any State, on February 21, 1997 at 3:30 P.M., pursuant to waiver of notice. The following directors, being all of the directors of the Corporation, were present:

Theodore C. Strickland
Patrick K. Strickland

Theodore C. Strickland called the meeting to order and, upon motion duly made, seconded, and carried, Theodore C. Strickland was chosen as Chair of the meeting and Patrick K. Strickland was chosen as Secretary. The Chair then stated that the meeting was to be held in compliance with the statutes of the State of Any State.

The Secretary presented the Minutes of the Organizational Meeting of the Incorporators of the Corporation held at 3:00 P.M. Upon motion duly made, seconded, and carried it was

RESOLVED, that the Minutes of the Organizational Meeting of the Incorporators of the Corporation be approved and that the bylaws adopted at said organizational meeting of the incorporators be approved and adopted by the Board of Directors as the bylaws of the Corporation.

The Chair then called for the nomination of officers of the Corporation and upon motion duly made, seconded, and carried the following persons were nominated to serve in the offices set forth below opposite their names:

Theodore C. Strickland   President and Treasurer
Patrick K. Strickland   Vice President and Secretary

Upon unanimous vote of the directors, the Chair then declared that Theodore C. Strickland and Patrick K. Strickland were elected to serve in the above respective offices in accordance with the provisions of the bylaws until their respective successors are elected and qualify.

EXHIBIT 9.4   *Continued*

The Secretary presented a proposed corporate seal conforming to the provisions of the statutes of Any State, the seal making the following impression:

(SEAL)

Upon motion duly made, seconded, and carried it was

RESOLVED, that the seal in the form presented to this meeting be and hereby is approved and adopted as the corporate seal of the Corporation.

The Secretary next presented a specimen form of stock certificate of the Corporation representing shares of the Corporation. Upon motion duly made, seconded, and carried it was

RESOLVED, that the form of stock certificate for shares of capital stock of the Corporation presented to the meeting be and hereby is approved and adopted as the stock certificate of the Corporation and a specimen copy of said certificate shall be inserted in the corporate minute book. Stock certificates in such form and appropriately completed shall be signed by the President and Secretary of the Corporation.

Further, it was

RESOLVED, that the Corporation's fiscal year shall commence on January 1 of each year and shall end on December 31 of each year.

The Treasurer then presented a banking resolution authorizing the opening of a corporate account at Patriot Bank and upon motion duly made, seconded, and carried it was

RESOLVED, that the banking resolution directed to Patriot Bank and presented at this meeting be adopted in its entirety, a copy of which shall be inserted in the corporate minute book.

The Chair then submitted statements of expenses incurred to date in connection with the organization of the Corporation, including but not limited to, all professional

EXHIBIT 9.4   *Continued*

services and taxes. Upon motion duly made, seconded, and carried, the Treasurer was directed to reimburse from corporate funds all persons for expenditures so incurred.

It was further

RESOLVED, that the President, Vice President, Treasurer or Secretary of the Corporation be, and each hereby is, authorized to sign for and on behalf of the Corporation and in its corporate name all documents necessary in the ordinary course of business; and that the Secretary hereby is authorized to affix the corporate seal to any such document and to certify under such seal and issue copies of any resolution adopted by the Board of Directors or shareholders of the Corporation.

The Chair next presented to the directors the advantages of adopting a plan for offering common stock in accordance with Section 1244 of the Internal Revenue Code available to small business corporations, permitting ordinary loss treatment for losses sustained on stock sold or exchanged. Upon motion duly made, seconded, and carried it was

RESOLVED, that the following plan for offering common stock under Section 1244 of the Internal Revenue Code be adopted:

PLAN TO ISSUE SECTION 1244 STOCK

Adopted on February 21, 1997

1. The Corporation is a "small business corporation" as defined in Section 1244(c)(2) of the Internal Revenue Code.
2. The common stock of the Corporation, none of which has yet been issued, will be offered for sale only in accordance with this plan while this plan remains in effect.
3. The Board of Directors of the Corporation shall sell and issue as many shares of common stock and at such prices, payable in cash or other property (other than capital stock, securities, or services rendered) as from time to time it deems to be in the best interests of the Corporation, subject to the following:
   a. The maximum amount to be received by the Corporation in consideration of the common stock to be issued pursuant to this plan shall be a maximum of $1,000,000 and the equity capital of the Corporation shall not exceed $1,000,000.

EXHIBIT 9.4 *Continued*

b. The offer to sell and issue common stock shall remain in full force and effect until said shares are sold or for a period of two years from the above indicated date of adoption of this plan by the Board of Directors, whichever occurs first.

4. This plan shall be interpreted and construed in such manner and the Corporation will take such further steps as will enable this plan to qualify under Section 1244 of the Internal Revenue Code, as amended, and as will enable the shares of common stock issued hereunder to qualify as "Section 1244 stock," as defined in said section.

The Chair next stated that certain subscriptions for shares of the corporate stock had been executed prior to the filing of the articles of incorporation, as follows:

Theodore C. Strickland	30,000 shares of common stock for $60,000
Adrienne B. Strickland	10,000 shares of common stock for $20,000
Patrick K. Strickland	25,000 shares of common stock for $50,000
Kristin R. Strickland	10,000 shares of common stock for $20,000

The Chair then stated that the laws of the State of Any State provide that it is the responsibility of the Board of Directors to determine whether the consideration offered for shares of stock is reasonable and to determine the time and manner of payment of stock subscriptions. Upon motion duly made, seconded, and carried it was

RESOLVED, that the Board of Directors of the Corporation having determined that the consideration offered by the subscribers was of a value at least equal to the par value of the stock to be issued and having further determined that the consideration offered was reasonable, that the subscription agreements be and hereby are accepted and that upon delivery of the total consideration indicated in the subscription agreements, stock certificates be issued to the subscribers for the number of shares indicated in the subscription agreements and that upon such issuance the subscribers shall then constitute shareholders of the Corporation.

There being no further business to come before the meeting, on motion duly made, seconded, and carried, the meeting was adjourned.

Dated: February 21, 1997

_____

Patrick K. Strickland, Secretary

In reviewing the above minutes, a certain logical order becomes apparent. In the minutes of the organizational meeting of the incorporators, the first order of the day is to ascertain whether the meeting is conducted lawfully. This entails ascertaining first whether proper notification was made or waivers obtained and whether the statutorily prescribed quorum is present. Once this is done a chairperson must be chosen to run the meeting and a secretary chosen to take down the minutes of the meeting (please note that once officers of the corporation are elected, the task of minute-taking shall fall upon the shoulders of the elected secretary). One task of a secretary is to maintain corporate records. Therefore, the secretary presents various documents for approval. The articles of incorporation, having been previously filed, are not submitted for approval as such; rather, the filing information is noted for the record to indicate that the corporation has been lawfully created. The bylaws regulate the conduct of meetings, the qualifications and terms of directors and officers, and other provisions pertaining to the formalities of corporate life. Thus, the approval of the bylaws typically occurs toward the beginning of the organizational meeting. Additionally, because the bylaws may dictate certain requirements to be met by the directors (i.e., must be a resident of the corporation's state of domicile, must be at least 21 years of age) it is logical that the bylaws be approved before the directors are elected by the incorporators to assure that the nominated directors meet these qualifications. Once a board of directors has been elected, the board is then authorized to issue stock.

The first meeting of the board of directors then directly follows the organizational meeting of the incorporators. Again, there is the preliminary business of ascertaining that notice and quorum requirements are met. After this is done and a chair and secretary are chosen, the secretary must officially report on the minutes of the prior meeting and the approval of the bylaws. The next order of business is the election of officers. This must be done before any stock is issued because the stock certificates must be signed by officers of the corporation. Once officers are elected, the corporate seal and form of stock certificates are approved. Although many states do not require that the impression of the corporate seal is necessary to validate contracts entered into by the corporation, some states require that the impression of the corporate seal appear on mortgage instruments and deeds executed by officers of the corporation. In addition, state statutes may require that the impression of the seal appear on stock certificates and on documents filed with state filing authorities. The banking resolution must then be approved so the officers can open a corporate bank account and deposit and distribute corporate funds. Once the account is approved, the treasurer can be authorized to reimburse from the corporate account those individuals who have incurred personal expense in the organization of the corporation and can pay any other bills that have thus far accrued. If the corporation wishes to adopt a 1244 stock plan, this should be done before any shares of stock are issued. As illustrated in Exhibit 9.4, once the plan is in place the board of directors can then determine whether offers for stock shares meet the Section 1244 requirements. In Exhibit 9.4, subscription agreements were signed prior to the filing of the articles of incorporation. Now that the corporation is legally created these subscribers can become shareholders upon paying the promised consideration for the corporate shares.

C. *Written Consent in Lieu of an Organizational Meeting*

As noted above, many states allow organizational matters to be handled by a written consent in lieu of an actual organizational meeting. Most states recognize corporations comprised of one person, that person being the sole shareholder, the sole director, and holding all official positions. Thus, a meeting under such circumstances would lack logic. Even in situations in which there are many shareholders, states will allow unanimous consent in lieu of a meeting.

Recall in the last chapter Karen was asked to assist a client in the process of incorporating. The client was an advertising, marketing, and public relations company incorporated under the name of The Graphic Image, Inc. If Karen were asked to prepare a written consent in lieu of an organizational meeting for the client, she could easily do so by referring back to the corporation formation worksheet completed during her meeting with Oliver Spires. The worksheet included the names of the directors and officers, information pertaining to bank accounts, the number of shares to be issued to the initial shareholders and the amount of consideration to be paid for the shares, the client's preference for qualification as a subchapter S corporation, for election of a Section 1244 stock plan, and for a Section 248 election. In addition, from conversations with Oliver, Karen knows that he signed a lease for office space on behalf of the corporation and has sent a copy of the lease to Karen to be inserted in the corporate file. This lease must be approved by the board of directors and a novation prepared (see earlier chapters) to transfer legal liability for the lease from Oliver to The Graphic Image, Inc. All these matters are to be addressed in the consent. Recall that Karen has already ordered the corporate kit and has prepared bylaws. She was also told by the client that the shareholders desired a shareholders' restrictive agreement (discussed in detail in Chapter 10). Assuming that such an agreement has been prepared, the consent in lieu of an organizational meeting will include a resolution approving the agreement.

Karen would also prepare a banking resolution, such as the one found later in the chapter in Exhibit 9.21, for signature and the resolution or a certified copy of it would be attached and inserted in the corporate minute book. Each bank may set forth its own requirements of the information to be contained in the resolution. Some banks even have prepared forms that may be completed by the paralegal. In addition to the resolutions, banks typically require the corporation's federal employer identification number and other proof of corporate existence, such as a copy of the certificate of incorporation or a certified copy of the filed articles. Some also want to see a copy of the corporate bylaws. Karen would have to check with the bank in question, in this instance Capitol Bank in Any City, to determine what information is required by the banking officials and what formalities must be observed as prerequisites for opening a corporate account. Karen would also request that Capitol Bank send her signature cards for the corporate officers to sign at the organizational meeting. Additionally, if the client's accountant has not already done so, she would prepare for signature by all the shareholders a 2553 form for "Election by Small Business Corporation" to qualify as a subchapter S corporation. Because the initial board of directors has been named in the articles of incorporation, the written consent Karen would prepare would be a consent of the board of directors, such as the one found in Exhibit 9.5 below.

EXHIBIT 9.5

**Unanimous Consent to Action Taken in Lieu of Organizational Meeting
by the Board of Directors of The Graphic Image, Inc.**

The undersigned, being the directors of The Graphic Image, Inc., a corporation duly organized under the laws of the State of Any State, hereby consent to and ratify the following actions taken to organize the Corporation:

RESOLVED, that the Articles of Incorporation filed with the Secretary of State of the State of Any State on February 21, 1997 was approved and a certified copy of the Articles of Incorporation, together with the Certificate of Incorporation were inserted in the corporate minute book.

RESOLVED, that bylaws regulating the business affairs of the Corporation were adopted and ordered inserted in the corporate minute book.

RESOLVED, that the following persons were elected to the offices of the Corporation set opposite their respective names to serve subject to the provisions of the bylaws until their respective successors are elected and qualify:

Oliver Spires	President
Amanda Spires	Vice President and Secretary
Lawrence Macklin	Treasurer

EXHIBIT 9.5 *Continued*

RESOLVED, that the seal, an impression of which is provided in the margin of this consent, was adopted as the seal of this Corporation.

(SEAL)

RESOLVED, that the specimen stock certificate for common stock of the Corporation attached hereto was adopted as the corporate stock certificate which, when completed, may be signed by any two (2) individuals listed as officers of the Corporation.

RESOLVED, that the Corporation's fiscal year shall commence on January 1 of each year and shall end on December 31 of each year.

RESOLVED, that the banking resolution required by Capitol Bank authorizing the opening of a corporate bank account was adopted and all drafts, checks, and notes of the Corporation, payable on said account were directed to be made in the name of the Corporation and signed by any two (2) individuals listed as officers. A copy of the resolution was ordered inserted in the corporate minute book.

RESOLVED, that the Treasurer was duly authorized to reimburse from the corporate account all parties for expenditures made by them in connection with the organization of the Corporation.

RESOLVED, that Gerald Moss be retained as the accountant for the Corporation and that the statement for his services rendered to date be paid by the Treasurer from the corporate account.

RESOLVED, that the President, Vice President, Secretary, and Treasurer of the Corporation each was authorized and empowered to sign for and on behalf of the Corporation all documents necessary in the ordinary course of business and to certify under seal any resolution adopted by the Board of Directors or shareholders of the Corporation.

RESOLVED, that a certain lease between Sinclair Property Management, Inc. and Oliver Spires on behalf of the Corporation for office space located at 1440 Adams Avenue, Any City, Any State, was approved and ratified by the Corporation and a copy of the lease inserted in the corporate records.

FURTHER RESOLVED, that a novation to substitute the Corporation for Oliver Spires as lessee on the above-mentioned lease was executed by the President of the Corporation with directions that it be forwarded to Sinclair Property Management, Inc. for signature. A copy of the novation was directed to be inserted in the corporate records.

EXHIBIT 9.5   °Continued

RESOLVED, that the Board of Directors was authorized, in its discretion, to issue the capital stock of the Corporation to the full amount or number of shares authorized by the Articles of Incorporation in such amounts and for such consideration as determined from time to time by the Board and as permitted by law.

RESOLVED, that the Corporation elected to be taxed as a small business corporation for income tax purposes under the provisions of Section 1362 of the Internal Revenue Code as it hereafter exists or is subsequently amended.

FURTHER RESOLVED, that the officers of the Corporation are to obtain and file within the required time the consent of all shareholders of the Corporation to this election and to do any other acts required for compliance with Section 1362 of the Internal Revenue Code.

FURTHER RESOLVED, that the officers of the Corporation are directed to file with the Internal Revenue Service a Form 2553 for the Corporation to be taxed as an S corporation and that a copy of Form 2553 be inserted in the corporate minute book.

RESOLVED, that the following plan for offering common stock under Section 1244 of the Internal Revenue Service be adopted:

PLAN TO ISSUE SECTION 1244 STOCK

Adopted March 4, 1997

1. The Corporation is a "small business corporation" as defined in Section 1244(c)(2) of the Internal Revenue Code.
2. The common stock of the Corporation, none of which has yet been issued, will be offered for sale only in accordance with this plan while this plan remains in effect.
3. The Board of Directors of the Corporation shall sell and issue as many shares of common stock and at such prices, payable in cash or other property (other than capital stock, securities, or services rendered) as from time to time it deems to be in the best interests of the Corporation, subject to the following:
    a. The maximum amount to be received by the Corporation in consideration of the common stock to be issued pursuant to this plan shall be a maximum of $1,000,000 and the equity capital of the Corporation shall not exceed $1,000,000.

EXHIBIT 9.5   *Continued*

    b. The offer to sell and issue common stock shall remain in full force and effect until said shares are sold or for a period of two (2) years from the above indicated date of adoption of this plan by the Board of Directors, whichever occurs first.

    4. This plan shall be interpreted and construed in such manner and the Corporation will take such further steps as will enable this plan to qualify under Section 1244 of the Internal Revenue Code, as amended, and as will enable the shares of common stock issued hereunder to qualify as "Section 1244 stock," as defined in said Section.

RESOLVED, that the directors approved the shareholders' restrictive agreement dated March 4, 1997 which sets forth the rights and restrictions imposed on the transferring of corporate shares and that a copy of the shareholders' restrictive agreement be inserted in the corporate minute book.

RESOLVED, that the Corporation accepted the offer of Oliver Spires to purchase 20,000 shares of the common stock of the Corporation under the terms and conditions of the above-mentioned shareholders' restrictive agreement, par value one dollar ($1) per share, and that the Corporation issue and deliver to Oliver Spires said 20,000 shares of common stock upon payment of twenty thousand dollars ($20,000) as full consideration for the stock, the directors having found this sum to be at least equal to the full par value of the stock and to be reasonable consideration for said shares.

RESOLVED, that the Corporation accepted the offer of Amanda Spires to purchase 20,000 shares of the common stock of the Corporation under the terms and conditions of the above-mentioned shareholders' restrictive agreement, par value one dollar ($1) per share, and that the Corporation issue and deliver to Amanda Spires said 20,000 shares of common stock upon payment of twenty thousand dollars ($20,000) as full consideration for the stock, the directors having found this sum to be at least equal to the full par value of the stock and to be reasonable consideration for said shares.

RESOLVED, that the Corporation accepted the offer of Lawrence Macklin to purchase 20,000 shares of the common stock of the Corporation under the terms and conditions of the above-mentioned shareholders' restrictive agreement, par value one dollar ($1) per share, and that the Corporation issue and deliver to Lawrence Macklin said 20,000 shares of common stock upon payment of twenty thousand dollars ($20,000) as full consideration for the stock, the directors having found this sum to be at least equal to the full par value of the stock and to be reasonable consideration for said shares.

EXHIBIT 9.5   *Continued*

RESOLVED, that the Corporation elected to amortize its organizational expenditures over a period of sixty (60) months or five (5) years as permitted under Section 248 of the Internal Revenue Code, commencing with the month of March 1997.

FURTHER RESOLVED, that the officers of the Corporation were directed to prepare a statement and attach said statement to the corporate return for the 1997 taxable year.

DATED: March 4, 1997

Oliver Spires
Director
Amanda Spires
Director
Lawrence Macklin
Director

SHAREHOLDERS' MEETINGS

A paralegal may be asked to arrange for and, at times, attend shareholders' meetings. Therefore, it is important for a paralegal to have an understanding of such topics as quorum and notice requirements, record date and record shareholders, voting lists, proxies, ballots, and inspectors' reports.

Shareholders' meetings fall into two categories: annual meetings and special meetings. Every corporation is required by state statute to hold an annual meeting of the shareholders. The principal purpose of this meeting is the election of directors to the corporation's board of directors, although other corporate business may be conducted at this meeting as well. The subject of shareholders' meetings is covered in the corporate bylaws, which may set the meeting date or specify that the date may be set by the board of directors. The annual meeting may be conducted at the corporate headquarters or at any other location specified in the bylaws or determined by the board.

To keep track of the corporate matters that occur on a regular basis, such as annual meetings, a paralegal may choose to keep a "tickler" system of index cards for each corporate client indicating important dates, similar to the example provided in Exhibit 9.6 below.

EXHIBIT 9.6

Corporate Tickler File

CLIENT NUMBER: _____

ATTORNEY: _____

NAME OF CORPORATION: _____

ADDRESS OF CORPORATION: _____

TELEPHONE: _____ FAX: _____

PRESIDENT: _____

VICE PRESIDENT: _____

SECRETARY: _____

TREASURER: _____

ANNUAL MEETING DATE: _____

NOTICE REQUIREMENTS FOR
ANNUAL MEETING: _____

DATE FOR ANNUAL RETURN: _____

DATE(S) FOR SUBMISSION OF REPORTS TO SHAREHOLDERS: _____

The paralegal can then file these index cards in a tickler file under a date which provides sufficient advance notice for preparation of all tasks that must be completed before the meeting. For example, if a corporation's annual meeting of the shareholders is to take place on March 30 and the bylaws indicate that notice of the meeting be sent not more than 60 days and not less than ten days prior to the meeting, the paralegal can insert the tickler card under the month of January behind the tab card numbered 30 and this will serve as a reminder to contact the corporate client on January 30 in order to begin coordinating all tasks necessary for the upcoming annual meeting.

A. Preparation for an Annual Meeting

Prior to the holding of the annual meeting, a determination must be made as to the shareholders entitled to vote at the meeting. To determine the shareholders entitled to vote the bylaws may fix, or provide a method of fixing, the **record date** (a fixed date upon which a corporation checks its records to verify the shareholders holding voting stock). All shareholders holding voting stock on that date, as reflected in the corporation's stock transfer books, are considered **record shareholders** and must receive notification of the meeting. In most states, if the bylaws do not fix a record date then the board of directors may fix the date. If the board of directors does not provide for the record date, then state statutes usually mandate that the record date for shareholders entitled to notice of and to vote at the annual meeting is the close of the business day before the first notice of the annual meeting is delivered to shareholders.

Once the record shareholders are determined, a **voting list** must be compiled, listing in alphabetical order the names and addresses of all record shareholders, together with the number, class, and series of corporate shares represented by each. This list must be available for inspection at the corporate offices for a statutorily prescribed period prior to the annual meeting (i.e., ten days) and must be made available at the meeting.

After the voting list is compiled, notices must be sent to all record shareholders. State statutes specify the time period within which notice of the annual meeting must be sent (e.g., no fewer than ten and no more than 60 days before the meeting date). If notice is sent by mail it is deemed delivered when deposited in the United States mail, postage prepaid, sent to the address last provided by the record shareholder to the corporation. The corporation's annual report is mailed to the record shareholders along with the notice. Some states require that the secretary of the corporation sign an affidavit swearing to the fact that the notices were mailed on the specified date in accordance with state statutes and the corporate bylaws. Exhibits 9.7 and 9.8 below provide examples of a notice to shareholders and affidavit of mailing of notice respectively.

EXHIBIT 9.7

Notice to Shareholders of Annual Meeting of
The Golden Llama Tea Company

TO: All Shareholders

The Annual Meeting of Shareholders of The Golden Llama Tea Company will be held on Monday, March 17, 1997 at 9:00 A.M. at the corporate offices located at

EXHIBIT 9.7 *Continued*

400 Waverly Road, Any City, Any State, for the purpose of electing directors and transacting such other business as may properly come before the meeting.

This notice was deposited, postage prepaid, in the United States mail on February 17, 1997.

Evelyn Lindstrom
─────────────────
Secretary

EXHIBIT 9.8

Affidavit of Mailing Notice of Annual Meeting of Shareholders of The Golden Llama Tea Company

STATE OF ANY STATE   )
                                          ss:
COUNTY OF ANY COUNTY   )

EVELYN LINDSTROM, being duly sworn according to law, deposes and says:

I am the Secretary of The Golden Llama Tea Company, and that on the seventeenth day of February, 1997, I personally deposited copies of the Notice of the Annual Meeting of the Shareholders in a post office box in the City of Any City, State of Any State.

Each copy of the notice was in a sealed, stamped envelope. One copy was addressed to each person whose name appears on the attached list and to the respective addresses shown on the list.

Evelyn Lindstrom
─────────────────
Secretary

Sworn to and subscribed before me this seventeenth day of February, 1997.

──────────────────────────
Notary Public, State of Any State
My Commission Expires:

Record shareholders may vote at the annual meeting in person or by proxy. As noted earlier in the text, a **proxy** is a shareholder's written authorization turning over to another his or her voting rights. A proxy is valid for the time period specified in the proxy form. If no time period is given then, in most states, the proxy will become invalid after 11 months from the date of the proxy. The secretary of the corporation usually sends a proxy form to record shareholders together with the notice of meeting, such as found in Exhibit 9.9.

EXHIBIT 9.9

Proxy

The undersigned shareholder hereby appoints _____ as the shareholder's general proxy to cast the votes of the shareholder at all regular and special meetings of the shareholders of The Golden Llama Tea Company, a corporation organized under the laws of the State of Any State, with all powers the shareholder would possess if personally present. This proxy shall be effective for one year from the date hereof unless revoked sooner by written notice given to the Secretary of the corporation.

DATED: _____   _____
                                                                          Shareholder

---

Shareholders may choose to waive notice of the annual meeting. For the waiver of notice to be valid it must be in writing, signed by the shareholder entitled to notice, and placed in the corporate minute book. If a shareholder fails to receive proper notice yet attends the meeting, that shareholder is considered to have waived his or her rights to object to lack of notice unless, at the beginning of the meeting, the shareholder objects to the transacting of any business at the meeting.

B.   Attending an Annual Meeting

The annual shareholders' meeting will follow a certain order. Sometimes a paralegal is asked to prepare a script or outline to be followed at the meeting. The order of business typically is as follows:

1.   The meeting is called to order.
2.   Appointment of inspectors or judges of election, if desired.
3.   Secretary reports on the service of notice to shareholders and, if required, submits an affidavit of mailing of notice. If waiver of notice is given, then the secretary submits the waiver to be inserted in the corporate minute book.
4.   Chair of the meeting is selected.
5.   Determination is made that a quorum is present either in person or by proxy.
6.   The minutes of the preceding meeting of shareholders is read or the reading of such minutes is waived.
7.   The annual report is read, unless such reading is waived.
8.   The reports of the officers are read.
9.   Nominations for directors are presented.
10.   Ballots are completed and tallied.
11.   Proposals for other actions to be taken at the meeting are presented and deliberated.
12.   Votes on these proposals are taken.
13.   The inspectors' report is read (if applicable).
14.   Adjournment.

To assure smooth sailing at the annual meeting, the paralegal should make sure that certain items are at hand. State statutes do not specify the rules to be followed at corporate meetings. Most corporations choose to conduct their meetings in accordance with *Robert's Rules of Order* and a copy should be on hand for consultation. Additionally, the chairperson of the meeting may, on occasion, need to consult the articles of incorporation, the bylaws, or the state statutes, so these should be available. The corporate minute book and corporate seal, the voting list, a copy of the notice (or waiver of notice), the affidavit of mailing of notice, ballots, annual report, and proposals to be voted on must all be taken to the meeting. If permitted, a paralegal assigned the task of attending the meeting and preparing the minutes should consider bringing along a tape recorder to aid in the reconstruction of the proceedings.

Exhibit 9.10 provides a sample of minutes of an annual meeting of shareholders and Exhibit 9.11 provides a sample ballot.

EXHIBIT 9.10

Minutes of the Annual Meeting of the Shareholders
of The Golden Llama Tea Company

The Annual Meeting of the Shareholders of The Golden Llama Tea Company was held at 400 Waverly Road, Any City, Any State, on the 17th day of March, 1997, at 9:00 A.M.

The President duly called the meeting to order and outlined its purposes. The Secretary indicated that notice of the meeting was properly served and a copy of an affidavit to that effect, together with a copy of said notice, were ordered inserted in the corporate minute book.

A motion was made, seconded, and carried that Mr. Keith Billingsly act as Chair of the meeting.

The Chair announced that the transfer books and alphabetical list of all shareholders entitled to vote in the election of directors (said list including the residential address of each shareholder and number of shares held by each), has been on file for inspection at the corporate offices since February 17, 1997 and that said list was available for inspection at the meeting.

The Secretary next stated that of the 300,000 shares of common stock entitled to vote at the meeting, the holders of 270,000 shares were present in person and the holder of 30,000 shares was represented by a valid proxy. The Chair then announced that an excess of the required quorum was represented either in person or by proxy and ordered the proxy to be filed with the Secretary and that the Secretary prepare a Certificate indicating the number of shares represented by proxies and insert said Certificate in the corporate minute book.

A motion was duly made, seconded, and carried that a reading of the minutes of the preceding meeting of shareholders be waived.

The Chair then presented the annual report, a copy of which had been mailed to every shareholder of record as of the record date. A motion was duly made, seconded, and carried that the report be received and filed.

The Secretary then presented her report. A motion was duly made, seconded, and carried that the report be received and filed.

The Treasurer next presented his report. A motion was duly made, seconded, and carried that the report be received and filed.

The Chair stated that the election of four directors, constituting the entire board of directors, was the next order of business. The following individuals were nominated as directors:

EXHIBIT 9.10   *Continued*

Keith Billingsly
Susan Harrison
Evelyn Lindstrom
Gregory Walker

There being no other nominations, upon motion duly made, seconded, and carried the nominations were closed. Each shareholder was asked to place his or her vote in a ballot, stating the number of shares voted, and signing the same.

After completing a tally of the vote, the Chair thereupon declared that Keith Billingsly, Susan Harrison, Evelyn Lindstrom, and Gregory Walker had been duly elected directors of the Corporation, to serve until the next annual meeting and until their successors shall be elected and qualify.

There being no further business, a motion was duly made, seconded and carried that the meeting be adjourned.

DATED: March 17, 1997

_____
Evelyn Lindstrom
Secretary

EXHIBIT 9.11

Ballot
Annual Meeting of the Shareholders of
The Golden Llama Tea Company
March 17, 1997

The undersigned, as holder of record of _____ shares of common stock of The Golden Llama Tea Company as of the above-stated date, being entitled to vote said shares at the annual meeting of the Corporation, does hereby vote said shares in the election of directors as follows:

Names of Directors	*Number of Shares in Favor*	*Number of Shares Against*
1. Keith Billingsly	_____	_____
2. Susan Harrison	_____	_____

EXHIBIT 9.11   *Continued*

Names of Directors	Number of Shares in Favor	Number of Shares Against
3. Evelyn Lindstrom	_____	_____
4. Gregory Walker	_____	_____

_____

Shareholder

C.   *Inspectors of Election*

To ensure impartiality, **inspectors** (sometimes referred to as **judges of election**) can be appointed to tally votes and report on the results at the meeting. Inspectors may be transfer agents or employees of the corporation or anyone other than nominees at the election. Should inspectors be appointed, they are often required to sign an oath, such as the one found in Exhibit 9.12. An inspectors' report appears in Exhibit 9.13.

EXHIBIT 9.12

Oath of Inspectors

We, the undersigned, constituting all the duly appointed Inspectors of The Golden Llama Tea Company, do solemnly swear that we will faithfully and impartially perform our duties at the annual meeting of the shareholders of The Golden Llama Tea Company to be held at 9:00 A.M. on March 17, 1997 at the corporate offices. We further swear that we will truthfully report the result of said election.

Maryann Salva
_____
Inspector

Robert Harcourt
_____
Inspector

Sworn to and subscribed before me this seventeenth day of March, 1997.

_____
Notary Public, State of Any State
My Commission Expires:

EXHIBIT 9.13

Inspectors' Report of the Annual Meeting of
Shareholders of The Golden Llama Tea Company

We, the undersigned, constituting all the duly appointed Inspectors at the annual meeting of the shareholders of The Golden Llama Tea Company held at the corporate offices at 9:00 A.M. on March 17, 1997, do submit the following report:

We certify that we took and subscribed to an oath to diligently and impartially execute our duties as Inspectors.

We examined the list of record shareholders, together with the submitted ballots and proxies and have determined that the record holders of 300,000 shares of common stock of the Corporation are represented in person or by proxy at the meeting, out of a total of 300,000 outstanding shares of common stock, this number constituting an excess of the shares required by law for a quorum.

The result of the vote for election of directors is as follows:

Names of Directors	Number of Shares in Favor	Number of Shares Against
1. Keith Billingsly	300,000	0
2. Susan Harrison	300,000	0
3. Evelyn Lindstrom	300,000	0
4. Gregory Walker	300,000	0

The record shareholders having unanimously voted in favor of the nominated directors, such nominated directors have been duly voted the directors of the Corporation.

DATED: March 17, 1997

Maryann Salva
Inspector

Robert Harcourt
Inspector

D.   *Written Consent in Lieu of a Shareholders' Meeting*

Unless otherwise provided in the articles of incorporation, state statutes permit any action to be taken without a meeting if consent in writing, setting forth the action to be so taken, is signed by the holders of the outstanding stock having the minimum number of votes required to authorize such action at a meeting. Thus, for example, if the holders of the requisite number of shares of The Golden Llama Tea Company consented to the election of Keith Billingsly, Susan Harrison, Evelyn Lindstrom, and Gregory Walker as directors, the action could be taken by written consent and the annual meeting need not be held.

E. Special Meetings

Special meetings of the shareholders may also be held. Corporate bylaws set forth the procedures for calling special meetings. Usually such meetings may be called by the board of directors or upon demand by shareholders holding a certain percentage of outstanding voting stock (e.g., 10 percent). Special meetings of the shareholders are commonly held when a shareholder vote is mandated to take action on certain proposals. These proposals may be proposed amendments to the articles of incorporation or fundamental changes in the corporate structure. For a detailed discussion, see Chapter 10. Requisite notice of the holding of a special meeting must be given, as provided in the corporate bylaws. The notice must not only specify the time, date, and location of the meeting, but must also include a statement of the purpose of the meeting. As is the case with annual meetings, voting shareholders may vote in person or by proxy. An example of a notice of special meeting of the shareholders can be found in Exhibit 9.14, while Exhibit 9.15 provides an example of consent to action without a meeting.

EXHIBIT 9.14

Notice of Special Meeting of the Shareholders of The Golden Llama Tea Company

TO: All Shareholders of The Golden Llama Tea Company

You are hereby notified that pursuant to Article II, Section 2 of the corporate bylaws, a Special Meeting of the Shareholders of The Golden Llama Tea Company will be held at 2:00 P.M. on Thursday, April 10, 1997 at the offices of the Corporation, located at 400 Waverly Road, for the purpose of voting on the proposed amendment to

EXHIBIT 9.14   *Continued*

the Articles of Incorporation. The proposed amendment has been recommended by the Board of Directors to Article IV of the Articles of Incorporation to increase the number of shares of capital stock of the Corporation. A copy of the proposed amendment is attached to this notice.

This notice was deposited, postage prepaid, in the United States mail on March 21, 1997.

_____
Evelyn Lindstrom, Secretary

EXHIBIT 9.15

Memorandum of Shareholder Action Without Meeting of The Golden Llama Tea Company

The undersigned, constituting all of the shareholders of The Golden Llama Tea Company, hereby unanimously consent to the following action of the shareholders taken in lieu of a special meeting of the shareholders:

RESOLVED, that the amendment to Article IV of the Articles of Incorporation of The Golden Llama Tea Company proposed and recommended by the Board of Directors to increase the number of shares of common stock in the corporation from 500,000 to 1,000,000 shares of common stock is approved and that counsel for the corporation be directed to amend the Articles of Incorporation accordingly and to file the Amendment of the Articles of Incorporation with the Secretary of State of the State of Any State. A copy of the approved amendment to be attached to this memorandum.

DATED: April 3, 1997

Keith Billingsly	_Gregory Walker_
Shareholder	Shareholder
Joan Trent	_Jack Winston_
Shareholder	Shareholder

EXHIBIT 9.15   *Continued*

Marsha Weiss	*Evelyn Lindstrom*
Shareholder	Shareholder
Margaret Farrell	*Neil Carter*
Shareholder	Shareholder
Susan Harrison	*Barbara Davidson*
Shareholder	Shareholder

CUMULATIVE VOTING

As noted above, the principal activity conducted at the annual meeting of the shareholders is the election of directors. When shareholders vote to elect directors to the board of directors they can do so in one of two ways: by straight voting or by cumulative voting. **Cumulative voting** is a method of applying votes to enhance the opportunity for minority shareholders to vote their representative onto the board. Under cumulative voting, a shareholder can cast as many votes as are equal to the number of his or her voting shares of stock multiplied by the number of directors to be elected at the annual meeting of the shareholders. The accumulated number of votes can then be cast for any one or more candidates. For example, if the election of directors calls for four persons to be elected to the board and a shareholder has 1,000 voting shares of stock, that shareholder may cast 4,000 votes (1,000 shares multiplied by four, the number of directors to be elected) for one candidate. Under straight voting, that shareholder would have to cast 1,000 votes for each of four separate candidates. Thus, under cumulative voting, a shareholder's votes carry more power. While applying votes under cumulative voting will not secure control of the board, it is more likely to assure that minority shareholders are represented by using the power of accumulated votes to vote in their candidate.

A formula has been devised to determine the number of voting shares a shareholder must have in order to elect a specific number of directors to the board under cumulative voting. The formula is as follows:

$$X = \frac{T \times D}{N + 1} + 1$$

X = the number of shares needed
T = total number of voting shares
D = number of directors desired to be elected
N = total number of directors to be elected

An example is in order here. Suppose there are four directors to be elected at the annual meeting of the shareholders. Further suppose that a shareholder wishes to determine how many votes would be needed to elect one candidate to the board. If there are 100,000 total voting shares outstanding in the corporation, the number of shares needed to elect one candidate can easily be determined by plugging these numbers into the formula as follows:

$$X = \frac{100,000 \times 1}{4 + 1} + 1 = 20,000 \ [100,000 \div 5] + 1 = 20,001$$

Thus, one candidate needs 20,001 votes to be elected to office. Although some state statutes make cumulative voting mandatory unless the articles of incorporation provide otherwise, in most states an affirmative statement must be included in the articles of incorporation indicating that cumulative voting is desired in order for cumulative voting to be allowed.

DIRECTORS' MEETINGS

Although state statutes may not require the holding of annual meetings of the board of directors, such meetings may be required by the corporation's bylaws. If annual meetings of the board are held, they typically are held directly following the annual meeting of the shareholders and their primary purpose is the election of corporate officers. Notice of the meeting may not be required because the board members are presumed to attend the annual meeting of the shareholders which directly precedes the board's meeting. However, should the annual meeting of the board of directors be held at some time other than directly after the shareholders' meeting, notice should be provided.

A.   Regular Meetings

Corporate bylaws provide for both regular and special meetings of the board of directors. The bylaws may be quite specific, stating that regular meetings of the board of directors are to be held each Tuesday at 9:00 A.M., or they may simply state that regular meetings may be held at such time as determined from time to time by the board. Further, the bylaws may detail notice procedures for regular meetings or indicate that regular meetings may be held without notice. It is common for state statutes to permit directors to participate in board meetings by means of conference calls if the requisite quorum cannot all come together in the same physical location. A notice of a regular meeting of the board of directors is found below in Exhibit 9.16.

EXHIBIT 9.16

**Notice to Directors of Regular Board Meeting of
The Golden Llama Tea Company**

TO: All Directors

    A meeting of the Board of Directors of The Golden Llama Tea Company will be held at the offices of the Corporation located at 400 Waverly Road, Any City, Any State, on April 9, 1997 at 10:00 A.M., for the purpose of transacting all such business as may properly come before the same.

    This notice was deposited, postage prepaid, in the United States mail, on April 3, 1997.

Evelyn Lindstrom
——————————————
Secretary

Most regular meetings of the board of directors follow a standard agenda:

1. Call to order.
2. Determination of a quorum.
3. Reading and approval (or correction) of the previous meeting's minutes, unless such reading is waived.
4. Reports by the directors and officers.
5. Reports by committee chairpersons.
6. Old business.
7. New business.
8. Adjournment.

A meeting agenda following this basic pattern and enumerating the items to be acted upon at the meeting (both old business and new business) should be prepared for review prior to the meeting. If documents are to be submitted for approval and/or discussion at the meeting, they should be prepared as well. Copies of the agenda and any submitted documents should be made for each attendee at the meeting. Exhibit 9.17 serves as an example of minutes of a regular meeting of the board of directors.

EXHIBIT 9.17

Minutes of the Regular Meeting of the Board of Directors of The Golden Llama Tea Company

A meeting of the Board of Directors of The Golden Llama Tea Company was held at 400 Waverly Road, Any City, Any State, on April 9, 1997 at 10:00 A.M., pursuant to call and notice by the Secretary.

The Secretary called the roll and a quorum of directors were present, namely:

Keith Billingsly
Susan Harrison
Evelyn Lindstrom
Gregory Walker

The President then stated that, a quorum being present, the meeting could transact business. The President called for the reading of the minutes of the previous meeting. Upon motion duly made, seconded, and carried the minutes were approved as read.

The President then called for the Treasurer to present his report to the Board. Upon motion duly made, seconded, and carried the Treasurer's report was approved and the President directed that a copy be inserted in the corporate records.

There being no old business to complete, the President directed that the Board consider any new business, whereupon the Vice President indicated that Mr. Andrew Jacobson desired to become a shareholder in the Corporation, desiring to purchase 100,000 shares of stock in the Corporation at the suggested purchase price of $2 per share.

After due deliberation, on motion duly made, seconded, and carried it was

RESOLVED, that the Corporation issue and deliver one hundred thousand (100,000) shares of common stock, par value one dollar ($1) per share, to Andrew Jacobson at the price of two dollars ($2) per share upon receipt of full consideration for said shares in the amount of two hundred thousand dollars ($200,000).

There being no further business, upon motion, the meeting adjourned.

Evelyn Lindstrom
Secretary

B.   *Written Consent in Lieu of a Directors' Meeting*

Unless otherwise provided in the articles of incorporation or the bylaws, an action may be taken by the board of directors without a meeting if a written consent setting forth the action to be taken is signed by all of the directors, such as in the example in Exhibit 9.18.

EXHIBIT 9.18

Memorandum of Board of Director Action Without Meeting of The Golden Llama Tea Company

The undersigned, constituting all of the directors of The Golden Llama Company, hereby unanimously consent to the following action of the Board of Directors taken in lieu of a meeting of the Board of Directors:

RESOLVED, that the Corporation issue and deliver One Hundred Thousand (100,000) shares of common stock, par value one dollar ($1) per share, to Andrew Jacobson at the price of two dollars ($2) per share upon receipt of full consideration for said shares in the amount of two hundred thousand dollars ($200,000).

DATED: April 19, 1997

Keith Billingsly
_____
Director

Susan Harrison
_____
Director

Evelyn Lindstrom
_____
Director

Gregory Walker
_____
Director

C.   *Special Meetings*

Special meetings of the board of directors require notice, unless it is waived. Unlike special meetings of the shareholders, some state statutes provide that the notice for a special meeting of the board of directors need not describe the purpose of the special meeting unless such description of purpose is required by the corporation's articles of incorporation or bylaws. Exhibit 9.19, a sample notice of special meeting in which the purpose of the meeting is described, is followed by Exhibit 9.20, which sets forth the minutes of the special meeting.

EXHIBIT 9.19

Notice of Special Meeting of the Board of Directors of The Golden Llama Tea Company

TO: All Directors of The Golden Llama Tea Company

You are hereby notified that pursuant to Article III, Section 2 of the corporate bylaws, a special meeting of the Board of Directors of The Golden Llama Tea Company will be held at 10:00 A.M., on Thursday, May 8, 1997 at the offices of the Corporation located at 400 Waverly Road, Any City, Any State, for the purpose of filling the vacancy of the position of Treasurer of the corporation and the transaction of any other lawful business.

This notice was deposited, postage prepaid, in the United States mail on April 25, 1997.

Evelyn Lindstrom
Secretary

EXHIBIT 9.20

Minutes of the Special Meeting of the Board of Directors of The Golden Llama Tea Company

---

The special meeting of the Board of Directors of The Golden Llama Tea Company was held at 400 Waverly Road, Any City, Any State, on May 8, 1997 at 10:00 A.M., pursuant to call and notice by the Secretary of the Corporation. Present at the meeting were the following persons, being designated directors of the Corporation:

Keith Billingsly
Susan Harrison
Evelyn Lindstrom

EXHIBIT 9.20 *Continued*

It being determined that a quorum was present, Keith Billingsly was elected Chair of the meeting. The Chair stated that the purpose of the special meeting was to fill the vacancy for the position of Treasurer caused by the serious illness of Gregory Walker, the current Treasurer, who can no longer serve in said position.

Upon motion duly made, seconded, and carried it was

RESOLVED, that Susan Harrison fill the vacant position of Treasurer as well as continuing in her current position as Vice President of the Corporation until the next election of officers at the meeting of the Board of Directors directly following the annual meeting of the shareholders.

There being no further or other business to come before the meeting, on motion duly made, seconded, and carried, the meeting was adjourned.

DATED: May 8, 1997

Evelyn Lindstrom
Secretary

RESOLUTIONS

As can be seen from the corporate minutes and written consents discussed above, corporate resolutions provide a well-documented record of approved corporate actions. All resolutions must accurately state the authorized corporate action and must clearly designate those persons empowered to carry out the approved actions. For example, a resolution approving the hiring of a key employee should accurately state the terms and conditions of an employment contract entered into between the corporation and the employee, or indicate that the president of the corporation or some other specifically designated officer negotiate the contract on such terms and conditions as he or she deems fit.

On various occasions, the board of directors or shareholders of a corporation may be required to issue **certified resolutions**. These are copies of resolutions passed at directors' or shareholders' meetings in which the secretary of the corporation certifies to third parties that the person acting on behalf of the corporation has the authority to so act. The corporate seal typically is affixed to certified resolutions and sometimes a notarization is included as well. A prospective seller of real property, for example, would require a certified resolution that the officer signing the contract for sale and purchase has authority to enter into the contract on behalf of the corporation. Likewise, banking resolutions are certified resolutions conclusively showing that the corporation has given certain officers the authority to draw checks, take out loans, and conduct other banking business on behalf of the corporation.

Recall in the discussion earlier that one of Karen's tasks to complete prior to the preparation of the written consent in lieu of the organizational meeting of the board of directors of The Graphic Image, Inc. was the drafting of a banking resolution certified to Capitol Bank. The corporation formation worksheet for the client corporation indicates that any two officers may sign checks, notes, and other instruments on behalf of the corporation. This statement is deceptively unclear, because the corporation has three individuals holding a total of four offices. Amanda Spires holds the offices of vice president and secretary. If the statement in the worksheet is to be taken literally, then Amanda has the authority to sign checks without any countersignature. The client may intend this result. More likely, the client intends that the signatures of any two individuals holding positions of officers are required. Precision in the language used in corporate resolutions is thus evidently of the utmost importance. Karen would have to consult further with the client to determine the client's true intentions.

Exhibits 9.21, 9.22, and 9.23 below provide three examples of certified resolutions. The first example, found in Exhibit 9.21, is a sample banking resolution prepared by Karen for The Graphic Image, Inc. Exhibit 9.22 is an example of a certified resolution approving the purchase of a parcel of real property by the corporation, while Exhibit 9.23 is a certified resolution approving a corporate president's negotiation of an equipment leasing agreement.

EXHIBIT 9.21

Banking Resolution of The Graphic Image, Inc.

I, the undersigned Secretary of The Graphic Image, Inc., a corporation duly organized and existing under the laws of the State of Any State, hereby certify that the following is a true copy of the banking resolution duly adopted by the Board of Directors of the Corporation and recorded in the written consent in lieu of the organizational meeting of the Board of Directors on March 4, 1997:

EXHIBIT 9.21   *Continued*

RESOLVED, that Capitol Bank is designated as the depository for The Graphic Image, Inc., a corporation duly organized and existing under the laws of the State of Any State. The Treasurer of the Corporation is directed to open a deposit account with Capitol Bank, the account to be subject to the rules and regulations of Capitol Bank, and to state and federal law.

FURTHER RESOLVED, that the Secretary is directed to certify to Capitol Bank a copy of the Articles of Incorporation and a copy of the bylaws of the Corporation and submit them, together with signature cards of all officers authorized to endorse or sign checks, notes, drafts, and other instruments drawn upon Capitol Bank, to the Treasurer for the opening of the aforementioned account.

FURTHER RESOLVED, that all checks, notes, and drafts against the corporate account shall be signed by any two individuals holding positions of officers of the Corporation. The signatures of any two individuals holding positions of officers of the Corporation are required as authorization of the following:

1. to make loans from the bank from time to time for credit to the account of the Corporation, and to transfer to the bank collateral securities or other corporate property of any character as may be required to secure any indebtedness to the bank;
2. to accept drafts and other instruments payable to the bank; and
3. to waive demand, protest and notice of protest or dishonor of any check, note, draft, or other instrument made, drawn, or endorsed by the Corporation.

FURTHER RESOLVED, that the bank is authorized to honor, receive, certify, or pay all instruments signed in accordance with this resolution and the bank shall not be under any obligation to inquire as to the circumstances of the issuance of any instrument signed in accordance with this resolution.

FURTHER RESOLVED, that the foregoing resolutions shall continue in full force and effect until written notice of revocation, duly signed by any officer of the Corporation on behalf of the Corporation, or a certified copy of a subsequent resolution be submitted to the bank.

FURTHER RESOLVED, that the following individuals have been duly elected to the offices of the Corporation set opposite their respective names and that any two of such individuals are authorized to sign for and on behalf of the Corporation:

Oliver Spires   President
Amanda Spires   Vice President and Secretary
Lawrence Macklin   Treasurer

EXHIBIT 9.21 *Continued*

IN WITNESS WHEREOF I have hereunto set my hand and affixed the corporate seal of this Corporation this 4th day of March, 1997.

(Corporate Seal)

<u>*Amanda Spires*</u>
Secretary

EXHIBIT 9.22

Resolution of the Board of Directors of RKM Corporation

I, the undersigned Secretary of RKM Corporation, a corporation duly organized and existing under the laws of the State of Any State, hereby certify that the following is a true copy of a resolution duly adopted by the Board of Directors at a special meeting held on March 20, 1997:

WHEREAS, Mathis Land Developers, Inc., owner of real property located at 650 Piedmont Street, Any City, Any State, has offered to sell said real property to the Corporation for the sum of two hundred thousand dollars ($200,000), and

WHEREAS, the Board of Directors deems it advisable that the Corporation purchase said real property for the aforementioned price, it is hereby

RESOLVED, that the Corporation purchase from Mathis Land Developers, Inc. that parcel of real property more particularly described as:

Lot 6, Block 2 of INDUSTRIAL PARK SUBDIVISION, according to the plat thereof, as recorded in Plat Book 12, Page 133 of the Public Records of the County of Any County, Any State

FURTHER RESOLVED, that the President of the Corporation is hereby authorized to enter into a contract for purchase on behalf of the Corporation pursuant to the terms and conditions contained in the contract presented to and read at this meeting, a copy of which is attached to the minutes of this meeting.

FURTHER RESOLVED, that the President of the Corporation is hereby authorized to execute all requisite instruments and make all payments to effectuate this resolution and to accept all duly executed documents necessary for the transfer and conveyance of the aforementioned real property to the Corporation.

EXHIBIT 9.22   *Continued*

IN WITNESS WHEREOF, I have affixed my name as Secretary and have caused the corporate seal of the Corporation to be hereunto affixed this 20th day of March, 1997.

(Corporate Seal)   _Joyce Newfield_
                                                                         Secretary

---

EXHIBIT 9.23

Resolution of the Board of Directors of Elite Staffing, Inc.

I, the undersigned Secretary of Elite Staffing, Inc., a corporation duly organized and existing under the laws of the State of Any State, hereby certify that the following is a true copy of a resolution duly adopted by the Board of Directors at a meeting held on April 21, 1997:

RESOLVED, that the President of the Corporation be and hereby is empowered and authorized on behalf of the Corporation to enter into a contract for the leasing of office equipment with Future Trends Computer Company, upon such terms and conditions as may be agreed upon between the President and said leasing company.

IN WITNESS WHEREOF, I have affixed my name as Secretary and have caused the corporate seal of said Corporation to be hereunto affixed this 21st day of April, 1997.

(Corporate Seal)   _Justin Michaels_
                                                                         Secretary

---

Chapter Summary

1. Corporate minutes and resolutions serve several important functions. First, they document the fact that the corporation has complied with all statu-

torily prescribed formalities, maintaining the legal fiction that the corporation is an entity separate and apart from its owners. Secondly, minutes and resolutions protect the directors and officers by providing evidence that certain actions taken by them were duly authorized by the corporation. Finally, minutes and resolutions provide evidence to third parties that corporate approval has been given to designated individuals to transact business with these third parties on behalf of the corporation.

2. A paralegal's responsibilities for corporate meetings can include sending notices of meetings or preparing waivers of notice for signature, preparing any documents or resolutions for approval at the meeting, preparing minutes of corporate meetings, and maintaining the corporate minute book by ensuring that all necessary documents are inserted and can be readily retrieved when required.

3. Organizational meetings typically are held shortly after the filing of the articles of incorporation. The business conducted at organizational meetings includes, but is not limited to, the election of directors (unless the initial board of directors is included in the articles), the approval of the articles of incorporation, the adoption of corporate bylaws, the election of corporate officers, the acceptance of the corporate seal and form of stock certificate, the approval of banking resolutions, and the issuance of shares of stock to the initial shareholders. Other matters that also may be addressed at organizational meetings include subchapter S election, Section 1244 stock election, and Section 248 election.

4. The annual meeting of the shareholders is attended by record shareholders whose names and addresses appear on the corporation's voting list compiled on the record date. Each record shareholder receives notice of the meeting, a copy of the corporation's annual report, and a proxy form, permitting the shareholder to attend in person or by proxy. The primary purpose of the annual meeting of the shareholders is the election of directors to the board of directors. The election may be supervised by inspectors (or judges of election) who submit a report of the election results.

5. Cumulative voting is a method of applying shareholder votes to facilitate the election of a representative of minority shareholders to the board of directors. In most states, if a corporation wishes to implement cumulative voting, a provision to that effect must be included in the articles of incorporation. Under cumulative voting, a shareholder's total number of voting shares are multiplied by the number of directors to be elected and the resulting number of votes may then be applied by the shareholder to one or more candidates.

6. The board of directors may hold an annual meeting directly following the annual meeting of the shareholders, at which the directors elect the corporate officers. Regular meetings of the board may be held more informally than

annual meetings, the times, location, and notice requirements (if any) specified in the bylaws. State statutes may permit board meetings to be conducted by telephone conference calls and also permit written consents of actions to be taken in lieu of meetings if such consents are signed by all of the directors.

7. A certified resolution is a statement certified by the secretary of a corporation to a third party that a particular resolution has been duly adopted by the board of directors or shareholders of the corporation. Such a statement provides evidence that a designated person is authorized to carry out certain actions on behalf of the corporation. Banking resolutions and resolutions approving contracts with third parties are examples of certified resolutions.

Review Questions

1. Describe: (a) the tasks to be done in preparation for an organizational meeting, and (b) the items of business conducted at an organizational meeting.
2. Explain the concept of cumulative voting.
3. List the items of business conducted at an annual shareholders' meeting.
4. Distinguish a resolution from a certified resolution.
5. Describe the standard agenda for a board of directors' meeting.

KEY TERMS

certified resolution   record date
inspector of election   record shareholder
minutes   resolution
organizational meeting   voting list

10

Shareholders' Rights and Liabilities

Overview of Objectives

Upon completion of this chapter, the student will:

- understand the basic rights shareholders have as owners of a corporation
- know how to draft a shareholders' restrictive agreement
- understand the similarities and differences between a voting trust and a shareholders' voting ("pooling") agreement
- know the various methods of valuing the stock of a closely held corporation
- understand the steps that must be taken to bring a shareholders' derivative suit
- understand the circumstances under which a shareholder may lose the protective shield of limited personal liability

INTRODUCTION

As discussed in previous chapters, a shareholder has an equity interest in a corporation which is reflected in the shares of stock the shareholder owns. As such, a shareholder is an owner of the corporation, managing the business indirectly through the corporation's board of directors. Nonetheless, there are certain rights which shareholders may directly exercise which are set forth in state statutes as well as the corporation's articles of incorporation and bylaws. One of the most important of these rights is voting rights, which may be exercised by voting in person or by proxy. The shareholders elect the directors who carry out corporate policies. They also vote on major corporate issues, such as **mergers** (two or more corporations combining in such a manner that assets are transferred to one **surviving corporation** which continues in existence with the other(s) terminated), **consolidations** (two or more corporations combining in such a manner that they create a new corporation, the others ceasing to exist), the sale of substantially all of the corporate assets, the removal of directors (with or without cause), and the dissolution of the corporation. Additionally, unless the articles of incorporation or bylaws indicate otherwise, a vote of the shareholders is required to amend the articles of incorporation and the bylaws.

As owners of the corporation, shareholders are entitled to inspect and copy corporate records. These records include accounting records; minutes of shareholder, board of director, and committee meetings; and records providing the names and addresses of all shareholders of the corporation. Most states allow these records to be kept in any form (including microfilm, microfiche, and computer disk) as long as the records are readily convertible to printed form. Although state statutes vary regarding shareholder inspection rights, they typically require that inspection and copying be done during regular business hours and that they be done in good faith and for a proper purpose. Some states require that a shareholder desiring to inspect and copy corporate records make a written demand indicating this desire and stating a proper purpose, such as determining the value of stock or determining availability of appropriate funds for the payment of dividends. Some statutes require that shareholders provide a certain stated period of notice, such as five business days, before records must be produced. In some states, only shareholders owning a certain percentage of shares of stock (e.g., 5 percent or more of the outstanding stock) have an automatic right to demand inspection and shareholders owning less than the stated percentage must make request of the court before inspection rights are permitted. Still others require that a shareholder own his or her shares of stock for a certain statutory time period before such inspection is allowed.

Shareholders purchase an equity interest in a corporate business in the hope of receiving a return on their investment. This return is paid out in dividends. All shareholders are entitled to dividends; however, it is the board of directors that decides when and how they are to be paid. Once the board of directors declares dividends, the shareholders are entitled to enforce their dividend rights as long as the dividends will be paid from legally available funds. Hand in hand with dividend rights, shareholders have liquidation rights in that they are entitled to receipt of return of capital and profits upon dissolution and liquidation of a corporation after all corporate obligations are met. Finally, shareholders have preemptive rights (if the articles of incorporation so provide) and derivative rights, both of which are discussed below.

This chapter focuses on all of the shareholder rights mentioned above. Additionally, it explores the ways in which shareholders may relinquish rights, such as voting rights or rights to freely transfer their shares of stock, to accomplish certain goals (e.g., increase the strength of their voting shares or retain management of the business in the hands of certain individuals). It also explains the documents you, as a paralegal, may draft in aiding clients in achieving these goals. Finally, the chapter discusses the ways in which shareholders and directors can lose their protective shield from liability if certain formalities are not kept.

PREEMPTIVE RIGHTS

Preemptive rights give original shareholders first rights in purchasing newly issued corporate shares of stock on a pro rata basis. This provides a method by which the original shareholders may protect their proportionate interests and exercise ownership control of the business. State statutes vary in their treatment of preemptive rights. Some states follow the traditional route of granting preemptive rights as a matter of law unless they are specifically waived in the articles of incorporation. Many state statutes, however, provide for the opposite result, recognizing preemptive rights only if the articles of incorporation specifically provide for them. In either instance, it is important to determine whether the client desires preemptive rights before the articles of incorporation are drafted. Closely held corporations are more likely to desire preemptive rights than publicly held corporations.

Should a client desire preemptive rights, it must be noted that such rights normally do not pertain to certain types of stock unless a carefully worded provision in the articles of incorporation specifically provides for their inclusion. For example, preemptive rights usually do not pertain to preferred stock or treasury stock (both discussed in Chapter 8), nor do they usually pertain to stock issued in exchange for property or services rendered to the corporation. Perhaps it is the intention of the client to provide preemptive rights for certain types or classes of stock and not for others. In this instance as well, the preemptive rights provision needs to clarify the client's intent. Do original holders of common stock have preemptive rights when the corporation decides to issue new shares of preferred stock, or vice versa? How are shareholders to exercise their preemptive rights? What time frame do they have within which to exercise their rights?

How is the purchase price of these new shares to be determined? All of these questions must be addressed when drafting preemptive rights provisions.

What recourse does a shareholder have if he or she is wrongfully denied the exercise of his or her preemptive rights? The shareholder has the right to sue the corporation in a direct suit asking for one or more alternative forms of relief. If the shares in question have yet to be issued by the corporation, the shareholder will want to seek an injunction against the corporation to prevent it from issuing those shares to an outsider. Further, it may request that the court order **specific performance** (compel a party to perform its legal obligation) from the corporation, requiring the corporation to issue the shares to the wronged shareholder. If the corporation has already issued the shares to another, the shareholder's preferred remedy is to seek monetary damages. Typically, these damages will be **compensatory** (designed to repay the plaintiff, in this case the shareholder, for his or her monetary loss), but if state statutes permit, the shareholder additionally may request **punitive damages** (designed to punish the wrongdoer, in this case the corporation).

SHAREHOLDERS' AGREEMENTS

In addition to preemptive rights, shareholders have other devices available to exercise control over corporate policies and corporate participants. The two major areas of concern are control of voting rights (thus exercising power over corporate policies) and control of share transfers (thus exercising power over corporate participants). If either of these areas are of concern to the client, they should be handled in the early stages of a corporation's existence and the appropriate documents should be drafted simultaneously with or shortly after the drafting of the articles of incorporation.

A.   Voting Trusts

If the client's main concern is control of voting rights, the client may want to consider one of two options: a voting trust or a shareholders' voting agreement. Both of these devices are designed as a way in which minority shareholders may exercise greater power by working together toward a common aim than they might otherwise have done.

The **voting trust** (sometimes referred to as a **voting trust agreement**) is the more complex and expensive of the two devices, yet it provides the greater degree of control. It is a formal mechanism permitted in most jurisdictions and it assures against divisiveness amongst the participatory shareholders by taking voting power out of their hands and placing it in the hands of one or more trustees. A voting trust works similarly to other trusts. The trust property (in this case, the participating shareholder's shares of stock) is placed in trust through assignment to the trustee(s). In a typical trust, legal title and equitable title to trust property are divided. The trustee is given **legal title** to exercise certain powers enumerated in the trust document. The **beneficiary** (the person or entity to be benefitted by the trust) is given **equitable title**, entitling the beneficiary to ownership rights in the trust property. At the termination of a trust, the legal and equitable titles merge in the beneficiary.

A voting trust is no exception to the norm. A trustee in a voting trust obtains legal title to the shares of stock when they are transferred by the shareholders to a trustee and registered in the corporate books in the trustee's name indicating the trustee as the record owner. In this manner, a trustee is given the power to vote the shares of stock in accordance with the terms of the trust document. In return, a voting trustee provides the shareholders with **voting trust certificates** (sometimes referred to as **trustees' certificates**) acknowledging the shareholders' equitable interests in the shares of stock (including the continued right to receipt of dividends). The shareholders issued these certificates may be allowed (unless the trust agreement specifies otherwise) to transfer these certificates to another, but the transferee will be subject to the terms of the voting trust until its termination. At the termination of a voting trust, the legal and equitable interests merge in the shareholder beneficiaries, who may then freely exercise all shareholder rights over their shares of stock.

State statutes set limitations on the duration of voting trusts, the usual time limitation being ten years' duration. Some states permit extensions of an additional ten-year period. When drafting a voting trust, the document should indicate its period of duration, the manner in which such period may be extended (if state law permits), and the manner in which the trust may be terminated prior to the expiration of the stated statutory period.

A voting trust should designate both the trustees and the shareholder-beneficiaries. It should state all powers given to the trustees as well as any limitations on those powers. Specifically, it should indicate whether the trustees must obtain consent of a designated percentage of the beneficiaries prior to exercising their voting rights or whether they may exercise their own judgment without obtaining such consent. If no such consent is required, consideration must be given to whether the trustees are allowed to vote on major corporate changes such as mergers and consolidations or whether these voting rights remain the province of the shareholders. In a situation where a voting trust designates more than one trustee, provision should be made for how disputes are to be settled if the trustees disagree with one another.

The agreement should provide a method by which the trust certificates are issued and transferred as well as a method for replacing and/or removing a trustee. Trustees usually are compensated for their duties. The voting trust should specify the terms of compensation. Some voting trusts allow the trustees to deduct their compensation from shareholder dividends prior to turning over the remaining dividends to the shareholder-beneficiaries. If this is agreeable to all parties, it should be so indicated in the voting trust. Most voting trusts include an indemnification provision which compensates the trustees for expenses incurred in the exercise of their trust duties. Additionally, it is common for voting trusts to include an **exculpatory clause** (which relieves a party from blame or guilt), excusing the trustees from all liability except in instances of willful misconduct or gross negligence. A sample voting trust agreement may be found in Exhibit 10.1.

EXHIBIT 10.1

Voting Trust Agreement

BY THIS AGREEMENT, made this _____ day of _____, 19_____, between _____, _____, and _____ (the Trustees) and _____, _____, _____, _____, _____, and _____, shareholders of _____ Corporation (the Beneficiaries), the parties hereby agree to the following terms and conditions.

I. *Term of the Trust.* Unless terminated sooner by a majority vote of the Trustees, this trust shall remain in full force and effect for a period of ten (10) years commencing from the date first above written. This trust may be extended for an additional ten-year period by written unanimous consent of all of the parties at any time within one (1) year prior to the expiration of the original term of the trust. The trust may be terminated any time prior to the above-stated period upon unanimous written agreement of the Beneficiaries.

II. *Delivery of Shares to Trustees.* Upon the execution of this Agreement, the Beneficiaries shall deliver to the Trustees stock certificates representing all the shares of _____ Corporation now owned or controlled by them. These certificates shall be accompanied by appropriate instruments of assignment. Should any

EXHIBIT 10.1 *Continued*

additional shares of stock be issued to any of the Beneficiaries during the period in which this trust is in force, the additional certificates shall be delivered in like manner.

III. *Voting Trust Certificates*. Upon receipt of the Beneficiaries' stock certificates, the Trustees shall have the certificates transferred on the books of the Corporation to themselves and shall deliver to each Beneficiary a Trustee's Certificate on which will be indicated: (1) the number of shares delivered, (2) the duration of the trust, (3) the voting rights of the Trustees, and (4) the conditions and procedures for transfer or assignment of the Trustee's Certificate.

IV. *Voting*. For the duration of this Agreement the Trustees shall have the exclusive right to vote the Beneficiaries' stock at any and all meetings and proceedings at which shareholder action is required. The manner in which such voting power is exercised shall be determined by agreement of the majority of the Trustees who, after having reached such agreement, shall all vote as a unit. The Trustees may use their own best judgment in reaching such agreement. The Trustees may not vote on the following major corporate changes without first obtaining the written consent of the majority of the Beneficiaries:

1. Corporate mergers
2. Corporate consolidations
3. Corporate dissolution

V. *Successor Trustees*. In the event of the death, resignation, or incapacity of any of the Trustees, a successor Trustee shall be determined by written agreement of the remaining Trustees. Any successor Trustee shall have all the rights and duties of the original Trustees heretofore named in this Agreement.

VI. *Removal of a Trustee*. A Trustee may be removed for cause by consent of the majority of the Beneficiaries. Any of the following circumstances are deemed appropriate grounds for removal for cause:

1. Willful misconduct of a Trustee
2. Gross negligence of a Trustee
3. Breach of statutory fiduciary duties by a Trustee
4. Failure to abide by the terms of this voting trust agreement

Should a Trustee be removed for cause, a successor Trustee shall be appointed according to the procedures indicated in paragraph V of this Agreement.

EXHIBIT 10.1   *Continued*

VII. *Dividends.* Before declaring any dividend, the Board of Directors of the Corporation shall request the Trustees to certify to the Board the names of all persons who are the owners of Trustees' Certificates and the number of shares to which each is entitled. Dividends shall be paid out based on the information so provided.

VIII. *Compensation of Trustees.* The Beneficiaries shall pay a reasonable compensation to the Trustees for their service under the terms of this Agreement, said compensation shall be paid according to the amounts indicated on a Schedule to be attached to this Agreement. In addition, the Beneficiaries shall reimburse all expenses and costs incurred by the Trustees in executing the trust.

IX. *Exculpation.* The Trustees shall not be liable or incur any responsibility by reason of their acts of omission or commission in the execution of the terms of the trust, except that said Trustees shall be liable for acts of wilful misconduct or gross negligence.

IN WITNESS WHEREOF, the parties have hereunto set their hands the day and year first above written.

TRUSTEES:

_____

_____

_____

SHAREHOLDER-BENEFICIARIES:

_____

_____

_____

_____

_____

_____

B.   *Shareholders' Voting Agreements*

A voting trust may not be the best solution for a client concerned about the costs of drafting and maintaining such a trust or a client reluctant to turn over stock shares to a trustee. If this is the case, and the client is nonetheless desirous of controlling shareholder voting rights, a **shareholders' voting agreement** (sometimes referred to as a **"pooling" agreement**) may be a possible option. These agreements are set up to concentrate shareholder voting power by having shareholders contractually agree to pool their votes and vote as a unit on various specified matters. The agreement may indicate in advance how the shareholders will vote on such matters, or may provide that such determinations will be made on an issue-by-issue basis as they arise. Unlike the case with voting trusts, many states do not place statutory time limitations on shareholders' voting agreements. It is therefore important to indicate within the body of the shareholders' voting agreement either a termination date or the circumstances under which the agreement may be terminated, or both. Some states have subjected shareholders' voting agreements to the same statutory time limitations as are imposed on voting trusts.

Under a shareholders' voting agreement, the parties to the agreement never give up their legal rights in their stock shares as they do under a voting trust. Thus, enforceability is more difficult than under a voting trust. Should a shareholder-signatory to the shareholders' voting agreement disagree with the other shareholder-signatories and refuse to vote according to the terms of the agreement, the shareholder-signatory may be in breach of contract. Little can be done in this situation, other than bringing suit for specific performance to make the shareholder-signatory tow the line, unless state statutes permit **self-executing shareholders' voting agreements.** In states that do permit such agreements, each shareholder-signatory gives a written, irrevocable proxy to a specified individual entitling that individual to vote those shares in accordance with the terms of the agreement. All shareholder-signatories may give their proxies to the same individual or each may give his or her proxy to another party to the agreement.

When drafting a shareholders' voting agreement, care should be taken not to draft provisions which impinge upon the powers of the board of directors. For example, it is the province of the board of directors to appoint the officers of the corporation. Therefore, a shareholder may not vote for officers nor dictate to the board of directors. However, they may agree to vote as a unit for the members of the board and may in that manner use their "best efforts" to help determine the individuals to be appointed as officers by the board. In closely held corporations, often the entire group of shareholders comprise the board of directors and usually have decided amongst themselves the individuals to be appointed to the various offices before the shareholder agreement is drafted. In this situation, a shareholders' voting agreement is unnecessary, but the shareholders may want a shareholders' restrictive agreement drafted and in such an agreement choose to include such matters as the composition of the first board of directors and other managerial provisions to officially acknowledge the like-mindedness of the parties.

C.   *Shareholders' Restrictive Agreements*

A **shareholders' restrictive agreement** (also known as **stock purchase agreements**, **buyout agreements**, and **buy-sell agreements**) often are used by shareholders who want to exercise control over stock transfers and thereby exercise control over corporate participants while maintaining the delicate balance of proportionate interests set up at the time of incorporation. This is particularly the case with closely held corporations in which the shareholders view their relationship to each other as partners might in a partnership. The addition of new parties to the business enterprise may upset the dynamics of the corporation, as might the interjection of family members either through lifetime transfers made by a shareholder to a spouse or child, or through the death of a shareholder and his or her replacement by a spouse or personal representative.

Please note that although these are the most common reasons for desiring a shareholders' restrictive agreement, the client may have other or additional reasons which must be explored, such as maintaining compliance with subchapter S requirements (i.e., limitations on the numbers and types of shareholders as discussed in Chapter 6) and other federal and state laws. Although stock transfer restrictions may be included in the articles of incorporation or the corporate bylaws, a separate written agreement is preferable, indicating the parties to the agreement (note that the corporation itself should be included as a party), detailing the restrictions on transfers of stock, and providing procedures for buyout during the lifetime or at the death of a shareholder.

1.   Permissible Restrictions

Most state statutes disallow absolute prohibitions on stock transfers and even if they did not, most shareholders would not agree to an absolute prohibition on the sale of his or her property. Several options are available without resorting to such drastic measures. One possibility is the concept of consent restrictions, whereby a shareholder may only sell or transfer his or her shares if the other shareholders or the corporation consent. In order for such a provision to work, the shareholders and/or the corporation may not unreasonably withhold their consent.

Another possibility is granting the corporation or other shareholders the **right of first refusal** in the purchase of the selling shareholder's shares of stock. The purchase price might be a fixed price or an amount determined by any of the means discussed below. This option provides flexibility for the corporation by allowing but not requiring the purchase of the shares, while assuring the selling shareholder of a means of disposing of his or her shares by selling to the corporation, the other shareholders, or an outside bona fide offeror if the right of first refusal is not exercised. Should the corporation choose to exercise its right, it must make sure that internal funds are not only available, but that they may be used. Some states have statutes pertaining to corporate surplus requirements and these must be checked to determine legally available funds. In addition, if the other shareholders are to exercise their purchase option, it is advisable to require all of them to exercise it or else none of them may do so. The reason for this harks back to the underlying reason for the agreement in the first place, namely to keep proportionate interests intact.

Yet another possibility is a mandatory buyout provision which mandates that the corporation must purchase a shareholder's shares either upon the occurrence of a triggering event, such as the death of a shareholder (typically funded by life insurance proceeds from policies purchased by the corporation or the shareholders in a cross-purchase plan), or upon a shareholder **put** (the exercise of the right to compel the corporation to purchase shares at a predetermined price). A put is most legitimately used in the circumstance of retirement or disability of a shareholder, but there may be other circumstances that warrant it. Note that life insurance funding may not only be used in the event of death. Some life insurance funding allows for use in a buyout situation brought about by the retirement or disability of a shareholder and should be researched. Disability insurance also may be available. Attention should be paid to the definitional sections of both life and disability insurance policies as they may define certain terms, such as disability, very specifically and may not cover all contingencies required by the client.

A shareholders' restrictive agreement may limit transfers of stock to certain individuals, such as family members or employees. Finally, an agreement may include elements of several or all of the above options. In any of the above situations, it is quite common for the transfer restrictions to require the selling (and purchasing) of all of the selling shareholder's shares to keep proportionate interests in the corporation intact.

Generally speaking, as long as the restrictions on the transfer or sale of stock are reasonable, they will be enforceable by the courts. The smaller the number of shareholders in a corporation, the greater the likelihood that a court will consider the purpose for transfer restrictions to be legitimate. Likewise, the lesser the degree of restraint on a shareholder desiring to sell or transfer his or her shares and the fairer the method of valuation of those shares, the greater the likelihood that the agreement will be enforceable.

In states that follow the Close Corporation Supplement to the Model Business Corporation Act, statutory law may indicate the types of restrictions that are permitted and prohibited for such corporations. Typically under such statutes, if a shareholder receives a bona fide offer to purchase his or her shares from an outsider, the corporation is given the right of first refusal to purchase the selling shareholder's shares of stock at the same price and on the same terms proffered by the bona fide offeror. In these states, this restriction usually does not apply to transfers of shares of stock to family members, other shareholders, a personal representative, or to transfers receiving the written approval of the other shareholders.

2. Valuation Methods of Stock in a Closely Held Corporation

As in the case of the sale of a partner's interest in a general or limited partnership, it is often difficult to determine the purchase price of stock in a closely held corporation because, like a partnership interest and unlike the stock of a publicly held corporation, there is no true market value for the stock and any valuation decided upon will be at best an estimation of value and at worst, purely fictional. Many of the same valuation methods discussed in Chapter 3 pertaining to general partnership agreements may be used in determining the valuation for purposes of a shareholders' restrictive agreement.

The simplest valuation method is setting a fixed value for the stock by mutual agreement of the shareholders at the execution of the shareholders' restrictive agreement with a caveat that this fixed value shall be redetermined on a periodic basis (i.e., quarterly, semiannually, annually). If this method is used, then the agreement should note that if the shareholders fail to reach an agreement during any periodic redetermination, the value of the stock shall remain at the previously agreed-upon price until the next redetermination.

Another common and simple valuation method is using the book value of the stock as the purchase price. To determine book value, the total assets of the corporation are divided by the number of outstanding shares of stock. If this method is chosen, a determination must be made whether to include intangible assets such as goodwill into the calculation. On the one hand, intangible assets may be the most prized assets of the corporation (for example, a patent for a new wonder drug or a copyright on state-of-the-art software). On the other hand, the valuation of intangible assets may be highly speculative. Further, if the intangible asset is the goodwill of the corporation, some of that asset may inevitably walk out the door with the departing shareholder. Whether or not intangibles are included in the calculations, if the book value method is used, its calculation should be done by an independent accountant or auditor.

The capitalization of earnings methods is another available option. This method is not only more complex, but also more appropriate for an established business with several years' track record than for a newly formed enterprise. Recall that with this method the average yearly net earnings of a business are calculated for a set period and then multiplied by a multiplier to calculate the current value of the business.

Rather than having the shareholders or the corporate accountant determine the value of the corporation's stock, the shareholders may choose to hire an appraiser or appraisers to appraise the business. If this route is chosen, the shareholders' restrictive agreement should detail the procedure for choosing the appraiser(s), the guidelines for the appraisal, and the manner in which compensation for the appraisal is to be paid.

Finally, the shareholders may decide not to place their own value on the stock but rather to use the best bona fide offer from an outsider to determine the purchase price which the corporation or other shareholders may meet within a specified time period. Should they fail to do so, the selling shareholder may proceed to sell the shares at the price and upon the terms of the offeror. If the shareholders choose this device, the provision should indicate that the offer must be made in good faith and in writing and the shareholders may even want to require an escrow deposit to be made as a good-faith deposit to be held in reserve during the prescribed period during which the corporation (or other shareholders) deliberates. These precautions increase the likelihood that both the offeror and the offer are legitimate. However, although this may be a possible solution for lifetime transfers of stock, this method poses a problem in the event of a shareholder's death if the corporation and remaining shareholders want to exclude the deceased shareholder's heirs from participation in the business. How is the buyout price in such a circumstance to be determined? A possible solution is to allow either the purchaser or the selling shareholder to choose between a fixed price or the bona fide offer price. In the case of death of the shareholder where no bona fide offer from an outsider exists, the fixed price governs.

3. Settlement Terms

Not only must a valuation method for the stock shares be determined when drafting a shareholders' restrictive agreement, but the settlement or closing terms should be detailed. Where life insurance proceeds are providing the funding of the purchase, a lump-sum cash settlement may be possible. In other instances, however, the corporation or other shareholders may not be able to come up with the total purchase price in one lump sum and an installment payment method may be more feasible. If such a method is chosen, the applicable provision should indicate how much of the total purchase price will be paid at settlement and should detail how the rest of the payments will be made (e.g., a set number of installments, quarterly installments). Further, any interest that is to be paid on the balance remaining at the time of settlement should be determined, as should the time of payment of this interest (e.g., with each payment of principal or in a lump sum at the end of the installments). In addition, it should be noted that in order to placate the selling shareholder in an installment payment scenario, the selling shareholder may want certain corporate assets to be pledged as collateral or may request that the shares be placed in escrow until the payment schedule is completed.

4.   Notice

A shareholders' restrictive agreement should include a provision specifying the notice procedure to be used when advising the corporation and other shareholders of an offer to purchase. This provision should also pertain to notice of acceptance or rejection of first refusal rights as well as notice procedures for exercising a put, if applicable.

5.   Transferees

The agreement should include a provision requiring any transferee of the shares of stock to take such shares subject to the terms of the shareholders' restrictive agreement. To this end, it also should require that all stock certificates bear a legend indicating that they are subject to transfer restrictions. If the corporation has made a subchapter S election, any transferee of shares of stock must consent to this election for it to remain in force. Therefore, a transferee should be required to sign any requisite documents as a condition of transfer. If the corporation has yet to make such an election, the shareholders may choose to indicate their desire to elect subchapter S by including a provision in the agreement. This inclusion does not substitute, however, for the filing of the necessary tax documents.

6.   Miscellaneous Provisions

A determination must be made as to whether a noncompetition clause will be included in the agreement. As noted in earlier chapters, such a provision generally is enforceable as long as it is reasonable in duration and geographic scope. State statutes and case law should be consulted in determining proper perimeters.

Discussions with the client should raise the question of whether managerial provisions (e.g., provisions pertaining to the composition of the board of directors, compensation of directors or officers, employment agreements, consent requirements for certain actions) are to be included.

Spouses should be included as signatories to a shareholders' restrictive agreement. In community property states, they have legal rights in their husbands' or wives' shares. Even in non-community property states, it is prudent to include the spouses as signatories since ownership rights may accrue in the spouses by inclusion of corporate shares in a will or other estate document.

Just as with any other agreement, a shareholders' restrictive agreement may include mediation and arbitration provisions, amendment procedure provisions, and the usual boilerplate provisions pertaining to the state law governing the agreement, the severability of unenforceable provisions, and the like. To assure thorough coverage, a worksheet should be used during client intake. A completed sample worksheet is provided in the Client Simulation at the end of the chapter.

DERIVATIVE ACTIONS

A shareholder may sue a corporation in his or her own right if the corporation has denied the shareholder any of the basic rights discussed in the beginning of this chapter (e.g., to recover dividends, to inspect corporate records). Additionally, a shareholder may, under certain circumstances, bring a **derivative action** in court. In the latter situation, the shareholder is not bringing suit against the corporation; rather, the shareholder is bringing suit on *behalf of* the corporation. The shareholder is not suing to enforce an individual right or redress a wrong done to the shareholder; the shareholder is suing to enforce a corporate right or redress a wrong done to the corporation. The distinction may, at times, seem difficult to comprehend, but one must remember that a corporation is a legal entity separate and apart from its owners. Nonetheless, a wrong done to the corporation is a wrong to the shareholders and that is why the courts allow for such actions. A derivative action may be brought by a single shareholder or a group of shareholders and typically is brought because the board of directors fails to act to enforce corporate rights, perhaps because the board itself has acted wrongfully and has brought about the events complained of.

Before a shareholder may bring a derivative action, some completed or threatened injury to the corporation must be present. Appropriate examples include actions taken by the board of directors beyond the scope of their authority or which promote self-interest and work against the interests of the corporation. Most states additionally require that prior to bringing a derivative action, a written demand be made to the board of directors asking the board to take appropriate action on the matter. If the board of directors fails to meet this demand within the statutorily prescribed time period, the shareholder(s) making such demand may then proceed with a derivative action suit. Even in states which have demand statutes, shareholders are not required to make written demand and wait for the prescribed period to expire if irreparable injury will result by such delay.

In addition to the above requirements, most courts will require a showing of standing before they will allow a shareholder to come before the court. Many states require a shareholder to prove that he or she owned shares of stock in the corporation at the time of the alleged wrongdoing. In some states, this is not sufficient: there is an additional requirement that the shareholder(s) bringing the suit must retain the shares of stock throughout the litigation in order to maintain standing in the court. To avoid frivolous suits, some courts demand that the shareholder post security for the expenses of the suit if the shareholder is a small shareholder (one owning less than a stated percentage or stated monetary value of stock). Should the shareholder's suit prove successful, the security is to be returned to the shareholder. In instances where security is required to be posted, it may take the form of a bond with sureties or it may take the form of cash or other marketable securities. States which have statutory security requirements do so to avoid situations in which actions are brought primarily in the hopes of obtaining large settlements rather than redressing an actual wrong. This is particularly understandable when one considers that most derivative actions suits are taken by law firms on a contingency basis and that the majority of such cases tend to be settled out of court prior to a final determination by a judge or jury. Finally, most courts require that the complaint filed in a derivative action suit be a **verified complaint** (one in which the plaintiff swears to the veracity of the allegations set forth in the complaint).

SHAREHOLDER LIABILITIES

One of the primary reasons that clients give for choosing to incorporate a business is the limited personal liability afforded to shareholders. As stated in earlier chapters, shareholders usually stand to lose no more than the purchase price for their shares of stock if a corporation meets with financial difficulties. Of course, shareholders who personally sign as guarantors on corporate loans (more and more typical these days as lending institutions are requiring such guarantees) put their personal assets at risk should the corporation fail to meet the terms of the loan agreement.

There are other instances in which a shareholder's protective shield of limited personal liability may be threatened. The most common instance occurs when a court deems it appropriate to **pierce the corporate veil**. The veil refers to the veil of protection accorded to shareholders when corporations are formed for legal purposes and meet all statutory requirements. When a corporation is formed for an improper purpose or fails to maintain corporate formalities, a court may pierce the corporate veil to allow a party doing business with the corporation to reach behind the veil and go after personal assets of the shareholders. Because courts generally are reluctant to pierce the corporate veil, they tend not to do so unless it is apparent that the corporation was formed for the purpose of income tax evasion or that the corporation has failed to maintain the most basic corporate requirements.

Corporations which may find their protective status in jeopardy include those that have failed to follow proper incorporation procedures, either because they have failed to complete all incorporation requirements or have filed improper articles of incorporation. Because such articles of incorporation typically are returned to the erring incorporator or result in the failure of a certificate of incorporation to be executed, it is highly improbable that the shareholders are unaware of such problems from a very early stage. If these problems go uncorrected and the business nonetheless holds itself out to the world as a corporation, it is committing fraud and the corporate veil will be pierced. Further, a corporation may be administratively dissolved for failure to pay requisite franchise taxes. Should this occur and the corporation nonetheless continues its operations, the corporate veil will be pierced.

More common situations in which the requisite formalities are found missing are those in which, once incorporated, the business tends to be run in the manner of a partnership or, in the instance of a one-person corporation, in the manner of a sole proprietorship. Unlike these business structures, many states have statutory capitalization requirements which must be met by a corporation because of the shareholders' limited liability status. These states seek to balance the interests of the shareholders and the interests of the corporation's creditors by mandating that a minimum amount of capital be retained in the corporation. Failure to maintain minimum capital requirements may be grounds for a court to pierce the corporate veil. Even in states which do not have minimum capitalization requirements, shareholders are at risk if the majority of corporate monies are paid out to the shareholders in dividends and inadequate resources are retained to pay debt obligations or tort claims. In like vein, the federal Bankruptcy Act allows a bankruptcy judge to pierce the corporate veil if it is clear that the corporation was undercapitalized yet the shareholders' assets are considerable. Here, the bankruptcy judge may consider whether the bankruptcy petition has been fraudulently filed or filed in bad faith, in which case the judge may dismiss the proceeding and disallow protection from creditors or, instead, may simply preserve the rights of certain creditors and not release those debts.

Commingling of corporate and personal funds is prohibited and if done, points to a situation in which the business is one which cannot be clearly separated from its owners. Again, this situation allows a court to pierce the corporate veil, as does the failure of the shareholders and directors to hold regular meetings and maintain proper corporate records.

There are certain other instances in which a shareholder may incur liability. Shareholders are obligated to pay for all shares of stock that they have agreed to purchase and, in the event a corporation finds itself insolvent, the corporation or its creditors may look to a shareholder who has failed to meet this contractual obligation for his or her pro rata share of the corporation's debt obligation. Additionally, if a shareholder is an employee of the corporation and commits a negligent act within the scope of such employment, a tort action may be brought not only against the corporation but also against the shareholder-employee personally. Finally, special requirements pertain to those corporations registered with the Securities and Exchange Commission. According to federal statutes, shareholders holding more than 10 percent of the corporate stock in such corporations must file ownership statements with the Commission. Failure to do so may lead to both civil and criminal proceedings brought against the shareholder and the directors of the corporation.

CLIENT SIMULATION

This morning, Karen's first priority is drafting a shareholders' restrictive agreement for a new client, EnviroCare, Inc. Karen has already taken care of certain initial procedures for the client, such as preparing the articles of incorporation, which have been reviewed, signed, and sent to the office of the Secretary of State. The client is a closely held corporation, comprised of three shareholders: Carl Lewis, Lillian Stone, and Victor Ferrera. All three have been friends for many years and have now come together to form a company providing environment-friendly household products which are marketed to supermarkets

and health food stores. Carl, Lillian, and Victor are all agreed that the future
success of their business depends on maintaining the close cooperation they
have established and want to keep tight control on the introduction of new
parties to the business. They all agree that spouses should not be allowed to
exercise any authority in the operation of the company and have discussed this
with their respective spouses. In keeping with their objectives, Karen included
a preemptive rights provision in the articles of incorporation and joined Thomas in sitting down with Carl to discuss various options for a shareholders'
restrictive agreement. Thomas explained to Carl that the spouses should join
as signatories to the agreement to assure that they understand its objectives and
consent to the restrictions. After this discussion, Karen met separately with
Carl to complete a worksheet upon which the agreement will be based, which
reads as follows in Exhibit 10.2:

EXHIBIT 10.2

Shareholders' Agreement Worksheet

DATE OF INTAKE: February 21, 1997

ATTORNEY: Thomas Trumbull

PARALEGAL: Karen Greer

CLIENT NUMBER: 1637

MATTER NUMBER: 0002

PERSON RESPONSIBLE

FOR INTAKE: Karen Greer

  1. CLIENT NAME: Carl Lewis for client company, EnviroCare, Inc.

  2. ADDRESS: 334 Stirling Street

                    Any City, Any State

  3. TELEPHONE: (000) 423-3613   FAX: (000) 423-1183

  4. TERM OF AGREEMENT: Shall remain in force unless terminated by
unanimous written agreement or death of next to the last
of shareholders.

EXHIBIT 10.2   *Continued*

---

5. AUTHORIZED CAPITALIZATION OF CORPORATION:

     100,000 shares of common stock with a par value of $1 per share.

6. PARTICIPATING SHAREHOLDERS (INDICATE NAMES, ADDRESSES, NUMBERS OF SHARES OF STOCK, AND TYPE OF STOCK):

     Carl Lewis   10,000 shares common stock

     278 Oakhill Drive, Any City, Any State

     Lillian Stone   10,000 shares common stock

     731 Verde Lane, Any City, Any State

     Victor Ferrera   10,000 shares common stock

     149 Arbor Place, Any City, Any State

7. ARE ALL SHAREHOLDERS OF THE CORPORATION PARTIES TO THIS AGREEMENT?   __X__ YES   _____ NO

8. IS THE CORPORATION A PARTY TO THIS AGREEMENT?

     __X__ YES   _____ NO

9. RESTRICTIONS ON LIFETIME TRANSFERS:

     (i) CIRCUMSTANCES: Shareholder receives bona fide written offer to purchase all of his/her shares of stock.

     (ii) PROCEDURES: Shareholder notifies Corporation and all other shareholders of receipt of offer within seven days. Corporation has 30 days from receipt of notice to exercise right of first refusal to purchase all the shares. If not exercised, the other shareholders have 15 days within which to exercise option of purchasing the shares on a pro rata basis to keep proportionate interests in the Corporation intact. If not exercised, selling shareholder may sell to offeror who takes subject to terms of this agreement.

EXHIBIT 10.2   *Continued*

(iii)   ARE INTERFAMILY TRANSFERS PERMITTED? <u>Provision not desired by client.</u>

(iv)   FORCED BUYOUT PROVISION: (IF DESIRED, SPECIFY TERMS): Not desired by client.

(v)   VALUATION METHOD FOR DETERMINING PRICE: <u>Purchaser has option of purchasing shares at either (a) the price in the bona fide written offer or (b) the book value of the shares. Book value will be determined by the Corporation's certified public accountant and shall be based on the net assets of the Corporation (goodwill not to be included) on the date of notification of the offer, divided by the number of shares of common stock outstanding on that date.</u>

(vi)   SOURCE OF FUNDS FOR STOCK PURCHASE: <u>Corporate capital accounts if Corporation purchases; individual funding if shareholders purchase.</u>

(vii)   PAYMENT METHOD: <u>Settlement shall occur within 60 days of notification by purchaser of exercising option to purchase. At option of purchaser, payment may be made (a) in lump-sum cash payment or (b) 25 percent of purchase price at settlement and the remainder in equal quarterly installments. If the latter option is chosen, interest shall be paid on the unpaid balance of the purchase price at the rate of 10 percent per annum, payable quarterly when payments of principal are due.</u>

10.   DEATH OF A SHAREHOLDER:

(i)   PROCEDURES: <u>Upon the death of a shareholder, the Corporation shall purchase all of the deceased shareholder's shares of stock.</u>

EXHIBIT 10.2   *Continued*

(ii)   VALUATION METHOD FOR DETERMINING PRICE OF STOCK:
         Book value at date of death as described above.

(iii)   SOURCE OF FUNDS FOR STOCK PURCHASE: The Corporation
         shall purchase life insurance policies on the life of each
         shareholder, insuring each shareholder for $100,000. The
         policies shall remain in force for the duration of this agree-
         ment. The Corporation shall increase the amount of life
         insurance as and when it is deemed appropriate to do so.
         Any life insurance proceeds remaining after payment of
         book value for a deceased shareholder's shares of stock
         shall belong to the Corporation.

(iv)   PAYMENT METHOD: Payment to the deceased shareholder's estate be
         made in lump sum cash payment within 15 days from
         receipt of insurance proceeds by the Corporation.

11.   MANAGEMENT PROVISIONS:

(i)   COMPOSITION OF THE BOARD OF DIRECTORS: The shareholders
         agree to elect Carl Lewis, Lillian Stone, and Victor Ferrera
         to the Board of Directors following the execution of this
         agreement.

(ii)   OFFICERS: The shareholders agree to use their best efforts to see that
         the following individuals are appointed to the following
         positions: Carl Lewis as President, Lillian Stone as Treas-
         urer, Victor Ferrera as Vice President and Secretary.

(iii)   COMPENSATION OF DIRECTORS: (IF DESIRED):   Not desired by
         client.

EXHIBIT 10.2 *Continued*

(iv) COMPENSATION OF OFFICERS: (IF DESIRED): <u>Not desired by</u> <u>client. Compensation shall be determined by provisions of</u> <u>employment agreements.</u>

(v) MERGERS: <u>Only by unanimous agreement of the shareholders.</u>

(vi) CONSOLIDATIONS: <u>Only by unanimous agreement of the share-</u> <u>holders.</u>

(vii) SALE OF CORPORATE ASSETS: <u>Only by unanimous agreement of</u> <u>the shareholders.</u>

(viii) AMENDMENT OF ARTICLES OF INCORPORATION: <u>Only by</u> <u>unanimous agreement of the shareholders.</u>

(ix) AMENDMENT OF BYLAWS: <u>By majority vote of the shareholders.</u>

2. NONCOMPETITION CLAUSE: (IF DESIRED): <u>No shareholder, as long as</u> <u>he or she remains a shareholder of the Corporation and</u> <u>for a period of two years thereafter shall engage, within</u> <u>the boundaries of the State of Any State, in any manner</u> <u>of business which is competitive with that of the Cor-</u> <u>poration.</u>

13. MEDIATION: <u>Not desired by client.</u>

14. ARBITRATION: <u>All disputes arising in connection with any provision of this</u> <u>agreement shall be resolved by arbitration in the City of</u> <u>Any City in accordance with the rules of the American</u> <u>Arbitration Association then in force.</u>

15. ADDITIONAL PROVISIONS: <u>Subchapter S election; spouses to join in sign-</u> <u>ing of the agreement acknowledging full knowledge and</u> <u>contents.</u>

Having reviewed the worksheet, Karen pulls up a skeletal shareholders' agreement on her computer. Because Karen has prepared so many shareholders' agreements in her role as corporate paralegal, she has drafted a number of alternative provisions (i.e., settlement provisions, management provisions, noncompetition provisions, arbitration provisions, and the like) from which she will pick and choose as she proceeds with the drafting process, merging the provisions with the skeletal agreement. Once she has done this, she will then customize each of the provisions to meet her client's needs. Upon completion, the draft agreement reads as follows:

EXHIBIT 10.3

Shareholders' Agreement

THIS AGREEMENT, dated this _____ day of _____, 19_____, by and between Carl Lewis, Lillian Stone, and Victor Ferrera (the Shareholders); Beth Lewis, Ronald Stone, and Anita Ferrera (the Spouses); and EnviroCare, Inc., a corporation organized under the laws of the State of Any State (the Corporation).

WHEREAS, the Corporation has an authorized capitalization of 100,000 shares of common stock having a par value of one dollar ($1) per share; and

WHEREAS, the Shareholders are the holders of all of the issued and outstanding capital stock of the Corporation, each Shareholder owning 10,000 shares of stock; and

WHEREAS, the Shareholders desire to enter into an agreement among themselves and with the Corporation establishing certain restrictions on transfer of their shares of stock as well as establishing certain other rights regarding the management of the Corporation;

NOW THEREFORE, in consideration of the mutual covenants contained herein, the Shareholders agree among themselves and with the Corporation as follows:

I. *Restrictions on Lifetime Transfers.* No Shareholder shall transfer or dispose, by any means, any of his or her shares of stock in the Corporation except as permitted by the terms of this Agreement. If a Shareholder receives a bona fide written offer to purchase all of his or her shares of stock, which offer he or she desires to accept, the Shareholder (referred to as the Selling Shareholder) shall, within seven (7) days of receipt of the offer, so inform the Corporation and each of the other Shareholders by providing written notice of said offer. The Corporation shall then have thirty (30) days within which

EXHIBIT 10.3   *Continued*

to exercise its right of first refusal to purchase all of the Selling Shareholder's shares. If the Corporation fails to notify the Selling Shareholder by written notice within this time period of its desire to exercise its right of first refusal, it shall be deemed to have not exercised its right. The other Shareholders shall then have fifteen (15) days within which to exercise their option of purchasing all the shares of the Selling Shareholder on a pro rata basis to keep their proportionate interests in the Corporation intact. Should they fail to exercise their option within this time period, the Selling Share-holder may sell his or her shares to the offeror who takes said shares subject to the terms of this Agreement.

II. *Purchase Price.* The Purchaser (be the Purchaser the Corporation or the other Shareholders) has the option of purchasing the Selling Shareholder's shares at either (a) the price in the bona fide written offer or (b) the book value of the shares. Book value will be determined by the Corporation's certified public accountant and shall be based on the net assets of the Corporation (goodwill shall not be included) on the date of notification of the offer, divided by the number of shares of common stock outstanding on that date.

III. *Settlement Terms.* Settlement shall occur within sixty (60) days of notification by the Purchaser of the Purchaser's decision to exercise the option to purchase. At the option of the Purchaser, payment may be made (a) in lump-sum cash payment or (b) twenty-five percent (25%) of the purchase price at settlement and the remainder in equal quarterly installments. If the latter option is chosen, interest shall be paid on the unpaid balance at the rate of ten percent (10%) per annum, payable quarterly when payments of principal are due.

IV. *Death of a Shareholder.* Upon the death of a Shareholder, the Corporation shall purchase all of the Deceased Shareholder's share of stock in the Corporation at the book value of said shares as of the date of death (book value defined as in paragraph II above).

To this end, the Corporation shall purchase life insurance policies on the life of each Shareholder, insuring each Shareholder for One Hundred Thousand Dollars ($100,000). The policies shall remain in force for the duration of this Agreement. The Corporation shall increase the amount of life insurance as and when it is deemed appropriate to do so. Any life insurance proceeds remaining after payment of book value for the Deceased Shareholder's shares of stock shall belong to the Corporation.

Payment to the Deceased Shareholder's estate shall be made in lump-sum cash

EXHIBIT 10.3   *Continued*

payment within fifteen (15) days from receipt of the insurance proceeds by the Corporation.

V. *Management of the Corporation.* The Shareholders agree to elect Carl Lewis, Lillian Stone, and Victor Ferrera to the Board of Directors following the execution of this Agreement. In addition, the Shareholders agree to use their best efforts to see that the following individuals are appointed to the following positions:

Carl Lewis	President
Victor Ferrera	Vice President and Secretary
Lillian Stone	Treasurer

VI. *Voting.* The following actions may only be taken by the Corporation with the unanimous agreement of the Shareholders:

(a)   Mergers
(b)   Consolidations
(c)   Sale of substantially all of the corporate assets
(d)   Amendment of the Articles of Incorporation

The bylaws of the Corporation may be amended by the majority vote of the Shareholders.

VII. *Subchapter S Qualification.* The Corporation shall file the necessary documents to qualify the Corporation as an "S" corporation under subchapter S of the Internal Revenue Code. The Shareholders agree to execute all necessary documents to obtain said qualification. The subchapter S election may only be revoked by the written consent of the majority of the Shareholders.

VIII. *Noncompetition.* No Shareholder, as long as he or she remains a Shareholder of the Corporation and for a period of two (2) years thereafter shall engage, within the boundaries of the State of Any State, in any manner of business which is competitive with that of the Corporation. Each Shareholder acknowledges that the restrictions contained herein are reasonable and necessary to protect the Corporation's legitimate interests.

IX. *Term of Agreement.* This Agreement shall remain in force unless terminated by the unanimous written agreement of the Shareholders or the death of the next to the last of the Shareholders.

EXHIBIT 10.3   *Continued*

X. *Arbitration.* All disputes arising in connection with any provision of this Agreement shall be resolved by arbitration in the City of Any City in accordance with the rules of the American Arbitration Association then in force.

XI. *Endorsement on Stock Certificates.* A notice of all transfer and other restrictions imposed by this Agreement shall appear on all stock certificates issued by the Corporation.

X. *Notices.* All notices relating to this Agreement shall be deemed to have been duly given or made if either (a) mailed by United States certified mail, return receipt requested, or (b) sent by facsimile machine, to the following addresses:

If to the Corporation:	EnviroCare, Inc. 334 Stirling Street Any City, Any State
If to Carl Lewis:	278 Oakhill Drive Any City, Any State
If to Lillian Stone:	731 Verde Lane Any City, Any State
If to Victor Ferrera:	149 Arbor Place Any City, Any State

Any addressee may designate a different address to which notices are to be sent by providing notice of the change of address in conformity with this provision.

XI. *Spousal Joinder.* The Spouses of the Shareholders have joined as signatories to this Agreement for the purpose of acknowledging that they have full knowledge of its contents and that they give approval to the terms of this Agreement.

XII. *Governing Law.* This Agreement shall be governed by and construed in accordance with the laws of the State of Any State.

XIII. *Binding Effect.* This Agreement shall be binding on the Corporation, all of the Shareholders, and their respective personal representatives, successors, and assigns.

XIV. *Amendment.* This Agreement may not be amended except by the written consent of all of the Shareholders then existing at the time of said amendment.

EXHIBIT 10.3 *Continued*

XV. *Severability.* In the event that any provision of this Agreement shall be unenforceable, the Agreement shall continue in full force and effect and shall be construed as if such unenforceable provision had never been contained herein.

IN WITNESS WHEREOF, the parties have executed this Agreement as of the day and year first above written.

Attest: EnviroCare, Inc.

_____ [Seal]   By: _____ [Seal]
            Secretary   *President*

                                                 Shareholders and Spouses:

                                                 _____ [Seal]
                                                            Carl Lewis

                                                 _____ [Seal]
                                                            Beth Lewis

                                                 _____ [Seal]
                                                           Lillian Stone

                                                 _____ [Seal]
                                                           Ronald Stone

                                                 _____ [Seal]
                                                          Victor Ferrera

                                                 _____ [Seal]
                                                           Anita Ferrera

Chapter Summary

1. Shareholders retain certain overseeing privileges as owners of a corporation while depending on the board of directors and officers to carry out corporate policies. Shareholders keep abreast of management decisions through the exercise of inspection rights. They oversee major corporate changes, such as mergers, consolidations, and amendments to corporate documents, through

the exercise of voting rights. They oversee the fiduciary responsibilities of the board of directors and the officers through the exercise of derivative action rights. In addition to these rights, shareholders may exercise some control over the addition of new shareholders through the exercise of preemptive rights, if so provided in the articles of incorporation.

2. Shareholders wishing to increase their voting power may band together under a voting trust agreement or a shareholders' voting agreement. A voting trust agreement, although more complex and expensive to initiate and maintain, provides the greatest degree of control over voting shares. Under such an arrangement, participating shareholders transfer their shares of stock to trustees who are given the power to vote those shares in accordance with the terms of the trust agreement. A shareholders' voting agreement, on the other hand, provides greater flexibility because fewer statutory restrictions apply, yet also provides fewer mechanisms for enforceability unless such agreements are made self-executing.

3. A shareholders' restrictive agreement is a useful tool in restricting stock transfers from a shareholder to an outside party and works best with closely held corporations. While the purpose of such agreements typically is to guarantee the proportionate interests and managerial control of the original shareholders, these agreements also may serve to assure that a corporation remains in compliance with pertinent state and federal statutory regulations.

4. A thorough shareholders' restrictive agreement includes provisions for both lifetime transfers and the purchase of a deceased shareholder's stock. The circumstances under which a transfer may take place, the valuation of the subject shares, and the settlement terms must be addressed. Additionally, noncompetition clauses may be included as well as desired managerial provisions.

5. Many of the valuation methods partnerships use to calculate the value of a partner's interest also may be used to value shares of stock in a closely held corporation. These methods range from setting a fixed value, to using book value or the capitalization of earnings methods, to hiring an outside appraiser, or simply matching the best offer of a bona fide offeror.

6. A derivative action suit is a lawsuit brought by one or more shareholders to enforce the rights of a corporation when the board of directors fails to do so. Typically, such actions are brought to redress a wrong perpetrated by the board or the officers. To avoid needless litigation, many states require that certain procedures be followed before courts will hear such cases. These procedures may include making written demand on the board before filing suit, proving proper standing in court, and posting security for expenses.

7. Shareholders enjoy limited personal liability for corporate debts. This protection may be stripped away under various circumstances. The most common of these circumstances are those in which corporate formalities have been

disregarded and the corporation cannot, in reality, be separated from its identification with the shareholders. In such instances a court, to avoid injustice to
an outside party, may deem it appropriate to pierce the corporate veil and allow
that party to pursue the shareholders personally. Other instances in which
shareholders may suffer personal liability include the negligent actions of a
shareholder-employee performed within the scope of employment, the signing
of a personal guarantee on corporate loan documents, the failure to pay the
agreed value for corporate shares, and the failure to file ownership statements
when required under Securities and Exchange Commission regulations.

Review Questions

1. Discuss the options available for placing restrictions on the transfer of
   stock.
2. Explain the difference between legal title and equitable title.
3. Discuss the respective strengths and weaknesses of voting trusts and
   shareholders' voting agreements.
4. Explain the concept of piercing the corporate veil.
5. What procedures must a shareholder follow to proceed with a derivative action suit?

KEY TERMS

beneficiary

equitable title

legal title

piercing the corporate
   veil

right of first refusal

shareholders' restrictive
   agreement

shareholders' voting
   agreement

voting trust

voting trust certificate

11

Employment and Compensation

Overview of Objectives

Upon completion of this chapter, the student will:

- understand the purpose of employee manuals and their various components
- know the circumstances under which employment agreements are necessary
- understand the various methods of compensating employees
- know how to draft an employment agreement

INTRODUCTION

A corporation is only as good as the people who make it run. Acknowledging this, successful corporations often invest considerable time and money in the hiring, training, and retention of their employees. Frequent employee turn-around leads to confusion, instability, and often duplication of effort. A corporation geared to high employee performance has an image of itself and an understanding of where each employee fits within this image. "Image" in this context refers to a combination of corporate philosophies, ethics, and goals.

Although all corporations must abide by state and federal employment statutes, they rarely negotiate contracts with each employee. A majority of employees hired by a corporation are **employees "at will,"** meaning they are not hired under the terms of a written contract and may leave, or may be fired by the corporation, without cause. To enable such employees to understand the corporate culture and expectations of their particular company, many corporations have corporate employment manuals to which employees may refer. Employees operating under an organized union rarely have individual employment agreements and work under the terms of an agreement between the union and the corporation.

To assure that a corporation acquires the best talent for its business enterprise, the hiring of key employees often requires more intricate employment arrangements. A **key employee** may be one retained in a senior executive or management position; or may be one hired for other special talents, such as research or marketing expertise. To assure continually high job performance and to reduce risk of loss of the employee (and along with the employee, the corporation's trade secrets) to a competitor, most corporations enter into written employment agreements with persons considered key employees. This is particularly the case when an employee may acquire valuable intangible property rights in a work product to which the corporation wishes to attain or retain title, such as a patent or copyright.

The concept of indentured servitude has long since been abolished. Thus, no court will force an employee to continue in the employ of an employer he or she no longer wishes to work for. The concept of employment at will recognizes the voluntary nature of employment relationships. Even an employer armed with a written employment agreement cannot force an employee to continue working until the end of the contract. However, an employee who leaves his or her employment prior to the expiration of the agreement may, in certain instances, be said to have breached the agreement and such breach may allow an employer other methods of legal recourse apart from forced continued employment.

A written agreement is a two-edged sword and many corporate employers are reluctant to enter into such an agreement because a court may require a corporation to specifically abide by the terms of the agreement and continue the employment of a no-longer desirable employee until the expiration of the agreement unless the corporation can show that the employee breached the agreement in some fashion. Moreover, the terms of compensation are set in an employment agreement and may prove to be a hardship if the corporation faces a financial setback.

The cost in terms of not only salary but other benefits has many corporations rethinking the hiring of squadrons of full-time employees. Many corporations in their "downsizing" efforts have found alternative solutions to their employment needs by reducing the number of full-time employees and utilizing more independent contractors and consultants. In such instances, independent contractor or consulting agreements may be advisable to clearly demarcate as well as limit each party's respective responsibilities to the other.

This chapter explores the ways in which corporations choose to project a particular corporate mind-frame or image to employees and set out guidelines for employees to follow which fit this mind-frame or image through the use of employee manuals. Additionally, this chapter looks at the various methods by which corporations compensate employees. Because you, as a corporate paralegal, may be asked to assist in drafting employment agreements for key corporate personnel, this chapter also discusses the various provisions that may be incorporated into an employment agreement.

EMPLOYEE MANUALS

Employee manuals, sometimes referred to as employee handbooks, are becoming customary in most large corporations. If properly drafted, they are mutually advantageous to both the employer and the employee. If improperly drafted, they can spawn protracted litigation. They can demonstrate corporate compliance with mandatory regulations. They can also provide a cost-effective means of providing basic training and orientation to employees. Many corporations have their personnel or human resources departments draft their manuals. Some put together their corporate employee manuals with a marketing slant to entice employees. Others put together employee manuals that read like a never-ending list of "Thou shalt nots." A combination of the two approaches is often most appropriate.

No employee manual should be distributed before it is reviewed by an attorney. It is the attorney's job to make sure that the manual complies with all federal and state employment statutes regarding such issues as sexual harassment, family and medical leave, and employment discrimination. Further, the attorney will ensure that various disclaimers are included, such as those permitting the employer to make changes to the manual and those stating that the manual should in no way be construed as an employment contract between the employer and the employee.

While an employee manual cannot, and should not, cover as many specifics as customized employment agreements, it can serve to set the tone for the employment relationship. Providing an employee manual to all employees gives an indication that a certain uniformity exists within the corporation, one that implies fairness in the application of personnel policies. It also provides the employee with the corporate agenda as to performance expectations.

A.   Mission Statement

Employee manuals commonly begin with an introductory section including a history of the corporation and its basic business philosophy. This section gives the new or prospective employee the first glimpse of the corporation's degree of formality or informality. A corporation whose manual begins "Once upon a time there were these two guys, Hank and Frank, who thought it would be a nifty idea to open vacation retreats all over the country" is going to have a more relaxed attitude than one which begins "As this corporation celebrates its twenty-fifth anniversary, its founders, Henry M. Pickering and Franklin T. Samuels, can look back with pride on their accomplishments. Founded in 1972, the P & S Company . . . ." Many companies phrase their business philosophies in the form of a **mission statement**. Such statements not only tell the employee about the corporation's aspirations, but also tell the employee how it expects these aspirations to be achieved. It may include a synopsis of the general corporate principles upon which the business is run. An effective mission statement draws the employee into the corporate fold, telling the employee how he or she fits into the corporate mission.

B.   Personnel Policies Section

Following the introductory section are sections pertaining to personnel policies, employee benefits, and employee conduct. The personnel policies section should include a discussion of such basic issues as equal opportunity, required work hours, overtime policies, leaves of absence including family leave, sick and personal days, vacations and holidays, and performance review. If not included in this section, mention of the Family and Medical Leave Act should be included somewhere in the manual.

C.   Employee Benefits Section

The employee benefits section should describe the various kinds of insurance coverage provided by the corporation, such as health, dental, and life insurance, as well as any contributions the employees must make to such plans. It also should describe workers' compensation and disability, employee assistance programs, tuition reimbursement programs, and company retirement plans.

D. Employee Conduct Section

Another section of the manual should be devoted to employee conduct. This can include anything from dress code requirements to smoking policies. The corporation's sexual harassment policy should be included as well. Other improper conduct may be addressed with guidelines for grievance and employee discharge procedures. A word of warning in the drafting of such procedures: if a corporation sets forth certain procedures to be followed prior to discharging an employee, this provision may be in conflict with a later disclaimer that the employer corporation may terminate employment without cause. Care should be taken to assure alignment between discharge procedures, if any, stated in the employee conduct section and disclaimers made at the beginning or end of the manual.

E. Additional Sections

Employee manuals may include additional sections as appropriate to the corporation, such as organizational charts and glossaries of terms particular to the corporation. Throughout each section of the manual, special care must be given to word choices. For example, a manual should not use the general term "employees" when it is meant to pertain only to certain workers, such as full-time employees. In the section pertaining to employee benefits, for instance, if the manual refers to health insurance coverage available to "employees," a part-time employee may assume that he or she is entitled to coverage when the corporation in fact may provide health insurance only for full-time employees. A lack of attention to word usage can amount to major litigation down the line.

Although precision and clarity are key, a manual should not be written so stringently as to prohibit an evolution in corporate policy as the corporation experiences growth or, conversely, downsizing, as well as other changes. Additionally, a disclaimer should appear in the manual indicating that the manual is not to be construed as an employment agreement and that the employment relationship between the employer and employee may be terminated at any time and for any reason, with or without cause. Further, should the corporation wish to reserve its rights regarding the payment of severance and other benefits that may be detailed in the manual, not only should a prominent disclaimer to that effect be included but care should be taken to assure that such a disclaimer does not contradict any federal or state statutes pertaining to employee benefits. It is good practice to require employees to sign a statement acknowledging their receipt of the manual, the statement to be filed in the employee's personnel file as evidence that the employee was made aware of various corporate policies and procedures.

CURRENT AND INCENTIVE COMPENSATION

The term **current compensation** refers to compensation paid to an employee for the present services provided to the corporation by the employee, such as salary. The term **incentive compensation** refers to compensation paid to an employee as motivation for continued high performance, such as commissions and bonuses. Although pensions and other deferred benefit plans may act as an incentive for such performance, in the context of this discussion incentive compensation will refer to compensation keyed directly to the employee's performance.

A major concern in deciding upon compensation to be paid to employees is the tax treatment of such compensation. The Internal Revenue Code imposes certain limitations on currently deductible compensation. For example, Section 162 of the Internal Revenue Code limits the deductibility of compensation paid to shareholder-employees to a reasonable allowance for personal services actually rendered by the shareholder-employee.

Compensation paid to shareholder-employees is looked upon with greater scrutiny than compensation paid to nonshareholder-employees (with certain exceptions, such as those for family members) because compensation to shareholder-employees may be a form of disguised dividend payments. In determining whether compensation is really a disguised dividend payment, the Internal Revenue Service will compare the percentage of corporate shares owned by the shareholder-employee with the amount and timing of the compensation paid. If a direct relationship is evident, the compensation will most likely be considered a constructive dividend and will be taxed as such. In addition, the reasonableness of the compensation will be scrutinized. The Internal Revenue Service will look at the qualifications possessed by the shareholder-employee, the duties to be performed by the shareholder-employee, and what is ordinarily paid to employees with similar qualifications and duties. Again, if compensation is deemed disproportionate it will not be deductible. Bonuses paid to shareholder-employees are usually suspect and will be treated as disguised dividends based on the theory that shareholder-employees, as owners of the corporation, do not need such incentives in return for performance; rather, their incentive is their proportionate share of the profits which most properly should be received in the form of dividends.

A. *Stock Option Plans versus Stock Purchase Agreements*

Besides the payment of salary and bonuses, other types of current compensation include stock option plans and fringe benefits. **Stock option plans** give the employee the opportunity to purchase a certain number of shares of stock within a defined period at a predetermined or determinable price. Although the employee is under no obligation to purchase these shares, the principle behind such a plan is that if the employee performs well, the stock's value will increase and the employee turned shareholder-employee will prosper. These stock option plans are referred to by the Internal Revenue Service under Section 422A as **incentive stock options**. If certain requirements are met, the employee pays taxes on these shares only when the shares are sold by the employee. The employee must hold on to the stock for at least one year after purchasing it and for at least two years from the date the option was granted in order to realize this tax benefit. The granting of these stock options must be approved by corporate resolution, typically by the board of directors, within 12 months before or after the adoption of the plan. An example of a resolution approving stock options is found in Exhibit 11.1 below.

EXHIBIT 11.1

Resolution of the Board of Directors of Garden of Eden Nurseries, Inc.

WHEREAS, the Board of Directors have voted to approve the Stock Option Plan annexed to this resolution, granting key employees the option to purchase shares under the provisions of said plan, it is

RESOLVED, that the Board of Directors of this corporation shall set aside a total of Fifty Thousand (50,000) shares of the common stock, without par value, of this corporation for sale to the executives and key employees under the terms of said Stock Option Plan.

I do hereby certify that I am the duly elected and qualified Secretary, and that the above is a true and correct copy of a resolution duly adopted at a meeting of the Board

EXHIBIT 11.1   *Continued*

of Directors thereof, convened and held in accordance with law and the bylaws of said corporation on January 10, 1997, and that such resolution is now in full force and effect.

IN WITNESS WHEREOF, I have affixed my name as Secretary and have caused the corporate seal of said corporation to be hereunto affixed, this 10th day of January, 1997.

A True Record

Attest   *Vera Green*
                                                                              Secretary

A stock purchase agreement differs from a stock option plan. Under a **stock purchase agreement**, the employee is contractually obligated to purchase a certain number of corporate shares at a predetermined or determinable price within a specified time period. These agreements are not tax-qualified.

B.   *Tax-Qualified Fringe Benefits*

Tax-qualified **fringe benefits** take many forms. In order for fringe benefits to be considered tax-qualified, they must be presented in the form of a written plan exclusively for the benefit of the employees to continue for an indefinite period. Please note that the term **"tax-qualified"** has been used rather than the term "tax deductible" because a tax-qualified plan not only is tax deductible for the corporation but also is nontaxable as income for the employee. For example, under Section 79 of the Internal Revenue Code, a corporation may provide group term life insurance under such a plan to its employees up to an amount of $50,000 per employee. This plan may be available to all employees except S corporation shareholder-employees owning 2 percent or more of the corporate stock. If such a plan is adopted, an eligible employee may have coverage in an amount greater than $50,000 but is taxed only on the excess. As with stock option plans, employee group life insurance plans should be adopted formally by resolution of the board of directors. An example of such a resolution is found below.

EXHIBIT 11.2

Resolution of the Board of Directors of Firelight Publishing Company

WHEREAS, the board of directors has voted to adopt a group life insurance program by providing eligible employees with life insurance at no cost to the employees, it is hereby

RESOLVED, that the Treasurer is authorized to contract for a group life insurance program, which shall provide that all employees having one or more years of service with the corporation shall receive life insurance. Each life insurance policy shall be in the amount of Fifty Thousand Dollars ($50,000) and the entire cost of the group insurance program shall be paid by the corporation.

I do hereby certify that I am the duly elected and qualified Secretary, and that the above is a true and correct copy of a resolution duly adopted at a meeting of the Board of Directors thereof, convened and held in accordance with law and the bylaws of said corporation on February 8, 1997, and that such resolution is now in full force and effect.

IN WITNESS WHEREOF, I have affixed my name as Secretary and have caused the corporate seal of said corporation to be hereunto affixed, this 8th day of February, 1997.

A True Record

Attest

_____
Leo Tompkins
Secretary

Sections 105 and 106 of the Internal Revenue Code permit tax-qualified employee health and accident insurance plans which may include not only employees, but their spouses and dependents. These plans may be set up either to provide for direct premium payments by the corporation or to provide corporate reimbursement to employees for expenses incurred. These plans are available to those employees eligible for the group term life insurance plan discussed above. Group term life insurance plans and employee health and accident plans must satisfy the Internal Revenue Code's nondiscriminatory requirements regarding eligibility to qualify.

A corporation is allowed to deduct other fringe benefits as well. These include reimbursement of certain expenses. For instance, under Section 217 of the Internal Revenue Code, reimbursement for moving expenses is tax deductible. This includes not only the costs of transporting the household goods of the employee to his or her new residence, but also travel expenses incurred by the employee and his or her dependents including food and lodging (not to exceed $1,500) as well as expenses (not to exceed $3,000) incurred in the termination of a lease or in the acquisition of a new lease or residence.

In addition to reimbursement for moving expenses, Section 162 of the Internal Revenue Code allows deductions for business-related travel expenses, including meals and lodging, while Section 274 allows deductions for 80 percent of business-related entertainment expenses (note that Section 274 imposes limitations on deductions for foreign travel). Meticulous expense account records should be kept by both the employee and the corporation to validate these deductible reimbursements. Other deductible fringe benefits include educational assistance programs and group legal services plans.

Contingent compensation is compensation dependent upon certain criteria, such as corporate growth or profit. Incentive compensation can include contingent compensation whereby the employee's compensation is contingent upon either individual or group performance. The Internal Revenue Service typically allows for larger corporate deductions for contingent compensation than it allows for straight salary deductions.

DEFERRED COMPENSATION

Deferred compensation is a broad term, used to describe all types of compensation whose payment to the employee is postponed until the happening of a future event, such as, but not limited to, retirement. There are two categories of deferred compensation plans: **qualified** and **nonqualified plans**. As noted in Chapter 2, these terms refer to plans which do (or do not, as the case may be) qualify for special tax treatment under the Internal Revenue Code. Those plans qualifying for special treatment are subject to certain employee eligibility, vesting, funding, and distribution requirements. Only qualified plans allow funding without contemporaneous assessment of reportable income to the employee. Under qualified plans, the employee does not pay taxes on the funds until the funds are distributed. Even then, if the funds are distributed in one lump sum, special tax rates may apply to lower the tax burden incurred by the employee. Further, contributions made by the employer; up to a limit of $100,000 can be paid to a deceased employee's beneficiary without subjection to federal estate tax. As an incentive to the employer, qualified plans have an added advantage of allowing the employer to deduct contributions against income for the tax year in which such contributions are made, regardless of when compensation is to be distributed to the employee.

A. Defined Contribution Plans versus Defined Benefit Plans

As stated earlier in Chapter 2, qualified plans can be divided into two categories: defined contribution plans and defined benefit plans. You may recall that a **defined contribution plan** is one which sets up individual accounts for each participating employee. The benefits incurred are based on the amount of contributions to the employee's account. **Stock bonus plans** and **profit-sharing plans** are examples of defined contribution plans. These two types of defined contribution plans actually are quite similar, with the exception that the employee receives a share of the profits paid out in shares of stock rather than cash under the stock bonus plan. As contrasted with a stock bonus plan, an **employee stock ownership plan (ESOP)** involves monetary contributions put into an employee stock ownership trust. These contributions are then used to purchase shares of corporate stock. These stock shares, or their monetary equivalent, are distributed to employees upon the happening of a specified event, such as retirement. In order to determine whether an ESOP meets the legal requirements for approval by the Internal Revenue Service, a corporation must file a Form 5309, *Application for Determination of Employee Stock Ownership Plan,* together with other specified applicable forms (see Exhibit 11.5 at the end of this chapter for Form 5309).

A qualified plan that does not fall into the category of defined contribution plan is considered a **defined benefit plan**. Annuity plans are considered defined benefit plans. An **annuity plan** is one in which contributions are used to buy annuity policies from an insurance company. Annuity policies provide that as of a stated date, the recipient receive fixed, period payments for the remainder of his or her life.

Pension plans may be either defined compensation or defined benefit plans. One type of pension plan discussed earlier in the text is a **simplified employee pension plan** in which the employer makes contributions into each employee's individual IRA account. This plan is considered a defined contribution plan for tax purposes. A **401(k) plan** is an elective deferral plan in which the employee elects to have the employer contribute a part of his or her before-tax salary to the plan, said part remaining tax-free until it is distributed under the plan. Some 401(k) plans permit matching contributions to be made by the employer. A **money purchase pension plan**, considered a deferred contribution plan, is one in which the employer's contributions are determined by a fixed formula based on the salary of the employee. **Integrated plans** can be either deferred compensation plans or deferred benefit plans and allow the employer to integrate contributions made to Social Security when calculating the amount of contribution or benefit to be received by the employee.

B.   *Statutory Criteria*

Both defined contribution plans and defined benefit plans have statutorily imposed limits, the defined contribution plan being limited in the amount of annual contributions that may be made versus the defined contribution plan being limited in the amount of annual benefits provided. At the time of this writing, the annual contribution limit for defined contribution plans made to an individual employee is the lesser of $30,000 or 25 percent of that employee's annual compensation and the benefits contributed to defined benefit plans are limited to the lesser of $120,000 or 100 percent of the employee's average annual compensation for the employee's highest consecutive three years. Please note that adjustments to these limits are made to reflect inflation as measured by the Consumer Price Index. Special limits apply to 401(k) plans as set forth by statute. However, this limit is indexed based on the Consumer Price Index (for example, this limit was $9,240 in 1995).

Section 401 of the Internal Revenue Code states that a plan may not discriminate either as to participants or benefits if the plan is to qualify for special tax treatment. Eligible employees are those who are at least 21 years of age or who have been employed for one year, whichever occurs latest. In addition, the plan must pass one of several tests for nondiscrimination. Many corporations apply the percentage test which requires that a plan cover at least 70 percent of all employees or 80 percent of all eligible employees, provided that at least 70 percent of all employees are eligible. Other corporations apply different tests to ensure a nondiscriminatory result.

Section 411 of the Internal Revenue Code enforces maximum time limits for **deferred vesting** (postponement of the time at which the employee's rights to the benefits become nonforfeitable). It allows a corporation to defer the vesting of benefits until the employee has worked for five years, at which time the entire amount of benefits vest in the employee. In the alternative, Section 411 also allows vesting in increments, with a certain percentage of the benefits to vest in the employee over a period of three to seven years. **Top heavy plans** are subject to special vesting requirements. A plan is considered "top heavy" if 60 percent or more of the plan benefits are to vest in key employees. The Internal Revenue Code defines key employees as corporate officers, a corporation's ten largest shareholders, persons holding 5 percent or more of the corporate stock, or persons holding 1 percent or more of the corporate stock and whose annual compensation exceeds $150,000 (this compensation amount to be adjusted according to cost of living changes).

In addition to the above requirements, qualified plans fall under the authority of the **Employee Retirement Income Security Act of 1974 (ERISA)**, the **Tax Equity and Fiscal Responsibility Act of 1982 (TEFRA)**, the **Retirement Equity Act of 1984 (REA)**, and the **Pension Protection Act of 1987 (PPA)**, just to mention a few of the legislative acts that must by researched by a corporate attorney or corporate paralegal prior to the attorney's advising a client on the feasibility of a deferred compensation plan. Please note that a corporation with an employee benefit plan subject to ERISA must file annual informational returns. Additionally, corporations maintaining certain fringe benefit plans as specified under Section 6039D of the Internal Revenue Code must file these returns as well. They may be filed using either form 5500-C/R (a plan with fewer than 100 participants) or Form 5500 (a plan with 100 or more participants). These forms may be found in Exhibits 11.6 and 11.7 at the end of this chapter.

EMPLOYMENT AGREEMENTS

A well-drafted employment agreement is one which is mutually advantageous to the parties. Although it typically is drafted by legal counsel for the employer corporation, it should reflect an arm's length negotiation process between the prospective employer and employee. An employment agreement entered into by the corporation must be approved by the corporation's board of directors. As is the case with other contracts, an employee agreement must be customized to suit the objectives of the parties to the agreement. Nonetheless, most employment agreements contain similar components.

A. *Term of Employment*

An employment agreement should clearly state the term of employment and the date upon which such term begins. Some agreements contain a provision for automatic renewal after the initial term expires while others do not. If an agreement includes an automatic renewal provision, included in the provision should be a notice requirement indicating the notice that must be given by either party should that party not wish to renew.

B.   Title and Duties

The title, if any, given to the employee should be indicated, and the duties to be performed by the employee should be outlined. Care should be taken in the title given to the employee's position. Corporate officers must be elected by a corporation's board of directors and therefore the granting of a title such as president or vice president should be avoided. Further, the wording of the employee's duties should be specific enough to inform the employee of the employer's expectations, but not so specific that it precludes room for growth of responsibilities. If the employee is expected to devote his or her full time to the fulfillment of these duties, this should be stated.

An employee performing duties on behalf of an employer is considered an agent of the employer-principal. An employee must be given adequate authority to act effectively on behalf of the corporation. Nonetheless, there may be limitations the corporation wishes to place on the employee's authority. If this is the case, the scope of the employee's authority to act on behalf of the corporation should be clearly demarcated. Although an employee's actions falling outside the scope of authority may, in some circumstances, bind the corporation with regard to third parties, such actions may be considered a breach of contract on the part of the employee and the corporation will be able to pursue legal remedies against the employee. Additionally, if the employee is to be precluded from involvement with other businesses while working for the employer, the provision should so indicate.

C.   Compensation

The compensation provision should present an attractive package to both the employer and employee. The employee will be looking for a compensation package that includes not only straight salary but incentive compensation and fringe benefits. The employer corporation will be looking to provide compensation that is tax deductible to the corporation. These objectives need not be mutually exclusive. Few employment agreements forego straight salary altogether. Often a salary amount is stated for the initial year of employment with a stated percentage increase for each subsequent year the agreement is in effect.

Occasionally, an employee is hired on straight commission or on a mixture of salary plus commission. If the employee is to receive commission, the provision should indicate not only the amount of commission to be paid but also the criteria that must be met before such commission is earned, as well as the timing of the payment of the commission. Typically, a commission will be a specified percentage of the sales generated by the individual employee, but a commission can be a percentage of the corporation's net profits. If the majority of the employee's compensation is based on commission it is common practice to allow an employee to make **draws** against the commission (i.e., receive a certain monetary sum weekly or monthly, the total of which is to be deducted from the commission due to the employee). Problems may arise if the employee's draws exceed the amount of commission earned. The agreement should specify whether the employer is entitled to reimbursement by the employee for all amounts drawn in excess of the commission earned or whether the draws are to stop at a fixed dollar amount.

In addition to or instead of commission, an agreement may provide for the payment of cash or stock bonuses to an employee. If a bonus is to be included as part of the employee's compensation, the amount of the bonus (whether fixed or a percentage) as well as the timing for the payment of the bonus should be indicated. Further, the agreement should provide for a method of determining the amount of incentive compensation owed to the employee if the agreement is terminated before it expires. For example, if the employee is to receive a certain percentage of the net profits of the business at the end of each business year and the employee's employment is terminated prematurely, the agreement should indicate whether the employee is entitled to any percentage of the profits for the year in which the termination has taken place and if so, how the amount due the employee shall be calculated.

D. Fringe Benefits

Any stock options and fringe benefits offered to the employee should be stated with specificity. Some of the fringe benefits offered may be available to all employees, such as health and life insurance. In this instance, the employment agreement need not go into detail about insurance coverage but rather should indicate that the employee is entitled to coverage under the group plan. If the employee is relocating to accept the position, the employer typically provides reimbursement for some or all of the employee's moving expenses. In positions requiring frequent travel on the part of the employee, the employer will reimburse the employee for travel expenses. A provision pertaining to such reimbursement should indicate that the employee will be reimbursed for "reasonable" business-related expenses and should require the employee to keep a detailed account of such expenses as a prerequisite to reimbursement. A common fringe benefit is the use of a company car. Some agreements state that the corporation shall provide the employee with a vehicle of the employee's choice up to a certain dollar value. Others state that the corporation shall provide the employee with an "appropriate" vehicle or simply indicate that a vehicle will be provided but omit the use of any descriptive language.

E.   Disability

Unforeseen illnesses and other potentially incapacitating events occur. The employment agreement should specify what compensation, if any, beyond pay for ordinary sick days, the employee is entitled to should the employee become disabled or incapacitated. If the employee is to continue to receive salary, the agreement should specify whether the employee is to receive full or partial salary and the duration of payment. Further, the agreement should indicate at what point the employer is allowed to terminate the employment of a disabled or incapacitated employee.

F.   Restrictive Covenants

The portion of the agreement that is of primary concern to most corporations is the portion containing restrictive covenants. A **restrictive covenant** is a provision restricting: (1) the use of work product, (2) the disclosure of trade secrets or other confidential information, or (3) the future engagement of the employee in a business competitive with the business of the corporation. An employment agreement can contain one or all three types of restrictive covenants.

1.   Trade Secrets

Trade secrets are protected by common and statutory law even in the absence of a restrictive provision in an employment agreement. A **trade secret** is confidential information, in whatever form, that gives the possessor of the information a business advantage over the competition. A trade secret can be as concrete as a patented formula or as abstract as a business method. When a court considers whether disclosed information is a trade secret worthy of legal protection, it looks at various factors. These factors include: (1) the scope of people who have access to the information (the larger the scope the less likely the information will be deemed protected), (2) the value of the information (the greater the value the more likely the information will be deemed protected), (3) the expenditure in time and money to acquire the information (the greater the expenditure the more likely the information will be deemed protected), (4) the difficulty in duplicating the information by other means (the greater the difficulty the more likely the information will be deemed protected), and (5) the measures taken to ensure confidentiality (the greater the measures the more likely the information will be deemed protected). Often an employment agreement will contain a trade secrets provision but will not define the term "trade secret." Should a dispute arise, the above factors come into play.

If trade secrets are disclosed by an employee to a third party, the employer will have a legal cause of action for breach of confidentiality. That breach may arise as a breach of a fiduciary duty or it may arise as a breach of an express or implied contract to retain confidentiality. A written employment agreement containing a trade secrets provision is an express contract which allows the employer to sue for breach. The employer will desire **injunctive relief** (an order by the court prohibiting further detrimental activity) and often will desire money damages as well. A trade secrets provision should not restrict the employer to any particular form of relief.

2. Work Product Provision

Some employees are hired for their technical or research skills. They often are hired to create formulas, processes, or other inventions. The employer seeking exclusive rights to these inventions and any patents or copyrights pertaining to them should include a **work product provision** in the employment agreement. Under common law, an employer owns the work product of the employee if the employee was specifically hired to create the work product. However, the employer does not own a work product that is created by an employee during his or her regular hours or employment but is not included as part of his or her job description. Under common law, an employer has **shop rights** to such a work product, meaning that the employer has a nonexclusive right to use the work product. To guard against the possibility that a court will determine that an employer merely has shop rights to a work product, a work product provision should indicate which inventions (or categories of inventions) shall be deemed the property of the employer. Often, an assignment of the inventions by the employee to the employer is required to vest full legal title to the invention (and applicable patent or copyright) in the employer. Thus, the provision should state that the employee agrees to execute all requisite documents to effectuate legal title vesting in the employer.

3.   Covenant Not to Compete

Common law provides no protection against competition. Therefore a **covenant not to compete** (sometimes referred to as a **noncompetition clause**) should be included in the employment agreement. Courts look at these provisions with much scrutiny and will only enforce those provisions deemed reasonable as to geographic scope and duration. What is reasonable can vary considerably. In some instances, prohibiting a former employee from engaging in a competitive business within the same state may be considered too restrictive to be enforced (as would be the case if the employee were a hair stylist) and may not be restrictive enough in other instances (as would be the case if the employee's duties and contacts were national in scope). Similarly, what is reasonable in terms of duration can vary greatly. Very rarely, if at all, will a court enforce a covenant not to compete that includes a duration longer than the term of the employment agreement. Some provisions provide that the covenant is not applicable if the employer terminates the agreement unless such termination is brought about by breach of the agreement by the employee.

G.   *Termination*

In addition to restrictive covenants, an employment agreement should address the circumstances under which the parties may terminate the agreement. Failure to include such a provision implies that termination of the agreement prior to its expiration date is a material breach of the agreement. Even if the parties wish to treat early termination of the agreement as a breach, it is still good practice to spell it out. In instances in which the parties desire to hold each other to the term of duration set forth in the agreement, the parties will want to provide for termination of employment for "good cause" and should indicate the grounds constituting "good cause." If the parties wish to allow for termination prior to the expiration of the agreement with or without cause, the agreement should so provide and should specify the applicable notice requirements to effectuate termination. Many corporations provide severance packages for an employee whose employment has been prematurely terminated. Severance packages can include the continuation of full or partial salary for a specified period of time, as well as the continuation of certain employee benefits. If a severance package is to be provided, it should be detailed in the agreement.

H.   Arbitration

It is becoming increasingly common for employment disputes to be settled through arbitration. Arbitration can save both employers and employees the considerable expense of court costs and other litigation-related expenses. Nonetheless, even arbitration can leave the parties with large attorney's fees. Under contract law, the losing party in litigation is not required to pay the successful party's legal fees unless the contract so provides. Therefore, it is good practice to include an attorney's fees provision in the employment agreement.

A paralegal can aid corporate legal counsel in various corporation-employee matters. Paralegals research federal and state statutes that pertain to tax treatment of employee compensation and benefit plans, as well as those statutes that pertain to employment discrimination and employee rights. Paralegals may aid in the drafting of employee manuals, corporate resolutions approving the hiring of or benefits provided to employees, and employment agreements. It is advisable to use an employment agreement worksheet when interviewing a client to assure that all pertinent provisions are covered. A completed sample worksheet follows in the Client Simulation.

CLIENT SIMULATION

Checking her tickler file, Karen notices that a client, William R. Davis of WRD Enterprises, Inc., is scheduled to meet with Thomas at the end of the week to review an employment contract between his company and Celia Cameron, a prospective employee. Last week, Thomas and Karen met with the client to discuss the drafting of the contract. Celia Cameron is presently working for a company in Los Angeles, California but is willing to relocate to Any State for the right incentives. Celia has been working in the field of computer software marketing for eight years and her name has become well known within the field. One of WRD Enterprises' newest activities is the assembly of computer software packages which it sells to computer hardware companies. These packages, called "bundles" are offered at no additional cost to the consumer when the consumer purchases a computer manufactured by the computer hardware company. Typically, these bundles include various computer games, a word processing program, a spreadsheet program, and other basic software. WRD Enterprises, Inc. does not produce the software itself; rather, it negotiates favorable price terms with software companies in return for buying in bulk with the understanding that the software will be used in bundling packages.

Celia has been performing these same activities for her present company but feels that her growth opportunities are limited with that company because it is a family operation. She has told William that she does not have a written employment agreement with her present company, and that she was hired as an employee "at will." Therefore, she is not operating under the constraints of a covenant not to compete.

William has met with his board of directors to discuss the hiring of Celia and has accepted salary and additional compensation recommendations made by the board. The board has passed a resolution authorizing William, as President, to enter into an employment agreement with Celia on behalf of WRD Enterprises, Inc. Should an acceptable agreement be reached with Celia, the board will pass a resolution permitting the granting of stock options to her (one of the incentive possibilities Thomas discussed with the client). Celia's present employer is providing her with the incentive of a percentage of the net business profits and William knows that in addition to straight salary, he will have to offer Celia the same kind of incentive if he hopes to hire her.

Of greatest concern to William is the protection of trade secrets and the possibility of Celia quitting WRD Enterprises, Inc. and using her expertise on behalf of a competitor. Providing a stock option is one way to encourage loyalty by indicating to Celia that she has a vested interest in WRD Enterprises, Inc. Additionally, trade secret and noncompetition provisions will be included in the agreement. Because Celia's duties with the client's corporation will require both national and international travel, her contacts will be broad. Therefore, the noncompetition clause will preclude Celia from working in the same field within the territory of the United States. Because such a broad territorial constraint will be imposed, Thomas believes that a time limitation of no longer than two years after the expiration of the agreement is reasonable. Additionally, he advises William that such constraints should not be imposed if the company has terminated the agreement prior to its expiration for some reason other than a breach of the contract by Celia. If Celia desires to terminate the agreement prior to its expiration, the noncompetition constraint will remain in effect.

Finally, although Celia's title will be Executive Director of Sales and Marketing, William wants assurance that any concepts Celia may develop as a result of her knowledge of the computer software business will become the property of WRD Enterprises, Inc. Karen met with the client after the initial discussion with Thomas to complete the employment agreement worksheet which follows in Exhibit 11.3.

EXHIBIT 11.3

Employment Agreement Worksheet

DATE OF INTAKE:	March 3, 1997
ATTORNEY:	Thomas Trumbull
PARALEGAL:	Karen Greer
CLIENT NUMBER:	1586
MATTER NUMBER:	0017
PERSON RESPONSIBLE FOR INTAKE:	Karen Greer
1. CLIENT NAME:	William R. Davis for client company WRD Enterprises, Inc.
2. ADDRESS:	253 Parkside Avenue Any City, Any State
3. TELEPHONE:	(000) 774-2228 FAX: (000) 774-3994
4. EMPLOYEE:	Celia Cameron
5. ADDRESS:	316 N.W. 20th Street Los Angeles, California
6. TERM OF AGREEMENT:	A term of three years commencing upon the signing of the agreement.
7. RENEWAL OPTION:	The agreement will be automatically renewed for a one-year period upon all the terms and conditions contained in the agreement unless written notice is given by either party at least 60 days prior to the expiration of the agree-

EXHIBIT 11.3   *Continued*

ment of that party's intention not to renew the agreement.

8. EMPLOYEE'S POSITION: Employee shall hold the position of executive director of sales and marketing.

9. EMPLOYEE'S DUTIES: Employee shall be in charge of all national and international "bundling" contracts. Employee shall devote her full time and energies to the negotiation and acquisition of software contracts from software manufacturers for software games and other programs to be used in the assembly of bundling packages. Employee shall also be in charge of the sale of bundling packages to computer hardware companies. Employee understands that her responsibilities will require her to travel at least two weeks out of each month and she is willing and able to adhere to this travel schedule.

10. SALARY: Employee shall be paid an annual salary of $100,000 for the first year of the contract, with a 5 percent salary increase the second year and another 5 percent salary increase the third year and each subsequent year this agreement remains in effect under the exercise of the renewal option.

11. PAY SCHEDULE: Employee's salary shall be paid on the fifteenth day and the last day of each month.

12. COMMISSION: Employee shall receive a commission of 3 percent per annum on the net profits of the Company. Employee shall

EXHIBIT 11.3 *Continued*

receive this commission within 90 days after the close of the business year.

13. DRAWING ACCOUNT: Not applicable

14. BONUSES: Not applicable

15. EXPENSES: Employer shall reimburse Employee for all reasonable travel and other business-related expenses incurred by Employee (and which have not been directly paid by Employer) upon receipt of an itemized expense account presented by Employee.

16. STOCK OPTIONS: Employer grants to Employee, by resolution of its Board of Directors, the option, exercisable at any time within five years after the granting of this option, to purchase up to a total of 5,000 shares of common stock of the Company at a purchase price not less than the fair market value of the stock, to be determined by mutual agreement of the parties or, should the parties fail to reach such an agreement, by arbitration as provided for in this agreement. In the event termination of employment occurs for any reason, Employee's option shall expire immediately upon such termination. This stock option is not assignable.

17. STOCK BONUS: Not applicable

18. FRINGE BENEFITS: Employee shall be entitled to the benefits of the Company's group life, medical, accident, disability, and other benefit plans as long as she is in the Company's em-

EXHIBIT 11.3   *Continued*

ploy. Additionally, Employer will provide Employee with the use of an automobile in connection with the performance of her duties.

19. RETIREMENT BENEFITS: Covered in fringe benefits above.

20. DEATH BENEFITS: Covered in fringe benefits above.

21. VACATIONS: The Employee will be entitled to three weeks of paid vacation time per year. Any accumulated vacation time not used shall not carry over into the following year.

22. DISABILITY: If Employee cannot perform her duties because of illness or incapacity, Employer shall continue payment of Employee's salary at the above-stated rate for a period of three months, after which time Employee's salary shall be reduced 25 percent for the next three months. Employee's full compensation shall be reinstated should she return to work at any time during this period. If, after the expiration of this six-month period, Employee remains unable to discharge her duties, Employer has the right to terminate this agreement and its obligations shall cease upon such termination.

23. EMPLOYEE WORK PRODUCT: All inventions, designs, procedures, and any other materials created, developed or improved by Employee in any way related to computer software or hardware during the course of her employment, shall be the sole property of the Employer, free from any legal or equitable title of the Employee. Employee agrees to execute

EXHIBIT 11.3 *Continued*

and deliver in a timely fashion all necessary documents for perfecting title in the Employer.

24. TRADE SECRETS: The Employee agrees that she will not, during or after the term of her employment with the Company, reveal directly or indirectly to any person or business entity, any information concerning the business of the Company, including but not limited to, customer names or lists; business methods, policies, and procedures; research and development projects; or any information covered in the work product provision of this agreement. If Employee does reveal this information, the Employer shall be entitled to an injunction restraining the Employee from making such disclosures or from rendering services to any person or entity to whom said information has been revealed. The right to injunctive relief is not exclusive; the Employer may pursue other remedies against Employee for breach of contract.

25. NONCOMPETITION CLAUSE: Employee agrees that she shall not, during the term this agreement remains in effect and for a period of two years thereafter, engage in activities within the territory of the United States, directly or indirectly, in any business competitive with the Employer. The term "engaging in business" shall include, but not be limited to, acting as owner, partner, shareholder, principal, agent, consultant, or employee in any business competitive with

EXHIBIT 11.3   *Continued*

the Employer. If this agreement is terminated by Employer before the expiration of its term for any reason other than breach of the agreement by Employee, the restrictions imposed upon Employee in this provision shall not apply. If this agreement is terminated by Employee before the expiration of its term, the restrictions imposed upon Employee in this provision shall remain in effect.

26. TERMINATION OF AGREEMENT BY EMPLOYEE:

Without cause, either party to this agreement may terminate it by providing 60 days' written notice of intent to terminate the agreement. In the event of termination of this agreement by either party, Employee shall receive the commission on net profits of the business stated above based on a calculation from the beginning of the Company's fiscal year up to and including Employee's last day of employment. Employee shall receive payment of said commission within 90 days of the close of the business year in which termination of this agreement has occurred. Employee agrees that immediately upon termination of her employment she will turn over to Employer all records, forms, contracts, customer lists and data, and any other documents that have come into her possession by reason of her employment with the Company.

27. TERMINATION OF AGREEMENT BY EMPLOYER:

Employer may terminate the agreement upon 30 days' written notice if any of the following events occur:

EXHIBIT 11.3 *Continued*

(a) the sale of substantially all of the Company's assets, (b) the sale, exchange, or other disposition in one transaction of the majority of the Company's outstanding shares of stock, (c) the merger or consolidation of the Company with another company, or (d) the Company's bona fide decision to terminate its business or liquidate its assets. Should Employer terminate the agreement under any of the conditions listed in (a) through (d) above, Employer shall pay Employee the equivalent of one additional month's salary upon Employee's last day of employment.

28. MEDIATION: Not desired by client.

29. ARBITRATION: Any claim or controversy that arises out of or relates to this agreement, or the breach of it, shall be settled by arbitration in accordance with the rules of the American Arbitration Association. Judgment upon the award may be entered in any court possessing jurisdiction of arbitration awards.

30. ADDITIONAL PROVISIONS:

(1) Employee agrees, during the term of employment as well as after termination of this agreement to provide such information and cooperation to the Company as it may reasonably require in connection with any litigation in which the Company is, or may become, a party. (2) Employer shall reimburse Employee for reasonable moving expenses incurred by Employee for relocation from California to Any State.

After completing the worksheet, Karen was instructed by Thomas to wait until the client called to say that Celia agreed to the basic terms before drafting the agreement. Having received the telephone call this morning, Karen is ready to proceed with the drafting of the agreement. She has a skeletal form for an employment agreement in her computer files which contains some of the provision headings she will incorporate into the client's agreement as well as many of the boilerplate provisions found in standard employment agreements. Using this form and her worksheet as guides, she drafts the following agreement.

EXHIBIT 11.4

Employment Agreement

AGREEMENT, effective as of this _____ day of _____, 19_____, by and between WRD ENTERPRISES, INC., a corporation duly organized and existing under the laws of the State of Any State (hereinafter referred to as "EMPLOYER") and CELIA CAMERON (hereinafter referred to as "EMPLOYEE").

In consideration of the mutual covenants herein contained, the parties agree as follows.

I. *TERM OF EMPLOYMENT*. EMPLOYER agrees to hire EMPLOYEE for a term of three (3) years commencing on the date hereof.

II. *RENEWAL*. This Agreement shall be automatically renewed for a one-year period upon all the terms and conditions contained in the Agreement unless written notice is given by either party at least sixty (60) days prior to the expiration of the Agreement of that party's intention not to renew the Agreement.

III. *TITLE AND DUTIES*. EMPLOYEE shall hold the position of Executive Director of Sales and Marketing. EMPLOYEE shall be in charge of all national and international "bundling" contracts. EMPLOYEE shall devote her full time and energies to the negotiation and acquisition of software contracts from software manufacturers for software games and other programs to be used in the putting together of bundling packages. EMPLOYEE shall also be in charge of the sale of bundling packages to computer hardware companies. EMPLOYEE understands that her responsibilities will require her to travel at least two (2) weeks out of each month and she is willing and able to adhere to this travel schedule.

EXHIBIT 11.4 *Continued*

IV. *SALARY AND PAY SCHEDULE*. EMPLOYEE shall be paid an annual salary of One Hundred Thousand Dollars ($100,000) for the first year of the Agreement, with a five percent (5%) salary increase the second year and another five percent (5%) salary increase the third year and each subsequent year this Agreement remains in effect under the exercise of the renewal option. EMPLOYEE's salary shall be paid on the fifteenth day and the last day of each month.

V. *COMMISSION*. EMPLOYEE shall receive a commission of three percent (3%) per annum on the net profits of the Company. EMPLOYEE shall receive this commission within ninety (90) days after the close of the business year.

VI. *EXPENSES*. EMPLOYER shall reimburse EMPLOYEE for all reasonable travel and other business-related expenses incurred by EMPLOYEE (and which have not been directly paid by EMPLOYER) upon receipt of an itemized expense account presented by EMPLOYEE. In addition, EMPLOYER shall reimburse EMPLOYEE for reasonable moving expenses incurred by EMPLOYEE for relocation from California to Any State.

VII. *STOCK OPTIONS*. EMPLOYER grants to EMPLOYEE, by resolution of its Board of Directors, the option, exercisable at any time within five years after the granting of this option, to purchase up to a total of Five Thousand (5,000) shares of common stock of the Company at a purchase price not less than the fair market value of the stock, to be determined by mutual agreement of the parties or, should the parties fail to reach such an agreement, by arbitration as provided for in this Agreement. In the event termination of employment occurs for any reason, EMPLOYEE's option shall expire immediately upon such termination. This stock option is not assignable.

VIII. *FRINGE BENEFITS*. EMPLOYEE shall be entitled to the benefits of the Company's group life, medical, accident, disability, and other benefit plans as long as she is in the Company's employ. Additionally, EMPLOYER will provide EMPLOYEE with the use of an automobile in connection with the performance of her duties.

IX. *VACATIONS*. EMPLOYEE shall be entitled to three (3) weeks of paid vacation time per year. Any accumulated vacation time not used shall not carry over into the following year.

X. *DISABILITY*. If EMPLOYEE cannot perform her duties because of illness or incapacity, EMPLOYER shall continue payment of EMPLOYEE's salary at the above-stated rate for a period of three (3) months, after which time EMPLOYEE's salary shall be reduced twenty-five percent (25%) for the next three months. EMPLOYEE's full com-

EXHIBIT 11.4   *Continued*

pensation shall be reinstated should she return to work at any time during this period. If, after the expiration of this six-month period, EMPLOYEE remains unable to discharge her duties, EMPLOYER has the right to terminate this Agreement and its obligations shall cease upon such termination.

XI. *EMPLOYEE WORK PRODUCT.* All inventions, designs, procedures, and any other materials created, developed, or improved by EMPLOYEE in any way related to computer software or hardware during the course of her employment, shall be the sole property of EMPLOYER, free from any legal or equitable title of EMPLOYEE. EMPLOYEE agrees to execute and deliver in a timely fashion all necessary documents for perfecting title in EMPLOYER.

XII. *TRADE SECRETS.* EMPLOYEE agrees that she will not, during or after the term of her employment with the Company, reveal directly or indirectly to any person or business entity, any information concerning the business of the Company, including but not limited to, customer names or lists; business methods, policies, and procedures; research and development projects; or any information covered in the work product provision of this Agreement. If EMPLOYEE does reveal this information, EMPLOYER shall be entitled to an injunction restraining EMPLOYEE from making such disclosures or from rendering services to any person or entity to whom said information has been revealed. The right to injunctive relief is not exclusive; EMPLOYER may pursue other remedies against EMPLOYEE for breach of this Agreement.

XIII. *COVENANT NOT TO COMPETE.* EMPLOYEE agrees that she shall not, during the term this Agreement remains in effect and for a period of two (2) years thereafter, engage in activities within the territory of the United States, directly or indirectly, in any business competitive with EMPLOYER. The term "engaging in business" shall include, but not be limited to, acting as owner, partner, shareholder, principal, agent, consultant, or employee in any business competitive with EMPLOYER. EMPLOYEE acknowledges that the restrictions contained in this provision are reasonable and necessary to protect EMPLOYER's legitimate interests. If this Agreement is terminated by EMPLOYER before the expiration of its term for any reason other than breach of the Agreement by EMPLOYEE, the restrictions imposed upon EMPLOYEE in this provision shall not apply. If this Agreement is terminated by EMPLOYEE before the expiration of its term, the restrictions imposed upon EMPLOYEE in this provision shall remain in effect.

XIV. *TERMINATION OF AGREEMENT.* Without cause, either party to this Agreement may terminate it by providing sixty (60) days' written notice of intent to termi-

EXHIBIT 11.4 *Continued*

nate the Agreement. In the event of termination of this Agreement by either party, EMPLOYEE shall receive the commission on net profits of the business stated above based on a calculation from the beginning of the Company's fiscal year up to and including EMPLOYEE's last day of employment. EMPLOYEE shall receive payment of said commission within ninety (90) days of the close of the business year in which termination of this Agreement has occurred.

Additionally, EMPLOYER may terminate the Agreement upon thirty (30) days' written notice if any of the following events occur:

(a) the sale of substantially all of the Company's assets,
(b) the sale, exchange, or other disposition in one transaction of the majority of the Company's outstanding shares of stock,
(c) the merger or consolidation of the Company with another company, or
(d) the Company's bona fide decision to terminate its business or liquidate its assets.

Should EMPLOYER terminate the Agreement under any of the conditions listed in (a) through (d) above, EMPLOYER shall pay EMPLOYEE the equivalent of one (1) additional month's salary upon EMPLOYEE's last day of employment.

EMPLOYEE agrees that immediately upon termination of her employment she shall turn over to EMPLOYER all records, forms, contracts, customer lists and data, and any other documents that have come into her possession by reason of her employment with the Company.

XV. *ARBITRATION.* Any claim or controversy that arises out of or relates to this Agreement, or the breach of it, shall be settled by arbitration in accordance with the rules of the American Arbitration Association. Judgment upon the award may be entered in any court possessing jurisdiction of arbitration awards.

XVI. *ASSISTANCE IN LITIGATION.* EMPLOYEE agrees, during the term of employment as well as after termination of this Agreement, to provide such information and cooperation to the Company as it may reasonably require in connection with any litigation in which the Company is, or may become, a party.

XVII. *NOTICES.* Any notices pursuant to this Agreement shall be validly served if in writing and delivered personally or sent by certified mail, return receipt requested to the respective address of each party.

EXHIBIT 11.4   *Continued*

XVIII. *ATTORNEY'S FEES.* In the event that any action is filed in relation to this Agreement, the unsuccessful party shall pay, in addition to all sums that either party may be required to pay, the attorney's fees of the successful party.

XIX. *WAIVER.* If EMPLOYER waives a breach of any provision of this Agreement by EMPLOYEE, said waiver shall not operate or be construed as a waiver of subsequent breaches by EMPLOYEE.

XX. *GOVERNING LAW.* This Agreement shall be construed and governed in accordance with the laws of the State of Any State.

XXI. *ENTIRE AGREEMENT.* This Agreement shall constitute the entire agreement between the parties and any prior understanding or representation of any kind prior to the date of this Agreement shall not be binding upon either party.

XXII. *MODIFICATION OF AGREEMENT.* Any modification to this Agreement shall be enforceable only by a written document signed by each party.

XXIII. *SEVERABILITY.* If, for any reason, any provision of this Agreement is held invalid, the other provisions of this Agreement shall remain in effect, insofar as is consistent with law.

    IN WITNESS WHEREOF, the parties have executed this Agreement under seal on the day and year first above written.

[Corporate Seal]   WRD ENTERPRISES, INC.

                                          By: _____
                                                            President

                                          Attest: _____
                                                            Secretary

                                          _____
                                              CELIA CAMERON

Chapter Summary

1. An employee manual does not act as an employment agreement between the employer and its employees. Rather, it sets forth the philosophies and expectations of the employer corporation. An employee manual enables a corporation to standardize personnel policies as well as to explain corporate "etiquette."

2. Most employee manuals are divided into sections covering general corporate philosophy, employment policies, employee conduct, and employee benefits. A manual should clearly indicate that the corporation reserves the right to make changes.

3. Although an employee manual is often drafted by the corporation rather than by an attorney, an attorney should be consulted to assure that the manual abides by all state and federal employment statutes, including the Americans with Disabilities Act and the Family and Medical Leave Act.

4. Written employment agreements commonly are used for key employees in executive or other positions in which restrictive covenants are advisable. A written agreement provides each party with assurances. The employee is assured of employment for a set term with an agreed-upon salary and possibly other forms of compensation. In return, the employer is assured of "damage control" upon termination of the agreement. Both parties are clear on their respective duties and obligations.

5. In addition to salary, corporations can offer employees various other forms of compensation, including fringe benefits; incentive compensation in the form of commissions, bonuses, and stock options; and deferred compensation benefits. Pertinent Internal Revenue Code sections should be reviewed to determine which deductions for compensation will be considered ordinary and necessary business expenses of a corporation. The Internal Revenue Service makes a distinction between shareholder-employees and other employees in this regard.

6. Fringe benefits available to most employees include group life insurance plans and employee health and accident plans. These plans typically must meet certain nondiscriminatory requirements. Other fringe benefits include death benefits and expense reimbursements for moving, travel, entertainment, and other business-related expenditures.

7. Deferred compensation refers to both qualified and nonqualified employee benefit plans. Qualified plans include profit-sharing plans, stock bonus or ownership plans, annuity plans, pension plans, and 401(k) plans. Qualified plans must meet certain eligibility, vesting, and distribution requirements.

8. Employment agreements for key employees often include severance

packages tailored to meet the objectives of both parties. Such packages may allow for the continuation of full or partial salary for a set period as well as continuation of various employee benefits.

9. A properly drafted employment agreement should contain, at a minimum, provisions outlining the term of the agreement, renewal options, duties of the employee, compensation (current and deferred), other granted benefits, restrictive covenants, and termination of the agreement.

Review Questions

1. What distinctions are made between shareholder-employees and other employees regarding a corporation's deduction of employee compensation as a business expense?
2. List the topics that should be included in an employee manual.
3. Compare and contrast the following:
   (i)   contingent compensation and deferred compensation;
   (ii) defined contribution plans and defined benefit plans;
   (iii) stock option plans and stock purchase agreements.
4. List the fringe benefits that are considered tax-qualified by the Internal Revenue Service.
5. Discuss the provisions that should be contained in an employment agreement.

KEY TERMS

annuity plan

contingent compensation

current compensation

deferred compensation

deferred vesting

draw

employee manual

employee stock
   ownership plan

401(k) plan

fringe benefits

incentive compensation

integrated plan

key employee

mission statement

restrictive covenant

shop right

stock option plan

stock purchase
   agreement

"top heavy" plan

trade secret

EXHIBIT 11.5

| Form **5309** (Rev. January 1994) Department of the Treasury Internal Revenue Service | **Application for Determination of Employee Stock Ownership Plan** (Under section 409 or 4975(e)(7) of the Internal Revenue Code) File with Form 5300 or 5303, whichever applies. | OMB No. 1545-0284 Expires 1-31-97 |

For IRS Use Only
File folder number ▶

1 Employer's name, address, and ZIP code

....
....

Telephone number ▶ ( )

2 Employer identification number

3 Date plan was adopted
Mo. Day Yr.

4 This application is for (complete one):

a ☐ A tax credit employee stock ownership plan under section 409
b ☐ An employee stock ownership plan under section 4975(e)(7)

5 Type of plan:

a ☐ Profit-sharing
b ☐ Stock bonus
c ☐ Money purchase and stock bonus

Show the section and page number in the plan document where the following provisions will appear.

| | | Section and page number |

6 Complete the following for all plans:

a The plan is designed to invest primarily in employer securities.

b Each participant must be entitled to direct the plan to vote the allocated securities as required in section 409(e)

c A participant entitled to a distribution from the plan may demand the entire distribution in employer securities, and if the securities are not readily tradable, the employer will repurchase the securities under a fair valuation formula

d A participant may elect to diversify a portion of his or her account's investment in employer securities as required under section 401(a)(28)

e A participant may begin distribution of his or her account balance after reaching normal retirement age, or after death, disability, or separation from service not later than required by section 409(o)

7 Only plans applying under section 409 complete the following:

a All employer securities transferred to or purchased by the plan for the employee plan credit or employee stock ownership credit will be allocated for the plan year to the accounts of all participants who are entitled to share in these allocations

b The allocation to each participant of the employer securities transferred or purchased for the employee plan credit or employee stock ownership credit is in substantially the same proportion as each employee's compensation is to the total compensation of all participants. For this allocation, compensation of any participant in excess of the first $100,000 per year is disregarded

c No allocated securities described in section 409(d) may be distributed to any participant before the end of the 84th month after the month the securities are allocated except for separation from service, death, disability, termination of the plan, or as otherwise stated in section 409(d).

d The participants have a nonforfeitable right to the securities allocated to them

e If any part of the employee plan credit or employee stock ownership credit is recaptured or redetermined, amounts transferred to the plan for such credit shall remain in the plan and if allocated shall remain allocated

8 Only plans applying under section 4975(e)(7) complete the following:

a The plan is designated as an employee stock ownership plan within the meaning of section 4975(e)(7)

b The plan provides for the establishment and maintenance of a suspense account as required under Regulations section 54.4975-11(c)

c Participants' rights to plan assets acquired by use of the exempt loan are protected as specified in Regulations section 54.4975-11(a)(3)(i) and (ii)

9 If the plan is applying under section 409(n) with respect to transactions under section 1042, the plan provides that the assets of the plan attributable to employer securities acquired by the plan in a sale to which section 1042 applies cannot accrue for the benefit of the persons specified in section 409(n) during the nonallocation period

Under penalties of perjury, I declare that I have examined this application, including accompanying statements, and to the best of my knowledge and belief it is true, correct, and complete.

Signature ▶   Title ▶   Date ▶

For Paperwork Reduction Act Notice, see back of form.   Cat. No. 11835F   Form **5309** (Rev. 1-94)

EXHIBIT 11.6

Form **5500-C/R**	**Return/Report of Employee Benefit Plan**	OMB Nos. 1210-0016

Form **5500-C/R**
Department of the Treasury
Internal Revenue Service
Department of Labor
Pension and Welfare Benefits Administration
Pension Benefit Guaranty Corporation

Return/Report of Employee Benefit Plan
(With fewer than 100 participants)
This form is required to be filed under sections 104 and 4065 of the Employee
Retirement Income Security Act of 1974 and sections 6039D, 6047(e),
6057(b), and 6058(a) of the Internal Revenue Code.
▶ See separate instructions.

OMB Nos. 1210-0016
1210-0089
1995
This Form Is Open
to Public Inspection.

For the calendar plan year 1995 or fiscal plan year beginning _____ **, 1995, and ending** _____ **, 19** ___

If **A**(1) through **A**(4), **B, C,** and/or **D** do not apply to this year's return/report,
leave the boxes unmarked.
You must check either box A(5) or A(6), whichever is applicable. See instructions.
A This return/report is:
(1) ☐ the first return/report filed for the plan;
(2) ☐ an amended return/report;
(3) ☐ the final return/report filed for the plan; or
(4) ☐ a short plan year return/report (less than 12 months).

For IRS Use Only
EP-ID

(5) **Form 5500-C filer check here** . . . . . ☐
(Complete only pages 1 and 3 through 6.) (Code section
6039D filers see instructions on page 5.)
(6) **Form 5500-R filer check here** . . . . . ☐
(Complete only pages 1 and 2. Detach pages 3 through 6
before filing. If you checked box (1) or (3), you must file a
Form 5500-C. (See page 6 of the instructions.)

**IF ANY INFORMATION ON A PREPRINTED PAGE 1 IS INCORRECT, CORRECT IT. IF ANY INFORMATION IS MISSING, ADD IT. PLEASE USE
RED INK WHEN MAKING THESE CHANGES AND INCLUDE THE PREPRINTED PAGE 1 WITH YOUR COMPLETED RETURN/REPORT.**

B Check here if any information reported in 1a, 2a, 2b, or 5a changed since the last return/report for this plan . . . . ▶ ☐
C If your plan year changed since the last return/report, check here . . . . ▶ ☐
D If you filed for an extension of time to file this return/report, check here and attach a copy of the approved extension . . . . . ▶ ☐

1a Name and address of plan sponsor (employer, if for a single-employer plan)
(Address should include room or suite no.)

1b Employer identification number (EIN)

1c Sponsor's telephone number

1d Business code (see instructions, page 19)

1e CUSIP issuer number

2a Name and address of plan administrator (if same as plan sponsor, enter "Same")

2b Administrator's EIN

2c Administrator's telephone number

3 If you are filing this page without the preprinted historical plan information and the name, address, and EIN of the plan sponsor or plan
administrator has changed since the last return/report filed for this plan, enter the information from the last return/report on lines 3a and/or
3b and complete line **3c.**
a Sponsor .... EIN .... Plan number ....
b Administrator .... EIN ....
c If line 3a indicates a change in the sponsor's name, address, and EIN, is this a change in sponsorship only? (See line 3c on page 9 of the
instructions for the definition of sponsorship.) Enter "Yes" or "No." ▶

4 **ENTITY CODE.** (If not shown, enter applicable code from page 9 of the instructions.) ▶

5a Name of plan ▶ ....
....

5b Effective date of plan (mo., day, yr.)

5c Three-digit
plan number ▶

All filers must complete 6a through 6d, as applicable.
6a ☐ Welfare benefit plan   **6b** ☐ Pension benefit plan
(If the correct codes are not preprinted below, enter the applicable codes from
page 9 of the instructions in the boxes.)

6c Pension plan features. (If the correct codes are not preprinted below, enter the applicable
pension plan feature codes from page 9 of the instructions in the boxes.)

6d ☐ Fringe benefit plan. Attach Schedule F (Form 5500). See instructions.

Caution: A penalty for the late or incomplete filing of this return/report will be assessed unless reasonable cause is established.

Under penalties of perjury and other penalties set forth in the instructions, I declare that I have examined this return/report, including accompanying schedules and
statements, and to the best of my knowledge and belief, it is true, correct, and complete.

Signature of employer/plan sponsor ▶ .... Date ▶ ....
Type or print name of individual signing for employer/plan sponsor ....
Signature of plan administrator ▶ .... Date ▶ ....
Type or print name of individual signing for plan administrator

For Paperwork Reduction Act Notice, see page 1 of the instructions.   Cat. No. 10957K   Form **5500-C/R** (1995)

EXHIBIT 11.6 *Continued*

Form 5500-C/R (1995)   **Form 5500-R filers, complete pages 1 and 2 only. Form 5500-C filers, complete page 1, skip page 2, and complete pages 3 through 6.**   Page **2**

		Yes	No
6e	Check investment arrangement(s): **(1)** ☐ Master trust **(2)** ☐ Common/Collective trust **(3)** ☐ Pooled separate account		
7a	Total participants: **(1)** At the beginning of plan year ▶ .... **(2)** At the end of plan year ▶		
b	Enter number of participants with account balances at the end of the plan year (defined benefit plans do not complete this item) ▶		
c	**(1)** Were any participants in the pension benefit plan separated from service with a deferred vested benefit for which a Schedule SSA (Form 5500) is required to be attached? (See instructions.) . . . . **7c(1)**		
	(2) If "Yes," enter the number of separated participants required to be reported ▶		
8a	Was this plan terminated during this plan year or any prior plan year? If "Yes," enter the year ▶ **8a**		
b	Were all the plan assets either distributed to participants or beneficiaries, transferred to another plan, or brought under the control of PBGC? **8b**		
c	If line **8a** is "Yes" and the plan is covered by PBGC, is the plan continuing to file PBGC Form 1 and pay premiums until the end of the plan year in which assets are distributed or brought under the control of PBGC? **8c**		
9	Is this a plan established or maintained pursuant to one or more collective bargaining agreements? **9**		
10	If any benefits are provided by an insurance company, insurance service, or similar organization, enter the number of Schedules A (Form 5500), Insurance Information, that are attached. If none, enter -0-. ▶		
11a	**(1)** Were any plan amendments adopted during this plan year? . . . . **11a(1)**		
	(2) Enter the date the most recent amendment was adopted ▶ Month............Day ....Year		
b	If line **11a** is "Yes," did any amendment result in a retroactive reduction of accrued benefits for any participant? . . . **11b**		
c	If line **11a** is "Yes," did any amendment change the information contained in the latest summary plan description or summary description of modifications available at the time of the amendment? **11c**		
d	If line **11c** is "Yes," has a summary plan description or summary description of modifications that reflects the plan amendments referred to on line **11c** been both furnished to participants and filed with the Department of Labor? . . . **11d**		
12a	If this is a pension benefit plan subject to the minimum funding standards, has the plan experienced a funding deficiency for this plan year? (See instructions.). **12a**		
b	If line **12a** is "Yes," have you filed Form 5330 to pay the excise tax? **12b**		
c	Is the plan administrator making an election under section 412(c)(8) for an amendment adopted after the end of the plan year? (See instructions.) **12c**		
d	If a change in the actuarial funding method was made for the plan year pursuant to a Revenue Procedure providing automatic approval for the change, indicate whether the plan sponsor/administrator agrees to the change **12d**		
13a	Total plan assets as of the beginning .... and end .... of the plan year		
b	Total liabilities as of the beginning .... and end .... of the plan year		
c	Net assets as of the beginning ▶ and end ▶ of the plan year		
14	For this plan year, enter: **a** Plan income .... **d** Plan contributions		
	b Expenses .... **e** Total benefits paid		
	c Net income (loss) (subtract **14b** from **14a**)		

			Yes	No	Amount
15	You may **NOT** use **N/A** in response to lines 15a through 15o. If you check "Yes," you must enter a dollar amount in the amount column. **During this plan year:**				
a	Was this plan covered by a fidelity bond?	**15a**			
b	If line **15a** is "Yes," enter the name of the surety company ▶				
c	Was there any loss to the plan, whether or not reimbursed, caused by fraud or dishonesty? . . .	**15c**			
d	Was there any sale, exchange, or lease of any property between the plan and the employer, any fiduciary, any of the five most highly paid employees of the employer, any owner of a 10% or more interest in the employer, or relatives of any such persons?	**15d**			
e	Was there any loan or extension of credit by the plan to the employer, any fiduciary, any of the five most highly paid employees of the employer, any owner of a 10% or more interest in the employer, or relatives of any such persons?	**15e**			
f	Did the plan acquire or hold any employer security or employer real property?	**15f**			
g	Has the plan granted an extension on any delinquent loan owed to the plan?	**15g**			
h	Were any participant contributions transmitted to the plan more than 31 days after receipt or withholding by the employer?	**15h**			
i	Were any loans by the plan or fixed income obligations due the plan classified as uncollectible or in default as of the close of the plan year?	**15i**			
j	Has any plan fiduciary had a financial interest in excess of 10% in any party providing services to the plan or received anything of value from any such party?	**15j**			
k	Did the plan at any time hold 20% or more of its assets in any single security, debt, mortgage, parcel of real estate, or partnership/joint venture interests?	**15k**			
l	Did the plan at any time engage in any transaction or series of related transactions involving 20% or more of the current value of plan assets?	**15l**			
m	Were any noncash contributions made to the plan the value of which was set without an appraisal by an independent third party?	**15m**			
n	Were there any purchases of nonpublicly traded securities by the plan the value of which was set without an appraisal by an independent third party?	**15n**			
o	Has the plan reduced or failed to provide any benefit when due under the plan because of insufficient assets?. .	**15o**			

16a Is the plan covered under the Pension Benefit Guaranty Corporation termination insurance program? ☐ Yes ☐ No ☐ Not determined
b If line **16a** is "Yes" or "Not determined," enter the employer identification number and the plan number used to identify it.
  Employer identification number ▶   Plan number ▶

EXHIBIT 11.6   *Continued*

Form 5500-C/R (1995)   **Complete page 1, and pages 3 through 6 only, if you are filing Form 5500-C. (See instructions on page 13.)**   Page **3**

6e Check all applicable investment arrangements below. (See instructions on page 13.):

(1) ☐ Master trust   **(2)** ☐ 103-12 investment entity

(3) ☐ Common/collective trust   **(4)** ☐ Pooled separate account

....

....

....

....

f Single-employer plans enter the tax year end of the employer in which this plan year ends ▶ Month .... Day .... Year ....

g Is any part of this plan funded by an insurance contract described in Code section 412(i)? . . . . ☐ **Yes** ☐ **No**

h If line **6g** is "Yes," was the part subject to the minimum funding standards for either of the prior 2 plan years? . . . ☐ **Yes** ☐ **No**

7a Total participants: **(1)** At the beginning of plan year ▶ .... **(2)** At the end of plan year ▶ ....

b Enter number of participants with account balances at the end of the plan year. (Defined benefits plans do not complete this item.) ▶ ....

c Number of participants that terminated employment during the plan year with accrued benefits that were less than 100% vested ▶ ....

	Yes	No
d **(1)** Were any participants in the pension benefit plan separated from service with a deferred vested benefit for which a Schedule SSA (Form 5500) is required to be attached? . . . . **7d(1)**		
(2) If "Yes," enter the number of separated participants required to be reported ▶		
8a Was this plan ever amended since its effective date? If "Yes," complete line **8b** and, if the amendment was adopted in this plan year, complete lines **8c** through **8e** **8a**		
b If line **8a** is "Yes," enter the date the most recent amendment was adopted ▶ Month ...... Day ...... Year		
c Did any amendment during the current plan year result in the retroactive reduction of accrued benefits for any participant? **8c**		
d During this plan year, did any amendment change the information contained in the latest summary plan description or summary description of modifications available at the time of amendment? **8d**		
e If line **8d** is "Yes," has a summary plan description or summary description of modifications that reflects the plan amendments referred to on line **8d** been both furnished to participants and filed with the Department of Labor? . . . **8e**		
9a Was this plan terminated during this plan year or any prior plan year? If "Yes," enter year ▶ **9a**		
b Were all plan assets either distributed to participants or beneficiaries, transferred to another plan, or brought under the control of PBGC? **9b**		
c Was a resolution to terminate this plan adopted during this plan year or any prior plan year? **9c**		
d If line **9a** or line **9c** is "Yes," have you received a favorable determination letter from the IRS for the termination? . . **9d**		
e If line **9d** is "No," has a determination letter been requested from the IRS? **9e**		
f If line **9a** or line **9c** is "Yes," have participants and beneficiaries been notified of the termination or the proposed termination?. **9f**		
g If line **9a** is "Yes" and the plan is covered by PBGC, is the plan continuing to file a PBGC Form 1 and pay premiums until the end of the plan year in which assets are distributed or brought under the control of PBGC? . . . **9g**		
h During this plan year, did any trust assets revert to the employer for which the Code section 4980 excise tax is due? . **9h**		
i If line **9h** is "Yes," enter the amount of tax paid with Form 5330 ▶ **$**		
10a Was this plan merged or consolidated into another plan(s), or were assets or liabilities transferred to another plan(s) since the end of the plan year covered by the last return/report Form 5500 or 5500-C that was filed for this plan (or during this plan year if this is the first return/report)? If "Yes," complete lines **10b** through **10e** **10a**		

If "Yes," identify the other plan(s):   **c** Employer identification number(s)   **d** Plan number(s)

b Name of plan(s) ▶ ....

e If required, has a Form 5310-A been filed? . . . . ☐ **Yes** ☐ **No**

11 Enter the plan funding arrangement code from page 14 of the instructions ▶	**12** Enter the plan benefit arrangement code from page 14 of the instructions ▶	Yes	No
13 Is this a plan established or maintained pursuant to one or more collective bargaining agreements? **13**			
14 If any benefits are provided by an insurance company, insurance service, or similar organization, enter the number of Schedules A (Form 5500), Insurance Information, that are attached. If none, enter -0-. ▶			

EXHIBIT 11.6 *Continued*

Form 5500-C/R (1995) **Complete page 1, and pages 3 through 6 only, if you are filing Form 5500-C.** Page **4**

Welfare Plans Do Not Complete Lines 15 Through 25. Skip To Line 26 on page 5.

			Yes	No
15a	If this is a defined benefit plan subject to the minimum funding standards for this plan year, is Schedule B (Form 5500) required to be attached? (If this is a defined contribution plan, leave blank.) (See instructions.) **15a**			

If "Yes," attach Schedule B (Form 5500).

b If this is a defined contribution plan (i.e., money purchase or target benefit), is it subject to the minimum funding standards (if a waiver was granted, see instructions)? (If this is a defined benefit plan, leave blank.) **15b**

If "Yes," complete **(1)**, **(2)**, and **(3)** below:

(1) Amount of employer contribution required for the plan year under Code section 412 | **15b(1)** $

(2) Amount of contribution paid by the employer for the plan year . . . . | **15b(2)** $

Enter date of last payment by employer ▶ Month ..... Day ...... Year .....

(3) If **(1)** is greater than **(2)**, subtract **(2)** from **(1)** and enter the funding deficiency here. Otherwise, enter -0-. (If you have a funding deficiency, file Form 5330.) . . | **15b(3)** $

			Yes	No
16	Has the annual compensation of each participant taken into account under the current plan year been limited as required by section 401(a)(17)? (See instructions.)	**16**		
17a	**(1)** Did the plan distribute any annuity contracts this year? (See instructions.)	**17a(1)**		
	(2) If **(1)** is "Yes," did these contracts contain a requirement that the spouse consent before any distributions under the contract are made in a form other than a qualified joint and survivor annuity?	**17a(2)**		
b	Did the plan make distributions or loans to married participants and beneficiaries without the required consent of the participant's spouse?	**17b**		
c	Upon plan amendment or termination, do the accrued benefits of every participant include the subsidized benefits that the participant may become entitled to receive subsequent to the plan amendment or termination?	**17c**		
18	Is the plan administrator making an election under section 412(c)(8) for an amendment adopted after the end of the plan year? (See instructions.)	**18**		
19	If a change in the actuarial funding method was made for the plan year pursuant to a Revenue Procedure providing automatic approval for the change, indicate whether the plan sponsor/administrator agrees to the change	**19**		
20	Have any contributions been made or benefits accrued in excess of the Code section 415 limits, as amended?. . .	**20**		

21 Check if you are applying either of the following in completing lines 21a through 21o (see instructions):

   (i) ☐ Reasonable, good-faith interpretation of the nondiscrimination provisions

   (ii) ☐ Substantiation guidelines

   If you checked box **21(ii)**, enter the first day of the plan year for which data is being submitted ▶ Month ...Day ...Year ...

			Yes	No
a	Does the employer apply the separate line of business rules of Code section 414(r) when testing this plan for the coverage and discrimination tests requirements of Code sections 410(b) and 401(a)(4)?	**21a**		

b If line **21a** is "Yes," enter the total number of separate lines of business claimed by the employer ▶ ....

If more than one separate line of business, see instructions for additional information to attach.

			Yes	No
c	Does the employer apply the mandatory disaggregation rules under Income Tax Regulations section 1.410(b)–7(c)? If "Yes," see instructions for additional information to attach	**21c**		
d	In testing whether this plan satisfies the coverage and discrimination tests of Code sections 410(b) and 401(a), does the employer aggregate plans?	**21d**		
e	Does the employer restructure the plan into component plans to satisfy the coverage and discrimination tests of Code sections 410(b) and 401(a)(4)?	**21e**		

f If you meet either one of the following exceptions, check the applicable box to tell us which exception you meet and DO NOT complete the rest of question 21:

   (1) ☐ No highly compensated employee benefited under the plan at any time during the plan year;

   (2) ☐ This is a collectively bargained plan that benefits only collectively bargained employees, no more than 2% of whom are professional employees.

			Yes	No
g	Did any leased employee perform services for the employer at any time during the plan year?	**21g**		
			Number	
h	Enter the total number of employees of the employer. Employer includes entities aggregated with the employer under Code section 414(b), (c), or (m). Include leased employees and self-employed individuals	**21h**	
i	Enter the total number of employees excludable under the plan because of: *(1)* failure to meet requirements for minimum age and years of service; *(2)* collectively bargained employees; *(3)* nonresident aliens who receive no earned income from U. S. sources; and *(4)* 500 hours of service/last day rule	**21i**	

EXHIBIT 11.6 *Continued*

Form 5500-C/R (1995)   **Complete page 1, and pages 3 through 6 only, if you are filing Form 5500-C.**   Page **5**

		Number

j Enter the number of nonexcludable employees. Subtract line **21i** from line **21h** **21j**

k Do 100% of the nonexcludable employees entered on line **21j** benefit under the plan? . . . . ☐ Yes ☐ No
   If line **21k** is "Yes," DO NOT complete lines **21l** through **21o.**

l Enter the number of nonexcludable employees (line **21j**) who are highly compensated employees **21l**

m Enter the number of nonexcludable employees who benefit under the plan **21m**

n Enter the number of employees entered on line **21m** who are highly compensated employees **21n**

o This plan satisfies the coverage requirements on the basis of (check one):
   (1) ☐ The average benefits test   **(2)** ☐ The ratio percentage test—enter percentage ▶ [   ] . [   ] %

		Yes	No

22a Is it or was it ever intended that this plan qualify under Code section 401(a)? If "Yes," complete lines **22b** and **22c** **22a**

b Enter the date of the most recent IRS determination letter . . . . ▶ Month . . . . Year . . . .

c Is a determination letter request pending with the IRS? **22c**

23a Does the plan hold any assets that have a fair market value that is not readily determinable on an established market?
   (If "Yes," complete line **23b**.) (See instructions.) **23a**

b Were all the assets referred to on line **23a** valued for the 1995 plan year by an independent third-party appraiser? . **23b**

c If line **23b** is "No," enter the value of the assets that were not valued by an independent
   third-party appraiser for the 1995 plan year . . . . ▶ | **23c** |

d Enter the most recent date the assets on line **23c** were valued by an independent third-party appraiser. (If more than
   one asset, see instructions.) ▶ Month . . . . Day . . . . Year . . . .
   (If this plan has NO ESOP features, leave line **23e** blank and go to line **24**.)

e If dividends paid on employer securities held by the ESOP were used to make payments
   on ESOP loans, enter the amount of the dividends used to make the payments . . ▶ | **23e** |

24 Does the employer/sponsor listed in 1a of this form maintain other qualified pension benefit plans? **24**
   If "Yes," enter the total number of plans, including this plan ▶

25a Is the plan covered under the Pension Benefit Guaranty Corporation termination insurance
   program? . . . . ☐ Yes ☐ No ☐ Not determined

b If line **25a** is "Yes" or "Not determined," enter the EIN and the plan number used to identify it.
   EIN ▶   Plan number ▶

		Yes	No	Amount

26 You may **NOT** use **N/A** in response to any line 26 item. If you check "Yes," you must enter a dollar
   amount in the amount column.

   During this plan year:

a Was this plan covered by a fidelity bond? **26a**

b If line **26a** is "Yes," enter the name of the surety company ▶ . . . .

c Was there any loss to the plan, whether or not reimbursed, caused by fraud or dishonesty? **26c**

d Was there any sale, exchange, or lease of any property between the plan and the employer, any fiduciary,
   any of the five most highly paid employees of the employer, any owner of a 10% or more interest in
   the employer, or relatives of any such persons? **26d**

e Was there any loan or extension of credit by the plan to the employer, any fiduciary, any of the five
   most highly paid employees of the employer, any owner of a 10% or more interest in the employer, or
   relatives of any such persons? **26e**

f Did the plan acquire or hold any employer security or employer real property? **26f**

g Has the plan granted an extension on any delinquent loan owed to the plan? **26g**

h Were any participant contributions transmitted to the plan more than 31 days after receipt or withholding
   by the employer? **26h**

i Were any loans by the plan or fixed income obligations due the plan classified as uncollectible or in
   default as of the close of the plan year? **26i**

j Has any plan fiduciary had a financial interest in excess of 10% in any party providing services to the
   plan or received anything of value from any such party? **26j**

k Did the plan at any time hold 20% or more of its assets in any single security, debt, mortgage, parcel
   of real estate, or partnership/joint venture interests? **26k**

l Did the plan at any time engage in any transaction or series of related transactions involving 20% or
   more of the current value of plan assets? **26l**

m Were there any noncash contributions made to the plan whose value was set without an appraisal by
   an independent third party? **26m**

n Were there any purchases of nonpublicly traded securities by the plan whose value was set without an
   appraisal by an independent third party? **26n**

o Has the plan reduced or failed to provide any benefit when due under the terms of the plan because
   of insufficient assets? **26o**

EXHIBIT 11.6 *Continued*

Form 5500-C/R (1995) **Complete page 1, and pages 3 through 6 only, if you are filing Form 5500-C.** Page **6**

27 Current value of plan assets and liabilities at the beginning and end of the plan year. Combine the value of plan assets held in more than one trust. Allocate the value of the plan's interest in a commingled trust containing the assets of more than one plan on a line-by-line basis unless the trust meets one of the specific exceptions described in the instructions. Do not enter the value of the portion of an insurance contract that guarantees during this plan year to pay a specific dollar benefit at a future date. **Round off amounts to the nearest dollar. Any other amounts are subject to rejection. Plans with no assets at the beginning and end of the plan year enter -0- on line 27f.**

Assets		(a) Beginning of year	(b) End of year
a Cash	27a		
b Receivables	27b		
c Investments:			
(1) U.S. Government securities	27c(1)		
(2) Corporate debt and equity instruments	27c(2)		
(3) Real estate and mortgages (other than to participants)	27c(3)		
(4) Loans to participants:			
A Mortgages	(4)A		
B Other	(4)B		
(5) Other	27c(5)		
(6) Total investments. Add lines 27c(1) through 27c(5) ▶	27c(6)		
d Buildings and other property used in plan operations	27d		
e Other assets	27e		
f Total assets. Add lines 27a, 27b, 27c(6), 27d, and 27e ▶	27f		
Liabilities			
g Payables	27g		
h Acquisition indebtedness	27h		
i Other liabilities	27i		
j Total liabilities. Add lines 27g through 27i ▶	27j		
k Net assets. Subtract line 27j from line 27f ▶	27k		

28 Plan income, expenses, and changes in net assets for the plan year. Include all income and expenses of the plan including any trust(s) or separately maintained fund(s) and any payments/receipts to/from insurance carriers. **Round off amounts to the nearest dollar. Any other amounts are subject to rejection.**

Income		(a) Amount	(b) Total
a Contributions received or receivable in cash from:			
(1) Employer(s) (including contributions on behalf of self-employed individuals)	28a(1)		
(2) Employees	28a(2)		
(3) Others	28a(3)		
(4) Add lines 28a(1) through 28a(3)	28a(4)		
b Noncash contributions. Enter the total of lines 28a(4) and lines 28b in column (b)	28b		
c Earnings from investments (interest, dividends, rents, royalties)	28c		
d Net realized gain (loss) on sale or exchange of assets	28d		
e Other income (specify) ▶	28e		
f Total income. Add lines 28b through 28e ▶	28f		
Expenses			
g Distribution of benefits and payments to provide benefits:			
(1) Directly to participants or their beneficiaries	28g(1)		
(2) Other	28g(2)		
(3) Total distribution of benefits and payments to provide benefits	28g(3)		
h Administrative expenses (salaries, fees, commissions, insurance premiums)	28h		
i Other expenses (specify) ▶	28i		
j Total expenses. Add lines 28g through 28i ▶	28j		
k Net income (loss). Subtract line 28j from line 28f ▶	28k		

EXHIBIT 11.7

| Form **5500** | **Annual Return/Report of Employee Benefit Plan** | OMB Nos. 1210-0016 |
| | | 1210-0089 |

Form **5500**
Department of the Treasury
Internal Revenue Service
Department of Labor
Pension and Welfare Benefits
Administration
Pension Benefit Guaranty Corporation

Annual Return/Report of Employee Benefit Plan
(With 100 or more participants)
This form is required to be filed under sections 104 and 4065 of the Employee Retirement Income Security Act of 1974 and sections 6039D, 6047(e), 6057(b), and 6058(a) of the Internal Revenue Code, referred to as the Code.
▶ See separate instructions.

OMB Nos. 1210-0016
1210-0089

1995

This Form Is Open to Public Inspection.

For the calendar plan year 1995 or fiscal plan year beginning _____ , 1995, and ending _____ , 19____

If A(1) through A(4), B, C, and/or D, do not apply to this year's return/report, leave the boxes unmarked.

For IRS Use Only
EP-ID

A   This return/report is: *(1)* ☐ the first return/report filed for the plan;   *(3)* ☐ the final return/report filed for the plan; or
                                 (2) ☐ an amended return/report;   *(4)* ☐ a short plan year return/report (less than 12 months).

IF ANY INFORMATION ON A PREPRINTED PAGE 1 IS INCORRECT, CORRECT IT. IF ANY INFORMATION IS MISSING, ADD IT. PLEASE USE RED INK WHEN MAKING THESE CHANGES AND INCLUDE THE PREPRINTED PAGE 1 WITH YOUR COMPLETED RETURN/REPORT.

B   Check here if any information reported in 1a, 2a, 2b, or 5a changed since the last return/report for this plan . . . . ▶ ☐
C   If your plan year changed since the last return/report, check here . . . . ▶ ☐
D   If you filed for an extension of time to file this return/report, check here and attach a copy of the approved extension . . . . . ▶ ☐

1a Name and address of plan sponsor (employer, if for a single-employer plan) (Address should include room or suite no.)

1b Employer identification number (EIN)

1c Sponsor's telephone number

1d Business code (see instructions, page 23)

1e CUSIP issuer number

2a Name and address of plan administrator (if same as plan sponsor, enter "Same")

2b Administrator's EIN

2c Administrator's telephone number

3   If you are filing this page without the preprinted historical plan information and the name, address, and EIN of the plan sponsor or plan administrator has changed since the last return/report filed for this plan, enter the information from the last return/report in line **3a** and/or line **3b** and complete line **3c.**
a   Sponsor ....   EIN .... Plan number..........
b   Administrator ....   EIN ....
c   If line **3a** indicates a change in the sponsor's name, address, and EIN, is this a change in sponsorship only? (See line 3c on page 9 of the instructions for the definition of sponsorship.) Enter "Yes" or "No." ▶

4   **ENTITY CODE.** (If not shown, enter the applicable code from page 9 of the instructions.) ▶

5a Name of plan ▶ ....

5b Effective date of plan (mo., day, yr.)

5c Three-digit plan number ▶

All filers must complete 6a through 6d, as applicable.

6a ☐ Welfare benefit plan   **6b** ☐ Pension benefit plan
(If the correct codes are not preprinted below, enter the applicable codes from page 9 of the instructions in the boxes.)

6c Pension plan features. (If the correct codes are not preprinted below, enter the applicable pension plan feature codes from page 9 of the instructions in the boxes.)

6d ☐ Fringe benefit plan. Attach Schedule F (Form 5500). See instructions.

Caution: *A penalty for the late or incomplete filing of this return/report will be assessed unless reasonable cause is established.*

Under penalties of perjury and other penalties set forth in the instructions, I declare that I have examined this return/report, including accompanying schedules and statements, and to the best of my knowledge and belief, it is true, correct, and complete.

Signature of employer/plan sponsor ▶..   Date ▶...........................
Type or print name of individual signing for the employer/plan sponsor...
Signature of plan administrator ▶..   Date ▶...........................
Type or print name of individual signing for the plan administrator

For Paperwork Reduction Act Notice, see page 1 of the instructions.   Cat. No. 13500F   Form **5500** (1995)

EXHIBIT 11.7

Form 5500 (1995)

Page **2**

6e Check all applicable investment arrangements below (see instructions on page 10):

(1) ☐ Master trust   *(2)* ☐ 103-12 investment entity

(3) ☐ Common/collective trust   *(4)* ☐ Pooled separate account

....

....

....

f Single-employer plans enter the tax year end of the employer in which this plan year ends ▶ Month .... Day .... Year ....

g Is any part of this plan funded by an insurance contract described in Code section 412(i)? . . . . ▶ ☐ Yes ☐ No

h If line **6g** is "Yes," was the part subject to the minimum funding standards for either of the prior 2 plan years? . . . . ☐ Yes ☐ No

7 Number of participants as of the end of the plan year (welfare plans complete only lines 7a(4), 7b, 7c, and 7d):

a Active participants: *(1)* Number fully vested . . . . **a(1)**

                (2) Number partially vested . . . . **a(2)**

                (3) Number nonvested. . . . . **a(3)**

                (4) Total . . . . **a(4)**

b Retired or separated participants receiving benefits . . . . **b**

c Retired or separated participants entitled to future benefits . . . . **c**

d Subtotal. Add lines **7a(4), 7b,** and **7c** . . . . **d**

e Deceased participants whose beneficiaries are receiving or are entitled to receive benefits . . . **e**

f Total. Add lines **7d** and **7e** . . . . **f**

g Number of participants with account balances. (Defined benefit plans do not complete this line item.). . . **g**

h Number of participants that terminated employment during the plan year with accrued benefits that were less than 100% vested . . . . **h**

i *(1)* Was any participant(s) separated from service with a deferred vested benefit for which a Schedule SSA (Form 5500) is required to be attached? (See instructions.) . . . . **i(1)**

    (2) If "Yes," enter the number of separated participants required to be reported ▶

	Yes	No

8a Was this plan ever amended since its effective date? If "Yes," complete line 8b **8a**

If the amendment was adopted in this plan year, complete lines 8c through 8e.

b If line **8a** is "Yes," enter the date the most recent amendment was adopted ▶ Month .... Day .... Year ....

c Did any amendment during the current plan year result in the retroactive reduction of accrued benefits for any participants? **c**

d During this plan year did any amendment change the information contained in the latest summary plan descriptions or summary description of modifications available at the time of amendment?. . . . . **d**

e If line **8d** is "Yes," has a summary plan description or summary description of modifications that reflects the plan amendments referred to on line **8d** been both furnished to participants and filed with the Department of Labor?. . . **e**

9a Was this plan terminated during this plan year or any prior plan year? If "Yes," enter the year ▶.................... **9a**

b Were all the plan assets either distributed to participants or beneficiaries, transferred to another plan, or brought under the control of PBGC?. . . . . **b**

c Was a resolution to terminate this plan adopted during this plan year or any prior plan year? . . . . **c**

d If line **9a** or line **9c** is "Yes," have you received a favorable determination letter from the IRS for the termination? **d**

e If line **9d** is "No," has a determination letter been requested from the IRS? . . . . **e**

f If line **9a** or line **9c** is "Yes," have participants and beneficiaries been notified of the termination or the proposed termination?. **f**

g If line **9a** is "Yes" and the plan is covered by PBGC, is the plan continuing to file a PBGC Form 1 and pay premiums until the end of the plan year in which assets are distributed or brought under the control of PBGC? . . . . . **g**

h During this plan year, did any trust assets revert to the employer for which the Code section 4980 excise tax is due? **h**

i If line **9h** is "Yes," enter the amount of tax paid with Form 5330 ▶ $

10a In this plan year, was this plan merged or consolidated into another plan(s), or were assets or liabilities transferred to another plan(s)? If "Yes," complete lines **10b** through **10e** . . . . ▶ ☐ Yes ☐ No

If "Yes," identify the other plan(s)

b Name of plan(s) ▶ ....   **c** Employer identification number(s)   **d** Plan number(s)

e If required, has a Form 5310-A been filed? . . . . ▶ ☐ Yes ☐ No

11 Enter the plan funding arrangement code from page 11 of the instructions . . . . ▶

12 Enter the plan benefit arrangement code from page 11 of the instructions ▶

	Yes	No

13a Is this a plan established or maintained pursuant to one or more collective bargaining agreements? **13a**

b If line **13a** is "Yes," enter the appropriate six-digit LM number(s) of the sponsoring labor organization(s) (see instructions):

(1)   *(2)*   *(3)*

14 If any benefits are provided by an insurance company, insurance service, or similar organization, enter the number of **Schedules A (Form 5500),** Insurance Information, attached. If none, enter "-0-:" ▶

EXHIBIT 11.7 *Continued*

Form 5500 (1995)   Page **3**

Welfare Plans Do Not Complete Lines 15 Through 24. Go To Line 25 On Page 4.

		Yes	No
15a	If this is a defined benefit plan subject to the minimum funding standards for this plan year, is **Schedule B** (Form 5500) required to be attached? (If this is a defined contribution plan leave blank.) (See instructions.) **15a**		
b	If this is a defined contribution plan (i.e., money purchase or target benefit), is it subject to the minimum funding standards? (If a waiver was granted, see instructions.) (If this is a defined benefit plan, leave blank.) . . . . **b**		

If "Yes," complete (1), (2), and (3) below:
- (1) Amount of employer contribution required for the plan year under Code section 412 — **b(1)** $
- (2) Amount of contribution paid by the employer for the plan year. . . . . . . — **b(2)** $
  Enter date of last payment by employer ▶ Month......... Day........ Year......
- (3) If (1) is greater than (2), subtract (2) from (1) and enter the funding deficiency here; otherwise, enter -0-. (If you have a funding deficiency, file Form 5330.) — **b(3)** $

		Yes	No
16	Has the annual compensation of each participant taken into account under the current plan year been limited as required by section 401(a)(17)? (See instructions.) **16**		
17a (1)	Did the plan distribute any annuity contracts this year? (See instructions.) . . . . **a(1)**		
(2)	If (1) is "Yes," did these contracts contain a requirement that the spouse consent before any distributions under the contract are made in a form other than a qualified joint and survivor annuity? . . . . . . **a(2)**		
b	Did the plan make distributions or loans to married participants and beneficiaries without the required consent of the participant's spouse? . . . . **b**		
c	Upon plan amendment or termination, do the accrued benefits of every participant include the subsidized benefits that the participant may become entitled to receive subsequent to the plan amendment or termination? . . . . . . **c**		
18	Is the plan administrator making an election under section 412(c)(8) for an amendment adopted after the end of the plan year? (See instructions.) **18**		
19	If a change in the actuarial funding method was made for the plan year pursuant to a Revenue Procedure providing automatic approval for the change, indicate whether the plan sponsor agrees to the change **19**		
20a	For purposes of the minimum funding requirements is the employer making an irrevocable election to compute the additional unfunded old liability using the Optional rule of Code section 412(l)(3)(E)? **20a**		
b	Is the employer electing to compute minimum funding for the plan year using the Transition rule of Code section 412(l)(11)? . . **b**		

21 Check if you are applying either of the following in completing lines **21a** through **21o** (see instructions):
- (i) ☐ Reasonable, good-faith interpretation of the nondiscrimination provisions.   (ii) ☐ Substantiation guidelines.
  If you checked box 21(ii), enter the first day of the plan year for which data is being submitted ▶ Month .... Day ....Year ....

		Yes	No
a	Does the employer apply the separate line of business rules of Code section 414(r) when testing this plan for the coverage and discrimination tests of Code sections 410(b) and 401(a)(4)? **21a**		
b	If line **21a** is "Yes," enter the total number of separate lines of business claimed by the employer ▶ .... If more than one separate line of business, see instructions for additional information to attach.		
c	Does the employer apply the mandatory disaggregation rules under Income Tax Regulations section 1.410(b)-7(c)? . If "Yes," see instructions for additional information to attach. **c**		
d	In testing whether this plan satisfies the coverage and discrimination tests of Code sections 410(b) and 401(a), does the employer aggregate plans? . . . . **d**		
e	Does the employer restructure the plan into component plans to satisfy the coverage and discrimination tests of Code sections 410(b) and 401(a)(4)? . . . . **e**		

f If you meet either of the following exceptions, check the applicable box to tell us which exception you meet and do NOT complete the rest of question **21**:
- (1) ☐ No highly compensated employee benefited under the plan at any time during the plan year;
- (2) ☐ This is a collectively bargained plan that benefits only collectively bargained employees, no more than 2% of whom are professional employees.

		Yes	No
g	Did any leased employee perform services for the employer at any time during the plan year? . . . . **g**		

		Number
h	Enter the total number of employees of the employer. Employer includes entities aggregated with the employer under Code section 414(b), (c), or (m). Include leased employees and self-employed individuals . . . . . **h**	
i	Enter the total number of employees excludable because of: (1) failure to meet requirements for minimum age and years of service; (2) collectively bargained employees; (3) nonresident aliens who receive no earned income from U.S. sources; and (4) 500 hours of service/last day rule . . . . **i**	
j	Enter the number of nonexcludable employees. Subtract line 21i from line 21h . . . . **j**	
k	Do 100% of the nonexcludable employees entered on line **21j** benefit under the plan? . . . . ☐ Yes ☐ No If line **21k** is "Yes," do NOT complete lines **21l** through **21o**.	
l	Enter the number of nonexcludable employees (line **21j**) who are highly compensated employees . . . . . . **l**	
m	Enter the number of nonexcludable employees (line **21j**) who benefit under the plan . . . . **m**	
n	Enter the number of employees entered on line **21m** who are highly compensated employees . . . . . . **n**	

o This plan satisfies the coverage requirements on the basis of (check one):
(1) ☐ The average benefits test   (2) ☐ The ratio percentage test—Enter percentage ▶ [   ].   %

EXHIBIT 11.7   *Continued*

Form 5500 (1995)　　　　　　　　　　　　　　　　　　　　　　　　　　　　　　　Page **4**

Welfare Plans Go To Line 25 On This Page.

			Yes	No

22a Is it or was it ever intended that this plan qualify under Code section 401(a)? If "Yes," complete lines **22b** and **22c.** | **22a** |

 b Enter the date of the most recent IRS determination letter . . . . ▶ Month . . . . Year . . . .

 c Is a determination letter request pending with the IRS? . . . . | **c** |

23a Does the plan hold any assets that have a fair market value that is not readily determinable on an established market?
(If "Yes," complete line **23b**) (See instructions) . . . . | **23a** |

 b Were all the assets referred to in line **23a** valued for the 1995 plan year by an independent third-party appraiser? . . | **b** |

 c If line **23b** is "No," enter the value of the assets that were not valued by an independent third-party appraiser for the 1995 plan year. ▶ _____

 d Enter the most recent date the assets on line **23c** were valued by an independent third-party appraiser. (If more than one asset, see instructions.) ▶ Month . . . . Day . . . . Year . . . .
(If this plan does not have ESOP features leave line **23e** blank and go to line **24**.)

 e If dividends paid on employer securities held by the ESOP were used to make payments
on ESOP loans, enter the amount of the dividends used to make the payments . . . | **23e** |

24 Does the employer/sponsor listed on line **1a** of this form maintain other qualified pension benefit plans? . . . . . | **24** |
If "Yes," enter the total number of plans, including this plan ▶

25a Did any person who rendered services to the plan receive directly or indirectly $5,000 or more in compensation from
the plan during the plan year (except for employees of the plan who were paid less than $1,000 in each month)? . . | **25a** |
If "Yes," complete Part I of **Schedule C** (Form 5500).

 b Did the plan have any trustees who must be listed in Part II of **Schedule C** (Form 5500)? . . . . | **b** |

 c Has there been a termination in the appointment of any person listed on line **25d** below? . . . . | **c** |

 d If line **25c** is "Yes," check the appropriate box(es), answer lines **25e** and **25f**, and complete Part III of **Schedule C** (Form 5500):
 (1) ☐ Accountant　(2) ☐ Enrolled actuary　(3) ☐ Insurance carrier　(4) ☐ Custodian
 (5) ☐ Administrator　(6) ☐ Investment manager　(7) ☐ Trustee

 e Have there been any outstanding material disputes or matters of disagreement concerning the above termination? . | **e** |

 f If an accountant or enrolled actuary has been terminated during the plan year, has the terminated accountant/actuary
been provided a copy of the explanation required by Part III of **Schedule C** (Form 5500) with a notice advising them of
their opportunity to submit comments on the explanation directly to the DOL? . . . . | **f** |

 g Enter the number of **Schedules C** (Form 5500) that are attached. If none, enter -0- ▶

26a Is this plan exempt from the requirement to engage an independent qualified public accountant? (see instructions) . | **26a** |

 b If line **26a** is "No," attach the accountant's opinion to this return/report and check the appropriate box. This opinion is:
 (1) ☐ Unqualified
 (2) ☐ Qualified/disclaimer per Department of Labor Regulations 29 CFR 2520.103-8 and/or 2520.103-12(d)
 (3) ☐ Qualified/disclaimer other　(4) ☐ Adverse　(5) ☐ Other (explain) . . . .
 . . . .

 c If line **26a** is "No," does the accountant's report, including the financial statements and/or notes required to be attached to this
return/report disclose (1) errors or irregularities; (2) illegal acts; (3) material internal control weaknesses; (4) a loss contingency indicating
that assets are impaired or a liability incurred; (5) significant real estate or other transactions in which the plan and (A) the sponsor,
(B) the plan administrator, (C) the employer(s), or (D) the employee organization(s) are jointly involved; (6) that the plan has participated
in any related party transactions; or (7) any unusual or infrequent events or transactions occurring subsequent to the plan year end
that might significantly affect the usefulness of the financial statements in assessing the plan's present or future ability to pay benefits? | **c** |

 d If line **26c** is "Yes," provide the total amount involved in such disclosure ▶

27 If line **26a** is "No," complete the following questions. (You may NOT use "N/A" in response to lines **27a** through **27i**):
If line **27a, 27b, 27c, 27d, 27e,** or **27f** is checked "Yes," schedules of these items in the format set forth in the instructions
are required to be attached to this return/report. **Schedule G** (Form 5500) may be used as specified in the instructions.
During the plan year:

 a Did the plan have assets held for investment? . . . . | **27a** |

 b Were any loans by the plan or fixed income obligations due the plan in default as of the close of the plan year or classified
during the year as uncollectible? . . . . | **b** |

 c Were any leases to which the plan was a party in default or classified during the year as uncollectible? . . . . . | **c** |

 d Were any plan transactions or series of transactions in excess of 5% of the current value of plan assets? . . . . . | **d** |

 e Do the notes to the financial statements accompanying the accountant's opinion disclose any nonexempt transactions
with parties-in-interest? . . . . | **e** |

 f Did the plan engage in any nonexempt transactions with parties-in-interest not reported on line **27e**? . . . . . . | **f** |

 g Did the plan hold qualifying employer securities that are not publicly traded? . . . . | **g** |

 h Did the plan purchase or receive any nonpublicly traded securities that were not appraised in writing by an unrelated
third party within 3 months prior to their receipt? . . . . | **h** |

 i Did any person manage plan assets who had a financial interest worth more than 10% in any party providing services
to the plan or receive anything of value from any party providing services to the plan? . . . . | **i** |

EXHIBIT 11.7   *Continued*

Form 5500 (1995)   Page **5**

			Yes	No

28 Did the plan acquire individual whole life insurance contracts during the plan year? **28**

29 During the plan year:

a (1) Was this plan covered by a fidelity bond? If "Yes," complete lines 29a(2) and 29a(3) . . . . **29a(1)**

  (2) Enter amount of bond ▶ $ ....

  (3) Enter the name of the surety company ▶ ....

b (1) Was there any loss to the plan, whether or not reimbursed, caused by fraud or dishonesty? . . . . . **29b(1)**

  (2) If line **29b(1)** is "Yes," enter amount of loss ▶ $

30a Is the plan covered under the Pension Benefit Guaranty Corporation termination insurance program?

  ☐ **Yes**   ☐ **No**   ☐ **Not determined**

b If line **30a** is "Yes" or "Not determined," enter the employer identification number and the plan number used to identify it.

  Employer identification number ▶   Plan number ▶

31 Current value of plan assets and liabilities at the beginning and end of the plan year. Combine the value of plan assets held in more than one trust. Allocate the value of the plan's interest in a commingled trust containing the assets of more than one plan on a line-by-line basis unless the trust meets one of the specific exceptions described in the instructions. Do not enter the value of that portion of an insurance contract that guarantees, during this plan year, to pay a specific dollar benefit at a future date. **Round off amounts to the nearest dollar; any other amounts are subject to rejection.** Plans with no assets at the beginning and the end of the plan year, enter -0- on line **31f**.

	Assets		(a) Beginning of Year	(b) End of Year
a	Total noninterest-bearing cash	**a**		
b	Receivables: **(1)** Employer contributions	**b(1)**		
	(2) Participant contributions	**(2)**		
	(3) Income	**(3)**		
	(4) Other	**(4)**		
	(5) Less allowance for doubtful accounts	**(5)**		
	(6) Total. Add lines **31b(1)** through **31b(4)** and subtract line **31b(5)** . . . . ▶	**(6)**		
c	General Investments: **(1)** Interest-bearing cash (including money market funds) . .	**c(1)**		
	(2) Certificates of deposit	**(2)**		
	(3) U.S. Government securities	**(3)**		
	(4) Corporate debt instruments: **(A)** Preferred	**(4)(A)**		
	(B) All other.	**(4)(B)**		
	(5) Corporate stocks: **(A)** Preferred	**(5)(A)**		
	(B) Common	**(5)(B)**		
	(6) Partnership/joint venture interests	**(6)**		
	(7) Real estate: **(A)** Income-producing	**(7)(A)**		
	(B) Nonincome-producing	**(7)(B)**		
	(8) Loans (other than to participants) secured by mortgages: **(A)** Residential . .	**(8)(A)**		
	(B) Commercial	**(8)(B)**		
	(9) Loans to participants: **(A)** Mortgages	**(9)(A)**		
	(B) Other	**(9)(B)**		
	(10) Other loans.	**(10)**		
	(11) Value of interest in common/collective trusts	**(11)**		
	(12) Value of interest in pooled separate accounts	**(12)**		
	(13) Value of interest in master trusts	**(13)**		
	(14) Value of interest in 103-12 investment entities	**(14)**		
	(15) Value of interest in registered investment companies	**(15)**		
	(16) Value of funds held in insurance company general account (unallocated contracts) .	**(16)**		
	(17) Other	**(17)**		
	(18) Total. Add lines **31c(1)** through **31c(17)** . . . . ▶	**(18)**		
d	Employer-related investments: **(1)** Employer securities	**d(1)**		
	(2) Employer real property	**(2)**		
e	Buildings and other property used in plan operation	**e**		
f	**Total** assets. Add lines **31a, 31b(6), 31c(18), 31d(1), 31d(2),** and **31e** . . . . ▶	**f**		
	Liabilities			
g	Benefit claims payable	**g**		
h	Operating payables	**h**		
i	Acquisition indebtedness	**i**		
j	Other liabilities	**j**		
k	**Total** liabilities. Add lines **31g** through **31j** . . . . ▶	**k**		
	Net Assets			
l	Subtract line **31k** from line **31f** . . . . ▶	**l**		

EXHIBIT 11.7 *Continued*

Form 5500 (1995)   Page **6**

32   Plan income, expenses, and changes in net assets for the plan year. *Include all income and expenses of the plan, including any trust(s) or separately maintained fund(s), and any payments/receipts to/from insurance carriers.* **Round off amounts to the nearest dollar; any other amounts are subject to rejection.**

Income	(a) Amount	(b) Total
a . **Contributions:**		
(1) Received or receivable from:		
(A) Employers	a(1)(A)	
(B) Participants	(B)	
(C) Others	(C)	
(2) Noncash contributions	(2)	
(3) Total contributions. Add lines **32a(1)(A), (B), (C)** and line **32a(2)** . . . . ▶	(3)	
b **Earnings on investments:**		
(1) Interest		
(A) Interest-bearing cash (including money market funds)	b(1)(A)	
(B) Certificates of deposit	(B)	
(C) U.S. Government securities	(C)	
(D) Corporate debt instruments	(D)	
(E) Mortgage loans	(E)	
(F) Other loans	(F)	
(G) Other interest	(G)	
(H) Total interest. Add lines **32b(1)(A)** through **(G)** . . . . . ▶	(H)	
(2) Dividends: **(A)** Preferred stock	b(2)(A)	
(B) Common stock	(B)	
(C) Total dividends. Add lines **32b(2)(A)** and **(B)** . . . . . ▶	(C)	
(3) Rents	(3)	
(4) Net gain (loss) on sale of assets: **(A)** Aggregate proceeds	(4)(A)	
(B) Aggregate carrying amount (see instructions)	(B)	
(C) Subtract **(B)** from **(A)** and enter result	(C)	
(5) Unrealized appreciation (depreciation) of assets	(5)	
(6) Net investment gain (loss) from common/collective trusts	(6)	
(7) Net investment gain (loss) from pooled separate accounts	(7)	
(8) Net investment gain (loss) from master trusts	(8)	
(9) Net investment gain (loss) from 103-12 investment entities	(9)	
(10) Net investment gain (loss) from registered investment companies . . .	(10)	
c Other income	c	
d Total income. Add all amounts in column **(b)** and enter total . . . . ▶	d	
Expenses		
e Benefit payment and payments to provide benefits:		
(1) Directly to participants or beneficiaries	e(1)	
(2) To insurance carriers for the provision of benefits	(2)	
(3) Other	(3)	
(4) Total payments. Add lines **32e(1)** through **32e(3)** . . . . . ▶	(4)	
f Interest expense	f	
g Administrative expenses: **(1)** Salaries and allowances	g(1)	
(2) Accounting fees	(2)	
(3) Actuarial fees	(3)	
(4) Contract administrator fees	(4)	
(5) Investment advisory and management fees	(5)	
(6) Legal fees	(6)	
(7) Valuation/appraisal fees	(7)	
(8) Trustees fees/expenses (including travel, seminars, meetings, etc.)	(8)	
(9) Other	(9)	
(10) Total administrative expenses. Add lines **32g(1)** through **32g(9)**	(10)	
h Total expenses. Add lines **32e(4), 32f,** and **32g(10)** . . . . . . ▶	h	
i Net income (loss). Subtract line **32h** from line **32d** . . . . ▶	i	
j Transfers to (from) the plan (see instructions)	j	
k Net assets at beginning of year (line **31l**, column **(a)**)	k	
l Net assets at end of year (line **31l**, column **(b)**) . . . . ▶	l	

	Yes	No
33 Did any employer sponsoring the plan pay any of the administrative expenses of the plan that were not reported on line **32g?**		

*U.S.GPO:1996-389-397

12 | *Trademark Registration*

Overview of Objectives

Upon completion of this chapter, the student will:

- understand the purpose of a trademark
- understand what constitutes a proper trademark
- understand the different types of trademark registration
- know how to draft federal trademark registration documents

INTRODUCTION

Some of a company's most valuable assets may be the intellectual property rights it possesses. Intellectual property includes copyrights, patents, and trademarks, all of which are governed by federal law. Unlike patents and copyrights, trademarks, the focus of this chapter, are governed by state law as well.

Lawmakers confront seemingly conflicting policy issues in their recognition of the importance of providing legal protection to intellectual property. On the one hand, they want to encourage a competitive marketplace in which the public is best served by access to the free flow of ideas. On the other hand, they recognize that unless certain protections are in place for the creators of new ideas, this access will eventually be curtailed because the economic incentive for new creations will be diminished if others are allowed to freely copy a creator's work. Present intellectual property law recognizes the balancing of these interests.

As a paralegal working in the field of corporate law, you must understand the value of intellectual property to a business client and become knowledgeable in aiding the client in protecting intellectual property rights. This chapter provides a fundamental discussion of the subject matter protected by intellectual property law and outlines the standards to be met before such protection is granted. Further, this chapter sets forth the steps to be taken to register a trademark.

TERMINOLOGY

A proper understanding of intellectual property begins with a clarification of terminology. The first category of terminology with which to acquaint oneself pertains to the distinction between the three basic areas of intellectual property: copyrights, patents, and trademarks. Each of these areas protects a different type of subject matter and provides for a different period of protection.

A.   Copyright

A **copyright** protects the authorship of literary, musical, and artistic works. Artistic works include dramatic works, choreography and pantomime, motion pictures, and architectural works, as well as pictorial, graphic, and audiovisual works. Copyright protection applies only to the protection of the author's method of expressing his or her ideas; ideas alone are not afforded protection. In order for a literary, musical, or artistic work to obtain copyright protection, the work must be deemed original. This does not mean that a work must be different in every aspect from anything that has ever been created before (a test that would be virtually impossible for one to meet), but it does mean that some amount of independent intellectual endeavor must be exhibited in the creation of the work.

Original works are afforded copyright protection from the moment of creation, which is the moment the idea of the author is put forth in some form of tangible expression. Thus, it is not necessary to submit a copyright application form to the federal Office of Copyrights to be afforded copyright protection, although submission of such a form serves well as evidentiary proof should a copyright infringement issue arise. The duration of protection of a copyrighted work is the life of the author plus 50 years, or 75 years from publication, or 100 years from creation, whichever expires first. Unauthorized copying of a work or substantial similarity to a copyrighted work are grounds for copyright infringement.

B. Patents

There are two categories of patents. A **utility patent** protects the functional characteristics of products and processes. A **design patent** protects ornamental designs of manufactured products. In order to be afforded the protection of a utility patent, the product function must be novel, useful, and nonobvious. In order to be afforded a design patent, the design of the product must be novel and nonobvious. Patent protection does not commence until the U.S. Patent and Trademark Office approves a patent application. If approval is granted, a utility patent will last for 17 years from the date issued and a design patent will last for 14 years from the date issued. A patent may not be renewed. Anyone who makes, uses, or sells the subject matter of a utility patent during the duration of the patent may be sued for patent infringement. Similarity of design to a product design protected by a design patent will constitute patent infringement as well.

C. Trademarks and Service Marks

Trademark protection provides protection to words, letters, numbers, names, phrases, symbols, or devices, or any combination of these that is associated with a product (e.g., Redken hair products, Easy Spirit shoes, Power Ranger dolls). If the mark is associated with a service rather than a product, it is called a **service mark** (e.g., Century 21 real estate brokers, Roto-Rooter septic tank service). Trademarks and service marks are afforded the same protection in the United States although there are some countries that afford no legal protection for service marks. The mark (as the enumeration of possibilities above will be referred to hereafter) may be protected if it can be shown to distinguish one's goods or services from those of others.

    Protection begins upon use of the mark and can continue indefinitely as long as the mark is properly used to distinguish itself as a trademark. As in the case of copyrights, legal rights in a trademark are not derived from the filing of a federal application, although there are distinct benefits from doing so. The legal rights are created in the mark upon first use.

    The purpose of a trademark is to establish consumer recognition of a company's products or services and through such recognition to enhance consumer goodwill and preference over competing products and services. To do so, it is important that the consumer not be confused by similar marks. Therefore, the standard for trademark infringement is likelihood of confusion.

While it is quite possible that the corporate paralegal may have occasion to work with clients in the areas of copyright and patent protection, by far most business clients will be concerned with trademark protection, which is why it is emphasized in this chapter.

In addition to knowledge of the distinctions between the major areas of intellectual property, there are other terms, some more commonly heard than others, with which one should be acquainted. One such example is trade names. **Trade names** are names used for a business. They cannot be registered as federal trademarks and therefore the only way to provide federal protection for a trade name is to use it as a trademark on products or in connection with services. Conversely, trade dress can be afforded federal protection. **Trade dress** refers to the look of a product (through color, shape, size) which is distinctive to that product. An example of trade dress is the Mrs. Butterworth maple syrup bottle.

Ingredient marks do precisely what the term implies, identifying an ingredient contained in a company's product the consumer considers desirable, such as triclene, a whitening agent in toothpaste, which is a trademark for sodium tripolyphosphate, or citrimax, a trademark of InterHealth Company, the active ingredient of which is hydrocitric acid. Although ingredient marks do not always lead to company name recognition, because the ingredient is perceived as beneficial a company producing products labelled with the ingredient mark has an advantage in the marketplace.

A **collective mark** is similar to a trademark or service mark in that it is composed of a words, letters, numbers, phrases, or symbols, but instead of distinguishing a product or service, it is used to indicate association within a group or membership body. An example of a collective mark is ILGWU.

A **certification mark** indicates that products or services meet certain objectively defined quality standards. An example of a certification mark is the Good Housekeeping Seal of Approval. Rather than a mark which is used by the owner of the mark to promote product recognition, a certification mark is licensed to manufacturers to use on their products (or to services to use in connection with their business) to certify that those products (or services) meet the requisite standards. Indeed, federal law clearly disallows the owner of a certification mark to use the mark on its own products and services, and requires that the owner police the mark to ensure no false or fraudulent use of it is made by other companies.

A **house mark** or **multi-product mark** is a mark which is used on many or all products of a company, such as Kraft or Kenmore. Because consumers already identify with the name, it is reasonably assumed that the consumer will gravitate toward any new product introduced with the name. Similar to the concept of a house mark is that of a **derivative mark**, which is a new mark created from and having aspects in common with an existing mark of a company. An example of a company which makes good and profitable use of derivative marks is Eastman Kodak, creating such derivative marks as Kodacolor and Kodachrome, each of which is immediately associated in the consumer's mind with Eastman Kodak.

TYPES OF MARKS

It makes business sense for a mark to be distinctive, certainly distinctive enough to distinguish in the consumer's mind one company's products from those of its competitors. It is also required, as noted above, for a mark to be distinctive to be afforded legal protection. Thus, it sounds like public relations and marketing staff would work in harmony with legal staff in formulating a winning trademark for a business client. In fact, they often butt heads because marks that are afforded the most protection legally sometimes take longer to establish a general recognition with the public. The reason for this lies in the fact that the more descriptive a mark is, the less protection it is afforded. The less an average person would associate a mark with the product sold, the more legal protection it is afforded! This seemingly contradictory concept relates back to the balancing test lawmakers are enforcing in intellectual property protection. It is asserted that rights to a term which is simply descriptive of what a product is or does, should not be given exclusively to one company in a general industry. Doing so would promote unfair competition. Therefore, when creating a mark, a company should bear in mind that certain types of marks are easier to protect. The primary criterion must always be distinctiveness.

Descriptive marks, considered the weakest, must show that they have attained a secondary meaning with the public before they can acquire trademark protection. Falling within this category are not only marks that simply describe a product or service but also marks which describe the geographical origins of a product, as well as marks which are someone's surname, such as Singer and Lipton. How does a descriptive mark obtain the requisite secondary meaning to be afforded protection? Usually it is a matter of time; the mark having been used consistently as a trademark may come to be associated with a company's product and thus acquire secondary meaning. Federal statutory law states that prima facie evidence of secondary meaning occurs when a descriptive mark is used for five years exclusively and consistently in association with a product.

A **suggestive mark** is not as weak as a purely descriptive mark because it merely suggests attributes of a product or service rather than clearly describing them. An example of a suggestive mark is Magic Chef for kitchen appliances, implying that through the use of Magic Chef appliances, the consumer will perform expertly in the kitchen.

Stronger than either descriptive or suggestive marks are **arbitrary** or **fanciful marks**. These marks are made up of commonly understood words, but of words not commonly associated with the nature of the product or service to which they are attached. Examples of these marks are Ace (hardware), Lotus (computer software), and Accent (pest control). These marks are considered more distinctive because the words comprising the marks are being used in a clearly distinctive way, i.e., they are not describing the nature of the product or service and therefore are not related to its nature, but rather to something not ordinarily associated with it.

Marks afforded the most protection are coined marks. **Coined marks** are invented words, words that have no meaning apart from that provided when associated with a product or service. Examples of coined marks are Esso and Rolex. Both of these marks immediately bring forth product associations now, but because they are invented words rather than descriptive words, consumer recognition has been built up over a period of time.

FORBIDDEN TRADEMARKS

The federal statutes pertaining to trademarks are collectively known as the **Lanham Act** (found in 15 United States Code Section 1051 et seq.). The Lanham Act sets forth a listing of marks which may not be federally registered as trademarks. The common denominator found with most of these "forbidden" marks are their lack of distinctiveness. For example, one type of forbidden mark is a mark which is considered descriptive and lacking in secondary meaning, another is a mark which is a surname and lacking in secondary meaning. Using a generic name of a product or a geographic name as a trademark, such as Hawaiian Pineapple (which would fit both the generic and geographic categories), is disallowed as well. It easily is argued that the mark could apply to all pineapples grown in Hawaii and therefore should not be given exclusive use to any one company. One should note that the use of geographic marks is allowed if the geographic region named has no instinctive connection with the product, such as Pacific Coast for bicycles.

Some marks which were once protected marks may be denied protection because the trademark owner's lack of policing of the mark has permitted the mark to become generic, and thus the public considers the mark the name of the product rather than a way in which to distinguish a company's version of a product. The occurrence of this seemingly unfortunate incident is a double-edged sword. The mark has become generic because the product has attained such widespread popularity with the public. Aspirin, thermos, shredded wheat, and escalator were at one time trademarks but have subsequently lost that status. Trademarks soon to be in jeopardy are Xerox (which is used to mean photocopy) and Rollerblade (a trademark for a particular in-line skate). As soon as a trademark becomes generic, it loses its favored status and may be used by anyone. A company must make sure that all users of the mark use it appropriately, by using the trademark as an adjective followed by the generic name of the product, e.g., Kleenex facial tissues.

In addition to marks which lack distinctiveness, the Lanham Act denies federal registration of any mark considered disparaging of a national symbol, a belief, an institution, or a person. Even if not meant disparagingly, the use of flags or other insignia of any city, county, state, or country is prohibited. Similarly, one cannot use the name, signature, or likeness of a living person as a mark without his or her written consent. In the case of a deceased president, one cannot use his name, signature, or likeness during his widow's lifetime without obtaining the consent of the widow.

Marks which are immoral or deceptive are denied federal registration. A mark may be deceptive if it implies a product originates somewhere other than its place of origin, such as Sunshine State for produce which would imply it comes from Florida when in fact the produce in question is cultivated in Texas.

TYPES OF REGISTRATION

Trademark law has its origins in common law and to this day common law principles protect trademark owners. Under common law, an unregistered trademark is afforded legal recourse against infringement by the courts, and a trademark holder of an unregistered mark whose goods or services are being palmed off by another may sue under the legal theories of common law trademark infringement and common law unfair competition. Nonetheless, most companies recognize that federally registering their trademarks on the Principal Register presents certain advantages.

One of these advantages is the right to sue in a federal court because federal trademark infringement is a violation of federal statutes. In a suit under this cause of action, the plaintiff may ask to be awarded the infringing party's profits, triple damages, attorney's fees, and costs. An important tactical advantage for suing under the federal statutes is the advantage that federal registration of a trademark puts everyone on "constructive notice" of the registered owner's priority of use of the mark dating back to the filing of the federal registration application. Thus, the infringing party cannot claim lack of notice as a defense. This priority of use applies to all parties except those who used the mark themselves prior to the registered owner's filing date and continue to do so or a party who filed an application prior to the registered owner's filing date that is still pending. Together with constructive notice, federal registration serves as prima facie evidence of exclusive right to the mark and therefore this right does not have to be proved by the plaintiff. Additionally, the owner of a federally registered mark has the right to stop importation of products with an infringing mark from entering the United States. Criminal penalties may be imposed as well upon anyone who counterfeits a federally registered mark. A first offender can face fines up to $250,000 or five years in prison, subsequent offenses can bring fines of $1 million or 15 years in prison.

Two distinct trademark registers are maintained by the U.S. Patent and Trademark Office (hereafter referred to as the PTO): the Principal Register and the Supplemental Register. It is the Principal Register which provides the numerous advantages discussed above in federally registering a mark. If a mark fails to meet the criteria set forth by the PTO for acceptance on the Principal Register, it may be possible to amend a federal trademark application to register the mark on the Supplemental Register. Marks failing to meet Principal Register criteria are those which are geographic, descriptive, or surnames and fail to evidence sufficient secondary meaning to prove distinctiveness. If a mark falls within this category, it is advisable to register it on the Supplemental Register because doing so will prevent another from federally registering the same or a deceptively similar mark. Once the mark has acquired sufficient secondary meaning, another attempt can be made to have it accepted on the Principal Register.

To fully understand the implications of federally registering a mark, it is helpful to imagine a conflict between two companies' marks. In a contest between conflicting trademarks, the two preliminary questions asked are: (1) Was your company the first to federally register the mark?, and (2) Was your company first to use the mark? If your company was both the first to federally register and the first to use the mark, your company is entitled to exclusive nationwide use of the mark.

If your company was the first to federally register the mark, but not the first to use it, then the relevant question is whether your company knew or should have known of the other mark's prior use. If yes, then your company's right to use the mark is contestable. If no, your company has the exclusive right to use the mark nationwide except in areas in which the other mark is already in use.

If your company was not the first to federally register, but was the first to actually use the mark, the question then turns on whether the other company knew or should have known of your first use. If yes, then your company can challenge the other company's right to the mark. If the other company did not or could not know of your company's first use of the mark, your company is limited to using it locally and may be prevented from using it nationally.

If your company was neither the first to use nor the first to register a mark, the test to be applied is whether the public would be deceived and/or there would be public confusion caused by dual use of the mark. If the likelihood is yes, the other company has a right to object to your use of the mark, and can legally prevent you from doing so.

In addition to federal registration on the Principal or Supplemental Registers, a trademark can be registered locally under state registration procedures. Some companies having no future plans of expanding outside state boundaries prefer to register under state registration because the procedure is ordinarily simpler and less expensive. State registration will provide statutory protection within the boundaries of the state. If a company plans nationwide expansion but its mark cannot be afforded the full rights of the Principal Register and it managed to be listed on the Supplemental Register, it is advisable to obtain state registration which may provide additional legal relief, such as statutory anti-dilution causes of action. Further, state registration may provide tactical advantages in shifting the burden of proof in a lawsuit. Typically, a plaintiff has the burden of going forward and proving each element of a cause of action. In many states, if a mark has acquired state registration, this serves as prima facie evidence of ownership of a mark and shifts the burden of proof to the alleged infringing party. This type of tactical advantage makes the process of bringing an infringement suit much easier than it would be if the mark was unregistered.

PROCEDURES FOR FILING AN APPLICATION

A corporate paralegal may become involved in the trademark registration process prior to the actual filing of an application. A prudent company will involve in-house legal staff or hire a law firm at the very inception of the trademark creation process to assure that vast sums of money are not invested in a mark that may be denied protection. Prior to formal adoption of a mark, two major considerations must be addressed: (1) devising a mark that is distinctive, and (2) clearing the mark to be sure the same or similar mark is not already in use.

A.   Trademark Search

Legal counsel might not become actively involved in the creation process of the mark, but may advise as to what attributes would be helpful to meet distinctiveness standards under the Lanham Act. As noted above, coined marks are most likely to meet this standard, descriptive marks the least likely, with arbitrary and suggestive marks falling in the midrange of the spectrum. Additional considerations in choosing a mark are ease in spelling and pronunciation. Remember, the purpose of a trademark is the attainment of product recognition with the consumer. If a mark is difficult to spell or pronounce, it will also be difficult to remember, thus defeating its intended purpose. Legal counsel should inquire into the scope of use projected for the mark; for example, will it be used in foreign countries as well as within the United States. If a mark will be used abroad, it is important to make sure that any meaning the words or design comprising the mark may have in another language will not be considered derogatory in foreign markets. If not brought into the picture prior to the selection process, legal counsel certainly should be called upon to review the selection and to write an advisory letter evaluating the strength of the proposed mark.

When a trademark search is conducted, the mark is searched by the international class number and separate searches must be conducted under each pertinent international class number. The international class number corresponds to a description of the type of goods or services to which the mark will be affixed. The international classifications and their corresponding numbers are found on Exhibit 12.1. Note that prior to September 1, 1973 a separate classification system existed for trademark classifications within the United States. While this system is no longer used for the registering of new trademarks, it may still pertain to the renewal of old ones (see Exhibit 12.2).

Once a preliminary selection of a mark is made and the classification or classifications are determined, the next step is searching the mark to find out if the mark is already in use and/or registered. There are many different searches which may be done. An initial search can be made by checking the *Trade Names Directory*, which can be found in most public libraries, as well as the yellow pages for major U.S. cities. Searching these materials may lead to marks that are not federally registered but nonetheless properly used and thus valid trademarks.

It is important to conduct a search of registered marks. In addition, the

EXHIBIT 12.1

International schedule of classes of goods and services

Goods

1 Chemicals used in industry, science and photography, as well as in agriculture, horticulture and forestry; unprocessed artificial resins, unprocessed plastics; manures; fire extinguishing compositions; tempering and soldering preparations; chemical substances for preserving foodstuffs; tanning substances; adhesives used in industry.

2 Paints, varnishes, lacquers; preservatives against rust and against deterioration of wood; colorants; mordants; raw natural resins; metals in foil and powder form for painters, decorators, printers and artists.

3 Bleaching preparations and other substances for laundry use; cleaning polishing, scouring and abrasive preparations; soaps; perfumery, essential oils, cosmetics, hair lotions; dentifrices.

4 Industrial oils and greases; lubricants; dust absorbing, wetting and binding compositions; fuels (including motor spirit) and illuminants; candles, wicks.

5 Pharmaceutical, veterinary and sanitary preparations; dietetic substances adapted for medical use, food for babies; plasters, materials for dressings; material for stopping teeth, dental wax; disinfectants; preparations for destroying vermin; fungicides, herbicides.

6 Common metals and their alloys; metal building materials; transportable buildings of metal; materials of metal for railway tracks; non-electric cables and wires of common metal; ironmongery, small items of metal hardware; pipes and tubes of metal; safes; goods of common metal not included in other classes; ores.

7 Machines and machine tools; motors and engines (except for land vehicles); machine coupling and transmission components (except for land vehicles); agricultural implements; incubators for eggs.

8 Hand tools and implements (hand operated); cutlery; side arms; razors.

9 Scientific, nautical, surveying, electric, photographic, cinematographic, optical, weighing, measuring, signalling, checking (supervision), life-saving and teaching apparatus and instruments; apparatus for recording, transmission or reproduction of sound or images; magnetic data carriers, recording discs; automatic vending machines and mechanisms for coin operated apparatus; cash registers, calculating machines, data processing equipment and computers; fire-extinguishing apparatus.

10 Surgical, medical, dental and veterinary apparatus and instruments, artificial limbs, eyes and teeth; orthopedic articles; suture materials.

11 Apparatus for lighting, heating, steam generating, cooking, refrigerating, drying, ventilating, water supply and sanitary purposes.

12 Vehicles; apparatus for locomotion by land, air or water.

13 Firearms; ammunition and projectiles; explosives; fireworks.

14 Precious metals and their alloys and goods in precious metals or coated therewith, not included in other classes; jewellery, precious stones; horological and chronometric instruments.

15 Musical instruments.

16 Paper, cardboard and goods made from these materials, not included in other classes; printed matter; bookbinding material; photographs; stationery; adhesives for stationery or household purposes; artists' materials; paint brushes; typewriters and office requisites (except furniture); instructional and teaching material (except apparatus); playing cards; printers' type; printing blocks.

17 Rubber, gutta-percha, gum asbestos, mica and goods made from these materials and not included in other classes; plastics in extruded form for use in manufacture; packing, stopping and insulating materials; flexible pipes, not of metal.

18 Leather and imitations of leather, and goods made of these materials and not included in other classes; animal skins, hides; trunks and travelling bags; umbrellas, parasols and walking sticks; whips, harness and saddlery.

19 Building materials (non-metallic); non-metallic rigid pipes for building; asphalt, pitch and bitumen; non-metallic transportable buildings; monuments, not of metal.

20 Furniture, mirrors, picture frames; goods (not included in other classes) of wood, cork, reed, cane, wicker, horn, bone, ivory, whalebone, shell, amber, mother-of-pearl, meerschaum and substitutes for all these materials, or of plastics.

21 Household or kitchen utensils and containers (not of precious metal or coated therewith); combs and sponges; brushes (except paint brushes); brush-making materials; articles for cleaning purposes; steelwool; unworked or semi-worked glass (except glass used in building); glassware, porcelain and earthenware not included in other classes.

22 Ropes, string, nets, tents, awnings, tarpaulins, sails, sacks and bags (not included in other classes); padding and stuffing materials (except of rubber or plastics); raw fibrous textile materials.

23 Yarns and threads, for textile use.

24 Textiles and textile goods, not included in other classes; bed and table covers.

25 Clothing, footwear, headgear.

26 Lace and embroidery, ribbons and braid; buttons, hooks and eyes, pins and needles; artificial flowers.

27 Carpets, rugs, mats and matting, linoleum and other materials for covering existing floors; wall hangings (non-textile).

28 Games and playthings; gymnastic and sporting articles not included in other classes; decorations for Christmas trees.

29 Meat, fish, poultry and game; meat extracts; preserved, dried and cooked fruits and vegetables; jellies, jams, fruit sauces; eggs, milk and milk products; edible oils and fats.

30 Coffee, tea, cocoa, sugar, rice, tapioca, sago, artificial coffee; flour and preparations made from cereals, bread, pastry and confectionery, honey, treacle; yeast, baking-powder; salt, mustard; vinegar, sauces (condiments); spices; ice.

31 Agricultural, horticultural and forestry products and grains not included in other classes; live animals; fresh fruits and vegetables; seeds, natural plants and flowers; foodstuffs for animals, malt.

32 Beers; mineral and aerated waters and other non-alcoholic drinks; fruit drinks and fruit juices; syrups and other preparations for making beverages.

33 Alcoholic beverages (except beers).

34 Tobacco; smokers' articles; matches.

Services

35 Advertising; business management; business administration; office functions.

36 Insurance; financial affairs; monetary affairs; real estate affairs.

37 Building construction; repair; installation services.

38 Telecommunications.

39 Transport; packaging and storage of goods; travel arrangement.

40 Treatment of materials.

41 Education; providing of training; entertainment; sporting and cultural activities.

42 Providing of food and drink; temporary accommodation; medical, hygienic and beauty care; veterinary and agricultural services; legal services; scientific and industrial research; computer programming; services that cannot be placed in other classes.

EXHIBIT 12.2

Classification of Goods and Service in International Classes Crossed with U.S. Classes

International Class	Prior U.S. Class
1	1, 5, 6, 10, 31, 34, 52
2	1, 6, 11, 14, 16
3	4, 51, 52
	(SHAMPOOS & DETERGENTS)
4	6, 15
5	6, 18, 44
6	2, 13, 14, 25
7	23, 24
8	23
9	21, 23, 26, 36, 38
10	44
11	13, 21, 31, 34
12	19, 35
13	9
14	8, 14, 27, 28
15	36
16	37, 38
17	1, 13, 35
18	3, 41
19	12, 33
20	2, 13, 32, 50
21	2, 29, 30, 33, 40
	(BRUSHES, CLEANING INSTRUMENTS)
22	1, 7, 50
23	43
24	42
25	39
26	40
27	20, 42
	(LINOLEUM)
28	22
29	46
30	46

EXHIBIT 12.2   *Continued*

International Class	Prior U.S. Class
31	1, 46
32	45, 46, 48
	(SODAS, NON-ALCOHOLIC DRINKS)
33	47, 49
	(LIQUEURS)
34	8, 17

SERVICES

35	101
36	102
37	103
38	104
39	105
40	106
41	107
42	100, 101

PTO has a search library available to the public and there are many libraries designated as Patent and Trademark Depository Libraries (PTDLs) across the country which are supplied with search materials from the PTO, including the patent and trademark sections of the *Official Gazette of the U.S. Patent and Trademark Office*, in which all federally registered trademarks are published. A complete listing of PTDLs can be found in the student workbook accompanying this text. Additional search resources include the *Trademark Register*, which contains a list of existing U.S. registered marks classified by goods and services; on-line sources such as LEXIS-NEXIS, Compu-Mark, and Trademark-scan; and *Shepard's Patent and Trademark Citations*, which provides a listing of trademarks subject to previous litigation or PTO proceedings.

Before a mark can acquire either common law or statutory protection it must be affixed in some manner to the product and must be used. Affixation may be made by placing the mark on the goods themselves or through the use of labels, tags, or a prominent display of the mark in the advertisement of the product. For federal statutory protection, the mark must be affixed, used in "commerce," and registered with the PTO. The PTO defines **commerce** as interstate commerce or commerce between the United States and another country.

B.   Use and Intent-to-Use Applications

After a mark is searched and cleared in the manner described above, the client has two options available: (1) file a "use" application, where the client uses the product in commerce and then federally registers the mark under 15 United States Code Section 1051(a), or (2) file an "intent-to-use" application, where the client files a federal registration application indicating a bona fide intention to use the mark under Section 1051(b) and after using the mark in commerce supplements the application with a Statement of Use under 37 Code of Federal Regulations Section 2.88 or an Amendment to Allege Use under Section 2.76 (discussed further below). If the second option is chosen, the mark will not be federally protected until the Statement of Use or Amendment to Allege Use has been filed and accepted. However, once accepted by the PTO, the protection will be deemed to have commenced from the filing of the initial registration application.

If the client chooses to file an intent-to-use application, an important point to remember is that trademark search updates may be necessary if there is a considerable delay between the initial search report and the actual use of the mark. As soon as the client begins use of the mark, be it before or after filing a federal registration application, the client may and should use the designation TM in association with the mark if the mark is used with a product (or SM if used with a service) from the onset of use. These designations indicate ownership of the mark.

1.   Information Gathering

Before filing under either option noted above, all pertinent filing information must be obtained from the client. The Client Simulation at the end of the chapter provides a completed form. Note that information must be requested with regard to specimens. A **specimen** is a sample of how the mark is being used in commerce. Before the PTO will grant registration, it requires three specimens of the mark to be provided.

If the client has registered the mark abroad, it is not necessary to use it in interstate commerce within the United States to obtain registration with the PTO; instead, a certified copy of the foreign registration must be included with the application.

2. Application Form

Once the requisite information has been supplied by the client, the application process can commence. The same application, *Trademark/Service Mark Application, Principal Register, with Declaration*, can be used by an applicant as either a use application or an intent-to-use application (see Exhibit 12.3). The application form and instruction pamphlet can be obtained by writing or calling the PTO (a listing of PTO information numbers is provided in the student workbook accompanying this text). Many corporate law firms keep a supply on file. The back of the application form provides cursory instructions and a reminder that application fees are subject to change, with changes usually taking effect on October 1, so it is advisable to keep a tickler to call the PTO just prior to October of each year.

A complete trademark application includes the application form, the **drawing page** (a drawing of the mark according to precise PTO instructions), three specimens (if a use application), the applicable filing fee, and a cover letter. These materials should be sent certified mail, return receipt requested. At first glance, the application form appears straightforward and simple to fill out, but a cautionary word is in order. It is quite common for applications to be sent back by the PTO for errors, so time and care is required to prevent this occurrence. The PTO pamphlet provides line-by-line instructions for completing the form and should be followed to the letter. A separate application must be filed for each mark the client wants to register. Additionally, a separate application must be filed for each version of the mark if the client wants to register more than one version of the same mark.

The first item asked for is the mark. Whatever is written here must be checked for proper spelling and must conform with the information supplied on the drawing page. The classification number(s) box refers to the international classifications, not the prior U.S. domestic classifications. If the classifications are known, they should be included here. If this box is left blank, the PTO will make its own determination of the appropriate classifications. However, the filing fee is based on the number of classifications for the mark, so it truly is necessary to determine this before mailing the application.

Information about the owner must be completed including the name, address, type of business entity, and place of citizenship or domicile (for a partnership this would be where it was formed, for a corporation where it was incorporated, for a limited liability company where it was organized).

The box entitled "Goods and/or Services" must be completed even if the mark has not yet been used and an intent-to-use application is being filed. Special care must be taken here because what is listed in this box will determine the scope of protection of the mark. The tendency is to use overly broad terms (e.g. food, equipment, materials), or those used to identify international classi-

EXHIBIT 12.3

TRADEMARK/SERVICE MARK APPLICATION, PRINCIPAL REGISTER, WITH DECLARATION	MARK (Word(s) and/or Design)	CLASS NO. (If known)

TO THE ASSISTANT COMMISSIONER FOR TRADEMARKS:

APPLICANT'S NAME:

APPLICANT'S BUSINESS ADDRESS: _____
(Display address exactly as it   _____
should appear on registration)   _____

APPLICANT'S ENTITY TYPE: (Check one and supply requested information)

    Individual - Citizen of (Country):

    Partnership - State where organized (Country, if appropriate): _____
    Names and Citizenship (Country) of General Partners: _____
    _____
    _____

    Corporation - State (Country, if appropriate) of Incorporation:

    Other (Specific Nature of Entity and Domicile):

GOODS AND/OR SERVICES:

Applicant requests registration of the trademark/service mark shown in the accompanying drawing in the United States Patent and Trademark Office on the Principal Register established by the Act of July 5, 1946 (15 U.S.C. 1051 et. seq., as amended) for the following goods/services **(SPECIFIC GOODS AND/OR SERVICES MUST BE INSERTED HERE):**

_____
_____
_____
_____
_____

BASIS FOR APPLICATION: (Check boxes which apply, but never both the first AND second boxes, and supply requested information related to each box checked.)

[ ]   Applicant is using mark in commerce on or in connection with the above identified goods/services. (15 U.S.C. 1051(a), as amended.) Three specimens showing the mark as used in commerce are submitted with this application.
    ● Date of first use of the mark in commerce which the U.S. Congress may regulate (for example, interstate or between the U.S. and a foreign country): _____
    ● Specify the type of commerce: _____
            (for example, interstate or between the U.S. and a specified foreign country)
    ● Date of first use anywhere (the same as or before use in commerce date): _____
    ● Specify intended manner or mode of use of mark on or in connection with the goods/services: _____
    (for example, trademark is applied to labels, service mark is used in advertisements)

[ ]   Applicant has a bona fide intention to use the mark in commerce on or in connection with the above identified goods/services. (15 U.S.C. 1051(b), as amended.)
    ● Specify manner or mode of use of mark on or in connection with the goods/services: _____
    (for example, trademark will be applied to labels, service mark will be used in advertisements)

[ ]   Applicant has a bona fide intention to use the mark in commerce on or in connection with the above identified goods/services and asserts a claim of priority based upon a foreign application in accordance with 15 U.S.C. 1126(d), as amended.
    ● Country of foreign filing: _____   ● Date of foreign filing: _____

[ ]   Applicant has a bona fide intention to use the mark in commerce or in connection with the above identified goods/services, and, accompanying this application, submits a certification or certified copy of a foreign registration in accordance with 15 U.S.C 1126(e), as amended.
    ● Country of registration: _____   ● Registration number: _____

NOTE: Declaration, on Reverse Side, MUST be Signed

PTO Form 1478 (REV 10/94)   U.S. DEPARTMENT OF COMMERCE/Patent and Trademark Office
OMB No. 0651-0009 (Exp. 6/30/95)

EXHIBIT 12.3   *Continued*

If submitted on one page, side two of the form should be Upside Down" in relation to page 1.

DECLARATION

The undersigned being hereby warned that willful false statements and the like so made are punishable by fine or imprisonment, or both, under 18 U.S.C. 1001, and that such willful false statements may jeopardize the validity of the application or any resulting registration, declares that he/she is properly authorized to execute this application this application on behalf of the applicant; he/she believes the applicant to be owner of the trademark/service mark sought to be registered, or if the application is being files under 15 U.S.C. 1051(b), he/she believes applicant to be entitled to use such mark in commerce; to the best of his/her knowledge and belief no other person, firm, corporation, or association has the right to use the above identified mark in commerce, either in the identical form thereof or in such near resemblance thereto as to be likely, when used on or in connection with the goods/services of such other person, to cause confusion, or to cause mistake, or to deceive; and that all statements made of his/her own knowledge are true and that all statements made on information and belief are believed to be true.

DATE _____   SIGNATURE _____

TELEPHONE NUMBER _____   PRINT OR TYPE NAME _____

INSTRUCTIONS AND INFORMATION FOR APPLICANT

TO RECEIVE A FILING DATE, THE APPLICATION <u>MUST</u> BE COMPLETED AND SIGNED BY THE APPLICANT AND SUBMITTED ALONG WITH:

1. The prescribed **FEE of $245.00*** for each class of goods/services listed in the application;
2. A **DRAWING PAGE** displaying the mark in conformance with 37 CFR 2.52;
3. If the application is based on use of the mark in commerce, **THREE (3) SPECIMENS** (evidence) of the mark as used in commerce for each class of goods/services listed in the application. All three specimens may be in the nature of: (a) labels showing the mark which are placed on the goods; (b) photographs of the mark as it appears on the goods, (c) brochures or advertisements showing the mark as used in connection with the services.
4. An **APPLICATION WITH DECLARATION** (this form) - The application must be signed in order for the application to receive a filing date. Only the following person may sign the declaration, depending on the applicant's legal entity: (a) the individual applicant; (b) an officer of the corporate applicant; (c) one general partner of a partnership applicant; (d) all joint applicants.

SEND APPLICATION FORM, DRAWING PAGE, FEE AND SPECIMENS (IF APPROPRIATE) TO:
Assistant Commissioner for Trademarks
Box New App / Fee
2900 Crystal Drive
Arlington, VA 22202-3513

Additional information concerning the requirements for filing an application is available in a booklet entitled **Basic Facts About Registering a Trademark,** which may be obtained by writing to the above address or by calling: (703) 308-9000.

* Fees are subject to change; changes usually take effect on October 1. If filing on or after October 1, 1995, please call the PTO to confirm the correct fee.

This form is estimated to take an average of 1 hour to complete, including time required for reading and understanding instructions, gathering necessary information, recordkeeping, and actually providing the information. Any comments on this form, including the amount of time required to complete this form, should be sent to the Office of Management and Organizations, U.S. Patent and Trademark Office, U.S. Department of Commerce, Washington, D.C. 20231, and Paper Reduction Project 0651-0009, Office of Information and Regulatory Affairs, Office of Management and Budget, Washington, D.C. 20503. Do NOT send completed forms to either of these addresses.

fications, with the belief that this will afford the widest protection. What may happen, in fact, is that the application will be sent back to the applicant. Additionally, terminology should not be too specific because it may not be possible to later amend the application to add products or services. The rule of thumb is a term may be amended to narrow its scope but may not be amended to change or broaden its scope. For example, "computer software" could later be amended to "educational software" but could not be amended to include computer hardware.

The application form requires the applicant to indicate a basis for application (e.g., use, intent to use). Check only one box or the application will be sent back. Note that checking the first box will turn the application into a use application. Here one needs to supply the first date of use in commerce and the type of commerce, as well as the first date of use anywhere (which may or may not be the same as first use in commerce). Following this is the "method-of-use" clause where one indicates how the mark is affixed (e.g., used on labels, used on containers). If the client intends to file an intent to use application, the second box, not the first, should be checked and completed by supplying the method-of-use clause. The third and fourth basis-for-application boxes are pertinent only for those clients filing under the terms of an international treaty.

The declaration is supplied on the back of the application form. The declaration is simply a verification that the information provided is truthful and accurate and it must be signed by the appropriate individual. If the client is a sole proprietor, he or she signs in his or her own name. If the client is a general or limited partnership, any general partner may sign. If the client is a corporation, an officer of the corporation may sign. In addition, attached to the application must be a Power of Attorney signed by the client indicating that the client is giving the attorney the authority to act on its behalf with regard to the application process. It must include the mailing address and telephone number of the attorney. If the client is a foreign business entity (originating from a foreign country), the client must have a domestic representative. This person, similar to a registered agent, is a resident of the United States who accepts service of any notices regarding the application and may be an attorney hired by the entity. A Designation of Domestic Representative should be attached to the application form in this instance.

3. Drawing Page

A drawing page must be submitted with either a use or intent-to-use application. Special attention must be paid to the detailed PTO instructions. The drawing must be on 8½" by 11" white, non-shiny paper. Paper margins must be at least one inch on the sides, top, and bottom of the paper. There must be at least one inch between the heading and the display of the mark.

The first line of the heading is the applicant's name. The second line is the applicant's address. The third line lists the goods and/or services connected with the mark. If the application is a use application, this is followed by a fourth line indicating date of first use of the mark and a fifth line indicating date of first use in commerce. If a design is used, a short description of the design is then indicated.

At least one inch underneath this heading the mark should appear. If the mark consists only of words, letters, or numbers, one can simply type it on the drawing page entirely in capital letters (used even if the actual mark includes lower-case letters). If the mark consists of words and a design, the drawing page includes a **special-form drawing**, so called because of its exact specifications. The drawing must not be larger than 4″ by 4″ and must be done only in black and white. Color is indicated by the color linings shown in Exhibit 12.4 below.

EXHIBIT 12.4

Special-form Drawing Color Codes

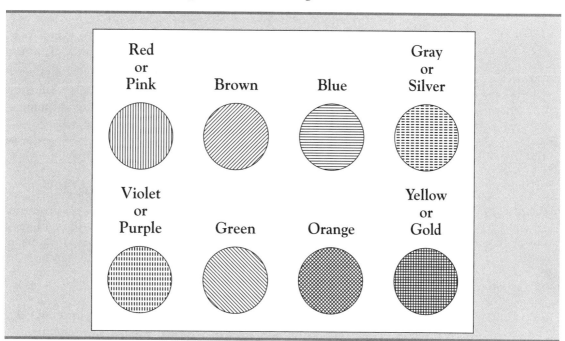

4. Specimens

If a use application is submitted, three specimens per class (e.g., international classification) must be included. As noted above, the specimens may be tags, labels, containers, displays, or photographs of the product showing how the mark actually is used in commerce. If the mark is a service mark, advertisements, business cards, brochures, and stationery may be used as specimens. (Note that advertisements, business cards, brochures, and stationery may not be submitted as specimens for a trademark). The specimens may be identical or each may be different. They must not be larger than 8½" by 11" and must be flat. If a label, business card, or other small item is used as a specimen, it may be stapled to a sheet of paper labeled SPECIMENS.

In the case of either a use or intent-to-use application, a filing fee must be sent. At the time of this writing, the filing fee is $245 for each class of goods and/or services listed on the application. If this fee is not submitted, the application will not be processed. The fee must be paid by check, certified check, or post office money order, made payable to The Assistant Commissioner for Trademarks and the application package posted to the same at 2900 Crystal Drive, Arlington, Virginia 22202-3513, directed to Box NEW APP/FEE.

5.   Post-Application Matters

Once the application has been received, it is reviewed to determine if it is in order. If so, it will receive a filing date and be given a serial number. The time lapse between mailing the application and receipt of a serial number is usually two months. Actually, two receipts will be sent: one receipt will show only the assigned serial number and the filing date, and the other will summarize material information regarding the application and request that any corrections be made. This second receipt should be reviewed carefully. Once a serial number has been issued, any correspondence regarding the application should include this number.

The application is then examined by a PTO attorney to determine if the mark can be registered. If, upon review, the PTO attorney finds no problems, or if problems are identified and subsequently remedied, the mark will be approved and published in the *Official Gazette*, a weekly publication of the PTO. The applicant will receive a Notice of Publication, which states the publication date. Once the mark is published in the *Official Gazette*, any party opposing registration of the mark has 30 days within which to so notify the PTO.

If the applicant has submitted an intent-to-use application to the PTO, a certificate of registration will not be issued until the mark is actually used in commerce. As soon as such use occurs, the applicant must make an additional submission to the PTO of: (1) three specimens per class, (2) an additional fee of $100 per class, and (3) either an Amendment to Allege Use or a Statement of Use (the forms appear as Exhibits 12.5 and 12.6). The applicant will file an

EXHIBIT 12.5

AMENDMENT TO ALLEGE USE UNDER 37 CFR 2.76, WITH DECLARATION	MARK (Identify the mark)
	SERIAL NO.

TO THE ASSISTANT COMMISSIONER FOR TRADEMARKS:

APPLICANT NAME:

Applicant requests registration of the above-identified trademarks/service mark in the United States Patent and Trademark Office on the Principal Register established by the Act of July 5, 1946 (15 U.S.C. 1051 et. seq., as amended). Three specimens per class showing the mark as used in commerce are submitted with this amendment.

☐ Check here if Request to Divide under 37 C.F.R. 2.87 is being submitted with this amendment.

Applicant is using the mark in commerce on or in connection with the following goods/services:

_____

_____

(NOTE: Goods/Services listed above may not be broader than the goods/services identified in this application currently)

Date of first use of mark in commerce
which the U.S. Congress may regulate: _____

Specify type of commerce: (e.g., interstate, between the U.S. and a specified foreign country) _____

_____

Date of first use anywhere: _____

(the same as or before use-in-commerce date)

Specify manner or mode of use of mark on or in connection with the goods/services: (e.g., trademark is applied to labels, service mark is used in advertisements) _____

_____

The undersigned being hereby warned that willful false statements and the like so made are punishable by fine or imprisonment, or both, under 18 U.S.C. 1001, and that such willful false statements may jeopardize the validity of the application or any resulting registration, declares that he/she is properly authorized to execute this Amendment to Allege Use on behalf of the applicant; he/she believes the applicant to be the owner of the trademark/service mark sought to be registered; the trademark/service mark is now in use in commerce; and that all statements made of his/her own knowledge are true and all statements made on information and belief are believed to be true.

_____   _____
Date   Signature

_____   _____
Telephone Number   Print or Type Name and Position

PTO Form 1579 (REV. 10-94)
OMB No. 0651-0009
Exp. 6-30-95

U.S. Department of Commerce/Patent and Trademark Office

EXHIBIT 12.6

STATEMENT OF USE UNDER 37 CFR 2.88, WITH DECLARATION	MARK (Identify the mark)
	SERIAL NO.

TO THE ASSISTANT COMMISSIONER FOR TRADEMARKS:

APPLICANT NAME:

NOTICE OF ALLOWANCE ISSUE DATE:

Applicant requests registration of the above-identified trademarks/service mark in the United States Patent and Trademark Office on the Principal Register established by the Act of July 5, 1946 (15 U.S.C. 1051 et. seq., as amended). Three specimens per class showing the mark as used in commerce are submitted with this statement.

☐   Check here if a Request to Divide under 37 C.F.R. 2.87 is being submitted with this statement.

Applicant is using the mark in commerce on or in connection with the following goods/services: (Check One)

☐   Those goods/services identified in the Notice of Allowance in this application.

☐   Those goods/services identified in the Notice of Allowance in this application except: (Identify goods/services to be deleted from application) _____

_____

_____

Date of first use of mark in commerce
which the U.S. Congress may regulate: _____

Specify type of commerce: (e.g., interstate, between the U.S. and a specified foreign country) _____

_____

Date of first use anywhere: _____
                                        (the same as or before use-in-commerce date)

Specify manner or mode of use of mark on or in connection with the goods/services: (e.g., trademark is applied to labels, service mark is used in advertisements) _____

The undersigned being hereby warned that willful false statements and the like so made are punishable by fine or imprisonment, or both, under 18 U.S.C. 1001, and that such willful false statements may jeopardize the validity of the application or any resulting registration, declares that he/she is properly authorized to execute this Statement of Use on behalf of the applicant; he/she believes the applicant to be the owner of the trademark/service mark sought to be registered; the trademark/service mark is now in use in commerce; and all statements made of his/her own knowledge are true and all statements made on information and belief are believed to be true.

_____   _____
Date   Signature

_____   _____
Telephone Number   Print or Type Name and Position

PTO Form 1580 (REV. 10-94)   U.S. Department of Commerce/Patent and Trademark Office
OMB No. 0651-0009
Exp. 6-30-95

Amendment to Allege Use if the mark has been used prior to PTO approval of its publication in the *Official Gazette*. The applicant will file a Statement of Use if the mark has been published and the applicant has received a Notice of Allowance before the mark has been used. If the latter is the case, the applicant must either use the mark and file a Statement of Use within six months of the issuance of the Notice of Allowance or file a Request for an Extension of Time to File a Statement of Use (see Exhibit 12.7). If this is not done, the application is considered abandoned.

Initial federal trademark registration lasts for ten years and can be renewed for ten-year periods. Between the fifth and sixth year after the date of registration, a **Section 8 affidavit** (also called an **affidavit of use**) must be filed with the PTO, together with a filing fee ($100 per class at time of this writing) to keep the trademark's registration active for the remainder of this ten-year term (see Exhibit 12.8). If this is not done, the mark's registration will be canceled. Additionally, a **Section 15 affidavit** (an **incontestability affidavit**) may be submitted (the filing fee to be submitted with the affidavit is $100 per class at time of this writing) to the PTO if the mark has been in continuous use (see Exhibit 12.9). This provides prima facie evidence of incontestability for most litigation purposes. If the mark has been in continuous use from first use through the time the Section 8 affidavit is to be filed, it is possible to file a combined Section 8 and Section 15 affidavit (see Exhibit 12.10.) At time of this writing, the filing fee was $200 per class. To assure continued federal registration, the mark must be renewed every ten years.

EXHIBIT 12.7

REQUEST FOR EXTENSION OF TIME UNDER 37 CFR 2.89, TO FILE A STATEMENT OF USE, WITH DECLARATION	MARK (Identify the mark)
	SERIAL NO.

TO THE ASSISTANT COMMISSIONER FOR TRADEMARKS:

APPLICANT NAME:

NOTICE OF ALLOWANCE MAILING DATE:

Applicant requests a six-month extension of time to file the Statement of Use under 37 CFR 2.89 in this application.

☐   Check here if a Request to Divide under 37 C.F.R. 2.87 is being submitted with this request.

Applicant has a continued bona fide intention to use the mark in commerce on in connection with the following goods/services: (Check One below)

☐ Those goods/services identified in the Notice of Allowance in this application.

☐ Those goods/services identified in the Notice of Allowance in this application except: (Identify goods/services to be **deleted** from application) _____

_____

_____

This is the _____ request for an Extension of Time following mailing of the Notice of Allowance.
(Specify: First - Fifth)

If this is not the first request for an Extension of Time, check one box below. If the first box is checked explain the circumstance(s) of the non-use in the space provided:

☐   Applicant has not used the mark in commerce yet on all goods/services specified in the Notice of Allowance; however, applicant has made the following ongoing efforts to use the mark in commerce on or in connection with each of the goods/services specified above:

_____

_____

If additional space is needed, please attach a separate sheet to this form

☐   Applicant believes that it has made valid use of the mark in commerce, as evidenced by the Statement of Use submitted with this request; however, if the Statement of Use does not meet minimum requirements under 37 CFR 2.88(e), applicant will need additional time in which to file a new statement.

The undersigned being hereby warned that willful false statements and the like so made are punishable by fine or imprisonment, or both, under 18 U.S.C. 1001, and that such willful false statements may jeopardize the validity of the application or any resulting registration, declares that he/she is properly authorized to execute this Request for an Extension of Time to File a Statement of Use on behalf of the applicant; and that all statements made of his/her own knowledge are true and all statements made on information and belief are believed to be true.

_____   _____
Date   Signature

_____   _____
Telephone Number   Print or Type Name and Position

PTO Form 1580 (REV. 10-94)   U.S. Department of Commerce/Patent and Trademark Office
OMB No. 0651-0009
Exp. 6-30-95

EXHIBIT 12.8

DECLARATION OF USE OF A MARK UNDER **SECTION 8** OF THE TRADEMARK ACT OF 1946, AS AMENDED	MARK (Identify the mark)	
	REGISTRATION NO.	DATE OF REGISTRATION:

TO THE ASSISTANT SECRETARY AND COMMISSIONER OF PATENTS AND TRADEMARKS:

REGISTRANT'S NAME:[1]

REGISTRANT'S CURRENT MAILING ADDRESS: _____

GOODS AND/OR SERVICES AND USE IN COMMERCE STATEMENT:

The mark shown in Registration No. _____ owned by the above-identified registrant is in use in

_____ commerce on or in connection with all of the goods and/or services identified in the
(type of)[2]

registration, (*except* for the following)[3] _____

_____ ;

as evidenced by the attached specimen(s)[4] showing the mark as currently used.

DECLARATION

The undersigned being hereby warned that willful false statements and the like so made are punishable by fine or imprisonment, or both, under 18 U.S.C. 1001, and that such willful false statements may jeopardize the validity of this document, declares that he/she is properly authorized to execute this document on behalf of the registrant; he/she believes the registrant to be the owner of the above identified registration; the trademark/service mark is in use in commerce; and all statements made of his/her own knowledge are true and all statements made on information and belief are believed to be true.

_____
Date

_____
Signature

_____
Telephone Number

_____
Print or Type Name and Position
[if applicable][5]

PTO Form 1583 (Rev. 1/93)   U.S. DEPARTMENT OF COMMERCE/Patent and Trademark Office
OMB No. 0651-0009 (Exp. 6/30/95)

EXHIBIT 12.9

DECLARATION OF INCONTESTABILITY OF A MARK UNDER **SECTION 15** OF THE TRADEMARK ACT OF 1946 AS AMENDED	MARK (Identify the mark)	
	REGISTRATION NO.	DATE OF REGISTRATION:

TO THE ASSISTANT SECRETARY AND COMMISSIONER OF PATENTS AND TRADEMARKS:

REGISTRANT'S NAME:[1]

REGISTRANT'S CURRENT MAILING ADDRESS: _____
_____
_____
_____

GOODS AND/OR SERVICES AND USE IN COMMERCE STATEMENT:

The mark shown in **Principal Register** Registration No. _____, owned by the above-identified

registrant has been incontinuous use in _____ commerce for five consecutive years from _____
                                              (type of)[2]   (date)

to the present on or in connection with all of the goods and/or services identified in the registration, (*except* for the following)[3]

_____

_____.

There has been no final decision adverse to registrant's claim of ownership of such mark for such goods or

services, or to registrant's right to register the same or to keep the same on the register; and there is no

proceeding involving said rights pending and not disposed of either in the Patent and Trademark Office or in

the courts.

DECLARATION

The undersigned being hereby warned that willful false statements and the like so made are punishable by fine or imprisonment, or both, under 18 U.S.C. 1001, and that such willful false statements may jeopardize the validity of this document, declares that he/she is properly authorized to execute this document on behalf of the registrant; he/she believes the registrant to be the owner of the above identified registration; the trademark/service mark is in use in commerce; and all statements made of his/her own knowledge are true and all statements made on information and belief are believed to be true.

_____   _____
Date   Signature

_____   _____
Telephone Number   Print or Type Name and Position
                                                                    [if applicable][4]

PTO Form 4.16 (Rev. 1/93)   U.S. DEPARTMENT OF COMMERCE/Patent and Trademark Office
OMB No. 0651-0009 (Exp. 6/30/95)

EXHIBIT 12.10

COMBINED DECLARATION OF USE AND INCONTESTABILITY UNDER SECTIONS 8 & 15[1] OF THE TRADEMARK ACT OF 1946, AS AMENDED	MARK (Identify the mark)
	REGISTRATION NO. DATE OF REGISTRATION:

TO THE ASSISTANT SECRETARY AND COMMISSIONER OF PATENTS AND TRADEMARKS:

REGISTRANT'S NAME:[2]

REGISTRANT'S CURRENT MAILING ADDRESS: _____

_____

_____

GOODS AND/OR SERVICES AND USE IN COMMERCE STATEMENT:

The mark shown in Registration No. _____, owned by the above-identified registrant, has been in

continuous use in _____ commerce for five consecutive years from the date of registration or the
_____(type of)[3]

date of publication under §12(c)[4] to the present, on or in connection with all of the goods and/or services

identified in the registration, (*except* for the following)[5]_____

_____ ;

as evidenced by the attached specimen(s)[6] showing the mark as currently used. There has been no final

decision adverse to registrant's claim of ownership of such mark for such goods or services, or to registrant's

right to register the same or to keep the same on the register; and there is no proceeding involving said

rights pending and not disposed of either in the Patent and Trademark Office or in the courts.

DECLARATION

The undersigned being hereby warned that willful false statements and the like so made are punishable by fine or imprisonment, or both, under 18 U.S.C. 1001, and that such willful false statements may jeopardize the validity of this document, declares that he/she is properly authorized to execute this document on behalf of the registrant; he/she believes the registrant to be the owner of the above identified registration; the trademark/service mark is in use in commerce; and all statements made of his/her own knowledge are true and all statements made on information and belief are believed to be true.

_____   _____
Date   Signature

_____   _____
Telephone Number   Print or Type Name and Position
                                                      [if applicable][7]

PTO-FB-TM (Combined 8 & 15) (Rev. 1/93)   U.S. DEPARTMENT OF COMMERCE/Patent and Trademark Office
OMB No. 0651-0009 (Exp. 6/30/95)

CLIENT SIMULATION

Karen has a trademark matter she has scheduled for this morning, the preparation of a "use" application for federal trademark registration for a corporate client. The client, Footprints Across America, Inc., a manufacturer of footwear and bags, is ready to register a new trademark, "Boot Camp," for its latest line, catering to a teens and twenties market. The line is being tested in an experimental market encompassing select stores in several cities nationwide, and so the client has used the mark in interstate commerce. The client, wanting to file its application before it invests considerable money in a nationwide advertising campaign, met with Thomas and Karen at an earlier date to supply the requisite information and specimens. Karen pulls the client file and takes out the completed registration worksheet, which reads as follows.

EXHIBIT 12.11

Trademark Registration Worksheet

DATE OF INTAKE: March 5, 1997

ATTORNEY: Thomas Trumbull

PARALEGAL: Karen Greer

CLIENT NUMBER: 1520

MATTER NUMBER: 0011

PERSON RESPONSIBLE
FOR INTAKE: Karen Greer

  1. CLIENT NAME: Footprints Across America, Inc.; Eric Wright, President

  2. ADDRESS: 3225 Newmarket Lane

                         Any City, Any State

  3. TELEPHONE: (000) 999-2646   FAX: (000) 999-3155

  4. NAME OF OWNER OF MARK: Footprints Across America, Inc.

EXHIBIT 12.11   *Continued*

5. BUSINESS ENTITY OF OWNER:

    _____ Sole Proprietorship; resident of: _____

    _____ General Partnership; formed in: _____

    _____ Limited Partnership; formed in: _____

    __X__ Corporation; incorporated in: Any State _____

    _____ Limited Liability Company; organized in: _____

    _____ Other (please describe): _____

6. SIGNATURE ON APPLICATION:

    Name: Eric Wright

    Title: President

7. THE MARK: Boot Camp

8. TYPE OF MARK: __X__ Trademark _____ Service Mark

    _____ Other (specify): _____

9. MEANING OF MARK (if applicable): military terminology used for place of indoctrination of new recruits

10. DESIGN: __X__ No

    _____ Yes _____ Sample attached

    _____ Need to get

11. HOW DESIGN IS USED: Not applicable

12. MARK TO BE USED FOR (Describe goods or services): Boots, shoes, handbags, backpacks

13. INTERNATIONAL CLASSIFICATION(S):

    Class 18 for handbags and backpacks

    Class 25 for boots and shoes

EXHIBIT 12.11   *Continued*

14. MARK ALREADY REGISTERED:

___X___ No

_____ Yes, state registration (indicate state):

_____

_____ Yes, abroad (indicate country or countries):

_____

15. MARK PRESENTLY USED:

___X___ Yes _____ No

(a) If yes, indicate:

Date of first use: 1/14/97: boots and shoes; 2/21/97: handbags and
backpacks

Location of first use: interstate (Boston, Chicago, San Francisco,
New York City)

Evidence of this use (if available, please attach to worksheet):

___X___ available _____ not available

Date of first use in interstate or foreign commerce: same as above

Location of first use in interstate or foreign commerce: same as above

Evidence of this use (if available, please attach to worksheet):

___X___ available _____ not available

(b) If no, indicate:

Expected date of first use: _____

Expected location of first use: _____

Expected date of first use in interstate or foreign commerce: _____

Expected location of first use in interstate or foreign commerce: _____

16. WHERE AND HOW WILL MARK BE USED IN THE FUTURE:
On labels affixed to boots, shoes, handbags, and
backpacks

| EXHIBIT 12.11 *Continued* |

17. SPECIMENS: __X__ Available and attached

_____ Available; client needs to provide

_____ Not available; availability date: _____

18. ADDITIONAL COMMENTS: <u>ready to file a "use" application</u>

With the above information, Karen can readily prepare the application package. Because the client's products on which the mark is used fall within two international classifications, Karen needs to include six instead of three specimens with the application. She must also be sure to include a Power of Attorney and attach it to the application to indicate that all correspondence and other notifications with regard to the application should be sent to the law firm. The completed package includes a cover letter, the application, the power of attorney, the drawing page, the six specimens (not shown here), and a check in the amount of $490 (recall that the fee at time of this writing is $245 per class). Karen pulls up on her computer a form cover letter to accompany the application. Because the letter is strictly administrative, containing no legal advice, Karen may sign it herself as long as she includes her title of legal assistant next to her name. The cover letter reads as follows.

CERTIFIED MAIL
RETURN RECEIPT REQUESTED

Commissioner of Patents and Trademarks
Patent and Trademark Office
Washington, D.C. 20231

Re: Federal Trademark Application for BOOT CAMP;
International Classes 18 & 25

Dear Sir:

Enclosed for filing please find trademark application of Footprints Across America, Inc. for the mark "BOOT CAMP" in International Classes 18 and 25 together with the drawing, six specimens and the filing fee of $490 for an original application in two classes at $245 per class. In addition, a copy of the

EXHIBIT 12.12

TRADEMARK/SERVICE MARK APPLICATION, PRINCIPAL REGISTER, WITH DECLARATION	MARK (Word(s) and/or Design) BOOT CAMP	CLASS NO. (If known) 18 and 25

TO THE ASSISTANT COMMISSIONER FOR TRADEMARKS:

APPLICANT'S NAME: Footprints Across America, Inc.

APPLICANT'S BUSINESS ADDRESS: 3225 Newmarket Lane
(Display address exactly as it should appear on registration)   Any City, Any State 98765

APPLICANT'S ENTITY TYPE: (Check one and supply requested information)

Individual - Citizen of (Country):

Partnership - State where organized (Country, if appropriate): _____

Names and Citizenship (Country) of General Partners: _____

Corporation - State (Country, if appropriate) of Incorporation: Any State

Other (Specific Nature of Entity and Domicile):

GOODS AND/OR SERVICES:

Applicant requests registration of the trademark/service mark shown in the accompanying drawing in the United States Patent and Trademark Office on the Principal Register established by the Act of July 5, 1946 (15 U.S.C. 1051 et. seq., as amended) for the following goods/services (SPECIFIC GOODS AND/OR SERVICES MUST BE INSERTED HERE):

Handbags and backpacks (Class 18); Boots and shoes (Class 25)

BASIS FOR APPLICATION: (Check boxes which apply, but never both the first AND second boxes, and supply requested information related to each box checked.)

kk Applicant is using mark in commerce on or in connection with the above identified goods/services. (15 U.S.C. 1051(a), as amended.) Three specimens showing the mark as used in commerce are submitted with this application.
 • Date of first use of the mark in commerce which the U.S. Congress may regulate (for example, interstate or between the U.S. and a foreign country): (Class 18) 2/21/97; (Class 25) 1/14/97
 • Specify the type of commerce: Interstate
    (for example, interstate or between the U.S. and a specified foreign country)
 • Date of first use anywhere (the same as or before use in commerce date): Cl 18-2/21/97; Cl 25-1/14/97
 • Specify intended manner or mode of use of mark on or in connection with the goods/services: Affixed to labels used with handbags, backpacks, boots, and shoes
    (for example, trademark is applied to labels, service mark is used in advertisements)

[ ] Applicant has a bona fide intention to use the mark in commerce on or in connection with the above identified goods/services. (15 U.S.C. 1051(b), as amended.)
 • Specify manner or mode of use of mark on or in connection with the goods/services: _____

    (for example, trademark will be applied to labels, service mark will be used in advertisements)

[ ] Applicant has a bona fide intention to use the mark in commerce on or in connection with the above identified goods/services and asserts a claim of priority based upon a foreign application in accordance with 15 U.S.C. 1126(d), as amended.

 • Country of foreign filing: _____   • Date of foreign filing: _____

[ ] Applicant has a bona fide intention to use the mark in commerce or in connection with the above identified goods/services, and, accompanying this application, submits a certification or certified copy of a foreign registration in accordance with 15 U.S.C 1126(e), as amended.

 • Country of registration: _____   • Registration number: _____

NOTE: Declaration, on Reverse Side, MUST be Signed

PTO Form 1478 (REV 10/94)
OMB No. 0651-0009 (Exp. 6/30/95)   U.S. DEPARTMENT OF COMMERCE/Patent and Trademark Office

EXHIBIT 12.12 *Continued*

If submitted on one page, side two of the form should be Upside Down" in relation to page 1

DECLARATION

The undersigned being hereby warned that willful false statements and the like so made are punishable by fine or imprisonment, or both, under 18 U.S.C. 1001, and that such willful false statements may jeopardize the validity of the application or any resulting registration, declares that he/she is properly authorized to execute this application this application on behalf of the applicant; he/she believes the applicant to be owner of the trademark/service mark sought to be registered, or if the application is being files under 15 U.S.C. 1051(b), he/she believes applicant to be entitled to use such mark in commerce; to the best of his/her knowledge and belief no other person, firm, corporation, or association has the right to use the above identified mark in commerce, either in the identical form thereof or in such near resemblance thereto as to be likely, when used on or in connection with the goods/services of such other person, to cause confusion, or to cause mistake, or to deceive; and that all statements made of his/her own knowledge are true and that all statements made on information and belief are believed to be true.

DATE	SIGNATURE
(000) 999 - 2646	Eric Wright, President
TELEPHONE NUMBER	PRINT OR TYPE NAME

INSTRUCTIONS AND INFORMATION FOR APPLICANT

TO RECEIVE A FILING DATE, THE APPLICATION MUST BE COMPLETED AND SIGNED BY THE APPLICANT AND SUBMITTED ALONG WITH:

1. The prescribed **FEE of $245.00*** for each class of goods/services listed in the application;
2. A **DRAWING PAGE** displaying the mark in conformance with 37 CFR 2.52;
3. If the application is based on use of the mark in commerce, **THREE (3) SPECIMENS** (evidence) of the mark as used in commerce for each class of goods/services listed in the application. All three specimens may be in the nature of: (a) labels showing the mark which are placed on the goods; (b) photographs of the mark as it appears on the goods, (c) brochures or advertisements showing the mark as used in connection with the services.
4. An **APPLICATION WITH DECLARATION** (this form) - The application must be signed in order for the application to receive a filing date. Only the following person may sign the declaration, depending on the applicant's legal entity: (a) the individual applicant; (b) an officer of the corporate applicant; (c) one general partner of a partnership applicant; (d) all joint applicants.

SEND APPLICATION FORM, DRAWING PAGE, FEE AND SPECIMENS (IF APPROPRIATE) TO:
Assistant Commissioner for Trademarks
Box New App / Fee
2900 Crystal Drive
Arlington, VA 22202-3513

Additional information concerning the requirements for filing an application is available in a booklet entitled **Basic Facts About Registering a Trademark,** which may be obtained by writing to the above address or by calling: (703) 308-9000.

* Fees are subject to change; changes usually take effect on October 1. If filing on or after October 1, 1995, please call the PTO to confirm the correct fee.

This form is estimated to take an average of 1 hour to complete, including time required for reading and understanding instructions, gathering necessary information, recordkeeping, and actually providing the information. Any comments on this form, including the amount of time required to complete this form, should be sent to the Office of Management and Organizations, U.S. Patent and Trademark Office, U.S. Department of Commerce, Washington, D.C. 20231, and Paper Reduction Project 0651-0009, Office of Information and Regulatory Affairs, Office of Management and Budget, Washington, D.C. 20503. Do NOT send completed forms to either of these addresses.

application is enclosed for return by you indicating receipt thereof, together with a stamped, self-addressed envelope.

Very truly yours,

Karen Greer, Legal Assistant

Enclosures

cc: Eric Wright

Karen goes to the file cabinet where extra copies of all PTO forms are kept, finds the form and completes it, leaving the signature and date lines blank. To the application, she attaches the following Power of Attorney.

POWER OF ATTORNEY

MARK: BOOT CAMP
APPLICANT: Footprints Across America, Inc.

Applicant hereby appoints:
Thomas Trumbull, Esquire
Trumbull and McDonald, P.A.
2500 Jefferson Street
Any City, Any State
(000) 856-3135

to prosecute this application to register, to transact all business in the Patent and Trademark Office in connection therewith, and to receive the certificate of registration.

Dated this _____ day of _____, 19_____.

_____
Eric Wright, President

Karen next turns her attention to the drawing page. If the trademark included a design, Karen might have asked the client to have its advertising staff prepare the drawing page, providing the staff with the PTO specifications. However, because no design is attached to the trademark, Karen can prepare it herself as follows.

EXHIBIT 12.13

Sample Drawing Page

APPLICANT'S NAME:	Footprints Across America, Inc.
APPLICANT'S ADDRESS:	3225 Newmarket Lane, Any City, Any State 98765
GOODS:	Handbags, backpacks, boots, and shoes
FIRST USE:	Handbags and backpacks (Class 18) February 21, 1997 Boots and shoes (Class 25) January 14, 1997
FIRST USE IN COMMERCE:	Handbags and backpacks (Class 18) February 21, 1997 Boots and shoes (Class 25) January 14, 1997

BOOT CAMP

Karen puts the application package together and leaves it on Thomas's desk for review and the client's signature, after which she will make copies of the application and include one copy and a self-addressed, stamped envelope with the package before sending it to the PTO.

Chapter Summary

1. The term "intellectual property" encompasses patents, copyrights, and trademarks (as well as service marks). A patent protects an invention, a copyright protects a work of authorship, and a trademark protects a term and/or design identifying a product. A service mark protects a term and/or design identifying a product.

2. The purpose of a trademark is to develop consumer recognition of the product or services of a business, and by so doing to establish an advantage over competitors.

3. Trademark protection begins when the mark is affixed to a product or service and used in connection with that product or service. Common law rights pertain to the mark from the first use of the mark. Statutory protection is provided when the mark is registered. The life of a trademark lasts as long as its proper use.

4. A mark's strength is measured by its distinctiveness. The strongest marks are coined marks. The weakest marks are those which are merely descriptive. A mark that starts out strong may be diluted over time through improper use. Care must be taken to police a mark, both in-house and externally.

5. To be afforded additional rights beyond those provided by common law, a mark should be federally registered. This may be done after the mark is used in interstate commerce through the filing of a "use" application, or before the mark is actually used in interstate commerce through the filing of an "intent-to-use" application. The latter must be followed up with either an Amendment to Allege Use or a Statement of Use once the mark has been used in interstate commerce.

6. A complete federal registration application package includes the application form, a drawing page, three specimens per applicable international classification, and the filing fee. The United States Patent and Trademark Office sets forth detailed requirements, which must be adhered to exactly in order for an application package to be processed.

7. If an application package is completed properly and passes review by a PTO examining attorney, a Notice of Publication will be sent indicating the

date on which the mark will appear in the *Official Gazette*. Anyone opposing registration of the mark has 30 days within which to file a letter of protest or opposition. If this is not done or if an opposition proceeding is won by the trademark applicant, a certificate of registration is issued.

8. In addition to federal trademark registration, a trademark may be registered under state law. State registration provides additional legal relief and tactical advantages in an infringement lawsuit.

Review Questions

1. Distinguish between a copyright, a patent, and a trademark.
2. List the types of marks which are considered "forbidden marks" under the Lanham Act.
3. What are the advantages of federally registering a trademark?
4. Compare and contrast the following:
   (i)   a collective mark and a house mark
   (ii) a descriptive mark and a suggestive mark
   (iii) an arbitrary mark and a coined mark
5. Outline the procedures for filing a federal trademark application.

KEY TERMS

arbitrary mark	Section 8 affidavit
certification mark	Section 15 affidavit
coined mark	service mark
collective mark	special-form drawing
copyright	specimen
derivative mark	suggestive mark
descriptive mark	trade dress
design patent	trademark
house mark	trade name
ingredient mark	use application
intent-to-use application	utility patent
Lanham Act	

13 Changing and Dissolving the Corporate Structure

Overview of Objectives

Upon completion of this chapter, the student will:

- know how to amend articles of incorporation
- understand the distinctions between various types of corporate reorganizations
- know the various tasks that may be assigned to a paralegal assisting in a corporate reorganization
- know how to draft articles of dissolution

INTRODUCTION

Throughout a corporation's "lifetime," there may be junctures when changes to the corporate structure become advisable or necessary. Such changes may include, but need not be limited to, the changing of the corporation's name, its purpose, or its stock structure. The latter change may involve changing the number of authorized shares of the corporation, changing the classes of stock, or changing the rights given to certain shareholders. When such changes are desired, the articles of incorporation must be amended to reflect these changes.

Some changes may be more dramatic in nature, such as when a corporation decides to reorganize through merger or consolidation. Perhaps a corporation is in a position to expand by acquiring the stock and/or assets of another corporation. Conversely, a corporation may decide to dissolve and liquidate the business. A corporate paralegal may be asked to assist in any of these transactions. You may be asked to set up board of directors' and shareholders' meetings at which such transactions are voted on. You may be asked to draft articles of amendment or articles of dissolution. Further, you may be asked to compile, draft, and organize pertinent documents for the closing of a merger or share exchange. This final chapter discusses both the small and major changes that impact a corporation, and the role of the paralegal in assisting in the process.

AMENDMENTS

Each state has its own statutes specifying when and how a corporation is to amend its articles of incorporation. Some states provide detailed lists of changes that require amendments to the articles, while other states more broadly state that amendments may be made to delete provisions not statutorily required or to include (or change) provisions statutorily permitted in the original articles of incorporation.

A.   Acquiring Approval for Amendment

State statutes typically indicate the circumstances under which shareholder approval is needed to amend a corporation's articles of incorporation. Additionally, the original articles themselves may include a provision indicating when shareholder approval must be obtained. If the articles do include such a provision, it must not be in conflict with state statutory law. Thus, the articles may provide that shareholder approval is necessary for any and all amendments to the articles of incorporation (even if state statute allows for some instances in which the board of directors may amend the articles without such approval because the provision will not violate shareholder rights), but they may not provide that shareholder approval is never required if state statutes indicate circumstances under which shareholder approval must be obtained.

The board of directors or the incorporators may amend the articles of incorporation at any time prior to the issuance of shares of corporate stock. This makes sense because there are no shareholders to grant approval to amendments prior to issuance of stock. Exhibit 13.1 below provides an example of articles of amendment to articles of incorporation prior to the issuance of shares.

EXHIBIT 13.1

Articles of Amendment to Articles of Incorporation of VR Games, Inc.

Pursuant to the provisions of Chapter 305 of the Statutes of Any State, the undersigned corporation adopts the following Articles of Amendment to its Articles of Incorporation, filed January 14, 1997, Certificate Number V780092,

FIRST: The name of the corporation is amended from VR GAMES, INC. to COMPU-GAMES, INC.

SECOND: The amendment was adopted by the Board of Directors on February 12, 1997.

THIRD: No stock has yet been issued in the corporation.

DATED: February 13, 1997

COMPU-GAMES

BY _____*Sheila Taylor*_____

Incorporator/Director

Subscribed and sworn to before me this thirteenth day of February, 1997, by Sheila Taylor, Incorporator/Director of COMPU-GAMES, INC., a corporation organized under the laws of the State of Any State.

_____

Notary Public

Note that in Exhibit 13.1 the corporation's articles of incorporation are amended to change the corporation's name. Prior to so doing, a name check for availability must be made in the state of domicile as well as in any other state in which the corporation is registered as a foreign corporation or may wish to register as a foreign corporation in the future.

In states whose statutes parallel the Model Business Corporation Act, the board of directors of a corporation, once stock is issued, is granted the authority to adopt certain amendments to the articles of incorporation without first obtaining shareholder approval. These amendments can be categorized as administrative in nature rather than as fundamental in nature. They may include an amendment to change the corporate name through deletion or addition of certain words, an amendment to extend the period of existence of the corporation if the corporation's original articles did not provide for perpetual duration, or an amendment to delete the names and addresses of initial directors (if included in the original articles) or the name and address of the initial registered agent and registered office (provided a change of registered agent and registered office has been filed with the appropriate filing authority). In addition, the board of directors typically may, without shareholder approval, amend the articles of incorporation to change each issued and unissued authorized share of an outstanding class into a greater number of whole shares if the corporation has only shares of that class outstanding. An example of articles of amendment adopted after the issuance of shares without requiring shareholder approval is provided by Exhibit 13.2.

EXHIBIT 13.2

Articles of Amendment to Articles of Incorporation of Lasalle Enterprises, Inc.

Pursuant to the provisions of Chapter 305 of the Statutes of Any State, the undersigned corporation adopts the following Articles of Amendment to its Articles of Incorporation, filed December 30, 1995, Certificate Number L174403.

FIRST: The name of the corporation is LASALLE ENTERPRISES, INC.

SECOND: The following amendment of the Articles of Incorporation was adopted by the corporation: The initial board of directors, stated below, is deleted.

Bernard Gramont	855 N.W. 16th Street Any City, Any State
Andre Valmont	994 S.W. 5th Terrace Any City, Any State
Marie Deveaux	140 Rosewood Lane Any City, Any State

THIRD: The amendment was adopted by the Board of Directors on January 7, 1997.

FOURTH: Shareholder action was not required.

DATED: January 8, 1997

LASALLE ENTERPRISES, INC.

BY _____*Danielle De Bourcy*_____
                    President

EXHIBIT 13.2 *Continued*

ATTEST:

_____Louis Vebert_____   (Seal)
            Secretary

    Subscribed and sworn to before me this eighth day of January, 1997, by Danielle De Bourcy, President, and Louis Vebert, Secretary, of LASALLE ENTERPRISES, INC., a corporation organized under the laws of the State of Any State.

_____
                                    Notary Public

    A proposed amendment may be initiated by the board of directors or, in some states, by the shareholders (usually a certain percentage of shareholders or of outstanding voting stock is required by statute or by the bylaws for such an action). When proposed by the shareholders, the shareholders may petition the board of directors to call a meeting of the shareholders to vote on the amendment. When an amendment is proposed by the board of directors, the proposed amendment will be set forth in the form of a resolution adopted by the board. If shareholder approval for amendment is required (such as in the case of merger, consolidation, or the adoption of some other fundamental corporate change), the resolution will not only set forth the proposed amendment, but will also direct that the proposed amendment be set to a shareholder vote. Proper written notice will then be provided to each record shareholder entitled to vote on the amendment. What constitutes proper notice is determined by state statute. Some states require that certain amendment proposals be submitted to vote at a special meeting. If this is the case, the notice must specify the reason for the special meeting. Other states allow amendment proposals to be voted on at annual shareholder meetings and in such a case the usual notice requirements for annual meetings will pertain. The articles of incorporation may require higher shareholder approval (i.e., a supermajority) for voting on certain amendments than is prescribed to vote on other matters or than is mandated by statute. In states that permit unanimous consent in lieu of a shareholder meeting, no actual meeting need be held. Provided with notice of the proposed amendment, the shareholders may unanimously approve the proposed amendment in a unanimous consent statement.

    Please note that if the proposed amendment will affect the rights of a certain class of shareholders, that affected class must vote to approve the amendment, regardless of what other voting rights that class may or may not have. Typically, shareholders of outstanding shares of a class entitled to vote must vote on the amendment if the amendment would:

1.   increase or decrease the aggregate number of authorized shares of the class;
2.   effect an exchange or reclassification of all or part of the shares of the class into shares of another class;
3.   effect an exchange or reclassification, or create a right of exchange, of all or part of the shares of another class into the shares of the class;
4.   change the designation, rights, preferences, or limitations of all or part of the shares of the class;
5.   change the shares of all or part of the class into a different number of shares of the same class;
6.   create a new class of shares having rights or preferences with respect to distributions or to dissolution that are prior, superior, or substantially equal to the shares of the class;
7.   increase the rights, preferences, or number of authorized shares of any class that, after giving effect to the amendment, has rights or preferences with respect to distributions or dissolution that are prior, superior, or substantially equal to the shares of the class;
8.   limit or deny an existing preemptive right of all or part of the shares of the class; or
9.   cancel or otherwise affect rights to distributions or dividends that have accumulated but not yet been declared on all or part of the shares.

B.   Articles of Amendment

Once an amendment is approved, it is necessary to draft articles of amendment which are filed with the appropriate governmental authority, together with the requisite filing fee. The articles of amendment typically will include the following:

1.   the name of the corporation;
2.   the text of each adopted amendment;
3.   the date each amendment was adopted;
4.   if an amendment provides for an exchange, reclassification, or cancellation of issued shares, provisions for implementing the amendment (if not provided in the text of the amendment);

5. if an amendment was adopted by the incorporators or board of directors without shareholder action, a statement to that effect and that shareholder action was not required; and
6. if an amendment was approved by the shareholders, the designation of each voting group entitled to vote separately on the amendment, and a statement that the number of votes cast for the amendment by each voting group was sufficient for approval by that group.

If the amendments are adopted prior to the issuance of shares, the articles of amendment are signed by the incorporator(s) or board of directors. If the amendments are adopted once shares have been issued, they typically are signed by the president or vice president of the corporation and attested to by the secretary. Some states require notarization. It is common practice to request a certified copy of the articles of amendment for the corporation's minute book. If this is desired, a copy of the articles of amendment must be sent together with the original and additional fees must be paid. Once the articles of amendment are filed, a certificate will be issued by the state filing authority. Exhibits 13.3 and 13.4 provide, respectively, examples of a board of directors resolution to adopt an amendment to the articles of incorporation and the articles of amendment in a situation in which (in this hypothetical) shareholder approval is required.

EXHIBIT 13.3

Resolution of the Board of Directors of American Data Systems Corporation

Upon a motion duly made and unanimously adopted, it was

RESOLVED, that Article IV of the Articles of Incorporation of the corporation be amended to provide as follows:

Authorized Shares and Par Value. The total number of shares that the corporation shall have authority to issue is 200,000 shares of common stock, which stock shall have a par value of One Dollar ($1) per share.

FURTHER RESOLVED, that this amendment be submitted to a vote of the shareholders at a special meeting of shareholders called for the purpose of considering this amendment, which meeting shall be held on April 16, 1997, pursuant to notice as provided in the Bylaws.

EXHIBIT 13.3   *Continued*

I do hereby certify that I am the duly elected and qualified Secretary, and that the above is a true and correct copy of a resolution duly adopted at a meeting of the Board of Directors thereof, convened and held in accordance with the law and the Bylaws of the corporation on March 5, 1997, and that such resolution is now in full force and effect.

IN WITNESS WHEREOF, I have affixed my name as Secretary and have caused the corporate seal of said corporation to be hereunto affixed, this fifth day of March, 1997.

A True Record

ATTEST:

Lawrence Mitchell
    Secretary

EXHIBIT 13.4

Articles of Amendment to Articles of Incorporation of
American Data Systems Corporation

Pursuant to the provisions of Chapter 305 of the Statutes of Any State, the undersigned corporation adopts the following Articles of Amendment to its Articles of Incorporation, filed November 12, 1993, Certificate Number A600809:

FIRST: The name of the corporation is AMERICAN DATA SYSTEMS CORPORATION.

SECOND: The following amendment to the Articles of Incorporation was adopted by the shareholders of the corporation on April 16, 1997, in the manner prescribed by Chapter 305 of the Statutes of the State of Any State:

Article IV is amended to provide as follows: **Authorized Shares and Par Value**. The total number of shares that the corporation is authorized to issue is 200,000 shares of common stock, which stock shall have a par value of One Dollar ($1) per share.

THIRD: The number of shares of common stock of the corporation outstanding at the time of the adoption of the above amendment was 80,000 and the number of shares entitled to vote on the amendment was 80,000.

EXHIBIT 13.4   *Continued*

FOURTH: The number of shares of common stock that voted for the above amendment was 80,000 and the number of shares of common stock that voted against the above amendment was 0.

FIFTH: The corporation only has one type of stock, that being common stock, and therefore all shareholders entitled to vote on the amendment did so vote.

DATED: April 17, 1997   AMERICAN DATA SYSTEMS CORPORATION

BY _____*Elliott Dunn*_____
                           President

ATTEST:

_____*Lawrence Mitchell*_____   (Seal)
              Secretary

Subscribed and sworn to before me this seventeenth day of April, 1997, by Elliott Dunn, President, and Lawrence Mitchell, Secretary, of AMERICAN DATA SYSTEMS CORPORATION, a corporation organized under the laws of the State of Any State.

_____
                           Notary Public

A paralegal's involvement in the amendment process both prior to and after the filing of the articles of amendment is considerable. As noted above, if a corporation amends its articles to change the corporate name, a name check for availability must be made in the state of domicile and in every other state in which the corporation presently does or intends in the future to do business. If the name is available, it must be reserved in each applicable state. This entails the filing of reservation forms with the applicable filing fees. Once the amendment is approved, the name of the corporation must be changed on the minute book and the bylaws and a new corporate seal must be ordered. Note that when ordering a new seal, the date to be used is the original date of incorporation. The corporate name must be changed on the corporation's annual reports as well. Some states may require the corporation to issue new stock certificates using the new name. A paralegal may be in charge of setting up the board of directors meeting at which the amendment will be proposed, as well as drafting the resolution containing the proposed amendment and the minutes of the meeting. In states allowing unanimous consent in lieu of a board of directors meeting, a paralegal may be asked to draft the consent statement. Should shareholder approval be required to adopt an amendment, a paralegal may draft the notice for the shareholders meeting and may be responsible for ensuring that all shareholders entitled to vote receive the notice. Again, the minutes for the meeting must be drafted and put into the corporate minute book. If the state allows for unanimous shareholder consent, a consent statement should be prepared. Once the amendment is approved, a paralegal may be asked to draft the articles of amendment for attorney review and client signature. The paralegal will then be responsible for filing the articles of amendment (with one copy for return of a certified copy) and the appropriate fees with the state filing authority. Once the certified copy is returned to the law office with the certificate, both must be placed in the corporate minute book. If the amendment creates additional classes of authorized stock, a notation should be made on the stock register and appropriate legends prepared for stock certificates. If the number of authorized shares of stock or the par value of the stock has been changed by the amendment, this also must be noted in the stock register and it may be advisable (or even required by state statute) to issue new certificates for outstanding shares. The following checklist may prove helpful.

Checklist for Amendment of Articles of Incorporation

1. Change of Name (if applicable)
   (i) Check availability of name in state of domicile and in any other state in which the corporation presently does or may in the future engage in business
   (ii) Reserve the name by filing reservation forms with requisite fees
   (iii) Change name on corporate minute book
   (iv) Order new corporate seal
   (v) Change name on bylaws, stock certificates (if required), and other appropriate materials
2. Set up board of directors meeting (if required)
   (i) Notice the meeting
   (ii) Prepare the resolution
   (iii) Draft the minutes
3. Prepare board of directors unanimous consent in lieu of meeting (if allowed)

4. Set up shareholders meeting (if required)
    (i) Notice the meeting
    (ii) Draft the minutes
5. Prepare shareholders unanimous consent in lieu of meeting (if allowed)
6. Draft articles of amendment
7. File original articles of amendment, together with one copy and applicable fees
8. Upon return of certified copy and certificate, place in minute book
9. Prepare new legends for stock certificates (if applicable)
10. Prepare and issue new stock certificates (if applicable)

Sometimes articles of incorporation have undergone several amendments. In this situation, it may be advisable to file a restated articles of incorporation. A **restated articles of incorporation** consolidates all of the amendments with the remaining original, unchanged provisions into one new document. The restated articles are then filed (together with one copy) along with the requisite fees to the state filing authority, which will issue a restated certificate of incorporation. Some states allow the board of directors to approve a restated articles of incorporation without requiring shareholder approval while other states do not.

C. *Foreign and Nonprofit Corporations*

Two other areas must be addressed before leaving the discussion of amendments to articles of incorporation. The first pertains to foreign corporations. Generally speaking, a corporation must amend its certificate of authority to transact business as a foreign corporation if it changes its name, its period of existence, or the state of domicile. Some states may require amending the certificate of authority if other changes are made, so state statutes should be carefully checked. The second area is nonprofit corporations. As noted in Chapter 6, nonprofit corporations do not have shareholders, they have members. If there are members entitled to vote on a proposed amendment, the board of directors must adopt a resolution setting forth the proposed amendment and directing that the amendment be submitted to a vote at a meeting of the members entitled to vote. Proper written notice must be provided to the members. If there are no members or if the members are not entitled to vote on the proposed amendment, the amendment may be adopted at a meeting of the board of directors of the nonprofit corporation. Exhibit 13.5 provides an example of articles of amendment of a nonprofit corporation.

EXHIBIT 13.5

Articles of Amendment to Articles of Incorporation
of Environment Conservation Centers, Inc.

Pursuant to Chapter 306 of the Statutes of the State of Any State, the undersigned corporation adopts the following Articles of Amendment to its Articles of Incorporation, filed September 4, 1994, Certificate Number E330218,

FIRST: The name of the corporation is ENVIRONMENT CONSERVATION CENTERS, INC.

SECOND: Article V, Section 1 is amended to provide as follows:

The affairs of the corporation shall be managed by a Board of Directors. The Board of Directors shall consist of not less than five (5) and not more than ten (10) persons. Directors shall be elected or removed in accordance with the procedure provided in the Bylaws.

THIRD: The amendment was adopted on March 10, 1997.

FOURTH: The amendment was adopted by the members and the number of votes cast for the amendment was sufficient for approval.

DATED: March 11, 1997

ENVIRONMENT CONSERVATION CENTERS, INC.

BY ___*Rosalind Larkin*___
                    President

ATTEST:

___*William Smith*___   (Seal)
      Secretary

Subscribed and sworn to before me this eleventh day of March, 1997, by Rosalind Larkin, President, and William Smith, Secretary, of ENVIRONMENT CONSERVATION CENTERS, INC., a nonprofit corporation organized under the laws of the State of Any State.

_____
                    Notary Public

TYPES OF CORPORATE REORGANIZATIONS

Corporations seeking to expand or restructure may do so in various ways. They may combine with other existing corporations through merger (two or more corporations unite into one already existing corporation) or through consolidation (two or more corporations combine to form a brand new corporation). Many states have revised their statutory references to consolidations, following the lead of the Revised Model Business Corporation Act, which no longer refers to consolidations. In the Revised Act and those statutes patterned after it, consolidations and mergers are treated in the same manner. Thus, corporations consolidating are considered to be "merging" into an entity with an already existing infrastructure, even if it chooses to give itself a refurbished identity by taking on a new name. Other states choose to consider a consolidation as a transaction distinct from a merger, and have separate statutory sections pertaining to each. In each of these instances, the remaining corporation (whether considered a new or surviving entity) acquires all of the assets and liabilities of the other, extinguished corporation(s). A third method for expansion is through a share exchange (sometimes referred to as the stock-purchase method or stock acquisition) in which a corporation acquires the stock of one or more classes or series of another corporation. While the terms stock-purchase method and stock acquisition imply that one corporation purchases some or all of the shares of another corporation, the term share exchange implies that a corporation exchanges some or all of its stock for some or all of the stock of another corporation and, indeed, some states may consider stock purchases and share exchanges to be two different methods of acquisition. Additionally, a corporation may expand by purchasing all of the assets of another corporation through asset acquisition.

A.   Mergers

A merger is one type of corporate reorganization. In a **merger**, one or more corporations join another existing corporation, which becomes the **surviving corporation**, while the others cease to exist. The shareholders of the absorbed corporation(s) become shareholders in the surviving corporation or are paid cash for their shares. The process of merger usually begins when the board of directors of each corporation pass a resolution in favor of adopting a **plan of merger** to be placed before each corporation's shareholders for approval.

Most state statutory laws consider a merger a fundamental corporate change requiring shareholder approval. Therefore, although most states allow the initiative to come from the board of directors, they require a shareholder vote on a plan of merger. However, the Revised Model Business Corporation Act recognizes two exceptions to the requirement of shareholder approval. States that have modeled their corporate statutes after the Revised Act may recognize these exceptions as well. Under the Revised Act, the board of directors of the corporation that is to be surviving corporation in the merger may adopt a resolution approving a plan of merger without bringing the plan to a shareholder vote if the merger is deemed a either a short-form merger or a small-impact merger.

Under the Revised Act, a merger is considered a **short-form merger** if a subsidiary corporation is to merge into a parent corporation and the parent corporation owns at least 90 percent of the outstanding shares of the subsidiary corporation. Note that some states acknowledge short-form mergers, but require a different percentage of parent ownership of subsidiary stock, such as 80 percent. A **small-impact merger** may or may not be a merger between a parent corporation and a subsidiary corporation. A small-impact merger is one which leaves the shareholders, with respect to their shares and rights, virtually unaffected. Under the Revised Act, this occurs if the following conditions exist:

1. the surviving corporation's articles of incorporation will not change as a result of the merger;
2. each shareholder of the surviving corporation will have the same number of shares with the same rights after the merger;
3. the number of voting shares outstanding after the merger (plus the number issued as a result of the merger) will not exceed 20 percent of the total number of voting shares of the surviving corporation immediately before the merger; and
4. the number of participating shares outstanding immediately after the merger (plus the number of participating shares issued as a result of the merger) will not exceed 20 percent of the total number of participating shares outstanding immediately before the merger.

While each state's statutes may differ in some particulars, the information that generally is contained in a plan of merger includes:

1. the name and authorized capitalization of each corporation;
2. designation of the surviving corporation;
3. all the terms and conditions of the merger;
4. the method of converting and exchange rate of stock shares;
5. the rights to acquire shares;
6. the method of handling existing obligations;

7. amendments to the articles of incorporation of the surviving corporation (if applicable); and

8. closing date of the merger.

Needless to say, the time involved in getting to the point where the board of directors of each involved corporation is amenable to all terms of a merger is considerable. A lengthy negotiation process followed by drafting and redrafting of the plan will involve not only the directors but the legal counsel of each corporation. During the negotiation period, each corporation may send **letters of intent** to the other parties expressing their proposals and/or outlining their understanding of the agreed-upon terms and conditions. The directors of each board have a fiduciary duty to uphold to their respective corporations and their shareholders, and must believe that the agreed-upon plan is in the best interests of their shareholders. This means looking out for the interests of minority as well as majority shareholders. The directors of each board as well as the officers of each corporation additionally will be concerned about their own positions in the surviving corporation. While some may be willing to relinquish titles and the commensurate responsibilities accompanying those titles, others will not. Employment issues regarding employees of both the merging corporation(s) and the surviving corporation must be discussed. Financial reports must be compiled and the accounts of each corporation must be analyzed by financial advisors and ultimately reconciled. Tax considerations must be addressed. State and federal securities and antitrust laws must be reviewed. Any **executory contracts** (a contract under which the obligations of one or more parties are not yet fulfilled) entered into by the corporation to be absorbed must be reviewed to determine the feasibility of **novation agreements** (an agreement to substitute a new party, in this case the surviving corporation, for an original party, in this case the absorbed corporation, to the contract). In the interim period between the initial concept of merger and the finalization of a plan, it may be advisable that each corporation place certain restrictions on corporate transactions, such as the sale of stock and the payment of dividends. By the time the plan of merger is presented for shareholder vote, assuming such vote is required, all of these considerations should be worked out. Should the proposed merger be between a parent corporation and its subsidiary, the planning and closing process are simplified.

As with any other change requiring shareholder approval, the appropriate shareholders of each involved corporation must receive proper written notice of a meeting at which the merger will be voted upon. Some states allow all shareholders to vote on a plan of merger, whether or not they have voting rights, because a merger is a fundamental corporate change which can impact all shareholders. Other states only require that record shareholders with voting rights be permitted to vote on the plan. Further, some states only require a majority vote for approval (be it a majority of all shareholders or a majority of shareholders with voting rights), while others require a supermajority vote for approval. The notice sent to the shareholders must include details about the proposed merger and may be required, depending on state statute, to inform the shareholders of dissenting shareholders' rights. In states permitting unanimous written consents in lieu of shareholders' meetings, a merger may be approved by this method.

Before proceeding further, a note regarding dissenting shareholders' rights is in order. Shareholders entitled to vote on a plan of merger have **dissenter's rights**. The extent of these rights vary. Generally, if a plan of merger is approved, any dissenting shareholders have the right to demand payment of fair value their shares. Each dissenting shareholder must set forth his or her demand in a written notice of demand of payment, state statute indicating the time period within which a demand must be made. Often, a dispute arises between dissenting shareholders and the corporation with regard to what constitutes fair value for the stock. If such a dispute arises, a judicial appraisal may be necessary. Under the Revised Model Business Corporation Act (and in states whose statutes are modeled after it), dissenting shareholders' rights are not applicable in short-form mergers. In some states, dissenting shareholders' rights are not applicable to shareholders of corporations registered on a national securities exchange or to shareholders of corporations having more than a statutorily specified number of shareholders of record.

Should a plan of merger be approved by the shareholders, the surviving corporation must draft **articles of merger** to be filed with the surviving corporation's state of domicile. Typically, the articles of merger are signed by the president or vice president of each corporation as well as each corporation's secretary. Notarization of articles of merger is required by many states. Although variation exists among state statutes, articles of merger generally are required to set forth the following information:

1. The effective date of the merger, which may be the same as or different from the date the articles of merger, is filed. Should the articles of merger fail to specify an effective date, most state statutes provide the effective date will, in that event, be the date on which the articles of merger are filed.
2. The name of the surviving corporation. (Note that this is not always stated expressly as a requirement because the plan of merger indicates the name of the surviving corporation.)
3. The plan of merger. The copy of the plan is often included as an exhibit attached to the articles of merger to meet this requirement.
4. If shareholder approval was not required, a statement to that effect.

5. If shareholder approval was required, the following information with regard to each corporation:
    (i)   the date the plan of merger was adopted by the shareholders;
    (ii)   the number of shares of stock outstanding;
    (iii) the designation and number of outstanding shares of each class of stock entitled to vote as a class;
    (iv)   the total number of shares voting in favor of the merger;
    (v)   the total number of shares voting against the merger;
    (vi)   the number of shares in each class voting in favor of the merger; and
    (vii) the number of shares in each class voting against the merger.

Exhibit 13.6 below provides an example of articles of merger.

EXHIBIT 13.6

Articles of Merger

Pursuant to Section 305.711 of the Statutes of the State of Any State, the undersigned corporations have adopted the following articles of merger.

FIRST: The merger shall become effective upon the filing of these articles of merger.

SECOND: The surviving Corporation is COMPREHENSIVE HEALTH PLANS, INC., a domestic corporation lawfully incorporated under the laws of the State of Any State.

THIRD: A plan of merger was approved by the shareholders of each of the undersigned corporations in the manner prescribed by statute, a copy of said plan is attached hereto as Exhibit A.

FOURTH: As to each of the undersigned corporations, the number of shares outstanding, and the designation and number of outstanding shares of each class entitled to vote as a class on the plan of merger are as follows:

Name of Corporation	Number of Shares Outstanding	Entitled to Vote as a Class	
		Designation of Class	Number of Shares
Comprehensive Health Plans, Inc.	300,000	A	150,000
		B	150,000
UniMed Corp.	100,000	A	100,000

EXHIBIT 13.6   *Continued*

FIFTH: As to each of the undersigned corporations, the date of adoption of the plan of merger, the total number of shares voted for and against the plan of merger, respectively, and, as to each class entitled to vote thereon as a class, the number of shares of such class voted for and against the plan, respectively, are as follows:

	Number of Shares			Entitled to Vote as a Class		
Name of Corporation	Total Voted For	Total Voted Against	Class	Voted For	Voted Against	Date of Adoption
Comprehensive Health Plans, Inc.	260,000	40,000	A	127,000	23,000	3/7/97
			B	133,000	17,000	3/7/97
UniMed Corp.	85,000	15,000	A	85,000	15,000	3/10/97

DATED: March 21, 1997   COMPREHENSIVE HEALTH PLANS, INC.

BY   _Marcus MacKenzie_
              President

(Seal)   and

              Nancy Clifton
              Secretary

                                UNIMED CORPORATION

BY   _Charlene Bremen_
              President

(Seal)   and

              Jeffrey Adler
              Secretary

Subscribed and sworn to before me this twenty-first day of March, 1997, by Marcus MacKenzie, President, and Nancy Clifton, Secretary, of COMPREHENSIVE HEALTH PLANS, INC., a corporation organized under the laws of the State of Any State; and by Charlene Bremen, President, and Jeffrey Adler, Secretary, of UNIMED CORPORATION, a corporation organized under the laws of the State of Any State.

                                        _____
                                             Notary Public

A paralegal is invaluable in assisting in the myriad mechanics of a merger. At the closing, all documents necessary to finalize the transaction between or among the parties change hands. Each party will be responsible for the preparation of various documents to be exchanged. A paralegal is often responsible for keeping track of which party is responsible for producing each of these documents at closing. Additionally, paralegals may themselves be involved in the drafting of documents, in the preliminary legal and factual research that is crucial in formulating and carrying out a plan of merger, an in such post-closing matters as filing documents with the appropriate authorities. A paralegal's tasks may include (but need not be limited to) the following:

1. researching applicable state and federal law;
2. compiling and organizing various documents for review (e.g., financial reports, tax returns, stock ledgers, employment agreements, employee benefit plans);
3. assisting attorneys in plan drafting;
4. drafting the resolution of the board of directors;
5. drafting the minutes of the meeting of the board of directors;
6. drafting the notices to shareholders (if applicable);
7. drafting the minutes of the meeting of the shareholders;
8. drafting the articles of merger;
9. filing the articles of merger and requisite fees with the state filing authority;
10. filing the articles of merger with the Securities and Exchange Commission and state securities authority (if applicable);
11. drafting and, upon review and signature, filing articles of amendment to the articles of incorporation of the surviving corporation (if articles of amendment are not included in the plan of merger);
12. ordering a new corporate kit (if applicable);
13. preparing new stock certificates;
14. amending of the bylaws of the surviving corporation (if applicable);
15. drafting appropriate documents of transfer of property from the absorbed corporation(s) to the surviving corporation (e.g., deeds, title documents, leases);
16. drafting novations or assignments of security agreements and insurance policies for any transferred property (if applicable); and
17. drafting and filing any requisite Uniform Commercial Code forms for any transferred collateralized property (if applicable).

A postscript about mergers pertaining to the merger of nonprofit corporations is in order. Should nonprofit corporations wish to merge, the procedure in most states is quite similar to that of other, for-profit corporations. A plan of merger must be proposed and adopted by each corporation's board of directors. If a member vote on the plan is statutorily required (or required by the articles of incorporation or bylaws), proper written notice must be given to all members or, depending on state statute, all members entitled to vote. Because a nonprofit corporation does not have shares or shareholders, dissenting rights do not apply. The plan of merger will also tend to be simpler because the corporations do not have to address such issues as share conversions and exchange rates.

B.   Consolidations

A consolidation is very similar to a merger and, as stated above, many state statutes have been revised, treating consolidations in the same manner as they treat mergers and excluding statutory provisions which refer to consolidations as reorganizations distinct from mergers. Indeed, a **consolidation** *is* a type of merger, whereby two or more corporations merge to create a new corporation. Unlike the mergers discussed above, there is no surviving corporation, as all involved corporations disappear with the creation of the new corporation. In most other respects, however, the process of consolidation coincides with that of a merger. The board of directors of each corporation exchange letters of intent regarding a plan to consolidate, ultimately leading to a resolution to adopt the plan. This plan is typically put to a shareholder vote (unless not required by statute). Most of the paralegal's tasks required to be performed in a merger would be applicable in a consolidation.

C.   Share Exchanges

A **share exchange** may occur if one corporation (the **acquiring corporation**) desires to acquire the outstanding shares of one or more classes or series of stock in another corporation (the **target corporation**). In a share exchange, the shareholders of the target corporation receive shares of stock in the acquiring corporation or a cash payment for their shares. The board of directors of each corporation must agree on a **plan of share exchange** (sometimes referred to as a **plan of exchange**), set forth in a resolution passed by each corporation's board of directors. As is the case with mergers and consolidations, letters of intent are exchanged between the corporations and the negotiation and investigatory phase is often lengthy before a plan of share exchange is finalized. Although state statutes vary, a plan of share exchange usually contains the following elements:

1.   the name and authorized capitalization of each corporation;
2.   designation of the acquiring corporation;

3. all the terms and conditions of the exchange;
4. the manner of exchanging the shares;
5. the method of handling existing obligations;
6. amendments to the articles of incorporation of the acquiring corporation; and
7. the closing date of the share exchange.

A share exchange generally will require a shareholder vote of approval of the plan. Again, as with mergers and consolidations, proper written notice is required, including details of the plan of share exchange. Dissenting shareholders may demand fair value for their shares rather than receive shares in the acquiring corporation. In states so permitting, the shareholders may approve a share exchange by signing a unanimous consent. An example of such a consent is found in Exhibit 13.7 below.

EXHIBIT 13.7

Certificate of Shareholders' Unanimous Consent of Share Exchange

We, the undersigned shareholders of TRS ELECTRONICS, INC., a corporation duly organized under the laws of the State of Any State, and holders of the number of shares set opposite our names, amounting in total to Fifty Thousand (50,000) shares, the entire capital stock of said corporation, hereby agree for value received, and in consideration of the same number of shares and of the same par value of the stock of GRAF ELECTRONICS CORPORATION as existing on this date, subject, however, to the agreement of said GRAF ELECTRONICS CORPORATION to assume and pay all outstanding debts and obligations of TRS ELECTRONICS, INC., and consent to the exchange of the stock now held by us in TRS ELECTRONICS, INC. for the same number of shares of GRAF ELECTRONICS CORPORATION.

Shareholder Name	Shareholder Signature	Date	Number of Shares
Theresa R. Simmons		2/20/97	30,000
Andrew Simmons		2/20/97	10,000
Kevin Keeler		2/20/97	5,000
Noreen Torman		2/20/97	5,000

Should the plan be approved, the acquiring corporation drafts, signs, and files **articles of share exchange** with the appropriate state filing authority. State statute dictates the required contents of the articles. Articles of share exchange typically contain the following:

1. The effective date of the share exchange, which may be the date of filing of the articles or a different date specified in the articles.
2. The plan of share exchange (this may be attached as an exhibit to the articles).
3. If shareholder approval was not required, the date the plan of share exchange was adopted by the board of directors of each corporation.
4. If shareholder approval was not required, a statement to that effect.
5. If shareholder approval was required, the following information with regard to each corporation:
    (i) the date the plan of share exchange was adopted by the shareholders;
    (ii) the number of shares of stock outstanding;
    (iii) the designation and number of outstanding shares of each class of stock entitled to vote as a class;
    (iv) the total number of shares voting in favor of the share exchange;
    (v) the total number of shares voting against the share exchange;
    (vi) the number of shares in each class voting in favor of the share exchange; and
    (vii) the number of shares in each class voting against the share exchange.

The articles of share exchange are then filed with the appropriate state filing authority (and, when applicable, with the Securities and Exchange Commission and the state securities authority). Finally, as with mergers and consolidations, various documents are exchanged between the acquiring and target corporations, particularly new stock certificates reflecting the exchange of stock. Many of the tasks performed by paralegals both before and after a merger closing are applicable to a share exchange. Note that nonprofit corporations may not engage in share exchanges, as they have neither shareholders nor stock.

D.　Stock and Asset Acquisitions

In a **stock purchase**, one corporation (the acquiring corporation) purchases all, or substantially all, of the stock of another corporation (the target corporation) with the target corporation merging with or becoming a subsidiary corporation of the acquiring corporation. In an **asset purchase**, one corporation purchases all, or substantially all, of the assets of another business, be that business another corporation or some other business entity. In either instance, the target business legally continues to exist, albeit as a "shell." Which acquisition method is preferable is determined by various factors. If the majority of the target corporation's assets are tangible assets, such as real estate or equipment, an asset purchase may be preferable. However, if the majority of the target corporation's assets are intangible assets (for example, the goodwill the corporation has accumulated over a period of time), a stock purchase may be preferable. This is especially true if the major asset of the target corporation is a nonassignable asset (e.g., a nonassignable license agreement), which makes it impossible for the acquiring corporation to acquire the asset through an asset purchase. In this instance, the acquiring corporation must acquire rights to this asset indirectly by purchasing stock in the selling corporation. The number of shareholders in the target corporation may be a factor. The fewer the shareholders, the easier it is to effectuate a stock purchase. Further, the **bulk transfer laws** of Article 6 of the Uniform Commercial Code (laws intending to prevent the defrauding of creditors when a business sells substantially all of its assets) have been incorporated into many state statutes. These laws typically pertain to asset purchases, but not stock purchases. While some states have abandoned these laws, believing them to be outdated and no longer necessary, they remain in effect in other states.

Nonetheless, as stated above, an asset purchase is the only way for a corporation to acquire a noncorporate business entity unless the business entity is incorporated just prior to acquisition. The liabilities of the target corporation are yet another consideration. In a stock purchase, the acquiring corporation assumes the liabilities of the target corporation. The acquiring corporation in an asset purchase, however, does not have to assume the liabilities of the target corporation unless a court considers the target corporation's identity completely merged with that of the acquiring corporation so as to make their identities indistinguishable.

As is the case with all of the other methods of reorganization discussed thus far, stock purchases and asset purchases may be initiated by a corporation's board of directors, but usually must be approved by shareholder vote before they may be effectuated. Most state statutes do not include specific provisions regarding procedures for stock and asset purchases. Nonetheless, they typically do indicate that the sale of substantially all of a corporation's assets is a fundamental change requiring approval by the shareholders of the target corporation. Both state and federal statutes must be consulted to determine applicability and compliance procedures (e.g., state and federal security laws, bulk transfer laws).

An asset purchase agreement is similar, in many ways, to other sales contracts. The assets to be sold are described, the purchase price and pay-out terms are indicated, delivery time and method is specified, any applicable warranties are detailed, and remedies available for breach of contract by either party are included. A stock purchase agreement will not list the assets of the target corporation. Rather, it will include the number, classes, and series of stock to be sold, the purchase price and pay-out method, warranties regarding good standing of the target corporation and any representations made, and the agreement of the acquiring corporation to assume the liabilities of the target corporation.

Paralegals may be as actively involved in stock and asset purchases as they are in the other reorganizations discussed. They may be called upon to research state and federal laws; draft resolutions, meeting minutes, and stock or asset purchase agreements; amend corporate documents to reflect the stock or asset purchase; draft promissory notes, deeds, and bills of sale (if applicable); prepare new stock certificates (if applicable); draft assignments or novations for loans, security agreements, bank account transfers, and insurance policies (if applicable); and file documents with appropriate filing authorities.

E.   Tax Treatment of Reorganizations

The Internal Revenue Code uses the term "reorganization" to refer broadly to the types of transactions discussed here. The Code then distinguishes between these transactions by classifying them into types, each given an alphabetic classification, such as type A transactions, type B transactions, and so forth. For example, a **type A transaction** is a merger or consolidation. A **type B transaction** is the acquisition by the acquiring corporation of at least 80 percent of the total combined voting power of all classes of voting stock, and at least 80 percent of the total number of shares of all classes of stock in the target corporation in exchange for voting stock in the acquiring corporation. (Thus, it refers to a form of share exchange.) A **type C transaction** is the acquisition of substantially all of the assets of another corporation in exchange for shares of the acquiring corporation (sometimes referred to as a **stocks-for-assets transaction**). Several other transaction types are specified as well. Under Section 368(a)(1) of the Internal Revenue Code, type A, type B, and type C transactions are considered tax-free transactions for both the acquiring and target corporations. In order for the transaction to be treated as tax-free, strict compliance with Code provisions is mandatory. Further, the Code requires that the transactions have a valid business purpose and not simply be used to avoid taxes on the reorganization.

There is an exception to the tax-free treatment if boot is given in a type A or type C transaction. **Boot** is a term used by the Internal Revenue Service to refer to cash or types of property not included in the definition of a nontaxable

EXHIBIT 13.8

| Form **8023-A**
(Rev. May 1994)
Department of the Treasury
Internal Revenue Service | **Corporate Qualified Stock Purchases**
▶ See separate instructions. | OMB No. 1545-1428
Expires 4-30-97 |

Section A—Purchasing Corporation

1a Name and address of purchasing corporation	1b Employer identification number (see instructions)
	1c Tax year ending	1d State or country of incorporation

Section B—Target Corporation

2a Name and address of target corporation	2b Employer identification number
	2c Tax year ending	2d Acquisition date
	2e Service Center where income tax return filed and date filed (see instructions)
	2f State or country of incorporation

Section C—Common Parent, Selling Affiliate, or S Corporation Shareholder
(Complete only for a section 338(h)(10) election.)

3a Name and address of common parent, selling affiliate, or S corporation shareholder	3b Identifiying number
	3c Tax year ending
	3d Service Center where income tax return filed and date filed

Section D—General Information

		Yes	No
4	Was the purchasing corporation listed in Section A, above, a member of an affiliated group of corporations before the acquisition date?		
5	Was the target corporation listed in Section B, above, before the acquisition date:		
a	A member of an affiliated group?		
b	A member of a consolidated group?		
6	Is the target corporation or any target affiliate:		
a	A controlled foreign corporation?		
b	A foreign corporation with income, gain, or loss effectively connected with the conduct of a trade or business within the United States (including U.S. real property interests)?		
c	A qualifying foreign target?		
d	A corporation to which section 936 applies?		
e	A corporation electing under section 1504(d) or section 953(d)?		
f	A domestic international sales corporation (DISC)?		
g	A passive foreign investment company (PFIC)?		
h	If the answer to item 6g is "Yes," is the PFIC a pedigreed qualified electing fund?		

For Paperwork Reduction Act Notice, see separate instructions.   Cat. No. 15083V   Form **8023-A** (Rev. 5-94)

EXHIBIT 13.8   *Continued*

Form 8023-A (Rev. 5-94)   Page **2**

Section E—Elections under section 338

7   Check here to make a section 338(h)(10) election for the target corporation listed in Section B on page 1 . . . . ▶ ☐

8   Check here to make a section 338 election (other than a section 338(h)(10) election) for the target corporation listed in Section B on page 1 . . . . ▶ ☐

9   If the box on line 8 is checked for the target corporation listed in Section B on page 1, check here to make a gain recognition election for that corporation . . . . ▶ ☐

10 Check here if this form is filed to make a section 338 election for any target corporation, in addition to the one listed in Section B on page 1 . . . . ▶ ☐

Under penalties of perjury, I state and declare that I am authorized to make the election(s) on line 7, 8, 9 or 10 on behalf of the purchasing corporation(s).

▶ _____ | _____   ▶ _____
  Signature of Authorized Person for Purchasing Corporation(s)   Date   Title

Under penalties of perjury, I state and declare that I am authorized to make the section 338(h)(10) election on line 7 on behalf of the common parent of the selling group, the selling affiliate, or S corporation shareholder.

▶ _____ | _____   ▶ _____
  Signature of Authorized Person for the Common Parent, selling   Date   Title
  affiliate, or S corporation shareholder.

  (Applicable only if a section 338(h)(10) election is made.)

✪ *Printed on recycled paper*   *U.S. Government Printing Office: 1994 — 301-628/00167 exchange. If boot is given in a type A or type C transaction, it is taxable to the target corporation.

Reorganizations not falling into one of the above three categories are typically taxable transactions. Section 338 of the Internal Revenue Code permits qualifying stock purchases to be treated by the Internal Revenue Service as asset purchases. In some situations, a target corporation's assets have a low **tax basis** (the amount assigned to an asset for income tax purposes) and the acquiring corporation wishes to allocate the purchase price to these assets rather than to the acquired stock for more advantageous tax treatment. To qualify for a section 338 election, the following requirements must be met:

1. at least 80 percent of the target corporation's total voting stock and at least 80 percent of its total shares must be purchased in one transaction or in a series of transactions during a twelve-month period, and
2. the acquiring corporation must make the election not later than the fifteenth day of the ninth month after the acquisition date.

The election is made by filing form 8023-A (see Exhibit 13.8) with the Internal Revenue Service.

CORPORATE DISSOLUTION

A.   *Voluntary Dissolution*

A corporation may be dissolved any time after its legal creation. It may be dissolved voluntarily or by administrative or judicial proceedings. A voluntary dissolution may occur either before or after a corporation has issued shares to shareholders or has commenced business. If a corporation's incorporators or directors choose to dissolve the corporation before shares have been issued or business commenced, they may do so by filing **articles of dissolution** with the state filing authority. Although state statutes vary, articles of dissolution filed before issuance of shares or commencement of business generally contain the following:

1. the name of the corporation;
2. the date the articles of incorporation were filed;
3. a statement that no corporate shares have been issued and/or that the corporation has not commenced business;

4. a statement that there are no outstanding corporate debts;
5. if shares have been issued (but business not commenced), a statement that the corporation's net assets remaining after winding up have been distributed to the shareholders; and
6. A statement that the majority of the incorporators or the directors have authorized the dissolution.

Once shares of stock have been issued and the corporation is an ongoing concern, a voluntary dissolution must be approved by the shareholders. The board of directors may initiate the dissolution and pass a resolution proposing that corporate dissolution be put to a shareholder vote or, in some states, the initiative may come from the shareholders. In states that so allow, unanimous shareholder consent in lieu of a meeting will suffice. Some states require that all shareholders be permitted to vote on the matter of dissolution, even if not allowed to vote on other corporate issues, while other states require only a vote of record shareholders with general voting rights. If an actual meeting to vote on the dissolution is to be held, written notice must be sent to the shareholders (all shareholders or only voting shareholders, depending on state statute) indicating the subject matter of the meeting.

Upon shareholder approval (by either a majority or a supermajority vote, depending on the state), a number of states require that the corporation, prior to filing articles of dissolution, file a statement of **intent to dissolve**. The purpose of this statement is to put creditors of the corporation on notice. In states requiring this preliminary statement, there is often the requirement that it be published in a newspaper of general circulation rather than, or in addition to, filing with the state filing authority. Some states require that the corporation send notices of intent to dissolve personally to each creditor of the corporation rather than publish the statement in the newspaper. Other states do not require a statement of intent to be published, filed, or sent to creditors, and require only the filing of articles of dissolution. Once the statement is filed (in applicable states), the only business that the corporation may engage in is the business of winding down and liquidation. During this process, articles of dissolution will be drafted containing the following information:

1. the name of the corporation;
2. the date the dissolution was authorized;
3. a statement that the number of shareholder votes cast in favor of dissolution was sufficient for approval; and
4. if voting groups were required, a statement indicating the number of votes cast in each voting group, showing sufficient votes cast in favor of dissolution.

Once the articles of dissolution are drafted, reviewed, and signed, they are filed, together with the requisite fees, with the state filing authority. The corporation is legally dissolved on the effective date of its articles of dissolution. It is common for the state to issue a **certificate of dissolution**. Please note that in many states in which a notice of intent to resolve is required, dissolution will not be granted until liquidation occurs, all corporate debts and liabilities are paid, and all remaining corporate assets appropriately distributed. In states not requiring such notice, liquidation generally may occur after the articles of dissolution are filed. Further note that in many states a corporation remains liable for claims for a certain period of time after liquidation and dissolution (e.g., five years after publication of notice of intent to dissolve). Should a creditor make a claim against the corporation after dissolution but within the statutorily prescribed time period, the shareholders of the corporation are liable to the creditor up to the amount of their proportionate distribution of liquidated assets. However, creditors cannot reach other assets of the shareholders.

For tax reasons, it is advisable for the dissolving corporation to adopt a **plan of liquidation**. If such a plan is not adopted, the Internal Revenue Service may consider the distribution of liquidated assets as dividends and tax them accordingly. If a plan of liquidation is adopted there is less likelihood of this happening. A plan of liquidation is usually adopted by a board of directors resolution and then ratified by the shareholders, but in many states consents in lieu of actual meetings will satisfy statutory requirements.

In addition to filing articles of dissolution, a dissolving corporation must file a 966 form with the Internal Revenue Service. This form asks for information concerning the number of outstanding stock shares at the time of liquidation or at the time of adoption of a resolution authorizing dissolution; the citation of the statute under which the corporation is being dissolved; dates of any amendments to a plan of dissolution; and attachment of a certified copy of the resolution authorizing dissolution. The form must be filed with the Internal Revenue Service within 30 days after the resolution or plan of liquidation is adopted to dissolve the corporation. A copy of Form 966 is found in Exhibit 13.9.

If a corporation voluntarily dissolves, most states allow the corporation to revoke its dissolution within a statutorily prescribed time period (e.g., 120 days from the effective date of dissolution). If shareholder approval is required to dissolve the corporation, then generally it also must be obtained to revoke the dissolution. To effectuate revocation, a corporation must file **articles of revocation**, which usually include:

1. the name of the corporation;
2. the effective date of the dissolution that is revoked;

EXHIBIT 13.9

Form **966**	**Corporate Dissolution or Liquidation**	
(Rev. December 1995) Department of the Treasury Internal Revenue Service	**(Required under section 6043(a) of the Internal Revenue Code)**	OMB No. 1545-0041

Please type or print

Name of corporation	Employer identification number
Number, street, and room or suite no. (If a P.O. box number, see instructions below.)	Check type of return ☐ 1120 ☐ 1120-L ☐ 1120-IC-DISC ☐ 1120S ☐ Other ▶
City or town, state, and ZIP code	

1 Date incorporated	2 Place incorporated	3 Type of liquidation ☐ Complete ☐ Partial	4 Date resolution or plan of complete or partial liquidation was adopted
5 Service Center where corporation filed its immediately preceding tax return	6 Last month, day, and year of immediately preceding tax year	7a Last month, day, and year of final tax year	7b Was corporation's final tax return filed as part of a consolidated income tax return? If "Yes," complete 7c, 7d, and 7e. ☐ Yes ☐ No
7c Name of common parent		7d Employer identification number of common parent	7e Service Center where consolidated return was filed

		Common	Preferred
8	Total number of shares outstanding at time of adoption of plan of liquidation		
9	Date(s) of any amendments to plan of dissolution		
10	Section of the Code under which the corporation is to be dissolved or liquidated . . .		
11	If this return concerns an amendment or supplement to a resolution or plan, enter the date the previous Form 966 was filed		

Attach a certified copy of the resolution or plan and all amendments or supplements not previously filed.

Under penalties of perjury, I declare that I have examined this return, including accompanying schedules and statements, and to the best of my knowledge and belief it is true, correct, and complete.

▶ | Signature of officer | Title | Date |
|---|---|---|

Instructions

Who Must File.—A corporation must file Form 966 if its adopts a resolution or plan to dissolve the corporation or liquidate any of its stock. Exempt organizations are not required to file Form 966. These organizations should see the Instructions for Form 990 or 990-PF.

When and Where To File.—File Form 966 within 30 days after the resolution or plan is adopted to dissolve the corporation or liquidate any of its stock. If the resolution or plan is amended or supplemented after Form 966 is filed, file another Form 966 within 30 days after the amendment or supplement is adopted. The additional form will be sufficient if the date the earlier form was filed is entered on line 11 and a certified copy of the amendment or supplement is attached. Include all information required by Form 966 that was not given in the earlier form.

File Form 966 with the Internal Revenue Service Center where the corporation is required to file its income tax return.

Distribution of Property.—A corporation must recognize gain or loss on the distribution of its assets in the complete liquidation of its stock. For purposes of determining gain or loss, the distributed assets are valued at fair market value. Exceptions to this rule apply to liquidation of a subsidiary and to a distribution that is made pursuant to a plan of reorganization.

Address.—Include the suite, room, or other unit number after the street address. If mail is not delivered to the street address and the corporation has a P.O. box, enter the box number instead of the street address.

Signature.—The return must be signed and dated by the president, vice president, treasurer, assistant treasurer, chief accounting officer, or any other corporate officer (such as tax officer) authorized to sign. A receiver, trustee, or assignee must sign and date any return required to be filed on behalf of a corporation.

3. the date the revocation of dissolution was authorized;
4. if revocation is authorized by incorporator or director action, a statement to that effect; and
5. if revocation is authorized by shareholder action, a statement setting forth the particulars of voting groups voting in favor of the revocation and a statement that the votes cast in favor of revocation is sufficient.

B.   *Administrative Dissolution*

An **administrative dissolution** is one form of involuntary dissolution. Many states allow the secretary of state or other appropriate authority to administratively dissolve a corporation for failure to comply with various statutory requirements. In most states, a corporation may be administratively dissolved under the following circumstances:

1. the corporation fails to file its annual report or pay the annual report filing fee within the prescribed time period;
2. the corporation fails to pay any requisite franchise fees;
3. the corporation is without a registered agent or registered office in the state of domicile for a prescribed time period;
4. the corporation fails to notify the secretary of state's office of a change in registered agent, a change in registered office, or the resignation of a registered agent;
5. the corporation fails to truthfully and fully answer interrogatories propounded by the state government within the prescribed time period; and
6. the corporation's period of existence as set forth in its articles of incorporation has expired (this happens rarely, as most states allow a corporation to exist perpetually and most articles of incorporation so provide).

Before an administrative dissolution takes place, the secretary of state's office serves the corporation with written notice stating the grounds for the proposed dissolution and its intentions to dissolve the corporation. The transgressing corporation is given a stated time period within which to correct its transgressions or demonstrate to the state's satisfaction that the transgressions do not exist. Should a corporation fail to do so within the prescribed time period, it will be administratively dissolved and a certificate of dissolution will be issued. As is the case in a voluntary dissolution, the only business an administratively dissolved corporation may engage in is the business of winding up its affairs and liquidating. Should a director or officer continue to act in any other business transaction on behalf of the corporation after the corporation has been administratively dissolved, that director or officer will be held personally liable for all debts and obligations incurred after the dissolution of the corporation.

If an administratively dissolved corporation wishes to continue its business, it may apply to the secretary of state for **reinstatement**. Although state law varies, an **application for reinstatement** generally includes the following information:

1. the name of the corporation;
2. the effective date of its administrative dissolution;
3. a statement either that the grounds for dissolution did not exist or that they have been eliminated and no further grounds exist for dissolution; and
4. a statement that all fees owed by the corporation computed at the rate provided by law have been paid.

In some states, an administratively dissolved corporation may submit a current annual report with the reinstatement fee and other penalty fees rather than filing an application for reinstatement. Should a corporation wish reinstatement, it should act quickly, for in most states the name of a dissolved corporation becomes generally available after a statutorily determined time period.

C.   *Judicial Dissolution*

A **judicial dissolution** is usually an involuntary dissolution supervised by the court if sufficient grounds for dissolution exist. A shareholder may initiate a judicial dissolution if the shareholder establishes any of the following:

1. corporate assets are being wasted or misapplied;
2. the directors of the corporation are deadlocked in the management of corporate affairs, the shareholders are unable to break the deadlock, and the corporation will suffer irreparable injury as a result; or
3. the shareholders are deadlocked and thus cannot elect successors to directors whose terms have expired.

In addition, a creditor of a corporation may initiate a judicial dissolution if a creditor's claim against a corporation results in a court judgment, the execution of which cannot be satisfied because the corporation is insolvent. Similarly, a creditor may initiate a judicial dissolution if the corporation has admitted in writing that the creditor's claim is due and that the corporation is insolvent. Finally, a court may dissolve a corporation on its own initiative if it believes the corporation has exceeded or abused the authority conferred upon it by law or has perpetrated fraud. A court-appointed **receiver** manages the judicially dissolved corporation during its winding up and liquidation process.

CLIENT SIMULATION

Yesterday one of Thomas's clients, Shari Davidson, met with him and indicated that she wished to dissolve her three-year-old corporation. The corporation, Smooch Pooch Confections, Inc., is in the business of creating and selling gourmet pet treats. Although the original market study looked promising, the business has yet to realize profits. Neither Shari, nor the other two shareholders, Terrence Avery and Melanie Morris, have additional capital to put into the business. They have been unsuccessful in attaining additional investors to become shareholders and do not want the obligations of additional business loans. Therefore, the three shareholders have agreed that their best option is to dissolve the corporation and have sent Shari to discuss the mechanics with Thomas. During the meeting, Thomas and Shari discussed a possible plan of liquidation to conform with Internal Revenue Service requirements. Thomas apprised Karen of the client's situation, gave her the file with notes from the meeting, and he has requested that she prepare the requisite documents for review and client signature. The first document Karen prepares is a unanimous shareholder consent to dissolve, permitted by state statute.

EXHIBIT 13.10

**Action by Unanimous Consent of the Shareholders of
Smooch Pooch Confections, Inc.**

We, the undersigned, being all of the shareholders of SMOOCH POOCH CONFECTIONS, INC., a corporation organized and operating under the laws of the State of Any State hereby agree, by this unanimous written consent, to the following matters with the same force and effect as if they had been unanimously adopted at a duly convened meeting of the shareholders.

EXHIBIT 13.10   *Continued*

We agree that for the benefit of the said Corporation and its shareholders that the Corporation be dissolved and that articles of dissolution be filed in accordance with the laws of the State of Any State.

We authorize the directors and officers of the Corporation to satisfy all notice requirements as may be required by statute; further, we agree that within thirty (30) days from the date inscribed below a Form 966 be filed with the Internal Revenue Service, together with a certified copy of this unanimous consent, and that all other forms required by state and federal law be filed in connection with the dissolution of the Corporation.

DATED: _____

_____
Shari Davidson

_____
Terrence Avery

_____
Melanie Morris

According to the statutes of Any State, a dissolving corporation must file a notice of intent to dissolve with the secretary of state and publish it once in either a newspaper of general circulation in the county in which the corporation is located or in a legal newspaper circulated in that county. Individual notice to creditors is not required. Karen pulls up a notice form already on file in her computer which, upon customization for the client, reads as follows:

EXHIBIT 13.11

Notice of Intent to Dissolve Smooch Pooch Confections, Inc.

Pursuant to Section 305. 962 of the statutes of the State of Any State, the undersigned hereby provides the following notice of intent to dissolve SMOOCH POOCH CONFECTIONS, INC.

EXHIBIT 13.11   *Continued*

I.
The name of the Corporation is SMOOCH POOCH CONFECTIONS, INC.

II.
On the _____ day of _____, 19_____, the shareholders of the Corporation unanimously consented to a voluntary dissolution of the Corporation.

III.
The board of directors and officers of the Corporation are hereby authorized to take any and all actions necessary to wind up the business of the Corporation, and distribute the corporation's assets in accordance with statute.

DATED: _____   SMOOCH POOCH CONFECTIONS, INC.

BY _____
Shari Davidson, President

Subscribed and sworn to before me this _____ day of _____, 19_____, by Shari Davidson, President of SMOOCH POOCH CONFECTIONS,INC., a corporation organized under the laws of the State of Any State.

_____
Notary Public

Finally, Karen prepares the articles of dissolution. Again, the skeletal form is readily retrievable from her computer files. According to state statutes, the articles must include the name of the corporation, the date the dissolution was authorized, a statement providing the particulars on shareholder action approving the dissolution, and a statement that all corporate obligations have been satisfied or provision for their satisfaction has been made. Although the client will not file the articles of dissolution with the state until it has liquidated and paid off all corporate obligations, Karen prepares the document now to be signed and filed at a later date. Upon completion, the articles read as follows:

EXHIBIT 13.12

Articles of Dissolution of Smooch Pooch Confections, Inc.

Pursuant to Section 305.962 of the statutes of the State of Any State, the undersigned do hereby adopt the following Articles of Dissolution:

I.

The name of the Corporation is SMOOCH POOCH CONFECTIONS, INC.

II.

Dissolution of the Corporation was authorized on _____.

III.

Dissolution was approved by unanimous consent of the shareholders of said Corporation.

IV.

All debts and obligations of said Corporation have been paid and discharged, or adequate provision has been made therefor.

DATED: _____   SMOOCH POOCH CONFECTIONS, INC.

BY _____
Shari Davidson, President
and

_____
Terrence Avery, Secretary

Subscribed and sworn to before me this _____ day of _____, 19_____, by Shari Davidson, President, and Terrence Avery, Secretary, of SMOOCH POOCH CONFECTIONS,INC., a corporation organized under the laws of the State of Any State.

_____
Notary Public

Upon review and signature, Karen will put the unanimous consent to dissolve in the corporate minute book and will send the original and one copy (for a certified copy) of the notice of intent to the secretary of state's office for filing and one copy plus applicable fees to the newspaper for publication. Shari informed Thomas that her accountant will file the 966 form with the Internal Revenue Service, so Karen will provide Shari with a certified copy of the unanimous consent for the accountant to attach to the form. Once liquidation has begun, the client will sign the articles of dissolution and Karen will file the original plus one copy with the Secretary of State. Upon receiving the certified copy of the articles and a certificate of dissolution, Karen will place them in the corporate minute book.

Chapter Summary

1. A corporation may amend its articles of incorporation to reflect changes in the corporate name, purpose, or stock structure or, in general, to add any statutorily permissible provision or to delete any provision not statutorily required. Some amendments require shareholder approval while others do not. Amendments typically not requiring shareholder approval are those considered administrative in nature. Amendments requiring shareholder approval include, but are not limited to, those that change the aggregate number, rights, limitations, or classification of corporate shares of stock.

2. In most states, articles of amendment must include the name of the corporation, the text of each amendment, the date of adoption, and a statement pertaining to authorization which indicates whether the amendments were adopted by incorporator, director, or shareholder action. In the latter instance, the voting particulars are included in the articles of amendment.

3. A paralegal's tasks in the amendment process may include the drafting of meeting notices, board resolutions, meeting minutes, and articles of amendment; the filing of the articles with appropriate filing authorities; and the preparation of new stock legends or certificates, if applicable.

4. Corporate reorganizations may take various forms. A merger occurs when two or more corporations unite, leaving one surviving corporation. A consolidation occurs when two or more corporations merge to form a brand new corporation. The statutes of many states do not distinguish between mergers and consolidations. A share exchange occurs when a target corporation exchanges some or all of its shares of stock for some or all of the stock of an acquiring corporation. A stock purchase occurs when an acquiring corporation purchases all or substantially all of the stock of a target corporation. An asset

purchase occurs when an acquiring corporation purchases all or substantially all of the assets of another business, be that business another corporation or some other business entity.

5. In every type of corporate reorganization, considerable time is taken to review the legal and financial positions of the parties before and as a result of the proposed transaction. Applicable state and federal laws are researched, financial reports are reviewed, organizational shuffling of directors and officers is appraised, and the impact on employees of all participating corporations is considered.

6. The tasks to be performed by paralegals assisting in any type of corporate reorganization are similar. These tasks include conducting legal and factual research; organizing documents for review; assisting in the drafting of reorganization plans; drafting notices, resolutions, minutes, and articles; preparing transfer documents; and filing articles with appropriate filing authorities.

7. A corporation may be dissolved voluntarily by filing articles of dissolution, or it may be dissolved involuntarily through administrative or judicial dissolution. Should a voluntarily dissolved corporation wish to revoke its articles of dissolution and continue business, it may file articles of revocation. Should an administratively dissolved corporation wish to continue in business, it must file an application for reinstatement.

8. Voluntary dissolution of a corporation may occur before or after shares of stock are issued and business commences. In the former situation, the incorporators or directors approve the dissolution. In the latter situation, shareholder approval typically is required. Upon approval, many states require the dissolving corporation to put creditors on notice by filing and publishing a notice of intent to dissolve. Articles of dissolution are subsequently filed with the state filing authority and a 966 form is filed with the Internal Revenue Service.

Review Questions

1. What is the difference between a merger and a consolidation?
2. List the items to be included in:
   (i)   articles of merger
   (ii) articles of dissolution
3. List the tasks a paralegal might perform in the corporate amendment process.

4. Compare and contrast the following:
    (i)   a short-form merger and a small-impact merger
    (ii) a stock purchase and an asset purchase
    (iii) reinstated articles of incorporation and articles of revocation
5. List the tasks a paralegal might perform in a merger closing.

KEY TERMS
---

administrative
   dissolution
application for
   reinstatement
articles of dissolution
articles of merger
articles of revocation
articles of share
   exchange
asset purchase
boot
bulk transfer laws
certificate of dissolution
consolidation
intent to dissolve

judicial dissolution
letters of intent
merger
plan of liquidation
plan of share exchange
reinstated articles of
   incorporation
share exchange
short-form merger
small-impact merger
stock purchase
type A transaction
type B transaction
type C transaction

Uniform Partnership Act (1994) with Limited Liability Partnership Act (1996)*

*The Uniform Partnership Act (1994), as amended, has been reprinted through permission of the National Conference of Commissioners on Uniform State Laws.

ARTICLE 1
GENERAL PROVISIONS

§101.   Definitions.

In this [Act]:

(1) "Business" includes every trade, occupation, and profession.

(2) "Debtor in bankruptcy" means a person who is the subject of:

(i) an order for relief under Title 11 of the United States Code or a comparable order under a successor statute of general application; or

(ii) a comparable order under federal, state, or foreign law governing insolvency.

(3) "Distribution" means a transfer of money or other property from a partnership to a partner in the partner's capacity as a partner or to the partner's transferee.

(4) "Foreign limited liability partnership" means a partnership that:

(i) is formed under laws other than the laws of this State; and

(ii) has the status of a limited liability partnership under those laws.

(5) "Limited liability partnership" means a partnership that has filed a statement of qualification under Section 1001 and does not have a similar statement in effect in any other jurisdiction.

(6) "Partnership" means an association of two or more persons to carry on as co-owners a business for profit formed under Section 202, predecessor law, or comparable law of another jurisdiction.

(7) "Partnership agreement" means the agreement, whether written, oral, or implied, among the partners concerning the partnership, including amendments to the partnership agreement.

(8) "Partnership at will" means a partnership in which the partners have not agreed to remain partners until the expiration of a definite term or the completion of a particular undertaking.

(9) "Partnership interest" or "partner's interest in the partnership" means all of a partner's interests in the partnership, including the partner's transferable interest and all management and other rights.

(10) "Person" means an individual, corporation, business trust, estate, trust, partnership, association, joint venture, government, governmental subdivision, agency, or instrumentality, or any other legal or commercial entity.

(11) "Property" means all property, real, personal, or mixed, tangible or intangible, or any interest therein.

(12) "State" means a State of the United States, the District of Columbia, the Commonwealth of Puerto Rico, or any territory or insular possession subject to the jurisdiction of the United States.

(13) "Statement" means a statement of partnership authority under Section 303, a statement of denial under Section 304, a statement of dissociation under Section 704, a statement of dissolution under Section 805, a statement of merger under Section 907, a statement of qualification under Section 1001, a statement of foreign qualification under Section 1102, or an amendment or cancellation of any of the foregoing.

(14) "Transfer" includes an assignment, conveyance, lease, mortgage, deed, and encumbrance.

§102. Knowledge and Notice.

(a) A person knows a fact if the person has actual knowledge of it.

(b) A person has notice of a fact if the person:

(1) knows of it;

(2) has received a notification of it; or

(3) has reason to know it exists from all of the facts known to the person at the time in question.

(c) A person notifies or gives a notification to another by taking steps reasonably required to inform the other person in ordinary course, whether or not the other person learns of it.

(d) A person receives a notification when the notification:

(1) comes to the person's attention; or

(2) is duly delivered at the person's place of business or at any other place held out by the person as a place for receiving communications.

(e) Except as otherwise provided in subsection (f), a person other than an individual knows, has notice, or receives a notification of a fact for purposes of a particular transaction when the individual conducting the transaction knows, has notice, or receives a notification of the fact, or in any event when the fact would have been brought to the individual's attention if the person had exercised reasonable diligence. The person exercises reasonable diligence if it maintains reasonable routines for communicating significant information to the individual conducting the transaction and there is reasonable compliance with the routines. Reasonable diligence does not require an individual acting for the person to communicate information unless the communication is part of the individual's regular duties or the individual has reason to know of the transaction and that the transaction would be materially affected by the information.

(f) A partner's knowledge, notice, or receipt of a notification of a fact relating to the partnership is effective immediately as knowledge by, notice to, or receipt of a notification by the partnership, except in the case of a fraud on the partnership committed by or with the consent of that partner.

§103. Effect of Partnership Agreement; Nonwaivable Provisions.

(a) Except as otherwise provided in subsection (b), relations among the partners and between the partners and the partnership are governed by the partnership agreement. To the extent the partnership agreement does not otherwise provide, this [Act] governs relations among the partners and between the partners and the partnership.

(b) The partnership agreement may not:

(1) vary the rights and duties under Section 105 except to eliminate the duty to provide copies of statements to all of the partners;

(2) unreasonably restrict the right of access to books and records under Section 403(b);

(3) eliminate the duty of loyalty under Section 404(b) or 603(b)(3), but:

(i) the partnership agreement may identify specific types or categories of activities that do not violate the duty of loyalty, if not manifestly unreasonable; or

(ii) all of the partners or a number or percentage specified in the partnership agreement may authorize or ratify, after full disclosure of all material facts, a specific act or transaction that otherwise would violate the duty of loyalty;

(4) unreasonably reduce the duty of care under Section 404(c) or 603(b)(3);

(5) eliminate the obligation of good faith and fair dealing under Section 404(d), but the partnership agreement may prescribe the standards by which the performance of the obligation is to be measured, if the standards are not manifestly unreasonable;

(6) vary the power to dissociate as a partner under Section 602(a), except to require the notice under Section 601(1) to be in writing;

(7) vary the right of a court to expel a partner in the events specified in Section 601(5);

(8) vary the requirement to wind up the partnership business in cases specified in Section 801(4), (5), or (6);

(9) vary the law applicable to a limited liability partnership under Section 106(b); or

(10) restrict rights of third parties under this [Act].

§104. Supplemental Principles of Law.

(a) Unless displaced by particular provisions of this [Act], the principles of law and equity supplement this [Act].

(b) If an obligation to pay interest arises under this [Act] and the rate is not specified, the rate is that specified in [applicable statute].

§105. Execution, Filing, and Recording of Statements.

(a) A statement may be filed in the office of [the Secretary of State]. A certified copy of a statement that is filed in an office in another State may be filed in the office of [the Secretary of State]. Either filing has the effect provided in this [Act] with respect to partnership property located in or transactions that occur in this State.

(b) A certified copy of a statement that has been filed in the office of the [Secretary of State] and recorded in the office for recording transfers of real property has the effect provided for recorded statements in this [Act]. A recorded statement that is not a certified copy of a statement filed in the office of the [Secretary of State] does not have the effect provided for recorded statements in this [Act].

(c) A statement filed by a partnership must be executed by at least two partners. Other statements must be executed by a partner or other person authorized by this [Act]. An individual who executes a statement as, or on behalf of, a partner or other person named as a partner in a statement shall personally declare under penalty of perjury that the contents of the statement are accurate.

(d) A person authorized by this [Act] to file a statement may amend or cancel the statement by filing an amendment or cancellation that names the partnership, identifies the statement, and states the substance of the amendment or cancellation.

(e) A person who files a statement pursuant to this section shall promptly send a copy of the statement to every nonfiling partner and to any other person named as a partner in the statement. Failure to send a copy of a statement to a partner or other person does not limit the effectiveness of the statement as to a person not a partner.

(f) The [Secretary of State] may collect a fee for filing or providing a certified copy of a statement. The [officer responsible for recording transfers of real property] may collect a fee for recording a statement.

§106. Governing Law.

(a) Except as otherwise provided in subsection (b), the law of the jurisdiction in which a partnership has its chief executive office governs relations among the partners and between the partners and the partnership.

(b) The law of this State governs relations among the partners and between the partners and the partnership and the liability of partners for an obligation of a limited liability partnership.

§107.   Partnership Subject to Amendment or Repeal of [Act].

A partnership governed by this [Act] is subject to any amendment to or repeal of this [Act].

ARTICLE 2
NATURE OF PARTNERSHIP

§201.   Partnership as Entity.

(a) A partnership is an entity distinct from its partners.

(b) A limited liability partnership continues to be the same entity that existed before the filing of a statement of qualification under Section 1001.

§202.   Formation of Partnership.

(a) Except as otherwise provided in subsection (b), the association of two or more persons to carry on as co-owners a business for profit forms a partnership, whether or not the persons intend to form a partnership.

(b) An association formed under a statute other than this [Act], a predecessor statute, or a comparable statute of another jurisdiction is not a partnership under this [Act].

(c) In determining whether a partnership is formed, the following rules apply:

(1) Joint tenancy, tenancy in common, tenancy by the entireties, joint property, common property, or part ownership does not by itself establish a partnership, even if the co-owners share profits made by the use of the property.

(2) The sharing of gross returns does not by itself establish a partnership, even if the persons sharing them have a joint or common right or interest in property from which the returns are derived.

(3) A person who receives a share of the profits of a business is presumed to be a partner in the business, unless the profits were received in payment:

(i) of a debt by installments or otherwise;

(ii) for services as an independent contractor or of wages or other compensation to an employee;

(iii) of rent;

(iv) of an annuity or other retirement or health benefit to a beneficiary, representative, or designee of a deceased or retired partner;

(v) of interest or other charge on a loan, even if the amount of payment varies with the profits of the business, including a direct or indirect present or future ownership of the collateral, or rights to income, proceeds, or increase in value derived from the collateral; or

(vi) for the sale of the goodwill of a business or other property by installments or otherwise.

§203.   Partnership Property.

Property acquired by a partnership is property of the partnership and not of the partners individually.

§204.   When Property is Partnership Property.

(a) Property is partnership property if acquired in the name of:

(1) the partnership; or

(2) one or more partners with an indication in the instrument transferring title to the property of the person's capacity as a partner or of the existence of a partnership but without an indication of the name of the partnership.

(b) Property is acquired in the name of the partnership by a transfer to:

(1) the partnership in its name; or

(2) one or more partners in their capacity as partners in the partnership, if the name of the partnership is indicated in the instrument transferring title to the property.

(c) Property is presumed to be partnership property if purchased with partnership assets, even if not acquired in the name of the partnership or of one or more partners with an indication in the instrument transferring title to the property of the person's capacity as a partner or of the existence of a partnership.

(d) Property acquired in the name of one or more of the partners, without an indication in the instrument transferring title to the property of the person's capacity as a partner or of the existence of a partnership and without use of partnership assets, is presumed to be separate property, even if used for partnership purposes.

ARTICLE 3
RELATIONS OF PARTNERS TO
PERSONS DEALING WITH PARTNERSHIP

§301.   Partner Agent of Partnership.

Subject to the effect of a statement of partnership authority under Section 303:

(1) Each partner is an agent of the partnership for the purpose of its business. An act of a partner, including the execution of an instrument in the partnership name, for apparently carrying on in the ordinary course the partnership business or business of the kind carried on by the partnership binds the partnership, unless the partner had no authority to act for the partnership in the particular matter and the person with whom the partner was dealing knew or had received a notification that the partner lacked authority.

(2) An act of a partner which is not apparently for carrying on in the ordinary course the partnership business or business of the kind carried on by the partnership binds the partnership only if the act was authorized by the other partners.

§302.   Transfer of Partnership Property.

(a) Partnership property may be transferred as follows:

(1) Subject to the effect of a statement of partnership authority under Section 303, partnership property held in the name of the partnership may be transferred by an instrument of transfer executed by a partner in the partnership name.

(2) Partnership property held in the name of one or more partners with an indication in the instrument transferring the property to them of their capacity as partners or of the existence of a partnership, but without an indication of the name of the partnership, may be transferred by an instrument of transfer executed by the persons in whose name the property is held.

(3) Partnership property held in the name of one or more persons other than the partnership, without an indication in the instrument transferring the property to them of their capacity as partners or of the existence of a partnership, may be transferred by an instrument of transfer executed by the persons in whose name the property is held.

(b) A partnership may recover partnership property from a transferee only if it proves that execution of the instrument of initial transfer did not bind the partnership under Section 301 and:

(1) as to a subsequent transferee who gave value for property transferred under subsection (a)(1) and (2), proves that the subsequent transferee knew or had received a notification that the person who executed the instrument of initial transfer lacked authority to bind the partnership; or

(2) as to a transferee who gave value for property transferred under subsection (a)(3), proves that the transferee knew or had received a notification that the property was partnership property and that the person who executed the instrument of initial transfer lacked authority to bind the partnership.

(c) A partnership may not recover partnership property from a subsequent transferee if the partnership would not have been entitled to recover the property, under subsection (b), from any earlier transferee of the property.

(d) If a person holds all of the partners' interests in the partnership, all of the partnership property vests in that person. The person may execute a document in the name of the partnership to evidence vesting of the property in that person and may file or record the document.

§303.   Statement of Partnership Authority.

(a) A partnership may file a statement of partnership authority, which:

(1) must include:

(i) the name of the partnership;

(ii) the street address of its chief executive office and of one office in this State, if there is one;

(iii) the names and mailing addresses of all of the partners or of an agent appointed and maintained by the partnership for the purpose of subsection (b); and

(iv) the names of the partners authorized to execute an instrument transferring real property held in the name of the partnership; and

(2) may state the authority, or limitations on the authority, of some or all of the partners to enter into other transactions on behalf of the partnership and any other matter.

(b) If a statement of partnership authority names an agent, the agent shall maintain a list of the names and mailing addresses of all of the partners and make it available to any person on request for good cause shown.

(c) If a filed statement of partnership authority is executed pursuant to Section 105(c) and states the name of the partnership but does not contain all of the other information required by subsection (a), the statement nevertheless operates with respect to a person not a partner as provided in subsections (d) and (e).

(d) Except as otherwise provided in subsection (g), a filed statement of partnership authority supplements the authority of a partner to enter into transactions on behalf of the partnership as follows:

(1) Except for transfers of real property, a grant of authority contained in a filed statement of partnership authority is conclusive in favor of a person who gives value without knowledge to the contrary, so long as and to the extent that a limitation on that authority is not then contained in another filed statement. A filed cancellation of a limitation on authority revives the previous grant of authority.

(2) A grant of authority to transfer real property held in the name of the partnership contained in a certified copy of a filed statement of partnership authority recorded in the office for recording transfers of that real property is conclusive in favor of a person who gives value without knowledge to the contrary, so long as and to the extent that a certified copy of a filed statement containing a limitation on that authority is not then of record in the office for recording transfers of that real property. The recording in the office for recording transfers of that real property of a certified copy of a filed cancellation of a limitation on authority revives the previous grant of authority.

(e) A person not a partner is deemed to know of a limitation on the authority of a partner to transfer real property held in the name of the partnership if a certified copy of the filed statement containing the limitation on authority is of record in the office for recording transfers of that real property.

(f) Except as otherwise provided in subsections (d) and (e) and Sections 704 and 805, a person not a partner is not deemed to know of a limitation on the authority of a partner merely because the limitation is contained in a filed statement.

(g) Unless earlier canceled, a filed statement of partnership authority is canceled by operation of law

five years after the date on which the statement, or the most recent amendment, was filed with the [Secretary of State].

§304.   Statement of Denial.

A partner or other person named as a partner in a filed statement of partnership authority or in a list maintained by an agent pursuant to Section 303(b) may file a statement of denial stating the name of the partnership and that fact that is being denied, which may include denial of a person's authority or status as a partner. A statement of denial is a limitation on authority as provided in Section 303(d) and (e).

§305.   Partnership Liable for Partner's Actionable Conduct.

(a) A partnership is liable for loss or injury caused to a person, or for a penalty incurred, as a result of a wrongful act or omission, or other actionable conduct, of a partner acting in the ordinary course of business of the partnership or with authority of the partnership.

(b) If, in the course of the partnership's business or while acting with authority of the partnership, a partner receives or causes the partnership to receive money or property of a person not a partner, and the money or property is misapplied by a partner, the partnership is liable for the loss.

§306.   Partner's Liability.

(a) Except as otherwise provided in subsections (b) and (c), all partners are liable jointly and severally for all obligations of the partnership unless otherwise agreed by the claimant or provided by law.

(b) A person admitted as a partner into an existing partnership is not personally liable for any partnership obligation incurred before the person's admission as a partner.

(c) An obligation of a partnership incurred while the partnership is a limited liability partnership, whether arising in contract, tort, or otherwise, is solely the obligation of the partnership. A partner is not personally liable, directly or indirectly, by way of contribution or otherwise, for such a partnership obligation solely by reason of being or so acting as a partner. This subsection applies notwithstanding anything inconsistent in the partnership agreement that existed immediately before the vote required to become a limited liability partnership under Section 1001(b).

§307.   Actions By and Against Partnership and Partners.

(a) A partnership may sue and be sued in the name of the partnership.

(b) An action may be brought against the partnership and, to the extent not inconsistent with Section 306, any or all of the partners in the same action or in separate actions.

(c) A judgment against a partnership is not by itself a judgment against a partner. A judgment against a partnership may not be satisfied from a partner's assets unless there is also a judgment against the partner.

(d) A judgment creditor of a partner may not levy execution against the assets of the partner to satisfy a judgment based on a claim against the partnership unless the partner is personally liable for the claim under Section 306 and:

(1) a judgment based on the same claim has been obtained against the partnership and a writ of execution on the judgment has been returned unsatisfied in whole or in part;

(2) the partnership is a debtor in bankruptcy;

(3) the partner has agreed that the creditor need not exhaust partnership assets;

(4) a court grants permission to the judgment creditor to levy execution against the assets of a partner based on a finding that partnership assets subject to execution are clearly insufficient to satisfy the judgment, that exhaustion of partnership assets is excessively burdensome, or that the grant of permission is an appropriate exercise of the court's equitable powers; or

(5) liability is imposed on the partner by law or contract independent of the existence of the partnership.

(e) This section applies to any partnership liability or obligation resulting from a representation by a partner or purported partner under Section 308.

§308.   Liability of Purported Partner.

(a) If a person, by words or conduct, purports to be a partner, or consents to being represented by another as a partner, in a partnership or with one or more persons not partners, the purported partner is liable to a person to whom the representation is made, if that person, relying on the representation, enters into a transaction with the actual or purported partnership. If the representation, either by the purported partner or by a person with the purported partner's consent, is made in a public manner, the purported partner is liable to a person who relies upon the purported partnership even if the purported partner is not aware of being held out as a partner to the claimant. If partnership liability results, the purported partner is liable with respect to that liability as if the purported partner were a partner. If no partnership liability results, the purported partner is liable with respect to that liability jointly and severally with any other person consenting to the representation.

(b) If a person is thus represented to be a partner in an existing partnership, or with one or more persons not partners, the purported partner is an agent of persons consenting to the representation to bind them to the same extent and in the same manner as if the purported partner were a partner, with respect to persons who enter into transactions in reliance upon the representation. If all of the partners of the existing partnership consent to the representation, a partnership act or obligation results. If fewer than all of the partners of the existing partnership consent to the representation, the person acting and the partners consenting to the representation are jointly and severally liable.

(c) A person is not liable as a partner merely because the person is named by another in a statement of partnership authority.

(d) A person does not continue to be liable as a partner merely because of a failure to file a statement of dissociation or to amend a statement of partnership authority to indicate the partner's dissociation from the partnership.

(e) Except as otherwise provided in subsections (a) and (b), persons who are not partners as to each other are not liable as partners to other persons.

ARTICLE 4
RELATIONS OF PARTNERS TO EACH OTHER AND TO PARTNERSHIP

§401.   Partner's Rights and Duties.

(a) Each partner is deemed to have an account that is:

(1) credited with an amount equal to the

money plus the value of any other property, net of the amount of any liabilities, the partner contributes to the partnership and the partner's share of the partnership profits; and

(2) charged with an amount equal to the money plus the value of any other property, net of the amount of any liabilities, distributed by the partnership to the partner and the partner's share of the partnership losses.

(b) Each partner is entitled to an equal share of the partnership profits and is chargeable with a share of the partnership losses in proportion to the partner's share of the profits.

(c) A partnership shall reimburse a partner for payments made and indemnify a partner for liabilities incurred by the partner in the ordinary course of the business of the partnership or for the preservation of its business or property.

(d) A partnership shall reimburse a partner for an advance to the partnership beyond the amount of capital the partner agreed to contribute.

(e) A payment or advance made by a partner which gives rise to a partnership obligation under subsection (c) or (d) constitutes a loan to the partnership which accrues interest from the date of the payment or advance.

(f) Each partner has equal rights in the management and conduct of the partnership business.

(g) A partner may use or possess partnership property only on behalf of the partnership.

(h) A partner is not entitled to remuneration for services performed for the partnership, except for reasonable compensation for services rendered in winding up the business of the partnership.

(i) A person may become a partner only with the consent of all of the partners.

(j) A difference arising as to a matter in the ordinary course of business of a partnership may be decided by a majority of the partners. An act outside the ordinary course of business of a partnership and an amendment to the partnership agreement may be undertaken only with the consent of all of the partners.

(k) This section does not affect the obligations of a partnership to other persons under Section 301.

§402.   Distributions in Kind.

A partner has no right to receive, and may not be required to accept, a distribution in kind.

§403.   Partner's Rights and Duties with Respect to Information.

(a) A partnership shall keep its books and records, if any, at its chief executive office.

(b) A partnership shall provide partners and their agents and attorneys access to its books and records. It shall provide former partners and their agents and attorneys access to books and records pertaining to the period during which they were partners. The right of access provides the opportunity to inspect and copy books and records during ordinary business hours. A partnership may impose a reasonable charge, covering the costs of labor and material, for copies of documents furnished.

(c) Each partner and the partnership shall furnish to a partner, and to the legal representative of a deceased partner or partner under legal disability:

(1) without demand, any information concerning the partnership's business and affairs reasonably required for the proper exercise of the partner's rights and duties under the partnership agreement or this [Act]; and

(2) on demand, any other information concerning the partnership's business and affairs, except to the extent the demand or the information demanded is unreasonable or otherwise improper under the circumstances.

§404.   General Standards of Partner's Conduct.

(a) The only fiduciary duties a partner owes to the partnership and the other partners are the duty of loyalty and the duty of care set forth in subsections (b) and (c).

(b) A partner's duty of loyalty to the partnership and the other partners is limited to the following:

(1) to account to the partnership and hold as trustee for it any property, profit, or benefit derived by the partner in the conduct and winding up of the partnership business or derived from a use by the partner of partnership property, including the appropriation of a partnership opportunity;

(2) to refrain from dealing with the partnership in the conduct or winding up of the partnership business as or on behalf of a party having an interest adverse to the partnership; and

(3) to refrain from competing with the partnership in the conduct of the partnership business before the dissolution of the partnership.

(c) A partner's duty of care to the partnership and the other partners in the conduct and winding up of the partnership business is limited to refraining from engaging in grossly negligent or reckless conduct, intentional misconduct, or a knowing violation of law.

(d) A partner shall discharge the duties to the partnership and the other partners under this [Act] or under the partnership agreement and exercise any rights consistently with the obligation of good faith and fair dealing.

(e) A partner does not violate a duty or obligation under this [Act] or under the partnership agreement merely because the partner's conduct furthers the partner's own interest.

(f) A partner may lend money to and transact other business with the partnership, and as to each loan or transaction the rights and obligations of the partner are the same as those of a person who is not a partner, subject to other applicable law.

(g) This section applies to a person winding up the partnership business as the personal or legal representative of the last surviving partner as if the person were a partner.

§405.   Actions by Partnership and Partners.

(a) A partnership may maintain an action against a partner for a breach of the partnership agreement, or for the violation of a duty to the partnership, causing harm to the partnership.

(b) A partner may maintain an action against the partnership or another partner for legal or equitable relief, with or without an accounting as to partnership business, to:

(1) enforce the partner's rights under the partnership agreement;

(2) enforce the partner's rights under this [Act], including:

(i) the partner's rights under Sections 401, 403, or 404;

(ii) the partner's right on dissociation to have the partner's interest in the partnership purchased pursuant to Section 701 or enforce any other right under [Article] 6 or 7; or

(iii) the partner's right to compel a dissolution and winding up of the partnership business under Section 801 or enforce any other right under [Article] 8; or

(3) enforce the rights and otherwise protect the interests of the partner, including rights and interests arising independently of the partnership relationship.

(c) The accrual of, and any time limitation on, a right of action for a remedy under this section is governed by other law. A right to an accounting upon a dissolution and winding up does not revive a claim barred by law.

§406.   Continuation of Partnership Beyond Definite Term or Particular Undertaking.

(a) If a partnership for a definite term or particular undertaking is continued, without an express agreement, after the expiration of the term or completion of the undertaking, the rights and duties of the partners remain the same as they were at the expiration or completion, so far as is consistent with a partnership at will.

(b) If the partners, or those of them who habitually acted in the business during the term or undertaking, continue the business without any settlement or liquidation of the partnership, they are presumed to have agreed that the partnership will continue.

ARTICLE 5
TRANSFEREES AND CREDITORS OF PARTNER

§501.   Partner Not Co-Owner of Partnership Property.

A partner is not a co-owner of partnership property and has no interest in partnership property which can be transferred, either voluntarily or involuntarily.

§502.   Partner's Transferable Interest in Partnership.

The only transferable interest of a partner in the partnership is the partner's share of the profits and losses of the partnership and the partner's right to receive distributions. The interest is personal property.

§503.   Transfer of Partner's Transferable Interest.

(a) A transfer, in whole or in part, of a partner's transferable interest in the partnership:

(1) is permissible;

(2) does not by itself cause the partner's dissociation or a dissolution and winding up of the partnership business; and

(3) does not, as against the other partners or the partnership, entitle the transferee, during the continuance of the partnership, to participate in the management or conduct of the partnership business, to require access to information concerning partnership transactions, or to inspect or copy the partnership books or records.

(b) A transferee of a partner's transferable interest in the partnership has a right:

(1) to receive, in accordance with the transfer, distributions to which the transferor would otherwise be entitled;

(2) to receive upon the dissolution and winding up of the partnership business, in accordance with the transfer, the net amount otherwise distributable to the transferor; and

(3) to seek under Section 801(6) a judicial determination that it is equitable to wind up the partnership business.

(c) In a dissolution and winding up, a transferee is entitled to an account of partnership transactions only from the date of the latest account agreed to by all of the partners.

(d) Upon transfer, the transferor retains the rights and duties of a partner other than the interest in distributions transferred.

(e) A partnership need not give effect to a transferee's rights under this section until it has notice of the transfer.

(f) A transfer of a partner's transferable interest in the partnership in violation of a restriction on transfer contained in the partnership agreement is ineffective as to a person having notice of the restriction at the time of transfer.

§504.   Partner's Transferable Interest Subject to Charging Order.

(a) On application by a judgment creditor of a partner or of a partner's transferee, a court having jurisdiction may charge the transferable interest of the judgment debtor to satisfy the judgment. The court may appoint a receiver of the share of the distributions due or to become due to the judgment debtor in respect of the partnership and make all other orders, directions, accounts, and inquiries the judgment debtor might have made or which the circumstances of the case may require.

(b) A charging order constitutes a lien on the judgment debtor's transferable interest in the partnership. The court may order a foreclosure of the interest subject to the charging order at any time. The purchaser at the foreclosure sale has the rights of a transferee.

(c) At any time before foreclosure, an interest charged may be redeemed:

(1) by the judgment debtor;

(2) with property other than partnership property, by one or more of the other partners; or

(3) with partnership property, by one or more of the other partners with the consent of all of the partners whose interests are not so charged.

(d) This [Act] does not deprive a partner of a right under exemption laws with respect to the partner's interest in the partnership.

(e) This section provides the exclusive remedy by which a judgment creditor of a partner or partner's transferee may satisfy a judgment out of the judgment debtor's transferable interest in the partnership.

ARTICLE 6
PARTNER'S DISSOCIATION

§601.   Events Causing Partner's Dissociation.

A partner is dissociated from a partnership upon the occurrence of any of the following events:

(1) the partnership's having notice of the partner's express will to withdraw as a partner or on a later date specified by the partner;

(2) an event agreed to in the partnership agreement as causing the partner's dissociation;

(3) the partner's expulsion pursuant to the partnership agreement;

(4) the partner's expulsion by the unanimous vote of the other partners if:

(i) it is unlawful to carry on the partnership business with that partner;

(ii) there has been a transfer of all or substantially all of that partner's transferable interest in the partnership, other than a transfer for security purposes, or a court order charging the partner's interest, which has not been foreclosed;

(iii) within 90 days after the partnership notifies a corporate partner that it will be expelled because it has filed a certificate of dissolution or the equivalent, its charter has been revoked, or its right to conduct business has been suspended by the jurisdiction of its incorporation, there is no revocation of the certificate of dissolution or no reinstatement of its charter or its right to conduct business; or

(iv) a partnership that is a partner has been dissolved and its business is being wound up;

(5) on application by the partnership or another partner, the partner's expulsion by judicial determination because:

(i) the partner engaged in wrongful conduct that adversely and materially affected the partnership business;

(ii) the partner willfully or persistently committed a material breach of the partnership agreement or of a duty owed to the partnership or the other partners under Section 404; or

(iii) the partner engaged in conduct relating to the partnership business which makes it not reasonably practicable to carry on the business in partnership with the partner;

(6) the partner's:

(i) becoming a debtor in bankruptcy;

(ii) executing an assignment for the benefit of creditors;

(iii) seeking, consenting to, or acquiescing in the appointment of a trustee, receiver, or liquidator of that partner or of all or substantially all of that partner's property; or

(iv) failing, within 90 days after the appointment, to have vacated or stayed the appointment of a trustee, receiver, or liquidator of the partner or of all or substantially all of the partner's property obtained without the partner's consent or acquiescence, or failing within 90 days after the expiration of a stay to have the appointment vacated;

(7) in the case of a partner who is an individual:

(i) the partner's death;

(ii) the appointment of a guardian or general conservator for the partner; or

(iii) a judicial determination that the partner has otherwise become incapable of performing the partner's duties under the partnership agreement;

(8) in the case of a partner that is a trust or is acting as a partner by virtue of being a trustee of a trust, distribution of the trust's entire transferable interest in the partnership, but not merely by reason of the substitution of a successor trustee;

(9) in the case of a partner that is an estate or is acting as a partner by virtue of being a personal representative of an estate, distribution of the estate's entire transferable interest in the partnership, but not merely by reason of the substitution of a successor personal representative; or

(10) termination of a partner who is not an individual, partnership, corporation, trust, or estate.

§602.   Partner's Power to Dissociate; Wrongful Dissociation.

(a) A partner has the power to dissociate at any time, rightfully or wrongfully, by express will pursuant to Section 601(1).

(b) A partner's dissociation is wrongful only if:

(1) it is in breach of an express provision of the partnership agreement; or

(2) in the case of a partnership for a definite term or particular undertaking, before the expiration of the term or the completion of the undertaking:

(i) the partner withdraws by express will, unless the withdrawal follows within 90 days after another partner's dissociation by death or otherwise under Section 601(6) through (10) or wrongful dissociation under this subsection;

(ii) the partner is expelled by judicial determination under Section 601(5);

(iii) the partner is dissociated by becoming a debtor in bankruptcy; or

(iv) in the case of a partner who is not an individual, trust other than a business trust, or estate, the partner is expelled or otherwise dissociated because it willfully dissolved or terminated.

(c) A partner who wrongfully dissociates is liable to the partnership and to the other partners for damages caused by the dissociation. The liability is in addition to any other obligation of the partner to the partnership or to the other partners.

§603.   Effect of Partner's Dissociation.

(a) If a partner's dissociation results in a dissolution and winding up of the partnership business, [Article] 8 applies; otherwise, [Article] 7 applies.

(b) Upon a partner's dissociation:

(1) the partner's right to participate in the management and conduct of the partnership busi-

ness terminates, except as otherwise provided in Section 803;

(2) the partner's duty of loyalty under Section 404(b)(3) terminates; and

(3) the partner's duty of loyalty under Section 404(b)(1) and (2) and duty of care under Section 404(c) continue only with regard to matters arising and events occurring before the partner's dissociation, unless the partner participates in winding up the partnership's business pursuant to Section 803.

ARTICLE 7
PARTNER'S DISSOCIATION WHEN BUSINESS NOT WOUND UP

§701.   Purchase of Dissociated Partner's Interest.

(a) If a partner is dissociated from a partnership without resulting in a dissolution and winding up of the partnership business under Section 801, the partnership shall cause the dissociated partner's interest in the partnership to be purchased for a buyout price determined pursuant to subsection (b).

(b) The buyout price of a dissociated partner's interest is the amount that would have been distributable to the dissociating partner under Section 807(b) if, on the date of dissociation, the assets of the partnership were sold at a price equal to the greater of the liquidation value or the value based on a sale of the entire business as a going concern without the dissociated partner and the partnership were wound up as of that date. Interest must be paid from the date of dissociation to the date of payment.

(c) Damages for wrongful dissociation under Section 602(b), and all other amounts owing, whether or not presently due, from the dissociated partner to the partnership, must be offset against the buyout price. Interest must be paid from the date the amount owed becomes due to the date of payment.

(d) A partnership shall indemnify a dissociated partner whose interest is being purchased against all partnership liabilities, whether incurred before or after the dissociation, except liabilities incurred by an act of the dissociated partner under Section 702.

(e) If no agreement for the purchase of a dissociated partner's interest is reached within 120 days after a written demand for payment, the partnership

shall pay, or cause to be paid, in cash to the dissociated partner the amount the partnership estimates to be the buyout price and accrued interest, reduced by any offsets and accrued interest under subsection (c).

(f) If a deferred payment is authorized under subsection (h), the partnership may tender a written offer to pay the amount it estimates to be the buyout price and accrued interest, reduced by any offsets under subsection (c), stating the time of payment, the amount and type of security for payment, and the other terms and conditions of the obligation.

(g) The payment or tender required by subsection (e) or (f) must be accompanied by the following:

(1) a statement of partnership assets and liabilities as of the date of dissociation;

(2) the latest available partnership balance sheet and income statement, if any;

(3) an explanation of how the estimated amount of the payment was calculated; and

(4) written notice that the payment is in full satisfaction of the obligation to purchase unless, within 120 days after the written notice, the dissociated partner commences an action to determine the buyout price, any offsets under subsection (c), or other terms of the obligation to purchase.

(h) A partner who wrongfully dissociates before the expiration of a definite term or the completion of a particular undertaking is not entitled to payment of any portion of the buyout price until the expiration of the term or completion of the undertaking, unless the partner establishes to the satisfaction of the court that earlier payment will not cause undue hardship to the business of the partnership. A deferred payment must be adequately secured and bear interest.

(i) A dissociated partner may maintain an action against the partnership, pursuant to Section 405(b)(2)(ii), to determine the buyout price of that partner's interest, any offsets under subsection (c), or other terms of the obligation to purchase. The action must be commenced within 120 days after the partnership has tendered payment or an offer to pay or within one year after written demand for payment if no payment or offer to pay is tendered. The court shall determine the buyout price of the dissociated partner's interest, any offset due under subsection (c), and accrued interest, and enter judgment for any additional payment or refund. If deferred payment is authorized under subsection (h), the court shall also determine the security for payment and other terms of the obligation to purchase. The court may assess reasonable attorney's fees and the fees and expenses of appraisers or other experts for a party to the action, in amounts the court finds equitable, against a party that the court finds acted arbitrarily, vexatiously, or not in good faith. The finding may be based on the partnership's failure to tender payment or an offer to pay or to comply with subsection (g).

§702.   Dissociated Partner's Power to Bind and Liability to Partnership.

(a) For two years after a partner dissociates without resulting in a dissolution and winding up of the partnership business, the partnership, including a surviving partnership under [Article] 9, is bound by an act of the dissociated partner which would have bound the partnership under Section 301 before dissociation only if at the time of entering into the transaction the other party:

(1) reasonably believed that the dissociated partner was then a partner;

(2) did not have notice of the partner's dissociation; and

(3) is not deemed to have had knowledge under Section 303(e) or notice under Section 704(c).

(b) A dissociated partner is liable to the partnership for any damage caused to the partnership arising from an obligation incurred by the dissociated partner after dissociation for which the partnership is liable under subsection (a).

§703.   Dissociated Partner's Liability to Other Persons.

(a) A partner's dissociation does not of itself discharge the partner's liability for a partnership obligation incurred before dissociation. A dissociated partner is not liable for a partnership obligation incurred after dissociation, except as otherwise provided in subsection (b).

(b) A partner who dissociates without resulting in a dissolution and winding up of the partnership business is liable as a partner to the other party in a transaction entered into by the partnership, or a surviving partnership under [Article] 9, within two years after the partner's dissociation, only if the partner is liable for the obligation under Section 306 and at the time of entering into the transaction the other party:

(1) reasonably believed that the dissociated partner was then a partner;

(2) did not have notice of the partner's dissociation; and

(3) is not deemed to have had knowledge under Section 303(e) or notice under Section 704(c).

(c) By agreement with the partnership creditor and the partners continuing the business, a dissociated partner may be released from liability for a partnership obligation.

(d) A dissociated partner is released from liability for a partnership obligation if a partnership creditor, with notice of the partner's dissociation but without the partner's consent, agrees to a material alteration in the nature or time of payment of a partnership obligation.

§704.   Statement of Dissociation.

(a) A dissociated partner or the partnership may file a statement of dissociation stating the name of the partnership and that the partner is dissociated from the partnership.

(b) A statement of dissociation is a limitation on the authority of a dissociated partner for the purposes of Section 303(d) and (e).

(c) For the purposes of Sections 702(a)(3) and 703(b)(3), a person not a partner is deemed to have notice of the dissociation 90 days after the statement of dissociation is filed.

§705.   Continued Use of Partnership Name.

Continued use of a partnership name, or a dissociated partner's name as part thereof, by partners continuing the business does not of itself make the dissociated partner liable for an obligation of the partners or the partnership continuing the business.

ARTICLE 8
WINDING UP PARTNERSHIP BUSINESS

§801.   Events Causing Dissolution and Winding Up of Partnership Business.

A partnership is dissolved, and its business must be wound up, only upon the occurrence of any of the following events:

(1) in a partnership at will, the partnership's

having notice from a partner, other than a partner who is dissociated under Section 601(2) through (10), of that partner's express will to withdraw as a partner, or on a later date specified by the partner;

(2) in a partnership for a definite term or particular undertaking:

(i) the expiration of 90 days after a partner's dissociation by death or otherwise under Section 601(6) through (10) or wrongful dissociation under Section 602(b), unless before that time a majority in interest of the remaining partners, including partners who have rightfully dissociated pursuant to Section 602(b)(2)(i), agree to continue the partnership;

(ii) the express will of all of the partners to wind up the partnership business; or

(iii) the expiration of the term or the completion of the undertaking;

(3) an event agreed to in the partnership agreement resulting in the winding up of the partnership business;

(4) an event that makes it unlawful for all or substantially all of the business of the partnership to be continued, but a cure of illegality within 90 days after notice to the partnership of the event is effective retroactively to the date of the event for purposes of this section;

(5) on application by a partner, a judicial determination that:

(i) the economic purpose of the partnership is likely to be unreasonably frustrated;

(ii) another partner has engaged in conduct relating to the partnership business which makes it not reasonably practicable to carry on the business in partnership with that partner; or

(iii) it is not otherwise reasonably practicable to carry on the partnership business in conformity with the partnership agreement; or

(6) on application by a transferee of a partner's transferable interest, a judicial determination that it is equitable to wind up the partnership business:

(i) after the expiration of the term or completion of the undertaking, if the partnership was for a definite term or particular undertaking at the time of the transfer or entry of the charging order that gave rise to the transfer; or

(ii) at any time, if the partnership was a partnership at will at the time of the transfer or entry of the charging order that gave rise to the transfer.

§802.   Partnership Continues After Dissolution.

(a) Subject to subsection (b), a partnership continues after dissolution only for the purpose of winding up its business. The partnership is terminated when the winding up of its business is completed.

(b) At any time after the dissolution of a partnership and before the winding up of its business is completed, all of the partners, including any dissociating partner other than a wrongfully dissociating partner, may waive the right to have the partnership's business wound up and the partnership terminated. In that event:

(1) the partnership resumes carrying on its business as if dissolution had never occurred, and any liability incurred by the partnership or a partner after the dissolution and before the waiver is determined as if dissolution had never occurred; and

(2) the rights of a third party accruing under Section 804(1) or arising out of conduct in reliance on the dissolution before the third party knew or received a notification of the waiver may not be adversely affected.

§803.   Right to Wind Up Partnership Business.

(a) After dissolution, a partner who has not wrongfully dissociated may participate in winding up the partnership's business, but on application of any partner, partner's legal representative, or transferee, the [designate the appropriate court], for good cause shown, may order judicial supervision of the winding up.

(b) The legal representative of the last surviving partner may wind up a partnership's business.

(c) A person winding up a partnership's business may preserve the partnership business or property as a going concern for a reasonable time, prosecute and defend actions and proceedings, whether civil, criminal, or administrative, settle and close the partnership's business, dispose of and transfer the partnership's property, discharge the partnership's liabilities, distribute the assets of the partnership pursuant to Section 807, settle disputes by mediation or arbitration, and perform other necessary acts.

§804.   Partner's Power to Bind Partnership After Dissolution.

Subject to Section 805, a partnership is bound by a partner's act after dissolution that:

(1) is appropriate for winding up the partnership business; or

(2) would have bound the partnership under Section 301 before dissolution, if the other party to the transaction did not have notice of the dissolution.

§805.   Statement of Dissolution.

(a) After dissolution, a partner who has not wrongfully dissociated may file a statement of dissolution stating the name of the partnership and that the partnership has dissolved and is winding up its business.

(b) A statement of dissolution cancels a filed statement of partnership authority for the purposes of Section 303(d) and is a limitation on authority for the purposes of Section 303(e).

(c) For the purposes of Sections 301 and 804, a person not a partner is deemed to have notice of the dissolution and the limitation on the partners' authority as a result of the statement of dissolution 90 days after it is filed.

(d) After filing and, if appropriate, recording a statement of dissolution, a dissolved partnership may file and, if appropriate, record a statement of partnership authority which will operate with respect to a person not a partner as provided in Section 303(d) and (e) in any transaction, whether or not the transaction is appropriate for winding up the partnership business.

§806.   Partner's Liability to Other Partners After Dissolution.

(a) Except as otherwise provided in subsection (b) and Section 306, after dissolution a partner is liable to the other partners for the partner's share of any partnership liability incurred under Section 804.

(b) A partner who, with knowledge of the dissolution, incurs a partnership liability under Section 804(2) by an act that is not appropriate for winding up the partnership business is liable to the partnership for any damage caused to the partnership arising from the liability.

§807.   Settlement of Accounts and Contributions Among Partners.

(a) In winding up a partnership's business, the assets of the partnership, including the contributions of the partners required by this section, must be applied to discharge its obligations to creditors, including, to the extent permitted by law, partners who are creditors. Any surplus must be applied to pay in cash the net amount distributable to partners in accordance with their right to distributions under subsection (b).

(b) Each partner is entitled to a settlement of all partnership accounts upon winding up the partnership business. In settling accounts among the partners, profits and losses that result from the liquidation of the partnership assets must be credited and charged to the partners' accounts. The partnership shall make a distribution to a partner in an amount equal to any excess of the credits over the charges in the partner's account. A partner shall contribute to the partnership an amount equal to any excess of the charges over the credits in the partner's account but excluding from the calculation charges attributable to an obligation for which the partner is not personally liable under Section 306.

(c) If a partner fails to contribute the full amount required under subsection (b), all of the other partners shall contribute, in the proportions in which those partners share partnership losses, the additional amount necessary to satisfy the partnership obligations for which they are personally liable under Section 306. A partner or partner's legal representative may recover from the other partners any contributions the partner makes to the extent the amount contributed exceeds that partner's share of the partnership obligations for which the partner is personally liable under Section 306.

(d) After the settlement of accounts, each partner shall contribute, in the proportion in which the partner shares partnership losses, the amount necessary to satisfy partnership obligations that were not known at the time of the settlement and for which the partner is personally liable under Section 306.

(e) The estate of a deceased partner is liable for the partner's obligation to contribute to the partnership.

(f) An assignee for the benefit of creditors of a partnership or a partner, or a person appointed by a court to represent creditors of a partnership or a partner, may enforce a partner's obligation to contribute to the partnership.

ARTICLE 9
CONVERSIONS AND MERGERS

§901.   Definitions.

In this [article]:

(1) "General partner" means a partner in a partnership and a general partner in a limited partnership.

(2) "Limited partner" means a limited partner in a limited partnership.

(3) "Limited partnership" means a limited partnership created under the [State Limited Partnership Act], predecessor law, or comparable law of another jurisdiction.

(4) "Partner" includes both a general partner and a limited partner.

§902.   Conversion of Partnership to Limited Partnership.

(a) A partnership may be converted to a limited partnership pursuant to this section.

(b) The terms and conditions of a conversion of a partnership to a limited partnership must be approved by all of the partners or by a number or percentage specified for conversion in the partnership agreement.

(c) After the conversion is approved by the partners, the partnership shall file a certificate of limited partnership in the jurisdiction in which the limited partnership is to be formed. The certificate must include:

(1) a statement that the partnership was converted to a limited partnership from a partnership;

(2) its former name; and

(3) a statement of the number of votes cast by the partners for and against the conversion and, if the vote is less than unanimous, the number or percentage required to approve the conversion under the partnership agreement.

(d) The conversion takes effect when the certificate of limited partnership is filed or at any later date specified in the certificate.

(e) A general partner who becomes a limited partner as a result of the conversion remains liable as a general partner for an obligation incurred by the partnership before the conversion takes effect. If the other party to a transaction with the limited partnership reasonably believes when entering the transaction that the limited partner is a general partner, the limited partner is liable for an obligation incurred by the limited partnership within 90 days after the conversion takes effect. The limited partner's liability for all other obligations of the limited partnership incurred after the conversion takes effect is that of a limited partner as provided in the [State Limited Partnership Act].

§903.   Conversion of Limited Partnership to Partnership.

(a) A limited partnership may be converted to a partnership pursuant to this section.

(b) Notwithstanding a provision to the contrary in a limited partnership agreement, the terms and conditions of a conversion of a limited partnership to a partnership must be approved by all of the partners.

(c) After the conversion is approved by the partners, the limited partnership shall cancel its certificate of limited partnership.

(d) The conversion takes effect when the certificate of limited partnership is canceled.

(e) A limited partner who becomes a general partner as a result of the conversion remains liable only as a limited partner for an obligation incurred by the limited partnership before the conversion takes effect. Except as otherwise provided in Section 306, the partner is liable as a general partner for an obligation of the partnership incurred after the conversion takes effect.

§904.   Effect of Conversion; Entity Unchanged.

(a) A partnership or limited partnership that has been converted pursuant to this [article] is for all purposes the same entity that existed before the conversion.

(b) When a conversion takes effect:

(1) all property owned by the converting partnership or limited partnership remains vested in the converted entity;

(2) all obligations of the converting partnership or limited partnership continue as obligations of the converted entity; and

(3) an action or proceeding pending against the converting partnership or limited partnership

may be continued as if the conversion had not occurred.

§905.   Merger of Partnerships.

(a) Pursuant to a plan of merger approved as provided in subsection (c), a partnership may be merged with one or more partnerships or limited partnerships.

(b) The plan of merger must set forth:

(1) the name of each partnership or limited partnership that is a party to the merger;

(2) the name of the surviving entity into which the other partnerships or limited partnerships will merge;

(3) whether the surviving entity is a partnership or a limited partnership and the status of each partner;

(4) the terms and conditions of the merger;

(5) the manner and basis of converting the interests of each party to the merger into interests or obligations of the surviving entity, or into money or other property in whole or part; and

(6) the street address of the surviving entity's chief executive office.

(c) The plan of merger must be approved:

(1) in the case of a partnership that is a party to the merger, by all of the partners, or a number or percentage specified for merger in the partnership agreement; and

(2) in the case of a limited partnership that is a party to the merger, by the vote required for approval of a merger by the law of the State or foreign jurisdiction in which the limited partnership is organized and, in the absence of such a specifically applicable law, by all of the partners, notwithstanding a provision to the contrary in the partnership agreement.

(d) After a plan of merger is approved and before the merger takes effect, the plan may be amended or abandoned as provided in the plan.

(e) The merger takes effect on the later of:

(1) the approval of the plan of merger by all parties to the merger, as provided in subsection (c);

(2) the filing of all documents required by law to be filed as a condition to the effectiveness of the merger; or

(3) any effective date specified in the plan of merger.

§906.   Effect of Merger.

(a) When a merger takes effect:

(1) the separate existence of every partnership or limited partnership that is a party to the merger, other than the surviving entity, ceases;

(2) all property owned by each of the merged partnerships or limited partnerships vests in the surviving entity;

(3) all obligations of every partnership or limited partnership that is a party to the merger become the obligations of the surviving entity; and

(4) an action or proceeding pending against a partnership or limited partnership that is a party to the merger may be continued as if the merger had not occurred, or the surviving entity may be substituted as a party to the action or proceeding.

(b) The [Secretary of State] of this State is the agent for service of process in an action or proceeding against a surviving foreign partnership or limited partnership to enforce an obligation of a domestic partnership or limited partnership that is a party to a merger. The surviving entity shall promptly notify the [Secretary of State] of the mailing address of its chief executive office and of any change of address. Upon receipt of process, the [Secretary of State] shall mail a copy of the process to the surviving foreign partnership or limited partnership.

(c) A partner of the surviving partnership or limited partnership is liable for:

(1) all obligations of a party to the merger for which the partner was personally liable before the merger;

(2) all other obligations of the surviving entity incurred before the merger by a party to the merger, but those obligations may be satisfied only out of property of the entity; and

(3) except as otherwise provided in Section 306, all obligations of the surviving entity incurred after the merger takes effect, but those obligations may be satisfied only out of property of the entity if the partner is a limited partner.

(d) If the obligations incurred before the merger by a party to the merger are not satisfied out of the property of the surviving partnership or limited partnership, the general partners of that party immediately before the effective date of the merger shall contribute the amount necessary to satisfy that party's obligations to the surviving entity, in the manner provided in Section 807 or in the [Limited Partnership Act] of the jurisdiction in which the party was formed, as the case may be, as if the merged party were dissolved.

(e) A partner of a party to a merger who does not become a partner of the surviving partnership or limited partnership is dissociated from the entity, of which that partner was a partner, as of the date the merger takes effect. The surviving entity shall cause the partner's interest in the entity to be purchased under Section 701 or another statute specifically applicable to that partner's interest with respect to a merger. The surviving entity is bound under Section 702 by an act of a general partner dissociated under this subsection, and the partner is liable under Section 703 for transactions entered into by the surviving entity after the merger takes effect.

§907.   Statement of Merger.

(a) After a merger, the surviving partnership or limited partnership may file a statement that one or more partnerships or limited partnerships have merged into the surviving entity.

(b) A statement of merger must contain:

(1) the name of each partnership or limited partnership that is a party to the merger;

(2) the name of the surviving entity into which the other partnerships or limited partnership were merged;

(3) the street address of the surviving entity's chief executive office and of an office in this State, if any; and

(4) whether the surviving entity is a partnership or a limited partnership.

(c) Except as otherwise provided in subsection (d), for the purposes of Section 302, property of the surviving partnership or limited partnership which before the merger was held in the name of another party to the merger is property held in the name of the surviving entity upon filing a statement of merger.

(d) For the purposes of Section 302, real property of the surviving partnership or limited partnership which before the merger was held in the name of another party to the merger is property held in the name of the surviving entity upon recording a certified copy of the statement of merger in the office for recording transfers of that real property.

(e) A filed and, if appropriate, recorded statement of merger, executed and declared to be accurate pursuant to Section 105(c), stating the name of a partnership or limited partnership that is a party to the merger in whose name property was held before the merger and the name of the surviving entity, but not containing all of the other information required by subsection (b), operates with respect to the partnerships or limited partnerships named to the extent provided in subsections (c) and (d).

§908.   Nonexclusive.

This [article] is not exclusive. Partnerships or limited partnerships may be converted or merged in any other manner provided by law.

ARTICLE 10
LIMITED LIABILITY PARTNERSHIP

§1001.   Statement of Qualification.

(a) A partnership may become a limited liability partnership pursuant to this section.

(b) The terms and conditions on which a partnership becomes a limited liability partnership must be approved by the vote necessary to amend the partnership agreement except, in the case of a partnership agreement that expressly considers contribution obligations, the vote necessary to amend those provisions.

(c) After the approval required by subsection (b), a partnership may become a limited liability partnership by filing a statement of qualification. The statement must contain:

(1) the name of the partnership;

(2) the street address of the partnership's chief executive office and, if different, the street address of an office in this State, if any;

(3) if there is no office in this State, the name and street address of the partnership's agent for service of process who must be an individual resident of this State or any other person authorized to do business in this State;

(4) a statement that the partnership elects to be a limited liability partnership; and

(5) a deferred effective date, if any.

(d) The status of a partnership as a limited liability partnership is effective on the later of the filing of the statement or a date specified in the statement. The status remains effective, regardless of changes in the partnership, until it is canceled pursuant to Section 105(d) or revoked pursuant to Section 1003.

(e) The status of a partnership as a limited liability partnership and the liability of its partners is not affected by errors or later changes in the information required to be contained in the statement of qualification under subsection (c).

(f) The filing of a statement of qualification establishes that a partnership has satisfied all conditions precedent to the qualification of the partnership as a limited liability partnership.

(g) An amendment or cancellation of a statement of qualification is effective when it is filed or on a deferred effective date specified in the amendment or cancellation.

§1002.   Name.

The name of a limited liability partnership must end with "Registered Limited Liability Partnership," "Limited Liability Partnership," "R.L.L.P.," "L.L.P.," "RLLP," or "LLP."

§1003.   Annual Report.

(a) A limited liability partnership, and a foreign limited liability partnership authorized to transact business in this State, shall file an annual report in the office of the [Secretary of State] which contains:

(1) the name of the limited liability partnership and the State or other jurisdiction under whose laws the foreign limited liability partnership is formed;

(2) the current street address of the partnership's chief executive office and, if different, the current street address of an office in this State, if any; and

(3) if there is no current office in this State, the name and street address of the partnership's current agent for service of process who must be an individual resident of this State or any other person authorized to do business in this State.

(b) An annual report must be filed between [January 1 and April 1] of each year following the calendar year in which a partnership files a statement of qualification or a foreign partnership becomes authorized to transact business in this State.

(c) The [Secretary of State] may administratively revoke the statement of qualification of a partnership that fails to file an annual report when due or to pay the required filing fee. The [Secretary of State] shall provide the partnership at least 60 days' written notice of intent to revoke the statement. The notice must be mailed to the partnership at its chief executive office set forth in the last filed statement of qualification or annual report. The notice must specify the annual report that has not been filed, the fee that has not been paid, and the effective date of the revocation. The revocation is not effective if the annual report is filed and the fee is paid before the effective date of the revocation.

(d) A revocation under subsection (c) only affects a partnership's status as a limited liability partnership and is not an event of dissolution of the partnership.

(e) A partnership whose statement of qualification has been administratively revoked may apply to the [Secretary of State] for reinstatement within two years after the effective date of the revocation. The application must state:

(1) the name of the partnership and the effective date of the revocation; and

(2) that the ground for revocation either did not exist or has been corrected.

(f) A reinstatement under subsection (e) relates back to and takes effect as of the effective date of the revocation, and the partnership's status as a limited liability partnership continues as if the revocation had never occurred.

ARTICLE 11
FOREIGN LIMITED LIABILITY PARTNERSHIP

§1101.   Law Governing Foreign Limited Liability Partnership.

(a) The laws under which a foreign limited liability partnership is formed govern relations among the partners and between the partners and the partnership and the liability of partners for obligations of the partnership.

(b) A foreign limited liability partnership may not be denied a statement of foreign qualification by reason of any difference between the laws under which the partnership was formed and the laws of this State.

(c) A statement of foreign qualification does not authorize a foreign limited liability partnership to engage in any business or exercise any power that a partnership may not engage in or exercise in this State as a limited liability partnership.

§1102.   Statement of Foreign Qualification.

(a) Before transacting business in this State, a foreign limited liability partnership must file a statement of foreign qualification. The statement must contain:

(1) the name of the foreign limited liability partnership which satisfies the requirements of the State or other jurisdiction under whose laws it is formed and ends with "Registered Limited Liability Partnership," "Limited Liability Partnership," "R.L.L.P.," "L.L.P.," "RLLP," or "LLP."

(2) the street address of the partnership's chief executive office and, if different, the street address of an office in this State, if any;

(3) if there is no office in this State, the name and street address of the partnership's agent for service of process who must be an individual resident of this State or any other person authorized to do business in this State; and

(4) a deferred effective date, if any.

(b) The status of a partnership as a foreign limited liability partnership is effective on the later of the filing of the statement of foreign qualification or a date specified in the statement. The status remains effective, regardless of changes in the partnership, until it is canceled pursuant to Section 105(d) or revoked pursuant to Section 1003.

(c) An amendment or cancellation of a statement of foreign qualification is effective when it is filed or on a deferred effective date specified in the amendment or cancellation.

§1103.   Effect of Failure to Qualify.

(a) A foreign limited liability partnership transacting business in this State may not maintain an action or proceeding in this State unless it has in effect a statement of foreign qualification.

(b) The failure of a foreign limited liability partnership to have in effect a statement of foreign qualification does not impair the validity of a contract or act of the foreign limited liability partnership or preclude it from defending an action or proceeding in this State.

(c) Limitations on personal liability of partners are not waived solely by transacting business in this State without a statement of foreign qualification.

(d) If a foreign limited liability partnership transacts business in this State without a statement of foreign qualification, the [Secretary of State] is its agent for service of process with respect to [claims for relief] arising out of the transaction of business in this State.

§1104.   Activities Not Constituting Transacting Business.

(a) Activities of a foreign limited liability partnership which do not constitute transacting business within the meaning of this [article] include:

(1) maintaining, defending, or settling an action or proceeding;

(2) holding meetings of its partners or carrying on any other activity concerning its internal affairs;

(3) maintaining bank accounts;

(4) maintaining offices or agencies for the transfer, exchange, and registration of the partnership's own securities or maintaining trustees or depositories with respect to those securities;

(5) selling through independent contractors;

(6) soliciting or obtaining orders, whether by mail or through employees or agents or otherwise, if the orders require acceptance outside this State before they become contracts;

(7) creating or acquiring indebtedness, mortgages, or security interests in real or personal property;

(8) securing or collecting debts or foreclosing mortgages or other security interests in property securing the debts, and holding, protecting, and maintaining property so acquired;

(9) conducting an isolated transaction that is completed within 30 days and is not one in the course of similar transactions of like nature; and

(10) transacting business in interstate commerce.

(b) For purposes of this [article], the ownership in this State of income-producing real property or tangible personal property, other than property excluded under subsection (a), constitutes transacting business in this State.

(c) This section does not apply in determining the contacts or activities that may subject a foreign limited liability partnership to service of process, taxation, or regulation under any other law of this State.

§1105.   Action by [Attorney General].

The [Attorney General] may maintain an action to restrain a foreign limited liability partnership from transacting business in this State in violation of this [article].

ARTICLE 12
MISCELLANEOUS PROVISIONS

§1201.   Uniformity of Application and Construction.

This [Act] shall be applied and construed to effectuate its general purpose to make uniform the law with respect to the subject of this [Act] among States enacting it.

§1202.   Short Title.

This [Act] may be cited as the Uniform Partnership Act (1994).

§1203.   Severability Clause.

If any provision of this [Act] or its application to any person or circumstance is held invalid, the invalidity does not affect other provisions or applications of this [Act] which can be given effect without the invalid provision or application, and to this end the provisions of this [Act] are severable.

§1204.   Effective Date.

This [Act] takes effect _____.

§1205.   Repeals.

Effective January 1, 199__, the following acts and parts of acts are repealed: [the State Partnership Act as amended and in effect immediately before the effective date of this [Act]].

§1206.   Applicability.

(a) Before January 1, 199__, this [Act] governs only a partnership formed:

(1) after the effective date of this [Act], unless that partnership is continuing the business of a dissolved partnership under [Section 41 of the prior Uniform Partnership Act]; and

(2) before the effective date of this [Act], that elects, as provided by subsection (c), to be governed by this [Act].

(b) After January 1, 199__, this [Act] governs all partnerships.

(c) Before January 1, 199__, a partnership voluntarily may elect, in the manner provided in its partnership agreement or by law for amending the partnership agreement, to be governed by this [Act]. The provisions of this [Act] relating to the liability of the partnership's partners to third parties apply to limit those partners' liability to a third party who had done business with the partnership within one year preceding the partnership's election to be governed by this [Act], only if the third party knows or has received a notification of the partnership's election to be governed by this [Act].

§1207.   Savings Clause.

This [Act] does not affect an action or proceeding commenced or right accrued before this [Act] takes effect.

[Sections 1208 through 1211 are necessary only for jurisdictions adopting Uniform Limited Liability Partnership Act Amendments after previously adopting Uniform Partnership Act (1994)]

§1208.   Effective Date.

These [Amendments] take effect _____.

§1209.   Repeals.

Effective January 1, 199__, the following acts and parts of acts are repealed: [the Limited Liability Partnership amendments to the State Partnership Act as amended and in effect immediately before the effective date of these [Amendments]].

§1210.   Applicability.

(a) Before January 1, 199__, these [Amendments] govern only a limited liability partnership formed:

(1) after the effective date of these [Amend-

ments], unless that partnership is continuing the business of a dissolved limited liability partnership; and

(2) before the effective date of these [Amendments], that elects, as provided by subsection (c), to be governed by these [Amendments].

(b) After January 1, 199___, these [Amendments] govern all partnerships.

(c) Before January 1, 199___, a partnership voluntarily may elect, in the manner provided in its partnership agreement or by law for amending the partnership agreement, to be governed by these [Amendments]. The provisions of these [Amendments] relating to the liability of the partnership's partners to third parties apply to limit those partners' liability to a third party who had done business with the partnership within one year preceding the partnership's election to be governed by these [Amendments], only if the third party knows or has received a notification of the partnership's election to be governed by these [Amendments].

(d) The existing provisions for execution and filing a statement of qualification of a limited liability partnership continue until either the limited liability partnership elects to have this [Act] apply or January 1, 199___.

§1211.   Savings Clause.

These [Amendments] do not affect an action or proceeding commenced or right accrued before these [Amendments] take effect.

Uniform Limited Partnership Act (1976) with 1985 Amendments*

* The Uniform Limited Partnership Act has been reprinted through the permission of the National Conference of Commissioners on Uniform State Laws.

ARTICLE 1
GENERAL PROVISIONS

§101.   Definitions

As used in this [Act], unless the context otherwise requires:

(1) "Certificate of limited partnership" means the certificate referred to in Section 201, and the certificate as amended or restated.

(2) "Contribution" means any cash, property, services rendered, or a promissory note or other binding obligation to contribute cash or property or to per-

form services, which a partner contributes to a limited partnership in his capacity as a partner.

(3) "Event of withdrawal of a general partner" means an event that causes a person to cease to be a general partner as provided in Section 402.

(4) "Foreign limited partnership" means a partnership formed under the laws of any state other than this State and having as partners one or more general partners and one or more limited partners.

(5) "General partner" means a person who has been admitted to a limited partnership as a general partner in accordance with the partnership agreement and named in the certificate of limited partnership as a general partner.

(6) "Limited partner" means a person who has been admitted to a limited partnership as a limited partner in accordance with the partnership agreement.

(7) "Limited partnership" and "domestic limited partnership" mean a partnership formed by two or more persons under the laws of this State and having one or more general partners and one or more limited partners.

(8) "Partner" means a limited or general partner.

(9) "Partnership agreement" means any valid agreement, written or oral, of the partners as to the affairs of a limited partnership and the conduct of its business.

(10) "Partnership interest" means a partner's share of the profits and losses of a limited partnership and the right to receive distributions of partnership assets.

(11) "Person" means a natural person, partnership, limited partnership (domestic or foreign), trust, estate, association, or corporation.

(12) "State" means a state, territory, or possession of the United States, the District of Columbia, or the Commonwealth of Puerto Rico.

§102.   Name

The name of each limited partnership as set forth in its certificate of limited partnership:

(1) shall contain without abbreviation the words "limited partnership";

(2) may not contain the name of a limited partner unless (i) it is also the name of a general partner or the corporate name of a corporate general partner, or (ii) the business of the limited partnership had been

carried on under that name before the admission of that limited partner;

(3) may not be the same as, or deceptively similar to, the name of any corporation or limited partnership organized under the laws of this State or licensed or registered as a foreign corporation or limited partnership in this State; and

(4) may not contain the following words [here insert prohibited words].

§103. Reservation of Name

(a) The exclusive right to the use of a name may be reserved by:

(1) any person intended to organize a limited partnership under this [Act] and to adopt that name;

(2) any domestic limited partnership or any foreign limited partnership registered in this State which, in either case, intends to adopt that name;

(3) any foreign limited partnership intending to register in this State and adopt that name; and

(4) any person intending to organize a foreign limited partnership and intending to have it register in this State and adopt that name.

(b) The reservation shall be made by filing with the Secretary of State an application, executed by the applicant, to reserve a specified name. If the Secretary of State finds that the name is available for use by a domestic or foreign limited partnership, he [or she] shall reserve the name for the exclusive use of the applicant for a period of 120 days. Once having so reserved a name, the same applicant may not again reserve the same name until more than 60 days after the expiration of the last 120-day period for which that applicant reserved that name. The right to the exclusive use of a reserved name may be transferred to any other person by filing in the office of the Secretary of State a notice of the transfer, executed by the applicant for whom the name was reserved and specifying the name and address of the transferee.

§104. Specified Office and Agent

Each limited partnership shall continuously maintain in this State:

(1) an office, which may but need not be a place of its business in this State, at which shall be kept the records required by Section 105 to be maintained; and

(2) an agent for service of process on the limited partnership, which agent must be an individual resident of this State, a domestic corporation, or a foreign corporation authorized to do business in this State.

§105. Records to be Kept

(a) Each limited partnership shall keep at the office referred to in Section 104(1) the following:

(1) a current list of the full name and last known business address of each partner, separately identifying the general partners (in alphabetical order) and the limited partners (in alphabetical order);

(2) a copy of the certificate of limited partnership and all certificates of amendment thereto, together with executed copies of any powers of attorney pursuant to which any certificate has been executed;

(3) copies of the limited partnership's federal, state and local income tax returns and reports, if any, for the three most recent years;

(4) copies of any then effective written partnership agreements and of any financial statements of the limited partnership for the three most recent years; and

(5) unless contained in a written partnership agreement, a writing setting out:

(i) the amount of cash and a description and statement of the agreed value of the other property or services contributed by each partner and which each partner has agreed to contribute;

(ii) the times at which or events on the happening of which any additional contributions agreed to be made by each partner are to be made;

(iii) any right of a partner to receive, or of a general partner to make, distributions to a partner which include a return of all or any part of the partner's contribution; and

(iv) any events upon the happening of which the limited partnership is to be dissolved and its affairs wound up.

(b) Records kept under this section are subject to inspection and copying at the reasonable request and at the expense of any partner during ordinary business hours.

§106. Nature of Business

A limited partnership may carry on any business that a partnership without limited partners may carry on except [here designate prohibited activities].

§107. Business Transactions of Partner with Partnership

Except as provided in the partnership agreement, a partner may lend money to and transact other business with the limited partnership and, subject to other applicable law, has the same rights and obligations with respect thereto as a person who is not a partner.

ARTICLE 2
FORMATION; CERTIFICATE OF LIMITED PARTNERSHIP

§201. Certificate of Limited Partnership

(a) In order to form a limited partnership, a certificate of limited partnership must be executed and filed in the office of the Secretary of State. The certificate shall set forth:

(1) the name of the limited partnership;

(2) the address of the office and the name and address of the agent for service of process required to be maintained by Section 104;

(3) the name and the business address of each general partner;

(4) the latest date upon which the limited partnership is to dissolve; and

(5) any other matters the general partners determine to include therein.

(b) A limited partnership is formed at the time of the filing of the certificate of limited partnership in the office of the Secretary of State or at any later time specified in the certificate of limited partnership if, in either case, there has been substantial compliance with the requirements of this section.

§202. Amendment to Certificate

(a) A certificate of limited partnership is amended by filing a certificate of amendment thereto in the office of the Secretary of State. The certificate shall set forth:

(1) the name of the limited partnership;

(2) the date of filing the certificate; and

(3) the amendment to the certificate.

(b) Within 30 days after the happening of any of the following events, an amendment to a certificate of limited partnership reflecting the occurrence of the event or events shall be filed:

(1) the admission of a new general partner;

(2) the withdrawal of a general partner; or

(3) the continuation of the business under Section 801 after an event of withdrawal of a general partner.

(c) A general partner who becomes aware that any statement in a certificate of limited partnership was false when made or that any arrangements or other facts described have changed, making the certificate inaccurate in any respect, shall promptly amend the certificate.

(d) A certificate of limited partnership may be amended at any time for any other proper purpose the general partners determine.

(e) No person has any liability because an amendment to a certificate of limited partnership has not been filed to reflect the occurrence of any event referred to in subsection (b) of this section if the amendment is filed within the 30-day period specified in subsection (b).

(f) A restated certificate of limited partnership may be executed and filed in the same manner as a certificate of amendment.

§203. Cancellation of Certificate

A certificate of limited partnership shall be cancelled upon the dissolution and the commencement of winding up of the partnership or at any other time there are no limited partners. A certificate of cancellation shall be filed in the office of the Secretary of State and set forth:

(1) the name of the limited partnership;

(2) the date of filing of its certificate of limited partnership;

(3) the reason for filing the certificate of cancellation;

(4) the effective date (which shall be a date certain) of cancellation if it is not to be effective upon the filing of the certificate; and

(5) any other information the general partners filing the certificate determine.

§204. Execution of Certificates

(a) Each certificate required by this Article to be filed in the office of the Secretary of State shall be executed in the following manner:

(1) an original certificate of limited partnership must be signed by all general partners;

(2) a certificate of amendment must be signed by at least one general partner and by each other general partner designated in the certificate as a new general partner; and

(3) a certificate of cancellation must be signed by all general partners.

(b) Any person may sign a certificate by an attorney-in-fact, but a power of attorney to sign a certificate relating to the admission of a general partner must specifically describe the admission.

(c) The execution of a certificate by a general partner constitutes an affirmation under the penalties of perjury that the facts stated therein are true.

§205.   Execution by Judicial Act

If a person required by Section 204 to execute any certificate fails or refuses to do so, any other person who is adversely affected by the failure or refusal may petition the [designate the appropriate court] to direct the execution of the certificate. If the court finds that it is proper for the certificate to be executed and that any person so designated has failed or refused to execute the certificate, it shall order the Secretary of State to record an appropriate certificate.

§206.   Filing in Office of Secretary of State

(a) Two signed copies of the certificate of limited partnership and of any certificates of amendment or cancellation (or of any judicial decree of amendment or cancellation) shall be delivered to the Secretary of State. A person who executes a certificate as an agent or fiduciary need not exhibit evidence of his [or her] authority as a prerequisite to filing. Unless the Secretary of State finds that any certificate does not conform to law, upon receipt of all filing fees required by law he [or she] shall:

(1) endorse on each duplicate original the word "Filed" and the day, month, and year of the filing thereof;

(2) file one duplicate original in his [or her] office; and

(3) return the other duplicate original to the person who filed it or his [or her] representative.

(b) Upon the filing of a certificate of amendment (or judicial decree of amendment) in the office of the Secretary of State, the certificate of limited partnership shall be amended as set forth therein, and upon the effective date of a certificate of cancellation (or a judicial decree thereof), the certificate of limited partnership is cancelled.

§207.   Liability for False Statement in Certificate

If any certificate of limited partnership or certificate of amendment or cancellation contains a false statement, one who suffers loss by reliance on the statement may recover damages for the loss from:

(1) any person who executes the certificate, or causes another to execute it on his behalf, and knew, and any general partner who knew or should have known, the statement to be false at the time the certificate was executed; and

(2) any general partner who thereafter knows or should have known that any arrangement or other fact described in the certificate has changed, making the statement inaccurate in any respect within a sufficient time before the statement was relied upon reasonably to have enabled that general partner to cancel or amend the certificate, or to file a petition for its cancellation or amendment under Section 205.

§208.   Scope of Notice

The fact that a certificate of limited partnership is on file in the office of the Secretary of State is notice that the partnership is a limited partnership and the persons designated therein as general partners are general partners, but it is not notice of any other fact.

§209.   Delivery of Certificates to Limited Partners

Upon the return by the Secretary of State pursuant to Section 206 of a certificate marked "Filed," the general partners shall promptly deliver or mail a copy of the certificate of limited partnership and each certificate of amendment or cancellation to each limited partner unless the partnership agreement provides otherwise.

ARTICLE 3
LIMITED PARTNERS

§301.   Admission of Limited Partners

(a) A person becomes a limited partner:

(1) at the time the limited partnership is formed; or

(2) at any later time specified in the records of the limited partnership for becoming a limited partner.

(b) After the filing of a limited partnership's original certificate of limited partnership, a person may be admitted as an additional limited partner:

(1) in the case of a person acquiring a partnership interest directly from the limited partnership, upon compliance with the partnership agreement or, if the partnership agreement does not so provide, upon the written consent of all partners; and

(2) in the case of an assignee of a partnership interest of a partner who has the power, as provided in Section 704, to grant the assignee the right to become a limited partner, upon the exercise of that power and compliance with any conditions limiting the grant or exercise of the power.

§302.   Voting

Subject to Section 303, the partnership agreement may grant to all or a specified group of the limited partners the right to vote (on a per capita or other basis) upon any matter.

§303.   Liability to Third Parties

(a) Except as provided in subsection (d), a limited partner is not liable for the obligations of a limited partnership unless he [or she] is also a general partner or, in addition to the exercise of his [or her] rights and powers as a limited partner, he [or she] participates in the control of the business. However, if the limited partner participates in the control of the business, he [or she] is liable only to persons who transact business with the limited partnership reasonably believing, based upon the limited partner's conduct, that the limited partner is a general partner.

(b) A limited partner does not participate in the control of the business within the meaning of subsection (a) solely by doing one or more of the following:

(1) being a contractor for or an agent or employee of the limited partnership or of a general partner or being an officer, director, or shareholder of a general partner that is a corporation;

(2) consulting with and advising a general partner with respect to the business of the limited partnership;

(3) acting as surety for the limited partnership or guaranteeing or assuming one or more specific obligations of the limited partnership;

(4) taking any action required or permitted by law to bring or pursue a derivative action in the right of the limited partnership;

(5) requesting or attending a meeting of partners;

(6) proposing, approving, or disapproving, by voting or otherwise, one or more of the following matters:

(i) the dissolution and winding up of the limited partnership;

(ii) the sale, exchange, lease, mortgage, pledge, or other transfer of all or substantially all of the assets of the limited partnership;

(iii) the incurrence of indebtedness by the limited partnership other than in the ordinary course of its business;

(iv) a change in the nature of the business;

(v) the admission or removal of a general partner;

(vi) the admission or removal of a limited partner;

(vii) a transaction involving an actual or potential conflict of interest between a general partner and the limited partnership or the limited partners;

(viii) an amendment to the partnership agreement or certificate of limited partnership; or

(ix) matters related to the business of the limited partnership not otherwise enumerated in this subsection (b), which the partnership agreement states in writing may be subject to the approval or disapproval of limited partners;

(7) winding up the limited partnership pursuant to Section 803; or

(8) exercising any right or power permitted to limited partners under this [Act] and not specifically enumerated in this subsection (b).

(c) The enumeration in subsection (b) does not mean that the possession or exercise of any other powers by a limited partner constitutes participation by him [or her] in the business of the limited partnership.

(d) A limited partner who knowingly permits his [or her] name to be used in the name of the limited partnership, except under circumstances permitted by Section 102(2), is liable to creditors who extend credit to the limited partnership without actual knowledge that the limited partner is not a general partner.

§304.   Person Erroneously Believing Himself [or Herself] Limited Partner

(a) Except as provided in subsection (b), a person who makes a contribution to a business enterprise and erroneously but in good faith believes that he [or she] has become a limited partner in the enterprise is not a general partner in the enterprise and is not bound by its obligations by reason of making the contribution, receiving distributions from the enterprise, or exercising any rights of a limited partner, if, on ascertaining the mistake, he [or she]:

(1) causes an appropriate certificate of limited partnership or a certificate of amendment to be executed and filed; or

(2) withdraws from future equity participation in the enterprise by executing and filing in the office of the Secretary of State a certificate declaring withdrawal under this section.

(b) A person who makes a contribution of the kind described in subsection (a) is liable as a general partner to any third party who transacts business with the enterprise (i) before the person withdraws and an appropriate certificate is filed to show withdrawal, or (ii) before an appropriate certificate is filed to show that he [or she] is not a general partner, but in either case only if the third party actually believed in good faith that the person was a general partner at the time of the transaction.

§305.   Information

Each limited partner has the right to:

(1) inspect and copy any of the partnership records required to be maintained by Section 105; and

(2) obtain from the general partners from time to time upon reasonable demand (i) true and full information regarding the state of the business and financial condition of the limited partnership, (ii) promptly after becoming available, a copy of the limited partnership's federal, state, and local income tax returns for each year, and (iii) other information regarding the affairs of the limited partnership as is just and reasonable.

ARTICLE 4
GENERAL PARTNERS

§401.   Admission of Additional General Partners

After the filing of a limited partnership's original certificate of limited partnership, additional general partners may be admitted as provided in writing in the partnership agreement or, if the partnership agreement does not provide in writing for the admission of additional general partners, with the written consent of all partners.

§402.   Events of Withdrawal

Except as approved by the specific written consent of all partners at the time, a person ceases to be a general partner of a limited partnership upon the happening of any of the following events:

(1) the general partner withdraws from the limited partnership as provided in Section 602;

(2) the general partner ceases to be a member of the limited partnership as provided in Section 702;

(3) the general partner is removed as a general partner in accordance with the partnership agreement;

(4) unless otherwise provided in writing in the partnership agreement, the general partner: (i) makes an assignment for the benefit of creditors; (ii) files a voluntary petition in bankruptcy; (iii) is adjudicated a bankrupt or insolvent; (iv) files a petition or answer seeking for himself [or herself] any reorganization, arrangement, composition, readjustment, liquidation, dissolution, or similar relief under any statute, law, or regulation; (v) files an answer or other pleading admitting or failing to contest the material allegations of a petition filed against him [or her] in any proceeding of this nature; or (vi) seeks, consents to, or acquiesces in the appointment of a trustee, receiver, or liquidator of the general partner or of all or any substantial part of his [or her] properties;

(5) unless otherwise provided in writing in the partnership agreement, [120] days after the commencement of any proceeding against the general partner seeking reorganization, arrangement, composition, readjustment, liquidation, dissolution, or similar relief under any statute, law, or regulation, the proceeding has not been dismissed, or if within [90] days after the appointment without his [or her] consent or acquiescence of a trustee, receiver, or liquidator of the general partner or of all or any substantial part of his [or her] properties, the appointment is not vacated or stayed or within [90] days after the expiration of any such stay, the appointment is not vacated;

(6) in the case of a general partner who is a natural person,

(i) his [or her] death; or

(ii) the entry of an order by a court of competent jurisdiction adjudicating him [or her] incompetent to manage his [or her] person or his [or her] estate;

(7) in the case of a general partner who is acting as a general partner by virtue of being a trustee of a trust, the termination of the trust (but not merely the substitution of a new trustee);

(8) in the case of a general partner that is a separate partnership, the dissolution and commencement of winding up of the separate partnership;

(9) in the case of a general partner that is a corporation, the filing of a certificate of dissolution, or its equivalent, for the corporation or the revocation of its charter; or

(10) in the case of an estate, the distribution by the fiduciary of the estate's entire interest in the partnership.

§403.   General Powers and Liabilities

(a) Except as provided in this [Act] or in the partnership agreement, a general partner of a limited partnership has the rights and powers and is subject to the restrictions of a partner in a partnership without limited partners.

(b) Except as provided in this [Act], a general partner of a limited partnership has the liabilities of a partner in a partnership without limited partners to persons other than the partnership and the other partners. Except as provided in this [Act] or in the partnership agreement, a general partner of a limited partnership has the liabilities of a partner in a partnership without limited partners to the partnership and to the other partners.

§404.   Contributions by General Partner

A general partner of a limited partnership may make contributions to the partnership and share in the profits and losses of, and in distributions from, the limited partnership as a general partner. A general partner also may make contributions to and share in profits, losses, and distributions as a limited partner. A person who is both a general partner and a limited partner has the rights and powers, and is subject to the restrictions and liabilities, of a general partner and, except as provided in the partnership agreement, also has the powers, and is subject to the restrictions, of a limited partner to the extent of his [or her] participation in the partnership as a limited partner.

§405.   Voting

The partnership agreement may grant to all or certain identified general partners the right to vote (on a per capita or any other basis), separately or with all or any class of the limited partners, on any matter.

ARTICLE 5
FINANCE

§501.   Form of Contribution

The contribution of a partner may be in cash, property, or services rendered, or a promissory note or other obligation to contribute cash or property or to perform services.

§502.   Liability for Contribution

(a) A promise by a limited partner to contribute to the limited partnership is not enforceable unless set out in a writing signed by the limited partner.

(b) Except as provided in the partnership agreement, a partner is obligated to the limited partnership to perform any enforceable promise to contribute cash or property or to perform services, even if he [or she] is unable to perform because of death, disability, or any other reason. If a partner does not make the required contribution of property or services, he [or she] is obligated at the option of the limited partnership to contribute cash equal to that portion of the value, as stated in the partnership records required to be kept pursuant to Section 105, of the stated contribution which has not been made.

(c) Unless otherwise provided in the partnership agreement, the obligation of a partner to make a contribution or return money or other property paid or distributed in violation of this [Act] may be compromised only by consent of all partners. Notwithstanding the compromise, a creditor of a limited partnership who extends credit or otherwise acts in reliance on that obligation after the partner signs a writing which reflects the obligation and before the amendment or cancellation thereof to reflect the compromise, may enforce the original obligation.

§503.   Sharing of Profits and Losses

The profits and losses of a limited partnership shall be allocated among the partners, and among classes of partners, in the manner provided in writing in the partnership agreement. If the partnership agreement does not so provide in writing, profits and losses shall be allocated on the basis of the value, as stated in the partnership records required to be kept pursuant to Section 105, of the contributions made by each partner to the extent they have been received by the partnership and have not been returned.

§504.   Sharing of Distributions

Distributions of cash or other assets of a limited partnership shall be allocated among the partners and among classes of partners in the manner provided in writing in the partnership agreement. If the partnership agreement does not so provide in writing, distributions shall be made on the basis of the value, as stated in the partnership records required to be kept pursuant to Section 105, of the contributions made by each partner to the extent they have been received by the partnership and have not been returned.

ARTICLE 6
DISTRIBUTIONS AND WITHDRAWAL

§601.   Interim Distributions

Except as provided in this Article, a partner is entitled to receive distributions from a limited partnership before his [or her] withdrawal from the limited partnership and before the dissolution and winding up thereof to the extent and at the times or upon the happening of the events specified in the partnership agreement.

§602.   Withdrawal of General Partner

A general partner may withdraw from a limited partnership at any time by giving written notice to the other partners, but if the withdrawal violates the partnership agreement, the limited partnership may recover from the withdrawing general partner damages for breach of the partnership agreement and offset the damages against the amount otherwise distributable to him [or her].

§603.   Withdrawal of Limited Partner

A limited partner may withdraw from a limited partnership at the time or upon the happening of events specified in writing in the partnership agreement. If the agreement does not specify in writing the time or the events upon the happening of which a limited partner may withdraw or a definite time for the dissolution and winding up of the limited partnership, a limited partner may withdraw upon not less than six months' prior written notice to each general partner at his [other] address on the books of the limited partnership at its office in this State.

§604.   Distribution Upon Withdrawal

Except as provided in this Article, upon withdrawal any withdrawing partner is entitled to receive any distribution to which he [or she] is entitled under the partnership agreement and, if not otherwise provided in the agreement, he [or she] is entitled to receive, within a reasonable time after withdrawal, the fair value of his [or her] interest in the limited partnership as of the date of withdrawal based upon his [or her] right to share in distributions from the limited partnership.

§605.   Distribution in Kind

Except as provided in writing in the partnership agreement, a partner, regardless of the nature of his [or her] contribution, has no right to demand and receive any distribution from a limited partnership in any form other than cash. Except as provided in writing in the partnership agreement, a partner may not be compelled to accept a distribution of any asset in kind from a limited partnership to the extent that the percentage of the asset distributed to him [or her] exceeds a percentage of that asset which is equal to the percentage in which he [or she] shares in distributions from the limited partnership.

§606.   Right to Distribution

At the time a partner becomes entitled to receive a distribution, he [or she] has the status of, and is entitled to all remedies available to, a creditor of the limited partnership with respect to the distribution.

§607.   Limitations on Distribution

A partner may not receive a distribution from a limited partnership to the extent that, after giving effect to the distribution, all liabilities of the limited partnership, other than liabilities to partners on account of their partnership interests, exceed the fair value of the partnership assets.

§608.   Liability Upon Return of Contribution

(a) If a partner has received the return of any part of his [or her] contribution without violation of the partnership agreement or this [Act], he [or she] is liable to the limited partnership for a period of one year thereafter for the amount of the returned contribution, but only to the extent necessary to discharge the limited partnership's liabilities to creditors who extended credit to the limited partnership during the period the contribution was held by the partnership.

(b) If a partner has received the return of any part of his [or her] contribution in violation of the partnership agreement or this [Act], he [or she] is liable to the limited partnership for a period of six years thereafter for the amount of the contribution wrongfully returned.

(c) A partner receives a return of his [or her] contribution to the extent that a distribution to him [or her] reduces his [or her] share of the fair value of the net assets of the limited partnership below the value, as set forth in the partnership records required to be kept pursuant to Section 105, of his contribution which has not been distributed to him [or her].

ARTICLE 7
ASSIGNMENT OF PARTNERSHIP INTERESTS

§701.   Nature of Partnership Interest

A partnership interest is personal property.

§702.   Assignment of Partnership Interest

Except as provided in the partnership agreement, a partnership interest is assignable in whole or in part. An assignment of a partnership interest does not dissolve a limited partnership or entitle the assignee to become or to exercise any rights of a partner. An assignment entitles the assignee to receive, to the extent assigned, only the distribution to which the assignor would be entitled. Except as provided in the partnership agreement, a partner ceases to be a partner upon assignment of all his [or her] partnership interest.

§703.   Rights of Creditor

On application to a court of competent jurisdiction by any judgment creditor of a partner, the court may charge the partnership interest of the partner with payment of the unsatisfied amount of the judgment with interest. To the extent so charged, the judgment creditor has only the rights of an assignee of the partnership interest. This [Act] does not deprive any partner of the benefit of any exemption laws applicable to his [or her] partnership interest.

§704.   Right of Assignee to Become Limited Partner

(a) An assignee of a partnership interest, including an assignee of a general partner, may become a limited partner if and to the extent that (i) the assignor gives the assignee that right in accordance with authority described in the partnership agreement, or (ii) all other partners consent.

(b) An assignee who has become a limited partner has, to the extent assigned, the rights and powers, and is subject to the restrictions and liabilities, of a limited partner under the partnership agreement and this [Act]. An assignee who becomes a limited partner also is liable for the obligations of his [or her] assignor to make and return contributions as provided in Articles 5 and 6. However, the assignee is not obligated for liabilities unknown to the assignee at the time he [or she] became a limited partner.

(c) If an assignee of a partnership interest becomes a limited partner, the assignor is not released from his [or her] liability to the limited partnership under Sections 207 and 502.

§705.   Power of Estate of Deceased or Incompetent Partner

If a partner who is an individual dies or a court of competent jurisdiction adjudges him [or her] to be incompetent to manage his [or her] person or his [or her] property, the partner's executor, administrator, guardian, conservator, or other legal representative may exercise all of the partner's rights for the purpose of settling his [or her] estate or administering his [or her] property, including any power the partner had to give an assignee the right to become a limited partner. If a partner is a corporation, trust, or other entity and is dissolved or terminated, the powers of that partner may be exercised by its legal representative or successor.

ARTICLE 8
DISSOLUTION

§801.   Nonjudicial Dissolution

A limited partnership is dissolved and its affairs shall be wound up upon the happening of the first to occur of the following:

(1) at the time specified in the certificate of limited partnership;

(2) upon the happening of events specified in writing in the partnership agreement;

(3) written consent of all partners;

(4) an event of withdrawal of a general partner unless at the time there is at least one other general partner and the written provisions of the partnership agreement permit the business of the limited partnership to be carried on by the remaining general partner and that partner does so, but the limited partnership is not dissolved and is not required to be wound up by reason of any event of withdrawal if, within 90 days after the withdrawal, all partners agree in writing to continue the business of the limited partnership and to the appointment of one or more additional general partners if necessary or desired; or

(5) entry of a decree of judicial dissolution under Section 802.

§802.   Judicial Dissolution

On application by or for a partner the [designate the appropriate court] court may decree dissolution of a limited partnership whenever it is not reasonably practicable to carry on the business in conformity with the partnership agreement.

§803.   Winding Up

Except as provided in the partnership agreement, the general partners who have not wrongfully dissolved a limited partnership or, if none, the limited partners, may wind up the limited partnership's affairs; but the [designate the appropriate court] court may wind up the limited partnership's affairs upon application of any partner, his [or her] legal representative, or assignee.

§804.   Distribution of Assets

Upon the winding up of a limited partnership, the assets shall be distributed as follows:

(1) to creditors, including partners who are creditors, to the extent permitted by law in satisfaction of liabilities of the limited partnership other than liabilities for distributions to partners under Section 601 or 604;

(2) except as provided in the partnership agreement, to partners and former partners in satisfaction of liabilities for distributions under Section 601 and 604; and

(3) except as provided in the partnership agreement, to partners first for the return of their contri-

butions and secondly respecting their partnership interests, in the proportions in which the partners share in distributions.

ARTICLE 9
FOREIGN LIMITED PARTNERSHIPS

§901.   Law Governing

Subject to the Constitution of this State, (i) the laws of the state under which a foreign limited partnership is organized govern its organization and internal affairs and the liability of its limited partners, and (ii) a foreign limited partnership may not be denied registration by reason of any difference between those laws and the laws of this State.

§902.   Registration

Before transacting business in this State, a foreign limited partnership shall register with the Secretary of State. In order to register, a foreign limited partnership shall submit to the Secretary of State, in duplicate, an application for registration as a foreign limited partnership, signed and sworn to by a general partner and setting forth:

(1) the name of the foreign limited partnership and, if different, the name under which it proposes to register and transact business in this State;

(2) the State and date of its formation;

(3) the name and address of any agent for service of process on the foreign limited partnership whom the foreign limited partnership elects to appoint; the agent must be an individual resident of this State, a domestic corporation, or a foreign corporation having a place of business in, and authorized to do business in, this State;

(4) a statement that the Secretary of State is appointed the agent of the foreign limited partnership for service of process if no agent has been appointed under paragraph (3) or, if appointed, the agent's authority has been revoked or if the agent cannot be found or served with the exercise of reasonable diligence;

(5) the address of the office required to be maintained in the state of its organization by the laws of that state or, if not so required, of the principal office of the foreign limited partnership;

(6) the name and business address of each general partner; and

(7) the address of the office at which is kept a list of the names and addresses of the limited partners and their capital contributions, together with an undertaking by the foreign limited partnership to keep those records until the foreign limited partnership's registration in this State is cancelled or withdrawn.

§903.   Issuance of Registration

(a) If the Secretary of State finds that an application for registration conforms to law and all requisite fees have been paid, he [or she] shall:

(1) endorse on the application the word "Filed", and the month, day, and year of the filing thereof;

(2) file in his [or her] office a duplicate original of the application; and

(3) issue a certificate of registration to transact business in this State.

(b) The certificate of registration, together with a duplicate original of the application, shall be returned to the person who filed the application or his [or her] representative.

§904.   Name

A foreign limited partnership may register with the Secretary of State under any name, whether or not it is the name under which it is registered in its state of organization, that includes without abbreviation the words "limited partnership" and that could be registered by a domestic limited partnership.

§905.   Changes and Amendments

If any statement in the application for registration of a foreign limited partnership was false when made or any arrangements or other facts described have changed, making the application inaccurate in any respect, the foreign limited partnership shall promptly file in the office of the Secretary of State a certificate, signed and sworn to by a general partner, correcting such statement.

§906.   Cancellation of Registration

A foreign limited partnership may cancel its registration by filing with the Secretary of State a certificate of cancellation signed and sworn to by a general partner. A cancellation does not terminate the authority of the Secretary of State to accept service of process on the foreign limited partnership with respect to [claims for relief]

[causes of action] arising out of the transactions of business in this State.

§907.   Transaction of Business Without Registration

(a) A foreign limited partnership transacting business in this State may not maintain any action, suit, or proceeding in any court of this State until it has registered in this State.

(b) The failure of a foreign limited partnership to register in this State does not impair the validity of any contract or act of the foreign limited partnership or prevent the foreign limited partnership from defending any action, suit, or proceeding in any court of this State.

(c) A limited partner of a foreign limited partnership is not liable as a general partner of the foreign limited partnership solely by reason of having transacted business in this State without registration.

(d) A foreign limited partnership, by transacting business in this State without registration, appoints the Secretary of State as its agent for service of process with respect to [claims for relief] [causes of action] arising out of the transaction of business in this State.

§908.   Action by [Appropriate Official]

The [designate the appropriate official] may bring an action to restrain a foreign limited partnership from transacting business in this State in violation of this Article.

ARTICLE 10
DERIVATIVE ACTIONS

§1001.   Right of Action

A limited partner may bring an action in the right of a limited partnership to recover a judgment in favor if general partners with authority to do so have refused to bring the action or if an effort to cause those general partners to bring the action is not likely to succeed.

§1002.   Proper Plaintiff

In a derivative action, the plaintiff must be a partner at the time of bringing the action and (i) must have been a partner at the time of the transaction of which he [or she] complains or (ii) his [or her] status as a partner must have devolved upon him [or her] by operation of law or pursuant to the terms of the partnership agreement from a person who was a partner at the time of the transaction.

§1003.   Pleading

In a derivative action, the complaint shall set forth with particularity the effort of the plaintiff to secure initiation of the action by a general partner or the reasons for not making the effort.

§1004.   Expenses

If a derivative action is successful, in whole or in part, or if anything is received by the plaintiff as a result of a judgment, compromise, or settlement of an action or claim, the court may award the plaintiff reasonable expenses, including reasonable attorney's fees, and shall direct him [or her] to remit to the limited partnership the remainder of those proceeds received by him [or her].

ARTICLE 11
MISCELLANEOUS

§1101.   Construction and Application

This [Act] shall be so applied and construed to effectuate its general purpose to make uniform the law with respect to the subject of this [Act] among states enacting it.

§1102.   Short Title

This [Act] may be cited as the Uniform Limited Partnership Act.

§1103.   Severability

If any provision of this [Act] or its application to any person or circumstance is held invalid, the invalidity does not affect other provisions or applications of the [Act] which can be given effect without the invalid provision or application, and to this end the provisions of this [Act] are severable.

§1104.   Effective Date, Extended Effective Date and Repeal

Except as set forth below, the effective date of this [Act] is _____ and the following acts [list existing limited partnership acts] are hereby repealed:

(1) The existing provisions for execution and filing of certificates of limited partnerships and amendments thereunder and cancellations thereof continue in effect until [specify time required to create central filing system], the extended effective date, and Sections 102, 103, 104, 105, 201, 202, 203, 204 and 206 are not effective until the extended effective date.

(2) Section 402, specifying the conditions under which a general partner ceases to be a member of a limited partnership, is not effective until the extended effective date, and the applicable provisions of existing law continue to govern until the extended effective date.

(3) Sections 501, 502 and 608 apply only to contributions and distributions made after the effective date of this [Act].

(4) Section 704 applies only to assignments made after the effective date of this [Act].

(5) Article 9, dealing with registration of foreign limited partnerships, is not effective until the extended effective date.

(6) Unless otherwise agreed by the partners, the applicable provisions of existing law governing allocation of profits and losses (rather than the provisions of Section 503), distributions to a withdrawing partner (rather than the provisions of Section 604), and distributions of assets upon the winding up of a limited partnership (rather than the provisions of Section 804) govern limited partnerships formed before the effective date of this [Act].

§1105.   Rules for Cases Not Provided for in This [Act]

In any case not provided for in this [Act] the provisions of the Uniform Partnership Act govern.

§1106.   Savings Clause

The repeal of any statutory provision by this [Act] does not impair, or otherwise affect, the organization or the continued existence of a limited partnership existing at the effective date of this [Act], nor does the repeal of any existing statutory provision by this [Act] impair any contract or affect any right accrued before the effective date of this [Act].

Uniform Limited Liability Company Act (1995)*

*The Uniform Limited Liability Company Act (1995) has been reprinted through permission of the National Conference of Commissioners on Uniform State Laws.

ARTICLE 1   GENERAL PROVISIONS

Section 101.   Definitions.

In this [Act]:

(1) "Articles of organization" means initial, amended, and restated articles of organization and articles of merger. In the case of a foreign limited liabil-

ity company, the term includes all records serving a similar function required to be filed in the office of the [Secretary of State] or other official having custody of company records in the State or country under whose law it is organized.

(2) "At-will company" means a limited liability company other than a term company.

(3) "Business" includes every trade, occupation, profession, and other lawful purpose, whether or not carried on for profit.

(4) "Debtor in bankruptcy" means a person who is the subject of an order for relief under Title 11 of the United States Code or a comparable order under a successor statute of general application or a comparable order under federal, state, or foreign law governing insolvency.

(5) "Distribution" means a transfer of money, property, or other benefit from a limited liability company to a member in the member's capacity as a member or to a transferee of the member's distributional interest.

(6) "Distributional interest" means all of a member's interest in distributions by the limited liability company.

(7) "Entity" means a person other than an individual.

(8) "Foreign limited liability company" means an unincorporated entity organized under laws other than the laws of this State which afford limited liability to its owners comparable to the liability under Section 303 and is not required to obtain a certificate of authority to transact business under any law of this State other than this [Act].

(9) "Limited liability company" means a limited liability company organized under this [Act].

(10) "Manager" means a person, whether or not a member of a manager-managed company, who is vested with authority under Section 301.

(11) "Manager-managed company" means a limited liability company which is so designated in its articles of organization.

(12) "Member-managed company" means a limited liability company other than a manager-managed company.

(13) "Operating agreement" means the agreement under Section 103 concerning the relations among the members, managers, and limited liability company. The term includes amendments to the agreement.

(14) "Person" means an individual, corporation, business trust, estate, trust, partnership, limited liability company, association, joint venture, government, governmental subdivision, agency, or instrumentality, or any other legal or commercial entity.

(15) "Principal office" means the office, whether or not in this State, where the principal executive office of a domestic or foreign limited liability company is located.

(16) "Record" means information that is inscribed on a tangible medium or that is stored in an electronic or other medium and is retrievable in perceivable form.

(17) "Sign" means to identify a record by means of a signature, mark, or other symbol, with intent to authenticate it.

(18) "State" means a State of the United States, the District of Columbia, the Commonwealth of Puerto Rico, or any territory or insular possession subject to the jurisdiction of the United States.

(19) "Term company" means a limited liability company in which its members have agreed to remain members until the expiration of a term specified in the articles of organization.

(20) "Transfer" includes an assignment, conveyance, deed, bill of sale, lease, mortgage, security interest, encumbrance, and gift.

Section 102.   Knowledge and Notice.

(a) A person knows a fact if the person has actual knowledge of it.

(b) A person has notice of a fact if the person:

(1) knows the fact;

(2) has received a notification of the fact; or

(3) has reason to know the fact exists from all of the facts known to the person at the time in question.

(c) A person notifies or gives a notification of a fact to another by taking steps reasonably required to inform the other person in ordinary course, whether or not the other person knows the fact.

(d) A person receives a notification when the notification:

(1) comes to the person's attention; or

(2) is duly delivered at the person's place of business or at any other place held out by the person as a place for receiving communications.

(e) An entity knows, has notice, or receives a notification of a fact for purposes of a particular transaction when the individual conducting the transaction for the entity knows, has notice, or receives a notification of the fact, or in any event when the fact would have been brought to the individual's attention had the entity exercised reasonable diligence. An entity exercises reasonable diligence if it maintains reasonable routines for communicating significant information to the individual conducting the transaction for the entity and there is reasonable compliance with the routines. Reasonable diligence does not require an individual acting for the entity to communicate information unless the communication is part of the individual's regular duties or the individual has reason to know of the transaction and that the transaction would be materially affected by the information.

Section 103.   Effect of Operating Agreement; Nonwaivable Provisions.

(a) Except as otherwise provided in subsection (b), all members of a limited liability company may enter into an operating agreement, which need not be in writing, to regulate the affairs of the company and the conduct of its business, and to govern relations among the members, managers, and company. To the extent the operating agreement does not otherwise provide, this [Act] governs relations among the members, managers, and company.

(b) The operating agreement may not:

(1) unreasonably restrict a right to information or access to records under Section 408;

(2) eliminate the duty of loyalty under Section 409(b) or 603(b)(3), but the agreement may:

(i) identify specific types or categories of activities that do not violate the duty of loyalty, if not manifestly unreasonable; and

(ii) specify the number or percentage of members or disinterested managers that may authorize or ratify, after full disclosure of all material facts, a specific act or transaction that otherwise would violate the duty of loyalty;

(3) unreasonably reduce the duty of care under Section 409(c) or 603(b)(3);

(4) eliminate the obligation of good faith and fair dealing under Section 409(d), but the operating agreement may determine the standards by which the performance of the obligation is to be measured, if the standards are not manifestly unreasonable;

(5) vary the right to expel a member in an event specified in Section 601(6);

(6) vary the requirement to wind up the limited liability company's business in a case specified in Section 801(b)(4) or (b)(5); or

(7) restrict rights of a person, other than a manager, member, and transferee of a member's distributional interest, under this [Act].

Section 104.   Supplemental Principles of Law.

(a) Unless displaced by particular provisions of this [Act], the principles of law and equity supplement this [Act].

(b) If an obligation to pay interest arises under this [Act] and the rate is not specified, the rate is that specified in [applicable statute].

Section 105.   Name.

(a) The name of a limited liability company must contain "limited liability company" or "limited company" or the abbreviation "L.L.C.," "LLC," "L.C.," or "LC." "Limited" may be abbreviated as "Ltd.," and "company" may be abbreviated as "Co.".

(b) Except as authorized by subsections (c) and (d), the name of a limited liability company must be distinguishable upon the records of the [Secretary of State] from:

(1) the name of any corporation, limited partnership, or company incorporated, organized or authorized to transact business, in this State;

(2) a name reserved or registered under Section 106 or 107;

(3) a fictitious name approved under Section 1005 for a foreign company authorized to transact business in this State because its real name is unavailable.

(c) A limited liability company may apply to the [Secretary of State] for authorization to use a name that is not distinguishable upon the records of the [Secretary of State] from one or more of the names described in subsection (b). The [Secretary of State] shall authorize use of the name applied for if:

(1) the present user, registrant, or owner of a reserved name consents to use in a record and submits an undertaking in form satisfactory to the [Secretary of State] to change the name to a name that is distinguishable upon the records of the [Secretary of State] from the name applied for; or

(2) the applicant delivers to the [Secretary of State] a certified copy of the final judgment of a court of competent jurisdiction establishing the applicant's right to use the name applied for in this State.

(d) A limited liability company may use the name, including a fictitious name, of another domestic or foreign company which is used in this State if the other company is organized or authorized to transact business in this State and the company proposing to use the name has:

(1) merged with the other company;

(2) been formed by reorganization with the other company; or

(3) acquired substantially all of the assets, including the name, of the other company.

Section 106.   Reserved Name.

(a) A person may reserve the exclusive use of the name of a limited liability company, including a fictitious name for a foreign company whose name is not available, by delivering an application to the [Secretary of State] for filing. The application must set forth the name and address of the applicant and the name proposed to be reserved. If the [Secretary of State] finds that the name applied for is available, it must be reserved for the applicant's exclusive use for a nonrenewable 120-day period.

(b) The owner of a name reserved for a limited liability company may transfer the reservation to another person by delivering to the [Secretary of State] a signed notice of the transfer which states the name and address of the transferee.

Section 107.   Registered Name.

(a) A foreign limited liability company may register its name subject to the requirements of Section 1005, if the name is distinguishable upon the records of the [Secretary of State] from names that are not available under Section 105(b).

(b) A foreign limited liability company registers its name, or its name with any addition required by Section 1005, by delivering to the [Secretary of State] for filing an application:

(1) setting forth its name, or its name with any addition required by Section 1005, the State or country and date of its organization, and a brief de-

scription of the nature of the business in which it is engaged; and

(2) accompanied by a certificate of existence, or a record of similar import, from the State or country of organization.

(c) A foreign limited liability company whose registration is effective may renew it for successive years by delivering for filing in the office of the [Secretary of State] a renewal application complying with subsection (b) between October 1 and December 31, of the preceding year. The renewal application renews the registration for the following calendar year.

(d) A foreign limited liability company whose registration is effective may qualify as a foreign company under its name or consent in writing to the use of its name by a limited liability company later organized under this [Act] or by another foreign company later authorized to transact business in this State. The registered name terminates when the limited liability company is organized or the foreign company qualifies or consents to the qualification of another foreign company under the registered name.

Section 108.   Designated Office and Agent for Service of Process.

(a) A limited liability company and a foreign limited liability company authorized to do business in this State shall designate and continuously maintain in this State:

(1) an office, which need not be a place of its business in this State; and

(2) an agent and street address of the agent for service of process on the company.

(b) An agent must be an individual resident of this State, a domestic corporation, another limited liability company, or a foreign corporation or foreign company authorized to do business in this State.

Section 109.   Change of Designated Office or Agent for Service of Process.

A limited liability company may change its designated office or agent for service of process by delivering to the [Secretary of State] for filing a statement of change which sets forth:

(1) the name of the company;

(2) the street address of its current designated office;

(3) if the current designated office is to be changed, the street address of the new designated office;

(4) the name and address of its current agent for service of process; and

(5) if the current agent for service of process or street address of that agent is to be changed, the new address or the name and street address of the new agent for service of process.

Section 110.   Resignation of Agent for Service of Process.

(a) An agent for service of process of a limited liability company may resign by delivering to the [Secretary of State] for filing a record of the statement of resignation.

(b) After filing a statement of resignation, the [Secretary of State] shall mail a copy to the designated office and another copy to the limited liability company at its principal office.

(c) An agency is terminated on the 31st day after the statement is filed in the office of the [Secretary of State].

Section 111.   Service of Process.

(a) An agent for service of process appointed by a limited liability company or a foreign limited liability company is an agent of the company for service of any process, notice, or demand required or permitted by law to be served upon the company.

(b) If a limited liability company or foreign limited liability company fails to appoint or maintain an agent for service of process in this State or the agent for service of process cannot with reasonable diligence be found at the agent's address, the [Secretary of State] is an agent of the company upon whom process, notice, or demand may be served.

(c) Service of any process, notice, or demand on the [Secretary of State] may be made by delivering to and leaving with the [Secretary of State], the [Assistant Secretary of State], or clerk having charge of the limited liability company department of the [Secretary of State's] office duplicate copies of the process, notice, or demand. If the process, notice, or demand is served on the [Secretary of State], the [Secretary of State] shall forward one of the copies by registered or certified mail, return receipt requested, to the company at its designated office. Service is effected under this subsection at the earliest of:

(1) the date the company receives the process, notice, or demand;

(2) the date shown on the return receipt, if signed on behalf of the company; or

(3) five days after its deposit in the mail, if mailed postpaid and correctly addressed.

(d) The [Secretary of State] shall keep a record of all processes, notices, and demands served pursuant to this section and record the time of and the action taken regarding the service.

(e) This section does not affect the right to serve process, notice, or demand in any manner otherwise provided by law.

Section 112.   Nature of Business and Powers.

(a) A limited liability company may be organized under this [Act] for any lawful purpose, subject to any law of this State governing or regulating business.

(b) Unless its articles of organization provide otherwise, a limited liability company has the same powers as an individual to do all things necessary or convenient to carry on its business or affairs, including power to:

(1) sue and be sued, and defend in its name;

(2) purchase, receive, lease, or otherwise acquire, and own, hold, improve, use, and otherwise deal with real or personal property, or any legal or equitable interest in property, wherever located;

(3) sell, convey, mortgage, grant a security interest in, lease, exchange, and otherwise encounter or dispose of all or any part of its property;

(4) purchase, receive, subscribe for, or otherwise acquire, own, hold, vote, use, sell, mortgage, lend, grant a security interest in, or otherwise dispose of and deal in and with, shares or other interests in or obligations of any other entity;

(5) make contracts and guarantees, incur liabilities, borrow money, issue its notes, bonds, and other obligations, which may be convertible into or include the option to purchase other securities of the limited liability company, and secure any of its obligations by a mortgage on or a security interest in any of its property, franchises, or income;

(6) lend money, invest and reinvest its funds, and receive and hold real and personal property as security for repayment;

(7) be a promoter, partner, member, associate, or manager of any partnership, joint venture, trust, or other entity;

(8) conduct its business, locate offices, and exercise the powers granted by this [Act] within or without this State;

(9) elect managers and appoint officers, employees, and agents of the limited liability company, define their duties, fix their compensation, and lend them money and credit;

(10) pay pensions and establish pension plans, pension trusts, profit sharing plans, bonus plans, option plans, and benefit or incentive plans for any or all of its current or former members, managers, officers, employees, and agents;

(11) make donations for the public welfare or for charitable, scientific, or educational purposes; and

(12) make payments or donations, or do any other act, not inconsistent with law, that furthers the business of the limited liability company.

ARTICLE 2   ORGANIZATION

Section 201.   Limited Liability Company as Legal Entity.

A limited liability company is a legal entity distinct from its members.

Section 202.   Organization.

(a) One or more persons may organize a limited liability company, consisting of one or more members, by delivering articles of organization to the office of the [Secretary of State] for filing.

(b) Unless a delayed effective date is specified, the existence of a limited liability company begins when the articles of organization are filed.

(c) The filing of the articles of organization by the [Secretary of State] is conclusive proof that the organizers satisfied all conditions precedent to the creation of a limited liability company.

Section 203.   Articles of Organization.

(a) Articles of organization of a limited liability company must set forth:

(1) the name of the company;

(2) the address of the initial designated office;

(3) the name and street address of the initial agent for service of process;

(4) the name and address of each organizer;

(5) whether the company is to be a term company and, if so, the term specified;

(6) whether the company is to be manager-managed, and, if so, the name and address of each initial manager; and

(7) whether one or more of the members of the company are to be liable for its debts and obligations under Section 303(c).

(b) Articles of organization of a limited liability company may set forth:

(1) provisions permitted to be set forth in an operating agreement; or

(2) other matters not inconsistent with law.

(c) Articles of organization of a limited liability company may not vary the nonwaivable provisions of Section 103(b). As to all other matters, if any provision of an operating agreement is inconsistent with the articles of organization:

(1) the operating agreement controls as to managers, members, and members' transferees; and

(2) the articles of organization control as to persons, other than managers, members and their transferees, who reasonably rely on the articles to their detriment.

Section 204.   Amendment or Restatement of Articles of Organization.

(a) Articles of organization of a limited liability company may be amended at any time by delivering articles of amendment to the [Secretary of State] for filing. The articles of amendment must set forth the:

(1) name of the limited liability company;

(2) date of filing of the articles of organization; and

(3) amendment to the articles.

(b) A limited liability company may restate its articles of organization at any time. Restated articles of organization must be signed and filed in the same manner as articles of amendment. Restated articles of organization must be designated as such in the heading and state in the heading or in an introductory paragraph the limited liability company's present name and, if it has been changed, all of its former names and the date of the filing of its initial articles of organization.

Section 205.   Signing of Records.

(a) Except as otherwise provided in this [Act], a record to be filed by or on behalf of a limited liability company in the office of the [Secretary of State] must be signed in the name of the company by a:

(1) manager of a manager-managed company;

(2) member of a member-managed company;

(3) person organizing the company, if the company has not been formed; or

(4) fiduciary, if the company is in the hands of a receiver, trustee, or other court-appointed fiduciary.

(b) A record signed under subsection (a) must state adjacent to the signature the name and capacity of the signer.

(c) Any person may sign a record to be filed under subsection (a) by an attorney-in-fact. Powers of attorney relating to the signing of records to be filed under subsection (a) by an attorney-in-fact need not be filed in the office of the [Secretary of State] as evidence of authority by the person filing but must be retained by the company.

Section 206.   Filing in Office of [Secretary of State].

(a) Articles of organization or any other record authorized to be filed under this [Act] must be in a medium permitted by the [Secretary of State] and must be delivered to the office of the [Secretary of State]. Unless the [Secretary of State] determines that a record fails to comply as to form with the filing requirements of this [Act], and if all filing fees have been paid, the [Secretary of State] shall file the record and send a receipt for the record and the fees to the limited liability company or its representative.

(b) Upon request and payment of a fee, the [Secretary of State] shall send to the requester a certified copy of the requested record.

(c) Except as otherwise provided in subsection (d) and Section 207(c), a record accepted for filing by the [Secretary of State] is effective:

(1) at the time of filing on the date it is filed, as evidenced by the [Secretary of State's] date and time endorsement on the original record; or

(2) at the time specified in the record as its effective time on the date it is filed.

(d) A record may specify a delayed effective time and date, and if it does so the record becomes effective at the time and date specified. If a delayed effective date but no time is specified, the record is effective at the close of business on that date. If a delayed effective date is later than the 90th day after the record is filed, the record is effective on the 90th day.

Section 207.   Correcting Filed Record.

(a) A limited liability company or foreign limited liability company may correct a record filed by the [Secretary of State] if the record contains a false or erroneous statement or was defectively signed.

(b) A record is corrected:

(1) by preparing articles of correction that:

(i) describe the record, including its filing date, or attach a copy of it to the articles of correction;

(ii) specify the incorrect statement and the reason it is incorrect or the manner in which the signing was defective; and

(iii) correct the incorrect statement or defective signing; and

(2) by delivering the corrected record to the [Secretary of State] for filing.

(c) Articles of correction are effective retroactively on the effective date of the record they correct except as to persons relying on the uncorrected record and adversely affected by the correction. As to those persons, articles of correction are effective when filed.

Section 208.   Certificate of Existence or Authorization.

(a) A person may request the [Secretary of State] to furnish a certificate of existence for a limited liability company or a certificate of authorization for a foreign limited liability company.

(b) A certificate of existence for a limited liability company must set forth:

(1) the company's name;

(2) that it is duly organized under the laws of this State, the date of organization, whether its duration is at-will or for a specified term, and, if the latter, the period specified;

(3) if payment is reflected in the records of the [Secretary of State] and if nonpayment affects the existence of the company, that all fees, taxes, and penalties owed to this State have been paid;

(4) whether its most recent annual report required by Section 211 has been filed with the [Secretary of State];

(5) that articles of termination have not been filed; and

(6) other facts of record in the office of the [Secretary of State] which may be requested by the applicant.

(c) A certificate of authorization for a foreign limited liability company must set forth:

(1) the company's name used in this State;

(2) that it is authorized to transact business in this State;

(3) if payment is reflected in the records of the [Secretary of State] and if nonpayment affects the authorization of the company, that all fees, taxes, and penalties owed to this State have been paid;

(4) whether its most recent annual report required by Section 211 has been filed with the [Secretary of State];

(5) that a certificate of cancellation has not been filed; and

(6) other facts of record in the office of the [Secretary of State] which may be requested by the applicant.

(d) Subject to any qualification stated in the certificate, a certificate of existence or authorization issued by the [Secretary of State] may be relied upon as conclusive evidence that the domestic or foreign limited liability company is in existence or is authorized to transact business in this State.

Section 209. Liability for False Statement in Filed Record.

If a record authorized or required to be filed under this [Act] contains a false statement, one who suffers loss by reliance on the statement may recover damages for the loss from a person who signed the record or caused

another to sign it on the person's behalf and knew the statement to be false at the time the record was signed.

Section 210. Filing by Judicial Act.

If a person required by Section 205 to sign any record fails or refuses to do so, any other person who is adversely affected by the failure or refusal may petition the [designate the appropriate court] to direct the signing of the record. If the court finds that it is proper for the record to be signed and that a person so designated has failed or refused to sign the record, it shall order the [Secretary of State] to sign and file an appropriate record.

Section 211. Annual Report for [Secretary of State].

(a) A limited liability company, and a foreign limited liability company authorized to transact business in this State, shall deliver to the [Secretary of State] for filing an annual report that sets forth:

(1) the name of the company and the State or country under whose law it is organized;

(2) the address of its designated office and the name and address of its agent for service of process in this State;

(3) the address of its principal office; and

(4) the names and business addresses of any managers.

(b) Information in an annual report must be current as of the date the annual report is signed on behalf of the limited liability company.

(c) The first annual report must be delivered to the [Secretary of State] between [January 1 and April 1] of the year following the calendar year in which a limited liability company was organized or a foreign company was authorized to transact business. Subsequent annual reports must be delivered to the [Secretary of State] between [January 1 and April 1] of the ensuing calendar years.

(d) If an annual report does not contain the information required in subsection (a), the [Secretary of State] shall promptly notify the reporting limited liability company or foreign limited liability company and return the report to it for correction. If the report is corrected to contain the information required in subsection (a) and delivered to the [Secretary of State] within 30 days after the effective date of the notice, it is timely filed.

ARTICLE 3   RELATIONS OF MEMBERS AND MANAGERS TO PERSONS DEALING WITH LIMITED LIABILITY COMPANY

Section 301.   Agency of Members and Managers.

(a) Subject to subsections (b) and (c):

(1) Each member is an agent of the limited liability company for the purpose of its business, and an act of a member, including the signing of an instrument in the company's name, for apparently carrying on in the ordinary course the company's business or business of the kind carried on by the company binds the company, unless the member had no authority to act for the company in the particular matter and the person with whom the member was dealing knew or had notice that the member lacked authority.

(2) An act of a member which is not apparently for carrying on in the ordinary course the company's business or business of the kind carried on by the company binds the company only if the act was authorized by the other members.

(b) Subject to subsection (c), in a manager-managed company:

(1) A member is not an agent of the company for the purpose of its business solely by reason of being a member. Each manager is an agent of the company for the purpose of its business, and an act of a manager, including the signing of an instrument in the company's name, for apparently carrying on in the ordinary course the company's business or business of the kind carried on by the company binds the company, unless the manager had no authority to act for the company in the particular matter and the person with whom the manager was dealing knew or had notice that the manager lacked authority.

(2) An act of a manager which is not apparently for carrying on in the ordinary course the company's business or business of the kind carried on by the company binds the company only if the act was authorized under Section 404.

(c) Unless the articles of organization limit their authority, any member of a member-managed company or manager of a manager-managed company may sign and deliver any instrument transferring or affecting the company's interest in real property. The instrument is conclusive in favor of a person who gives value without knowledge of the lack of the authority of the person signing and delivering the instrument.

Section 302.   Limited Liability Company Liable for Member's or Manager's Actionable Conduct.

A limited liability company is liable for loss or injury caused to a person, or for a penalty incurred, as a result of a wrongful act or omission, or other actionable conduct, of a member or manager acting in the ordinary course of business of the company or with authority of the company.

Section 303.   Liability of Members and Managers.

(a) Except as otherwise provided in subsection (c), the debts, obligations, and liabilities of a limited liability company, whether arising in contract, tort, or otherwise, are solely the debts, obligations, and liabilities of the company. A member or manager is not personally liable for a debt, obligation, or liability of the company solely by reason of being or acting as a member or manager.

(b) The failure of a limited liability company to observe the usual company formalities or requirements relating to the exercise of its company powers or management of its business is not a ground for imposing personal liability on the members or managers for liabilities of the company.

(c) All or specified members of a limited liability company are liable in their capacity as members for all or specified debts, obligations, or liabilities of the company if:

(1) a provision to that effect is contained in the articles of organization; and

(2) a member so liable has consented in writing to the adoption of the provision or to be bound by the provision.

ARTICLE 4   RELATIONS OF MEMBERS TO EACH OTHER AND TO LIMITED LIABILITY COMPANY

Section 401.   Form of Contribution.

A contribution of a member of a limited liability company may consist of tangible or intangible property or other benefit to the company, including money, promissory notes, services performed, or other agreements to contribute cash or property, or contracts for services to be performed.

Section 402.   Member's Liability for Contributions.

(a) A member's obligation to contribute money, property, or other benefit to, or to perform services for, a limited liability company is not excused by the member's death, disability, or other inability to perform personally. If a member does not make the required contribution of property or services, the member is obliged at the option of the company to contribute money equal to the value of that portion of the stated contribution which has not been made.

(b) A creditor of a limited liability company who extends credit or otherwise acts in reliance on an obligation described in subsection (a), and without notice of any compromise under Section 404(c)(5), may enforce the original obligation.

Section 403.   Member's and Manager's Rights to Payments and Reimbursement.

(a) A limited liability company shall reimburse a member or manager for payments made and indemnify a member or manager for liabilities incurred by the member or manager in the ordinary course of the business of the company or for the preservation of its business or property.

(b) A limited liability company shall reimburse a member for an advance to the company beyond the amount of contribution the member agreed to make.

(c) A payment or advance made by a member which gives rise to an obligation of a limited liability company under subsection (a) or (b) constitutes a loan to the company upon which interest accrues from the date of the payment or advance.

(d) A member is not entitled to remuneration for services performed for a limited liability company, except for reasonable compensation for services rendered in winding up the business of the company.

Section 404.   Management of Limited Liability Company.

(a) In a member-managed company:

(1) each member has equal rights in the management and conduct of the company's business; and

(2) except as otherwise provided in subsection (c) or in Section 801(b)(3)(i), any matter relating to the business of the company may be decided by a majority of the members.

(b) In a manager-managed company:

(1) each manager has equal rights in the management and conduct of the company's business;

(2) except as otherwise provided in subsection (c) or in Section 801(b)(3)(i), any matter relating to the business of the company may be exclusively decided by the manager or, if there is more than one manager, by a majority of the managers; and

(3) a manager:

(i) must be designated, appointed, elected, removed, or replaced by a vote, approval, or consent of a majority of the members; and

(ii) holds office until a successor has been elected and qualified, unless the manager sooner resigns or is removed.

(c) The only matters of a member or manager-managed company's business requiring the consent of all of the members are:

(1) the amendment of the operating agreement under Section 103;

(2) the authorization or ratification of acts or transactions under Section 103(b)(2)(ii) which would otherwise violate the duty of loyalty;

(3) an amendment to the articles of organization under Section 204;

(4) the compromise of an obligation to make a contribution under Section 402(b);

(5) the compromise, as among members, of an obligation of a member to make a contribution or return money or other property paid or distributed in violation of this [Act];

(6) the making of interim distributions under Section 405(a), including the redemption of an interest;

(7) the admission of a new member;

(8) the use of the company's property to redeem an interest subject to a charging order;

(9) the consent to dissolve the company under Section 801(b)(2);

(10) a waiver of the right to have the company's business wound up and the company terminated under Section 802(b);

(11) the consent of members to merge with another entity under Section 904(c)(1); and

(12) the sale, lease, exchange, or other disposal of all, or substantially all, of the company's property with or without goodwill.

(d) Action requiring the consent of members or managers under this [Act] may be taken without a meeting.

(e) A member or manager may appoint a proxy to vote or otherwise act for the member or manager by signing an appointment instrument, either personally or by the member's or manager's attorney-in-fact.

Section 405.   Sharing of and Right to Distributions.

(a) Any distributions made by a limited liability company before its dissolution and winding up must be in equal shares.

(b) A member has no right to receive, and may not be required to accept, a distribution in kind.

(c) If a member becomes entitled to receive a distribution, the member has the status of, and is entitled to all remedies available to, a creditor of the limited liability company with respect to the distribution.

Section 406.   Limitations on Distributions.

(a) A distribution may not be made if:

(1) the limited liability company would not be able to pay its debts as they become due in the ordinary course of business; or

(2) the company's total assets would be less than the sum of its total liabilities plus the amount that would be needed, if the company were to be dissolved, wound up, and terminated at the time of the distribution, to satisfy the preferential rights upon dissolution, winding up, and termination of members whose preferential rights are superior to those receiving the distribution.

(b) A limited liability company may base a determination that a distribution is not prohibited under subsection (a) on financial statements prepared on the basis of accounting practices and principles that are reasonable in the circumstances or on a fair valuation or other method that is reasonable in the circumstances.

(c) Except as otherwise provided in subsection (e), the effect of a distribution under subsection (a) is measured:

(1) in the case of distribution by purchase, redemption, or other acquisition of a distributional interest in a limited liability company, as of the date money or other property is transferred or debt incurred by the company; and

(2) in all other cases, as of the date the:

(i) distribution is authorized if the payment occurs within 120 days after the date of authorization; or

(ii) payment is made if it occurs more than 120 days after the date of authorization.

(d) A limited liability company's indebtedness to a member incurred by reason of a distribution made in accordance with this section is at parity with the company's indebtedness to its general, unsecured creditors.

(e) Indebtedness of a limited liability company, including indebtedness issued in connection with or as part of a distribution, is not considered a liability for purposes of determinations under subsection (a) if its terms provide that payment of principal and interest are made only if and to the extent that payment of a distribution to members could then be made under this section. If the indebtedness is issued as a distribution, each payment of principal or interest on the indebtedness is treated as a distribution, the effect of which is measured on the date the payment is made.

Section 407.   Liability for Unlawful Distributions.

(a) A member of a member-managed company or a member or manager of a manager-managed company who votes for or assents to a distribution made in violation of Section 406, the articles of organization, or the operating agreement is personally liable to the company for the amount of the distribution which exceeds the amount that could have been distributed without violating Section 406, the articles of organization, or the operating agreement if it is established that the member or manager did not perform the member's or manager's duties in compliance with Section 409.

(b) A member of a manager-managed company who knew a distribution was made in violation of Section 406, the articles of organization, or the operating agreement is personally liable to the company, but only to the extent that the distribution received by the member exceeded the amount that could have been properly paid under Section 406.

(c) A member or manager against whom an action is brought under this section may implead in the action all:

(1) other members or managers who voted for or assented to the distribution in violation of subsection (a) and may compel contribution from them; and

(2) members who received a distribution in violation of subsection (b) and may compel contribution from the member in the amount received in violation of subsection (b).

(d) A proceeding under this section is barred unless it is commenced within two years after the distribution.

Section 408.   Member's Right to Information.

(a) A limited liability company shall provide members and their agents and attorneys access to its records, if any, at the company's principal office or other reasonable locations specified in the operating agreement. The company shall provide former members and their agents and attorneys access for proper purposes to records pertaining to the period during which they were members. The right of access provides the opportunity to inspect and copy records during ordinary business hours. The company may impose a reasonable charge, limited to the costs of labor and material, for copies of records furnished.

(b) A limited liability company shall furnish to a member, and to the legal representative of a deceased member or member under legal disability:

(1) without demand, information concerning the company's business or affairs reasonably required for the proper exercise of the member's rights and performance of the member's duties under the operating agreement or this [Act]; and

(2) on demand, other information concerning the company's business or affairs, except to the extent the demand or the information demanded is unreasonable or otherwise improper under the circumstances.

(c) A member has the right upon written demand given to the limited liability company to obtain at the company's expense a copy of any written operating agreement.

Section 409.   General Standards of Member's and Manager's Conduct.

(a) The only fiduciary duties a member owes to a member-managed company and its other members are the duty of loyalty and the duty of care imposed by subsections (b) and (c).

(b) A member's duty of loyalty to a member-managed company and its other members is limited to the following:

(1) to account to the company and to hold as trustee for it any property, profit, or benefit derived by the member in the conduct or winding up of the company's business or derived from a use by the member of the company's property, including the appropriation of a company's opportunity;

(2) to refrain from dealing with the company in the conduct or winding up of the company's business as or on behalf of a party having an interest adverse to the company; and

(3) to refrain from competing with the company in the conduct of the company's business before the dissolution of the company.

(c) A member's duty of care to a member-managed company and its other members in the conduct of and winding up of the company's business is limited to refraining from engaging in grossly negligent or reckless conduct, intentional misconduct, or a knowing violation of law.

(d) A member shall discharge the duties of a member-managed company and its other members under this [Act] or under the operating agreement and exercise any rights consistently with the obligation of good faith and fair dealing.

(e) A member of a member-managed company does not violate a duty or obligation under this [Act] or under the operating agreement merely because the member's conduct furthers the member's own interest.

(f) A member of a member-managed company may lend money to and transact other business with the company. As to each loan or transaction, the rights and obligations of the member are the same as those of a person who is not a member, subject to other applicable law.

(g) This section applies to a person winding up the limited liability company's business as the personal or legal representative of the last surviving member as if the person were a member.

(h) In a manager-managed company:

(1) a member who is not also a manager owes no duties to the company or to the other members solely by reason of being a member;

(2) a manager is held to the same standards of conduct prescribed for members in subsections (b) through (f);

(3) a member who pursuant to the operating

agreement exercises some or all of the rights of a manager in the management and conduct of the company's business is held to the standards of conduct in subsections (b) through (f) to the extent that the member exercises the managerial authority vested in a manager by this [Act]; and

(4) a manager is relieved of liability imposed by law for violation of the standards prescribed by subsections (b) through (f) to the extent of the managerial authority delegated to the members by the operating agreement.

Section 410.   Actions by Members.

(a) A member may maintain an action against a limited liability company or another member for legal or equitable relief, with or without an accounting as to the company's business, to enforce:

(1) the member's rights under the operating agreement;

(2) the member's rights under this [Act]; and

(3) the rights and otherwise protect the interests of the member, including rights and interests arising independently of the member's relationship to the company.

(b) The accrual, and any time limited for the assertion, of a right of action for a remedy under this section is governed by other law. A right to an accounting upon a dissolution and winding up does not revive a claim barred by law.

Section 411.   Continuation of Term Company after Expiration of Specified Term.

(a) If a term company is continued after the expiration of the specified term, the rights and duties of the members and managers remain the same as they were at the expiration of the term except to the extent inconsistent with rights and duties of members and managers of an at-will company.

(b) If the members in a member-managed company or the managers in a manager-managed company continue the business without any winding up of the business of the company, it continues as an at-will company.

ARTICLE 5   TRANSFEREES AND CREDITORS OF MEMBER

Section 501.   Member's Distributional Interest.

(a) A member is not a co-owner of, and has no transferable interest in, property of a limited liability company.

(b) A distributional interest in a limited liability company is personal property and, subject to Sections 502 and 503, may be transferred in whole or in part.

(c) An operating agreement may provide that a distributional interest may be evidenced by a certificate of the interest issued by the limited liability company and, subject to Section 503, may also provide for the transfer of any interest represented by the certificate.

Section 502.   Transfer of Distributional Interest.

A transfer of a distributional interest does not entitle the transferee to become or to exercise any rights of a member. A transfer entitles the transferee to receive, to the extent transferred, only the distributions to which the transferor would be entitled.

Section 503.   Rights of Transferee.

(a) A transferee of a distributional interest may become a member of a limited liability company if and to the extent that the transferor gives the transferee the right in accordance with authority described in the operating agreement or all other members consent.

(b) A transferee who has become a member, to the extent transferred, has the rights and powers, and is subject to the restrictions and liabilities, of a member under the operating agreement of a limited liability company and this [Act]. A transferee who becomes a member also is liable for the transferor member's obligations to make contributions under Section 402 and for obligations under Section 407 to return unlawful distributions, but the transferee is not obligated for the transferor member's liabilities unknown to the transferee at the time the transferee becomes a member.

(c) Whether or not a transferee of a distributional interest becomes a member under subsection (a), the transferor is not released from liability to the limited liability company under the operating agreement or this [Act].

(d) A transferee who does not become a member is not entitled to participate in the management or conduct of the limited liability company's business, require access to information concerning the company's transactions, or inspect or copy any of the company's records.

(e) A transferee who does not become a member is entitled to:

(1) receive, in accordance with the transfer, distributions to which the transferor would otherwise be entitled;

(2) receive, upon dissolution and winding up of the limited liability company's business:

(i) in accordance with the transfer, the net amount otherwise distributable to the transferor;

(ii) a statement of account only from the date of the latest statement of account agreed to by all the members;

(3) seek under Section 801(b)(6) a judicial determination that it is equitable to dissolve and wind up the company's business.

(f) A limited liability company need not give effect to a transfer until it has notice of the transfer.

Section 504.   Rights of Creditor.

(a) On application by a judgment creditor of a member of a limited liability company or of a member's transferee, a court having jurisdiction may charge the distributional interest of the judgment debtor to satisfy the judgment. The court may appoint a receiver of the share of the distributions due or to become due to the judgment debtor and make all other orders, directions, accounts, and inquiries the judgment debtor might have made or which the circumstances may require to give effect to the charging order.

(b) A charging order constitutes a lien on the judgment debtor's distributional interest. The court may order a foreclosure of a lien on a distributional interest subject to the charging order at any time. A purchaser at the foreclosure sale has the rights of a transferee.

(c) At any time before foreclosure, a distributional interest in a limited liability company which is charged may be redeemed:

(1) by the judgment debtor;

(2) with property other than the company's property, by one or more of the other members; or

(3) with the company's property, but only if permitted by the operating agreement.

(d) This [Act] does not affect a member's right under exemption laws with respect to the member's distributional interest in a limited liability company.

(e) This section provides the exclusive remedy by which a judgment creditor of a member or a transferee may satisfy a judgment out of the judgment debtor's distributional interest in a limited liability company.

ARTICLE 6   MEMBER'S DISSOCIATION

Section 601.   Events Causing Member's Dissociation.

A member is dissociated from a limited liability company upon the occurrence of any of the following events:

(1) the company's having notice of the member's express will to withdraw upon the date of notice or on a later date specified by the member;

(2) an event agreed to in the operating agreement as causing the member's dissociation;

(3) upon transfer of all of a member's distributional interest, other than a transfer for security purposes or a court order charging the member's distributional interest which has not been foreclosed;

(4) the member's expulsion pursuant to the operating agreement;

(5) the member's expulsion by unanimous vote of the other members if:

(i) it is unlawful to carry on the company's business with the member;

(ii) there has been a transfer of substantially all of the member's distributional interest, other than a transfer for security purposes or a court order charging the member's distributional interest which has not been foreclosed;

(iii) within 90 days after the company notifies a corporate member that it will be expelled because it has filed a certificate of dissolution or the equivalent, its charter has been revoked, or its right to conduct business has been suspended by the jurisdiction of its incorporation, the member fails to obtain a revocation of the certificate of dissolution or a reinstatement of its charter or its right to conduct business; or

(iv) a partnership or a limited liability company that is a member has been dissolved and its business is being wound up;

(6) on application by the company or another member, the member's expulsion by judicial determination because the member:

(i) engaged in wrongful conduct that adversely and materially affected the company's business;

(ii) willfully or persistently committed a material breach of the operating agreement or of a duty owed to the company or the other members under Section 409; or

(iii) engaged in conduct relating to the company's business which makes it not reasonably practicable to carry on the business with the member;

(7) the member's:

(i) becoming a debtor in bankruptcy;

(ii) executing an assignment for the benefit of creditors;

(iii) seeking, consenting to, or acquiescing in the appointment of a trustee, receiver, or liquidator of the member or of all or substantially all of the member's property; or

(iv) failing, within 90 days after the appointment, to have vacated or stayed the appointment of a trustee, receiver, or liquidator of the member or of all or substantially all of the member's property obtained without the member's consent or acquiescence, or failing within 90 days after the expiration of a stay to have the appointment vacated;

(8) in the case of a member who is an individual:

(i) the member's death;

(ii) the appointment of a guardian or general conservator for the member; or

(iii) a judicial determination that the member has otherwise become incapable of performing the member's duties under the operating agreement;

(9) in the case of a member that is a trust or is acting as a member by virtue of being a trustee of a trust, distribution of the trust's entire rights to receive distributions from the company, but not merely by reason of the substitution of a successor trustee;

(10) in the case of a member that is an estate or is acting as a member by virtue of being a personal representative of an estate, distribution of the estate's en-

tire rights to receive distributions from the company, but not merely the substitution of a successor personal representative; or

(11) termination of the existence of a member if the member is not an individual, estate, or trust other than a business trust.

Section 602.   Member's Power to Dissociate; Wrongful Dissociation.

(a) Unless otherwise provided in the operating agreement, a member has the power to dissociate from a limited liability company at any time, rightfully or wrongfully, by express will pursuant to Section 601(1).

(b) If the operating agreement has not eliminated a member's power to dissociate, the member's dissociation from a limited liability company is wrongful only if:

(1) it is in breach of an express provision of the agreement; or

(2) before the expiration of the specified term of a term company:

(i) the member withdraws by express will;

(ii) the member is expelled by judicial determination under Section 601(6);

(iii) the member is dissociated by becoming a debtor in bankruptcy; or

(iv) in the case of a member who is not an individual, trust other than a business trust, or estate, the member is expelled or otherwise dissociated because it willfully dissolved or terminated its existence.

(c) A member who wrongfully dissociates from a limited liability company is liable to the company and to the other members for damages caused by the dissociation. The liability is in addition to any other obligation of the member to the company or to the other members.

(d) If a limited liability company does not dissolve and wind up its business as a result of a member's wrongful dissociation under subsection (b), damages sustained by the company for the wrongful dissociation must be offset against distributions otherwise due the member after the dissociation.

Section 603.   Effect of Member's Dissociation.

(a) If under Section 801 a member's dissociation from a limited liability company results in a dissolution and winding up of the company's business, [Article] 8 applies. If a member's dissociation from the company does not result in a dissolution and winding up of the company's business under Section 801:

(1) in an at-will company, the company must cause the dissociated member's distributional interest to be purchased under [Article] 7; and

(2) in a term company:

(i) if the company dissolves and winds up its business on or before the expiration of its specified term, [Article] 8 applies to determine the dissociated member's rights to distributions; and

(ii) if the company does not dissolve and wind up its business on or before the expiration of its specified term, the company must cause the dissociated member's distributional interest to be purchased under [Article] 7 on the date of the expiration of the term specified at the time of the member's dissociation.

(b) Upon a member's dissociation from a limited liability company:

(1) the member's right to participate in the management and conduct of the company's business terminates, except as otherwise provided in Section 803, and the member ceases to be a member and is treated the same as a transferee of a member;

(2) the member's duty of loyalty under Section 409(b)(3) terminates; and

(3) the member's duty of loyalty under Section 409(b)(1) and (2) and duty of care under Section 409(c) continue only with regard to matters arising and events occurring before the member's dissociation, unless the member participates in winding up the company's business pursuant to Section 803.

ARTICLE 7   MEMBER'S DISSOCIATION WHEN BUSINESS NOT WOUND UP

Section 701.   Company Purchase of Distributional Interest.

(a) A limited liability company shall purchase a distributional interest of a:

(1) member of an at-will company for its fair value determined as of the date of the member's dissociation if the member's dissociation does not result in a dissolution and winding up of the company's business under Section 801; or

(2) member of a term company for its fair value determined as of the date of the expiration of the specified term that existed on the date of the member's dissociation if the expiration of the specified term does not result in a dissolution and winding up of the company's business under Section 801.

(b) A limited liability company must deliver a purchase offer to the dissociated member whose distributional interest is entitled to be purchased not later than 30 days after the date determined under subsection (a). The purchase offer must be accompanied by:

(1) a statement of the company's assets and liabilities as of the date determined under subsection (a):

(2) the latest available balance sheet and income statement, if any; and

(3) an explanation of how the estimated amount of the payment was calculated.

(c) If the price and other terms of a purchase of a distributional interest are fixed or are to be determined by the operating agreement, the price and terms so fixed or determined govern the purchase unless the purchaser defaults. If a default occurs, the dissociated member is entitled to commence a proceeding to have the company dissolved under Section 801(b)(5)(iv).

(d) If an agreement to purchase the distributional interest is not made within 120 days after the date determined under subsection (a), the dissociated member, within another 120 days, may commence a proceeding against the limited liability company to enforce the purchase. The company at its expense shall notify in writing all of the remaining members, and any other person the court directs, of the commencement of the proceeding. The jurisdiction of the court in which the proceeding is commenced under this subsection is plenary and exclusive.

(e) The court shall determine the fair value of the distributional interest in accordance with the standards set forth in Section 702 together with the terms for the purchase. Upon making these determinations, the court shall order the limited liability company to purchase or cause the purchase of the interest.

(f) Damages for wrongful dissociation under Section 602(b), and all other amounts owing, whether or not currently due, from the dissociated member to a limited liability company, must be offset against the purchase price.

Section 702.   Court Action to Determine Fair Value of Distributional Interest.

(a) In an action brought to determine the fair value of a distributional interest in a limited liability company, the court shall:

(1) determine the fair value of the interest, considering among other relevant evidence the going concern value of the company, any agreement among some or all of the members fixing the price or specifying a formula for determining value of distributional interests for any other purpose, the recommendations of any appraiser appointed by the court, and any legal constraints on the company's ability to purchase the interest;

(2) specify the terms of the purchase, including, if appropriate, terms for installment payments, subordination of the purchase obligation to the rights of the company's other creditors, security for a deferred purchase price, and a covenant not to compete or other restriction on a dissociated member; and

(3) require the dissociated member to deliver an assignment of the interest to the purchaser upon receipt of the purchase price or the first installment of the purchase price.

(b) After the dissociated member delivers the assignment, the dissociated member has no further claim against the company, its members, officers, or managers, if any, other than a claim to any unpaid balance of the purchase price and a claim under any agreement with the company or the remaining members that is not terminated by the court.

(c) If the purchase is not completed in accordance with the specified terms, the company is to be dissolved upon application under Section 801(b)(5)(iv). If a limited liability company is so dissolved, the dissociated member has the same rights and priorities in the company's assets as if the sale had not been ordered.

(d) If the court finds that a party to the proceeding acted arbitrarily, vexatiously, or not in good faith, it may award one or more other parties their reasonable expenses, including attorney's fees and the expenses of appraisers or other experts, incurred in the proceeding. The finding may be based on the company's failure to make an offer to pay or to comply with Section 701(b).

(e) Interest must be paid on the amount awarded from the date determined under Section 701(a) to the date of payment.

Section 703.   Dissociated Member's Power to Bind Limited Liability Company.

For two years after a member dissociates without the dissociation resulting in a dissolution and winding up of a limited liability company's business, the company, including a surviving company under [Article] 9, is bound by an act of the dissociated member which would have bound the company under Section 301 before dissociation only if at the time of entering into the transaction the other party:

(1) reasonably believed that the dissociated member was then a member;

(2) did not have notice of the member's dissociation; and

(3) is not deemed to have had notice under Section 704.

Section 704.   Statement of Dissociation.

(a) A dissociated member or a limited liability company may file in the office of the [Secretary of State] a statement of dissociation stating the name of the company and that the member is dissociated from the company.

(b) For the purposes of Sections 301 and 703, a person not a member is deemed to have notice of the dissociation 90 days after the statement of dissociation is filed.

ARTICLE 8   WINDING UP COMPANY'S BUSINESS

Section 801.   Events causing Dissolution and Winding up of Company's Business.

(a) In this section, "future distributions" means the total distributions that, as of the date of dissociation, are reasonably estimated to be made to the remaining members if the company were continued until the projected date of its termination, reduced by the amount of distributions that would have been made to the remaining members if the business of the company were dissolved and wound up on the date of dissociation.

(b) A limited liability company is dissolved, and its business must be wound up, upon the occurrence of any of the following events:

(1) an event specified in the operating agreement;

(2) consent of the number or percentage of members specified in the operating agreement;

(3) dissociation of a member who is also a manager or, if none, a member of an at-will company, and dissociation of a member who is also a manager or, if none, a member of a term company but only if the dissociation was for a reason provided in Section 601(7) through (11) and occurred before the expiration of the specified term, but the company is not dissolved and required to be wound up by reason of the dissociation if:

(i) within 90 days after the dissociation, the business of the company is continued by the agreement of:

(A) the remaining members that would be entitled to receive a majority of any distributions that would be made to them assuming the business of the company were dissolved and wound up on the date of the dissociation; and

(B) the remaining members that would be entitled to receive a majority of any future distributions that would be made to them assuming the business of the company were continued after the date of the dissociation; or

(ii) the business of the company is continued under a right to continue stated in the operating agreement;

(4) an event that makes it unlawful for all or substantially all of the business of the company to be continued, but any cure of illegality within 90 days after notice to the company of the event is effective retroactively to the date of the event for purposes of this section;

(5) on application by a member or a dissociated member, upon entry of a judicial decree that:

(i) the economic purpose of the company is likely to be unreasonably frustrated;

(ii) another member has engaged in conduct relating to the company's business that makes it not reasonably practicable to carry on the company's business with that member;

(iii) it is not otherwise reasonably practicable to carry on the company's business in conformity with the articles of organization and the operating agreement;

(iv) the company failed to purchase the pe-

titioner's distributional interest as required by Section 701; or

(v) the managers or members in control of the company have acted, are acting, or will act in a manner that is illegal, oppressive, fraudulent, or unfairly prejudicial to the petitioner; or

(6) on application by a transferee of a member's interest, a judicial determination that it is equitable to wind up the company's business:

(i) after the expiration of the specified term, if the company was for a specified term at the time the applicant became a transferee by member dissociation, transfer, or entry of a charging order that gave rise to the transfer; or

(ii) at any time, if the company was at will at the time the applicant became a transferee by member dissociation, transfer, or entry of a charging order that gave rise to the transfer.

Section 802.   Limited Liability Company Continues after Dissolution.

(a) Subject to subsection (b), a limited liability company continues after dissolution only for the purpose of winding up its business.

(b) At any time after the dissolution of a limited liability company and before the winding up of its business is completed, the members, including a dissociated member whose dissociation caused the dissolution, may unanimously waive the right to have the company's business wound up and the company terminated. In that case:

(1) the limited liability company resumes carrying on its business as if dissolution had never occurred and any liability incurred by the company or a member after the dissolution and before the waiver is determined as if the dissolution had never occurred; and

(2) the rights of a third party accruing under Section 804(a) or arising out of conduct in reliance on the dissolution before the third party knew or received a notification of the waiver are not adversely affected.

Section 803.   Right to Wind up Limited Liability Company's Business.

(a) After dissolution, a member who has not wrongfully dissociated may participate in winding up a limited liability company's business, but on application of any member, member's legal representative, or transferee, the [designate the appropriate court], for good cause shown, may order judicial supervision of the winding up.

(b) A legal representative of the last surviving member may wind up a limited liability company's business.

(c) A person winding up a limited liability company's business may preserve the company's business or property as a going concern for a reasonable time, prosecute and defend actions and proceedings, whether civil, criminal, or administrative, settle and close the company's business, dispose of and transfer the company's property, discharge the company's liabilities, distribute the assets of the company pursuant to Section 806, settle disputes by mediation or arbitration, and perform other necessary acts.

Section 804.   Member's or Manager's Power and Liability as Agent after Dissolution.

(a) A limited liability company is bound by a member's or manager's act after dissolution that:

(1) is appropriate for winding up the company's business; or

(2) would have bound the company under Section 301 before dissolution, if the other party to the transaction did not have notice of the dissolution.

(b) A member or manager who, with knowledge of the dissolution, subjects a limited liability company to liability by an act that is not appropriate for winding up the company's business is liable to the company for any damage caused to the company arising from the liability.

Section 805.   Articles of Termination.

(a) At any time after dissolution and winding up, a limited liability company may terminate its existence by filing with the [Secretary of State] articles of termination stating:

(1) the name of the company;

(2) the date of the dissolution; and

(3) that the company's business has been wound up and the legal existence of the company has been terminated.

(b) The existence of a limited liability company is terminated upon the filing of the articles of termination, or upon a later effective date, if specified in the articles of termination.

Section 806.   Distribution of Assets in Winding up Limited Liability Company's Business.

(a) In winding up a limited liability company's business, the assets of the company must be applied to discharge its obligations to creditors, including members who are creditors. Any surplus must be applied to pay in money the net amount distributable to members in accordance with their right to distributions under subsection (b).

(b) Each member is entitled to a distribution upon the winding up of the limited liability company's business consisting of a return of all contributions which have not previously been returned and a distribution of any remainder in equal shares.

Section 807.   Known Claims Against Dissolved Limited Liability Company.

(a) A dissolved limited liability company may dispose of the known claims against it by following the procedure described in this section.

(b) A dissolved limited liability company shall notify its known claimants in writing of the dissolution. The notice must:

(1) specify the information required to be included in a claim;

(2) provide a mailing address where the claim is to be sent;

(3) state the deadline for receipt of the claim, which may not be less than 120 days after the date the written notice is received by the claimant; and

(4) state that the claim will be barred if not received by the deadline.

(c) A claim against a dissolved limited liability company is barred if the requirements of subsection (b) are met, and:

(1) the claim is not received by the specified deadline; or

(2) in the case of a claim that is timely received but rejected by the dissolved company, the claimant does not commence a proceeding to enforce the claim within 90 days after the receipt of the notice of the rejection.

(d) For the purposes of this section, "claim" does

not include a contingent liability or a claim based on an event occurring after the effective date of dissolution.

Section 808.   Other Claims against Dissolved Limited Liability Company.

(a) A dissolved limited liability company may publish notice of its dissolution and request persons having claims against the company to present them in accordance with the notice.

(b) The notice must:

(1) be published at least once in a newspaper of general circulation in the [county] in which the dissolved limited liability company's principal office is located or, if none in this State, in which its designated office is or was last located;

(2) describe the information required to be contained in a claim and provide a mailing address where the claim is to be sent; and

(3) state that a claim against the limited liability company is barred unless a proceeding to enforce the claim is commenced within five years after publication of the notice.

(c) If a dissolved limited liability company publishes a notice in accordance with subsection (b), the claim of each of the following claimants is barred unless the claimant commences a proceeding to enforce the claim against the dissolved company within five years after the publication date of the notice:

(1) a claimant who did not receive written notice under Section 807;

(2) a claimant whose claim was timely sent to the dissolved company but not acted on; and

(3) a claimant whose claim is contingent or based on an event occurring after the effective date of dissolution.

(d) A claim not barred under this section may be enforced:

(1) against the dissolved limited liability company, to the extent of its undistributed assets; or

(2) if the assets have been distributed in liquidation, against a member of the dissolved company to the extent of the member's proportionate share of the claim or the company's assets distributed to the member in liquidation, whichever is less, but a member's total liability for all claims under this section may not exceed the total amount of assets distributed to the member.

Section 809.   Grounds for Administrative Dissolution.

The [Secretary of State] may commence a proceeding to dissolve a limited liability company administratively if the company does not:

(1) pay any fees, taxes, or penalties imposed by this [Act] or other law within 60 days after they are due; or

(2) deliver its annual report to the [Secretary of State] within 60 days after it is due.

Section 810.   Procedure for and Effect of Administrative Dissolution.

(a) If the [Secretary of State] determines that a ground exists for administratively dissolving a limited liability company, the [Secretary of State] shall enter a record of the determination and serve the company with a copy of the record.

(b) If the company does not correct each ground for dissolution or demonstrate to the reasonable satisfaction of the [Secretary of State] that each ground determined by the [Secretary of State] does not exist within 60 days after service of the notice, the [Secretary of State] shall administratively dissolve the company by signing a certification of the dissolution that recites the ground for dissolution and its effective date. The [Secretary of State] shall file the original of the certificate and serve the company with a copy of the certificate.

(c) A company administratively dissolved continues its existence but may carry on only business necessary to wind up and liquidate its business and affairs under Section 802 and to notify claimants under Sections 807 and 808.

(d) The administrative dissolution of a company does not terminate the authority of its agent for service of process.

Section 811.   Reinstatement Following Administrative Dissolution.

(a) A limited liability company administratively dissolved may apply to the [Secretary of State] for reinstatement within two years after the effective date of dissolution. The application must:

(1) recite the name of the company and the effective date of its administrative dissolution;

(2) state that the grounds for dissolution either did not exist or have been eliminated;

(3) state that the company's name satisfies the requirements of Section 105; and

(4) contain a certificate from the [taxing authority] reciting that all taxes owed by the company have been paid.

(b) If the [Secretary of State] determines that the application contains the information required by subsection (a) and that the information is correct, the [Secretary of State] shall cancel the certificate of dissolution and prepare a certificate of reinstatement that recites this determination and the effective date of reinstatement, file the original of the certificate, and serve the company with a copy of the certificate.

(c) When reinstatement is effective, it relates back to and takes effect as of the effective date of the administrative dissolution and the company may resume its business as if the administrative dissolution had never occurred.

Section 812.   Appeal from Denial of Reinstatement.

(a) If the [Secretary of State] denies a limited liability company's application for reinstatement following administrative dissolution, the [Secretary of State] shall serve the company with a record that explains the reason or reasons for denial.

(b) The company may appeal the denial of reinstatement to the [name appropriate] court within 30 days after service of the notice of denial is perfected. The company appeals by petitioning the court to set aside the dissolution and attaching to the petition copies of the [Secretary of State's] certificate of dissolution, the company's application for reinstatement, and the [Secretary of State's] notice of denial.

(c) The court may summarily order the [Secretary of State] to reinstate the dissolved company or may take other action the court considers appropriate.

(d) The court's final decision may be appealed as in other civil proceedings.

ARTICLE 9   CONVERSIONS AND MERGERS

Section 901.   Definitions.

In this [article]:

(1) "Corporation" means a corporation under [the State Corporation Act], a predecessor law, or comparable law of another jurisdiction.

(2) "General partner" means a partner in a part-nership and a general partner in a limited partnership.

(3) "Limited partner" means a limited partner in a limited partnership.

(4) "Limited partnership" means a limited partnership created under [the State Limited Partnership Act], a predecessor law, or comparable law of another jurisdiction.

(5) "Partner" includes a general partner and a limited partner.

(6) "Partnership" means a general partnership under [the State Partnership Act], a predecessor law, or comparable law of another jurisdiction.

(7) "Partnership agreement" means an agreement among the partners concerning the partnership or limited partnership.

(8) "Shareholder" means a shareholder in a corporation.

Section 902.   Conversion of Partnership or Limited Partnership to Limited Liability Company.

(a) A partnership or limited partnership may be converted to a limited liability company pursuant to this section.

(b) The terms and conditions of a conversion of a partnership or limited partnership to a limited liability company must be approved by all of the partners or by a number or percentage of the partners required for conversion in the partnership agreement.

(c) An agreement of conversion must set forth the terms and conditions of the conversion of the interests of partners of a partnership or of a limited partnership, as the case may be, into interests in the converted limited liability company or the cash or other consideration to be paid or delivered as a result of the conversion of the interests of the partners, or a combination thereof.

(d) After a conversion is approved under subsection (b), the partnership or limited partnership shall file articles of organization in the office of the [Secretary of State] which satisfy the requirements of Section 203 and contain:

(1) a statement that the partnership or limited partnership was converted to a limited liability company from a partnership or limited partnership, as the case may be;

(2) its former name;

(3) a statement of the number of votes cast by the partners entitled to vote for and against the con-

version and, if the vote is less than unanimous, the number or percentage required to approve the conversion under subsection (b); and

(4) in the case of a limited partnership, a statement that the certificate of limited partnership is to be canceled as of the date the conversion took effect.

(e) In the case of a limited partnership, the filing of articles of organization under subsection (d) cancels its certificate of limited partnership as of the date the conversion took effect.

(f) A conversion takes effect when the articles of organization are filed in the office of the [Secretary of State] or at any later date specified in the articles of organization.

(g) A general partner who becomes a member of a limited liability company as a result of a conversion remains liable as a partner for an obligation incurred by the partnership or limited partnership before the conversion takes effect.

(h) A general partner's liability for all obligations of the limited liability company incurred after the conversion takes effect is that of a member of the company. A limited partner who becomes a member as a result of a conversion remains liable only to the extent the limited partner was liable for an obligation incurred by the limited partnership before the conversion takes effect.

Section 903.   Effect of Conversion; Entity Unchanged.

(a) A partnership or limited partnership that has been converted pursuant to this [article] is for all purposes the same entity that existed before the conversion.

(b) When a conversion takes effect:

(1) all property owned by the converting partnership or limited partnership vests in the limited liability company;

(2) all debts, liabilities, and other obligations of the converting partnership or limited partnership continue as obligations of the limited liability company;

(3) an action or proceeding pending by or against the converting partnership or limited partnership may be continued as if the conversion had not occurred;

(4) except as prohibited by other law, all of the rights, privileges, immunities, powers, and purposes of the converting partnership or limited partnership vest in the limited liability company; and

(5) except as otherwise provided in the agreement of conversion under Section 902(c), all of the partners of the converting partnership continue as members of the limited liability company.

Section 904.   Merger of Entities.

(a) Pursuant to a plan of merger approved under subsection (c), a limited liability company may be merged with or into one or more limited liability companies, foreign limited liability companies, corporations, foreign corporations, partnerships, foreign partnerships, limited partnerships, foreign limited partnerships, or other domestic or foreign entities.

(b) A plan of merger must set forth:

(1) the name of each entity that is a party to the merger;

(2) the name of the surviving entity into which the other entities will merge;

(3) the type of organization of the surviving entity;

(4) the terms and conditions of the merger;

(5) the manner and basis for converting the interests of each party to the merger into interests or obligations of the surviving entity, or into money or other property in whole or in part; and

(6) the street address of the surviving entity's principal place of business.

(c) A plan of merger must be approved:

(1) in the case of a limited liability company that is a party to the merger, by all of the members or by a number or percentage of members specified in the operating agreement;

(2) in the case of a foreign limited liability company that is a party to the merger, by the vote required for approval of a merger by the law of the State or foreign jurisdiction in which the foreign limited liability company is organized;

(3) in the case of a partnership or domestic limited partnership that is a party to the merger, by the vote required for approval of a conversion under Section 902(b); and

(4) in the case of any other entities that are parties to the merger, by the vote required for approval of a merger by the law of this State or of the State or foreign jurisdiction in which the entity is

organized and, in the absence of such a requirement, by all the owners of interests in the entity.

(d) After a plan of merger is approved and before the merger takes effect, the plan may be amended or abandoned as provided in the plan.

(e) The merger is effective upon the filing of the articles of merger with the [Secretary of State], or at such later date as the articles may provide.

Section 905.   Articles of Merger.

(a) After approval of the plan of merger under Section 904(c), unless the merger is abandoned under Section 904(d), articles of merger must be signed on behalf of each limited liability company and other entity that is a party to the merger and delivered to the [Secretary of State] for filing. The articles must set forth:

(1) the name and jurisdiction of formation or organization of each of the limited liability companies and other entities that are parties to the merger;

(2) for each limited liability company that is to merge, the date its articles of organization were filed with the [Secretary of State];

(3) that a plan of merger has been approved and signed by each limited liability company and other entity that is to merge;

(4) the name and address of the surviving limited liability company or other surviving entity;

(5) the effective date of the merger;

(6) if a limited liability company is the surviving entity, such changes in its articles of organization as are necessary by reason of the merger;

(7) if a party to a merger is a foreign limited liability company, the jurisdiction and date of filing of its initial articles of organization and the date when its application for authority was filed by the [Secretary of State] or, if an application has not been filed, a statement to that effect; and

(8) if the surviving entity is not a limited liability company, an agreement that the surviving entity may be served with process in this State and is subject to liability in any action or proceeding for the enforcement of any liability or obligation of any limited liability company previously subject to suit in this State which is to merge, and for the enforcement, as provided in this [Act], of the right of members of any limited liability company to re-

ceive payment for their interest against the surviving entity.

(b) If a foreign limited liability company is the surviving entity of a merger, it may not do business in this State until an application for that authority is filed with the [Secretary of State].

(c) The surviving limited liability company or other entity shall furnish a copy of the plan of merger, on request and without cost, to any member of any limited liability company or any person holding an interest in any other entity that is to merge.

(d) Articles of merger operate as an amendment to the limited liability company's articles of organization.

Section 906.   Effect of Merger.

(a) When a merger takes effect:

(1) the separate existence of each limited liability company and other entity that is a party to the merger, other than the surviving entity, terminates;

(2) all property owned by each of the limited liability companies and other entities that are party to the merger vests in the surviving entity;

(3) all debts, liabilities, and other obligations of each limited liability company and other entity that is party to the merger become the obligations of the surviving entity;

(4) an action or proceeding pending by or against a limited liability company or other party to a merger may be continued as if the merger had not occurred or the surviving entity may be substituted as a party to the action or proceeding; and

(5) except as prohibited by other law, all the rights, privileges, immunities, powers, and purposes of every limited liability company and other entity that is a party to a merger vest in the surviving entity.

(b) The [Secretary of State] is an agent for service of process in an action or proceeding against the surviving foreign entity to enforce an obligation of any party to a merger if the surviving foreign entity fails to appoint or maintain an agent designated for service of process in this State or the agent for service of process cannot with reasonable diligence be found at the designated office. Upon receipt of process, the [Secretary of State] shall send a copy of the process by registered or certified mail, return receipt requested, to the surviving entity at the address set forth in the articles of merger. Service is effected under this subsection at the earliest of:

(1) the date the company receives the process, notice, or demand;

(2) the date shown on the return receipt, if signed on behalf of the company; or

(3) five days after its deposit in the mail, if mailed postpaid and correctly addressed.

(c) A member of the surviving limited liability company is liable for all obligations of a party to the merger for which the member was personally liable before the merger.

(d) Unless otherwise agreed, a merger of a limited liability company that is not the surviving entity in the merger does not require the limited liability company to wind up its business under this [Act] or pay its liabilities and distribute its assets pursuant to this [Act].

(e) Articles of merger serve as articles of dissolution for a limited liability company that is not the surviving entity in the merger.

Section 907.   [Article] Not Exclusive.

This [article] does not preclude an entity from being converted or merged under other law.

ARTICLE 10   FOREIGN LIMITED LIABILITY COMPANIES

Section 1001.   Law Governing Foreign Limited Liability Companies.

(a) The laws of the State or other jurisdiction under which a foreign limited liability company is organized govern its organization and internal affairs and the liability of its managers, members, and their transferees.

(b) A foreign limited liability company may not be denied a certificate of authority by reason of any difference between the laws of another jurisdiction under which the foreign company is organized and the laws of this State.

(c) A certificate of authority does not authorize a foreign limited liability company to engage in any

business or exercise any power that a limited liability company may not engage in or exercise in this State.

Section 1002.   Application for Certificate of Authority.

(a) A foreign limited liability company may apply for a certificate of authority to transact business in this State by delivering an application to the [Secretary of State] for filing. The application must set forth:

(1) the name of the foreign company or, if its name is unavailable for use in this State, a name that satisfies the requirements of Section 1005;

(2) the name of the State or country under whose law it is organized;

(3) the street address of its principal office;

(4) the address of its initial designated office in this State;

(5) the name and street address of its initial agent for service of process in this State;

(6) whether the duration of the company is for a specified term and, if so, the period specified;

(7) whether the company is manager-managed, and, if so, the name and address of each initial manager; and

(8) whether the members of the company are to be liable for its debts and obligations under a provision similar to Section 303(c).

(b) A foreign limited liability company shall deliver with the completed application a certificate of existence or a record of similar import authenticated by the secretary of state or other official having custody of company records in the State or country under whose law it is organized.

Section 1003.   Activities Not Constituting Transacting Business.

(a) Activities of a foreign limited liability company that do not constitute transacting business in this State within the meaning of this [article] include:

(1) maintaining, defending, or settling an action or proceeding;

(2) holding meetings of its members or managers or carrying on any other activity concerning its internal affairs;

(3) maintaining bank accounts;

(4) maintaining offices or agencies for the transfer, exchange, and registration of the foreign

company's own securities or maintaining trustees or depositories with respect to those securities;

(5) selling through independent contractors;

(6) soliciting or obtaining orders, whether by mail or through employees or agents or otherwise, if the orders require acceptance outside this State before they become contracts;

(7) creating or acquiring indebtedness, mortgages, or security interests in real or personal property;

(8) securing or collecting debts or enforcing mortgages or other security interests in property securing the debts, and holding, protecting, and maintaining property so acquired;

(9) conducting an isolated transaction that is completed within 30 days and is not one in the course of similar transactions of a like manner; and

(10) transacting business in interstate commerce.

(b) for purposes of this [article], the ownership in this State of income-producing real property or tangible personal property, other than property excluded under subsection (a), constitutes transacting business in this State.

(c) This section does not apply in determining the contacts or activities that may subject a foreign limited liability company to service of process, taxation, or regulation under any other law of this State.

Section 1004. Issuance of Certificate of Authority.

Unless the [Secretary of State] determines that an application for a certificate of authority fails to comply as to form with the filing requirements of this [Act], the [Secretary of State], upon payment of all filing fees, shall file the application and send a receipt for it and the fees to the limited liability company or its representative.

Section 1005. Name of Foreign Limited Liability Company.

(a) If the name of a foreign limited liability company does not satisfy the requirements of Section 105, the company, to obtain or maintain a certificate of authority to transact business in this State, must use a fictitious name to transact business in this State if its real name is unavailable and it delivers to the [Secretary of State] for filing a copy of the resolution of its managers, in the case of a manager-managed company,

or of its members, in the case of a member-managed company, adopting the fictitious name.

(b) Except as authorized by subsections (c) and (d), the name, including a fictitious name to be used to transact business in this State, of a foreign limited liability company must be distinguishable upon the records of the [Secretary of State] from:

(1) the name of any corporation, limited partnership, or company incorporated, organized, or authorized to transact business in this State;

(2) a name reserved or registered under Section 106 or 107; and

(3) the fictitious name of another foreign limited liability company authorized to transact business in this State.

(c) A foreign limited liability company may apply to the [Secretary of State] for authority to use in this State a name that is not distinguishable upon the records of the [Secretary of State] from a name described in subsection (b). The [Secretary of State] shall authorize use of the name applied for if:

(1) the present user, registrant, or owner of a reserved name consents to the use in a record and submits an undertaking in form satisfactory to the [Secretary of State] to change its name to a name that is distinguishable upon the records of the [Secretary of State] from the name of the foreign applying liability company; or

(2) the applicant delivers to the [Secretary of State] a certified copy of a final judgment of a court establishing the applicant's right to use the name applied for in this State.

(d) A foreign limited liability company may use in this State the name, including the fictitious name, of another domestic or foreign entity that is used in this State if the other entity is incorporated, organized, or authorized to transact business in this State and the foreign limited liability company:

(1) has merged with the other entity;

(2) has been formed by reorganization of the other entity; or

(3) has acquired all or substantially all of the assets, including the name, of the other entity.

(e) If a foreign limited liability company authorized to transact business in this State changes its name to one that does not satisfy the requirements of Section 105, it may not transact business in this State under the name as changed until it adopts a name satisfying the requirements of Section 105 and obtains an amended certificate of authority.

Section 1006.   Revocation of Certificate of Authority.

(a) A certificate of authority of a foreign limited liability company to transact business in this State may be revoked by the [Secretary of State] in the manner provided in subsection (b) if:

(1) the company fails to:

(i) pay any fees, taxes, and penalties owed to this State;

(ii) deliver its annual report required under Section 211 to the [Secretary of State] within 60 days after it is due;

(iii) appoint and maintain an agent for service of process as required by this [article]; or

(iv) file a statement of a change in the name or business address of the agent as required by this [article]; or

(2) a misrepresentation has been made of any material matter in any application, report, affidavit, or other record submitted by the company pursuant to this [article].

(b) The [Secretary of State] may not revoke a certificate of authority of a foreign limited liability company unless the [Secretary of State] sends the company notice of the revocation, at least 60 days before its effective date, by a record addressed to its agent for service of process in this State, or if the company fails to appoint and maintain a proper agent in this State, addressed to the office required to be maintained by Section 108. The notice must specify the cause for the revocation of the certificate of authority. The authority of the company to transact business in this State ceases on the effective date of the revocation unless the foreign limited liability company cures the failure before that date.

Section 1007.   Cancellation of Authority.

A foreign limited liability company may cancel its authority to transact business in this State by filing in the office of the [Secretary of State] a certificate of cancellation. Cancellation does not terminate the authority of the [Secretary of State] to accept service of process on the company for [claims for relief] arising out of the transactions of business in this State.

Section 1008.   Effect of Failure to Obtain Certificate of Authority.

(a) A foreign limited liability company transacting business in this State may not maintain an action or proceeding in this State unless it has a certificate of authority to transact business in this State.

(b) The failure of a foreign limited liability company to have a certificate of authority to transact business in this State does not impair the validity of a contract or act of the company or prevent the foreign limited liability company from defending an action or proceeding in this State.

(c) Limitations on personal liability of managers, members, and their transferees are not waived solely by transacting business in this State without a certificate of authority.

(d) If a foreign limited liability company transacts business in this State without a certificate of authority, it appoints the [Secretary of State] as its agent for service of process for [claims for relief] arising out of the transaction of business in this State.

Section 1009.   Action by [Attorney General].

The [Attorney General] may maintain an action to restrain a foreign limited liability company from transacting business in this State in violation of this [article].

ARTICLE 11   DERIVATIVE ACTIONS

Section 1101.   Right of Action.

A member of a limited liability company may maintain an action in the right of the company if the members or managers having authority to do so have refused to commence the action or an effort to cause those members or managers to commence the action is not likely to succeed.

Section 1102.   Proper Plaintiff.

In a derivative action for a limited liability company, the plaintiff must be a member of the company when the action is commenced; and:

(1) must have been a member at the time of the transaction of which the plaintiff complains; or

(2) the plaintiff's status as a member must have devolved upon the plaintiff by operation of law or pur-

suant to the terms of the operating agreement from a person who was a member at the time of the transaction.

Section 1103.   Pleading.

In a derivative action for a limited liability company, the complaint must set forth with particularity the effort of the plaintiff to secure initiation of the action by a member or manager or the reasons for not making the effort.

Section 1104.   Expenses.

If a derivative action for a limited liability company is successful, in whole or in part, or if anything is received by the plaintiff as a result of a judgment, compromise, or settlement of an action or claim, the court may award the plaintiff reasonable expenses, including reasonable attorney's fees, and shall direct the plaintiff to remit to the limited liability company the remainder of the proceeds received.

ARTICLE 12   MISCELLANEOUS PROVISIONS

Section 1201.   Uniformity of Application and Construction.

This [Act] shall be applied and construed to effectuate its general purpose to make uniform the law with respect to the subject of this [Act] among States enacting it.

Section 1202.   Short Title.

This [Act] may be cited as the Uniform Limited Liability Company Act (1995).

Section 1203.   Severability Clause.

If any provision of this [Act] or its application to any person or circumstance is held invalid, the invalidity does not affect other provisions or applications of this [Act] which can be given effect without the invalid provision or application, and to this end the provisions of this [Act] are severable.

Section 1204.   Effective Date.

This [Act] takes effect [_____].

Section 1205.   Transitional Provisions.

(a) Before January 1, 199___, this [Act] governs only a limited liability company organized:

(1) after the effective date of this [Act], unless the company is continuing the business of a dissolved limited liability company under [Section of the existing Limited Liability Company Act]; and

(2) before the effective date of this [Act], which elects, as provided by subsection (c), to be governed by this [Act].

(b) On and after January 1, 199___, this [Act] governs all limited liability companies.

(c) Before January 1, 199___, a limited liability company voluntarily may elect, in the manner provided in its operating agreement or by law for amending the operating agreement, to be governed by this [Act].

Section 1206.   Savings Clause.

This [Act] does not affect an action or proceeding commenced or right accrued before the effective date of this [Act].

Revised Model Business Corporation Act (1984)

CHAPTER 1   GENERAL PROVISIONS

Short Title and Reservation of Power

Section 1.01.   Short Title

This Act shall be known and may be cited as the "[name of state] Business Corporation Act."

Section 1.02.   Reservation of Power to Amend or Repeal

The [name of state legislature] has power to amend or repeal all or part of this Act at any time and all domestic and foreign corporations subject to this Act are governed by the amendment or repeal.

Filing Documents

Section 1.20.   Filing Requirements

(a) A document must satisfy the requirements of this section, and of any other section that adds to or varies from these requirements, to be entitled to filing by the secretary of state.

(b) This Act must require or permit filing the document in the office of the secretary of state.

(c) The document must contain the information required by this Act. It may contain other information as well.

(d) The document must be typewritten or printed.

(e) The document must be in the English language. A corporate name need not be in English if written in English letters or Arabic or Roman numerals, and the certificate of existence required of foreign corporations need not be in English if accompanied by a reasonably authenticated English translation.

(f) The document must be executed:

(1) by the chairman of the board of directors of a domestic or foreign corporation, by its president, or by another of its officers;

(2) if directors have not been selected or the corporation has not been formed, by an incorporator; or

(3) if the corporation is in the hands of a receiver, trustee, or other court-appointed fiduciary, by that fiduciary.

(g) The person executing the document shall sign it and state beneath or opposite his signature his name and the capacity in which he signs. The document may but need not contain: (1) the corporate seal, (2) an attestation by the secretary or an assistant secretary, (3) an acknowledgement, verification, or proof.

(h) If the secretary of state has prescribed a mandatory form for the document under section 1.21, the document must be in or on the prescribed form.

(i) The document must be delivered to the office of the secretary of state for filing and must be accompanied by one exact or conformed copy (except as provided in sections 5.03 and 15.09), the correct filing fee, and any franchise tax, license fee, or penalty required by this Act or other law.

Section 1.21.   Forms

(a) The secretary of state may prescribe and furnish on request forms for: (1) an application for a certificate of existence, (2) a foreign corporation's application for a certificate of authority to transact business in this state, (3) a foreign corporation's application for a certificate of withdrawal, and (4) the annual report. If the secretary of state so requires, use of these forms is mandatory.

(b) The secretary of state may prescribe and furnish on request forms for other documents required or permitted to be filed by this Act but their use is not mandatory.

Section 1.22.   Filing, Service, and Copying Fees

(a) The secretary of state shall collect the following fees when the documents described in this subsection are delivered to him for filing:

	Document	Fee
(1)	Articles of incorporation	$_____.
(2)	Application for use of indistinguishable name	$_____.
(3)	Application for reserved name	$_____.
(4)	Notice of transfer of reserved name	$_____.
(5)	Application for registered name	$_____.
(6)	Application for renewal of registered name	$_____.
(7)	Corporation's statement of change of registered agent or registered office or both	$_____.
(8)	Agent's statement of change of registered office for each affected corporation not to exceed a total of	$_____.
(9)	Agent's statement of resignation	No fee.
(10)	Amendment of articles of incorporation	$_____.
(11)	Restatement of articles of incorporation with amendment of articles	$_____.
(12)	Articles of merger or share exchange	$_____.
(13)	Articles of dissolution	$_____.
(14)	Articles of revocation of dissolution	$_____.
(15)	Certificate of administrative dissolution	No fee.
(16)	Application for reinstatement following administrative dissolution	$_____.
(17)	Certificate of reinstatement	No fee.
(18)	Certificate of judicial dissolution	No fee.
(19)	Application for certificate of authority	$_____.
(20)	Application for amended certificate of authority	$_____.
(21)	Application for certificate of withdrawal	$_____.
(22)	Certificate of revocation of authority to transact business	No fee.
(23)	Annual report	$_____.
(24)	Articles of correction	$_____.
(25)	Application for certificate of existence or authorization	$_____.
(26)	Any other document required or permitted to be filed by this Act	$_____.

(b) The secretary of state shall collect a fee of $_____ each time process is served on him under this Act. The party to a proceeding causing service of process is entitled to recover this fee as costs if he prevails in the proceeding.

(c) The secretary of state shall collect the following fees for copying and certifying the copy of any filed document relating to a domestic or foreign corporation:

(1) $_____ a page for copying; and
(2) $_____ for the certificate.

Section 1.23.   Effective Time and Date of Document

(a) Except as provided in subsection (b) and section 1.24(c), a document accepted for filing is effective:

(1) at the time of filing on the date it is filed, as evidenced by the secretary of state's date and time endorsement on the original document; or

(2) at the time specified in the document as its effective time on the date it is filed.

(b) A document may specify a delayed effective time and date, and if it does so the document becomes effective at the time and date specified. If a delayed effective date but no time is specified, the document is effective at the close of business on that date. A delayed effective date for a document may not be later than the 90th day after the date it is filed.

Section 1.24.　Correcting Filed Document

(a) A domestic or foreign corporation may correct a document filed by the secretary of state if the document (1) contains an incorrect statement or (2) was defectively executed, attested, sealed, verified, or acknowledged.

(b) A document is corrected:

(1) by preparing articles of correction that (i) describe the document (including its filing date) or attach a copy of it to the articles, (ii) specify the incorrect statement and the reason it is incorrect or the manner in which the execution was defective, and (iii) correct the incorrect statement or defective execution; and

(2) by delivering the articles to the secretary of state for filing.

(c) Articles of correction are effective on the effective date of the document they correct except as to persons relying on the uncorrected document and adversely affected by the correction. As to those persons, articles of correction are effective when filed.

Section 1.25.　Filing Duty of Secretary of State

(a) If a document delivered to the office of the secretary of state for filing satisfies the requirements of section 1.20, the secretary of state shall file it.

(b) The secretary of state files a document by stamping or otherwise endorsing "Filed," together with his name and official title and the date and time of receipt, on both the original and the document copy and on the receipt for the filing fee. After filing a document, except as provided in sections 5.03 and 15.10, the secretary of state shall deliver the document copy, with the filing fee receipt (or acknowledgement of receipt if no fee is required) attached, to the domestic or foreign corporation or its representative.

(c) If the secretary of state refuses to file a document, he shall return it to the domestic or foreign corporation or its representative within five days after the document was delivered, together with a brief, written explanation of the reason for his refusal.

(d) The secretary of state's duty to file documents under this section is ministerial. His filing or refusing to file a document does not:

(1) affect the validity or invalidity of the document in whole or part;

(2) relate to the correctness or incorrectness of information contained in the document;

(3) create a presumption that the document is valid or invalid or that information contained in the document is correct or incorrect.

Section 1.26.　Appeal from Secretary of State's Refusal to File Document

(a) If the secretary of state refuses to file a document delivered to his office for filing, the domestic or foreign corporation may appeal the refusal within 30 days after the return of the document to the [name or describe] court [of the county where the corporation's principal office (or, if none in this state, its registered office) is or will be located] [of county]. The appeal is commenced by petitioning the court to compel filing the document and by attaching to the petition the document and the secretary of state's explanation of his refusal to file.

(b) The court may summarily order the secretary of state to file the document or take other action the court considers appropriate.

(c) The court's final decision may be appealed as in other civil proceedings.

Section 1.27.　Evidentiary Effect of Copy of Filed Document

A certificate attached to a copy of a document filed by the secretary of state, bearing his signature (which may be in facsimile) and the seal of this state, is conclusive evidence that the original document is on file with the secretary of state.

Section 1.28.　Certificate of Existence

(a) Anyone may apply to the secretary of state to furnish a certificate of existence for a domestic corporation or a certificate of authorization for a foreign corporation.

(b) A certificate of existence or authorization sets forth:

(1) the domestic corporation's corporate name or the foreign corporation's corporate name used in this state;

(2) that (i) the domestic corporation is duly incorporated under the law of this state, the date of its incorporation, and the period of its duration if less than perpetual; or (ii) that the foreign corporation is authorized to transact business in this state;

(3) that all fees, taxes, and penalties owed to

this state have been paid, if (i) payment is reflected in the records of the secretary of state and (ii) nonpayment affects the existence or authorization of the domestic or foreign corporation;

(4) that its most recent annual report required by section 16.22 has been delivered to the secretary of state;

(5) that articles of dissolution have not been filed; and

(6) other facts of record in the office of the secretary of state that may be requested by the applicant.

(c) Subject to any qualification stated in the certificate, a certificate of existence or authorization issued by the secretary of state may be relied upon as conclusive evidence that the domestic or foreign corporation is in existence or is authorized to transact business in this state.

Section 1.29. Penalty for Signing False Document

(a) A person commits an offense if he signs a document he knows is false in any material respect with intent that the document be delivered to the secretary of state for filing.

(b) An offense under this section is a [_____] misdemeanor [punishable by a fine of not to exceed $_____].

Secretary of State

Section 1.30. Powers

The secretary of state has the power reasonably necessary to perform the duties required of him by this Act.

Definitions

Section 1.40. Act Definitions

In this Act:

(1) "Articles of incorporation" include amended and restated articles of incorporation and articles of merger.

(2) "Authorized shares" means the shares of all classes a domestic or foreign corporation is authorized to issue.

(3) "Conspicuous" means so written that a reasonable person against whom the writing is to operate should have noticed it. For example, printing in italics or boldface or contrasting color, or typing in capitals or underlined, is conspicuous.

(4) "Corporation" or "domestic corporation" means a corporation for profit, which is not a foreign corporation, incorporated under or subject to the provisions of this Act.

(5) "Deliver" includes mail.

(6) "Distribution" means a direct or indirect transfer of money or other property (except its own shares) or incurrence of indebtedness by a corporation to or for the benefit of its shareholders in respect of any of its shares. A distribution may be in the form of a declaration or payment of a dividend; a purchase, redemption, or other acquisition of shares; a distribution of indebtedness; or otherwise.

(7) "Effective date of notice" is defined in section 1.41.

(8) "Employee" includes an officer but not a director. A director may accept duties that make him also an employee.

(9) "Entity" includes corporation and foreign corporation; not-for-profit corporation; profit and not-for-profit unincorporated association; business trust, estate, partnership, trust, and two or more persons having a joint or common economic interest; and state, United States, and foreign government.

(10) "Foreign corporation" means a corporation for profit incorporated under a law other than the law of this state.

(11) "Governmental subdivision" includes authority, county, district, and municipality.

(12) "Includes" denotes a partial definition.

(13) "Individual" includes the estate of an incompetent or deceased individual.

(14) "Means" denotes an exhaustive definition.

(15) "Notice" is defined in section 1.41.

(16) "Person" includes individual and entity.

(17) "Principal office" means the office (in or out of this state) so designated in the annual report where the principal executive offices of a domestic or foreign corporation are located.

(18) "Proceeding" includes civil suit and criminal, administrative, and investigatory action.

(19) "Record date" means the date established under chapter 6 or 7 on which a corporation determines the identity of its shareholders for purposes of this Act.

(20) "Secretary" means the corporate officer to whom the board of directors has delegated responsibility under section 8.40(c) for custody of the minutes of the meetings of the board of directors and of the shareholders and for authenticating records of the corporation.

(21) "Shares" means the units into which the proprietary interests in a corporation are divided.

(22) "Shareholder" means the person in whose name shares are registered in the records of a corporation or the beneficial owner of shares to the extent of the rights granted by a nominee certificate on file with a corporation.

(23) "State," when referring to a part of the United States, includes a state and commonwealth (and their agencies and governmental subdivisions) and a territory and insular possession (and their agencies and governmental subdivisions) of the United States.

(24) "Subscriber" means a person who subscribes for shares in a corporation, whether before or after incorporation.

(25) "United States" includes district, authority, bureau, commission, department, and any other agency of the United States.

(26) "Voting group" means all shares of one or more classes or series that under the articles of incorporation or this Act are entitled to vote and be counted together collectively on a matter at a meeting of shareholders. All shares entitled by the articles of incorporation or this Act to vote generally on the matter are for that purpose a single voting group.

Section 1.41. Notice

(a) Notice under this Act must be in writing unless oral notice is reasonable under the circumstances.

(b) Notice may be communicated in person; by telephone, telegraph, teletype, or other form of wire or wireless communication; or by mail or private carrier. If these forms of personal notice are impracticable, notice may be communicated by a newspaper of general circulation in the area where published; or by radio, television, or other form of public broadcast communication.

(c) Written notice by a domestic or foreign corporation to its shareholder, if in a comprehensible form, is effective when mailed, if mailed postpaid and correctly addressed to the shareholder's address shown in the corporation's current record of shareholders.

(d) Written notice to a domestic or foreign corporation (authorized to transact business in this state) may be addressed to its registered agent at its registered office or to the corporation or its secretary at its principal office shown in its most recent annual report or, in the case of a foreign corporation that has not yet delivered an annual report, in its application for a certificate of authority.

(e) Except as provided in subsection (c), written notice, if in a comprehensible form, is effective at the earliest of the following:

(1) when received;

(2) five days after its deposit in the United States Mail, as evidenced by the postmark, if mailed postpaid and correctly addressed;

(3) on the date shown on the return receipt, if sent by registered or certified mail, return receipt requested, and the receipt is signed by or on behalf of the addressee.

(f) Oral notice is effective when communicated if communicated in a comprehensible manner.

(g) If this Act prescribes notice requirements for particular circumstances, those requirements govern. If articles of incorporation or bylaws prescribe notice requirements, not inconsistent with this section or other provisions of this Act, those requirements govern.

Section 1.42. Number of Shareholders

(a) For purposes of this Act, the following identified as a shareholder in a corporation's current record of shareholders constitutes one shareholder:

(1) three or fewer coowners;

(2) a corporation, partnership, trust, estate, or other entity;

(3) the trustees, guardians, custodians, or other fiduciaries of a single trust, estate, or account.

(b) For purposes of this Act, shareholdings registered in substantially similar names constitute one shareholder if it is reasonable to believe that the names represent the same person.

CHAPTER 2   INCORPORATION

Section 2.01. Incorporators

One or more persons may act as the incorporator or incorporators of a corporation by delivering articles of incorporation to the secretary of state for filing.

Section 2.02. Articles of Incorporation

(a) The articles of incorporation must set forth:

(1) a corporate name for the corporation that satisfies the requirements of section 4.01;

(2) the number of shares the corporation is authorized to issue;

(3) the street address of the corporation's initial registered office and the name of its initial registered agent at that office; and

(4) the name and address of each incorporator.

(b) The articles of incorporation may set forth:

(1) the names and addresses of the individuals who are to serve as the initial directors;

(2) provisions not inconsistent with law regarding:

(i) the purpose or purposes for which the corporation is organized;

(ii) managing the business and regulating the affairs of the corporation;

(iii) defining, limiting, and regulating the powers of the corporation, its board of directors, and shareholders;

(iv) a par value for authorized shares or classes of shares;

(v) the imposition of personal liability on shareholders for the debt of the corporation to a specified extent and upon specified conditions; and

(3) any provision that under this Act is required or permitted to be set forth in the bylaws.

(c) The articles of incorporation need not set forth any of the corporate powers enumerated in this Act.

Section 2.03. Incorporation

(a) Unless a delayed effective date is specified, the corporate existence begins when the articles of incorporation are filed.

(b) The secretary of state's filing of the articles of incorporation is conclusive proof that the incorporators satisfied all conditions precedent to incorporation except in a proceeding by the state to cancel or revoke the incorporation or involuntarily dissolve the corporation.

Section 2.04. Liability for Preincorporation Transactions

All persons purporting to act as or on behalf of a corporation, knowing there was no incorporation under this Act, are jointly and severally liable for all liabilities created while so acting.

Section 2.05. Organization of Corporation

(a) After incorporation:

(1) if initial directors are named in the articles of incorporation, the initial directors shall hold an organizational meeting, at the call of a majority of the directors, to complete the organization of the corporation by appointing officers, adopting bylaws, and carrying on any other business brought before the meeting;

(2) if initial directors are not named in the articles, the incorporator or incorporators shall hold an organizational meeting at the call of a majority of the incorporators:

(i) to elect directors and complete the organization of the corporation; or

(ii) to elect a board of directors who shall complete the organization of the corporation.

(b) Action required or permitted by this Act to be taken by incorporators at an organizational meeting may be taken without a meeting if the action taken is evidenced by one or more written consents describing the action taken and signed by each incorporator.

(c) An organizational meeting may be held in or out of this state.

Section 2.06. Bylaws

(a) The incorporators or board of directors of a corporation shall adopt initial bylaws for the corporation.

(b) The bylaws of a corporation may contain any provision for managing the business and regulating the affairs of the corporation that is not inconsistent with law or the articles of incorporation.

Section 2.07. Emergency Bylaws

(a) Unless the articles of incorporation provide otherwise, the board of directors of a corporation may adopt bylaws to be effective only in an emergency defined in subsection (d). The emergency bylaws, which are subject to amendment or repeal by the shareholders, may make all provisions necessary for managing the corporation during the emergency, including:

(1) procedures for calling a meeting of the board of directors;

(2) quorum requirements for the meeting; and

(3) designation of additional or substitute directors.

(b) All provisions of the regular bylaws consistent with the emergency bylaws remain effective during the emergency. The emergency bylaws are not effective after the emergency ends.

(c) Corporate action taken in good faith in accordance with the emergency bylaws:

(1) binds the corporation; and

(2) may not be used to impose liability on a corporate director, officer, employee, or agent.

(d) An emergency exists for purposes of this section if a quorum of the corporation's directors cannot readily be assembled because of some catastrophic event.

CHAPTER 3   PURPOSES AND POWERS

Section 3.01.   Purposes

(a) Every corporation incorporated under this Act has the purpose of engaging in any lawful business unless a more limited purpose is set forth in the articles of incorporation.

(b) A corporation engaging in a business that is subject to regulation under another statute of this state may incorporate under this Act only if permitted by, and subject to all limitations of, the other statute.

Section 3.02.   General Powers

Unless its articles of incorporation provide otherwise, every corporation has perpetual duration and succession in its corporate name and has the same powers as an individual to do all things necessary or convenient to carry out its business and affairs, including without limitation power:

(1) to sue and be sued, complain and defend in its corporate name;

(2) to have a corporate seal, which may be altered at will, and to use it, or a facsimile of it, by impressing or affixing it or in any other manner reproducing it;

(3) to make and amend bylaws, not inconsistent with its articles of incorporation or with the laws of this state, for managing the business and regulating the affairs of the corporation;

(4) to purchase, receive, lease, or otherwise acquire, and own, hold, improve, use, and otherwise deal with, real or personal property, or any legal or equitable interest in property, wherever located;

(5) to sell, convey, mortgage, pledge, lease, exchange, and otherwise dispose of all or any part of its property;

(6) to purchase, receive, subscribe for, or otherwise acquire; own, hold, vote, use, sell, mortgage, lend, pledge, or otherwise dispose of; and deal in and with shares or other interests in, or obligations of, any other entity;

(7) to make contracts and guarantees, incur liabilities, borrow money, issue its notes, bonds, and other obligations (which may be convertible into or include the option to purchase other securities of the corporation), and secure any of its obligations by mortgage or pledge of any of its property, franchises, or income;

(8) to lend money, invest and reinvest its funds, and receive and hold real and personal property as security for repayment;

(9) to be a promoter, partner, member, associate, or manager of any partnership, joint venture, trust, or other entity;

(10) to conduct its business, locate offices, and exercise the powers granted by this Act within or without this state;

(11) to elect directors and appoint officers, employees, and agents of the corporation, define their duties, fix their compensation, and lend them money and credit;

(12) to pay pensions and establish pension plans, pension trusts, profit sharing plans, share bonus plans, share option plans, and benefit or incentive plans for any or all of its current or former directors, officers, employees, and agents;

(13) to make donations for the public welfare or for charitable, scientific, or educational purposes;

(14) to transact any lawful business that will aid governmental policy;

(15) to make payments or donations, or do any other act, not inconsistent with law, that furthers the business and affairs of the corporation.

Section 3.03.   Emergency Powers

(a) In anticipation of or during an emergency defined in subsection (d), the board of directors of a corporation may:

(1) modify lines of succession to accommodate the incapacity of any director, officer, employee, or agent; and

(2) relocate the principal office, designate alternative principal offices or regional offices, or authorize the officers to do so.

(b) During an emergency defined in subsection (d), unless emergency bylaws provide otherwise:

(1) notice of a meeting of the board of directors need be given only to those directors whom it is practicable to reach and may be given in any

practicable manner, including by publication and radio; and

(2) one or more officers of the corporation present at a meeting of the board of directors may be deemed to be directors for the meeting, in order of rank and within the same rank in order of seniority, as necessary to achieve a quorum.

(c) Corporate action taken in good faith during an emergency under this section to further the ordinary business affairs of the corporation:

(1) binds the corporation; and

(2) may not be used to impose liability on a corporate director, officer, employee, or agent.

(d) An emergency exists for purposes of this section if a quorum of the corporation's directors cannot readily be assembled because of some catastrophic event.

Section 3.04.   Ultra Vires

(a) Except as provided in subsection (b), the validity of corporate action may not be challenged on the ground that the corporation lacks or lacked power to act.

(b) A corporation's power to act may be challenged:

(1) in a proceeding by a shareholder against the corporation to enjoin the act;

(2) in a proceeding by the corporation, directly, derivatively, or through a receiver, trustee, or other legal representative, against an incumbent or former director, officer, employee, or agent of the corporation; or

(3) in a proceeding by the Attorney General under section 14.30.

(c) In a shareholder's proceeding under subsection (b)(1) to enjoin an unauthorized corporate act, the court may enjoin or set aside the act, if equitable and if all affected persons are parties to the proceeding, and may award damages for loss (other than anticipated profits) suffered by the corporation or another party because of enjoining the unauthorized act.

CHAPTER 4   NAME

Section 4.01.   Corporate Name

(a) A corporate name:

(1) must contain the word "corporation," "incorporated," "company," or "limited," or the abbreviation "corp.," "inc.," "co.," or "ltd.," or

words or abbreviations of like import in another language; and

(2) may not contain language stating or implying that the corporation is organized for a purpose other than that permitted by section 3.01 and its articles of incorporation.

(b) Except as authorized by subsections (c) and (d), a corporate name must be distinguishable upon the records of the secretary of state from:

(1) the corporate name of a corporation incorporated or authorized to transact business in this state;

(2) a corporate name reserved or registered under section 4.02 or 4.03;

(3) the fictitious name adopted by a foreign corporation authorized to transact business in this state because its real name is unavailable; and

(4) the corporate name of a not-for-profit corporation incorporated or authorized to transact business in this state.

(c) A corporation may apply to the secretary of state for authorization to use a name that is not distinguishable upon his records from one or more of the names described in subsection (b). The secretary of state shall authorize use of the name applied for if:

(1) the other corporation consents to the use in writing and submits an undertaking in form satisfactory to the secretary of state to change its name to a name that is distinguishable upon the records of the secretary of state from the name of the applying corporation; or

(2) the applicant delivers to the secretary of state a certified copy of the final judgment of a court of competent jurisdiction establishing the applicant's right to use the name applied for in this state.

(d) A corporation may use the name (including the fictitious name) of another domestic or foreign corporation that is used in this state if the other corporation is incorporated or authorized to transact business in this state and the proposed user corporation:

(1) has merged with the other corporation;

(2) has been formed by reorganization of the other corporation; or

(3) has acquired all or substantially all of the assets, including the corporate name, of the other corporation.

(e) This Act does not control the use of fictitious names.

Section 4.02.   Reserved Name

(a) A person may reserve the exclusive use of a corporate name, including a fictitious name for a foreign corporation whose corporate name is not available, by delivering an application to the secretary of state for filing. The application must set forth the name and address of the applicant and the name proposed to be reserved. If the secretary of state finds that the corporate name applied for is available, he shall reserve the name for the applicant's exclusive use for a nonrenewable 120-day period.

(b) The owner of a reserved corporate name may transfer the reservation to another person by delivering to the secretary of state a signed notice of the transfer that states the name and address of the transferee.

Section 4.03.   Registered Name

(a) A foreign corporation may register its corporate name, or its corporate name with any addition required by section 15.06, if the name is distinguishable upon the records of the secretary of state from the corporate names that are not available under section 4.01(b)(3).

(b) A foreign corporation registers its corporate name, or its corporate name with any addition required by section 15.06, by delivering to the secretary of state for filing an application:

(1) setting forth its corporate name, or its corporate name with any addition required by section 15.06, the state or country and date of its incorporation, and a brief description of the nature of the business in which it is engaged; and

(2) accompanied by a certificate of existence (or a document of similar import) from the state or country of incorporation.

(c) The name is registered for the applicant's exclusive use upon the effective date of the application.

(d) A foreign corporation whose registration is effective may renew it for successive years by delivering to the secretary of state for filing a renewal application, which complies with the requirements of subsection (b), between October 1 and December 31 of the preceding year. The renewal application when filed renews the registration for the following calendar year.

(e) A foreign corporation whose registration is effective may thereafter qualify as a foreign corpora-

tion under the registered name or consent in writing to the use of that name by a corporation thereafter incorporated under this Act or by another foreign corporation thereafter authorized to transact business in this state. The registration terminates when the domestic corporation is incorporated or the foreign corporation qualifies or consents to the qualification of another foreign corporation under the registered name.

CHAPTER 5   OFFICE AND AGENT

Section 5.01.   Registered Office and Registered Agent

Each corporation must continuously maintain in this state:

(1) a registered office that may be the same as any of its places of business; and

(2) a registered agent, who may be:

(i) an individual who resides in this state and whose business office is identical with the registered office;

(ii) a domestic corporation or not-for-profit domestic corporation whose business office is identical with the registered office; or

(iii) a foreign corporation or not-for-profit foreign corporation authorized to transact business in this state whose business office is identical with the registered office.

Section 5.02.   Change of Registered Office
or Registered Agent

(a) A corporation may change its registered office or registered agent by delivering to the secretary of state for filing a statement of change that sets forth:

(1) the name of the corporation;

(2) the street address of its current registered office;

(3) if the current registered office is to be changed, the street address of the new registered office;

(4) the name of its current registered agent;

(5) if the current registered agent is to be changed, the name of the new registered agent and the new agent's written consent (either on the statement or attached to it) to the appointment; and

(6) that after the change or changes are

made, the street addresses of its registered office and the business office of its registered agent will be identical.

(b) If a registered agent changes the street address of his business office, he may change the street address of the registered office of any corporation for which he is the registered agent by notifying the corporation in writing of the change and signing (either manually or in facsimile) and delivering to the secretary of state for filing a statement that complies with the requirements of subsection (a) and recites that the corporation has been notified of the change.

Section 5.03.   Resignation of Registered Agent

(a) A registered agent may resign his agency appointment by signing and delivering to the secretary of state for filing the signed original and two exact or conformed copies of a statement of resignation. The statement may include a statement that the registered office is also discontinued.

(b) After filing the statement the secretary of state shall mail one copy to the registered office (if not discontinued) and the other copy to the corporation at its principal office.

(c) The agency appointment is terminated, and the registered office discontinued if so provided, on the 31st day after the date on which the statement was filed.

Section 5.04.   Service on Corporation

(a) A corporation's registered agent is the corporation's agent for service of process, notice, or demand required or permitted by law to be served on the corporation.

(b) If a corporation has no registered agent, or the agent cannot with reasonable diligence be served, the corporation may be served by registered or certified mail, return receipt requested, addressed to the secretary of the corporation at its principal office. Service is perfected under this subsection at the earliest of:

(1) the date the corporation receives the mail;

(2) the date shown on the return receipt, if signed on behalf of the corporation; or

(3) five days after its deposit in the United States Mail, as evidenced by the postmark, if mailed postpaid and correctly addressed.

(c) This section does not prescribe the only means, or necessarily the required means, of serving a corporation.

CHAPTER 6   SHARES AND DISTRIBUTIONS

Shares

Section 6.01.   Authorized Shares

(a) The articles of incorporation must prescribe the classes of shares and the number of shares of each class that the corporation is authorized to issue. If more than one class of shares is authorized, the articles of incorporation must prescribe a distinguishing designation for each class, and, prior to the issuance of shares of a class, the preferences, limitations, and relative rights of that class must be described in the articles of incorporation. All shares of a class must have preferences, limitations, and relative rights identical with those of other shares of the same class except to the extent otherwise permitted by section 6.02.

(b) The articles of incorporation must authorize (1) one or more classes of shares that together have unlimited voting rights, and (2) one or more classes of shares (which may be the same class or classes as those with voting rights) that together are entitled to receive the net assets of the corporation upon dissolution.

(c) The articles of incorporation may authorize one or more classes of shares that:

(1) have special, conditional, or limited voting rights, or no right to vote; except to the extent prohibited by this Act;

(2) are redeemable or convertible as specified in the articles of incorporation (i) at the option of the corporation, the shareholder, or another person or upon the occurrence of a designated event; (ii) for cash, indebtedness, securities, or other property; (iii) in a designated amount or in an amount determined in accordance with a designated formula or by reference to extrinsic data or events;

(3) entitle the holders to distributions calculated in any manner, including dividends that may be cumulative, noncumulative, or partially cumulative;

(4) have preference over any other class of shares with respect to distributions, including dividends and distributions upon the dissolution of the corporation.

(d) The description of the designations, preferences, limitations, and relative rights of share classes in subsection (c) is not exhaustive.

Section 6.02.   Terms of Class or Series Determined by Board of Directors

(a) If the articles of incorporation so provide, the board of directors may determine, in whole or part, the preferences, limitations, and relative rights (within the limits set forth in section 6.01) of (1) any class of shares before the issuance of any shares of that class or (2) one or more series within a class before the issuance of any shares of that series.

(b) Each series of a class must be given a distinguishing designation.

(c) All shares of a series must have preferences, limitations, and relative rights identical with those of other shares of the same series and, except to the extent otherwise provided in the description of the series, with those of other series of the same class.

(d) Before issuing any shares of a class or series created under this section, the corporation must deliver to the secretary of state for filing articles of amendment, which are effective without shareholder action, that set forth:

(1) the name of the corporation;

(2) the text of the amendment determining the terms of the class or series of shares;

(3) the date it was adopted; and

(4) a statement that the amendment was duly adopted by the board of directors.

Section 6.03.   Issued and Outstanding Shares

(a) A corporation may issue the number of shares of each class or series authorized by the articles of incorporation. Shares that are issued are outstanding shares until they are reacquired, redeemed, converted, or cancelled.

(b) The reacquisition, redemption, or conversion of outstanding shares is subject to the limitations of subsection (c) of this section and to section 6.40.

(c) At all times that shares of the corporation are outstanding, one or more shares that together have unlimited voting rights and one or more shares that together are entitled to receive the net assets of the corporation upon dissolution must be outstanding.

Section 6.04.   Fractional Shares

(a) A corporation may:

(1) issue fractions of a share or pay in money the value of fractions of a share;

(2) arrange for disposition of fractional shares by the shareholders;

(3) issue scrip in registered or bearer form entitling the holder to receive a full share upon surrendering enough scrip to equal a full share.

(b) Each certificate representing scrip must be conspicuously labeled "scrip" and must contain the information required by section 6.25(b).

(c) The holder of a fractional share is entitled to exercise the rights of a shareholder, including the right to vote, to receive dividends, and to participate in the assets of the corporation upon liquidation. The holder of scrip is not entitled to any of these rights unless the scrip provides for them.

(d) The board of directors may authorize the issuance of scrip subject to any condition considered desirable, including:

(1) that the scrip will become void if not exchanged for full shares before a specified date; and

(2) that the shares for which the scrip is exchangeable may be sold and the proceeds paid to the scripholders.

Issuance of Shares

Section 6.20.   Subscription for Shares Before Incorporation

(a) A subscription for shares entered into before incorporation is irrevocable for six months unless the subscription agreement provides a longer or shorter period or all the subscribers agree to revocation.

(b) The board of directors may determine the payment terms of subscriptions for shares that were entered into before incorporation, unless the subscription agreement specifies them. A call for payment by the board of directors must be uniform so far as practicable as to all shares of the same class or series, unless the subscription agreement specifies otherwise.

(c) Shares issued pursuant to subscriptions entered into before incorporation are fully paid and nonassessable when the corporation receives the consideration specified in the subscription agreement.

(d) If a subscriber defaults in payment of money or property under a subscription agreement entered into before incorporation, the corporation may collect the amount owed as any other debt. Alternatively, unless the subscription agreement provides otherwise, the corporation may rescind the agreement and may sell the shares if the debt remains unpaid more than 20 days after the corporation sends written demand for payment to the subscriber.

(e) A subscription agreement entered into after incorporation is a contract between the subscriber and the corporation subject to section 6.21.

Section 6.21.   Issuance of Shares

(a) The powers granted in this section to the board of directors may be reserved to the shareholders by the articles of incorporation.

(b) The board of directors may authorize shares to be issued for consideration consisting of any tangible or intangible property or benefit to the corporation, including cash, promissory notes, services performed, contracts for services to be performed, or other securities of the corporation.

(c) Before the corporation issues shares, the board of directors must determine that the consideration received or to be received for shares to be issued is adequate. That determination by the board of directors is conclusive insofar as the adequacy of consideration for the issuance of shares relates to whether the shares are validly issued, fully paid, and nonassessable.

(d) When the corporation receives the consideration for which the board of directors authorized the issuance of shares, the shares issued therefor are fully paid and nonassessable.

(e) The corporation may place in escrow shares issued for a contract for future services or benefits or a promissory note, or make other arrangements to restrict the transfer of the shares, and may credit distributions in respect of the shares against their purchase price, until the services are performed, the note is paid, or the benefits received. If the services are not performed, the note is not paid, or the benefits are not received, the shares escrowed or restricted and the distributions credited may be cancelled in whole or part.

Section 6.22.   Liability of Shareholders

(a) A purchaser from a corporation of its own shares is not liable to the corporation or its creditors with respect to the shares except to pay the consideration for which the shares were authorized to be issued

(section 6.21) or specified in the subscription agreement (section 6.20).

(b) Unless otherwise provided in the articles of incorporation, a shareholder of a corporation is not personally liable for the acts or debts of the corporation except that he may become personally liable by reason of his own acts or conduct.

Section 6.23.   Share Dividends

(a) Unless the articles of incorporation provide otherwise, shares may be issued pro rata and without consideration to the corporation's shareholders or to the shareholders of one or more classes or series. An issuance of shares under this subsection is a share dividend.

(b) Shares of one class or series may not be issued as a share dividend in respect of shares of another class or series unless (1) the articles of incorporation so authorize, (2) a majority of the votes entitled to be cast by the class or series to be issued approve the issue, or (3) there are no outstanding shares of the class or series to be issued.

(c) If the board of directors does not fix the record date for determining shareholders entitled to a share dividend, it is the date the board of directors authorizes the share dividend.

Section 6.24.   Share Options

A corporation may issue rights, options, or warrants for the purchase of shares of the corporation. The board of directors shall determine the terms upon which the rights, options, or warrants are issued, their form and content, and the consideration for which the shares are to be issued.

Section 6.25.   Form and Content of Certificates

(a) Shares may but need not be represented by certificates. Unless this Act or another statute expressly provides otherwise, the rights and obligations of shareholders are identical whether or not their shares are represented by certificates.

(b) At a minimum each share certificate must state on its face:

(1) the name of the issuing corporation and that it is organized under the law of this state;

(2) the name of the person to whom issued; and

(3) the number and class of shares and the designation of the series, if any, the certificate represents.

(c) If the issuing corporation is authorized to issue different classes of shares or different series within a class, the designations, relative rights, preferences, and limitations applicable to each class and the variations in rights, preferences, and limitations determined for each series (and the authority of the board of directors to determine variations for future series) must be summarized on the front or back of each certificate. Alternatively, each certificate may state conspicuously on its front or back that the corporation will furnish the shareholder this information on request in writing and without charge.

(d) Each share certificate (1) must be signed (either manually or in facsimile) by two officers designated in the bylaws or by the board of directors and (2) may bear the corporate seal of its facsimile.

(e) If the person who signed (either manually or in facsimile) a share certificate no longer holds office when the certificate is issued, the certificate is nevertheless valid.

Section 6.26.   *Shares without Certificates*

(a) Unless the articles of incorporation or bylaws provide otherwise, the board of directors of a corporation may authorize the issue of some or all of the shares of any or all of its classes or series without certificates. The authorization does not affect shares already represented by certificates until they are surrendered to the corporation.

(b) Within a reasonable time after the issue or transfer of shares without certificates, the corporation shall send the shareholder a written statement of the information required on certificates by section 6.25(b) and (c), and, if applicable, section 6.27.

Section 6.27.   *Restriction on Transfer of Shares and Other Securities*

(a) The articles of incorporation, bylaws, an agreement among shareholders, or an agreement between shareholders and the corporation may impose restrictions on the transfer or registration of transfer of shares of the corporation. A restriction does not affect shares issued before the restriction was adopted unless the holders of the shares are parties to the restriction agreement or voted in favor of the restriction.

(b) A restriction on the transfer or registration of transfer of shares is valid and enforceable against the holder or a transferee of the holder if the restriction is authorized by this section and its existence is noted conspicuously on the front or back of the certificate or is contained in the information statement required by section 6.26(b). Unless so noted, a restriction is not enforceable against a person without knowledge of the restriction.

(c) A restriction on the transfer or registration of transfer of shares is authorized:

(1) to maintain the corporation's status when it is dependent on the number or identity of its shareholders;

(2) to preserve exemptions under federal or state securities law;

(3) for any other reasonable purpose.

(d) A restriction on the transfer or registration of transfer of shares may:

(1) obligate the shareholder first to offer the corporation or other persons (separately, consecutively, or simultaneously) an opportunity to acquire the restricted shares;

(2) obligate the corporation or other persons (separately, consecutively, or simultaneously) to acquire the restricted shares;

(3) require the corporation, the holders of any class of its shares, or another person to approve the transfer of the restricted shares, if the requirement is not manifestly unreasonable;

(4) prohibit the transfer of the restricted shares to designated persons or classes of persons, if the prohibition is not manifestly unreasonable.

(e) For purposes of this section, "shares" includes a security convertible into or carrying a right to subscribe for or acquire shares.

Section 6.28.   *Expense of Issue*

A corporation may pay the expenses of selling or underwriting its shares, and of organizing or reorganizing the corporation, from the consideration received for shares.

Subsequent Acquisition of Shares by Shareholders and Corporation

Section 6.30.   *Shareholders' Preemptive Rights*

(a) The shareholders of a corporation do not have a preemptive right to acquire the corporation's unissued shares except to the extent the articles of incorporation so provide.

(b) A statement included in the articles of incorporation that "the corporation elects to have preemptive rights" (or words of similar import) means that the following principles apply except to the extent the articles of incorporation expressly provide otherwise:

(1) The shareholders of the corporation have a preemptive right, granted on uniform terms and conditions prescribed by the board of directors to provide a fair and reasonable opportunity to exercise the right, to acquire proportional amounts of the corporation's unissued shares upon the decision of the board of directors to issue them.

(2) A shareholder may waive his preemptive right. A waiver evidenced by a writing is irrevocable even though it is not supported by consideration.

(3) There is no preemptive right with respect to:

(i) shares issued as compensation to directors, officers, agents, or employees of the corporation, its subsidiaries or affiliates;

(ii) shares issued to satisfy conversion or option rights created to provide compensation to directors, officers, agents, or employees of the corporation, its subsidiaries or affiliates;

(iii) shares authorized in articles of incorporation that are issued within six months from the effective date of incorporation;

(iv) shares sold otherwise than for money.

(4) Holders of shares of any class without general voting rights but with preferential rights to distributions or assets have no preemptive rights with respect to shares of any class.

(5) Holders of shares of any class with general voting rights but without preferential rights to distributions or assets have no preemptive rights with respect to shares of any class with preferential rights to distributions or assets unless the shares with preferential rights are convertible into or carry a right to subscribe for or acquire shares without preferential rights.

(6) Shares subject to preemptive rights that are not acquired by shareholders may be issued to any person for a period of one year after being offered to shareholders at a consideration set by the board of directors that is not lower than the consideration set for the exercise of preemptive rights. An

offer at a lower consideration or after the expiration of one year is subject to the shareholders' preemptive rights.

(c) For purposes of this section, "shares" includes a security convertible into or carrying a right to subscribe for or acquire shares.

Section 6.31. Corporation's Acquisition of its Own Shares

(a) A corporation may acquire its own shares and shares so acquired constitute authorized but unissued shares.

(b) If the articles of incorporation prohibit the reissue of acquired shares, the number of authorized shares is reduced by the number of shares acquired, effective upon amendment of the articles of incorporation.

(c) The board of directors may adopt articles of amendment under this section without shareholder action and deliver them to the secretary of state for filing. The articles must set forth:

(1) the name of the corporation;

(2) the reduction in the number of authorized shares, itemized by class and series; and

(3) the total number of authorized shares, itemized by class and series, remaining after reduction of the shares.

Distributions

Section 6.40. Distributions to Shareholders

(a) A board of directors may authorize and the corporation may make distributions to its shareholders subject to restriction by the articles of incorporation and the limitation in subsection (c).

(b) If the board of directors does not fix the record date for determining shareholders entitled to a distribution (other than one involving a repurchase or reacquisition of shares), it is the date the board of directors authorizes the distribution.

(c) No distribution may be made if, after giving it effect:

(1) the corporation would not be able to pay its debts as they become due in the usual course of business; or

(2) the corporation's total assets would be less than the sum of its total liabilities plus (unless the articles of incorporation permit otherwise) the amount that would be needed, if the corporation were to be dissolved at the time of the distribution,

to satisfy the preferential rights upon dissolution of shareholders whose preferential rights are superior to those receiving the distribution.

(d) The board of directors may base a determination that a distribution is not prohibited under subsection (c) either on financial statements prepared on the basis of accounting practices and principles that are reasonable in the circumstances or on a fair valuation or other method that is reasonable in the circumstances.

(e) Except as provided in subsection (c), the effect of a distribution under subsection (c) is measured:

(1) in the case of distribution by purchase, redemption, or other acquisition of the corporation's shares, as of the earlier of (i) the date money or other property is transferred or debt incurred by the corporation or (ii) the date the shareholder ceases to be a shareholder with respect to the acquired shares;

(2) in the case of any other distribution of indebtedness, as of the date the indebtedness is distributed;

(3) in all other cases, as of (i) the date the distribution is authorized if the payment occurs within 120 days after the date of authorization or (ii) the date the payment is made if it occurs more than 120 days after the date of authorization.

(f) A corporation's indebtedness to a shareholder incurred by reason of a distribution made in accordance with this section is at parity with the corporation's indebtedness to its general, unsecured creditors except to the extent subordinated by agreement.

CHAPTER 7   SHAREHOLDERS

Meetings

Section 7.01.   Annual Meeting

(a) A corporation shall hold a meeting of shareholders annually at a time stated in or fixed in accordance with the bylaws.

(b) Annual shareholders' meetings may be held in or out of this state at the place stated in or fixed in accordance with the bylaws. If no place is stated in or fixed in accordance with the bylaws, annual meetings shall be held at the corporation's principal office.

(c) The failure to hold an annual meeting at the time stated in or fixed in accordance with a corporation's bylaws does not affect the validity of any corporate action.

Section 7.02.   Special Meeting

(a) A corporation shall hold a special meeting of shareholders:

(1) on call of its board of directors or the person or persons authorized to do so by the articles of incorporation or bylaws; or

(2) if the holders of at least 10 percent of all the votes entitled to be cast on any issue proposed to be considered at the proposed special meeting sign, date, and deliver to the corporation's secretary one or more written demands for the meeting describing the purpose or purposes for which it is to be held.

(b) If not otherwise fixed under section 7.03 or 7.07, the record date for determining shareholders entitled to demand a special meeting is the date the first shareholder signs the demand.

(c) Special shareholders' meetings may be held in or out of this state at the place stated in or fixed in accordance with the bylaws. If no place is stated or fixed in accordance with the bylaws, special meetings shall be held at the corporation's principal office.

(d) Only business within the purpose or purposes described in the meeting notice required by section 7.05(c) may be conducted at a special shareholders' meeting.

Section 7.03.   Court-Ordered Meeting

(a) The [name or describe] court of the county where a corporation's principal office (or, if none in this state, its registered office) is located may summarily order a meeting to be held:

(1) on application of any shareholder of the corporation entitled to participate in an annual meeting if an annual meeting was not held within the earlier of 6 months after the end of the corporation's fiscal year or 15 months after its last annual meeting; or

(2) on application of a shareholder who signed a demand for a special meeting valid under section 7.02, if;

(i) notice of the special meeting was not given within 30 days after the date the demand was delivered to the corporation's secretary; or

(ii) the special meeting was not held in accordance with the notice.

(b) The court may fix the time and place of the meeting, determine the shares entitled to participate in the meeting, specify a record date for determining shareholders entitled to notice of and to vote at the meeting, prescribe the form and content of the meeting notice, fix the quorum required for specific matters to be considered at the meeting (or direct that the votes represented at the meeting constitute a quorum for action on those matters), and enter other orders necessary to accomplish the purpose or purposes of the meeting.

Section 7.04.   Action without Meeting

(a) Action required or permitted by this Act to be taken at a shareholders' meeting may be taken without a meeting if the action is taken by all the shareholders entitled to vote on the action. The action must be evidenced by one or more written consents describing the action taken, signed by all the shareholders entitled to vote on the action, and delivered to the corporation for inclusion in the minutes or filing with the corporate records.

(b) If not otherwise fixed under section 7.03 or 7.07, the record date for determining shareholders entitled to take action without a meeting is the date the first shareholder signs the consent under subsection (a).

(c) A consent signed under this section has the effect of a meeting vote and may be described as such in any document.

(d) If this Act requires that notice of proposed action be given to nonvoting shareholders and the action is to be taken by unanimous consent of the voting shareholders, the corporation must give its nonvoting shareholders written notice of the proposed action at least 10 days before the action is taken. The notice must contain or be accompanied by the same material that, under this Act, would have been required to be sent to nonvoting shareholders in a notice of meeting at which the proposed action would have been submitted to the shareholders for action.

Section 7.05.   Notice of Meeting

(a) A corporation shall notify shareholders of the date, time, and place of each annual and special shareholders' meeting no fewer than 10 nor more than 60 days before the meeting date. Unless this Act or the articles of incorporation require otherwise, the corporation is required to give notice only to shareholders entitled to vote at the meeting.

(b) Unless this Act or the articles of incorporation require otherwise, notice of an annual meeting

need not include a description of the purpose or purposes for which the meeting is called.

(c) Notice of a special meeting must include a description of the purpose or purposes for which the meeting is called.

(d) If not otherwise fixed under section 7.03 or 7.07, the record date for determining shareholders entitled to notice of and to vote at an annual or special shareholders' meeting is the close of business on the day before the first notice is delivered to shareholders.

(e) Unless the bylaws require otherwise, if an annual or special shareholders' meeting is adjourned to a different date, time, or place, notice need not be given of the new date, time, or place if the new date, time, or place is announced at the meeting before adjournment. If a new record date for the adjourned meeting is or must be fixed under section 7.07, however, notice of the adjourned meeting must be given under this section to persons who are shareholders as of the new record date.

Section 7.06.   Waiver of Notice

(a) A shareholder may waive any notice required by this Act, the articles of incorporation, or bylaws before or after the date and time stated in the notice. The waiver must be in writing, be signed by the shareholder entitled to the notice, and be delivered to the corporation for inclusion in the minutes or filing with the corporate records.

(b) A shareholder's attendance at a meeting:

(1) waives objection to lack of notice or defective notice of the meeting, unless the shareholder at the beginning of the meeting objects to holding the meeting or transacting business at the meeting;

(2) waives objection to consideration of a particular matter at the meeting that is not within the purpose or purposes described in the meeting notice, unless the shareholder objects to considering the matter when it is presented.

Section 7.07.   Record Date

(a) The bylaws may fix or provide the manner of fixing the record date for one or more voting groups in order to determine the shareholders entitled to notice of a shareholders' meeting, to demand a special meeting, to vote, or to take any other action. If the bylaws do not fix or provide for fixing a record date, the board of directors of the corporation may fix a future date as the record date.

(b) A record date fixed under this section may not be more than 70 days before the meeting or action requiring a determination of shareholders.

(c) A determination of shareholders entitled to notice of or to vote at a shareholders' meeting is effective for any adjournment of the meeting unless the board of directors fixes a new record date, which it must do if the meeting is adjourned to a date more than 120 days after the date fixed for the original meeting.

(d) If a court orders a meeting adjourned to a date more than 120 days after the date fixed for the original meeting, it may provide that the original record date continues in effect or it may fix a new record date.

Voting

Section 7.20.   Shareholders' List for Meeting

(a) After fixing a record date for a meeting, a corporation shall prepare an alphabetical list of the names of all its shareholders who are entitled to notice of a shareholders' meeting. The list must be arranged by voting group (and within each voting group by class or series of shares) and show the address of and number of shares held by each shareholder.

(b) The shareholders' list must be available for inspection by any shareholder, beginning two business days after notice of the meeting is given for which the list was prepared and continuing through the meeting, at the corporation's principal office or at a place identified in the meeting notice in the city where the meeting will be held. A shareholder, his agent, or attorney is entitled on written demand to inspect and, subject to the requirements of section 16.02(c), to copy the list, during regular business hours and at his expense, during the period it is available for inspection.

(c) The corporation shall make the shareholders' list available at the meeting, and any shareholder, his agent, or attorney is entitled to inspect the list at any time during the meeting or any adjournment.

(d) If the corporation refuses to allow a shareholder, his agent, or attorney to inspect the shareholders' list before or at the meeting (or copy the list as permitted by subsection (b)), the [name or describe] court of the county where a corporation's principal office (or, if none in this state, its registered office) is located, on application of the shareholder, may summarily order the inspection or copying at the corporation's expense and may postpone the meeting for which the list was prepared until the inspection or copying is complete.

(e) Refusal or failure to prepare or make available the shareholders' list does not affect the validity of action taken at the meeting.

Section 7.21.   Voting Entitlement of Shares

(a) Except as provided in subsections (b) and (c) or unless the articles of incorporation provide otherwise, each outstanding share, regardless of class, is entitled to one vote on each matter voted on at a shareholders' meeting. Only shares are entitled to vote.

(b) Absent special circumstances, the shares of a corporation are not entitled to vote if they are owned, directly or indirectly, by a second corporation, domestic or foreign, and the first corporation owns, directly or indirectly, a majority of the shares entitled to vote for directors of the second corporation.

(c) Subsection (b) does not limit the power of a corporation to vote any shares, including its own shares, held by it in a fiduciary capacity.

(d) Redeemable shares are not entitled to vote after notice of redemption is mailed to the holders and a sum sufficient to redeem the shares has been deposited with a bank, trust company, or other financial institution under an irrevocable obligation to pay the holders the redemption price on surrender of the shares.

Section 7.22.   Proxies

(a) A shareholder may vote his shares in person or by proxy.

(b) A shareholder may appoint a proxy to vote or otherwise act for him by signing an appointment form, either personally or by his attorney-in-fact.

(c) An appointment of a proxy is effective when received by the secretary or other officer or agent authorized to tabulate votes. An appointment is valid for 11 months unless a longer period is expressly provided in the appointment form.

(d) An appointment of a proxy is revocable by the shareholder unless the appointment form conspicuously states that it is irrevocable and the appointment is coupled with an interest. Appointments coupled with an interest include the appointment of:

(1) a pledge;

(2) a person who purchased or agreed to purchase the shares;

(3) a creditor of the corporation who extended it credit under terms requiring the appointment;

(4) an employee of the corporation whose employment contract requires the appointment; or

(5) a party to a voting agreement created under section 7.31.

(e) The death or incapacity of the shareholder appointing a proxy does not affect the right of the corporation to accept the proxy's authority unless notice of the death or incapacity is received by the secretary or other officer or agent authorized to tabulate votes before the proxy exercises his authority under the appointment.

(f) An appointment made irrevocable under subsection (d) is revoked when the interest with which it is coupled is extinguished.

(g) A transferee for value of shares subject to an irrevocable appointment may revoke the appointment if he did not know of its existence when he acquired the shares and the existence of the irrevocable appointment was not noted conspicuously on the certificate representing the shares or on the information statement for shares without certificates.

(h) Subject to section 7.24 and to any express limitation on the proxy's authority appearing on the face of the appointment form, a corporation is entitled to accept the proxy's vote or other action as that of the shareholder making the appointment.

Section 7.23.   Shares Held by Nominees

(a) A corporation may establish a procedure by which the beneficial owner of shares that are registered in the name of a nominee is recognized by the corporation as the shareholder. The extent of this recognition may be determined in the procedure.

(b) The procedure may set forth:

(1) the types of nominees to which it applies;

(2) the rights or privileges that the corporation recognizes in a beneficial owner;

(3) the manner is which the procedure is selected by the nominee;

(4) the information that must be provided when the procedure is selected;

(5) the period for which selection of the procedure is effective; and

(6) other aspects of the rights and duties created.

Section 7.24.   Corporation's Acceptance of Votes

(a) If the name signed on a vote, consent, waiver, or proxy appointment corresponds to the name of a shareholder, the corporation if acting in good faith is entitled to accept the vote, consent, waiver, or proxy appointment and give it effect as the act of the shareholder.

(b) If the name signed on a vote, consent, waiver, or proxy appointment does not correspond to the name of its shareholder, the corporation if acting in good faith is nevertheless entitled to accept the vote, consent, waiver, or proxy appointment and give it effect as the act of the shareholder if:

(1) the shareholder is an entity and the name signed purports to be that of an officer or agent of the entity;

(2) the name signed purports to be that of an administrator, executor, guardian, or conservator representing the shareholder and, if the corporation requests, evidence of fiduciary status acceptable to the corporation has been presented with respect to the vote, consent, waiver, or proxy appointment;

(3) the name signed purports to be that of a receiver or trustee in bankruptcy of the shareholder and, if the corporation requests, evidence of this status acceptable to the corporation has been presented with respect to the vote, consent, waiver, or proxy appointment;

(4) the name signed purports to be that of a pledgee, beneficial owner, or attorney-in-fact of the shareholder and, if the corporation requests, evidence acceptable to the corporation of the signatory's authority to sign for the shareholder has been presented with respect to the vote, consent, waiver, or proxy appointment;

(5) two or more persons are the shareholder as cotenants or fiduciaries and the name signed purports to be the name of at least one of the coowners and the person signing appears to be acting on behalf of all the coowners.

(c) The corporation is entitled to reject a vote, consent, waiver, or proxy appointment if the secretary or other officer or agent authorized to tabulate votes, acting in good faith, has reasonable basis for doubt about the validity of the signature on it or about the signatory's authority to sign for the shareholder.

(d) The corporation and its officer or agent who accepts or rejects a vote, consent, waiver, or proxy appointment in good faith and in accordance with the standards of this section are not liable in damages to the shareholder for the consequences of the acceptance or rejection.

(e) Corporate action based on the acceptance or rejection of a vote, consent, waiver, or proxy appointment under this section is valid unless a court of competent jurisdiction determines otherwise.

Section 7.25. *Quorum and Voting Requirements for Voting Groups*

(a) Shares entitled to vote as a separate voting group may take action on a matter at a meeting only if a quorum of those shares exists with respect to that matter. Unless the articles of incorporation or this Act provide otherwise, a majority of the votes entitled to be cast on the matter by the voting group constitutes a quorum of that voting group for action on that matter.

(b) Once a share is represented for any purpose at a meeting, it is deemed present for quorum purposes for the remainder of the meeting and for any adjournment of that meeting unless a new record date is or must be set for that adjourned meeting.

(c) If a quorum exists, action on a matter (other than the election of directors) by a voting group is approved if the votes cast within the voting group favoring the action exceed the votes cast opposing the action, unless the articles of incorporation or this Act require a greater number of affirmative votes.

(d) An amendment of articles of incorporation adding, changing, or deleting a quorum or voting requirement for a voting group greater than specified in subsection (a) or (c) is governed by section 7.27.

(e) The election of directors is governed by section 7.28.

Section 7.26. *Action by Single and Multiple Voting Groups*

(a) If the articles of incorporation or this Act provide for voting by a single voting group on a matter, action on that matter is taken when voted upon by that voting group as provided in section 7.25.

(b) If the articles of incorporation or this Act provide for voting by two or more voting groups on a matter, action on that matter is taken only when voted upon by each of those voting groups counted separately as provided in section 7.25. Action may be taken by one voting group on a matter even though no action is taken by another voting group entitled to vote on the matter.

Section 7.27. *Greater Quorum or Voting Requirements*

(a) The articles of incorporation may provide for a greater quorum or voting requirement for shareholders (or voting groups of shareholders) than is provided for by this Act.

(b) An amendment to the articles of incorporation that adds, changes, or deletes a greater quorum or voting requirement must meet the same quorum requirement and be adopted by the same vote and voting groups required to take action under the quorum and voting requirements then in effect or proposed to be adopted, whichever is greater.

Section 7.28. *Voting for Directors; Cumulative Voting*

(a) Unless otherwise provided in the articles of incorporation, directors are elected by a plurality of the votes cast by the shares entitled to vote in the election at a meeting at which a quorum is present.

(b) Shareholders do not have a right to cumulate their votes for directors unless the articles of incorporation so provide.

(c) A statement included in the articles of incorporation that "[all] [a designated voting group of] shareholders are entitled to cumulate their votes for directors" (or words of similar import) means that the shareholders designated are entitled to multiply the number of votes they are entitled to cast by the number of directors for whom they are entitled to vote and cast the product for a single candidate or distribute the product among two or more candidates.

(d) Shares otherwise entitled to vote cumulatively may not be voted cumulatively at a particular meeting unless:

(1) the meeting notice or proxy statement accompanying the notice states conspicuously that cumulative voting is authorized; or

(2) a shareholder who has the right to cumulate his votes gives notice to the corporation not less than 48 hours before the time set for the meeting of his intent to cumulate his votes during the meeting, and if one shareholder gives this notice all other shareholders in the same voting group participating in the election are entitled to cumulate their votes without giving further notice.

Voting Trusts and Agreements

Section 7.30.   Voting Trusts

(a) One or more shareholders may create a voting trust, conferring on a trustee the right to vote or otherwise act for them, by signing an agreement setting out the provisions of the trust (which may include anything consistent with its purpose) and transferring their shares to the trustee. When a voting trust agreement is signed, the trustee shall prepare a list of the names and addresses of all owners of beneficial interests in the trust, together with the number and class of shares each transferred to the trust, and deliver copies of the list and agreement to the corporation's principal office.

(b) A voting trust becomes effective on the date the first shares subject to the trust are registered in the trustee's name. A voting trust is valid for not more than 10 years after its effective date unless extended under subsection (c).

(c) All or some of the parties to a voting trust may extend it for additional terms of not more than 10 years each by signing an extension agreement and obtaining the voting trustee's written consent to the extension. An extension is valid for 10 years from the date the first shareholder signs the extension agreement. The voting trustee must deliver copies of the extension agreement and list of beneficial owners to the corporation's principal office. An extension agreement binds only those parties signing it.

Section 7.31.   Voting Agreements

(a) Two or more shareholders may provide for the manner in which they will vote their shares by signing an agreement for that purpose. A voting agreement created under this section is not subject to the provisions of section 7.30.

(b) A voting agreement created under this section is specifically enforceable.

Derivative Proceedings

Section 7.40.   Procedure in Derivative Proceedings

(a) A person may not commence a proceeding in the right of a domestic or foreign corporation unless he was a shareholder of the corporation when the transaction complained of occurred or unless he became a shareholder through transfer by operation of law from one who was a shareholder at that time.

(b) A complaint in a proceeding brought in the right of a corporation must be verified and allege with particularity the demand made, if any, to obtain action by the board of directors and either that the demand was refused or ignored or why he did not make the demand. Whether or not a demand for action was made, if the corporation commences an investigation of the changes made in the demand or complaint, the court may stay any proceeding until the investigation is completed.

(c) A proceeding commenced under this section may not be discontinued or settled without the court's approval. If the court determines that a proposed discontinuance or settlement will substantially affect the interest of the corporation's shareholders or a class of shareholders, the court shall direct that notice be given the shareholders affected.

(d) On termination of the proceeding the court may require the plaintiff to pay any defendant's reasonable expenses (including counsel fees) incurred in defending the proceeding if it finds that the proceeding was commenced without reasonable cause.

(e) For purposes of this section, "shareholder" includes a beneficial owner whose shares are held in a voting trust or held by a nominee on his behalf.

CHAPTER 8   DIRECTORS AND OFFICERS

Board of Directors

*Section 8.01.   Requirement for and Duties
of Board of Directors*

(a) Except as provided in subsection (c), each corporation must have a board of directors.

(b) All corporate powers shall be exercised by or under the authority of, and the business and affairs of the corporation managed under the direction of, its board of directors, subject to any limitation set forth in the articles of incorporation.

(c) A corporation having 50 or fewer shareholders may dispense with or limit the authority of a board of directors by describing in its articles of incorporation who will perform some or all of the duties of a board of directors.

Section 8.02.   Qualifications of Directors

The articles of incorporation or bylaws may prescribe qualifications for directors. A director need not be a resident of this state or a shareholder of the corporation unless the articles of incorporation or bylaws so prescribe.

Section 8.03.　Number and Election of Directors

(a) A board of directors must consist of one or more individuals, with the number specified in or fixed in accordance with the articles of incorporation or bylaws.

(b) If a board of directors has power to fix or change the number of directors, the board may increase or decrease by 30 percent or less the number of directors last approved by the shareholders, but only the shareholders may increase or decrease by more than 30 percent the number of directors last approved by the shareholders.

(c) The articles of incorporation or bylaws may establish a variable range for the size of the board of directors by fixing a minimum and maximum number of directors. If a variable range is established, the number of directors may be fixed or changed from time to time, within the minimum and maximum, by the shareholders or the board of directors. After shares are issued, only the shareholders may change the range for the size of the board or change from a fixed to a variable-range size board or vice versa.

(d) Directors are elected at the first annual shareholders' meeting and at each annual meeting thereafter unless their terms are staggered under section 8.06.

Section 8.04.　Election of Directors by Certain Classes of Shareholders

If the articles of incorporation authorize dividing the shares into classes, the articles may also authorize the election of all or a specified number of directors by the holders of one or more authorized classes of shares. A class (or classes) of shares entitled to elect one or more directors is a separate voting group for purposes of the election of directors.

Section 8.05.　Terms of Directors Generally

(a) The terms of the initial directors of a corporation expire at the first shareholders' meeting at which directors are elected.

(b) The terms of all other directors expire at the next annual shareholders' meeting following their election unless their terms are staggered under section 8.06.

(c) A decrease in the number of directors does not shorten an incumbent director's term.

(d) The term of a director elected to fill a vacancy expires at the next shareholders' meeting at which directors are elected.

(e) Despite the expiration of a director's term, he continues to serve until his successor is elected and qualifies or until there is a decrease in the number of directors.

Section 8.06.　Staggered Terms for Directors

If there are nine or more directors, the articles of incorporation may provide for staggering their terms by dividing the total number of directors into two or three groups, with each group containing one half or one-third of the total, as near as may be. In that event, the terms of directors in the first group expire at the first annual shareholders' meeting after their election, the terms of the second group expire at the second annual shareholders' meeting after their election, and the terms of the third group, if any, expire at the third annual shareholders' meeting after their election. At each annual shareholders' meeting held thereafter, directors shall be chosen for a term of two years or three years, as the case may be, to succeed those whose terms expire.

Section 8.07.　Resignation of Directors

(a) A director may resign at any time by delivering written notice to the board of directors, its chairman, or to the corporation.

(b) A resignation is effective when the notice is delivered unless the notice specifies a later effective date.

Section 8.08.　Removal of Directors by Shareholders

(a) The shareholders may remove one or more directors with or without cause unless the articles of incorporation provide that directors may be removed only for cause.

(b) If a director is elected by a voting group of shareholders, only the shareholders of that voting group may participate in the vote to remove him.

(c) If cumulative voting is authorized, a director may not be removed if the number of votes sufficient to elect him under cumulative voting is voted against his removal. If cumulative voting is not authorized, a director may be removed only if the number of votes cast to remove him exceeds the number of votes cast not to remove him.

(d) A director may be removed by the shareholders only at a meeting called for the purpose of removing him and the meeting notice must state that the purpose, or one of the purposes, of the meeting is removal of the director.

Section 8.09. *Removal of Directors by Judicial Proceeding*

(a) The [name or describe] court of the county where a corporation's principal office (or, if none in this state, its registered office) is located may remove a director of the corporation from office in a proceeding commenced either by the corporation or by its shareholders holding at least 10 percent of the outstanding shares of any class if the court finds that (1) the director engaged in fraudulent or dishonest conduct, or gross abuse of authority or discretion, with respect to the corporation and (2) removal is in the best interest of the corporation.

(b) The court that removes a director may bar the director from reelection for a period prescribed by the court.

(c) If shareholders commence a proceeding under subsection (a), they shall make the corporation a party defendant.

Section 8.10. *Vacancy on Board*

(a) Unless the articles of incorporation provide otherwise, if a vacancy occurs on a board of directors, including a vacancy resulting from an increase in the number of directors:

(1) the shareholders may fill the vacancy;

(2) the board of directors may fill the vacancy; or

(3) if the directors remaining in office constitute fewer than a quorum of the board, they may fill the vacancy by the affirmative vote of a majority of all the directors remaining in office.

(b) If the vacant office was held by a director elected by a voting group of shareholders, only the holders of shares of that voting group are entitled to vote to fill the vacancy if it is filled by the shareholders.

(c) A vacancy that will occur at a specific later date (by reason of a resignation effective at a later date under section 8.07(b) or otherwise) may be filled before the vacancy occurs but the new director may not take office until the vacancy occurs.

Section 8.11. *Compensation of Directors*

Unless the articles of incorporation or bylaws provide otherwise, the board of directors may fix the compensation of directors.

Meetings and Action of the Board

Section 8.20. *Meetings*

(a) The board of directors may hold regular or special meetings in or out of this state.

(b) Unless the articles of incorporation or bylaws provide otherwise, the board of directors may permit any or all directors to participate in a regular or special meeting by, or conduct the meeting through the use of, any means of communication by which all directors participating may simultaneously hear each other during the meeting. A director participating in a meeting by this means is deemed to be present in person at the meeting.

Section 8.21. *Action without Meeting*

(a) Unless the articles of incorporation or bylaws provide otherwise, action required or permitted by this Act to be taken at a board of directors' meeting may be taken without a meeting if the action is taken by all members of the board. The action must be evidenced by one or more written consents describing the action taken, signed by each director, and included in the minutes or filed with the corporate records reflecting the action taken.

(b) Action taken under this section is effective when the last director signs the consent, unless the consent specifies a different effective date.

(c) A consent signed under this section has the effect of a meeting vote and may be described as such in any document.

Section 8.22. *Notice of Meeting*

(a) Unless the articles of incorporation or bylaws provide otherwise, regular meetings of the board of directors may be held without notice of the date, time, place, or purpose of the meeting.

(b) Unless the articles of incorporation or bylaws provide for a longer or shorter period, special meetings of the board of directors must be preceded by at least two days' notice of the date, time, and place of the meeting. The notice need not describe the purpose of the special meeting unless required by the articles of incorporation or bylaws.

Section 8.23. *Waiver of Notice*

(a) A director may waive any notice required by this Act, the articles of incorporation, or bylaws before or after the date and time stated in the notice. Except as provided by subsection (b), the waiver must be in writing, signed by the director entitled to the notice, and filed with the minutes or corporate records.

(b) A director's attendance at or participation in a meeting waives any required notice to him of the meeting unless the director at the beginning of the meeting (or promptly upon his arrival) objects to holding the meeting or transacting business at the meeting and does not thereafter vote for or assent to action taken at the meeting.

Section 8.24.   Quorum and Voting

(a) Unless the articles of incorporation or bylaws require a greater number, a quorum of a board of directors consists of:

(1) a majority of the fixed number of directors if the corporation has a fixed board size; or

(2) a majority of the number of directors prescribed, or if no number is prescribed the number in office immediately before the meeting begins, if the corporation has a variable-range size board.

(b) The articles of incorporation or bylaws may authorize a quorum of a board of directors to consist of no fewer than one-third of the fixed or prescribed number of directors determined under subsection (a).

(c) If a quorum is present when a vote is taken, the affirmative vote of a majority of directors present is the act of the board of directors unless the articles of incorporation or bylaws require the vote of a greater number of directors.

(d) A director who is present at a meeting of the board of directors or a committee of the board of directors when corporate action is taken is deemed to have assented to the action taken unless: (1) he objects at the beginning of the meeting (or promptly upon his arrival) to holding it or transacting business at the meeting; (2) his dissent or abstention from the action taken is entered in the minutes of the meeting; or (3) he delivers written notice of his dissent or abstention to the presiding officer of the meeting before its adjournment or to the corporation immediately after adjournment of the meeting. The right of dissent or abstention is not available to a director who votes in favor of the action taken.

Section 8.25.   Committees

(a) Unless the articles of incorporation or bylaws provide otherwise, a board of directors may create one or more committees and appoint members of the board of directors to serve on them. Each committee must

have two or more members, who serve at the pleasure of the board of directors.

(b) The creation of a committee and appointment of members to it must be approved by the greater of (1) a majority of all the directors in office when the action is taken or (2) the number of directors required by the articles of incorporation or bylaws to take action under section 8.24.

(c) Sections 8.20 through 8.24, which govern meetings, action without meetings, notice and waiver of notice, and quorum and voting requirements of the board of directors, apply to committees and their members as well.

(d) To the extent specified by the board of directors or in the articles of incorporation or bylaws, each committee may exercise the authority of the board of directors under section 8.01.

(e) A committee may not, however:

(1) authorize distributions;

(2) approve or propose to shareholders action that this Act requires be approved by shareholders;

(3) fill vacancies on the board of directors or on any of its committees;

(4) amend articles of incorporation pursuant to section 10.02;

(5) adopt, amend, or repeal bylaws;

(6) approve a plan of merger not requiring shareholder approval;

(7) authorize or approve reacquisition of shares, except according to a formula or method prescribed by the board of directors; or

(8) authorize or approve the issuance or sale or contract for sale of shares, or determine the designation and relative rights, preferences, and limitations of a class or series of shares, except that the board of directors may authorize a committee (or a senior executive officer of the corporation) to do so within limits specifically prescribed by the board of directors.

(f) The creation of, delegation of authority to, or action by a committee does not alone constitute compliance by a director with the standards of conduct described in section 8.30.

Standards of Conduct

Section 8.30.   General Standards for Directors

(a) A director shall discharge his duties as a director, including his duties as a member of a committee:

(1) in good faith;

(2) with the care an ordinary prudent person in a like position would exercise under similar circumstances; and

(3) in a manner he reasonably believes to be in the best interests of the corporation.

(b) In discharging his duties a director is entitled to rely on information, opinions, reports, or statements, including financial statements and other financial data, if prepared or presented by:

(1) one or more officers or employees of the corporation whom the director reasonably believes to be reliable and competent in the matters presented;

(2) legal counsel, public accountants, or other persons as to matters the director reasonably believes are within the person's professional or expert competence; or

(3) a committee of the board of directors of which he is not a member if the director reasonably believes the committee merits confidence.

(c) A director is not acting in good faith if he has knowledge concerning the matter in question that makes reliance otherwise permitted by subsection (b) unwarranted.

(d) A director is not liable for any action taken as a director, or any failure to take any action, if he performed the duties of his office in compliance with this section.

Section 8.31.   Director Conflict of Interest

(a) A conflict of interest transaction is a transaction with the corporation in which a director of the corporation has a direct or indirect interest. A conflict of interest transaction is not voidable by the corporation solely because of the director's interest in the transaction if any one of the following is true:

(1) the material facts of the transaction and the director's interest were disclosed or known to the board of directors or a committee of the board of directors and the board of directors or committee authorized, approved, or ratified the transaction;

(2) the material facts of the transaction and the director's interest were disclosed or known to the shareholders entitled to vote and they authorized, approved, or ratified the transaction; or

(3) the transaction was fair to the corporation.

(b) For purposes of this section, a director of the corporation has an indirect interest in a transaction if

(1) another entity in which he has a material financial interest or in which he is a general partner is a party to the transaction or (2) another entity of which he is a director, officer, or trustee is a party to the transaction and the transaction is or should be considered by the board of directors of the corporation.

(c) For purposes of subsection (a)(1), a conflict of interest transaction is authorized, approved, or ratified if it receives the affirmative vote of a majority of the directors on the board of directors (or on the committee) who have no direct or indirect interest in the transaction, but a transaction may not be authorized, approved, or ratified under this section by a single director. If a majority of the directors who have no direct or indirect interest in the transaction voted to authorize, approve, or ratify the transaction, a quorum is present for the purpose of taking action under this section. The presence of, or a vote cast by, a director with a direct or indirect interest in the transaction does not affect the validity of any action taken under subsection (a)(1) if the transaction is otherwise authorized, approved, or ratified as provided in that subsection.

(d) For purposes of subsection (a)(2), a conflict of interest transaction is authorized, approved, or ratified if it receives the vote of a majority of the shares entitled to be counted under this subsection. Shares owned by or voted under the control of a director who has a direct or indirect interest in the transaction, and shares owned by or voted under the control of an entity described in subsection (b)(1), may not be counted in a vote of shareholders to determine whether to authorize, approve, or ratify a conflict of interest transaction under subsection (a)(2). The vote of those shares, however, is counted in determining whether the transaction is approved under other sections of this Act. A majority of the shares, whether or not present, that are entitled to be counted in a vote on the transaction under this subsection constitutes a quorum for the purpose of taking action under this section.

Section 8.32.   Loans to Directors

(a) Except as provided by subsection (c), a corporation may not lend money to or guarantee the obligation of a director of the corporation unless:

(1) the particular loan or guarantee is approved by a majority of the votes represented by the outstanding voting shares of all classes, voting as a single voting group, except the votes of shares

owned by or voted under the control of the benefitted director; or

(2) the corporation's board of directors determines that the loan or guarantee benefits the corporation and either approves the specified loan or guarantee or a general plan authorizing loans and guarantees.

(b) The fact that a loan or guarantee is made in violation of this section does not affect the borrower's liability on the loan.

(c) This section does not apply to loans and guarantees authorized by statute regulating any special class of corporations.

Section 8.33.   *Liability for Unlawful Distributions*

(a) Unless he complies with the applicable standards of conduct described in section 8.30, a director who votes for or assents to a distribution made in violation of this Act or the articles of incorporation is personally liable to the corporation for the amount of the distribution that exceeds what could have been distributed without violating this Act or the articles of incorporation.

(b) A director held liable for an unlawful distribution under subsection (a) is entitled to contribution:

(1) from every other director who voted for or assented to the distribution without complying with the applicable standards of conduct described in section 8.30; and

(2) from each shareholder for the amount the shareholder accepted knowing the distribution was made in violation of this Act or the articles of incorporation.

Officers

Section 8.40.   *Required Officers*

(a) A corporation has the officers described in its bylaws or appointed by the board of directors in accordance with the bylaws.

(b) A duly appointed officer may appoint one or more officers or assistant officers if authorized by the bylaws or the board of directors.

(c) The bylaws or the board of directors shall delegate to one of the officers responsibility for preparing minutes of the directors' and shareholders' meetings and for authenticating records of the corporation.

(d) The same individual may simultaneously hold more than one office in a corporation.

Section 8.41.   *Duties of Officers*

Each officer has the authority and shall perform the duties set forth in the bylaws or, to the extent consistent with the bylaws, the duties prescribed by the board of directors or by direction of an officer authorized by the board of directors to prescribe the duties of other officers.

Section 8.42.   *Standards of Conduct for Officers*

(a) An officer with discretionary authority shall discharge his duties under that authority:

(1) in good faith;

(2) with the care an ordinarily prudent person in a like position would exercise under similar circumstances; and

(3) in a manner he reasonably believes to be in the best interests of the corporation.

(b) In discharging his duties an officer is entitled to rely on information, opinions, reports, or statements, including financial statements and other financial data, if prepared or presented by:

(1) one or more officers or employees of the corporation whom the officer reasonably believes to be reliable and competent in the matters presented; or

(2) legal counsel, public accountants, or other persons as to matters the officer reasonably believes are within the person's professional or expert competence.

(c) An officer is not acting in good faith if he has knowledge concerning the matter in question that makes reliance otherwise permitted by subsection (b) unwarranted.

(d) An officer is not liable for any action taken as an officer, or any failure to take any action, if he performed the duties of his office in compliance with this section.

Section 8.43.   *Resignation and Removal of Officers*

(a) An officer may resign at any time by delivering notice to the corporation. A resignation is effective when the notice is delivered unless the notice specifies a later effective date. If a resignation is made effective at a later date and the corporation accepts the future effective date, its board of directors may fill the pending vacancy before the effective date if the board of directors provides that the successor does not take office until the effective date.

(b) A board of directors may remove any officer at any time with or without cause.

Section 8.44.   *Contract Rights of Officers*

(a) The appointment of an officer does not itself create contract rights.

(b) An officer's removal does not affect the officer's contract rights, if any, with the corporation. An officer's resignation does not affect the corporation's contract rights, if any, with the officer.

Indemnification

Section 8.50.   *Subchapter Definitions*

In this subchapter:

(1) "Corporation" includes any domestic or foreign predecessor entity of a corporation in a merger or other transaction in which the predecessor's existence ceased upon consummation of the transaction.

(2) "Director" means an individual who is or was a director of a corporation or an individual who, while a director of a corporation, is or was serving at the corporation's request as a director, officer, partner, trustee, employee, or agent of another foreign or domestic corporation, partnership, joint venture, trust, employee benefit plan, or other enterprise. A director is considered to be serving an employee benefit plan at the corporation's request if his duties to the corporation also impose duties on, or otherwise involve services by, him to the plan or to participants in or beneficiaries of the plan. "Director" includes, unless the context requires otherwise, the estate or personal representative of a director.

(3) "Expenses" include counsel fees.

(4) "Liability" means the obligation to pay a judgment, settlement, penalty, fine (including an excise tax assessed with respect to an employee benefit plan), or reasonable expenses incurred with respect to a proceeding.

(5) "Official capacity" means: (i) when used with respect to a director, the office of director in a corporation; and (ii) when used with respect to an individual other than a director, as contemplated in section 8.56, the office in a corporation held by the officer or the employment or agency relationship undertaken by the employee or agent on behalf of the corporation. "Official capacity" does not include service for any other

foreign or domestic corporation or any partnership, joint venture, trust, employee benefit plan, or other enterprise.

(6) "Party" includes an individual who was, is, or is threatened to be made a named defendant or respondent in a proceeding.

(7) "Proceeding" means any threatened, pending, or completed action, suit, or proceeding, whether civil, criminal, administrative, or investigative and whether formal or informal.

Section 8.51.   *Authority to Indemnify*

(a) Except as provided in subsection (d), a corporation may indemnify an individual made a party to a proceeding because he is or was a director against liability incurred in the proceeding if:

(1) he conducted himself in good faith; and

(2) he reasonably believed:

(i) in the case of conduct in his official capacity with the corporation, that his conduct was in its best interests; and

(ii) in all other cases, that his conduct was at least not opposed to its best interests; and

(3) in the case of a criminal proceeding, he had no reasonable cause to believe his conduct was unlawful.

(b) A director's conduct with respect to an employee benefit plan for a purpose he reasonably believed to be in the interests of the participants in and beneficiaries of the plan is conduct that satisfies the requirement of subsection (a)(2)(ii).

(c) The termination of a proceeding by judgment, order, settlement, conviction, or upon a plea of nolo contendere or its equivalent is not, of itself, determinative that the director did not meet the standard of conduct described in this section.

(d) A corporation may not indemnify a director under this section:

(1) in connection with a proceeding by or in the right of the corporation in which the director was adjudged liable to the corporation; or

(2) in connection with any other proceeding charging improper personal benefit to him, whether or not involving action in his official capacity, in which he was adjudged liable on the basis that personal benefit was improperly received by him.

(e) Indemnification permitted under this section in connection with a proceeding by or in the right of the corporation is limited to reasonable expenses incurred in connection with the proceeding.

Section 8.52.   *Mandatory Indemnification*

Unless limited by its articles of incorporation, a corporation shall indemnify a director who was wholly successful, on the merits or otherwise, in the defense of any proceeding to which he was a party because he is or was a director of the corporation against reasonable expenses incurred by him in connection with the proceeding.

Section 8.53.   *Advance for Expenses*

(a) A corporation may pay for or reimburse the reasonable expenses incurred by a director who is a party to a proceeding in advance of final disposition of the proceeding if:

(1) the director furnishes the corporation a written affirmation of his good faith belief that he has met the standard of conduct described in section 8.51;

(2) the director furnishes the corporation a written undertaking, executed personally or on his behalf, to repay the advance if it is ultimately determined that he did not meet the standard of conduct; and

(3) a determination is made that the facts then known to those making the determination would not preclude indemnification under this subchapter.

(b) The undertaking required by subsection (a)(2) must be an unlimited general obligation of the director but need not be secured and may be accepted without reference to financial ability to make repayment.

(c) Determinations and authorizations of payments under this section shall be made in the manner specified in section 8.55.

Section 8.54.   *Court-Ordered Indemnification*

Unless a corporation's articles of incorporation provide otherwise, a director of the corporation who is a party to a proceeding may apply for indemnification to the court conducting the proceeding or to another court of competent jurisdiction. On receipt of an application, the court after giving any notice the court considers necessary may order indemnification if it determines:

(1) the director is entitled to mandatory indemnification under section 8.52, in which case the court shall also order the corporation to pay the director's

reasonable expenses incurred to obtain court-ordered indemnification; or

(2) the director is fairly and reasonably entitled to indemnification in view of all the relevant circumstances, whether or not he met the standard of conduct set forth in section 8.51 or was adjudged liable as described in section 8.51(d), but if he was adjudged so liable his indemnification is limited to reasonable expenses incurred.

Section 8.55.   *Determination and Authorization*
of Indemnification

(a) A corporation may not indemnify a director under section 8.51 unless authorized in the specific case after a determination has been made that indemnification of the director is permissible in the circumstances because he has met the standard of conduct set forth in section 8.51.

(b) The determination shall be made:

(1) by the board of directors by majority vote of a quorum consisting of directors not at the time parties to the proceeding;

(2) if a quorum cannot be obtained under subdivision (1), by majority vote of a committee duly designated by the board of directors (in which designation directors who are parties may participate), consisting solely of two or more directors not at the time parties to the proceeding;

(3) by special legal counsel:

(i) selecteed by the board of directors or its committee in the manner prescribed in subdivision (1) or (2); or

(ii) if a quorum of the board of directors cannot be obtained under subdivision (1) and a committee cannot be designated under subdivision (2), selected by majority vote of the full board of directors (in which selection directors who are parties may participate); or

(4) by the shareholders, but shares owned by or voted under the control of directors who are at the time parties to the proceeding may not be voted on the determination.

(c) Authorization of indemnification and evaluation as to reasonableness of expenses shall be made in the same manner as the determination that indemnification is permissible, except that if the determination is made by special legal counsel, authorization of indemnification and evaluation as to reasonableness of expenses shall be made by those entitled under subsection (b)(3) to select counsel.

Section 8.56.   *Indemnification of Officers, Employees, and Agents*

Unless a corporation's articles of incorporation provide otherwise:

(1) an officer of the corporation who is not a director is entitled to mandatory indemnification under section 8.52, and is entitled to apply for court-ordered indemnification under section 8.54, in each case to the same extent as a director;

(2) the corporation may indemnify and advance expenses under this subchapter to an officer, employee, or agent of the corporation who is not a director to the same extent as to a director; and

(3) a corporation may also indemnify and advance expenses to an officer, employee, or agent who is not a director to the extent, consistent with public policy, that may be provided by its articles of incorporation, bylaws, general or special action of its board of directors, or contract.

Section 8.57.   *Insurance*

A corporation may purchase and maintain insurance on behalf of an individual who is or was a director, officer, employee, or agent of the corporation, or who, while a director, officer, employee, or agent of the corporation, is or was serving at the request of the corporation as a director, officer, partner, trustee, employee, or agent of another foreign or domestic corporation, partnership, joint venture, trust, employee benefit plan, or other enterprise, against liability asserted against or incurred by him in that capacity or arising from his status as a director, officer, employee, or agent, whether or not the corporation would have power to indemnify him against the same liability under section 8.51 or 8.52.

Section 8.58.   *Application of Subchapter*

(a) A provision treating a corporation's indemnification of or advance for expenses to directors that is contained in its articles of incorporation, bylaws, a resolution of its shareholders or board of directors, or in a contract or otherwise, is valid only if and to the extent the provision is consistent with this subchapter. If articles of incorporation limit indemnification or advance for expenses, indemnification and advance for expenses are valid only to the extent consistent with the articles.

(b) This subchapter does not limit a corporation's power to pay or reimburse expenses incurred by a director in connection with his appearance as a witness in a proceeding at a time when he has not been made a named defendant or respondent to the proceeding.

CHAPTER 9   [RESERVED]

CHAPTER 10   AMENDMENT OF ARTICLES OF INCORPORATION AND BYLAWS

Amendment of Articles of Incorporation

Section 10.01.   *Authority to Amend*

(a) A corporation may amend its articles of incorporation at any time to add or change a provision that is required or permitted in the articles of incorporation or to delete a provision not required in the articles of incorporation. Whether a provision is required or permitted in the articles of incorporation is determined as of the effective date of the amendment.

(b) A shareholder of the corporation does not have a vested property right resulting from any provision in the articles of incorporation, including provisions relating to management, control, capital structure, dividend entitlement, or purpose or duration of the corporation.

Section 10.02.   *Amendment by Board of Directors*

Unless the articles of incorporation provide otherwise, a corporation's board of directors may adopt one or more amendments to the corporation's articles of incorporation without shareholder action:

(1) to extend the duration of the corporation if it was incorporated at a time when limited duration was required by law;

(2) to delete the names and addresses of the initial directors;

(3) to delete the name and address of the initial registered agent or registered office, if a statement of change is on file with the secretary of state;

(4) to change each issued and unissued authorized share of an outstanding class into a greater number of whole shares if the corporation has only shares of that class outstanding;

(5) to change the corporate name by substituting the word "corporation," "incorporated," "company," "limited," or the abbreviation "corp.," "inc.," "co.," or

"ltd.," for a similar word or abbreviation in the name, or by adding, deleting, or changing a geographical attribution for the name; or

(6) to make any other change expressly permitted by this Act to be made without shareholder action.

Section 10.03.   *Amendment by Board of Directors and Shareholders*

(a) A corporation's board of directors may propose one or more amendments to the articles of incorporation for submission to the shareholders.

(b) For the amendment to be adopted:

(1) the board of directors must recommend the amendment to the shareholders unless the board of directors determines that because of conflict of interest or other special circumstances it should make no recommendation and communicate the basis for its determination to the shareholders with the amendment; and

(2) the shareholders entitled to vote on the amendment must approve the amendment as provided in subsection (e).

(c) The board of directors may condition its submission of the proposed amendment on any basis.

(d) The corporation shall notify each shareholder, whether or not entitled to vote, of the proposed shareholders' meeting in accordance with section 7.05. The notice of meeting must also state that the purpose, or one of the purposes, of the meeting is to consider the proposed amendment and contain or be accompanied by a copy or summary of the amendment.

(e) Unless this Act, the articles of incorporation, or the board of directors (acting pursuant to subsection (c)) require a greater vote or a vote by voting groups, the amendment to be adopted must be approved by:

(1) a majority of the votes entitled to be cast on the amendment by any voting group with respect to which the amendment would create dissenters' rights; and

(2) the votes required by sections 7.25 and 7.26 by every other voting group entitled to vote on the amendment.

Section 10.04.   *Voting on Amendments by Voting Groups*

(a) The holders of the outstanding shares of a class are entitled to vote as a separate voting group (if shareholder voting is otherwise required by this Act)

on a proposed amendment if the amendment would:

(1) increase or decrease the aggregate number of authorized shares of the class;

(2) effect an exchange or reclassification of all or part of the shares of the class into shares of another class;

(3) effect an exchange or reclassification, or create the right of exchange, of all or part of the shares of another class into shares of the class;

(4) change the designation, rights, preferences, or limitations of all or part of the shares of the same class;

(5) change the shares of all or part of the class into a different number of shares of the same class;

(6) create a new class of shares having rights or preferences with respect to distributions or to dissolution that are prior, superior, or substantially equal to the shares of the class;

(7) increase the rights, preferences, or number of authorized shares of any class that, after giving effect to the amendment, having rights or preferences with respect to distributions or to dissolution that are prior, superior, or substantially equal to the shares of the class;

(8) limit or deny an existing preemptive right of all or part of the shares of the class; or

(9) cancel or otherwise affect rights to distributions or dividends that have accumulated but not yet been declared on all or part of the shares of the class.

(b) If a proposed amendment would affect a series of a class of shares in one or more of the ways described in subsection (a), the shares of that series are entitled to vote as a separate voting group on the proposed amendment.

(c) If a proposed amendment that entitles two or more series of shares to vote as separate voting groups under this section would affect those two or more series in the same or a substantially similar way, the shares of all the series so affected must vote together as a single voting group on the proposed amendment.

(d) A class or series of shares is entitled to the voting rights granted by this section although the articles of incorporation provide that the shares are nonvoting shares.

Section 10.05.   *Amendment before Issuance of Shares*

If a corporation has not yet issued shares, its incorporators or board of directors may adopt one or more amendments to the corporation's articles of incorporation.

Section 10.06.   Articles of Amendment

A corporation amending its articles of incorporation shall deliver to the secretary of state for filing articles of amendment setting forth:

(1) the name of the corporation;

(2) the text of each amendment adopted;

(3) if an amendment provides for an exchange, reclassification, or cancellation of issued shares, provisions for implementing the amendment if not contained in the amendment itself;

(4) the date of each amendment's adoption;

(5) if an amendment was adopted by the incorporators or board of directors without shareholder action, a statement to that effect and that shareholder action was not required;

(6) if an amendment was approved by the shareholders:

(i) the designation, number of outstanding shares, number of votes entitled to be cast by each voting group entitled to vote separately on the amendment, and number of votes of each voting group indisputably represented at the meeting;

(ii) either the total number of votes cast for and against the amendment by each voting group entitled to vote separately on the amendment or the total number of undisputed votes cast for the amendment by each voting group and a statement that the number cast for the amendment by each voting group was sufficient for approval by that voting group.

Section 10.07.   Restated Articles of Incorporation

(a) A corporation's board of directors may restate its articles of incorporation at any time with or without shareholder action.

(b) The restatement may include one or more amendments to the articles. If the restatement includes an amendment requiring shareholder approval, it must be adopted as provided in section 10.03.

(c) If the board of directors submits a restatement for shareholder action, the corporation shall notify each shareholder, whether or not entitled to vote, of the proposed shareholders' meeting in accordance with section 7.05. The notice must also state that the purpose, or one of the purposes, of the meeting is to consider the proposed restatement and contain or be accompanied by a copy of the restatement that identifies any amendment or other change it would make in the articles.

(d) A corporation restating its articles of incorporation shall deliver to the secretary of state for filing articles of restatement setting forth the name of the corporation and the text of the restated articles of incorporation together with a certificate setting forth:

(1) whether the restatement contains an amendment to the articles requiring shareholder approval and, if it does not, that the board of directors adopted the restatement; or

(2) if the restatement contains an amendment to the articles requiring shareholder approval, the information required by section 10.06.

(e) Duly adopted restated articles of incorporation supersede the original articles of incorporation and all amendments to them.

(f) The secretary of state may certify restated articles of incorporation, as the articles of incorporation currently in effect, without including the certification information required by subsection (d).

Section 10.08.   Amendment Pursuant to Reorganization

(a) A corporation's articles of incorporation may be amended without action by the board of directors or shareholders to carry out a plan of reorganization ordered or decreed by a court of competent jurisdiction under federal statute if the articles of incorporation after amendment contain only provisions required or permitted by section 2.02.

(b) The individual or individuals designated by the court shall deliver to the secretary of state for filing articles of amendment setting forth:

(1) the name of the corporation;

(2) the text of each amendment approved by the court;

(3) the date of the court's order or decree approving the articles of amendment;

(4) the title of the reorganization proceeding in which the order or decree was entered; and

(5) a statement that the court has jurisdiction of the proceeding under federal statute.

(c) Shareholders of a corporation undergoing reorganization do not have dissenters' rights except as and to the extent provided in the reorganization plan.

(d) This section does not apply after entry of a final decree in the reorganization proceeding even though the court retains jurisdiction of the proceeding for limited purposes unrelated to consummation of the reorganization plan.

Section 10.09.   *Effect of Amendment*

An amendment to articles of incorporation does not affect a cause of action existing against or in favor of the corporation, a proceeding to which the corporation is a party, or the existing rights of persons other than shareholders of the corporation. An amendment changing a corporation's name does not abate a proceeding brought by or against the corporation in its former name.

Amendment of Bylaws

Section 10.20.   *Amendment by Board of Directors or Shareholders*

(a) A corporation's board of directors may amend or repeal the corporation's bylaws unless:

(1) the articles of incorporation or this Act reserve this power exclusively to the shareholders in whole or part; or

(2) the shareholders in amending or repealing a particular bylaw provide expressly that the board of directors may not amend or repeal that bylaw.

(b) A corporation's shareholders may amend or repeal the corporation's bylaws even though the bylaws may also be amended or repealed by its board of directors.

Section 10.21.   *Bylaw Increasing Quorum or Voting Requirement for Shareholders*

(a) If authorized by the articles of incorporation, the shareholders may adopt or amend a bylaw that fixes a greater quorum or voting requirement for shareholders (or voting groups of shareholders) than is required by this Act. The adoption or amendment of a bylaw that adds, changes, or deletes a greater quorum or voting requirement for shareholders must meet the same quorum requirement and be adopted by the same vote and voting groups required to take action under the quorum and voting requirement then in effect or proposed to be adopted, whichever is greater.

(b) A bylaw that fixes a greater quorum or voting requirement for shareholders under subsection (a) may not be adopted, amended, or repealed by the board of directors.

Section 10.22.   *Bylaw Increasing Quorum or Voting Requirement for Directors*

(a) A bylaw that fixes a greater quorum or voting requirement for the board of directors may be amended or repealed:

(1) if originally adopted by the shareholders, only by the shareholders;

(2) if originally adopted by the board of directors, either by the shareholders or by the board of directors.

(b) A bylaw adopted or amended by the shareholders that fixes a greater quorum or voting requirement for the board of directors may provide that it may be amended or repealed only by a specified vote of either the shareholders or the board of directors.

(c) Action by the board of directors under subsection (a)(2) to adopt or amend a bylaw that changes the quorum or voting requirement for the board of directors must meet the same quorum requirement and be adopted by the same vote required to take action under the quorum and voting requirement then in effect or proposed to be adopted, whichever is greater.

CHAPTER 11   MERGER AND SHARE EXCHANGE

Section 11.01.   *Merger*

(a) One or more corporations may merge into another corporation if the board of directors of each corporation adopts and its shareholders (if required by section 11.03) approve a plan of merger.

(b) The plan of merger must set forth:

(1) the name of each corporation planning to merge and the name of the surviving corporation into which each other corporation plans to merge;

(2) the terms and conditions of the merger; and

(3) the manner and basis of converting the shares of each corporation into shares, obligations, or other securities of the surviving or any other corporation or into cash or other property in whole or part.

(c) The plan of merger may set forth:

(1) amendments to the articles of incorporation of the surviving corporation; and

(2) other provisions relating to the merger.

Section 11.02.   Share Exchange

(a) A corporation may acquire all of the outstanding shares of one or more classes or series of another corporation if the board of directors of each corporation adopts and its shareholders (if required by section 11.03) approve the exchange.

(b) The plan of exchange must set forth:

(1) the name of the corporation whose shares will be acquired and the name of the acquiring corporation;

(2) the terms and conditions of the exchange;

(3) the manner and basis of exchanging the shares to be acquired for shares, obligations, or other securities of the acquiring or any other corporation or for cash or other property in whole or part.

(c) The plan of exchange may set forth other provisions relating to the exchange.

(d) This section does not limit the power of a corporation to acquire all or part of the shares of one or more classes or series of another corporation through a voluntary exchange or otherwise.

Section 11.03.   Action on Plan

(a) After adopting a plan of merger or share exchange, the board of directors of each corporation party to the merger, and the board of directors of the corporation whose shares will be acquired in the share exchange, shall submit the plan of merger (except as provided in subsection (g)) or share exchange for approval by its shareholders.

(b) For a plan of merger or share exchange to be approved:

(1) the board of directors must recommend the plan of merger or share exchange to the shareholders, unless the board of directors determines that because of conflict of interest or other special circumstances it should make no recommendation and communicates the basis for its determination to the shareholders with the plan; and

(2) the shareholders entitled to vote must approve the plan.

(c) The board of directors may condition its submission of the proposed merger or share exchange on any basis.

(d) The corporation shall notify each shareholder, whether or not entitled to vote, of the proposed shareholders' meeting in accordance with section 7.05. The notice must also state that the purpose, or one of the purposes, of the meeting is to consider the plan of merger or share exchange and contain or be accompanied by a copy or summary of the plan.

(e) Unless this Act, the articles of incorporation, or the board of directors (acting pursuant to subsection (c)) require a greater vote or a vote by voting groups, the plan of merger or share exchange to be authorized must be approved by each voting group entitled to vote separately on the plan by a majority of all the votes entitled to be cast on the plan by that voting group.

(f) Separate voting by voting groups is required:

(1) on a plan of merger if the plan contains a provision that, if contained in a proposed amendment to articles of incorporation, would require action by one or more separate voting groups on the proposed amendment under section 10.04;

(2) on a plan of share exchange by each class or series of shares included in the exchange, with each class or series constituting a separate voting group.

(g) Action by the shareholders of the surviving corporation on a plan of merger is not required if:

(1) the articles of incorporation of the surviving corporation will not differ (except for amendments enumerated in section 10.02) from its articles before the merger;

(2) each shareholder of the surviving corporation whose shares were outstanding immediately before the effective date of the merger will hold the same number of shares, with identical designations, perferences, limitations, and relative rights, immediately after;

(3) the number of voting shares outstanding immediately after the merger, plus the number of voting shares issuable as a result of the merger (either by the conversion of securities issued pursuant to the merger or the exercise of rights and warrants issued pursuant to the merger), will not exceed by more than 20 percent the total number of voting shares of the surviving corporation outstanding immediately before the merger; and

(4) the number of participating shares outstanding immediately after the merger, plus the number of participating shares issuable as a result of the merger (either by the conversion of securities issued pursuant to the merger or the exercise of rights and warrants issued pursuant to the merger),

will not exceed by more than 20 percent the total number of participating shares outstanding immediately before the merger.

(h) As used in subsection (g):

(1) "Participating shares" means shares that entitle their holders to participate without limitation in distributions.

(2) "Voting shares" means shares that entitle their holders to vote unconditionally in elections of directors.

(i) After a merger or share exchange is authorized, and at any time before articles of merger or share exchange are filed, the planned merger or share exchange may be abandoned (subject to any contractual rights), without further shareholder action, in accordance with the procedure set forth in the plan of merger or share exchange or, if none is set forth, in the manner determined by the board of directors.

Section 11.04.   Merger of Subsidiary

(a) A parent corporation owning at least 90 percent of the outstanding shares of each class of a subsidiary corporation may merge the subsidiary into itself without approval of the shareholders of the parent or subsidiary.

(b) The board of directors of the parent shall adopt a plan of merger that sets forth:

(1) the names of the parent and subsidiary; and

(2) the manner and basis of converting the shares of the subsidiary into shares, obligations, or other securities of the parent or any other corporation or into cash or other property in whole or part.

(c) The parent shall mail a copy or summary of the plan of merger to each shareholder of the subsidiary who does not waive the mailing requirement in writing.

(d) The parent may not deliver articles of merger to the secretary of state for filing until at least 30 days after the date it mailed a copy of the plan of merger to each shareholder of the subsidiary who did not waive the mailing requirement.

(e) Articles of merger under this section may not contain amendments to the articles of incorporation of the parent corporation (except for amendments enumerated in section 10.02).

Section 11.05.   Articles of Merger or Share Exchange

(a) After a plan of merger or share exchange is approved by the shareholders, or adopted by the board of directors if shareholder approval is not required, the surviving or acquiring corporation shall deliver to the secretary of state for filing articles of merger or share exchange setting forth:

(1) the plan of merger or share exchange;

(2) if shareholder approval was not required, a statement to that effect;

(3) if approval of the shareholders of one or more corporations party to the merger or share exchange was required:

(i) the designation, number of outstanding shares, and number of votes entitled to be cast by each voting group entitled to vote separately on the plan as to each corporation; and

(ii) either the total number of votes cast for and against the plan by each voting group entitled to vote separately on the plan or the total number of undisputed votes cast for the plan separately by each voting group and a statement that the number cast for the plan by each voting group was sufficient for approval by that voting group.

(b) A merger or share exchange takes effect upon the effective date of the articles of merger or share exchange.

Section 11.06.   Effect of Merger or Share Exchange

(a) When a merger takes effect:

(1) every other corporation party to the merger merges into the surviving corporation and the separate existence of every corporation except the surviving corporation ceases;

(2) the title to all real estate and other property owned by each corporation party to the merger is vested in the surviving corporation without reversion or impairment;

(3) the surviving corporation has all liabilities of each corporation party to the merger;

(4) a proceeding pending against any corporation party to the merger may be continued as if the merger did not occur or the surviving corporation may be substituted in the proceeding for the corporation whose existence ceased;

(5) the articles of incorporation of the surviving corporation are amended to the extent provided in the plan of merger; and

(6) the shares of each corporation party to the merger that are to be converted into shares, obligations, or other securities of the surviving or any other corporation or into cash of other property are

converted, and the former holders of the shares are entitled only to the rights provided in the articles of merger or to their rights under chapter 13.

(b) When a share exchange takes effect, the shares of each acquired corporation are exchanged as provided in the plan, and the former holders of the shares are entitled only to the exchange rights provided in the articles of share exchange or to their rights under chapter 13.

Section 11.07.   Merger or Share Exchange with
                     Foreign Corporation

(a) One or more foreign corporations may merge or enter into a share exchange with one or more domestic corporations if:

(1) in a merger, the merger is permitted by the law of the state or country under whose law each foreign corporation is incorporated and each foreign corporation complies with that law in effecting the merger;

(2) in a share exchange, the corporation whose shares will be acquired is a domestic corporation, whether or not a share exchange is permitted by the law of the state or country under whose law the acquiring corporation is incorporated;

(3) the foreign corporation complies with section 11.05 if it is the surviving corporation of the merger or acquiring corporation of the share exchange; and

(4) each domestic corporation complies with the applicable provisions of sections 11.01 through 11.04 and, if it is the surviving corporation of the merger or acquiring corporation of the share exchange, with section 11.05.

(b) Upon the merger or share exchange taking effect, the surviving foreign corporation of a merger and the acquiring foreign corporation of a share exchange is deemed:

(1) to appoint the secretary of state as its agent for service of process in a proceeding to enforce any obligation or the rights of dissenting shareholders of each domestic corporation party to the merger or share exchange; and

(2) to agree that it will promptly pay to the dissenting shareholders of each domestic corporation party to the merger or share exchange the amount, if any, to which they are entitled under chapter 13.

(c) This section does not limit the power of a foreign corporation to acquire all or part of the shares of one or more classes or series of a domestic corporation through a voluntary exchange or otherwise.

CHAPTER 12   SALE OF ASSETS

Section 12.01.   Sale of Assets in Regular Course
                     of Business and Mortgage of Assets

(a) A corporation may, on the terms and conditions and for the consideration determined by the board of directors:

(1) sell, lease, exchange, or otherwise dispose of all, or substantially all, of its property in the usual and regular course of business;

(2) mortgage, pledge, dedicate to the repayment of indebtedness (whether with or without recourse), or otherwise encumber any or all of its property whether or not in the usual and regular course of business; or

(3) transfer any or all of its property to a corporation all the shares of which are owned by the corporation.

(b) Unless the articles of incorporation require it, approval by the shareholders of a transaction described in subsection (a) is not required.

Section 12.02.   Sale of Assets Other than in Regular
                     Course of Business

(a) A corporation may sell, lease, exchange, or otherwise dispose of all, or substantially all, of its property (with or without the good will), otherwise than in the usual and regular course of business, on the terms and conditions and for the consideration determined by the corporation's board of directors, if the board of directors proposes and its shareholders approve the proposed transaction.

(b) For a transaction to be authorized:

(1) the board of directors must recommend the proposed transaction to the shareholders unless the board of directors determines that because of conflict of interest or other special circumstances it should make no recommendation and communicates the basis for its determination to the shareholders with the submission of the proposed transaction; and

(2) the shareholders entitled to vote must approve the transaction.

(c) The board of directors may condition its submission of the proposed transaction on any basis.

(d) The corporation shall notify each shareholder, whether or not entitled to vote, of the proposed shareholders' meeting in accordance with section 7.05. The notice must also state that the purpose, or one of the purposes, of the meeting is to consider the sale, lease, exchange, or other disposition of all, or substantially all, the property of the corporation and contain or be accompanied by a description of the transaction.

(e) Unless the articles of incorporation or the board of directors (acting pursuant to subsection (c)) require a greater vote or a vote by voting groups, the transaction to be authorized must be approved by a majority of all the votes entitled to be cast on the transaction.

(f) After a sale, lease, exchange, or other disposition of property is authorized, the transaction may be abandoned (subject to any contractual rights) without further shareholder action.

(g) A transaction that constitutes a distribution is governed by section 6.40 and not by this section.

CHAPTER 13   DISSENTERS' RIGHTS

Right to Dissent and Obtain Payment for Shares

Section 13.01.   Definitions

In this chapter:

(1) "Corporation" means the issuer of the shares held by a dissenter before the corporate action, or the surviving or acquiring corporation by merger or share exchange of that issuer.

(2) "Dissenter" means a shareholder who is entitled to dissent from corporate action under section 13.02 and who exercises that right when and in the manner required by sections 13.20 through 13.28.

(3) "Fair value," with respect to a dissenter's shares, means the value of the shares immediately before the effectuation of the corporate action to which the dissenter objects, excluding any appreciation or depreciation in anticipation of the corporate action unless exclusion would be inequitable.

(4) "Interest" means interest from the effective date of the corporate action until the date of payment, at the average rate currently paid by the corporation on its principal bank loans or, if none, at a rate that is fair and equitable under all the circumstances.

(5) "Record shareholder" means the person in whose name shares are registered in the records of a corporation or the beneficial owner of shares to the extent of the rights granted by a nominee certificate on file with a corporation.

(6) "Beneficial shareholder" means the person who is a beneficial owner of shares held by a nominee as the record shareholder.

(7) "Shareholder" means the record shareholder or the beneficial shareholder.

Section 13.02.   Right to Dissent

(a) A shareholder is entitled to dissent from, and obtain payment of the fair value of his shares in the event of, any of the following corporate actions:

(1) consummation of a plan of merger to which the corporation is a party (i) if shareholder approval is required for the merger by section 11.03 or the articles of incorporation and the shareholder is entitled to vote on the merger or (ii) if the corporation is a subsidiary that is merged with its parent under section 11.04;

(2) consummation of a plan of share exchange to which the corporation is a party as the corporation whose shares will be acquired, if the shareholder is entitled to vote on the plan;

(3) consummation of a sale or exchange of all, or substantially all, of the property of the corporation other than in the usual and regular course of business, if the shareholder is entitled to vote on the sale or exchange, including a sale in dissolution, but not including a sale pursuant to court order or a sale for cash pursuant to a plan by which all or substantially all of the net proceeds of the sale will be distributed to the shareholders within one year after the date of sale;

(4) an amendment of the articles of incorporation that materially and adversely affects rights in respect of a dissenter's shares because it:

(i) alters or abolishes a preferential right of the shares;

(ii) creates, alters, or abolishes a right in respect of redemption, including a provision respecting a sinking fund for the redemption or repurchase, of the shares;

(iii) alters or abolishes a redemptive right of the holder of the shares to acquire shares or other securities;

(iv) excludes or limits the right of the shares

to vote on any matter, or to cumulate votes, other than a limitation by dilution through issuance of shares or other securities with similar voting rights; or

(v) reduces the number of shares owned by the shareholder to a fraction of a share if the fractional share so created is to be acquired for cash under section 6.04; or

(5) any corporate action taken pursuant to a shareholder vote to the extent the articles of incorporation, bylaws, or a resolution of the board of directors provides that voting or nonvoting shareholders are entitled to dissent and obtain payment for their shares.

(b) A shareholder entitled to dissent and obtain payment for his shares under this chapter may not challenge the corporate action creating his entitlement unless the action is unlawful or fraudulent with respect to the shareholder or the corporation.

Section 13.03.   Dissent by Nominees and Beneficial Owners

(a) A record shareholder may assert dissenters' rights as to fewer than all the shares registered in his name only if he dissents with respect to all shares beneficially owned by any one person and notifies the corporation in writing of the name and address of each person on whose behalf he asserts dissenters' rights. The rights of a partial dissenter under this subsection are determined as if the shares as to which he dissents and his other shares are registered in the names of different shareholders.

(b) A beneficial shareholder may assert dissenters' rights as to shares held on his behalf only if:

(1) he submits to the corporation the record shareholder's written consent to the dissent not later than the time the beneficial shareholder asserts dissenters' rights; and

(2) he does so with respect to all shares of which he is the beneficial shareholder or over which he has power to direct the vote.

Procedure for Exercise of Dissenters' Rights

Section 13.20.   Notice of Dissenters' Rights

(a) If proposed corporate action creating dissenters' rights under section 13.02 is submitted to a vote at a shareholders' meeting, the meeting notice must state

that shareholders are or may be entitled to assert dissenters' rights under this chapter and be accompanied by a copy of this chapter.

(b) If corporate action creating dissenters' rights under section 13.02 is taken without a vote of shareholders, the corporation shall notify in writing all shareholders entitled to assert dissenters' rights that the action was taken and send them the dissenters' notice described in section 13.22.

Section 13.21.   Notice of Intent to Demand Payment

(a) If proposed corporate action creating dissenters' rights under section 13.02 is submitted to a vote at a shareholders' meeting, a shareholder who wishes to assert dissenters' rights (1) must deliver to the corporation before the vote is taken written notice of his intent to demand payment for his shares if the proposed action is effectuated and (2) must not vote his shares in favor of the proposed action.

(b) A shareholder who does not satisfy the requirements of subsection (a) is not entitled to payment for his shares under this chapter.

Section 13.22.   Dissenters' Notice

(a) If proposed corporate action creating dissenters' rights under section 13.02 is authorized at a shareholders' meeting, the corporation shall deliver a written dissenters' notice to all shareholders who satisfied the requirements of section 13.21.

(b) The dissenters' notice must be sent no later than 10 days after the corporate action was taken, and must:

(1) state where the payment demand must be sent and where and when certificates for certificated shares must be deposited;

(2) Inform holders of uncertificated shares to what extent transfer of the shares will be restricted after the payment demand is received;

(3) supply a form for demanding payment that includes the date of the first announcement to news media or to shareholders of the terms of the proposed corporate action and requires that the person asserting dissenters' rights certify whether or not he acquired beneficial ownership of the shares before that date;

(4) set a date by which the corporation must receive the payment demand, which date may not

be fewer than 30 nor more than 60 days after the date the subsection (a) notice is delivered; and

(5) be accompanied by a copy of this chapter.

Section 13.23. *Duty to Demand Payment*

(a) A shareholder sent a dissenters' notice described in section 13.22 must demand payment, certify whether he acquired beneficial ownership of the shares before the date required to be set forth in the dissenters' notice pursuant to section 13.22(b)(3), and deposit his certificates in accordance with the terms of the notice.

(b) The shareholder who demands payment and deposits his share certificates under section (a) retains all other rights of a shareholder until these rights are cancelled or modified by the taking of the proposed corporate action.

(c) A shareholder who does not demand payment or deposit his share certificates where required, each by the date set in the dissenters' notice, is not entitled to payment for his shares under this chapter.

Section 13.24. *Share Restrictions*

(a) The corporation may restrict the transfer of uncertificated shares from the date the demand for their payment is received until the proposed corporate action is taken or the restrictions released under section 13.26.

(b) The person for whom dissenters' rights are asserted as to uncertificated shares retains all other rights of a shareholder until these rights are cancelled or modified by the taking of the proposed corporate action.

Section 13.25. *Payment*

(a) Except as provided in section 13.27, as soon as the proposed corporate action is taken, or upon receipt of a payment demand, the corporation shall pay each dissenter who complied with section 13.23 the amount the corporation estimates to be the fair value of his shares, plus accrued interest.

(b) The payment must be accompanied by:

(1) the corporation's balance sheet as of the end of a fiscal year ending not more than 16 months before the date of payment, an income statement for that year, a statement of changes in shareholders' equity for that year, and the latest available interim financial statements, if any;

(2) a statement of the corporation's estimate of the fair value of the shares;

(3) an explanation of how the interest was calculated;

(4) a statement of the dissenter's right to demand payment under section 13.28; and

(5) a copy of this chapter.

Section 13.26. *Failure to Take Action*

(a) If the corporation does not take the proposed action within 60 days after the date set for demanding payment and depositing share certificates, the corporation shall return the deposited certificates and release the transfer restrictions imposed on uncertificated shares.

(b) If after returning deposited certificates and releasing transfer restrictions, the corporation takes the proposed action, it must send a new dissenters' notice under section 13.22 and repeat the payment demand procedure.

Section 13.27. *After-Acquired Shares*

(a) A corporation may elect to withhold payment required by section 13.25 from a dissenter unless he was the beneficial owner of the shares before the date set forth in the dissenters' notice as the date of the first announcement to news media or to shareholders of the terms of the proposed corporate action.

(b) To the extent the corporation elects to withhold payment under subsection (a), after taking the proposed corporate action, it shall estimate the fair value of the shares, plus accrued interest, and shall pay this amount to each dissenter who agrees to accept it in full satisfaction of his demand. The corporation shall send with its offer a statement of its estimate of the fair value of the shares, an explanation of how the interest was calculated, and a statement of the dissenter's right to demand payment under section 13.28.

Section 13.28. *Procedure if Shareholder Dissatisfied with Payment or Offer*

(a) A dissenter may notify the corporation in writing of his own estimate of the fair value of his shares and amount of interest due, and demand payment of his estimate (less any payment under section 13.25), or reject the corporation's offer under section 13.27 and demand payment of the fair value of his shares and interest due, if:

(1) the dissenter believes that the amount paid under section 13.25 or offered under section 13.27 is less than the fair value of his shares or that the interest due is incorrectly calculated;

(2) the corporation fails to make payment under section 13.25 within 60 days after the date set for demanding payment; or

(3) the corporation, having failed to take the proposed action, does not return the deposited certificates or release the transfer restrictions imposed on uncertificated shares within 60 days after the date set for demanding payment.

(b)   A dissenter waives his right to demand payment under this section unless he notifies the corporation of his demand in writing under subsection (a) within 30 days after the corporation made or offered payment for his shares.

Judicial Appraisal of Shares

Section 13.30.   Court Action

(a) If a demand for payment under section 13.28 remains unsettled, the corporation shall commence a proceeding within 60 days after receiving the payment demand and petition the court to determine the fair value of the shares and accrued interest. If the corporation does not commence the proceeding within the 60-day period, it shall pay each dissenter whose demand remains unsettled the amount demanded.

(b) The corporation shall commence the proceeding in the [name or describe] court of the county where a corporation's principal office (or, if none in this state, its registered office) is located. If the corporation is a foreign corporation without a registered office in this state, it shall commence the proceeding in the county in this state where the registered office of the domestic corporation merged with or whose shares were acquired by the foreign corporation was located.

(c) The corporation shall make all dissenters (whether or not residents of this state) whose demands remain unsettled parties to the proceeding as in an action against their shares and all parties must be served with a copy of the petition. Nonresidents may be served by registered or certified mail or by publication as provided by law.

(d) The jurisdiction of the court in which the proceeding is commenced under subsection (b) is plenary and exclusive. The court may appoint one or more persons as appraisers to receive evidence and recommend decision on the question of fair value. The appraisers have the powers described in the order appointing them, or in any amendment to it. The dissenters are entitled to the same discovery rights as parties in other civil proceedings.

(e) Each dissenter made a party to the proceeding is entitled to judgment (1) for the amount, if any, by which the court finds the fair value of his shares, plus interest, exceeds the amount paid by the corporation or (2) for the fair value, plus accrued interest, of his after-acquired shares for which the corporation elected to withhold payment under section 13.27.

Section 13.31.   Court Costs and Counsel Fees

(a) The court in an appraisal proceeding commenced under section 13.30 shall determine all costs of the proceeding, including the reasonable compensation and expenses of appraisers appointed by the court. The court shall assess the costs against the corporation, except that the court may assess costs against all or some of the dissenters, in amounts the court finds equitable, to the extent the court finds the dissenters acted arbitrarily, vexatiously, or not in good faith in demanding payment under section 13.28.

(b) The court may also assess the fees and expenses of counsel and experts for the respective parties, in amounts the court finds equitable:

(1) against the corporation and in favor of any or all dissenters if the court finds the corporation did not substantially comply with the requirements of sections 13.20 through 13.28; or

(2) against either the corporation or a dissenter, in favor of any other party, if the court finds that the party against whom the fees and expenses are assessed acted arbitrarily, vexatiously, or not in good faith with respect to the rights provided by this chapter.

(c) If the court finds that the services of counsel for any dissenter were of substantial benefit to other dissenters similarly situated, and that the fees for those services should not be assessed against the corporation, the court may award to these counsel reasonable fees to be paid out of the amounts awarded the dissenters who were benefited.

CHAPTER 14   DISSOLUTION
Voluntary Dissolution

*Section 14.01.   Dissolution by Incorporators
            or Initial Directors*

A majority of the incorporators or initial directors of a corporation that has not issued shares or has not commenced business may dissolve the corporation by delivering to the secretary of state for filing articles of dissolution that set forth:

(1) the name of the corporation;

(2) the date of its incorporation;

(3) either (i) that none of the corporation's shares has been issued or (ii) that the corporation has not commenced business;

(4) that no debt of the corporation remains unpaid;

(5) that the net assets of the corporation remaining after winding up have been distributed to the shareholders, if shares were issued; and

(6) that a majority of the incorporators or initial directors authorized the dissolution.

Section 14.02.　Dissolution by Board of Directors and Shareholders

(a) A corporation's board of directors may propose dissolution for submission to the shareholders.

(b) For a proposal to dissolve to be adopted:

(1) the board of directors must recommend dissolution to the shareholders unless the board of directors determines that because of conflict of interest or other special circumstances it should make no recommendation and communicates the basis for its determination to the shareholders; and

(2) the shareholders entitled to vote must approve the proposal to dissolve as provided in subsection (e).

(c) the board of directors may condition its submission of the proposal for dissolution on any basis.

(d) The corporation shall notify each shareholder, whether or not entitled to vote, of the proposed shareholders' meeting in accordance with section 7.05. The notice must also state that the purpose, or one of the purposes, of the meeting is to consider dissolving the corporation.

(e) Unless the articles of incorporation or the board of directors (acting pursuant to subsection (c)) require a greater vote or a vote by voting groups, the proposal to dissolve to be adopted must be approved by a majority of all the votes entitled to be cast on that proposal.

Section 14.03.　Articles of Dissolution

(a) At any time after dissolution is authorized, the corporation may dissolve by delivering to the secretary of state for filing articles of dissolution setting forth:

(1) the name of the corporation;

(2) the date dissolution was authorized;

(3) if dissolution was approved by the shareholders:

(i) the number of votes entitled to be cast on the proposal to dissolve; and

(ii) either the total number of votes cast for and against dissolution or the total number of undisputed votes cast for dissolution and a statement that the number cast for dissolution was sufficient for approval.

(4) If voting by voting groups was required, the information required by subparagraph (3) must be separately provided for each voting group entitled to vote separately on the plan to dissolve.

(b) A corporation is dissolved upon the effective date of its articles of dissolution.

Section 14.04.　Revocation of Dissolution

(a) A corporation may revoke its dissolution within 120 days of its effective date.

(b) Revocation of dissolution must be authorized in the same manner as the dissolution was authorized unless that authorization permitted revocation by action of the board of directors alone, in which event the board of directors may revoke the dissolution without shareholder action.

(c) After the revocation of dissolution is authorized, the corporation may revoke the dissolution by delivering to the secretary of state for filing articles of revocation of dissolution, together with a copy of its articles of dissolution, that set forth:

(1) the name of the corporation;

(2) the effective date of the dissolution that was revoked;

(3) the date that the revocation of dissolution was authorized;

(4) if the corporation's board of directors (or incorporators) revoked the dissolution, a statement to that effect;

(5) if the corporation's board of directors revoked a dissolution authorized by the shareholders, a statement that revocation was permitted by action by the board of directors alone pursuant to that authorization; and

(6) if shareholder action was required to revoke the dissolution, the information required by section 14.03(a)(3) or (4).

(d) Revocation of dissolution is effective upon

the effective date of the articles or revocation of dissolution.

(e) When the revocation of dissolution is effective, it relates back to and takes effect as of the effective date of the dissolution and the corporation resumes carrying on its business as if dissolution had never occurred.

Section 14.05. Effect of Dissolution

(a) A dissolved corporation continues its corporate existence but may not carry on any business except that appropriate to wind up and liquidate its business and affairs, including:

(1) collecting its assets;

(2) disposing of its properties that will not be distributed in kind to its shareholders;

(3) discharging or making provision for discharging its liabilities;

(4) distributing its remaining property among its shareholders according to their interests; and

(5) doing every other act necessary to wind up and liquidate its business and affairs.

(b) Dissolution of a corporation does not:

(1) transfer title to the corporation's property;

(2) prevent transfer of its shares or securities, although the authorization to dissolve may provide for closing the corporation's share transfer records;

(3) subject its directors or officers to standards of conduct different from those prescribed in chapter 8;

(4) change quorum or voting requirements for its board of directors or shareholders; change provisions for selection, resignation, or removal of its directors or officers or both; or change provisions for amending its bylaws;

(5) prevent commencement of a proceeding by or against the corporation in its corporate name;

(6) abate or suspend a proceeding pending by or against the corporation on the effective date of dissolution; or

(7) terminate the authority of the registered agent of the corporation.

Section 14.06. Known Claims against Dissolved Corporation

(a) A dissolved corporation may dispose of the known claims against it by following the procedure described in this section.

(b) The dissolved corporation shall notify its known claimants in writing of the dissolution at any time after its effective date. The written notice must:

(1) describe information that must be included in a claim;

(2) provide a mailing address where a claim may be sent;

(3) state the deadline, which may not be fewer than 120 days from the effective date of the written notice, by which the dissolved corporation must receive the claim; and

(4) state that the claim will be barred if not received by the deadline.

(c) A claim against the dissolved corporation is barred:

(1) if a claimant who was given written notice under subsection (b) does not deliver the claim to the dissolved corporation by the deadline;

(2) if a claimant whose claim was rejected by the dissolved corporation does not commence a proceeding to enforce the claim within 90 days from the effective date of the rejection notice.

(d) For purposes of this section, "claim" does not include a contingent liability or a claim based on an event occurring after the effective date of dissolution.

Section 14.07. Unknown Claims against Dissolved Corporation

(a) A dissolved corporation may also publish notice of its dissolution and request that persons with claims against the corporation present them in accordance with the notice.

(b) The notice must:

(1) be published one time in a newspaper of general circulation in the county where the dissolved corporation's principal office (or, if none in this state, its registered office) is or was last located;

(2) describe the information that must be included in a claim and provide a mailing address where the claim may be sent; and

(3) state that a claim against the corporation will be barred unless a proceeding to enforce the claim is commenced within five years after the publication of the notice.

(c) If the dissolved corporation publishes a newspaper notice in accordance with subsection (b), the claim of each of the following claimants is barred unless the claimant commences a proceeding to enforce the claim against the dissolved corporation within five years after the publication date of the newspaper notice:

    (1) a claimant who did not receive written notice under section 14.06;

    (2) a claimant whose claim was timely sent to the dissolved corporation but not acted on;

    (3) a claimant whose claim is contingent or based on an event occurring after the effective date of dissolution.

    (d) A claim may be enforced under this section:

    (1) against the dissolved corporation, to the extent of its undistributed assets; or

    (2) if the assets have been distributed in liquidation, against a shareholder of the dissolved corporation to the extent of his pro rata share of the claim or the corporate assets distributed to him in liquidation, whichever is less, but a shareholder's total liability for all claims under this section may not exceed the total amount of assets distributed to him.

Administrative Dissolution

Section 14.20.   Grounds for Administrative Dissolution

    The secretary of state may commence a proceeding under section 14.21 to administratively dissolve a corporation if:

    (1) the corporation does not pay within 60 days after they are due any franchise taxes or penalties imposed by this Act or other law;

    (2) the corporation does not deliver its annual report to the secretary of state within 60 days after it is due;

    (3) the corporation is without a registered agent or registered office in this state for 60 days or more;

    (4) the corporation does not notify the secretary of state within 60 days that its registered agent or registered office has been changed, that its registered agent has resigned, or that its registered office has been discontinued; or

    (5) the corporation's period of duration stated in its articles of incorporation expires.

Section 14.21.   Procedure for and Effect
of Administrative Dissolution

    (a) If the secretary of state determines that one or more grounds exist under section 14.20 for dissolving a corporation, he shall serve the corporation with written notice of his determination under section 5.04.

    (b) If the corporation does not correct each ground for dissolution or demonstrate to the reasonable satisfaction of the secretary of state that each ground determined by the secretary of state does not exist within 60 days after service of the notice is perfected under section 5.04, the secretary of state shall administratively dissolve the corporation by signing a certificate of dissolution that recites the ground or grounds for dissolution and its effective date. The secretary of state shall file the original of the certificate and serve a copy on the corporation under section 5.04.

    (c) A corporation administratively dissolved continues its corporate existence but may not carry on business except that necessary to wind up and liquidate its business and affairs under section 14.05 and notify claimants under sections 14.06 and 14.07.

    (d) The administrative dissolution of a corporation does not terminate the authority of its registered agent.

Section 14.22.   Reinstatement Following
Administrative Dissolution

    (a) A corporation administratively dissolved under section 14.21 may apply to the secretary of state for reinstatement within two years after the effective date of dissolution. The application must:

    (1) recite the name of the corporation and the effective date of its administrative dissolution;

    (2) state that the ground or grounds for dissolution either did not exist or have been eliminated;

    (3) state that the corporation's name satisfies the requirements of section 4.01; and

    (4) contain a certificate from the [taxing authority] reciting that all taxes owed by the corporation have been paid.

    (b) If the secretary of state determines that the application contains the information required by subsection (a) and that the information is correct, he shall cancel the certificate of dissolution and prepare a certificate of reinstatement that recites his determination and the effective date of reinstatement, file the original of the certificate, and serve a copy on the corporation under section 5.04.

    (c) When the reinstatement is effective, it relates back to and takes effect as of the effective date of the administrative dissolution and the corporation resumes carrying on its business as if the administrative dissolution had never occurred.

Section 14.23.   Appeal from Denial of Reinstatement

(a) If the secretary of state denies a corporation's application for reinstatement following administrative dissolution, he shall serve the corporation under section 5.04 with a written notice that explains the reason or reasons for denial.

(b) The corporation may appeal the denial of reinstatement to the [name or describe] court within 30 days after service of the notice of denial is perfected. The corporation appeals by petitioning the court to set asisde the dissolution and attaching to the petition copies of the secretary of state's certificate of dissolution, the corporation's application for reinstatement, and the secretary of state's notice of denial.

(c) The court may summarily order the secretary of state to reinstate the dissolved corporation or may take other action the court considers appropriate.

(d) The court's final decision may be appealed as in other civil proceedings.

Judicial Dissolution

Section 14.30.   Grounds for Judicial Dissolution

The [name or describe court or courts] may dissolve a corporation:

(1) In a proceeding by the attorney general if it is established that:

(i) the corporation obtained its articles of incorporation through fraud; or

(ii) the corporation has continued to exceed or abuse the authority conferred upon it by law;

(2) in a proceeding by a shareholder if it is established that:

(i) the directors are deadlocked in the management of the corporate affairs, the shareholders are unable to break the deadlock, and irreparable injury to the corporation is threatened or being suffered, or the business and affairs of the corporation can no longer be conducted to the advantage of the shareholders generally, because of the deadlock;

(ii) the directors or those in control of the corporation have acted, are acting, or will act in a manner that is illegal, oppressive, or fraudulent;

(iii) the shareholders are deadlocked in voting power and have failed, for a period that includes at least two consecutive annual meeting dates, to elect successors to directors whose terms have expired; or

(iv) the corporate assets are being misapplied or wasted;

(3) in a proceeding by a creditor if it is established that:

(i) the creditor's claim has been reduced to judgment, the execution on the judgment returned unsatisfied, and the corporation is insolvent; or

(ii) the corporation has admitted in writing that the creditor's claim is due and owing and the corporation is insolvent; or

(4) in a proceeding by the corporation to have its voluntary dissolution continued under court supervision.

Section 14.31.   Procedure for Judicial Dissolution

(a) Venue for a proceeding by the attorney general to dissolve a corporation lies in [name the county or counties]. Venue for a proceeding brought by any other party named in section 14.30 lies in the county where a corporation's principal office (or, if none in this state, its registered office) is or was last located.

(b) It is not necessary to make shareholders parties to a proceeding to dissolve a corporation unless relief is sought against them individually.

(c) A court in a proceeding brought to dissolve a corporation may issue injunctions, appoint a receiver or custodian pendente lite with all powers and duties the court directs, take other action required to preserve the corporate assets wherever located, and carry on the business of the corporation until a full hearing can be held.

Section 14.32.   Receivership or Custodianship

(a) A court in a judicial proceeding brought to dissolve a corporation may appoint one or more receivers to wind up and liquidate, or one or more custodians to manage, the business and affairs of the corporation. The court shall hold a hearing, after notifying all parties to the proceeding and any interested persons designated by the court, before appointing a receiver or custodian. The court appointing a receiver or custodian has exclusive jurisdiction over the corporation and all of its property wherever located.

(b) The court may appoint an individual or a domestic or foreign corporation (authorized to transact business in this state) as a receiver or custodian. The court may require the receiver or custodian to post bond, with or without sureties, in an amount the court directs.

(c) The court shall describe the powers and duties of the receiver or custodian in its appointing order, which may be amended from time to time. Among other powers:

(1) the receiver (i) may dispose of all or any part of the assets of the corporation wherever located, at a public or private sale, if authorized by the court; and (ii) may sue and defend in his own name as receiver of the corporation in all courts of this state;

(2) the custodian may exercise all of the powers of the corporation, through or in place of its board of directors or officers, to the extent necessary to manage the affairs of the corporation in the best interests of its shareholders and creditors.

(d) The court during a receivership may redesignate the receiver a custodian, and during a custodianship may redesignate the custodian a receiver, if doing so is in the best interests of the corporation, its shareholders, and creditors.

(e) The court from time to time during the receivership or custodianship may order compensation paid and expense disbursements or reimbursements made to the receiver or custodian and his counsel from the assets of the corporation or proceeds from the sale of the assets.

Section 14.33.   *Decree of Dissolution*

(a) If after a hearing the court determines that one or more grounds for judicial dissolution described in section 14.30 exist, it may enter a decree dissolving the corporation and specifying the effective date of the dissolution, and the clerk of the court shall deliver a certified copy of the decree to the secretary of state, who shall file it.

(b) After entering the decree of dissolution, the court shall direct the winding up and liquidation of the corporation's business and affairs in accordance with section 14.05 and the notification of claimants in accordance with sections 14.06 and 14.07.

Miscellaneous

Section 14.40.   *Deposit with State Treasurer*

Assets of a dissolved corporation that should be transferred to a creditor, claimant, or shareholder of the corporation who cannot be found or who is not competent to receive them shall be reduced to cash and deposited with the state treasurer or other appropriate state official for safekeeping. When the creditor, claimant, or shareholder furnishes satisfactory proof of entitlement to the amount deposited, the state treasurer or other appropriate state official shall pay him or his representative that amount.

CHAPTER 15   FOREIGN CORPORATIONS

Certificate of Authority

Section 15.01.   *Authority to Transact Business Required*

(a) A foreign corporation may not transact business in this state until it obtains a certificate of authority from the secretary of state.

(b) The following activities, among others, do not constitute transacting business within the meaning of subsection (a):

(1) maintaining, defending, or settling any proceeding;

(2) holding meetings of the board of directors or shareholders or carrying on other activities concerning internal corporate affairs;

(3) maintaining bank accounts;

(4) maintaining offices or agencies for the transfer, exchange, and registration of the corporation's own securities or maintaining trustees or depositaries with respect to those securities;

(5) selling through independent contractors;

(6) soliciting or obtaining orders, whether by mail or through employees or agents or otherwise, if the orders require acceptance outside this state before they become contracts;

(7) creating or acquiring indebtedness, mortgages, and security interests in real or personal property;

(8) securing or collecting debts or enforcing mortgages and security interests in property securing the debts;

(9) owning, without more, real or personal property;

(10) conducting an isolated transaction that is completed within 30 days and that is not one in the course of repeated transactions of a like nature;

(11) transacting business in interstate commerce.

(c) The list of activities in subsection (b) is not exhaustive.

Section 15.02. Consequences of Transacting Business Without Authority

(a) A foreign corporation transacting business in this state without a certificate of authority may not maintain a proceeding in any court in this state until it obtains a certificate of authority.

(b) The successor to a foreign corporation that transacted business in this state without a certificate of authority and the assignee of a cause of action arising out of that business may not maintain a proceeding based on that cause of action in any court in this state until the foreign corporation or its successor obtains a certificate of authority.

(c) A court may stay a proceeding commenced by a foreign corporation, its successor, or assignee until it determines whether the foreign corporation or its successor requires a certificate of authority. If it so determines, the court may further stay the proceeding until the foreign corporation or its successor obtains the certificate.

(d) A foreign corporation is liable for a civil penalty of $ _____ for each day, but not to exceed a total of $ _____ for each year, it transacts business in this state without a certificate of authority. The attorney general may collect all penalties due under this subsection.

(e) Notwithstanding subsections (a) and (b), the failure of a foreign corporation to obtain a certificate of authority does not impair the validity of its corporate acts or prevent it from defending any proceeding in this state.

Section 15.03. Application for Certificate of Authority

(a) A foreign corporation may apply for a certificate of authority to transact business in this state by delivering an application to the secretary of state for filing. The application must set forth:

(1) the name of the foreign corporation or, if its name is unavailable for use in this state, a corporate name that satisfies the requirements of section 15.06;

(2) the name of the state or country under whose law it is incorporated;

(3) its date of incorporation and period of duration;

(4) the street address of its principal office;

(5) the address of its registered office in this state and the name of its registered agent at that office; and

(6) the names and usual business addresses of its current directors and officers.

(b) The foreign corporation shall deliver with the completed application a certificate of existence (or a document of similar import) duly authenticated by the secretary of state or other official having custody of corporate records in the state or country under whose law it is incorporated.

Section 15.04. Amended Certificate of Authority

(a) A foreign corporation authorized to transact business in this state must obtain an amended certificate of authority from the secretary of state if it changes:

(1) its corporate name;

(2) the period of its duration; or

(3) the state or country of its incorporation.

(b) The requirements of section 15.03 for obtaining an original certificate of authority apply to obtaining an amended certificate under this section.

Section 15.05. Effect of Certificate of Authority

(a) A certificate of authority authorizes the foreign corporation to which it is issued to transact business in this state subject, however, to the right of the state to revoke the certificate as provided in this Act.

(b) A foreign corporation with a valid certificate of authority has the same but no greater rights and has the same but no greater privileges as, and except as otherwise provided by this Act is subject to the same duties, restrictions, penalties, and liabilities now or later imposed on, a domestic corporation of like character.

(c) This Act does not authorize this state to regulate the organization or internal affairs of a foreign corporation authorized to transact business in this state.

Section 15.06. Corporate Name of Foreign Corporation

(a) If the corporate name of a foreign corporation does not satisfy the requirements of section 4.01, the foreign corporation to obtain or maintain a certificate of authority to transact business in this state:

(1) may add the word "corporation," "incorporated," "company," or "limited," or the abbrevia-

tion "corp.," "inc.," "co.," or "ltd.," to its corporate name for use in this state; or

(2) may use a fictitious name to transact business in this state if its real name is unavailable and it delivers to the secretary of state for filing a copy of the resolution of its board of directors, certified by its secretary, adopting the fictitious name.

(b) Except as authorized by subsections (c) and (d), the corporate name (including a fictitious name) of a foreign corporation must be distinguishable upon the records of the secretary of state from:

(1) the corporate name of a corporation incorporated or authorized to transact business in this state;

(2) a corporate name reserved or registered under section 4.02 or 4.03;

(3) the fictitious name of another foreign corporation authorized to transact business in this state; and

(4) the corporate name of a not-for-profit corporation incorporated or authorized to transact business in this state.

(c) A foreign corporation may apply to the secretary of state for authorization to use in this state the name of another corporation (incorporated or authorized to transact business in this state) that is not distinguishable upon his records from the name applied for. The secretary of state shall authorize use of the name applied for if:

(1) the other corporation consents to the use in writing and submits an undertaking in form satisfactory to the secretary of state to change its name to a name that is distinguishable upon the records of the secretary of state from the name of the applying corporation; or

(2) the applicant delivers to the secretary of state a certified copy of a final judgment of a court of competent jurisdiction establishing the applicant's right to use the name applied for in this state.

(d) A foreign corporation may use in this state the name (includng the fictitious name) of another domestic or foreign corporation that is used in this state if the other corporation is incorporated or authorized to transact business in this state and the foreign corporation:

(1) has merged with the other corporation;

(2) has been formed by reorganization of the other corporation; or

(3) has acquired all or substantially all of the assets, including the corporate name, of the other corporation.

(e) If a foreign corporation authorized to transact business in this state changes its corporate name to one that does not satisfy the requirements of section 4.01, it may not transact business in this state under the changed name until it adopts a name satisfying the requirements of section 4.01 and obtains an amended certificate of authority under section 15.04.

Section 15.07.   Registered Office and Registered Agent of Foreign Corporation

Each foreign corporation authorized to transact business in this state must continuously maintain in this state:

(1) a registered office that may be the same as any of its places of business; and

(2) a registered agent, who may be:

(i) an individual who resides in this state and whose business office is identical with the registered office;

(ii) a domestic corporation or not-for-profit domestic corporation whose business office is identical with the registered office; or

(iii) a foreign corporation or foreign not-for-profit corporation authorized to transact business in this state whose business office is identical with the registered office.

Section 15.08.   Change of Registered Office or Registered Agent of Foreign Corporation

(a) A foreign corporation authorized to transact business in this state may change its registered office or registered agent by delivering to the secretary of state for filing a statement of change that sets forth:

(1) its name;

(2) the street address of its current registered office;

(3) if the current registered office is to be changed, the street address of its new registered office;

(4) the name of its current registered agent;

(5) if the current registered agent is to be changed, the name of its new registered agent and the new agent's written consent (either on the statement or attached to it) to the appointment; and

(6) that after the change or changes are made, the street addresses of its registered office and the business office of its registered agent will be identical.

(b) If a registered agent changes the street address of his business office, he may change the street address of the registered office of any foreign corporation for which he is the registered agent by notifying the corporation in writing of the change and signing (either manually or in facsimile) and delivering to the secretary of state for filing a statement of change that complies with the requirements of subsection (a) and recites that the corporation has been notified of the change.

Section 15.09.   Resignation of Registered Agent of Foreign Corporation

(a) The registered agent of a foreign corporation may resign his agency appointment by signing and delivering to the secretary of state for filing the original and two exact or conformed copies of a statement of resignation. The statement of resignation may include a statement that the registered office is also discontinued.

(b) After filing the statement, the secretary of state shall attach the filing receipt to one copy and mail the copy and receipt to the registered office if not discontinued. The secretary of state shall mail the other copy to the foreign corporation at its principal office address shown in its most recent annual report.

(c) The agency appointment is terminated, and the registered office discontinued if so provided, on the 31st day after the date on which the statement was filed.

Section 15.10.   Service on Foreign Corporation

(a) The registered agent of a foreign corporation authorized to transact business in this state is the corporation's agent for service of process, notice, or demand required or permitted by law to be served on the foreign corporation.

(b) A foreign corporation may be served by registered or certified mail, return receipt requested, addressed to the secretary of the foreign corporation at its principal office shown in its application for a certificate of authority or in its most recent annual report if the foreign corporation:

(1) has no registered agent or its registered agent cannot with reasonable diligence be served;

(2) has withdrawn from transacting business in this state under section 15.20; or

(3) has had its certificate of authority revoked under section 15.31.

(c) Service is perfected under subsection (b) at the earliest of:

(1) the date the foreign corporation receives the mail;

(2) the date shown on the return receipt, if signed on behalf of the foreign corporation; or

(3) five days after its deposit in the United States Mail, as evidenced by the postmark, if mailed postpaid and correctly addressed.

(d) This section does not prescribe the only means, or necessarily the required means, of serving a foreign corporation.

Withdrawal

Section 15.20.   Withdrawal of Foreign Corporation

(a) A foreign corporation authorized to transact business in this state may not withdraw from this state until it obtains a certificate of withdrawal from the secretary of state.

(b) A foreign corporation authorized to transact business in this state may apply for a certificate of withdrawal by delivering an application to the secretary of state for filing. The application must set forth:

(1) the name of the foreign corporation and the name of the state or country under whose law it is incorporated;

(2) that it is not transacting business in this state and that it surrenders its authority to transact business in this state;

(3) that it revokes the authority of its registered agent to accept service on its behalf and appoints the secretary of state as its agent for service of process in any proceeding based on a cause of action arising during the time it was authorized to transact business in this state;

(4) a mailing address to which the secretary of state may mail a copy of any process served on him under subdivision (3); and

(5) a commitment to notify the secretary of state in the future of any change in its mailing address.

(c) After the withdrawal of the corporation is effective, service of process on the secretary of state under this section is service on the foreign corporation. Upon receipt of process, the secretary of state shall mail a copy of the process to the foreign corporation at the mailing address set forth under subsection (b).

Revocation of Certificate of Authority

Section 15.30.   Grounds for Revocation

The secretary of state may commence a proceeding under section 15.31 to revoke the certificate of authority of a foreign corporation authorized to transact business in this state if:

(1) the foreign corporation does not deliver its annual report to the secretary of state within 60 days after it is due;

(2) the foreign corporation does not pay within 60 days after they are due any franchise taxes or penalties imposed by this Act or other law;

(3) the foreign corporation is without a registered agent or registered office in this state for 60 days or more;

(4) the foreign corporation does not inform the secretary of state under section 15.08 or 15.09 that its registered agent or registered office has changed, that its registered agent has resigned, or that its registered office has been discontinued within 60 days of the change, resignation, or discontinuance;

(5) an incorporator, director, officer, or agent of the foreign corporation signed a document he knew was false in any material respect with intent that the document be delivered to the secretary of state for filing;

(6) the secretary of state receives a duly authenticated certificate from the secretary of state or other official having custody of corporate records in the state or country under whose law the foreign corporation is incorporated stating that it has been dissolved or disappeared as the result of a merger.

Section 15.31.   Procedure for and Effect of Revocation

(a) If the secretary of state determines that one or more grounds exist under section 15.30 for revocation of a certificate of authority, he shall serve the foreign corporation with written notice of his determination under section 15.10.

(b) If the foreign corporation does not correct each ground for revocation or demonstrate to the reasonable satisfaction of the secretary of state that each ground determined by the secretary of state does not exist within 60 days after service of the notice is perfected under section 15.10, the secretary of state may revoke the foreign corporation's certificate of authority by signing a certificate of revocation that recites the ground or grounds for revocation and its effective date.

The secretary of state shall file the original of the certificate and serve a copy on the foreign corporation under section 15.10.

(c) The authority of a foreign corporation to transact business in this state ceases on the date shown on the certificate revoking its certificate of authority.

(d) The secretary of state's revocation of a foreign corporation's certificate of authority appoints the secretary of state the foreign corporation's agent for service of process in any proceeding based on a cause of action which arose during the time the foreign corporation was authorized to transact business in this state. Service of process on the secretary of state under this subsection is service on the foreign corporation. Upon receipt of process, the secretary of state shall mail a copy of the process to the secretary of the foreign corporation at its principal office shown on its most recent annual report or in any subsequent communication received from the corporation stating the current mailing address of its principal office or, if none are on file, in its application for a certificate of authority.

(e) Revocation of a foreign corporation's certificate of authority does not terminate the authority of the registered agent of the corporation.

Section 15.32.   Appeal from Revocation

(a) A foreign corporation may appeal the secretary of state's revocation of its certificate of authority to the [name or describe] court within 30 days after service of the certificate of revocation is perfected under section 15.10. The foreign corporation appeals by petitioning the court to set aside the revocation and attaching to the petition copies of its certificate of authority and the secretary of state's certificate of revocation.

(b) The court may summarily order the secretary of state to reinstate the certificate of authority or may take any other action the court considers appropriate.

(c) The court's final decision may be appealed as in other civil proceedings.

CHAPTER 16   RECORDS AND REPORTS

Records

Section 16.01.   Corporate Records

(a) A corporation shall keep as permanent records minutes of all meetings of its shareholders and board of directors, a record of all actions taken by the shareholders or board of directors without a meeting, and a record of all actions taken by a committee of the board of directors in place of the board of directors on behalf of the corporation.

(b) A corporation shall maintain appropriate accounting records.

(c) A corporation or its agent shall maintain a record of its shareholders, in a form that permits preparation of a list of the names and addresses of all shareholders, in alphabetical order by class of shares showing the number and class of shares held by each.

(d) A corporation shall maintain its records in written form or in another form capable of conversion into written form within a reasonable time.

(e) A corporation shall keep a copy of the following records at its principal office:

(1) its articles or restated articles of incorporation and all amendments to them currently in effect;

(2) its bylaws or restated bylaws and all amendments to them currently in effect;

(3) resolutions adopted by its board of directors creating one or more classes or series of shares, and fixing their relative rights, preferences, and limitations, if shares issued pursuant to those resolutions are outstanding;

(4) the minutes of all shareholders' meetings, and records of all action taken by shareholders without a meeting, for the past three years;

(5) all written communications to shareholders generally within the past three years, including the financial statements furnished for the past three years under section 16.20;

(6) a list of the names and business addresses of its current directors and officers; and

(7) its most recent annual report delivered to the secretary of state under section 16.22.

Section 16.02.   Inspection of Records by Shareholders

(a) A shareholder of a corporation is entitled to inspect and copy, during regular business hours at the corporation's principal office, any of the records of the corporation described in section 16.01(e) if he gives the corporation written notice of his demand at least five business days before the date on which he wishes to inspect and copy.

(b) A shareholder of a corporation is entitled to inspect and copy, during regular business hours at a reasonable location specified by the corporation, any of the following records of the corporation if the shareholder meets the requirements of subsection (c) and gives the corporation written notice of his demand at least five business days before the date on which he wishes to inspect and copy:

(1) excerpts from minutes of any meeting of the board of directors, records of any action of a committee of the board of directors while acting in place of the board of directors on behalf of the corporation, minutes of any meeting of the shareholders, and records of action taken by the shareholders or board of directors without a meeting, to the extent not subject to inspection under section 16.02(a);

(2) accounting records of the corporation; and

(3) the record of shareholders.

(c) A shareholder may inspect and copy the records described in subsection (b) only if:

(1) his demand is made in good faith and for a proper purpose;

(2) he describes with reasonable particularity his purpose and the records he desires to inspect; and

(3) the records are directly connected with his purpose.

(d) The right of inspection granted by this section may not be abolished or limited by a corporation's articles of incorporation or bylaws.

(e) This section does not affect:

(1) the right of a shareholder to inspect records under section 7.20 or, if the shareholder is in litigation with the corporation, to the same extent as any other litigant;

(2) the power of a court, independently of this Act, to compel the production of corporate records for examination.

Section 16.03.   Scope of Inspection Right

(a) A shareholder's agent or attorney has the same inspection and copying rights as the shareholder he represents.

(b) The right to copy records under section 16.02 includes, if reasonable, the right to receive copies made by photographic, xerographic, or other means.

(c) The corporation may impose a reasonable charge, covering the costs of labor and material, for copies of any documents provided to the shareholder. The charge may not exceed the estimated cost of production or reproduction of the records.

(d) The corporation may comply with a shareholder's demand to inspect the record of shareholders under section 16.02(b)(3) by providing him with a list of its shareholders that was compiled no earlier than the date of the shareholder's demand.

Section 16.04.   Court-Ordered Inspection

(a) If a corporation does not allow a shareholder who complies with section 16.02(a) to inspect and copy any records required by that subsection to be available for inspection, the [name or describe court] of the county where the corporation's principal office (or, if none in this state, its registered office) is located may summarily order inspection and copying of the records demanded at the corporation's expense upon application of the shareholder.

(b) If a corporation does not within a reasonable time allow a shareholder to inspect and copy any other record, the shareholder who complies with section 16.02(b) and (c) may apply to the [name or describe court] in the county where the corporation's principal office (or, if none in this state, its registered office) is located for an order to permit inspection and copying of the records demanded. The court shall dispose of an application under this subsection on an expedited basis.

(c) If the court orders inspection and copying of the records demanded, it shall also order the corporation to pay the shareholder's costs (including reasonable counsel fees) incurred to obtain the order unless the corporation proves that it refused inspection in good faith because it had a reasonable basis for doubt about the right of the shareholder to inspect the records demanded.

(d) If the court orders inspection and copying of the records demanded, it may impose reasonable restrictions on the use or distribution of the records by the demanding shareholder.

Reports

Section 16.20.   Financial Statements for Shareholders

(a) A corporation shall furnish its shareholders annual financial statements, which may be consolidated or combined statements of the corporation and one or more of its subsidiaries, as appropriate, that include a balance sheet as of the end of the fiscal year, an income statement for that year, and a statement of changes in shareholders' equity for the year unless that information appears elsewhere in the financial state-

ments. If financial statements are prepared for the corporation on the basis of generally accepted accounting principles, the annual financial statements must also be prepared on that basis.

(b) If the annual financial statements are reported upon by a public accountant, his report must accompany them. If not, the statements must be accompanied by a statement of the president or the person responsible for the corporation's accounting records:

(1) stating his reasonable belief whether the statements were prepared on the basis of generally accepted accounting principles and, if not, describing the basis of preparation; and

(2) describing any respects in which the statements were not prepared on a basis of accounting consistent with the statements prepared for the preceding year.

(c) A corporation shall mail the annual financial statements to each shareholder within 120 days after the close of each fiscal year. Thereafter, on written request from a shareholder who was not mailed the statements, the corporation shall mail him the latest financial statements.

Section 16.21.   Other Reports to Shareholders

(a) If a corporation indemnifies or advances expenses to a director under section 8.51, 8.52, 8.53, or 8.54 in connection with a proceeding by or in the right of the corporation, the corporation shall report the indemnification or advance in writing to the shareholders with or before the notice of the next shareholders' meeting.

(b) If a corporation issues or authorizes the issuance of shares for promissory notes or for promises to render services in the future, the corporation shall report in writing to the shareholders the number of shares authorized or issued, and the consideration received by the corporation, with or before the notice of the next shareholders' meeting.

Section 16.22.   Annual Report for Secretary of State

(a) Each domestic corporation, and each foreign corporation authorized to transact business in this state, shall deliver to the secretary of state for filing an annual report that sets forth:

(1) the name of the corporation and the state or country under whose law it is incorporated;

(2) the address of its registered office and the name of its registered agent at that office in this state;

(3) the address of its principal office;

(4) the names and business addresses of its directors and principal officers;

(5) a brief description of the nature of its business;

(6) the total number of authorized shares, itemized by class and series, if any, within each class; and

(7) the total number of issued and outstanding shares, itemized by class and series, if any, within each class.

(b) Information in the annual report must be current as of the date the annual report is executed on behalf of the corporation.

(c) The first annual report must be delivered to the secretary of state between January 1 and April 1 of the year following the calendar year in which a domestic corporation was incorporated or a foreign corporation was authorized to transact business. Subsequent annual reports must be delivered to the secretary of state between January 1 and April 1 of the following calendar years.

(d) If an annual report does not contain the information required by this section, the secretary of state shall promptly notify the reporting domestic or foreign corporaiton in writing and return the report to it for correction. If the report is corrected to contain the information required by this section and delivered to the secretary of state within 30 days after the effective date of notice, it is deemed to be timely filed.

CHAPTER 17   TRANSITION PROVISIONS

Section 17.01.   *Application to Existing
                    Domestic Corporations*

This Act applies to all domestic corporations in existence on its effective date that were incorporated under any general statute of this state providing for incorporation of corporations for profit if power to amend or repeal

the statute under which the corporation was incorporated was reserved.

Section 17.02.   *Application to Qualified
                    Foreign Corporations*

A foreign corporation authorized to transact business in this state on the effective date of this Act is subject to this Act but is not required to obtain a new certificate of authority to transact business under this Act.

Section 17.03.   *Saving Provisions*

(a) Except as provided in subsection (b), the repeal of a statute by this Act does not affect:

(1) the operation of the statute or any action taken under it before its repeal;

(2) any ratification, right, remedy, privilege, obligation, or liability acquired, accrued, or incurred under the statute before its repeal;

(3) any violation of the statute, or any penalty, forfeiture, or punishment incurred because of the violation, before its repeal;

(4) any proceeding, reorganization, or dissolution commenced under the statute before its repeal, and the proceeding, reorganization, or dissolution may be completed in accordance with the statute as if it had not been repealed.

(b) If a penalty or punishment imposed for violation of a statute repealed by this Act is reduced by this Act, the penalty or punishment if not already imposed shall be imposed in accordance with this Act.

Section 17.04.   *Severability*

If any provision of this Act or its application to any person or circumstance is held invalid by a court of competent jurisdiction, the invalidity does not affect other provisions or applications of the Act that can be given effect without the invalid provision or application, and to this end the provisions of the Act are severable.

Section 17.05.   *Repeal*

The following laws and parts of laws are repealed: [to be inserted].

Section 17.06.   *Effective Date*

This Act takes effect _____.

Glossary

ABA standards: standards of ethical conduct for persons in the legal profession set forth in the American Bar Association's Model Code of Professional Responsibility and Model Code of Professional Conduct.

accountant's report: a report which verifies that the figures presented in an annual report have been reviewed by an independent certified accountant.

accounting: a formal rendition of account.

accounts receivable financing: a method of obtaining a short-term bank loan by pledging a business's receivables as collateral for the loan. It is based on a discounted value of the pledged receivables.

accrual method: an accounting method in which income is recorded as received when the customer is billed and expenses are recorded when incurred rather than when paid.

accumulated earnings: earnings that are retained by a corporation rather than paid out as dividends to the shareholders. If accumulated for the purpose of avoiding income tax imposed on shareholders, a corporation may be subject to an accumulated earnings tax.

actual authority: authority given by consent.

administrative dissolution: an involuntary dissolution of a corporation by the secretary of state or other appropriate authority for failure to comply with various statutory requirements.

agency: relation in which one party is given the authority to act for or to represent another.

agent: a party authorized to act for or represent another.

aggregate theory: a theory stating that a partnership is an association of persons.

amortization: a method of deducting the cost of certain intangible properties by spreading the cost over a certain number of years.

annual report: a corporation's financial statement, issued yearly and sent to shareholders.

annuity plan: a type of defined benefit pension plan in which contributions are used to buy retirement annuities for the benefit of employees.

apparent authority: authority a principal either knowingly or negligently allows an agent to assume or authority which a principal holds an agent out as possessing.

application for reinstatement: an application made to the appropriate state filing authority requesting reinstatement of articles of incorporation.

arbitrary mark: a mark made up of commonly understood words, but of words not commonly associated with the nature of a product or service.

articles of amendment: a document filed with the appropriate state filing authority amending the articles of organization of a limited liability company or the articles of incorporation of a corporation.

articles of dissolution: a document filed with the appropriate state filing authority legally dissolving a corporation.

articles of incorporation: a document filed with the appropriate state filing authority legally creating the existence of a corporation.

articles of merger: a document formally merging two or more business entities.

articles of organization: a document legally creating a limited liability company.

articles of partnership: *see* partnership agreement.

articles of revocation: a document filed with the appropriate state filing authority to revoke a dissolution.

articles of share exchange: a document filed by an acquiring corporation with the appropriate state filing authority containing the plan of share exchange.

articles of termination: a document filed with the appropriate state filing authority indicating the dissolution of a business entity.

asset purchase: a transaction in which one corporation purchases all, or substantially all, of the assets of another business.

attorney service bureau: *see* corporate service company.

at-will companies: limited liability companies existing for an unspecified duration.

authorized capital: *see* authorized shares.

authorized shares: the maximum amount of stock a corporation may issue, as set forth in the corporation's articles of incorporation.

balance sheet: that part of a corporate annual report which provides a "snapshot" of the corporation on a designated day as an indicator of the corporation's financial condition.

balance sheet test: a test commonly used to determine whether a corporation is solvent and therefore in the position to issue dividends to shareholders.

beneficiary: a person or entity to be benefitted by a trust.

blue sky laws: state statutes regulating securities offerings and sales.

board of directors: the governing body of a corporation which creates and implements a corporation's policies.

board of governors: a board, similar to a board of directors, which governs a limited liability company in some states.

boilerplate: standard language found in a contract.

bond: a long-term, secured debt instrument issued by a corporation.

book value method: a process for determining the value of a business by looking at its assets and liabilities as they appear in the business accounting records.

boot: a term used by the Internal Revenue Service to refer to cash or types of property not included in the definition of a nontaxable exchange.

bulk transfer laws: laws intending to prevent the defrauding of creditors when a business sells substantially all of its assets.

business judgment rule: a doctrine which holds that a director will be shielded from liability for a poor business decision if, at the time the decision was made, the decision was reasonable, rational, and informed, even if other reasonable persons might disagree with the decision.

business plan: a document which presents a detailed analysis of the estimated start-up expenses, market research, and profit objectives of a business.

bylaws: the rules by which the internal affairs of the corporation are governed.

call: an agreement permitting an individual or entity to buy stock at a specified price.

callable bond: *see* redeemable bond.

callable preferred stock: *see* redeemable preferred stock.

call date: the date upon which a corporation may recall redeemable preferred stock or redeemable bonds.

call premium: a premium paid by a corporation for the option of calling a bond prior to its maturity date.

capital expense: an expense which is incurred in getting started in a business.

capital stock: all common stock and preferred stock a corporation is authorized to issue.

capital structure: a combination of all equity securities authorized to be issued by a corporation and all debt securities of a corporation.

capital surplus: monies paid over the par value for par value stock plus the monies paid for no par stock that are not allocated by the board of directors to the stated capital account.

capitalization of earnings method: a process for determining the value of a business by calculating its average yearly net earnings and then multiplying this figure by a multiplier.

cash method: accounting method in which expenses and income are listed in the appropriate ledger when paid or received.

C corporation: a regular corporation which is subject to double taxation.

certificate of authority: a certificate from the secretary of state evidencing the good-standing status of a foreign business entity.

certificate of cancellation: a certificate from the appropriate state filing authority terminating the legal existence of a business entity.

certificate of dissolution: a certificate from the appropriate state filing authority legally dissolving a corporation.

certificate of existence: a certificate from the secretary of state evidencing the good-standing status of a domestic business entity.

certificate of good standing: *see* certificate of existence.

certificate of incorporation: a certificate from the secretary of state recognizing a corporation as duly authorized under state law.

certificate of limited partnership: a document filed with the appropriate state filing authority which creates the legal existence of a limited partnership.

certificate of registration: *see* certificate of authority.

certification mark: a mark which indicates that products or services meet certain objectively defined quality standards.

certified resolution: a statement certified by the secretary of a corporation to a third party that a particular resolution has been duly adopted by the corporation.

charter: *see* articles of incorporation.

client number: a numeric or alphanumeric number assigned to each client file which identifies the client.

client trust account: a special bank account set aside for the depositing of retainer fees or other advances, settlement checks, and monies not to be commingled with a law firm's regular business account.

closely held corporation (also called a **close corporation**): a corporation owned by a few shareholders which typically imposes restrictions on transfers of shares.

coined mark: a mark comprised of invented words.

collapsible corporation: a corporation used primarily for the manufacture, construction, production, or purchase of certain kinds of property with the principal aim of distribution to the corporation's shareholders prior to the realization by the corporation of a substantial portion of taxable income from the property.

collective mark: a mark that indicates association within a group or membership body.

common stock: ordinary stock which does not confer preferences to the shareholder.

confidentiality: the ethical responsibility to keep all communication with potential, present, and former clients strictly confidential.

conflict of interest: any situation in which an attorney's professional judgment might be affected because of business or personal interests.

consolidated balance sheet: a balance sheet combining figures for all subsidiaries plus the parent corporation.

consolidation: two or more corporations combining in such a manner that they create a new corporation, the other(s) ceasing to exist.

contingency fees: attorney's fees which are contingent upon the client reaching settlement or winning in court. The payment the attorney receives is set forth as a percentage of the settlement or court award.

contingent compensation: compensation contingent upon certain criteria, such as corporate growth or profit.

convertible bond: a bond which may be converted into a stated number of shares of stock in a corporation at a specified time.

convertible preferred stock: preferred stock which may be converted into a stated amount of common stock under specified conditions.

copyright: protection of the authorship of literary, musical, and artistic works.

corporate kit: a kit containing the corporate seal, stock certificates, and a minute book in which minutes of corporate meetings and corporate documents are kept.

corporate opportunity doctrine: a doctrine which requires a director or officer to inform the corporation of any business opportunity that comes the director's or officer's way which the corporation may deem valuable.

corporate service company: a company providing various services for attorneys and corporate clients, including the preparation and filing of corporate documents.

corporation: a legal entity separate from the owners of the business that is created according to the dictates of state statutes.

coupon rate: interest rate paid on a bond, as represented by an attached coupon presented by the bondholder in order to collect the interest.

cross-purchase plan: life insurance arrangement whereby the owners of a business take out life insurance policies on each others' lives in order to use the proceeds to purchase a deceased owner's interest in the business from his or her estate.

cumulative preferred stock: preferred stock entitled to any accumulated back dividends.

cumulative voting: a method of applying votes to enhance the opportunity for minority shareholders to vote their representative onto the board of directors.

current assets: cash and all other assets that are easily convertible into cash within the course of the year.

current compensation: compensation paid for the current services provided to the corporation by an employee, such as salary.

current liabilities: obligations that should be paid by a corporation within the year.

debenture: an unsecured debt instrument issued by a corporation.

debt financing: securing a loan to raise capital for a business.

debt securities: instruments evidencing a loan made to a corporation, such as a bond or a debenture.

deferred compensation: compensation to the employee postponed until the happening of a future event such as, but not limited to, retirement.

deferred vesting: the postponement of the time at which the employee's rights to benefits become nonforfeitable.

delectus personae: choice of persons. Refers to the right of a partner to choose any new partners in a business.

depletion: a method of deducting costs relating to the acquisition and utilization of mineral property.

depreciation: a method of deducting the cost of a business asset that has a useful life of more than one year by spreading the cost over the useful life of the asset.

derivative action: lawsuit brought to enforce rights derived from ownership of the injured entity.

derivative mark: a new mark created from and having aspects in common with an existing mark of a company.

descriptive mark: a mark which describes a product or service, the geographical origins of a product or service, or someone's surname.

design patent: protection of ornamental designs of manufactured products.

disclosed principal: a principal known by a third party to be the principal in an agency relationship.

discount stock: *see* watered stock.

discounted bond: a bond which is sold for less than the face amount of the principal.

dissociation: the termination of a person's (or entity's) association with a business entity.

dissolution: the act of terminating or dissolving.

dividends: profits paid out to shareholders in proportion to each shareholder's interest in the corporation.

documentary stamp tax: a tax imposed when original certificates of stock are issued.

domicile: the permanent residence of a person or state of formation of a business.

double taxation: a feature of C corporations in which the profits of a corporation are taxed twice: first, as income to the corporation, and second, when shareholders pay taxes on the profit paid out to them in the form of dividends.

draw: an advance payment of a certain monetary sum, the total of which is to be deducted from the commission due the employee.

earned surplus: the corporation's accumulated profits from the running of the business.

earnings report: *see* income statement.

emergency bylaws: bylaws which include all necessary provisions for managing a corporation during an emergency.

employee manual: a document setting forth the philosophies and expectations of the employer corporation.

employee stock ownership plan: one in which monetary contributions are put into an employee stock ownership trust.

entity plan: a life insurance policy purchased by a business entity on the lives of its owners in order to use the proceeds to purchase a deceased owner's interest in the business from his or her estate.

entity theory: a theory stating that a partnership is a legal entity with an identity separate and apart from the partners.

equitable title: title conferring the benefit interest in property.

equity financing: the raising of capital by selling ownership interest in the business.

equity securities: common or preferred stock of a corporation.

exercise price: *see* strike price.

factoring: a method of financing in which a business's accounts receivable are sold at a discounted value to a finance company or factoring company which then collects on the accounts.

family partnership: a partnership in which all partners are spouses, ancestors, and/or lineal descendants (or any trust for the primary benefit of those persons).

fanciful mark: *see* arbitrary mark.

fictitious name registration: registration made to operate under a name other than one's legal name.

fiduciary duty: a duty brought about by a special relationship of trust.

finance company: a lending company that lends money against the pledging of collateral such as equipment, inventory, accounts receivable, or a combination of these.

fiscal year: a consecutive twelve-month period selected by a business as its accounting period.

fixed assets: assets used to generate income for the corporation.

fixed liabilities: long-term loans, plus bonds and debentures issued by a corporation.

flat fees: attorney's fees set forth as a sum certain for the performance of a specified task.

floating rate bond: a bond with an adjustable interest rate.

foreign corporation: a corporation incorporated in one state which conducts business in another.

foreign limited partnership: a limited partnership created in one state which conducts business in another.

Form 8-K: a form filed with the Securities and Exchange Commission whenever any material information contained within a corporation's registration statement changes.

Form SS-4: a form used in acquiring a federal employer identification number.

Form 10-K: an annual report filed with the Securities and Exchange Commission.

Form 10-Q: a quarterly report filed with the Securities and Exchange Commission.

401(k) plan: an elective deferral plan in which the employee elects to have the employer contribute a part of his or her before-tax salary to the plan, said part remaining tax-free until it is distributed under the plan.

fractional share: a part or portion of a share of stock.

franchise tax: a tax imposed for the right to do business as a corporation in a particular state.

fringe benefits: benefits received by an employee in addition to salary.

general agent: an agent given authority to act on behalf of the principal in all matters concerning the principal's business.

general partnership: a business entity comprised of two or more persons who carry out a business as co-owners for profit.

going concern value: the price of selling a business as an existing, solvent enterprise.

goodwill: the continued customer patronage that results from a well-established reputation.

hourly fees: attorney's fees based upon the amount of time the attorney spends on a client matter.

house mark: a mark which is used on many or all products of a company.

incentive compensation: compensation paid to an employee as an incentive for continued high performance, such as commissions and bonuses.

income statement: a cumulative report of the profits and losses accrued by a corporation's operations for an entire year.

incorporator: a person who executes and files the articles of incorporation.

indemnification: reimbursement or compensation for loss or damage.

indenture: a statement setting forth the terms of a debt instrument.

ingredient mark: a mark which identifies an ingredient contained in a company's product.

insider trading: the sale or purchase of securities of a public corporation by a party with "insider" knowledge that gives that party a distinct advantage over a less informed public.

inspector of election: an individual chosen by the board of directors to make sure all election formalities are met.

integrated plan: a plan which allows the employer to integrate contributions made to Social Security when calculating the amount of contribution or benefit to be received by the employee.

intent to dissolve statement: a statement filed to put creditors of a corporation on notice that the corporation intends to dissolve.

intent-to-use application: a trademark application filed with the Patent and Trademark Office indicating a bona fide intention to use a mark in commerce at some time in the future.

intermediate-term financing: a loan term of one to five years.

Investment Advisors Act of 1940: a federal statute regulating activities of those who provide investment advice.

IRA: individual retirement arrangement or account, in which an employee may set aside a certain statutorily prescribed percentage of his or her income per year, said amount being deductible and tax-deferred.

issued shares: shares of stock sold to shareholders.

joint venture: a business entity designed to carry out a particular venture and then terminate upon its completion.

judicial dissolution: a corporate dissolution supervised by the court.

Keogh plan: a qualified retirement plan in which a certain percentage of an employee's taxable compensation is contributed and not taxed until the plan benefits are distributed.

key employee: an employee to be retained in a senior executive or management position, or one hired for other special talents.

Lanham Act: federal statutes collectively pertaining to trademarks.

legal title: title conferring rights of ownership and possession but not conferring any beneficial interest in property.

letter of intent: a letter expressing a corporation's merger proposal to another party.

limited liability company: a business entity combining characteristics of a partnership and a corporation.

limited liability partnership: a partnership designed for professionals in which the partners are treated as general partners but have no personal liability for certain partnership debts.

limited partner: a partner whose liability is limited to the partner's actual and promised contributions to the business.

limited partnership: a business entity comprised of at least one limited partner and at least one general partner, carrying out a business as co-owners for profit.

liquidation value: a hypothetical selling price presuming a willing and informed seller and a willing and informed buyer.

long-term financing: a loan term of more than five years.

manager: a person who oversees the daily operations of a limited liability company.

manager-managed companies: limited liability companies whose daily operations are managed by one or more managers.

market value method: determining the value of a business by looking to the current market value of all its assets and liabilities.

marshaling of assets: looking to partnership property first in the satisfaction of partnership debts.

matter number: a number assigned to each matter a firm handles for a particular client.

maturity date: the date upon which the principal amount of a debt instrument is repaid.

member: an owner of a limited liability company; also one of the persons constituting a nonprofit corporation.

member-managed companies: limited liability companies whose daily operations are directly managed by the owners of the business.

merger: two or more corporations combining in such a manner that assets are transferred to one surviving corporation which continues in existence, with the other(s) being terminated.

minute book: a binder in which minutes of corporate meetings and other corporate documents are kept.

minutes: a detailed record of all actions taken at a corporate meeting.

mission statement: a statement in an employee manual providing a synopsis of a corporation's general principles.

money purchase pension plan: one in which the employer's contributions are determined by a fixed formula based on the salary of the employee.

mortgage bond: a bond secured by a mortgage on real property.

multi-product mark: *see* house mark.

nonprofit corporation: a corporation which meets the requisite criteria set forth in Internal Revenue Code Section 501(c) so as to receive special tax status.

not-for-profit corporation: *see* nonprofit corporation.

novation: an agreement allowing the substitution of a party to a contract by releasing an original party from liability and substituting a new party in his or her place.

officer: a person appointed by the board of directors to manage the daily affairs of a corporation.

one-participant plan: a retirement plan set up by a sole proprietor which may also include the proprietor's spouse.

operating agreement: a contract between the members of a limited liability company.

option: a contract granting the right to buy or to sell a specific amount of securities at a fixed price for a specified period of time.

organizational meeting: a meeting held by the incorporators or directors after incorporation to attend to matters prerequisite to the transacting of corporate business.

organizer: a person who executes a limited liability company's articles of organization.

ostensible authority: *see* apparent authority.

outstanding shares: those shares of a corporation's authorized stock which have been issued to shareholders.

over-the-counter trading: trading of stocks through brokers utilizing computer networks.

paid-in capital: the amount above par value which a corporation receives from the sale of stock.

participating preferred stock: preferred stock providing fixed-rate dividends plus a pro rata portion of residual dividends.

partnership agreement: a contract between or among partners in a partnership which sets forth the manner in which partnership business will be conducted.

partnership at will: a partnership in which the partners have not agreed to remain partners until the expiration of a definite term or the completion of a particular undertaking.

partnership interest: a partner's share in the partnership.

par value: an arbitrary value assigned to stock.

personal holding company: a corporation in which more than 50 percent of outstanding corporate stock is owned by not more than five individuals, or one in which at least 60 percent of the corporation's adjusted gross income is derived from dividends, interest, royalties, annuities, trusts, estates, and certain personal service contracts.

piercing the corporate veil: allowing a party to ask a court to reach behind the protective veil of limited liability afforded shareholders and to go after the personal assets of shareholders.

plan of exchange: *see* plan of share exchange.

plan of liquidation: a plan outlining the procedures for liquidating a corporation.

plan of share exchange: a plan by which the shareholders of a target corporation receive shares in the acquiring corporation.

pooling agreement: *see* shareholders' voting agreement.

preemptive rights: original shareholders' rights to purchase newly issued corporate shares of stock on a pro rata basis before they are offered to others.

preferred stock: those shares of outstanding stock which are given priority in distribution of profits, or given other privileges over common stock.

president's report: the opening section of an annual report in which the president of a corporation provides an overview of the corporation's performance over the last year.

principal: a party who confers upon another the authority to act on his or her behalf.

professional association: a business entity which is similar to a professional partnership but is taxed like a corporation.

professional corporation: a legal entity created by state statute for the conduct of a statutorily recognized profession.

professional service corporation: *see* professional corporation.

profit and loss statement: *see* income statement.

profit-sharing plan: a plan for sharing employer profits with the employees of a business. The plan must set up systematic and substantial contributions as well as provide a definite formula for allocating contributions among participants.

promoter: a person who takes a business idea and develops it from the idea's inception to its birth as a newly created business.

prospectus: the document which goes out to the public for perusal and which is a part of a registration statement comprised of requisite disclosures of information on the corporate directors and officers, corporate assets, and other pertinent information.

proxy: a shareholder's authorization turning over to another his or her voting rights.

public corporation: a corporation whose shares of stock are traded in a public market and which is subject to state and federal securities regulations.

put: an option agreement permitting an individual or entity to sell stock at a specified price.

qualified plan: a written retirement plan that an employer establishes for the exclusive benefit of employees and their beneficiaries. The plan must meet the requirements of section 401 of the Internal Revenue Code and provide for deferred taxation of the employer's contribution until distribution is made to an employee.

quorum: the number of persons who must be present to conduct business at a meeting.

record date: the date a corporation closes its list of shareholders for purposes of determining the shareholders entitled to vote at a shareholders' meeting or determining the shareholders entitled to dividends.

record shareholder: a shareholder who owns shares of corporate stock on the record date.

redeemable bond: a bond which may be reacquired by a corporation prior to its maturity date.

redeemable preferred stock: preferred stock which may be reacquired by a corporation at a predetermined price.

red herring prospectus: a preliminary prospectus printed with a warning in red ink that registration is not yet effective.

registered agent: a person given the authority to accept service of process on behalf of a business.

registration statement: statement required by the Securities and Exchange Commission of a corporation desiring to make a transition from a private corporation to a public corporation.

regulations: a document, similar to corporate bylaws, which functions as the internal governing document of a limited liability company in some states.

resolution: a written statement authorizing certain actions to be taken by designated persons on behalf of the corporation.

restated articles of incorporation: a consolidation of all of the amendments with the remaining original, unchanged provisions into one new document.

restrictive covenant: a provision restricting (1) the use of work product, (2) the disclosure of trade secrets or other confidential information, or (3) the future engagement of the employee in a business competitive with the business of the corporation.

retained earnings: the profit earned by a corporation after paying dividends.

retainer agreement: a contract between an attorney and client which sets forth the manner in which the client will be billed for the attorney's work.

reverse stock split: the division of the number of authorized shares of a corporation into a lesser number.

RULPA: Revised Uniform Limited Partnership Act.

RUPA: Revised Uniform Partnership Act.

safe harbor list: a list of activities which a limited partner may undertake without losing limited liability status.

safe harbor rule: *see* safe harbor list.

salary reduction arrangement: an arrangement whereby employees choose to have their employer contribute part of their salaries to their SEPs.

S corporation: a corporation which qualifies for special tax status under the provisions of subchapter S of the Internal Revenue Code and is taxed similarly to a partnership.

scrip: a written certificate representing a fraction of a full share of stock.

Section 8 affidavit: an affidavit filed with the Patent and Trademark Office between the fifth and sixth year after the date of registration of a mark to keep the mark's registration active for the remainder of a ten-year term.

Section 15 affidavit: an affidavit filed with the Patent and Trademark Office that states that a mark has been in continuous use and that provides prima facie evidence of incontestability for litigation purposes.

Section 248 election: election to amortize certain organizational expenses over a period of not less than 60 months in accordance with Section 248 of the Internal Revenue Code.

Section 1244 election: election to treat a shareholder's financial investment in a corporation as an ordinary loss rather than a capital loss if certain qualifications are met in accordance with Section 1244 of the Internal Revenue Code.

secured loan: a loan in which collateral is required to secure the debt.

securities: instruments reflecting investments made by a corporation to earn a high rate of return,

Securities Act of 1933: federal act, enforced by the Securities and Exchange Commission, which requires registration of securities for public offering and the full disclosure of material information on security distributions.

Securities Exchange Act of 1934: federal act, enforced by the Securities and Exchange Commission, which regulates the selling of securities by securities exchanges and over-the-counter markets.

security: an investment in a business enterprise managed by others in which expectation of a profitable return depends on the efforts of others.

series: a subdivision of a class of stock.

service mark: protection of words, letters, numbers, names, phrases, symbols, or devices or any combination of these that is associated with a service.

set dollar amount method: a process for determining the value of a business by agreeing upon a set price which will be reevaluated and reset at specified intervals.

share certificate: *see* stock certificate.

share exchange: a transaction in which a corporation acquires the stock of one or more classes or series of another corporation.

shareholder: an owner of a corporation, receiving an equity interest in the corporation by purchasing shares of stock. Also referred to as a stockholder.

shareholders' equity: the combination of the par value of common stock, the par value of preferred stock, additional paid-in capital, and retained earnings.

shareholders' restrictive agreement: an agreement among the shareholders to restrict certain rights.

shareholders' voting agreement: an agreement whereby shareholders contractually agree to pool their votes and vote as a unit on specified matters.

share transfer tax: a tax imposed when stock transfers hands.

shop right: the nonexclusive right of an employer to use an employee's work product.

short-form merger: a merger in which a subsidiary corporation merges into a parent corporation and the parent corporation owns at least 90 percent of the outstanding shares of the subsidiary corporation.

short-term financing: a loan term of one year or less.

simplified employee pension (SEP): a retirement plan which sets up individual retirement arrangements for each participant with a bank, insurance company, or other qualified financial institution.

sinking fund: a reserve account set aside for the future redemption of redeemable preferred stock at a specified time.

small business corporation: an incorporated business that has fewer than 100 employees, 35 or fewer owners, and a net worth of less than $1 million.

small-impact merger: a merger which leaves the shareholders, with respect to their shares and rights, virtually unaffected.

sole proprietorship: an unincorporated business owned by one individual who is personally liable for business debts.

special agent: an agent given authority to act in a specific transaction or with regard to a specific matter only.

special-form drawing: a drawing submitted with a trademark application which must meet exact specifications.

specimen: a sample of how a trademark or service mark is being used in commerce.

stated capital: the par value of all shares issued by a corporation plus the portion of monies paid for all no par shares issued that the board of directors allocates to stated capital.

stated value: a minimum value for stock shares fixed by the board of directors.

statement of authority: a statement specifying the names of the partners authorized to carry out specified activities on behalf of the partnership.

statement of changes: a financial statement showing the increase or decrease in working capital.

statement of denial: a statement denying a factual allegation asserted in a statement of authority.

statement of foreign qualification: a document filed by a limited liability partnership seeking authorization to transact business in a state other than its state of domicile.

statement of qualification: a document filed with the appropriate state filing authority legally creating a limited liability partnership.

stock: a unit of ownership in a corporation. The two major types of stock are common stock and preferred stock.

stock bonus plan: a retirement plan available only to corporations in which stock of the employer corporation is invested.

stock certificate: a document evidencing the issuance of shares of stock.

stock dividend: a distribution to shareholders of extra shares of stock or extra fractions of shares of stock.

stock exchange: an organized market or similar facility at which stocks are traded by members of the exchange.

stockholder: *see* shareholder.

stock option plan: a plan giving an employee the option of purchasing a certain number of shares of stock within a defined period at a predetermined or determinable price.

stock purchase: a transaction in which one corporation purchases all, or substantially all, of the stock of another corporation.

stock purchase agreement: a contract under which an employee is obligated to purchase a certain number of corporate shares at a predetermined or determinable price within a specified time period.

stocks-for-assets transaction: *see* type C transaction.

stock split: a board of directors action which divides the shares of a corporation into a larger number of shares with each shareholder receiving his or her proportionate number of additional shares.

straight preferred stock: preferred stock conferring the right to fixed-rate dividends.

strike price: price at which the holder of a call may purchase stock.

subscriber: an individual or business entity agreeing to purchase shares of stock in a yet-to-be-created corporation.

suggestive mark: a mark which merely suggests attributes of a product or service.

tax basis: the amount assigned to an asset for income tax purposes.

term companies: limited liability companies whose legal duration is for a specified term.

term partnership: a partnership specifically structured to exist for a limited term.

time slip: a record detailing the time spent on a client matter and a description of the work done.

"top heavy" plan: an employee benefit plan in which 60 percent or more of the plan benefits are to vest in key employees.

trade credit: credit given to a business by its supplier which allows the business a specified period of time within which to pay its account.

trade dress: the look of a product which is distinctive to that product.

trademark: the protection of words, letters, numbers, names, phrases, symbols, or devices or any combination of these that is associated with a product or service.

trade name: a name descriptive of a manufacturer or service provider which applies to a business.

trade secret: confidential information, in whatever form, that gives the possessor of the information a business advantage over the competition.

treasury shares: stock that has been issued and then reacquired by the corporation.

trustee's certificate: *see* voting trust certificate.

trust indenture: *see* indenture.

type A transaction: a merger or consolidation.

type B transaction: a form of share exchange.

type C transaction: the acquisition of substantially all the assets of another corporation in exchange for shares of the acquiring corporation.

ULLCA: Uniform Limited Liability Company Act.

ULPA: Uniform Limited Partnership Act.

uncertified shares: stock issued without stock certificates.

underwriter: an individual or entity engaged in the business of purchasing and selling securities, often a securities broker or financial institution.

undisclosed principal: a principal unknown to a third party in a transaction.

uniform law: a law in a particular subject area that is approved by the Commissioners on Uniform State Laws and is adopted in whole or in part by individual states.

Uniform Securities Act of 1985: a uniform law adopted by several states providing for registration by filing of securities of public corporations.

Uniform Securities Act of 1956: a uniform law adopted by several states providing for registration by coordination of securities of public corporations.

unissued shares: shares of stock in a corporation which have yet to be issued to shareholders.

unsecured loan: a loan in which no collateral is required to secure the debt.

UPA: Uniform Partnership Act.

use application: a trademark application filed with the Patent and Trademark Office when one has used a product in commerce.

utility patent: protection of the functional characteristics of products and processes.

vicarious liability: indirect legal responsibility, such as the liability of an employer for the tortious acts of an employee commited within the scope of employment.

voting list: listing in alphabetical order of all record shareholders entitled to vote on a matter.

voting trust: a formal mechanism giving legal title to the stock of participating shareholders to the trustee authorized to vote those shares, with equitable title remaining with the participating shareholders.

voting trust agreement: *see* voting trust.

voting trust certificate: certificate acknowledging a shareholder's equitable interest in shares of stock.

watered stock: stock sold for a price below par value.

zero-coupon bond: a bond purchased at a discount which does not allow payment of interest until the maturity date of the bond.

Index